Accounting Reform in Transition and Developing Economies

Robert W. McGee
Editor

Accounting Reform in Transition and Developing Economies

 Springer

Robert W. McGee
School of Accounting
College of Business Administration
ACII 124
Florida International University
Biscayne Bay Campus
3000 NE 151st Street
North Miami, FL 33181

ISBN: 978-0-387-25707-5   e-ISBN: 978-0-387-25708-2
DOI: 10.1007/978-0-387-25708-2

Library of Congress Control Number: 2008930264

Printed on acid-free paper

springer.com

Preface

Much has been written about the economic and political problems of countries that are in the process of changing from centrally planned systems to market systems. Most studies have focused on the economic, legal, political, and sociological problems these economies have had to face during the transition period. However, not much has been written about the dramatic changes that have to be made to the accounting and financial system of a transition economy. This book was written to help fill that gap.

Accounting Reform in Transition and Developing Economies is the fourth in a series to examine accounting and financial system reform in transition and developing economies. The first volume used Russia as a case study. The second volume in the series examined some additional aspects of the reform in Russia and also looked at the accounting and financial system reform efforts that are being made in Ukraine, Bosnia & Herzegovina, Armenia, Eastern Europe, and Central Asia. The third volume examined taxation and public finance in transition and developing economies.

The present volume examines accounting reform in transition and developing economies. It is divided into five parts. Part I consists of 14 studies that examine various aspects of accounting reform in different transition economies. It is a series of country studies. Part II comprises ten chapters on how accounting education has been reformed in some former Soviet republics and countries in Central and Eastern Europe. Part III examines recent developments in accounting certification in Central Asia, the former Soviet Union, and Central and Eastern Europe. Part IV includes three studies on corporate governance and Part V examines the views on tax evasion in ten transition economies.

Contents

Part I
Country Studies

Chapter 1
Accounting Reforms in Bosnia and Herzegovina Since 1992

Meliha Basic

1.1 Introduction

Since 1992, Bosnia-Herzegovina (BiH) has been working not only on building state institutions but has also been working on its socio-economic recovery and development. Many processes related to modernizing the economy and society take place alongside the post-war recovery, with the vast assistance of the international community. The processes penetrate all fields and all levels, whereas the most important of them are the following:

- Shift from majority state-owned to privately owned property (this process is now nearly completed)
- Legislation on all administration levels and in all sectors (drafting and adopting of new laws that are fully harmonized with international law and European standards – process still ongoing)
- Development of the financial infrastructure (process aimed at development and modern operation of the Central Bank, plus creation of sound and strong financial institutions – process near completion)
- Finance and accounting reform on all levels (passing of appropriate regulations that provide for introduction and application of IFRS, trading securities, etc. – reform still ongoing)

These and other processes are all aiming to achieve one sole goal – creation of a modern and developed state that will be a member of the EU and that will have its place in the world.

During all these reforms, one very important factor in their implementation is always the constitutional structure, which in our case is the Dayton Agreement (developed under the close eye of the international community, mainly the USA). This Agreement has put an end to the war in BiH (1992–1995), and it established two constituent entities that together form the state of BiH:

M. Basic
University of Sarajevo

R. W. McGee (ed.), *Accounting Reform in Transition and Developing Economies,*
© Springer Science + Business Media LLC 2008

1. Federation of Bosnia-Herzegovina
2. Republic of Srpska (RS), plus
3. The District of Brcko

According to the Constitution, the entities consist of multiple Cantons, and the District of Brcko is a special section with no entity-like jurisdictions, but with an administration structure that is usual for a district.

Following the decision of the Council of Ministers (CoM) of BiH in 1999 to launch an initiative for our joining the EU, a whole series of events and tasks took place in trying to fulfill the accession criteria. The requirements of reform in the fields of accounting and tax policies are part of the aforementioned criteria. Thereby, the process initiated back in 1995, with the introduction of first accounting standards as of January 1, 1995, started gaining impetus. It was first expanded so as to include the tax policies, with a high accent on the agenda required for the eventual introduction of the value added tax (VAT). VAT became a state-level issue, being a requirement for the accession to the EU and an obligation that the CoM has pledged to fulfill by the year 2006 (the calculations, preparing of records and collecting of VAT on the entire territory of BiH are due to begin on January 1, 2006).

The reforming of the finance and accounting sectors, with the assistance of various international institutions and the United States Agency for International Development's (USAID's) unit for reforming of accounting in the private sector, was a twofold issue ever since it was started. It consisted of:

- Introducing new finance- and accounting-related regulations into state legislation and
- Education in the fields of finance and accounting

We will now look into the basic tasks and achievements in the field of accounting in BiH, and we will give an overview of the current situation in this field.

1.2 Reforms in Accounting Since 1992

The reform process is fueled by the general idea of introducing internationally accepted and recognized standards in the sectors of reporting, auditing and education in this field. The goal was to be able to offer security to both existing and future parties that invest in the BiH-economy, regardless of where they come from (domestic or foreign). Simplicity of accessing financial data and their accuracy, as well as reliable financial statements from domestic companies will provide adequate means for controlling companies they wish to invest in, or in which they already hold a share.

This goal was neither easy nor simple to achieve. The reforms were broken down to phases, the most important of which are as follows:

PHASE 1 – Initial phase – Raising awareness of the need to open up to the rest of the world in the field of accounting – Time span: 1992–1995

Key features of this phase:

- Overcoming the socialist economic system, and introducing and developing the market economy in all possible fields.
- Communication with Europe and the rest of the world was impossible because our standards and regulations were incompatible with their equivalents elsewhere. There was no internationally recognized system, and no obligation to present our data in the form of such, either.
- The accounting regulations were strict and with a firmly established code of conduct usual to the socialist economies and 'public-owned property'. When it comes to equity funds, they existed, but they implied state-owned equity etc. Selling and/ or buying were limited only to purchases that the State approved of.
- Then came the first ever market-oriented Law on Accounting, which embraced the market economy as the way of doing business, and it offered flexibility that former laws did not allow for.
- The new Law on Accounting uses international accounting standards for the first time ever (on a modest scale, though). This law entered into force on January 1, 1995.

PHASE 2 – Introduction of the accounting standards to the Federation and to the RS – Time span: 1995–2000

Key features:

- New regulations are introduced in terms of finance administration and legal framework for private companies (introduced: sole proprietorship, holdings [shareholder companies] with subsidiaries or limited liability [LTD/LLC]).
- New regulations are adopted with a view to privatization that featured specific requirements for preparation of balance sheets and mandatory audits prior to privatization. The term 'initial balance' is introduced for the first time. The initial balance, as the basis for privatization from the accountants' angle, consists of three parts: Active (assets), Passive (liabilities) and Neutral sub-balance. 'Active' stands for items in the initial balance that are eligible for sale. 'Passive' are items that are hard to sell, due to their being subject to the process of succession of the former Yugoslavia and the distribution of property of the former state union between the six republics that formed it (BiH was part of the former Yugoslavia). 'Neutral' stands for real estate that is now subject to purchase by employees to whom the real estate was allocated, and who are buying in accordance with the special Law on Privatization of Residential Apartments.
- The process of educating and issuing certificates to independent accountants began. The process is run through the Association, but it is not standardized according to international practice.
- Higher business schools and universities in BiH introduce new classes to the curriculum: financial management, finance, banking, accounting, basics of financial accounting, expenditure- and managerial accounting, audits and control. The classes are taught using IAS-based literature.
- Local and foreign experts work closely on defining the best method to introduce International Auditing Standards (IAS) and International Standards of Auditing (ISA) in BiH.

- A problem comes about: unequal regulations for certifying of independent accountants, and unequal qualifications of experts in this field that arose therefrom. This was a potential problem in terms of applying of IAS as well.

PHASE 3 – Adopting of IAS-based accounting and auditing standards in the Federation and in RS – Time span: 1995–2004

Key features:

- With the consent of USAID (as the lead coordinator in accounting and finance reforms), local accounting and auditing standards were adopted, separately for the Federation and for the RS, but both incorporating adjusted ISA and IAS.
- The Federation establishes the Federal Agency for Accounting and Auditing in 1997 to underpin the reforms in this field. The Federation Government and Federal Ministry of Finance authorize the Agency to define, adjust and issue accounting and auditing standards in the Federation.
- Although they were based on ISA and IAS, as a transitional phase in the process of switching entirely to these two, the adopted local standards differ from their international counterparts in one important feature: their adoption and interpretation, as well as corrections made thereto, are within the jurisdiction of government institutions, instead of that of International Accounting Standards Board in London (IASB). In the Federation, the Agency for Accounting and Auditing (established by a decision of the Federal Ministry of Finance) is also in charge of educating and attesting of independent accountants and auditors.
- The main shared (common) features and differences between IAS and the accounting standards in BiH are as follows.

1.2.1 Differences

(a) Bosnian standards consist of 38 items, whereas the IAS has 41, as well as several International Financial Reporting Standards (IFRS). At the time of introducing the Federal Codes of Accounting Principles and Standards (end of 1999, application starting on January 1, 2000), IAS standards #29, #40 and #41 were not included.
(b) International Standard #29 – Financial statements in economies w/hyperinflation – The reason given (by the State Expert Commission for the Definition of Standards) for not including this rule was that there was no inflation in BiH, due to the Currency Board's macroeconomic policy, which does not allow for inflation to come about (this policy slows down the economy and makes its development harder, but it provides for the stability of "KM" – the single BiH currency).
(c) International standard #40 – Investment in State – The reason behind failing to introduce this standard was the lack of existing regulations dealing with this issue, especially in accounting terms (before all, the uncompleted privatization process and the existence of special laws concerning foreign investments).

(d) International Standard #41 – Agriculture – The reason behind failing to introduce this standard is similar to that under #40, with the addition of agricultural reform at hand, that was being dealt with as a separate issue by the state authorities. Furthermore, this field requires more in-depth explanations and adjustments to facilitate a smooth transition to applying of new standards.
(e) The accounting standards in BiH, as compared to IAS, though the same in nature, are larger in volume. This is due to the fact that they incorporate the entire Law on Accounting and Auditing as their integral part.

1.2.2   Shared Features

(a) All accounting (and auditing) standards in BiH share the IAS numbering system and labeling.
(b) All accounting (and auditing) standards in BiH share the same content structure with IAS, i.e. all standards have *goals, purposes and definitions.*

  – The positive results yielded during this phase were in the fields of standardization, raising of the accounting profession on a generally higher level in the country, introduction of IAS through a domestic version thereof and embracing of a new, flexible approach to IAS application in managing business changes and financial reporting.
  – However, apart from the above listed achievements, it was the very manner of the standards' adoption and certification (attesting) methods that led to a series of problems and began to hinder further reforms in this field.

PHASE 4 – Transition to the direct application of IAS and to a single statewide method of education and attesting of accountants – Time span: September 2004 – until today

Key features:

- Adoption of the new Law on Accounting that is binding on the entire territory of the country, in September 2004
- Precisely defining of problems encountered during the implementation of reforms in the recent past and overcoming of such, through imposition of IAS on the entire territory of the country, in addition to appropriate education and attesting process, compliant with international standards.
- The application of IAS is mandatory in financial statements as of January 1, 2005, i.e. the system is adjusted so as to satisfy EU requirements (but only for companies that are listed on the stock market).
- Expert Commission is formed, chaired by a foreign coordinator tasked with monitoring of the education process (defining of the training curriculum, securing of continuous education and providing of adequate conditions for the trainers), and the attesting process on the state level (issuing of certificates and making a single record of certified experts in this field).

1.3   International Assessment of Current Conditions in Accounting

It was once again clear that the complex state structure defined by the Dayton Agreement and the BiH Constitution that envisages two entities with noteworthy powers and independence from one another, is an obstacle to the reforming process. It makes it harder to balance between separate approaches to the reforms that are present in the country. Huge powers vested in entities in terms of implementation of important reforms throughout phases 2 and 3 have resulted in the two adopting different approaches, different accounting standards and different attesting procedures.

The laws on accounting and the application of international accounting standards and other relevant regulations (in the taxation sector, financial reporting, etc.) were adopted in each of the entities independently, which ended up in the absurd situation where the two entities in the same country were operating with different accounting standards.[1] Accounting related laws and education in this field were different as well, again, within a single state.[2]

The Federal Agency for Accounting and Audits published a total of 32 accounting standards since 1998 to present. Some of them were released as separate materials, and some were published in the Official Gazette[3] of the Federation. These standards were implemented in 2000 in the form of various laws and reports. Despite the formal act of 'harmonizing' between local standards (both Federation and RS) and the IAS, it is still a fact that some of them deviate from the original. Furthermore, IAS is an ever-changing thing, which requires constant updating and adjustments, and neither the Federation nor the RS have actually followed this trend through. In the period of time between the years of 2000 and 2004, the Federal Agency did not publish one single amendment or a newly introduced standard. During the same period, the IASB released five standards, three of which were IAS (#29, #40 and #41), and two international financial reporting standards.

The World Bank's (WB) 'Report on observance of standards and codes' (ROSC) of October 2004, had also emphasized that the problems in the accounting sector were becoming ever more obvious, and that reforms were hindered instead of being implemented. Among other remarks in this sense, the report reads that the 'current arrangements in the field of accounting started to block the reforms in this field...', and that 'not only is a new law necessary, one that will be binding on the entire territory of BiH, but it is also necessary to harmonize between the entities...'. This report came after the new law was passed, but before its harmonization with entity laws. Some excerpts that illustrate the situation in the Federation are given below.[4]

---

[1] RS adopted the IAS rules that were in force at the time. The full version of the text was translated and published as the "Accounting Standards of RS."

[2] The accounting standards applied in the two entities were the same to a great extent, however, there were certain differences.

[3] Official Gazette of the Federation of BiH, #50/98, #52/99, and #54/00.

[4] ROSC – see http://www.worldbank.org/ifa/rosc

1.3.1 General Comments

The two entities have different regulatory frameworks in the fields of accounting and audits, which do not constitute a business-friendly environment, nor does this act in favour of future business development.

The accounting standards, attesting of accountants and issuing of auditing licenses are underlying the jurisdictions of two different regimes. The companies that are registered for business in both entities are required to do separate, i.e. different bookkeeping, they are subject to separate (and different) accounting laws and demands in terms of financial statements, etc. All this enormously increases the expenditures of running a business in BiH, and constitutes an obstacle to foreign investments and private sector growth.

1.3.2 Federation of BiH

The Agency for Accounting and Audits runs the process of adopting accounting and auditing policies in the territory of the Federation. Despite having the power to do so, the Agency failed to secure that the main principle in adopting of policies be the public interest. The Law on Accounting and Law on Audits are the most important regulatory frameworks, together with the Code. The Agency holds the exclusive power to regulate in the field of accounting and audits, but the existing arrangements within the Agency do not ensure that the key principles in adopting policies are professionalism, quality and public interest.

Even though it is based on international standards of financial reporting and EU Directives, the Law on Accounting actually puts the main focus on compliance with the Code and the accounting standards of the Federation, the quality of which does not meet the international standards in this field (IFRS). The accounting standards in the Federation are defined by the Agency for Accounting and Audits. Despite the fact that the Law on Accounting stipulates that Federal accounting standards be compliant to IAS, the team that prepared the ROSC established a few deficiencies in this sense (see Part III). Also, the Law on Accounting specifies certain accounting principles such as 'inequality', 'causing', 'individual assessment', 'inventory', or 'exclusivity of the initial balance', none of which are compliant with IFRS concepts. Therefore, we cannot say that financial statements prepared in accordance with Federal regulations are IFRS-compliant.

There is no public access to the financial statements. The Law on Accounting stipulates that companies submit their financial statements to the Agency for Money Transactions. Since this Agency ceased to exist in the year 2000, there is now no formal request for the public availability of companies' financial statements, except for those that appear on the stock market. The Federation has no central portal through which the interested parties could access the (reviewed) financial statements.

The right to perform mandatory audits of financial statements is reserved exclusively for individuals and auditing bureaus that are authorized for such by the Agency for Accounting and Audits. The Agency issued licenses to approximately 230 individual auditors, 60 auditing bureaus and 3,500 independent accountants.

The Federal Law on Accounting is accepting of the fact that this entire line of work is controlled and regulated by the Agency for Accounting and Audits, which is in fact a 'subsidiary' of the Ministry of Finance. Whereas the Law on Audits establishes the Agency as a separate and independent body, it still remains closely connected to the Ministry of Finance. Even though the Agency issues licenses to accountants and auditors, it does not operate as an association of professionals sharing the same line of work (auditors and accountants are not 'members' of the Agency and they do not have a say in how the Agency runs its business or in the selection of management). At the same time, the Agency is not responsible to the general public either.

Whereas the goals of the Federal Association of Professional Accountants could contribute to the development and improving of this profession, the Association lacks formal recognition of any kind (in legal terms), and therefore cannot effectively influence the quality of auditing. The Agency for Accounting and Audits is the only body in the Federation that is entitled to regulate the auditing sector. Should the Agency be abolished, the transfer of its resources and tasks to a professional union would come about, provided that the Independent Commission for Standards recognizes such a body first.

The regulations regarding the obligations, i.e. accountability of the auditors are poorly drafted and have never been tested so far. There is no proof whatsoever that all individuals to whom the Agency has issued certificates are appropriately qualified. The translation of IFRS into the local language does exist, but it is outdated, incomplete and inaccurate. There is no efficient mechanism for ensuring of application/ implementation of the requirements related to financial statements, except to a certain extent, those that apply to the banks.

The Federation lacks a sound mechanism for ensuring quality mandatory audits, which is crucial for a good auditing process. A good process would imply improved credibility and value of the disclosed financial data, and additional protection mechanisms offered to shareholders, investors, creditors and other stakeholders. However, the Federation failed to implement a quality protection mechanism, independent of the auditors and auditing bureaus mentioned above.

The accounting regulations and practices are on average so poor in quality that the investors and other users of financial statements are not able to establish if the companies' bonds are a sound investment or not, or to rely on the statements in decision-making. The accounting standards in the Federation reveal a number of shortcomings when compared with the IFRS. There are significant differences between Federal standards and the IFRS, which have a negative impact on the quality of the financial statements.

The ROSC team performed an evaluation of the 'compliance gap' by taking a sample of five sets of financial statements submitted as 'IFRS compliant', and another ten samples prepared 'in accordance with Federal accounting standards'.

The ROSC team evaluated five banks and ten companies (some of which were active in the stock exchange, and some not). Whereas the banks kept claiming that they comply with IFRS, none of them had really prepared a financial statement completely based on IFRS principles. The quality of financial statements of the companies was generally quite unsatisfactory.

The proofs of quality of the mandatory audits performed were quite contradictory to one another. The discussions that the ROSC team had held with individual auditors, small and big audit bureaus, and the Agency for Accounting and Audits made the following issues stand out as ones that have particularly bad impact on the auditing practice in BiH:

- Lack of documentation. Some auditors do not document all issues relevant for gathering of evidence to support their audit findings, i.e. evidence to support the assumption that the audit was performed in accordance with relevant standards.
- Fraud and error. In response to international scandals related to corporate financial statements, the international auditing standards dealing with issues of fraud and error were recently strengthened by a new amendment that is not yet incorporated in the Federal Auditing Guidelines. It is of even more concern that it appears that only a small number of auditors really understand the responsibility of paying extra attention to possible fraud indicators during their audit.
- Internal control systems. The auditors generally kick off with overall testing, without running in-depth checks of the accounting system in question, or the accompanying control system. As a result, many weaknesses in the system may remain undiscovered. It is therefore an oversight on their part to not inform the management of weak points in the basic accounting pattern/structure, or in the functioning of the accounting system and internal control. Thereby, a chance to improve financial management in the Federation is being missed.
- Related parties. It seems that a strict application of international standards when it comes to auditing of related parties' transactions generates tension between the auditor and the management, which may lead to inappropriate disclosure of transactions between the related parties.
- Lack of audit evidence. It appears that some auditors do not tend to be personally present when records of inventories are being made, regardless of being aware of the importance of such goods in terms of financial statements. Furthermore, some of the auditors apparently do not use 'outside' confirmations (ex from banks), even when circumstances point to the need for such.

The new state-level framework law was adopted in June 2004, and is expected to be endorsed in both entities. This is due to take place through two implementation laws that are already drafted, and through forming of the Independent Commission for Standards, i.e. appointing of a special international advisor.

All the above listed problems have encouraged our assistant in this matter, USAID, to take a new approach, which is the only right one, and is compliant with international practice. This new approach implies a new Law on Accounting to be adopted as binding on the entire territory of BiH, that the entity laws be adjusted to the state-level law, so as to include attesting and education in this field to be carried out equally in both entities, and in compliance with international standards. This is the only way we can have the same regulations valid in the entire territory of BiH, and the only way for the certified accountants and auditors to be able to practice their duties anywhere in the country. The direct application of IAS will also be secured to take place in the same manner throughout the country, and in accordance with procedures that are common to all those who choose to apply IAS.

This would also meet the criteria laid before BiH parties by the international institutions, in relation to the form in which the statements are to be submitted. This is also an EU accession requirement.

The adoption of the Law on Accounting and Audits in September 2004 launched this whole process and facilitated the accompanying reforms. Draft entity-level laws are currently reviewed in the Federation and in RS, pending their adoption. Preparations for the implementation of the state-level law are ongoing, and they envisage education issues, attesting, harmonization and direct application of IAS. This process will build on what was done so far while trying to improve it at the same time. A transition period of 1 year is envisaged. The implementation of new institutional frameworks for accounting in BiH started on January 1, 2005, whereas the application of the new Law on Accounting on the entire territory of BiH is expected to start as of January 1, 2006.

1.4   Differences Between Federal Accounting Standards and IAS 1999–2004

As outlined earlier, the key difference between Federal standards and IAS is the fact that 34 of IAS are being applied, together with 2 IFRS, and there are 31 Federal Accounting Standards that are adopted and in use.

Federal standards were adopted over several phases, and this overview of the differences between Federal Standards and IAS is presented according to those phases. This is how and in which order the standards were adopted:

1. **Phase 1** – by the end of March 1998 – 17 standards adopted. Namely: FS (Fed. Standard) #1, #2, #7, #8, #10, #11, #14, #16, #18, #20, #21, #23, #24, #25, #27, #28 and #31.
2. **Phase 2** – by the end of 1998 – eight standards adopted. Namely: FS #9, #12, #15, #17, #30, #32, #33 and #34.
3. **Phase 3** – during 1999 – seven standards adopted, the application of which started as of January 1, 2000. Namely: FS #19, #22, #26, #35, #36, #37 and #38. Partial change was made to three standards, namely FS #16, #28 and #31.
4. **Phase 4** – after Jan 1, 2000 to the end of 2004 – no new standards were adopted in the Federation, and no changes were made to the existing ones (there were 31 total standards in force). At the same time, the IASB had introduced three new IASs, namely IAS #39, #40 and #41, and two IFRSs, the adoption of which had

impact on changing of provisions of multiple other standards (IAS #25 was even withdrawn). Therefore, anything that has to do with these new standards constitutes a difference between Federal Standards and IAS.

Below is a phased comparison between FS and IAS.[5]

1. The differences in standards adopted in Phase 1, until the end of May 1998:

#	IAS	FS
1	IAS 1 prepares the grounds for the presentation of general purpose financial statements. Purpose and sections of financial statements, accounting policies, and the structure and contents of financial statements (balance sheets, income statement, statement of changes in equity, and notes, containing additional. comments) are outlined here. IAS 1 consists of 104 articles, and annexes such as the 'illustrations of the structure of financial statements'. Their purpose is to better explain the application of standards, offering examples of application of balance sheets, profit statement with two alternative classifications of income/ outcome (either according to their nature or to their function), and changes in capital (also with two alternative approaches offered).	FS 1 only has 33 articles, dealing with purpose and contents of financial statements, their key elements, accounting policies and accounting bases. The provisions do not include basic accounting principles, as these were incorporated in the Code of Ethics. Provisions on the contents of the Income Statement (balance of success) were omitted, and so were the contents of the Statement on Changes in Equity. Contents of balance sheets and additional comments were significantly shortened. The reason for omission of a great number of provisions is that the schemes of financial statements in the Federation were already established, i.e. it was impossible to apply the IAS provisions directly, especially when it comes to the alternative options offered. The balance sheet was based on function-wise distribution of costs, and sorting of data according to the nature of expenditure was thus disabled, or only possible if given under the 'Additional Comments' section. The alternative way of presenting of changes in equity was also impossible.
2	IAS 2 is one of the most important standards in practice. It deals with measuring and determining the costs of inventories (raw materials, work in process, products, finished goods, etc.), it defines costs of stock-keeping (basic and allowed alternative procedure), and calculating of expenses on basis of sell-off or write-down. When the costs are determined by the LIFO method, and in accordance with the allowed alternative proce dure, then IAS 2 demands	FS do not include article 9 of IAS #2, according to which the acquisition costs may only include the foreign exchange differences arising directly on the recent acquisition of inventories invoiced in a foreign currency, and under very specific (and rarely allowed) circumstances, according to the alternative procedure outlined under IAS #21. FS #2 also does not require that the difference resulting from alternative LIFO procedures be listed separately, as the LIFO method is

(continued)

[5] Z. Bosnjak: Compilation of Studies, 7th International Symposium, Accountants' Association of the Federation of BiH.

(continued)

#	IAS	FS
	that the difference between such amounts and the amounts calculated thru basic procedure be clearly outlined (disclosed). NOTE: The LIFO method is no longer an acceptable method.	considered to be "equal" to the basic IAS #2 procedure (FIFO and the weighted average cost formula). However, the use of the LIFO method is still limited in the Federation, due to specific provisions of the income tax regulations.
7	IAS #7 classifies cash flows according to operating, investing, and financial activities. The examples for all three are given, w/o cash receipts and interest or dividends paid. Article 31 stipulates that interest and dividends be listed consistently, from period to period, if classified as operating, investing, or financing cash flows. There are two reporting methods allowed: direct and indirect. Companies are encouraged to use the direct method in depicting cash flows resulting from business operations.	FS #7, under article 5 – 'the definitions' – precisely describes what 'cash' means, and what is understood as 'cash equivalents'. Examples of cash flows resulting from operating (business activities) also list cash receipts and interests paid, as well as dividends received, whereas cash dividends paid are listed under 'financial activities'. FS #7 envisages presenting of cash flow using the indirect model as obligatory. The obligatory financial statement for external users is to be made according to this model. The direct model is only allowed for internal use. FS #7 does not contain the 'net cash flow statements' section.
8	IAS #8 is about defining of financial results of regular business activities and atypical items, procedures related to cessation of business activities and changes in accounting estimations, basic errors and the correction thereof, and the procedure of changing of the accounting policy. IAS #8 was redefined in 1993, After IAS #35 was introduced on January 1, 1999, the provisions under articles 19–22 of IAS #8 were abolished. ('Discontinuing Operations' -cease of business activities). Note: IAS #35 has been changed with IFRS#5.	FS #8, although marked by fewer articles, is not really different from IAS #8, contents-wise. The only actual difference is that FS does not contain several articles that explain the standards in detail.[6] Although FS #8 is to be applied to financial statements covering the period from January 1, 1999 onwards, the initial version of this standard included the 'Discontinuing Operations' section. However, following the introduction of FS #35 (applicable to statements covering the period from January 1, 2000 onwards), articles 13–16 of FS #8 were abolished.
10	IAS #10 was adopted in 1999. It covers 'Events after the balance sheet date', and is applicable to annual financial statements covering the period from January 1, 2000 on. This standard supersedes all sections of the former #10 (unpredictable events and	FS #10 – Unpredictable events and developments that came about after the balance sheet was prepared. Defines 'unpredictable' and 'potential' developments that cause either profit or loss. Also explains accounting procedures and reporting on such. Once

(continued)

---

[6] All articles listed under IAS are not international standards as such. Standards are only the articles that are printed in bold italic font, whereas all the remaining text simply offers explanations related to the standard.

(continued)

#	IAS	FS
	the developments that took place after the balance was defined – 'Adjusting Event' & 'Non-Adjusting Event') that are not covered by the new IAS #37. The new #10 stipulates when to add adjustments due to events that took place after the balance was prepared, in the sense of their recognition and evaluation in financial statements. It also lists procedures for disclosing information related to events that occurred after the date stated on the balance sheet.	FS #37 became effective (January 1, 2000), it replaced all sections of #10 that dealt with unpredictable events, i.e. articles 3–17. Apart from not changing its title, the FS #10 also ended up poor in contents and too general, as compared to IAS #10.
11	IAS #11 deals with the specifics of construction contracts and construction related activities, with definitions of revenues and costs, retentions, and liabilities usual to the above. According to the way of revenue determining, i.e. defining of reimbursement due to the contractor (performer, customer), the difference is established between the fixed-price contracts and cost + contracts. The condition for recognition of revenues and costs in both types of contracts is that the results (costs) of contracts can be measured accurately.	FS #11 could be called the 'abbreviated IAS #11', as it contains all important provisions thereof, while lacking some of the explanations, such as articles 19 and 20 for example (these explain that contract costs cannot include general administrative costs and development costs). Articles 42 and 45 are also omitted. They require that the gross amount to be paid by the contract vendor for the works performed be presented both under assets and liabilities (due from customers – asset, due to customers – liability).
14	IAS #14 (Segment Reporting) deals with statements on business results according to the type of business and geographical area. Among other things, principles of presentation of financial data are defined, as well as elements thereof that are to be disclosed. IAS #14 is to be applied by companies-enterprises whose debt or equity securities are publicly traded.	FS #14 is no different from IAS #14, in terms of its structure and contents. However, here too the provisions are shortened, i.e. reduced so as to omit the explanations that accompany the standards. Even though FS #14 is shorter in all sections than IAS #14, the provisions on "primary" and "secondary" segments were the most reduced ones. FS #14 contains 56 articles, whereas IAS #14 has 84.
16	IAS #16 (Property, Plant and Equipment) describes the accounting procedures for real estate, machinery and equipment. The main issues here are timing of recognition of assets, determination of their carrying amounts, and the depreciation charges to be recognized in relation to them (related amortization costs). Property,	FS #16 covers other tangible assets as well. The most significant deviation from IAS #16 is the 'evaluation after the initial recognition', where article 22 of FS #16 demands presentation of the constant tangible asset according to the 'corrected historical cost'. FS #16 also gives precise instructions on depreciation charges, such as when

(continued)

(continued)

#	IAS	FS
	plant and equipment items that are recognized as assets should be valued according to their cost ('cost model'), whereby the asset is carried at cost less accumulated depreciation and impairment, or –alternatively- according to the revalued amount ('revaluation model'), i.e. the asset is carried at a revalued amount, being its fair value at the date of revaluation, less subsequent depreciation.	does it not apply, or when the calculation thereof begins, what methods of calculation are allowed, etc. Some of these provisions are obviously not standards, and should have been given in the form of a special act (ex Rulebook on Depreciation). The most disputable provision is the one defining minimum depreciation charges for state-owned companies.
18	IAS #18 (Revenue) is about measurement of revenue, recognition of operating (business) activities and transactions that result in income, recognition of profit from selling of goods, service-providing, interests, royalties and dividends, and disclosure-related demands.	FS #18 is quite similar to IAS #18, structure-wise and contents-wise. FS #18 even has two articles more, but this is because the provisions under article 30 are divided across three different articles (30, 33 and 35), whereas in IAS #18 they are all listed under a single article.
20	IAS #20 (Government Grants and Disclosure of Government Assistance) describes accounting in cases of government grants and the disclosure thereof, as well as other forms of state-provided assistance. Two approaches are allowed: the capital approach, whereby the aid is granted directly to the shareholder, and the profit approach, whereby the aid is added to the profit over a certain time span, or across multiple time spans. As for presenting of aid related to means, there are two methods allowed in financial statements: One defines the aid as deferred income, which is recognized in the profit statement, along system- and rationale-axes, and over the 'life-span' of the asset in question. The other one implies deduction of the grant from the asset's carrying amount (recognition during the use of asset thru reduction of depreciation costs/charges).	FS #20 is titled 'Donations', and it extends the range of accounting (and tax) procedures related to all kinds of grants and assistance. According to FS #2O, all donations received, be they tangibles, intangibles or cash, are recognized as deferred income, wherever there are no expenditures involved. The income from donations and aid is recognized in the calculation period up to the amount of expenditures that arose in relation thereto. As for financial statements, the asset-related donations, including non-monetary aid, should be presented as deferred income, whereby the amount of the deferred income is determined along system- and rationale-axes, and over the life-span of the asset in question. (The alternative method whereby the donation is recognized in the balance during the use of asset that is subject to depreciation, i.e. for which the depreciation costs are reduced, is not mentioned).
21	IAS #21 (Effects of Changes in Foreign Exchange Rates) is applied in transactions involving foreign currencies, and/or when	FS #21 is contents-wise and structure-wise pretty similar to IAS#21, and it outlines which exchange rate is to be used, in pretty much the same manner.

(continued)

(continued)

#	IAS	FS
	translating financial statements of foreign activities (into a presentation currency), if they are included in the company's financial statement thru consolidation, proportionate consolidation, or shares. When recognizing exchange differences, there is a basic procedure where the differences are recognized as either profit or loss in the given period; and there is an alternative procedure whereby the differences are (rarely, due to severe devaluation or depreciation of currency) recognized as the (carrying amount of the) asset, provided that such amount does not exceed the costs of exchange or the reimbursable value of the asset (depending on which figure is lower). Note: This IAS #21 has not been in use since 2003.	The instructions on recognizing the financial aspects of changes in foreign currency rates are also the same. The only difference is that FS #21 does not mention the alternative procedures for recognizing of exchange differences, so the difference generated by balance-settling (reconciliation) or reporting cash amounts according to rates different from those listed in the original entries, are to be presented either as income or outcome during the period. The exception is the exchange difference generated by monetary items that are part of investments made in a foreign party. Then it is expected that they be classified as head capital, until the time of disposing of the net investment.
23	IAS #23 (Borrowing Costs) is about costs of borrowings. It requires that such costs be expensed at the time they are incurred. The allowed alternate procedure is to recognize them as expenditures, excluding the amount up to which they can be capitalized. The standard is very detailed in terms of conditions and the manner of capitalization of costs of borrowing.	FS #23 corresponds to IAS #23. The only difference is that it specifically requires the alternate procedure described in IAS #23. Thereby, costs for borrowed financial assets are, in principal, recognized as expenditures during the reporting period. However, the borrowing costs that can be directly attributed to acquiring, construction, or producing of qualified assets, should be capitalized as part of acquisition costs of such asset.
24	IAS #24 is applied in 'related parties' activities and in transactions between the reporting party and their partner parties.	FS #24 is a 're-defined' IAS #24. The contents are identical, with 'minor rationalizations' (ex articles 13–16 of IAS #24 are compressed into one article in FS #24 – article 11 (a, b, c. d).
25	IAS #25 was redefined in 1994. It used to cover recognition and evaluation of debt and equity investments, as well as investments in both tangible and intangible permanent assets, that are considered to be investments. However, IAS #38 replaced #25 for investments in intangible assets. IAS #39 replaced it in terms of debt and equity investments, and IAS #40	FS #25 deals with investments in other parties' securities, as well as investments acquired thru exchange for another asset, in cases where the investor does not possess significant influence or control over the other party. The standard outlines forms and types of investments according to their deadlines, inventory costs, changes in the book value of the investment,

(continued)

(continued)

#	IAS	FS
	replaced it when it comes to objects of investment. Therefore, IASC had abolished the provisions of IAS #25 dealing with annual financial statements that cover the period starting January 1, 2002. Note: IAS #25 has been changed by IAS #39 and IAS#40, 2001	disclosure, etc. Since IAS #39 (Financial Instruments: recognition and evaluation) and IAS #40 (Investments in Real Estate) are not adopted in the Federation, FS #25 was applied to all financial statements covering the period from January 1, 1999 until December 31, 2004.
27	IAS #27 deals with accounting procedures to be applied in case of preparing and presenting of consolidated financial statements for a group of business parties controlled by one central party, as well as in investments in subsidiaries in separate financial statements prepared by the central party (mother company or so).	The initially adopted text of FS #27 contained certain provisions of IAS #22 concerning the acquisition of subsidiaries. However, once FS #22 was adopted, these provisions were withdrawn, whereas the remaining ones were compliant to IAS #27. Some differences occurred when certain articles of IAS #27 were harmonized so as to follow the introduction of IAS #39.
28	IAS #28 (Investments in Associates) is about investing in parties in which the investor had acquired significant influence, but not control. In that case, the consolidated financial statements should be prepared for the joint company using the 'equity method', except in cases where the investment is acquired and held exclusively with a view to its disposal in the future. In such case, the cost method should be used.	FS #28 outlines only the equity method for calculations involving the joint legal entity. The provisions of IAS #28 that allow the cost method are omitted. Once IAS #39 was released, the section pertaining to items in separate financial statements, the cross-references in #28 were adjusted so as to point to #39 instead to #25. As IAS #39 is not adopted in the Federation, FS #28 still contains cross-reference to #25.
31	IAS #31 (Interests in Joint Ventures) applies in accounting for all interests in joint ventures and in statements of assets, liabilities, incomes and expenses of the joint venture, in financial statements of the venturer and the investor, regardless of the structure and form of joint activities. Financial statements of the venturer should contain information for their part of the venture, using one of the two possible methods for proportionate consolidation (the basic one), or the equity method (the allowed alternative).	FS #31 defines jointly controlled activities, and jointly controlled entities in joint ventures, that represent the contractual arrangement between the parties involved. According to FS #31, the venturer should report to their part of the venture using the proportionate consolidation method. The possibility of using the alternative (equity) method is not given. When IAS #39 was released, the sections pertaining cross-references to equity-statements and disclosure were corrected so as to point to IAS #39, instead of to #25. In the Federation, the cross-references still point to #25.

2. The differences between IAS and FS in Phase 2 (until the end of May 1998): Back then (in 1999), there were no significant deviations in the provisions of FS #9, #12, #15, #17, #30, #32, #33 and #34, and their IAS counterparts.
3. The differences between IAS and FS in Phase 3 (during 1999): Out of 7 FS adopted, three were partially changed (#26, #28 and #31). Standards #28 and #31 needed to be changed so as to reflect the changes that took place in their IAS counterparts. FS #16 was expanded so as to include certain provisions on amortization.
4. The differences between IAS and FS after January 1, 2000 until the end of 2004: There were seven new FS that were to be applied in financial statements covering the period from January 1, 2000 onward. These are: #19, #22, #26, #35, #36, #37 and #38.

The adoption of FS #38 (Intangible Assets) meant that FS #9 was to be put out of order. It (#9) only lasted for 1 year (1999).

The adoption of FS #22 (Mergers) abolished the provisions contained in articles 22–39 of FS #27, that were taken over from IAS #22. Also, FS #37 (Reserves) suspended a large number of provisions from FS #10 (article 3), whereas FS #35 (Cessation of Activities) had abolished several provisions of FS #8 (article 11–16).

Therefore, there were 31 accounting standards in force in the Federation, on January 1, 2000. All of them were mainly compliant with IAS in all important aspects. However, deviations emerged over the next 5 years (2000–2004), not only due to the IASB's release of three new standards (IAS #39, #40, #41) and two new IFRSs, but also because these standards affected other existing standards, causing changes in their provisions (IAS #25 was even completely withdrawn). The Federation did not follow these changes through, but it preserved the status quo.

1.5 Applying the New Law on Accounting and Audits in BiH

1.5.1 Main Features of the New Law on Accounting and Audits in BiH from January 1, 2005

The process of transition is finally completed with the adoption of this new law. At the very least, the reforms in this field will now be able to yield results in terms of creating a suitable environment for keeping up with the rest of the world when it comes to accounting and accounting legislation. The process of implementation is of course yet to come, and so is the practical application of IAS, and the education of personnel that will provide us with expert staff to support the implementation.

The new Law on Accounting and Audits of BiH consists of the following sections:

I – BASIC PROVISIONS
II – STANDARDS

III – STATE COMMISSION FOR ACCOUNTING AND AUDITING
IV – VOCATION AND QUALIFICATIONS
V – IMPLEMENTATION MEASURES IN ENTITIES AND IN THE DISTRICT
VI – TRANSITIONAL AND FINAL PROVISIONS

The above listed problems are tackled by this law as follows.

1.5.1.1 Basic Provisions

Basic provisions outline the following:

- Purpose and object of the Law on Accounting and Audits. This directly enables homogeneous application of the Law on the entire territory of BiH, i.e. in both entities – Federation and RS, and in the District of Brcko. This is seen in the following excerpt[7]: 'This Law defines mandatory standards in accounting and auditing, includes the Code of Ethics for Professional Accountants and Auditors, makes their application to the entire territory of BiH obligatory, stipulates uniform requirements for obtaining qualifications and implementation of training, tests, certification and licensing of professional accountants and auditors that is obligatory for the entire territory of BiH, and establishes the obligation of harmonizing of implementation and other regulations enforced in the Federation, Republika Srpska and the Brcko District with the provisions of this Law.'
- Stipulates the formation of an independent expert commission chaired by a foreign expert who is to be chosen by means of the appropriate Decision of the Council of Ministers of BiH. The main task of the commission is to ensure the harmonization with IASs, proper application of regulations and professional development.
- Offers definitions of terms used in the Law (IFAC-compliant),[8] which can be seen from the following excerpt: 'The terms used in this Law shall mean:

  (a) Accounting profession shall mean the profession that provides accounting, auditing and other related services in BiH

  (b) Commission shall mean independent expert commission for accounting and auditing in BiH, that is in charge of accounting and auditing standards and accompanying instructions and practices, such as: International Accounting Standards (IAS), International Standards in Financial Statements, accompanying instructions, explanations and guidelines issued by the International Accounting Standards Board (IASB), International Standards in Auditing (ISA), Code of ethics for professional accountants, accompanying instructions, explanations and guidelines issued by the International Federation of

---

[7] Official Gazette of BiH, #42/04, Law on Accounting and Audits, Basic Provisions.

[8] Official Gazette of BiH, #42/04, Law on Accounting and Audits, Basic Provisions, article 1, paragraph 2.

Accountants (IFAC), as well as standards and instructions, explanations, guidelines and principles issued by IFAC and IASB after the entry into force of this Law

(c) standards shall mean accounting standards and auditing standards, together with the accompanying instructions, explanations and guidelines, as well as principles of professional ethics that are binding for the accounting profession on the entire territory of BiH

(d) professional bodies shall mean non-governmental, voluntary and expert associations in BiH that are recognized as good professional accounting organizations, enjoying good reputation, and fulfilling the following criteria[9]:

(a) cooperation with the Commission on all issues regulated by this Law
(b) implementing of uniform programme for obtaining qualifications, certificates and licenses for performing of accounting services in BiH'

1.5.1.2 Standards

This section of the Law secures the transition to the direct application of IASs for the entire territory of BiH, which can be seen from the following excerpt: 'Accounting Standards and Auditing Standards'

1. Accounting standards that apply to the entire territory of BiH shall mean:

(a) International accounting standards (IAS), i.e. international financial reporting standards (IFRS)
(b) Accompanying instructions, explanations and guidelines issued by the International Accounting Standards Board (IASB)

2. Auditing Standards and principles of professional ethics for professional accountants and auditors that are to be applied to the entire territory of BiH shall mean:

(a) International standards in auditing (ISA)
(b) Code of ethics for professional accountants
(c) Accompanying instructions, explanations and guidelines issued by the International Federation of Accountants (IFAC)

3. Standards, as understood in this Article, shall also include standards, instructions, explanations, guidelines and principles adopted by IFAC and IASB after this Law has entered into force

4. Standards from this Law shall apply to any and all private and public enterprises and all legal entities seated in BiH

---

[9] Official Gazette of BiH, #42/04, Law on Accounting and Audits, Basic Provisions, Article 11.

5. Budgets, budget users and non-budgetary funds in BiH shall be excluded from the provisions of Article 4 and shall use and apply the existing accounting and financial reporting regulations for the Institutions of BiH, entities and the District, pending the introduction of international accounting standards for governments and other public entities.

1.5.1.3 State Commission for Accounting and Auditing

Formation of the independent Commission for accounting and auditing of BiH is a specific feature of this Law. The Commission will oversee the implementation of standards and other activities required under the law if such activities underlie the accounting profession or practice. This is how the Law describes the forming of the Commission and its competencies:

'Forming and Competences of the Commission[10]

1. This Law stipulates the establishment of the Commission that is to be formed by a special international advisor, who shall in turn be appointed by the Council of Ministers of BiH.
2. The Commission will perform the following activities:

   (a) Translate and publish standards, accompanying instructions, explanations and guidelines, as well as principles of professional ethics for accountants and auditors.
   (b) Define the criteria and the uniform programme for obtaining qualifications, education, training, testing, certification and licensing for the accounting profession. The programme is to be fully harmonized with IFAC standards and guidelines and applied to the entire territory of BiH. The implementation of the programme is to be secured in the entities and in the District.
   (c) Monitor the implementation of the uniform programme for obtaining qualifications in the accounting profession, as well as issue-binding instructions that are necessary for securing of homogenous and proper application of the programme in the entire territory of BiH, in cooperation with appropriate professional bodies and training providers.
   (d) Establish a uniform testing plan for accountants-to-be (candidates), and implement such single plan in the entire territory of BiH.
   (e) Monitor the certification process carried out by appropriate professional bodies, verify if the conditions are met in terms of previous training/knowledge, exams taken, formal education and practical experience and other mandatory requirements that apply in the entire territory of BiH.

---

[10] Official Gazette of BiH, #42/04, Law on Accounting and Audits, Basic Provisions, article 3, paragraphs 1 & 2.

(f) Monitor licensing and certification of members of the accounting profession.

(g) Initiate and coordinate activities for the establishment of a common professional body on the state level, should such body be voluntarily established within 6 months of the day this Law had entered into force.

(h) Hold meetings on a regular basis, dedicated to controlling of standards' application, implementation of the uniform programme for obtaining qualifications and other related issues.

(i) Prepare the annual information memo to be submitted to the Council of Ministers of BiH, containing the Commission's income and expenditures, and secure public availability of such document at latest by February each year'.

Other activities of the Commission include[11]:

'The Commission shall be responsible for recognizing or refusing to recognize a certain association as a professional body. Appropriate Terms of Reference (ToR) will be drafted to that end. The Commission will define cooperation in a manner that will provide for efficient implementation of the uniform programme of certification for the accounting profession.

The Commission will establish procedures for settling of disputes that arise from the Commission's decision to refuse recognizing an association as the professional body. The appeals will be lodged at the Court of Bosnia-Herzegovina.

Ethnic-, gender-, or geographical location-based discrimination in case of any and all associations, individual accountant or auditor on part of the Commission is considered illegal'.

This section of the Law regulates financing of the Commission and raising funds for professional development of accounting in BiH, in the following manner[12]:

'Reasonable costs caused as the result of Commission's activities shall under this Law be financed by means of contributions paid by professional bodies, exam fees paid by the candidates, possible international donors' support, and from other available sources. The amounts and criteria for professional bodies' contribution to the work of the Commission will be established by the Commission, in coordination with professional bodies.

The exam fees and other Commission's income will be:

(a) independent and separate from the Budget of BiH, entity budgets, and District Budget.

(b) possible to use only for performing of Commission's activities and developing of the accounting profession in BiH.'

---

[11] Official Gazette of BiH, #42/04, Law on Accounting and Audits, Basic Provisions, article 5.

[12] Official Gazette of BiH, #42/04, Law on Accounting and Audits, Basic Provisions, article 3, paragraphs 3 and 4.

Members of the Commission

Under this Law, the Commission has seven (7) members, all of whom come from the accounting profession, whereas[13]:

- Three (3) members come from the Federation of BiH
- Three (3) members come from RS
- One (1) member comes from the District of Brcko

Each member of the Commission is appointed upon the proposal of the professional body. The professional body is responsible for ensuring that the nominated member represents the body's members appropriately. Should the Commission receive a petition signed by 10% or more of members of any professional body, within 9 onths of the day this Law enters into force, a special international advisor will monitor repeated voting of members of such body, thus establishing which of the candidates have the support of the body, on the basis of the simple majority principle. Members of the Commission are given a 2-year mandate. Member of the Commission cannot be nominated for election, if he/she has already spent 4 years in a row as the member of the Commission.

1.5.1.4   Vocation and Qualifications

This section of the Law deals with vocations, testing, certification and licensing. The following vocations are thereby recognized and certified in the (entire) territory of BiH[14]:

(a) Certified accounting technician (CRT)
(b) Certified Accountant (CR) {*abbreviations are given in Bosnian*}
(c) Licensed auditor (OR)

Testing of candidates for vocations, issuing of certificates to the successful candidates and licensing (issuing of work permits) are performed as follows[15]:

(a) Testing of candidates for CRT, CR and OR is done by the Commission. Testing is performed based on the uniform programme that is applied to the entire territory of BiH, and that is fully compliant with IFAC standards and guidelines. The Commission may transfer administrative tasks related to the testing to one or multiple professional bodies, whereby the Commission shall closely monitor the execution of such activities, while the responsibility for drafting and performing of tests remains with the Commission.

---

[13] Official Gazette of BiH, #42/04, Law on Accounting and Audits, Basic Provisions, article 4, paragraphs 1 and 2.

[14] Official Gazette of BiH, #42/04, Law on Accounting and Audits, Basic Provisions, article 5, paragraph 1.

[15] Official Gazette of BiH, #42/04, Law on Accounting and Audits, Basic Provisions, article 5, paragraph 2.

(b) Issuing of certificates for CRT and CR is done by professional bodies, under the Commission's supervision. The OR certificates are issued by the Commission.
(c) Licensing of CRTs and CRs who provide independent accounting services to third parties is done by professional associations. Licensing is not done in cases of CRTs and CRs who perform accounting tasks for internal needs of their companies or other legal entities they work for. Licensing of ORs is done by the entities and the District. Auditing in BiH can only be done by individuals who possess an appropriate license issued in BiH. Auditing reports can only be submitted by companies that possess an appropriate license issued in BiH.

Any use of vocation or title by parties who are not certified as such under this Law, any offering or providing of independent accounting or auditing services to third parties by persons who are not licensed for such under this Law, is illegal.

This section of the Law deals with the issue of individuals who possess certificates for earlier obtained qualifications in this profession (their certificates are obtained in line with regulations that were applied earlier, before this Law entered into force). They will be re-qualified as follows[16]:

(a) Accounting Technician – accountant receives the title of Certified Accounting Technician (CRT)
(b) Independent Accountant – accountant receives the title of Certified Accountant (CA)
(c) Authorized Accountant – accountant receives the title of Certified Accountant (CA)
(d) Assistant Auditor – accountant receives the title of Certified Accountant (CA)
(e) Licensed Auditor – keeps the title of Licensed Auditor

Following the request of individuals holding any of the above listed former titles, the professional bodies will, within 6 months of the day this Law enters into force, issue new certificates (w/new title) to such individuals. If a particular professional body is unable to fulfill this request, then the Commission will arrange appropriate procedures for their members. The Commission will recommend a standard administrative fee (nominal amount), the collecting of which shall enable the associations to reimburse the administrative costs inflicted upon them by the implementation of this provision.

Individuals with former titles of Assistant Auditor shall receive the title of Certified Accountant only provided that they take a special course in advanced auditing policies, with a syllabus of at least 40 classes, and provided that they pass the final exam. The course and the final exam will be taken care of by the Association of Accountants and Auditors of RS, under Commission's supervision.

---

[16] Official Gazette of BiH, #42/04, Law on Accounting and Audits, Basic Provisions, article 5, paragraph 4.

Qualifications[17]

1. New candidates for professional titles under this law must meet the criteria with regards to their formal education, practical experience, training and testing, which will be defined by the Commission. The criteria will be compliant with IFAC standards and guidelines. The pertinent body – the Commission – will issue certificates based on evidence of eligibility (if all the criteria are met).
2. All accounting professionals, including the individuals who obtained their titles under this Law, must attend a continuing professional education programme, in accordance with the criteria set by the Commission. The programme's syllabus must include at least 120 hours of training, over a 3-years span.
3. Licenses issued prior to the entry into force of this Law will be recognized, provided that holders of such licenses fulfill the continuing education criteria. Following a request on the part of license-holders under this provision, the entities or the District will issue a new license, in accordance with this Law.

State-Level Programme for Obtaining Qualifications and Training[18]

1. The uniform programme for obtaining qualifications in the accounting profession will be applied on the state level, in the same fashion and under the same conditions to the entire territory of BiH.
2. The Commission will define the programme, in accordance with IFAC standards and guidelines. A key component of the programme will be the uniform process of testing and certification for the titles of CRT, CR and OR. Differences between the entities and the District in terms of the testing will not be tolerated.
3. The Commission will announce the programme within 3 months of its formation, at the latest.
4. The Commission is responsible for adopting and publishing changes to the programme, if and when the IFAC changes or amends its standards and guidelines.
5. Individuals looking to become accounting professionals in BiH after the entry into force of this Law can obtain titles under this Law only if they meet the criteria specified by one or multiple sections of the programme.
6. Apart from the conditions for testing and certification, the programme will contain the criteria to be met by the candidates, in terms of:

   (a) Formal education and experience required for a specific certification level
   (b) Appropriate familiarity with the legal framework and taxation system in BiH, to be proved through a written exam.

7. Training services for the candidates, compliant with the programme, are provided by private companies, professional bodies and educational institutions in

---

[17] Official Gazette of BiH, #42/04, Law on Accounting and Audits, Basic Provisions, Art. 6, paragraphs 1–3.
[18] Official Gazette of BiH, #42/04, Law on Accounting and Audits, Basic Provisions, article 7, paragraphs 1–9.

BiH who meet the Commission's criteria. Upon completion of training, the instructor will provide the attendees with certificates that will display the number of classes taken and the contents of the syllabus. Attending courses is not obligatory for the candidates, but taking the test as part of the programme is necessary for obtaining the certificate.

8. The exams will take place along the lines (plan) defined by the Commission, and under the same conditions for all individuals in BiH. Drafting of tests is done by the Commission, whereas the activities on test administration can be transferred to one or multiple professional bodies, under the Commission's supervision.

9. Continuing professional education will be included in the programme in accordance with the Commission's instructions, and it will be carried out by appropriate professional bodies.

Recognition of Foreign Qualifications

1. By the powers vested in the Commission under this Law, the Commission will certify the individuals who obtained their qualifications outside of BiH, provided that such individuals submit proof of compliance with IFAC criteria for the education they received in the country that issued their certificate. They must also submit evidence of formal education, practical experience and familiarity with legislation and the taxation system of BiH, as outlined in the programme.

2. The Commission will define the conditions and procedures for certification of individuals from paragraph 1 of this article, within 6 months of the day this Law enters into force.

Mutual Recognition of Qualifications within BiH

1. All individuals holding a title acquired under this Law are entitled to the recognition of their title in the entire territory of BiH, without having to fulfill any additional requirements.

2. All individuals holding a title acquired under this Law are entitled to provide services listed in their certificate in the entire territory of BiH, without having to fulfill any additional requirements.

3. Completed audits and auditing reports will be recognized in the entire territory of BiH, without being subject to fulfillment of additional requirements.

4. The body authorized for issuing of licenses is considered to act in violation of the Law, should it refuse to license an eligible and certified candidate due to the fact that the candidate or his qualifications come from a certain entity or from the District, as well as any other type of additional condition-setting that is not stipulated by the letter of this Law.

5. The audits will be performed by auditing companies licensed in accordance with pertinent entity laws on accounting and audits. All auditing companies that are licensed in accordance with entity- or District laws, are entitled to provide auditing services listed in their license on the entire territory of BiH, without being subject to fulfilling additional requirements.

1.5.1.5   Implementation Measures in Entities
and in the District

Obligations of the Entities and of the District

1. Within 3 months of the day this Law enters into force, the entities and the District will undertake all necessary measures to implement it. All implementation bylaws in entities and in the District, as well as all other relevant laws and bylaws dealing with issues pertinent to this Law, will be adjusted so as to comply with this Law. Entity- and District laws on accounting will establish a uniform financial statements form and uniform forms of other accounting documents.
2. All individuals who provide independent accounting services are required to be certified and licensed under this Law. The implementation bylaws in entities and in the District will define the cessation of obligation to hold a certificate for accountants and financial assistants who provide accounting, bookkeeping and tax-related services to the companies they work for.

Recognition of Professional Bodies

Professional bodies in BiH must:

(a) Cooperate with the Commission
(b) Implement a uniform programme for obtaining qualifications, certificates and licenses in the accounting field in BiH

1.5.1.6   Transitional and Final Provisions

Special International Advisor

1. The Council of Ministers of BiH will appoint a special international advisor, skilled and experienced, in the field of accounting and auditing.
2. Within 6 months after the day this Law enters into force, the special international advisor will perform the following activities and tasks, respecting the order given hereunder:

   (a) Draft the Statute, action plan and internal Rulebook of the Commission
   (b) Draft the Code of Ethics for the Commission and the accounting profession
   (c) Coordinate the election of Commission members nominated by the professional bodies

3. The special international advisor will carry out the duties of the Commission's Director for the period of 6 months starting from the day the other members are elected. He/she can be kept for another 6 months as the special advisor to the Commission, if the Commission so decides, by majority vote.
4. Once the mandate of the special international advisor expires, all changes to the Statute and existing bylaws will be made only by unanimous decision of the Commission's seven members. All individuals who started their training

before this Law entered into force, are entitled to finish their training in accordance with entity- or District laws that were applicable when they started the training, provided that they complete the training within 1 year of the day this Law entered into force. Standards from article 2 of this Law will apply to financial statements covering the period from January 1, 2004 and on.

Entry into Force

This Law enters into force 8 days after being published in the Official Gazette of BiH, i.e. as of September 18, 2004.

1.5.2   Implementing the New Law on Accounting and Audits

Legal obligations and application of the new Law on Accounting and Auditing[19] are not properly taken care of, even though it should have happened as of January 1, 2005.

The Law on Accounting and Audits of BiH establishes mandatory standards in accounting and auditing, including the Code of Ethics for professional accountants and auditors, all of which are binding on the entire territory of BiH. Such standards are for example the IFRS and the accompanying instructions, explanations and guidelines issued by IASB.

According to the Law, the application of international standards is binding for all private and public enterprises and other legal entities (banks and other financial institutions, insurance companies, profit- and non-profit organizations, funds and associations) seated in BiH. The only exception are legal entities from the public sector such as the budgets, budget users and non-budgetary funds, that will apply the existing regulations of BiH institutions, entities and the District in the field of accounting, pending the introduction of the special international public sector accounting standards (IPSAS).

If we take a look at the legal entities in the EU, but only those appearing on the stock market since January 1, 2005, they are obliged to apply the IAS/IFRS, but there are only 7,000 such entities in the entire EU. In other words, there are millions of legal entities that are not obliged to apply the IAS/IFRS.

Most probably, it is not realistic to expect that all legal entities in BiH will have their statements harmonized with IAS in the upcoming balancing period (2005), as it was envisaged by the new Law on accounting and audits. There is obviously a difference in approach to IAS here and in the EU. Therefore, it is quite understandable to raise the issue of companies that do not appear in the stock market, and that are being obliged to respect the IAS, unlike their European counterparts. It is to be expected that companies do not meet the IAS requirements for preparing of financial statements, either because they do not want to, or they are not able to.

---

[19] Official Gazette of BiH, #42/04, Law on Accounting and Audits.

Such expectations are supported by the fact that ever since 1999, a huge number of companies did not respect these obligations, even though they were technically supposed to. As the tasks of the Taxation Authority do not include (and should not include) monitoring of the application of accounting standards, the behavior of the companies was never sanctioned in any way. The biggest thing that could happen to a company would be for them to be warned of not applying certain financial standards in an audit report. Having in mind that in BiH, the audits are only mandatory in shareholders' associations, it is easy to understand how poorly represented the monitoring of financial standard application is.

Besides, some provisions of certain tax regulations were contrary to the accounting standards, and the companies would rather avoid violation of the taxation rules (otherwise they would be subject to sanctions) than apply the accounting standards, even though they offered a better picture of the financial situation, and they were generally more suitable. Surveys even proved that smaller companies would usually have both records prepared, one for accounting purposes, and one for taxation purposes.

There is also the problem of translating and explaining the standards, as this material is pretty large in volume and uses complex and demanding terminology. Therefore, the standards were hard to comprehend, especially for accountants in small companies, who avoided even reading them, not to mention applying them. The conclusion is, without detailed explanations of IAS and methods and possibilities of their application, together with a continuing education on this sense, the problem with the lack of application will remain as present as ever.

Due to all of the above, we believe that the possible scenario for the upcoming period, in terms of the reform of accounting and auditing and the application of IAS, could be as follows:

- A huge number of 'LTD/LCC' companies (w/limited liabilities (*'d.o.o.'* in *Bosnian*) will either continue to avoid applying the IAS or they will apply it partially and occasionally.
- The holding (shareholders' associations – *'d.d.'* in *Bosnian*) will probably apply the IAS, fearing the audits, and so will some of LTDs that are fully or partially owned by foreign parties.
- Only a stronger professional development, before all through non-governmental professional associations, and in cooperation with educational institutions in the country, will over a certain period of time enable a higher rate of implementation of standards, thus resulting in higher reliability of financial statements in BiH.
- The role of the Commission will be extremely important throughout this process. The pace of reforming processes in the country will depend on their decisions and the implementation thereof.

1.6 Conclusion

The initial attempts to reform accounting in BiH were made in 1998 and 1999. These implied not only the transformation of state-owned property into privately owned property, as one of the most important reforms (privatization of companies) and the shift to a market economy, but also a whole series of other auxiliary reforms, including the reform of accounting. The latter should enable BiH to open up to the world, using a modern internationally recognized approach to recording of business developments and modern international methods of reporting that will reduce the feeling of risk on the part of international investors as much as possible, allowing them to feel at ease with investing their capital or providing credit in the BiH economy (an economy that is undergoing a development process, a transition process and in which market economy principles were so far unknown).

As the role of accounting and accountants in the market economy is quite an important one, especially in terms of the quality of financial statements, and the capability of providing assistance in maximizing of profits in contemporary business environments, the entire process was taken very seriously, and it was run under the close eye of the international community. The process was twofold: on one hand, legislation was drafted to secure the opening to the world through adoption of IAS, and on the other hand, education of both educators and accountants/auditors was initiated, aiming to end up with certified accountants that will constantly be re-educated in accordance with international standards (i.e. to ensure having quality personnel, trained to respond to current circumstances).

However, time has shown that the decision to implement domestic standards in the transitional period was a bad one, even though they were drafted on the basis of IAS standards. Domestic institutions were not too eager in harmonizing between the existing standards and the new ones, or in reflecting the changes that took place. Therefore, the gap between Federation Standards and IAS only kept growing, while the financial statements kept losing in terms of quality. With all this in mind, the new Law was adopted that requires direct transition to IAS/IFRS application.

The direct application of IAS to the entire territory of BiH should solve not only the problem of having internationally recognized financial statements, but it should also tackle the internal issue of the uniform certification process and uniform education in this field, all based on world-wide recognized standards and practices.

Nevertheless, having in mind that there were many difficulties in applying the accounting standards in both of the entities, especially in terms of understanding, interpreting and practical application thereof (in statements and audits), special attention needs to be given to education in this field. The process of certification and continuing education according to international standards should provide for further development of this profession. The said process has gone quite far already, but it is still not fully compliant with international standards. The adoption of the new law generated important preconditions for the representatives of the accounting profession in BiH to prove to the rest of the world that our education system includes international plans and programmes suitable for experts in this field to upgrade their knowledge. The independent testing that will take place in parallel with the education process should secure the adoption not only of IAS, but also of international reporting and management practices, and it should include both the present members of the accounting profession and the future ones.

References

Accounting. Standards of RS.

Bosnjak, Z. Compilation of Studies, 7th International Symposium, Accountants' Association of the Federation of Bosnia and Herzegovina.

Gazette of the Federation of Bosnia and Herzegovina, #50/98, #52/99 and #54/00.

Official Gazette of Bosnia and Herzegovina, #42/04, Law on Accounting and Audits, Basic Provisions.

ROSC – see http://www.worldbank.org/ifa/rosc

Chapter 2
Converting Enterprise Accounting Systems in Emerging Economies: A Case Study of Bosnia*

Robert W. McGee and Senad Pekmez

2.1 Introduction

This chapter discusses the process being used in Bosnia to convert the books of Bosnian enterprises so that they will comply with the new Bosnian accounting standards, which are identical to International Accounting Standards. Bosnian accountants were generally not familiar with the new rules, since most practicing accountants did not study them at the university. So the conversion process had to start by educating Bosnian accountants in the new rules. This process began with a series of seminars, followed by on-site visits to enterprises. Audit firms also had to be trained so that they would be able to audit the books of the enterprises. The process used to accomplish this task is similar in some respects to the process United States Agency for International Development (USAID) used in its other accounting reform projects. But the Bosnian case is also different in some important respects.

The USAID, EU-TACIS, the World Bank, and other groups have funded accounting reform projects in Eastern Europe, the CIS, and other parts of the world for several decades. Accounting reform projects have taken place in several African countries, Belarus (Sucher and Kemp, 1998; Pankov, 1998); Poland (Adams and McMillan, 1997; Jermakowicz and Rinke, 1996; Rolfe and Doupnik, 1995); the Czech Republic (Jermakowicz and Rinke, 1996; Rolfe and Doupnik, 1995); Hungary (Jermakowicz and Rinke, 1996; Rolfe and Doupnik, 1995); Uzbekistan, Turkmenistan, Kyrgyzstan, and Tajikistan (Crallan, 1997); Kazakhstan; Madagascar (Berry and Holzer, 1993); and Armenia (McGee, 1999b). In recent years there has been an increasing focus on accounting reform in developing and newly industrialized countries (Wallace, 1993; Larson and Kenny, 1996).

---

* An earlier version of this chapter was published in *Research in Accounting in Emerging Economies, Volume 6, Supplement 2: Accounting and Accountability in Emerging and Transition Economies*, 81–89 (2004).

R. W. McGee
Florida International University

S. Pekmez
KPMG, Bosnia

R. W. McGee (ed.), *Accounting Reform in Transition and Developing Economies*,
© Springer Science+Business Media LLC 2008

33

The main reason why these countries perceive a need to reform their accounting systems is so that they can attract badly needed foreign capital. They have to compete for capital with more than 100 other countries, and it is correctly perceived that international investors will not seriously consider investing in their country if the financial statements their companies publish are not credible to an international audience. This is where International Accounting Standards (IAS) come in. The adoption of IAS and their use in financial statements give instant credibility to a company's financial statements and also make them more intelligible to financial statement readers from other countries. Although it would be possible to adopt some other set of accounting standards, IAS is the only really internationally recognized set of standards. All other standards are either local or regional, at best.

Although the specifics vary depending on political and cultural differences and the strengths and knowledge set of the individuals conducting the reforms, there are some common threads that run through most or all accounting reform projects. For example, the early stage of most or all of the reforms involves helping the country in question adopt International Accounting Standards (IAS) and International Standards on Auditing (ISA), since at least partial adoption of these standards is necessary before other segments of the accounting reform project can proceed (McGee, 1999b).

There is also usually an effort to educate practicing accountants in the new accounting and auditing rules. This phase of the reform project has several aspects. Since most emerging economies either do not have any accounting associations in the private sector, or have private sector accounting organizations that are financially weak and perhaps lacking in direction, the private contractor that lands a USAID or other accounting reform contract is usually charged with the task of creating or strengthening accounting associations (Anon, 1999 [Ukraine]; Scopes, 1999 [Macedonia]; Kenzenkovic and Salihovic-Galijasevic, 1999 [Bosnia]). These associations are generally referred to as self-regulating organizations (SROs), and the existence of such organizations is essential if the private sector accounting profession is to prosper. Under the old, centrally planned systems, existing private institutions were destroyed and new ones were not permitted to be formed, so that the central planning authority would have a monopoly on control of economic activity. A market economy requires dispersion of control. Thus, part of most accounting reform projects involves institution building so that economic power can be more decentralized.

Funding and technical assistance are usually provided as a matter of course to ensure that these SROs are able to perform the functions that accounting associations in the developed world have been performing for years. The American Institute of Certified Public Accountants (AICPA) model or some variation of it is sometimes used as the starting point if the accounting reform project is USAID funded. The national SRO is aided in providing continuing professional education to its members. Various committees are formed, including an education committee and an ethics committee. Assistance is provided with instruction, training and the translation and publication of materials. However, the AICPA model is not always used, especially if the project is funded by a non-US entity, since such entities are both unfamiliar with the AICPA model and also prefer to create SROs that are structured more along the lines of the private accounting associations in their own country.

Another aspect of SRO development is professional certification. Certification of accountants and auditors is generally a governmental function in emerging economies, since centrally planned economies try to control everything. One aim of accounting reform projects is usually to shift at least a portion of that function to the private sector (McGee, 1999a, c) so that economic power will be less concentrated and so that a private sector institutional framework can be allowed to emerge and grow. In the USA, the AICPA, a private accounting organization, creates the certification exam and distributes it to the various state organizations, which administer the exam. AICPA then grades the exams and releases the scores to the state groups. The national SROs are encouraged to take on similar responsibilities, to the extent possible, although the various Finance Ministries and legislatures usually have to agree to the transfer of authority and administration. A model based upon the AICPA model is being proposed in Bosnia.

When a country adopts IAS and ISA, there is a need to teach the new rules to university students. Usually, the existing curriculum does not adequately prepare students for the new world of accounting they will face upon graduation, so the accounting reform project is charged with the task of helping the universities implement a new curriculum that adequately covers the new rules that their government has adopted. That usually means that texts have to be translated into the local language and professors have to be trained so that they will be able to convey the new information to their students. International Federation of Accountants (IFAC) Guideline No. 9 is often used as the basis for determining what the new accounting curriculum should look like (Needles et al., 2001).

Another aspect of most accounting reform projects is to provide training for users of financial statements, auditors, tax inspectors, and enterprise financial managers. A related but separate task is to help private enterprises convert their existing accounting systems to conform to IAS. It is this last task that is addressed in this article, using the USAID experience in Bosnia as a case study.

2.2   Political and Cultural Issues

Before the task of helping enterprises convert their accounting systems to comply with IAS can be discussed, it is necessary to address a few words about the political and cultural atmosphere in which Bosnian accountants work. Bosnia has a unique set of political and cultural factors that must be taken into consideration. A cookie-cutter approach to accounting reform might work in some countries, especially countries that are ethnically homogeneous, but such an approach would be a disaster in Bosnia, which consists of three ethnic groups who either hate or distrust each other. Cultural and political considerations play a crucial role in Bosnia's accounting reform process. Failure to take into account the unique situation in Bosnia would be a major mistake.

Bosnia – actually Bosnia and Herzegovina, but we will call it Bosnia for the sake of brevity – was one of Yugoslavia's six republics until the early 1990s, when several republics attempted to secede. Slovenia and Croatia seceded first, in June 1991 (Burg and Shoup, 1999, p. 69; Glenny, 1996, pp. 62–97). Their secession triggered a war. Bosnia declared independence in April 1992 (Dempsey and Fontaine, 2001, p. 87), triggering a longer and bloodier war. The Bosnian war ended with the Dayton Peace Accord, a document that has been both praised (Daalder, 2000) and criticized (Dempsey, 1998; Dempsey and Fontaine, 2001, pp. 85–121; Bandow, 2000, p. 35; Wilson, 1998).

But the situation is not so simple. The Croats and Muslims were not only fighting Serbs. Between 1992 and 1994 they were also fighting each other (Silber and Little, 1997, pp. 291–302). The war resulted in many personal tragedies (Sudetic, 1998) and also many stories of personal courage and kindness in the face of tragedy (Manuel, 1996). There were also many atrocities (Glenny, 1996, p. 182).

Before the war, the country consisted of 17% Roman Catholic Croats, 31% Eastern Orthodox Serbs, and 44% Bosniak Muslims (Dempsey and Fontaine, 2001, p. 87). The Croat part of the country wanted to merge with Croatia. The Serbian part of Bosnia wanted to merge with Serbia. The Bosniak Muslims wanted to maintain a single, multiethnic state (Dempsey and Fontaine, 2001, p. 87).

More than half of Bosnia's 4.4 million people were uprooted from their homes during the war (Kirking, 1999, p. 54; Zimmerman, 1999, p. 224). Nearly 300,000 people were killed between 1991 and 1995 in the various Yugoslav wars (Holbrooke, 1998, p. xv). The West has been criticized for allowing the slaughter to take place for several years before intervening (Rieff, 1995). America's last ambassador to the former Yugoslavia has stated that the failure to use air power early in the conflict prolonged the war by 3 years (Zimmerman, 1999, p. 232).

Post-war Bosnia is a multiethnic state having three ethnic groups and consisting of two separate entities. The Federation of Bosnia and Herzegovina (FBiH) comprises 51% of the total land area as a result of the Dayton Accord (Zimmerman, 1999, p. 233; Holbrooke, 1998, pp. 302–312) and consists of Roman Catholic Croats, who live mostly in Herzegovina, and Sunni Muslim Bosniaks, who live mostly in Bosnia. Orthodox Christian Serbs, who comprise less than 25% of the postwar population (Malcolm, 1996, p. 253), live mostly in the Republic of Srpska (RS), which accounts for the other 49% of the country's land area. However, the ethnic mix is more complicated than that.

For several generations before the war there were many mixed marriages (Rieff, 1995, pp. 73, 80), about 27% by one count (Bringa, 1995, p. 151), so it is not always easy to classify many people neatly into one ethnic group or another. One of the senior professors at the largest university in the country was born in Croatia but his father was Slovenian and his mother was Serbian. The bartender at one of our favorite restaurants in Sarajevo has a Muslim mother and a Roman Catholic father who died defending Sarajevo, which is now a Muslim city. Many of the people who work with the USAID Accounting Reform project have relatives from three or more of the six former Yugoslav republics. Such ethnic mixes are typical.

However, many of the people identify with one of the three main ethnic groups more strongly than with the others. Therein lies the source of the difficulty. Memories of the recent war are still firmly etched into the minds of the people, many of whom suffered greatly. People from one ethnic group are often apprehensive about working closely with individuals from other ethnic groups. There is also strong hesitation about voting for someone from one of the other ethnic groups. ". . . the vast majority of Bosnia's Muslims, Serbs and Croats still will not vote for each other's political candidates." (Dempsey and Fontaine, 2001, p. 85). In one poll, 85% of the Bosnians (which included Muslims, Catholics, and Orthodox Christians) surveyed said they would not vote for someone from one of the other ethnic groups (Dempsey and Fontaine, 2001, p. 92). As a result, there are strong voting blocs. Whichever group has the largest plurality in a given community tends to get the most votes.

One reason for the apprehension about voting for members of another ethnic group is because Serbs do not want to vote for Muslims. But Bosnia is probably the most secular Muslim country in the world (Zimmerman, 1999, p. 211). The threat that Samuel Huntington envisioned in his best-selling book, *The Clash of Civilizations* (1996) seems least likely to become reality in Bosnia.

2.2.1   Current Training

Because of the ethnic mix and the tensions that still persist, Bosnia really has two accounting reform programs, one in the Muslim and Croat Federation of Bosnia and Herzegovina (FBiH) and one in the Republika Srpska (RS), the Serbian part of the country. Both entities have their own legislatures and their lawmakers are not hesitant to enact different sets of laws, including accounting and auditing laws.

Although the goals of both programs are the same, and the methods used to achieve the goals are similar, two different groups of people have been selected to implement the accounting reforms. One group is headquartered in Sarajevo, which is the capital of both FBiH and Bosnia and Herzegovina (BiH), which includes the Republic of Srpska. The two accounting experts chosen to lead the conversion effort there are both Muslim. The other group is in Banja Luka, the capital of the RS. One of the two accounting experts leading the conversion effort there is a Serb. The other is a Hungarian who has had accounting reform experience in 11 other countries.

2.3   Converting Enterprise Accounting Systems

Both entities within Bosnia – FbiH and RS – are well-advanced in adopting IAS and ISA. The focus at this stage of the accounting reform is implementation of the reforms at the enterprise level. The enterprises in Bosnia still keep their books based on the system that existed before IAS and ISA were adopted. Those books have to be converted to be in compliance with the rules their country has recently adopted.

One of the initial problems to be overcome is to educate the accountants who work at those enterprises in the new rules. They never learned IAS and ISA in school and, until recently, there were no books or study materials available in their languages – Bosnian, Croatian, and Serbian – for them to refer to. So the first step in the conversion process was to create accounting materials that enterprise accountants could read, so they could learn the new rules and how to apply them.

The remainder of this section will discuss the approach to conversion training that took place in the FbiH. Training in the RS was slightly different, since the RS has slightly different accounting rules and a slightly different chart of accounts. Because of these differences, the training manuals used in the RS were custom-made for RS accountants, and were written by a different person than the individual who wrote the FbiH training manual. Training in the FbiH started sooner and was conducted by the two Muslims who were in charge of this aspect of the project. Training in the RS was delayed for many months for political reasons that we will not go into here, and was conducted by Serbs, for the most part, with a Hungarian thrown in for good measure. Training in both parts of the country is still in process, so a complete report cannot be given until a later time.

The accounting materials used for training in the FbiH consisted of a 220-page manual that gave an overview and comments on the new accounting standards, and another manual that dealt with the application and contents of the new Chart of Accounts that is used in FbiH. During the last 4 months of 2001 the two-person conversion team conducted a total of four 3-day seminars in Tuzla, Sarajevo, Zenica, and Mostar, all cities in the FbiH. The seminars were attended by more than 150 accountants from more than 60 enterprises. All participants received the training materials. Participants were asked to fill out evaluation forms at the end of the seminar, which were later collated and reviewed by the seminar leaders.

The evaluations showed that the participants were generally satisfied with the seminar. The training material was generally at the right level for them, neither too difficult nor too easy. The seminar material got very high grades for usefulness. About 40% of the material was new for the average participant, although 100% of the material was new for some of the respondents, a fact that indicates there was a great need for the seminar. The length of the seminar (3 days) was usually considered to be about right, neither too long nor too short. The 3-day length was chosen partly because it was thought that a longer seminar would draw fewer participants.

High marks were also given for various aspects of the presentation – visual equipment, the manner of presentation, the quality of the handouts, organization of the seminar, quality of the meeting facility, etc. The highest marks were given for the questions "Would you recommend this seminar to a colleague?" and "Would you attend another seminar presented by our organization?"

The fact that participants thought highly of the seminar and the seminar leaders was very important because the same two individuals who conducted the seminars also were assigned the task of visiting the enterprises to help them convert their books. The conversion process was conducted in two phases. During the first phase, the two individuals who led the seminar visited 11 enterprises. The visit to each enterprise lasted 3 days. By the time these visits were completed, a certain pattern began to emerge. It was found that companies tended to have the same difficulties, so future visits could be structured to anticipate these difficulties.

The two main difficulties they tended to have were how to allocate costs and how to get volume up to the break-even point. Participants did not have much of a problem understanding how to compute a breakeven point. The problem was that their companies were operating below that point. They wanted to know how to expand sales and tap into new markets so that they could achieve profitability. The other problem that kept coming up was that companies had a tendency to allocate all costs into the cost of their inventory, including selling and administrative costs, which did not belong there. As a result of this decision, it was difficult to make intelligent pricing decisions.

During the second phase of the conversion process, the two seminar leaders became team leaders. They started to work with eight FbiH audit firms. One of the eight audit firms was selected to perform the conversion at each of the other enterprises. The team leaders guided them through the process a few times so that the people at the eight audit firms would receive guided training in performing conversions. The reason for this approach was so that some FbiH audit firms would receive the training they would need to perform future audits. The various Bosnian private accounting associations were not able to provide this training because they did not have the expertise to guide the audit firms through the conversion process. But the team leaders did have the expertise because they created the training material for the initial seminars; they conducted the seminars and performed more than ten conversions themselves before training the audit firms to do it. At the conclusion of each conversion the audit firm prepared a report, which consisted of the following three parts:

1. General picture and history of the enterprise.
2. A discussion of accounting issues – accounting policies, review and recommendations, application of the new Chart of Accounts and correction entries, application of basic accounting principles in accordance with FbiH accounting standards (IAS), recommendations, etc.
3. Notes and conclusions.

The audit reports revealed some interesting facts. About 60% of the enterprises had intangible assets and had done the initial valuation properly. Of that group, about half amortized using the straight-line method. The other half did not amortize them. A small portion of the enterprises revalued intangibles if the price index increased by more than 10% per year since the last revaluation. Enterprises also tended to revalue their tangible assets if the price index increased by more than 10% annually since their last revaluation.

About 80% of the converted enterprises did not have research and development costs. Of those who did, the vast majority treated them as period costs. Enterprises did not have any goodwill or negative goodwill on their books. Almost all enterprises used the straight-line method to depreciate their tangible assets. The rules for impairment of assets were generally not followed, although some enterprises wrote down assets before the December 31, 2000 implementation date for their impairment of assets standard. Only about 20% of the enterprises recognized contingent assets or liabilities. The other 80% either did not have them or did not know what they were.

Practically none of the enterprises used the correct method to account for inventories. Although many of the enterprises adopted the lower of cost or market principle, they often did not apply it. Many accountants did not understand what net realizable value was. A small minority used an appropriate absorption costing system for their inventories. The vast majority of enterprises used a full costing system that loaded too many costs into the inventories. While such a system was perfectly acceptable under the old, central planning model, the new Bosnian rule for inventory, which is identical to the IAS on inventory, does not permit such a practice. Correcting journal entries were made to eliminate this problem.

Nearly half of the enterprises did not have any method for dealing with doubtful receivables. Firms tend to write-off doubtful accounts only after some court action because the tax law frowns on writing then off before a court action. About 20% of the enterprises did not know what an extraordinary item was. Other enterprises do not have extraordinary items. There was a tendency to include extraordinary items with other items of income and expense.

More than half of the enterprises did not have any leases. Of those that did, there was a tendency not to recognize financing leases because of a lack of understanding of the present value of money concept. Accountants did not know how to calculate the value of a financing lease, which is understandable, since the accounting materials they had in their university program did not include this topic. The treatment of borrowing costs was also a problem, since accountants were not familiar with the concept.

2.4   Concluding Comments

The conversion of enterprise books served a valuable function by upgrading the firms' books to comply with Bosnian accounting standards, which are the same as International Accounting Standards. The majority of enterprises had continued to apply the old accounting rules, which were replaced officially by new Bosnian/ International standards a few years before. Enterprise accountants who were not familiar with the new rules became familiar with them.

The conversion process served as an educational experience, both for the enterprise accountants and for the local audit firms that walked them through the conversion process. Mistakes that enterprise accountants had been making for years were corrected and the quality of enterprise books were upgraded, substantially in some cases, to comply with the standards the Bosnian government adopted a few years before.

The audit firms conducting the conversions recommended that the enterprises draft and adopt new bylaws that conform to the new rules their country adopted. The conversion team and audit firms provided enterprises with written guidelines from the accounting standards to help them make the necessary changes. The audit firms and conversion teams also assisted with making the necessary correcting entries so that the enterprises could properly apply the new Chart of Accounts.

Now that the conversion process is well underway, many Bosnian enterprises will be able to issue financial statements that have more credibility in international capital markets. FBiH now has several audit firms that are sufficiently trained to perform audits that meet international standards and expectations. It would not be fair to compare the expertise of those audit firms to the expertise of audit firms in Western Europe and America, but it also is not necessary to have the same level of expertise. Bosnian enterprises have no pension plans or financial derivatives, so there is no need to know how to account for such things at the moment.

One problem that Bosnian accountants and enterprises will have to face in the near future is how to account for joint ventures, share ownership, parent subsidiary relationships, etc. The Sarajevo stock exchange has opened for business and Bosnian enterprises must be able to clearly disclose their ownership structure. As of now, Bosnian accountants do not know how to construct consolidated financial statements. The 3-day seminar did not provide any instruction on this topic, since there were so many other, basic items that were in more urgent need of discussion. But the time is coming when Bosnian accountants will have to be able to construct consolidated financial statement and related footnotes that will meet stock exchange requirements.

It will take several years before the average Bosnian accountant will be as well-trained as accountants in Western Europe and USA. The accounting curriculum at Bosnian universities consisted of just two or three accounting courses, which is all anyone needed under the old system. Complying with the new Bosnian accounting standards will require the same level of training that accountants in Western Europe and USA receive.

All eight Bosnian universities are now in the process of upgrading their curriculum to meet IFAC and UNCTAD guidelines so that their graduates will be able to attain this level of expertise. Texts are being translated into the local language and professors are being trained to teach the new curriculum. Practicing accountants are to become exposed to the new rules through continuing education programs and instructors are being trained to lead these CPE seminars. Training is still in the early stages but it has begun.

References

Adams, Carol A. and Katarzyna M. McMillan (1997). Internationalizing Financial Reporting in a Newly Emerging Market Economy: The Polish Example. *Advances in International Accounting*, 10, 139–164.

Anonymous. (1999). Setting Up Shop in the Former Soviet Union. *Association Management*, 51(4), 105.

Bandow, Doug (2000). NATO's Hypocritical Humanitarianism. In Ted Galen Carpenter (ed.), *NATO's Empty Victory*, pp. 31–47, Washington, DC, The Cato Institute.

Berry, Maureen and Peter Holzer (1993). Restructuring the Accounting Function in the Third World: Madagascar's Approach. *Research in Third World Accounting*, 2, 225–244.

Bringa, Tone (1995). *Being a Muslim the Bosnian Way*, Princeton, NJ, Princeton University Press.

Burg, Steven L. and Paul S. Shoup (1999). *The War in Bosnia-Herzegovina: Ethnic Conflict and International Intervention*, Armonk, NY/London, M.E. Sharpe.

Crallan, Jocelyne (1997). Accounting Reform in the CIS, *Management Accounting* (January), p. 34.

Daalder, Ivo H. (2000). *Getting to Dayton: The Making of America's Bosnia Policy*, Washington, DC, The Brookings Institution.

Dempsey, Gary (1998). Rethinking the Dayton Peace Agreement: Bosnia Three Years Later, Cato Institute Policy Analysis No. 327. December 14.

Dempsey, Gary T. and Roger W. Fontaine (2001). *Fool's Errands: America's Recent Encounters with Nation Building*, Washington, DC, The Cato Institute.

Glenny, Misha (1996). *The Fall of Yugoslavia: The Third Balkan War*, New York, Penguin Books.

Holbrooke, Richard (1998). *To End a War*, New York, The Modern Library.

Huntington, Samuel P. (1996). *The Clash of Civilizations: Remaking the World Order*, New York, Simon & Schuster.

Jermakowicz, Eva and Dolores F. Rinke (1996). The New Accounting Standards in the Czech Republic, Hungary, and Poland vis-à-vis International Accounting Standards and European Union Directives. *Journal of International Accounting, Auditing and Taxation*, 5(1), 73–88.

Kenzenkovic, Kevin and Nedzida Salihovic-Galijasevic (1999). Association Building in Bosnia and Herzegovina. *Public Management*, 81(4), 21–23.

Kirking, Gale A. (1999). *Untangling Bosnia and Herzegovina: A Search for Understanding*, Madison, WI, Real World Press.

Larson, Robert K. and Sara York Kenny (1996). Accounting Standard-Setting Strategies and Theories of Economic Development: Implications for the Adoption of International Accounting Standards. *Advances in International Accounting*, 9, 1–20.

Malcolm, Noel. (1996). *Bosnia: A Short History*, New York, New York University Press.

Manuel, David. (1996). *Bosnia: Hope in the Ashes*, Brewster, MA, Paraclete Press.

McGee, Robert W. (1999a). Certification of Accountants and Auditors in the CIS: A Case Study of Armenia. *Journal of Accounting, Ethics & Public Policy*, 2(2), 338–353.

McGee, Robert W. (1999b). The Problem of Implementing International Accounting Standards: A Case Study of Armenia. *Journal of Accounting, Ethics & Public Policy*, 2(1), 38–41.

McGee, Robert W. (1999c). International Certification of Accountants in the CIS: A Case Study of Armenia. *Journal of Accounting, Ethics & Public Policy*, 2(1), 70–75.

Needles, Belverd E., Jr., Karen Cascini, Tatiana Krylova and Mohamed Moustafa. (2001). Strategy for Implementation of IFAC International Education Guideline No. 9: "Prequalification Education, Tests of Professional Competence and Practical Experience of Professional Accountants." *Journal of International Financial Management & Accounting*, 12(3), 317–353.

Pankov, Dmitri. (1998). Accounting for Change in Belarus. *Management Accounting* (London), 76(10), 56–58.

Rieff, David. (1995). *Slaughterhouse: Bosnia and the Failure of the West*, New York, Simon & Schuster.

Rolfe, Robert J. and Timothy S. Doupnik. (1995). Accounting Revolution in East Central Europe. *Advances in International Accounting*, 8, 223.

Scopes, Gary M. (1999). Mission Practically Impossible. *Association Management*, 51(8), 50–56.

Silber, Laura and Allan Little. (1997). *Yugoslavia: Death of a Nation*, New York, Penguin Books.

Sucher, Pat and Peter Kemp. (1998). Accounting and Auditing Reform in Belarus. *European Business Journal*, 10(3), 141–147.

Sudetic, Chuck. (1998). *Blood and Vengeance: One Family's Story of the War in Bosnia*, New York, Penguin Books.

Wallace, R.S. Olusegun. (1993). Development of Accounting Standards for Developing and Newly Industrialized Countries. *Research in Third World Accounting*, 2, 121–165.

Wilson, Gary. (1998). The Dayton Accords Reshape Europe. In Sara Flounders et al. (eds), *NATO in the Balkans*, pp. 141–162, New York, International Action Center.

Zimmerman, Warren. (1999). *Origins of a Catastrophe*, New York, Random House.

Chapter 3
Banking Reform in China

Belinda Bai and Jens Hölscher

3.1 Introduction

China's banking reform has achieved significant progress in the past decade; however, problems and challenges remain. Our chapter argues that the inefficiency in the banking industry is mainly due to the system problem, and separate financial sector regulation restricts further banking development. Accession to the World Trade Organization (WTO) will accelerate the speed of China's banking reform, even though with pain and at a price, and in turn, China will benefit from further integration into the world economy.

The past decades witnessed successful economic reform in China, with GDP growth at an average rate of almost 8%; per capita GDP from US$266 at the end of 1979 to US$1,081 at the end of 2003 increased more than four times (Table 3.1). Successful accession to WTO on 11 December, 2001, accelerating the pace of economic reform and opening up speed to the world, meanwhile led China's integration even more into the global economy, and "its share in world trade is now over 4 percent, compared with near zero in 1978" (Rodlauer and Heytnes, 2003, in 'Introduction and Overview'). Now, China has become the major driving force in the development of global economy and plays an important role. "China's historical record on globalization is very poor. China has almost always been either a strong opponent to this historical process when it was strong enough, or a reluctant follower when it was too weak to voice its opposition. However, given the size of China's population and its dynamic economy over the last 20 years, the integration of China into the world economy will be of far-reaching significance" (Wen, 2001). China could have a bigger impact on the global economy than the other economies in the future.

China's integration with the global economy represents its rapid expansion of international trade (Prasad, 2004). "Since the late 1970s, exports and inward foreign direct investment (FDI) in China have risen dramatically under the open-door policy. The contribution of FDI in China's exports has been widely recognized" (Zhang and Song, 2001, p. 385). "Attracting foreign direct investment (FDI) has been a strategic

B. Bai and J. Hölscher
Brighton Business School

R. W. McGee (ed.), *Accounting Reform in Transition and Developing Economies,*   45
© Springer Science+Business Media LLC 2008

Table 3.1 Rapid expanding international trade and FDI inflow in China 1993–2003. Unit: % (www.worldbank.org.cn/Chinese/Contents/ChinaEl.pdf)

Year	Export	Import	FDI
1993	(US$91.7 billion)	(US$104.0 billion)	(US$27.5 billion)
1994	31.9	11.2	22.9
1995	23.0	14.2	10.9
1996	1.5	5.1	11.2
1997	21.0	2.5	8.6
1998	0.5	−1.5	0.4
1999	6.1	18.2	−11.1
2000	27.8	35.8	0.9
2001	6.8	8.2	14.9
2002	22.3	21.2	12.6
2003	34.6	39.8	1.4

economic policy adopted by China to upgrade technology and boost economic growth. FDI inflows into China have increased rapidly in the past three decades, especially into the 1990s" (Wu, 2001). China became the most attractive FDI recipient country in the world. In 2002 it just took over the USA to become number one. Under the globalization environment associated with the joining of WTO, China has rapidly expanded its export from US$91.7 billion at the end of 1993 to US$438.4 billion by the end of 2003, and import from US$104.0 billion in 1993 to US$412.8 billion in 2003; it has grown at an average rate of 15% each year since 1979, compared with 7% annual expansion of world trade over the same period; and disbursements of FDI have increased from US$27.5 billion in 1993 to US$53.5 billion in 2003 (Table 3.1).[1]

Driven by the expansion of international trade and FDI influence, the financial system reform in China was carried out gradually and was integrated with the global financial system step by step (Wang, 2002). In April 1980, China resumed the membership of the International Monetary Fund (IMF); in May of the same year, the place in the World Bank had been resumed as well; after that China became the member of the Bank for International Settlements. The most important benchmark is the accession to WTO in 2001, which indicates that China will continue to be the key player in the global economy; but equally, China will face a lot of unprecedented challenges and risks, and of course have a lot of opportunities as well, especially to the used-to-be-tightly controlled and seldom-opened financial sector, respectively. It is expected that China will integrate into the global economy much more than before.

Under WTO accession commitments, the financial sector would be opened up to foreign financial investors without geographical and client restrictions in 2006, and the domestic financial sectors, particularly banking industry, will have an urgency to face the intense competition.

The rest of this chapter is organized as follows: Section 2 explains the current banking reform situation. Section 3 introduces the market structure. Section 4 analyzes the efficiency of banking industry. In Section 5, WTO's accession challenge is described. In Section 6, Basel I & II effect is discussed. And the final section explains China's banking regulation and supervision.

---

[1] In this chapter, all data from China sources are converted from RMB to US$ at exchange rate of US$1 = RMB8.27, otherwise stated respectively.

3.2   Current Banking Reform

The importance of improving financial intermediations has been recognized by the government and financial reform has become the top policy priority in recent years (Albert, 2001). Financial institutions being intermediations play important roles in resources allocation during the economic reform, especially in China. The Bank with its high saving and investment rate is the key player in the financial sector, as the stock and bond market is relatively small (Prasad, 2004). In 2003, the domestic and foreign loans made by financial institutions was US$0.36 trillion (26% of GDP), and the fund raised by the stock market was at US$16.44 billion (1% of GDP), and cooperate bond issuance was of only US$4.35 billion (0.3% of GDP).

China's banking reform has experienced state banking with administrative characteristics to commercial banking in the past years. In 1994, three policy banks were set up by the government, i.e., National Developing Bank, China Export and Import Bank, and China Agriculture Developing Bank, to carry out related scope of business respectively (Zhu and Wang, 2002). This indicates the starting of commercial banking in China. In 1995, the Commercial Bank Law was launched which stipulates that minimum capital adequacy for the commercial banks should not be less than 8%, which pushed the state banks' assets and liability management reform further. Granting all commercial banks operational independence apart from national emergency formed the important feature of the law (Wong and Wong, 2001). In 1998, the government withdrew the scope control to credit management, and the central bank applied a guide plan instead of an instructive plan. Furthermore, commercial bank risk control system was under reform, and an international five-category classification was applied instead of the traditional risk division, i.e., pass, special mention, substandard, doubtful, and loss. Also in the same year, the Ministry of Finance issued a special national bond of US$32.65 billion as capital to pump into the state commercial banks, so as to reach the capital adequacy required by Basel Accord I. In 1999, four Asset Management Companies (Table 3.2) were set up to solve the non-performing loans (NPL) problems. It was due to many reasons, such as history, system, poor management, unclear ownership, etc., that the NPL was accumulated high. The NPL ratio in

Table 3.2   Disposal of non-performing assets by the four AMCs in 2004. Unit: US$100 million; % (China Banking Regulatory Commission)

2004	Q1	Q2	Q3
Accumulated disposal	639.27	685.93	710.54
(cash recovered)	127.55	136.43	145.36
Disposal ratio	42.60%	45.70%	47.22%
Asset recovery ratio	27.61%	26.78%	26.79%
Cash recovery ratio	19.95%	19.89%	20.46%

1. Accumulated Disposal refers to the accumulated amount of cash and non-cash assets recovered as well as loss incurred by the end of the reporting period.
2. Disposal Ratio = Accumulated Disposal/Total NPAs purchased.
3. Asset Recovery Ratio = Total Assets Recovered/Accumulated Disposal.
4. Cash Recovery Ratio = Cash Recovered/Accumulated Disposal.

state banks reduced from an estimated 31.1% at the end of 2001 to 15.6% in June 2004 (BEA, 2004). However, the NPL amount still stands high, according to the official figure; NPL at state banks stood at US$184.16 billion at the end of the second quarter of 2004, and more than US$96.74 billion of non-performing assets remain to be processed at the four Asset Management Companies (AMCs). Chen and Shih (2004) consider that comparing with other countries' NPL disposal method, such as sale, reorganization, securitization, and conversion of debt to equity, China mainly replied on conversion of debt to equity. In 2001, the successful listing of Min Sheng Bank on the domestic stock market indicates that banks on the list will be the next step of reform. The list's aim is not only in domestic market but also in overseas equity markets, such as Hong Kong and New York, so as to broaden fund procurement channels for the banks and establish corporate governance structures suitable for a market economy as well.

3.3   Market Structure

Substantial progress has been made in recent years in the financial institution reform from central-planned to market-oriented; however, challenges still remain. The China government is still the main owner of the banks in one way or another. The banking sector comprises four wholly stated-owned commercial banks (Table 3.3), i.e., the Agriculture Bank of China (ABC), reestablished on 13 March, 1979, is the major bank handling the agriculture-related financial matters; Bank of China (BOC), which was separated from China People's Bank in 1979, mainly deals with foreign currency trading, raises and makes use of foreign fund, fosters export production and international monetary settlement, etc. On 23 August, 2004, Bank of China was relaunched as a 100% state-owned joint-stock commercial bank. China Construction Bank (CCB) was established in 1954 under the Ministry of Finance to pledge funds for construction projects supplied sufficiently and managed properly; it does not implement the function of bank, even though it is called a bank. In 1979, CCB was separated from the Finance Department and became an independent bank under the State Council. With the deepening of economic reform, China People's Bank implemented the function of a central bank in one way, and meanwhile carried out industrial and commercial credit; city and rural savings did not suit the need of reform and hence did not benefit the strengthening of macroeconomy control and management.

Table 3.3 China state-owned commercial banks as at the end of 2002.Unit: US$ million (PBOC)

Banks	Total assets	Total liabilities	NPL ratio	Profit before tax	Total capital ratio	Core capital ratio
ICBC	577,602.54	555,594.56	25.69%	834.58	5.54%	5.46%
CCB	372,816.81	359,849.94	15.17%	524.43	6.91%	5.78%
BOC	434,571.70	405,985.37	22.49%	1,667.59	8.15%	7.85%
ABC	359,923.34	343,473.52		352.72		

In 1983, the State Council decided that China People's Bank concentrated on implementing the function of a central bank, separate from commercial financial institutions, such as security company, fund raising company, etc., and its commercial function will be taken over by the Industrial and Commercial Bank of China (ICBC).

In March 2003, the First Plenum of the Tenth National People's Congress approved the Decision on Reform of the Organizational Structure of the State Council, separating the supervisory responsibilities of the PBC for the banking institutions, asset management companies, trust and investment companies and other depository financial institutions. Instead, the China Banking Regulatory Commission was established to supervise the financial industry.

On December 27, 2003, the Standing Committee of the Tenth National People's Congress approved at its Sixth Meeting the amendment to the Law of the People's Republic of China on the People's Bank of China, which has strengthened the role of the PBC in the making and implementation of monetary policy, in safeguarding the overall financial stability and in the provision of financial services.

Under the guidance of the State Council, the PBC formulates and implements monetary policy, prevents and resolves financial risks, and safeguards financial stability.

The Law of the People's Republic of China on the People's Bank of China provides that the PBC performs the following major functions: issuing and enforcing relevant orders and regulations; formulating and implementing monetary policy; issuing Renminbi and administering its circulation; regulating inter-bank lending market and inter-bank bond market; administering foreign exchange and regulating inter-bank foreign exchange market; regulating gold market; holding and managing official foreign exchange and gold reserves; managing the State treasury; maintaining normal operation of the payment and settlement system; guiding and organizing the anti-money laundering work of the financial sector and monitoring relevant fund flows; conducting financial statistics, surveys, analysis and forecasts; participating in international financial activities in the capacity of the central bank; performing other functions specified by the State Council. (www.pbc.gov.cn)

Under the leadership of the State Council, the PBC implements monetary policy, performs its functions, and carries out business operations independently according to laws and free from intervention by local governments, government departments at various levels, public organizations, or any individuals.

The PBC needs to report to the State Council its decisions concerning the annual money supply, interest rates, exchange rates and other important issues specified by the State Council for approval before they are put into effect. The PBC is also obliged to submit work report to the Standing Committee of the National People's Congress on the conduct of monetary policy and the performance of the financial industry.

All capital of the PBC is invested and owned by the State. Since the central bank has been set up, ICBC carried out industrial and commercial credit and city and rural savings. In 1984, ICBC was formally established.

China's economic reform started from the countryside in the late 1970s with the famous Bao Chan Dao Hu (meaning fixing of farm output quotas for each household), i.e., more plots for private use, more free market, more enterprises with sole responsibility for their own profit or loss, and fixing output quotas on a household basis (Shang, 2000). This kind of economic reform led some of the farmers to become the first rich group population in China. Given this situation, private or village and town enterprises operated by this group grew like mushrooms. From 1984, economic system reform changed from the countryside to the cities and towns, and the scope of non-state-owned economy has grown rapidly and their portion in GDP increased. In this situation, new financial institutions appeared and gradually formed new financial market structure: they are 11 commercial banks, also known as joint-stock commercial banks (JSCBs); local banks, including about 110 city commercial banks, such as Beijing City Commercial Bank, Shanghai City Commercial Bank; and also rural commercial banks and rural credit cooperatives (RCCs).

Along with the economic reform and opening the door to foreign financial institutions, the first foreign bank that was allowed to set up an operation branch here was the Hong Kong Nanyang Commercial Bank in 1981, which dealt with foreign currency business. Since then, many foreign-funded banks have been granted permission to operate in China from the Special Economic Zones and Eastern Coastal Cities to inland cities.

The state-owned commercial banks still occupy the major portion of the financial market share (Table 3.4). However, in recent years, this situation has changed, as joint-stock commercial banks have an increasing market share, from 11.3% in 2001, 12.7% in 2002 to 13.8% in 2003; thus, the state-owned commercial banks' share is falling, from 57.5% in 2001, 56.5% in 2002 to 55.0% in 2003, respectively. Foreign-funded financial institutions only hold a share of 1.4%, which indicates development of a lot of potential, particularly after 2006, when foreign financial institutions were allowed to enter the market without geographical and client barriers.

Concentration ratios of assets, deposits, and loans of four state-owned banks during 1994–1998 showed a slight decrease, Herfindahl indexes of assets, deposits, and loans of four state-owned banks indicated that domestic banking industry structure is oligopoly in nature with approximately equal size, and Herfindahl index for profits showed that the level of concentration in the industry decreased significantly (Wong and Wong, 2001).

Table 3.4 Balance sheet of banking institutions in China as on 31 December, 2003. Unit: US$ billion (PBOC)

| | Assets | | Liabilities | |
	Amount (US$ billion)	Proportion (%)	Amount (US$ billion)	Proportion (%)
State-owned commercial banks	18,372.50	55.0	17,625.39	54.9
Joint-stock banks	4,615.44	13.8	4,453.57	13,9
Policy banks	2,569.17	7.7	2,453.51	7.6
City commercial banks	1,768.04	5.3	1,707.68	5.3
Rural commercial banks	46.53	0.1	45.96	0.1
Urban credit cooperatives	177.55	0.5	177.06	0.6
Rural credit cooperatives	32,105.10	9.6	3,222.03	10.0
Non-bank financial institutions	1,100.36	3.3	928.97	2.9
Postal savings institutions	1,086.38	3.3	1,086.38	3.4
Foreign-funded financial institutions	479.93	1.4	432.62	1.3
Total	33,421.34	100.0	32,133.13	100.0

3.4   Efficiency of China's Banking Institutions

Chen and Shih (2004) argued that it is due to weak internal control and lack of effective risk management and incentive mechanisms associated with unclear ownership and government interference that state-owned commercial banks' operational performance is poor, and therefore they are not competitive enough compared with the commercial banks based on the market mechanism.

Based on Table 3.5, Banks in the Fortune Global 500, four state banks' ranking is on the front list. However, in terms of profit per employee, total assets, profit, and ROA ratio, the four banks are still far behind the top banks in the world. In terms of employee numbers, they are actually on the top front, which indicates that the efficiency and profit of the four banks are very low and they are not very competitive now, so further strengthening and deepening of the banking reform is required, and especially when foreign financial institutions enter the China market, domestic banking institutions will become strong competitors.

By using Spearman Rank Correlation for empirical testing to the operational performance of banks between 1995 and 2001, Chen and Shih (2004) found that in order to satisfy the customers' need, more branches are opened and the number of employee increased; however, professionalism is not improved and new areas of business are not further developed, and as a consequence, profitability is not increased.

Based on empirical tests by applying the model of profit maximization of banks restricted to interbank lending, Albert (2001, p. 636) found that "financial intermediation in China is far from efficient and that financial reforms in the mid-1990s have not reversed the trend of worsening bank performance."

Lin (2001) argued that high ratio of nonperforming loans, policy-lending burden to state banks, and low efficiency in state banks by monopolistic nature have resulted in the poor and uncompetitive quality of China's banking.

We can understand why it is low in profit and inefficient from the current situation of banking system. Most of the loans in the state banks have been given to the state-owned enterprises; however, most of the state-owned enterprises are high in debt and are nonprofitable, as unclear ownership exists; the major stock owners of the commercial banks are the country or local administration authorities, and they are under supervision from the central bank. However, the committee of stock owners cannot make their decisions alone and, as such, the motivation is not for the clients and not wholly from the stock owners either. Poor management system, employees' lack of profit-making motivation, and increase in the period of loan returncontributed to the accumulation of high NPLs in the banks. Furthermore, in order to reduce the high NPLs, the more supplementary capital is provided to the banks, the higher the cost will be. Even though in recent years, the ratio of NPLs has been reduced after government's hard effort and capital injection to the banks, the NPL amount still stands high.

Thus, apart from reducing the high NPLs, systemizing and modernizing the market, strengthening of the encouragement method, issuance of loans according to the potential return and risk control should be considered. Capital injection will not solve the NPL problem fundamentally, except increasing the cost.

Table 3.5 Banks in the Fortune Global 500 (Global 500, *Fortune* July 26, 2004)

Banking industry raking	Global 500 ranking	Company	Rev*	Total assets*	Pro*	ROA %	Emp	Rev Per	Pro Per
1	18	Citigroup	94,713	1,264,032	17,853	1.4	256,000	369,973	69,738
2	45	Credit Suisse	58,957	777,958	3,717	0.5	60,837	969,099	61,096
3	47	HSBC Holdings	57,608	1,034,216	8,774	0.8	218,000	264,257	40,248
4	48	BNP Parbas	27,272	987,717	4,257	0.4	89,071	306,180	47,789
5	51	Fortis	56,695	659,991	2,487	0.4	62,565	906,181	39,749
6	67	Deutsche Bank	48,670	1,013,623	1,545	0.2	67,682	719,104	22,826
7	71	Bank of America Corp.	48,065	736,445	10,810	1.5	133,549	359,905	80,944
8	72	UBS	47,741	1,120,650	4,747	0.4	65,929	724,127	72,008
9	78	Credit Agricole	45,928	1,103,964	2,971	0.3	136,446	336,603	21,773
10	81	JP Morgan Chase	44,363	770,912	6,719	0.9	93,453	474,709	71,897
29	243	Industrial and Commercial Bank of China	20,757	637,829	299	0.0	389,045	53,354	768
39	331	China Construction Bank	15,825	429,432	50	0.0	275,029	57,539	181
45	358	Bank of China	15,022	464,213	554	0.1	188,716	79,599	2,937
50	412	Agriculture Bank of China	13,303	359,632	232	0.1	511,425	26,012	454

Unit with * is in $ million.
Rev – Revenues; Emp – Employees; Pro – Profits; Rev Per – Revenues per employee $; Pro Per – Profits per employee $

The state-owned banks are still the major players in the market. Under this oligopoly situation, they concentrate on scope of the loans and savings, instead of making profit, increasing service quality, and reducing cost, which becomes a high-cost and low-profit situation.

Rapid expansion of branches and employee numbers also increase the management fee and cost. In terms of numbers of banks' branches and employees, China is in the top front; however, quite a few of the branches can be merged to reduce surplus labor and save cost.

Due to insufficient protection of the financial institutions and unawareness of the banking risks, and loose control, such as relationship loans, no-guarantee loans, fault-guarantee loans, etc., borrowers escaped by taking the advantages of reform, bankruptcy, etc., which led to unsuccessful recovery, high cost to solve the NPLs, high rate of nonprofit assets, and low profit.

Policy loans are too high. Most of these NPLs are actually government subsidies for loss-making state-owned enterprises, disbursed in the form of bank loans. These are in fact policy loans to enterprises not originally structured to operate profitably in a market economy.

This situation will harm the pay-off ability of the financial institutions, and affect the competitiveness of the banks and distribution of credit fund among different departments. The cost of policy loans will be complemented by the other loans, which increase the cost and hinder the potential enterprises' development.

Current separate institution supervision suits China's supervision- and management-level of the enterprises; however, it limits the banking development and competitiveness. With the capital market development, the scope of traditional credit business is reduced. Since cross-sector business is not allowed, a bank cannot enter the capital market to obtain new type of business and the bank's long credit fund cannot be securitized; this in turn restricts the capital flow and affects profit. Therefore, quite a bit of the capital is unused.

Interest rates for all kinds of deposits have been tightly controlled by the Central Bank, and thus, market competition is in a nonprice competition situation; consequently, banks with a large portion of deposit shares may not be the most profitable and efficient ones (Wong and Wong, 2001).

3.5   WTO's Accession Challenge

China's accession to the World Trade Organization (WTO) was a watershed event for both China and the WTO (World Bank Economic Review, 2004). "Based on an assessment of the coverage and depth of these commitments, Mattoo (2002) concludes that China's commitments under the General Agreement on Trade Services (GATS) represent the most radical reform program negotiated in the WTO" (see Yang, 2003, p. 7).

Under WTO commitments, after 5 years' accession, China's banking will be fully open to foreign financial institutions. Details can be summarized as follows:

in China a foreign country is allowed to set up a foreign bank's subsidiary branch, foreign bank branch, joint venture bank, foreign financial company, foreign financial representative office, etc. Requirement for establishing a foreign bank's subsidiary branch or a foreign wholly owned financial company is that the applicant is a financial institution, having a representative office in China for more than 2 years, with total assets as of the year before application more than US$10 billion. Requirement for establishing foreign banks is that the applicant is a financial institution, having a representative office in China for more than 2 years, with total assets as of the year before application more than US$20 billion. Requirement for a joint venture bank or financial institutions is that the applicant is a financial institution, having a representative office in China for more than 1 year, with total assets as of the year before application more than US$10 billion.

Geographical barriers will be gradually loosened. The cities that are allowed to set up foreign financial institutions are Shanghai, Shenzhen, Zhuhai, Hanan, Xiamen, etc. (Table 3.6). After 2 years of accession to WTO, foreign banks can carry out RMB business to domestic enterprises, and after 5 years, to individual residents.

The business which foreign banks are allowed to carry out under WTO Agreement involves as hereunder:

"*Banking and other financial (excluding insurance)*

(v)   *Acceptance of deposit and other repayable funds from the public;*
(vi)   *Lending of all types, including consumer credit, mortgage credit, factoring and financing of commercial transaction;*
(vii)   *Financial leasing;*
(viii) *All payment and money transmission services, including credit, charge and debit cards, travelers cheques and bankers drafts;*
(ix)   *Guarantees and commitments;*
(x)   *Trading for own account or for account of customers, whether on an exchange, in an over – the – counter market or otherwise, the following:*

(A) *money market instruments (including cheques, bills, certificates of deposits);*
(B) *foreign exchange;*
(C) *derivative products including, but not limited to, futures and options;*
(D) *exchange rate and interest rate instruments, including products such as swaps, forward rate agreements;*

Table 3.6 Time table for RMB currency opening to foreign financial institutions after WTO accession

Time	Withdraw geographical barriers	Withdraw clients barriers
On joining	Shenzhen, Shanghai, Dalian, Tianjing	–
Within 1 year	Guanghou, Qingdao, Nanjing, Wuhan	–
Within 2 years	Jinan, Fuzhou, Chengdu, Chongqing	China's Enterprises
Within 3 years	Kunming, Zhuhai, Beijing, Xiamen	–
Within 4 years	Shantou, Ningbo, Shenyang, Xian	–
Within 5 years	All	All China's individuals

(E) *transferable securities;*
(F) *other negotiable instruments and financial assets, including bullion.*

(xi) *Participation in issues of all kinds of securities, including underwriting and placement as agent (whether publicly or privately) and provision of services related to such issues;*
(xii) *Money broking;*
(xiii) *Asset management, such as cash or portfolio management, all forms of collective investment management, pension fund management, custodial, depository and trust services;*
(xiv) *Settlement and clearing services for financial assets, including securities, derivative products, and other negotiable instruments;*
(xv) *Provision and transfer of financial information, and financial data processing and related software by suppliers of other financial services;*
(xvi) *Advisory, intermediation and other auxiliary financial services on all the activities listed in subparagraphs (v) through (xv), including credit reference and analysis, investment and portfolio research and advice, advice on acquisitions and on corporate restructuring and strategy."* (Wu, 2001, pp. 349–351)

Given the experience of foreign countries and the existing foreign financial institutions in China, the competition between domestic and foreign banks will concentrate on the aspects of foreign currency, intermediation strengthening, human resources, etc.

Quite a number of the foreign banks are under operation of financial supermarket with flexible management, sufficient funds, high international prestige, consummated settlement, variable services, and products; their target is high-quality clients, for instance, joint-venture enterprises, global enterprises, and high-technology companies. In the short run, foreign banks' retail business may not threaten the domestic market, as domestic banks' number of branches and clients is still much more than that of the foreign banks. However, in the long run, it may become a threat, as foreign banks may target high-income clients by providing personal banking, credit card, online services, and phone banking to expand their client base, and attract RMB and foreign currency deposit savings by good services. Since they are foreign banks, they need local experts to operate the local business. Thus, fighting for the local experts by attractive salary, advanced facilities, etc., becomes very tense. Labor mobility will affect the already surplus labor in the domestic banks. About one quarter market share of foreign currency loans run by foreign banks and restrictions to foreign currency operation are deregulated after WTO accession; foreign banks will make use of their existing advantage to expand the market share and develop intermediations, for example, low-cost and low-risk and high-profit international settlement, credit card, and investment consultation.

WTO impact can be considered if China's domestic banks cannot improve efficiency of operation and prevention to risk, cannot increase services quality, quite a number of the clients are lost, and are going to face decreased market portion and increased risk. As lots of foreign banks enter, unemployment will increase due to reduction in the scale of financial institutions. After unification of accounting, reports and statistics, etc., to the international level, if the transparency cannot be improved, with strengthening of internal supervision, financial risks will be accumulated. Qualified personnel competition is due to the salary gap between foreign banks and domestic banks, so change jobs will become popular; meanwhile, it increases the personnel competition between foreign and domestic banks. China's supervision by institution is different from current foreign countries' supervision by function, and it will restrict domestic banks' development, as foreign banks will not limit their services as domestic banks do. Joint WTO will forcibly deepen China's financial reform. Under the opening of capital market, currency, and foreign currency, free capital flow will bring in difficulties of macroeconomy control and financial supervision; however, adopting step by step opening and sufficient opening policy and pace, as well as suitable system reform, this financial risk will not be converted to a financial disaster.

Oligopoly market structure will be changed by the entry of foreign financial institutions. Some of the market portion will be transferred to foreign financial institutions. It is estimated that after 10 years, foreign banking institutions will occupy about 20% market share. Profitability for domestic banks will decrease. Given the reducing portion of domestic market share and good-quality clients, profit will decrease and the output of domestic banks will be affected. Domestic banks' capital mobility will also change. The source of capital will transfer from domestic to foreign banks; particularly, domestic banks' NPLs will stand high, which will further worsen their risk, and if it gets worse, the existence of the domestic banks will be threatened. Domestic banks are also going to face the challenge of services and products by foreign financial institutions. They need to expand products from traditional saving deposit, loan, remittance and foreign currency to more variable products, particularly intermediation products. Capital adequacy in domestic banks is far behind foreign banks, which restrict their expansion. China's banking will turn to commercial banking with modernized management. The quality and efficiency of banking will be pushed to improve by saving cost, upgrading management skill, raising human resources' quality, and strengthening supervision. It will also advance the banking risk-control management, inter-control system, transparency system, regulated supervision, and eventually increase China bank's efficiency and competitiveness.

Saving deposit is the main capital resource for banks in China, which is what China's banks concentrate on. However, in recent years, the interest rate has been decreased severalfold, so, comparatively speaking, the portion of saving is reduced. Another profit source is from loans, and this is an area China's banks had not paid much attention to before. Current development trend in the international finance market is direct finance instead of indirect finance. In this case, the role of the commercial bank is decreasing, especially when China's banks are inefficient, and its market share will become less. Therefore, asset management and quality control will be the future target.

Table 3.7 Intermediation income ratio from 1994–1998. Unit: % (China Finance Yearbook 1995–1999)

	ICBC	BOC	CCB	ABC	Total
1994	3.16	19.11	5.43	2.79	7.55
1995	2.96	21.55	5.79	3.85	8.12
1996	3.2	22.97	5.65	11.64	9.54
1997	3.62	19.19	4.47	3.4	6.78
1998	3.31	22.05	3.09	2.51	7.25

Intermediation business is still at its infant stage (Table 3.7) and should be further developed, as it can enlarge the credit and loan business, increase profit, and reduce management risk. Banks need not take the risk of moral hazard and quality of credit from the clients; they can take the commission whilst providing the service, and thus, total management risk will be reduced. Break-separated management and business increase cross-sector business. Recent years' separated business management did not really reduce the system risk, but instead increased the risks. Cross-sector business will increase the services products and efficiency and reduce the disadvantages caused by separated management, and also benefit the supervision efficiency and quality. Based on the cross-sector business, improvement of the transparency of the financial system benefits supervision and reduces moral hazard. At present the profit from intermediation is still very low: in 1999, ICBC's interest income rate is 84.23% and commission income rate is 0.83%; BOC's interest income rate is 85.99% and commission income rate is 3.66%; CCB's interest income rate is 87.01% and commission income rate is 1.29%; ABC's interest income rate is 94.47% and commission income rate is 0.78% (Lu and Dai, 2002).

E-banking is another choice as information and Internet technology has developed very fast and become universalized. This high technology accelerates the globalization of economy and creation, and in turn accelerates competition; it further speeds up the usage of new technology in trading and finance. Additionally, by sharing and increasing information and data, it reduces the management cost and improves efficiency. Since e-banking is new in the market, cautious strategy and management and regulation are the key points to be paid attention to, especially in respect of similarity, individuality, and Internet market rules. Regularizing the future strategy well can grasp the market's developing opportunity and changes in the meantime.

In order to achieve the listed goals, management efficiency and profitability deepening reform in the banks are required, increasing management quality to meet the standards for listed firms, as at present, the revenue per employee and the return on assets are very low. Operations should be strengthened in comparison with the world's top banks, which will soon become strong competitors in the China market. The banks should obtain their own profit, instead of being supported by the government to achieve profit. Besides, raise in current low capital adequacy of the commercial banks to 8% based on the Basel I and II capital adequacy is done on an urgent basis.

3.6   Basel I and II Effect

New Basel Accord rules are regulated based on the information and data of well-developed western economic market and system, and the target is formed based on the developing model of western countries as well. For those undeveloped financial system countries, difference and not-well-fit remain; particularly in China, the level of banking management, efficiency of assets management, and banking software and hardware development appear as a big gap with those developed countries, and thus it is difficult to reach the target of Basel Accord in a short term.

The reasons behind it are, first, China state-owned commercial banks are always protected by the government policies, efficiency depends on the scale of assets instead of their development, management and quality control, and management concentrates on market share instead of improving the quality of assets. Second, Basel Accord II strengthens credit risk and market risk supervision, and risk management, which increases risk sensitiveness. In China, market efficiency is restricted by an inefficient system and unmatched and unharmonious efficiency that will increase the difficulty of supervision and weaken the rationalization and standardization of regulation, highlight the problem of capital inadequacy, and enlarge the gap between domestic banking and foreign banking; especially domestic banking will stand at an unfavorable position among the competition of WTO. The more advanced approaches under Basel are heavily dependent on data (The Banker, 2004). Significant work is involved in building the systems required for upfront data capture, linkage, storage, processing, and analysis. This is for sure a big challenge to China's banking system, given the current IT development level; in some remote countryside, electricity is still not sufficient for daily use, and even in the cities, electricity supply is not developed as fast as it is needed. One thing is certain – costs are expected to be heavily focused on IT spending across all regions and bank sizes (The Banker, 2004). The majority of banks expect 40–80% of costs to be for systems and interfaces and expect involvement of more IT than business headcount. Given the size and number of branches and staff involved, domestic banks' IT spending will meet a huge figure, which indicates that IT improvement has a long way to go.

However, with speed-up of China's banking supervision improvement and reform, Basel I & II will provide guidance to the reform of banking regulation and management, and eventually improve the banking quality.

In order to deepen banking reform and mature Chinese banking industry to an international level, CBRC issued "Regulation Governing Capital Adequacy of Commercial Banks" on 27 February, 2004, based on the combination of Basel Accord I & II. It is hoped that domestic banks will take about 3 years to reach the Basel I capital adequacy requirement.

CBRC hopes that the "Regulation" will strengthen validation of assets supervision. "Commercial Bank Law" has regulated that the capital adequacy of banks cannot be less than 8%; however, it does not regulate detailed measurement to those achieving less than the requirement, and loosens the calculation method of capital adequacy. In fact, China banks' capital adequacy is low, to set up capital regulation system and amend current capital adequacy. This method will strengthen the commercial banks' supervision and establish restrain system to commercial banks' capital enlargement, and further lay concrete foundation to the monetary policy application.

The "Regulation" will narrow the gap of capital regulation between China and the world. Besides, it will set up Chinese style capital supervision frame and connect Chinese banking supervision with the world, so as to accelerate fare competition in banking industry.

The "Regulation" also benefits to link with other newly applied regulations, such as "Commercial Bank Law". These regulations established the foundation of cautious capital management system. Amendment of measurement to capital adequacy will enhance the unanimity among different regulations, and furthermore, set up a complete cautious banking supervision system.

The larger are China's banking business types and scope year by year, the higher the risk it will face. Raise in the capital adequacy requirement will benefit the commercial banks' risk protection, so as to reduce risk as a whole. However, having considered the Chinese special situation, the "Regulation" issued its own capital adequacy measurement.

3.7 Regulations

China's financial regulation system is mainly formed by three parts. The basic part is laws formulated by the National People's Congress and its Standing Committee according to the legal procedure, such as, Commercial Bank Law, Insurance Law, Security Law, The People's Bank of China Law, etc. The second part is financial administrative regulations formulated by the State Council according to the legal procedure, for instance, Provisional Measures to Administrative Foreign Financial Institutions etc. The third part includes financial administrative rules issued by the People's Bank of China and ministries under the State Council according to the financial laws and financial administration regulations.

China's financial supervision is under separate sector supervision, i.e., China Banking Regulatory Commission, China Insurance Regulatory Commission, and China Securities Regulatory Commission. There are three main methods. Entry administration regulations: these will ensure the stability of development and provide sufficient prevention to the financial market. Operation regulations: strict rules to the entry administration are important; however, it will not guarantee that the participants will operate in accordance with the regulations. Thus, it finds out operation process and details so as to prevent risk. Whenever there is a problem, it can be solved sufficiently. For banks, it can be achieved by checking capital adequacy, quality of assets, mobility of capital, ability of profit, management level and internal risk control, etc. Regulations for disposal of troublesome financial institutions and withdrawal from the financial market: whenever a financial institution is in difficulty of capital flow, prestige, and affects stability of financial market, temporary loans will be lent to this institution for emergency use; however, if it does not work to the normal operation level, merger or buy out will be enforced. If this also does not work, cancellation of business permission certificate or force to leave the market will apply. Other risk-prevention supervision methods are non-spot check by annual reports, statistics analysis, etc.; spot check involves personal checking at the site according to the specific items.

In the past, the People's Bank of China, taking the role of financial regulator to banks, insurance, and security companies, also operated as a commercial bank. In 1995, the People's Bank of China Law promulgated and stipulated its role of financial supervision with independence, without interference of the local authorities, administrative departments, and individuals.

In 2003, the China Banking Regulatory Commission (CBRC) was established to take over the role of supervising commercial banks from PBOC. This indicates that China will distinguish clearly between monetary policy and bank supervision, and allow PBOC to become a central bank and be responsible for drafting and implementing the country's monetary policy through the 11-member Monetary Policy Committee (MPC), and improve operation rules of financial institutions.

The main functions of China Banking Regulatory Commission are to formulate supervisory rules and regulations governing the banking institutions; authorize the establishment, changes, termination and business scope of the banking institutions; conduct on-site examination and off-site surveillance of the banking institutions, and take enforcement actions against rule-breaking behaviors; conduct fit-and-proper tests on the senior managerial personnel of the banking institutions; compile and publish statistics and reports of the overall banking industry in accordance with relevant regulations; provide proposals on the resolution of problem deposit-taking institutions in consultation with relevant regulatory authorities; responsible for the administration of the supervisory boards of the major State-owned banking institutions; and other functions delegated by the State Council.

The regulatory objectives of the CBRC is to protect the interests of depositors and consumers through prudential and effective supervision; maintain market confidence through prudential and effective supervision; enhance public knowledge of modern finance though customer education and information disclosure; combat financial crimes.

The supervisory focuses of the CBRC is to conduct consolidated supervision to assess, monitor and mitigate the overall risks of each banking institution as a legal entity; stay focused on risk-based supervision and improvement of supervisory process and methods; urge banks to put in place and maintain a system of internal controls; enhance supervisory transparency in line with international standards and practices.

The supervisory and regulatory criteria of the CBRC is to promote the financial stability and facilitate financial innovation at the same time; enhance the international competitiveness of the Chinese banking sector; set appropriate supervisory and regulatory boundaries and refrain from unnecessary controls; encourage fair and orderly competition; clearly define the accountability of both the supervisor and the supervised institutions; and employ supervisory resources in an efficient and cost-effective manner. (www.cbrc.gov.cn)

The future supervision development will concentrate on several aspects of the overall and multilevel supervision system. Given the financial situation in China, separate sector regulation and supervision will be carried out for quite some time.

Future regulation and supervision will concentrate on several aspects. It will establish a multilevel supervision system, i.e., financial law system; regulatory committee; entry administration, operation supervision, and market withdrawal; financial institution internal control and external audit.

Deepening economic reform brings benefit and also increases the financial risk, which will affect the income of state finance. In recent years, the scope of banking has enlarged; however, the tax amount submitted to the state finance is decreasing, and the bank's profit after tax is dropping year by year. Since the gain and loss of banks, especially the four state-owned banks, directly relate to the state finance's income, supervision to internal control and external audit to the banks, prevent financial crisis, appear important and will ensure further health and continuous economic development.

Current commercial banks' finance supervision comprises established state-owned commercial banks' finance budget system, specialized fund management system, final accounts arrangement and final accounts approval system, selective examination to state-owned banks' accounts system.

China will use the experience of successful foreign banks' finance supervision to the domestic banking finance regulation and supervision so as to upgrade the current finance supervision method to the international level, particularly after accession of WTO, perfect domestic financial accounts system, improve banking competition, enhance the financial laws and regulations, based on the Basel Agreement and other international regulations; establish modern commercial bank system and operation system from stock system point of view, enhance the juridical administer system, improve efficiency of finance and its accounts supervision, prevent financial crisis, and maintain stability of finance. The experience will also be used to strengthen manager's operation responsibility, set up efficient internal risk control system, improve the standard of internal risks control, raise quality of credit, reduce NPLs etc., ensure e-banking, international settlement, e-payment, information, etc., up to the international level.

References

Albert, P. and Kaja, S. (2001), Tests of Financial Intermediation and Banking Reform in China, Journal of Comparative Economics, 29(4), December, 608–644.

Bank of East Asia (2004), Banking Reform in the Mainland, available at www.hkbea.com.

Chen, C.H. and Shih, H.T. (2004), Banking and Insurance in the New China: Competition and the Challenge of Accession to the WTO, Edward Elgar, Cheltenham.

Chang, C., Fleisher, B.M., and Parker, E. (2001), The Impact of China's entry to the WTO, China Economic Review, 11(4Winter), 319–322.

China Banking Regulatory Commission, available at www.cbrc.gov.cn.

China Finance Yearbook 1995–1999, China Finance Yearbook Editorial Section, People's China Publishing House. Global 500, Fortune, 26 July, 2004.

Lin, Y.F. Justin (2001), WTO Accession and Financial Reform in China, Cato Journal, 21(1, Spring/Summer).

Lu, S.M. and Dai, G.Q. (Ed.) (2002), 2002 China's Financial Development Report, Shanghai Finance and Economic University Press, Shanghai.

Prasad, E. (Ed.) (2004), China's Growth and Integration into the World Economy: Prospects and Challenges, IMF Occasional Paper 232.

Rodlauer, M. and Heytens, P. (2003), China Competing in the Global Economy, Tseng, W. and Rodlauer, M. (Eds.), International Monetary Fund, Washington, DC.

Shang, M. (Ed.) (2000). New China's Finance 50 Years, China Finance Economic Press, Beijing.

The Banker, (July, 2004), The Banker special supplement in association with Accenture, Mercer Oliver Wyman/SAP.

The People's Bank of China, available at www.pbc.gov.cn.

Wang, M.K. (2002), China: Accession to WTO and Financial Reform, Foreign Language Press, China.

Wen, G.J. (2001), New Frontier of Economic Globalization: The Significance of China's Accession to WTO, China Economic Review, 11(4), 432–436.

Wong, Y.C. Richard and Wong, M.L. Sonia (2001), Competition in China's Domestic Banking Industry, Cato Journal, 21(1, Spring/Summer).

World Bank, China Up Date 16 April, 2004, available at www.worldbank.org.cn.

World Bank Economic Review (2004), Economic Effects of China's Accession to the World Trade Organization, 18(1), Jan 2004. ISBN: 9780198530626.

Wu, X. (2001), Foreign Direct Investment, Intellectual Property rights, and Wage Inequality in China, China Economic Review, 11(4), 361–384.

Wu, X.P. (2001), Impact of WTO Accession on China's Life Insurance and Its Countermeasure, China Finance Publishing House, PRC.

Yang, Y.Z. (2003), China's Integration into the World's Economy: Implications for Developing Countries, IMF working paper No. 01/245.

Zhang, K.H. and Song, S. (2001), Promoting Exports: The Role of Inward FDI in China, China Economic Review, 11(4), 385–396.

Zhu, Y.F. and Wang, J.C. (2002), Opportunity and Gauntlet – Research on China's Financial Industry Development, Economic Science Press, Beijing.

Appendix

General Agreement on Trade in Services (China and WTO)
Annex on Financial Services

1. Scope and Definition

   (a) This Annex applies to measures affecting the supply of financial services. Reference to the supply of a financial service in this Annex shall mean the supply of a service as defined in paragraph 2 of Article I of the Agreement.

   (b) For the purpose of subparagraph 3 (b) of the Agreement, "services supplied in the exercise of governmental authority" means the following:

      (i)   Activities conducted by a central bank or monetary authority or by any other public entity in pursuit of monetary or exchange rate policies

      (ii) Activities forming part of a statutory system of social security or public retirement plans and

      (iii) Other activities conducted by a public entity for the account or with the guarantee or using the financial resources of the Government

(c) For the purpose of subparagraph 3 (b) of Article I of the Agreement, if a Member allows any of the activities referred to in subparagraphs (b) (ii) or (b) (iii) of this paragraph to be conducted by its financial service suppliers in competition with a public entity or a financial service supplier, "service" shall include such activities.

(d) Subparagraph 3(c) of Article I of Agreement shall not apply to services covered by this Annex.

2. Domestic Regulation

(a) Notwithstanding any other provisions of the Agreement, a Member shall not be prevented from taking measures for prudential reasons, including for the protection of investors, depositors, policy holders or persons to whom a fiduciary duty is owed by a financial service supplier, or to ensure the integrity and stability of the financial system. Where such measures do not conform to the provisions of the Agreement, they shall not be used as a means of avoiding the Member's commitments or obligations under the Agreement.

(b) Nothing in the Agreement shall be construed to require a Member to disclose information relating to the affairs and accounts of individual customers or any confidential or proprietary information in the possession of public entities.

3. Recognition

(a) A Member may recognize prudential measures of any other country in determining how the Member's Measures relating to financial services shall be applied. Such recognition, which may be achieved through harmonization or otherwise, may be based upon an agreement or arrangement with the country or may be accorded autonomously.

(b) A Member that is a party to such an agreement or arrangement referred to in subparagraph (a), whether future or existing, shall afford adequate opportunity for other interested Members to negotiate their accession to such agreements or arrangements, or to negotiate comparable ones with it, under circumstances in which there would be equivalent regulation, oversight, implementation of such regulation, and if appropriate, procedures concerning the sharing of information between the parties to the agreement or arrangement. Where a Member accords recognition autonomously, it shall afford adequate opportunity for any other Member to demonstrate that such circumstances exist.

(c) Where a Member is contemplating according recognition to prudential measures of any other country, paragraph 4(b) of Article VII shall not apply.

4. Dispute Settlement

Panels for dispute on prudential issues and other financial matters shall have the necessary expertise relevant to the specific financial service under dispute.

5. Definitions

For the purposes of this Annex:

(a) A financial service is any service of a financial nature offered by a financial service supplier of a Member. Financial services include all insurance and insurance – related services, and all banking and other financial services (excluding insurance). Financial services include the following activities:

Insurance and insurance-related services

(i)   Direct insurance (including co–insurance)
        (A) life
        (B) non-life
(ii)   Reinsurance and retrocession
(iii)   Insurance intermediation, such as brokerage and agency
(iv)   Services auxiliary to insurance, such as consultancy, actuarial, risk assessment and claim settlement services

Banking and other financial (excluding insurance)

(v)   Acceptance of deposit and other repayable funds from the public
(vi)   Lending of all types, including consumer credit, mortgage credit, factoring and financing of commercial transaction
(vii)   Financial leasing
(viii) All payment and money transmission services, including credit, charge and debit cards, traveler's cheques and bankers drafts
(ix)   Guarantees and commitments
(x)   Trading for own account or for account of customers, whether on an exchange, in an over-the-counter market or otherwise, the following:

        (G) Money market instruments (including cheques, bills, certificates of deposits)
        (H) Foreign exchange
        (I) Derivative products including, but not limited to, futures and options
        (J) Exchange rate and interest rate instruments, including products such as swaps, forward rate agreements
        (K) Transferable securities
        (L) Other negotiable instruments and financial assets, including bullion

(xi)   Participation in issues of all kinds of securities, including underwriting and placement as agent (whether publicly or privately) and provision of services related to such issues
(xii)   Money broking
(xiii) Asset management, such as cash or portfolio management, all forms of collective investment management, pension fund management, custodial, depository and trust services

(xiv) Settlement and clearing services for financial assets, including securities, derivative products, and other negotiable instruments

(xv) Provision and transfer of financial information, and financial data processing and related software by suppliers of other financial services

(xvi) Advisory, intermediation and other auxiliary financial services on all the activities listed in subparagraphs (v) through (xv), including credit reference and analysis, investment and portfolio research and advice, advice on acquisitions and on corporate restructuring and strategy

(b) A financial service supplier means any natural or juridical person of a Member wishing to supply or supplying financial services but the term "financial service supplier" does not include a public entity

(c) "Public entity" means:

(i) A government, a central bank or a monetary authority, of a Member, or an entity owned or controlled by a Member, that is principally engaged in carrying out governmental functions or activities for governmental purposes, not including an entity principally engaged in supplying financial services on commercial terms or

(ii) A private entity, performing functions normally performed by a central bank or monetary authority, when exercising those functions

Second Annex on Financial Services

1. Notwithstanding Article II of the Agreement and paragraph 1 and 2 of the Annex on Article II Exemptions, a Member may, during a period of 60 days beginning four months after the date of entry into force of the WTO Agreement, list in that Annex measures relating to financial services which are inconsistent with paragraph 1 of Article II of the Agreement.

2. Notwithstanding Article XXI of the Agreement, a Member may, during a period of 60 days beginning four months after the date of entry into force of the WTO Agreement, improve, modify or withdraw all or part of the specific commitments on financial services inscribed in its Schedule.

3. The Council for Trade in Services shall establish any procedures necessary for the application of paragraph 1 and 2.

Chapter 4
Accounting Reform in Croatia

Mira Dimitrić

4.1 Introduction

This chapter deals with the most important factors and difficulties that influence the accounting reform and harmonization process in Croatia. It analyzes the implementation of International Financial Reporting Standards (IFRS) and International Accounting Standards (IAS) in Croatian accounting practice and judges the degree of accounting development in financial institutions. The aim of this chapter is to provide a global framework for the Croatian corporate income tax system from the point of view of its accounting application and to judge the usefulness of traditional and modern costing systems in enterprises in transition and Croatian enterprises as well.

The first part of the chapter discusses the background of the accounting harmonization process in Croatia concerning the legal system, the prevailing capital market system, accounting organizations and board impact, and historical conditions. It describes some specific Croatian features, such as the consequences of the war, the privatization process, changes in the banking sector, economic development in the last few years, and the globalization process.

The second part researches four groups of difficulties connected with IFRS implementation in Croatia: difficulties connected with legal rules and regulations; difficulties connected with the concept, structure, and contents of IAS (IFRS); difficulties connected with undeveloped capital and financial markets; and difficulties connected with insufficiently experienced and numerous experts in the area of valuation and performance judgment.

The third part treats basic items concerning accounting in Croatian financial institutions and financial instruments accounting. The fourth part deals with accounting aspects of the corporate income tax system and compares it with IAS 12, which regulates corporate income tax recognition and reporting. And finally, the last part discusses the relationship between the internal costing system in enterprises and the managers' planning and control decision-making process. It analyzes the main difficulties to be faced in adjusting the process to modern production, marketing and organization by implementing and sustaining modern costing systems in Croatia.

M. Dimitrić
University of Rijeka

R. W. McGee (ed.), *Accounting Reform in Transition and Developing Economies,* 67
© Springer Science+Business Media LLC 2008

4.2 Background of the Accounting Harmonization Process

There are many factors that influence the accounting harmonization process in a particular country. The most important of them are:

- Belonging to a Roman or Anglo-Saxon legal system
- The prevailing capital market system and enterprise financing
- Accounting organizations and boards impact and
- Historical conditions

The Roman law system is built on prescribed rules that are stable, meaning the rules change infrequently. In contrast, the Anglo-Saxon system is based on individual cases and verdicts with precedent. The accounting system is more elastic and flexible in countries that belong to the Anglo-Saxon legal system. In these countries, financial statements are independent from tax reports and the accounting profession has autonomy in creating accounting principles and practices that do not depend on legal rules. Different accounting solutions in European countries are the consequence of different trade laws and further amendments that have been developed in these countries. The harmonization process based on IAS (IFRS) and the directives of the European Union (EU) is concerned with changing many rules and laws, which makes it very complex and slow.

The prevailing capital market system and enterprise financing are the most important factors in the accounting harmonization process. Accounting statement rules are directed toward enhancing stock investors' protection in countries where stock markets are independent of banks, for example, in the United Kingdom and the USA. In countries such as Germany and Japan, where universal banking markets exist and banks own equity shares, the accounting system is directed toward creditors' protection.

The implications of such a difference in philosophy on reported financial results could be very great. In so-called capital markets where a great number of small investors prevail, an interest for fair presentation of financial results, that influences stock prices, is much more prevalent than in universal banking markets. The focus of their interest is on profit and loss accounts, which can be called a dynamic approach to economic subject.

In countries with universal banking markets a small number of large investors or creditors prevail. Their risk is covered by the property of debtors and they are insured by fixed interest rates. They are focused on property accounts or balance sheet statements that can be called a static approach to the economic subject. European countries including transitional countries and excluding the United Kingdom have a system that tends toward universal banking and enterprises have a tendency to finance by credit.

The role of accounting organizations and boards in the process of harmonization is huge. The most important of them are the Financial Accounting Standards Board (FASB) in the USA and the International Accounting Standards Board (IASB) in the European Union (EU). They create accounting principles, standards, and recommendations that strongly influence accounting practice and they play a major role in the process of accounting and auditing profession internationalization and supervision.

The FASB is independent from the largest professional association in the USA, American Institute of Certified Public Accountants (AICPA). A significant role in American accounting regulation is played by the Securities and Exchange Commission (SEC), which protects investors from possible manipulation on stock markets, the American Accounting Association (AAA) and the Institute of Management Accountants (IMA). The IASB prescribes and publishes IFRS and has close relationships with the International Federation of Accountants (IFAC). The IASB and IFAC bring together and cooperate with more than 100 national professional associations from all over the world.

Historical conditions in a particular country play a significant role in the harmonization process. A crucial event in the USA was the economic crisis of 1929–1933. Generally Accepted Accounting Principles (GAAP) came into prominence after the creation of the SEC and the various private sector organizations that prescribed the accounting rules.

There was economic, political, and military integration in Europe after the Second World War. The EU prescribed some directives that concern the accounting area. The most important are the Fourth directive from 1978, which treats the annual accounts of certain types of companies, and the Seventh directive from 1983, which deals with consolidated accounts. These directives regulate all important financial statement areas for member states.

Besides the Fourth and Seventh directives, some rules prescribe the accounting process for financial institutions. The directive on the annual accounts of banks and other financial institutions from 1986 prescribes the layout, nomenclature and terminology for the balance sheet and the profit and loss account of all credit institutions in the community. It gives valuation rules for assets and liabilities, contents of the notes on the accounts and rules concerning publication and auditing.

The directive on the solvency ratio from 1989 considers risk of assets and activities of credit institutions and limits the solvency ratio to 8%. It prescribes the treatment of off-balance-sheet items and methods of measuring risk exposure. The directive on the capital adequacy from 1993 deals with investment firms and securities. It prescribes provisions against risks and reporting requirements. There are also other directives such as the Directive on the supervision of credit institutions on a consolidated basis from 1992 and the Directive on prudential supervision in the field of credit institutions, nonlife insurance, life assurance, investment firms, and undertakings for collective investment in transferable securities from 1995, which partly treat accounting area, too.

All of these factors concern Croatia. Belonging to a Roman law system, with the prevalence of a universal banking market, the influence of IASB and EU accounting directives are elements of the global background of the accounting harmonization process in Croatia. There are some specific conditions typical for Croatia, too. Among them are the war of 1991–1995, the privatization process, changes in the banking sector, economic development in the last few years, and the globalization process.

It is estimated that the total cost of war damage in Croatia exceeds US$21,000 million, equivalent to US$4,500 per capita of Croatia's population. Twelve percent of the housing stock in Croatia; about 10% of tourist facilities; and about 30% of industrial capacity were destroyed, burned down, or put out of action by destruction or occupation. The consequences of the war continue to constitute a considerable burden on domestic and economic development. The areas that were already economically underdeveloped before the war were subsequently depopulated and destroyed during the war.

During and after the war the privatization process did not contribute to the desired economic development. From 1991 to the end of 1999, the privatization process encompassed a total of 2,650 former socially owned companies, and 667 of these were industrial. It should be emphasized that the Croatian privatization model was primarily based on the case-by-case principle with preferential treatment to privileged buyers and with the approval of considerable discounts to former and current employees for the purchase of shares with a limited par value. They were allowed to purchase shares with payment in installments, on credit, first with repayment periods of 5 years and then later even of 20 years.

This approach created the "small shareholder" system that is specific to the Croatian transformation and privatization process. Contracts on the sale of shares were concluded with more than 650,000 former and current employees of formerly socially owned enterprises. Approximately 226,000 persons from the socially most-needy categories of the population that were hardest hit by the war (displaced persons, wartime and civilian disabled, families of missing persons, war veterans, etc.) were also introduced into the privatization process later.

On the other side, privileged owners, supported by the political elite have had only short-term goals. They made a purchase of shares from small shareholders and were not interested in employment expansion and survival of the enterprise, in many cases. Due to a specific privatization concept that formally preferred insiders (employees, managers) and enabled the de facto formation of a narrow "chosen" class of owners (tycoons), the degree of technological progress and innovation, and of investment in companies was inappropriate. After a very difficult year in 1999, the Croatian economy expanded modestly in 2000 with real GDP growth of 3.7%, compared with −0.4% a year earlier. Economic output in Croatia is now similar to that of any industrial market economy with manufacturing accounting for about 30% of GDP, agriculture accounting for about 10%, and services accounting for 30%.

Compared to other sectors of the Croatian economy in transition, the banking sector has been among the most exposed to mergers and acquisitions in its most recent economic history. In fact, during the 1990s there have been two mergers waves, the first one following the banking crisis in the mid-1990s (1995–1996), and the second one, at the turn of the century. This second wave led to a cross-border privatization of the largest national banks, opening new concerns about the structure and efficiency of the Croatian banking industry in the years to come.

Mergers in the Croatian banking sector and the entrance of foreign banks introduced many changes in banking activity regulation. Compared to other industries, mergers and acquisitions in the banking sector were marked by superior performances concerning both financial returns and rate of change. The process of basic EU principles implementation in the Croatian banking sector will be easy because the Croatian banking sector is more than 90% owned by foreign banks. Croatia has a higher share of foreign ownership in the banking sector than other transitional countries. For example, the rate in Hungary and Poland is almost 70%, and in other transition countries it is even less.

Croatia has a clear orientation toward a market economy with a structure largely aligned to private enterprise. The country's economic situation has been marked by an increasing recovery since 2000. In 2002 Croatia chalked up a remarkable 5.2% growth in GDP and 4.3% in 2003. Industrial production increased by 4.1% in 2003 compared to the previous year. Inflation continued to fall, dropping from 6.2% in 2000 to 2.1% in 2003.

Despite considerable macroeconomic successes in 2003, the economic situation is under strain. The unemployment rate is high, 19.1%, but in decline, as the budget is in a deficit position. The financial and capital markets are not at the level achieved in other transition countries. Widespread business closures, a lack of legal security, the deficit-ridden social insurance system, productivity shortfalls, and a still high number of state-owned companies all combine to form considerable reform pressure. This is further strengthened by the aim of bringing legislation and reality within a few years to a point that would enable Croatia to become a member of the EU.

The EU and its member states support this process on the basis of the interim trade agreement of the Stabilization and Association Agreement by providing comprehensive advice, measures to promote the private sector, particularly small and medium-sized businesses, credit from the European Investment Bank, and unilateral customs exemptions for Croatian exports. Recently, Croatia became a candidate country for full EU membership. Over the longer term, integration into the EU should help to accelerate Croatia's economic growth and its development in general. On the other hand, integration also implies high costs of adjustment and of building an appropriate administrative infrastructure.

As a future member Croatia must adopt the legal system of the EU. In the accounting area this means that some EU rules have to be adopted directly (regulations and decisions), some have to be respected indirectly by their implementation into domestic regulation in order to achieve their aims (directives), and some are not compulsory, but have to be taken into consideration (recommendations and statements). The areas of accounting and auditing belong under the EU classification into the so-called EU internal market that is regulated by financial reporting law rules and company law rules.

4.3 Difficulties Connected with IFRS Implementation

Croatia accepted IFRS (IAS) directly, by legal enforcement. Other republics from the former Yugoslavia have different approaches. Slovenia has national standards based on IFRS and the highest degree of accounting development. Other republics use IFRS indirectly, which means that they require harmonizing accounting practice and rules with IFRS (IAS). Difficulties connected with IFRS (former IAS) implementation are numerous despite their legal enforcement in Croatia. Some of them are common to most other transition countries. We can say that there are four groups of difficulties:

- Difficulties connected with law rules and regulations
- Difficulties connected with concepts, structure, and contents of IAS (IFRS)
- Difficulties connected with undeveloped capital and financial markets and
- Difficulties connected with insufficient experience and number of experts in the area of valuation and performance judgment

IASs were prescribed in Croatia in 1993 by its Accounting Act. This means that Croatia accepted IAS directly, as national standards. The Croatian board for accounting and accounting standards is in charge of standards translation, coordination, and explanation. The obligation of IAS application is prescribed for all enterprises regardless of their size or of their listing in financial markets. This means that the Croatian Accounting Act contains 30 articles of the Act and more than 2,000 articles of IAS. On the other hand, the Accounting Act prescribes some provisions that are not in accordance with the standards. Besides, plenty of sub-provisions derogate IAS application. Implementation of IAS and difficulties connected with law rules and regulations can be analyzed in the areas of: accounting reporting, tangible and intangible assets accounting, revenues, costs and profit, or loss accounting.

In the area of accounting presentation and statements the Accounting Act prescribes a minimum of enterprise balance sheet and profit and loss account items. These schemes are not the same as those prescribed by the EU Fourth Directive, although the directive offers two balance sheet proposals and four profit and loss account proposals. The differences are in the name and content of some items.

IAS 1 (Presentation of Financial Statements) does not prescribe financial statement schemes. The Accounting Act divides enterprises into small, middle, and large pursuant to criteria of revenues value, balance sheet total, and number of employees. In accordance with these criteria most Croatian enterprises are small, and it is not obvious that they make cash flow statements according to IAS 1 and IAS 7 (Cash Flow Statements). In accounting practice for large enterprises in Croatia the statement showing changes in equity, requested in accordance to IAS 1 was introduced. IFRS provides extended analysis and information of the various components of the financial statements in the notes to the accounts, while Croatian notes to the accounts are relatively condensed.

IAS 34 (*Interim Financial Reporting*) use is only recommended and obvious only under the request of any legal board or contract provision.

IAS 29 (*Financial Reporting in Hyperinflationary Economies*) was applied in Croatia in 1993, the last hyperinflationary year when the inflation price index was 1617.5. That year nonmonetary positions in balance sheets appreciated as the consequence of a static valuation method used in the privatization process. A price index was applied in nonmonetary assets revaluation linearly for all assets including appreciated and imported foreign-made equipment, although foreign exchange rates did not grow in accordance with the inflation price index.

IAS 26 (*Accounting and Reporting by Retirement Benefit Plans*) and IAS 19 (*Employee Benefits*) are awaiting Croatian retirement reform; after that their implementation will be possible in a wider range.

In the area of tangible and intangible assets accounting, enterprises do not use IAS 16 (*Property, Plant and Equipment*) in the articles of harmonizing between book value and fair value, and IAS 15 (*Information Reflecting the Effects of Changing Prices*), although there was single-digit inflation after the break of hyperinflation in 1993. There was no revaluation reserve growth in the balance sheets after 1993, because of undefined tax treatment of such reserves.

IAS 36 (*Impairment of Assets*) is not in use because the decline in value would not be a tax-recognized cost, except on the basis of relevant documentation that proves obsolescence and damage. Negative goodwill is regulated in IAS 38 (*Intangible Assets*) and IAS 22 (*Business Combinations*) but is not recognized in accounting practice, although there were cases of enterprise acquisition on price under the fair value of net property. Capitalization of research and development activities and borrowing costs are also not carried out in accounting practice.

IAS 17 (*Accounting for Leases*) prescribes several variants of lease accounting treatment. Finance leases are those that transfer substantially all risks and rewards to the lessee, without regard to ownership transfer. According to the prerogatives for finance lease recognition, most lease contracts would be classified as finance leases. Nevertheless, practice broadly uses accounting for operating leases, which substantially changes the disclosure of the leased object and revenues (cost) connected with lease contracts.

In the area of revenues, costs, profit, and loss accounting, IFRS (IAS) use is derogated with depreciation prescription, reserve recognition prescription, and accounts receivable estimate prescription. Temporary differences accrued by amortization are not recognized for tax purposes. It is obvious to increase the tax basis if amortization is higher than prescribed, but in the inverse case, the reduction of the tax basis is not permitted. Amortization rates and linear amortization methods are prescribed and in use.

Implementation difficulties connected with concepts, structure, and contents of IFRS (IAS) can be summarized as:

- Frequent changes of standards and new standards prescription
- Enforcement of new standards makes some parts of actual standards irrelevant
- Particular accounting areas are regulated by several standards
- Different standards suggest different solutions for particular accounting area
- Some accounting areas are not covered by standards and
- All standards are not in accordance with the EU directives

Almost all standards were modified in the last few years making outdated parts of effective standards and causing confusion in their understanding. IFRS are becoming something temporary, which is the opposite of what standards are supposed to be.

Some examples of differences of accounting solutions in the same area in various standards include recognition of restructuring cost provisions, regulated with IAS 22 (*Business Combinations*) and IAS 37 (*Provisions, Contingent Liabilities and Contingent Assets*). IAS 37 requires that a provision for restructuring costs should be recognized only when an enterprise has a detailed formal plan for the restructuring and requires a detailed formal plan to be in place at the balance sheet date.

IAS 22 (*Business Combinations*) requires a detailed formal plan to be in place no later than 3 months after the date of acquisition or the date when the annual financial statements are approved. This difference acknowledges that an acquirer may not have enough information to develop a detailed formal plan by the date of acquisition. It does not undermine the principle that no restructuring provision should be recognized if there is no obligation immediately following the acquisition.

Five standards deal with connected enterprises directly and a few others indirectly. IAS 27 (*Consolidated Financial Statements and Accounting for Investments in Subsidiaries*) defines a subsidiary as a company controlled by another enterprise. IAS 28 (*Accounting for Investments in Associates*) defines an associate as an enterprise, other than a subsidiary or joint venture, over which the investor has significant influence. Significant influence means the power to participate in financial and operating policy decisions and it is presumed to exist if the investor owns more than 20% of the associate. Both of these IASs treat the topic of consolidated statements, the equity method and the cost method, but IAS 27 stresses that it considers different areas than IAS 28.

On the other hand, IAS 24 (*Related Party Disclosures*) defines related parties as those able to control or exercise significant influence, which includes among others parent–subsidiary relationships and associates. Such regulation of particular accounting areas with more standards causes confusion in their understanding and application.

IASs cover the area of financial reporting and valuing assets, liabilities, revenues, and cost items. They do not treat areas of accounting analysis, accounting budgeting, and accounting control. These are accounting fields in a broader sense. Non-profit organizations and public sector companies are addressed in standards recently, but the Croatian Board for Accounting and Accounting Standards did not approve them yet, awaiting the public sector reform.

The EU accounting directives are not in accordance with all IFRS (IAS). The main difference is in the concept of fair value and recognition inaugurated by IFRS. The EU Fourth Directive promotes the inclusion of the possibility of financial instruments unrealized gains and losses into a special kind of equity (so-called fair value reserve), while IFRS promotes the inclusion of such effects in revenues or costs.

Undeveloped capital and financial markets have great difficulty implementing the fair value concept. Fair value is the present value of future cash flows discounted by the estimated risk adjusted rate, from the American FASB point of view. According to IAS, fair value is an amount that can be exchanged for an asset or liability settled between contractual parties.

The fair concept is mentioned in 19 standards, from financial instruments regulation to tangible and intangible assets and employee benefits. Fair value is used for market-active instruments and is measurable on the basis of similar instruments of comparative price and expert independent estimates. Croatia has neither of the circumstances for fair concept implementation – a developed financial market and independent estimators. Positive auditors' reports contain an assertion that financial statements are made on the basis of International Accounting Standards, without deeper use of analysis of particular standards.

IAS 2 (Inventories) instructs that inventories should be valued at the lower of cost or net realizable value and IFRS prescribes that LIFO is not acceptable. That provision implicitly includes a continual expert estimate of net realizable value. There are no experts, estimators for valuing net realizable value under circumstances of an undeveloped market. The same problem exists in estimation of fair value. Croatia makes significant efforts in the education of accounting and auditing experts. Accountants pass through the specialist education to obtain an expert's license. The limiting factor is insufficient experience and a system in which their knowledge and capabilities are not demanded and adequately rewarded.

The translation of IAS involved many new terms and words that are not compatible with their economic meaning. Surveys show that accountants consider IAS indistinct and confusing. Their opinion is that accommodation with IAS would be better through the development of national accounting standards. The direct use of IAS is appropriate only for companies listed in financial markets. According to IASC statistics for 2000, only four companies in Croatia prepare financial statements using IAS as the primary accounting basis.

4.4 Accounting in Financial Institutions

Croatian banking regulation is framed by the Banking Act and harmonized with EU banking directives more than any earlier act. Harmonization by EU directives led to the opening of the domestic banking industry to other countries implicitly, and made it possible for domestic banks to open locations in other countries. We find the first similarity in basic definitions. The First Council Directive (77/780/EEC) defines a credit institution as an undertaking whose business is to receive deposits or other repayable funds from the public and to grant credits for its own account, and the Second Council Directives (89/646/EEC) in the annex list defines activities subject to mutual recognition, so the Croatian Banking Act defines banking activities in accordance with the First EU Directive, and other financial activities, in global accordance with activities from the Second EU Directive.[1] Those activities,

---

[1] Second Council Directive (89/646/EEC) – Annex list of activities subject to mutual recognition: 1. Acceptance of deposits and other repayable funds from the public, 2. lending, 3. financial leasing, 4. money transmission services, 5. issuing and administering means of payment (e.g. credit cards, travellers' cheques and bankers' drafts), 6. guarantees and commitments, 7. trading for own

in accordance with the model of universal banking by broadly including securities activities in the banking sector, have meaningful consequences for the future development of the financial sector in Croatia.

The Croatian National Bank gives a license to banks or to branches of foreign banks for banking and also for other financial services, separately. Other financial services may be given by business entities that are not banks or banking branches and they are not under the Banking Act and Croatian National Bank regulation. The principle of mutual recognition is based on the belief that all member countries recognize home member state legal regulation concerning foreign banks although it differs from national regulation. In addition, it includes the principle of home country control and the principle of the single-banking license defined by the Second Banking directive of 1993.

Those principles result in questions for future members, especially Croatia. It can be expected that former domestic banks and existing bank subsidiaries with majority foreign ownership, now licensed in Croatia, will be converted into branches without legal personality and completely out of domestic jurisdiction and supervision. Indeed, the Second Directive permits the possibility of harmonization with host member national rules in some cases. The Directives rule on a single license place credit institutions in a better competitive position than other organizations that make financial services and activities.

Banks from member states that permit all financial activities under the Second Directive can do those activities in all other member countries even if there are domestic banks that are not in that position and vice versa, banks from members with more rigid regulation are limited in other countries where some activities are permitted. It will put pressure on all domestic financial entities not to be more restrictive than the minimum EU requirements.

In the area of financial statements Croatia has not adopted any scheme of balance sheet or profit and loss account prescribed in the Banking Accounting Directive (86/635/EEC) directly, but its statements include all prescribed items, classified by the principle of declining liquidity on the active (asset) side, and by the principle of arising maturity timing on the passive (liability) side in the balance sheet, and by the principle of vertical layout and separation concerning the kinds of activities in the profit and loss account. Contents of financial statements are harmonized with requests of directives and prescribed by Croatian Accounting Law.

IAS 30 – Disclosures in Banks and Similar Financial Institutions Financial Statements – regulates contents of basic financial statements, accounting policies

---

account or for account of customers in: (a) money market instruments (cheques, bills, CDs, etc.); (b) foreign exchange; (c) financial futures and options; (d) exchange and interest rate instruments; (e) transferable securities, 8. participation in share issues and the provision of services related to such issues, 9. advice to undertakings on capital structure, industrial strategy and related questions and advice and services relating to mergers and the purchase of undertakings, 10. money broking, 11. portfolio management and advice, 12. safekeeping and administration of securities, 13. credit reference services, 14. safe custody services; including inter alias: consumer credit, mortgage credit, factoring, with or without recourse, financing of commercial transactions (including forfeiting).

and disclosures connected with risks. A bank's income statement should group income and expenses by nature and should report the principal types of income and expenses. Specific minimum line items for assets and liabilities in banks' balance sheet are prescribed.

Disclosures are required of various kinds of contingencies and commitments, including off-balance-sheet items. Disclosures are required of information relating to losses on loans and advances and other required disclosures include: maturities of various kinds of liabilities, concentrations of assets, liabilities, and off-balance-sheet items, net foreign currency exposures, market values of investments, amounts set aside as appropriations of retained earnings for general banking risks, and secured liabilities and pledges of assets as security.

The Croatian Central Bank is revising the contents of financial statements continually and they are in accordance with IAS 30. The attitude of the Basel Committee is that IAS 30 has to be revised and updated until it is adjusted to new risk concerning issues that appeared during the last 10 years in the banking and financial sector.

IAS 32 – Financial Instruments: Presentation and Disclosures – regulates the accounting for financial instruments in accounting books (presentation) and in financial statements (disclosures). Financial instruments should be classified by issuers into liabilities and equity, which includes splitting compound instruments into these components. Classification has to reflect substance, not form. Split accounting is required for compound financial instruments, such as convertible securities. The standard regulates the treatment of the cost of a financial liability and the cost of equity financing. It prescribes that offsetting on the balance sheet is permitted only if the holder of the financial instrument can legally settle on a net basis.

Disclosure rules require all information on financial instruments relevant to influence the financial position to be disclosed. They include information disclosure of all terms and conditions connected with financial instruments, interest rate risk (reprising and maturity dates, fixed and floating interest rates, maturities), credit risk (maximum exposure and significant concentration), fair values of financial instruments, assets below fair value, and hedges of anticipated transactions.

IAS 39 – Financial Instruments: Recognition and Measurement – with an implementation date of 1 January 2001 is the newest of the "banking" international accounting standards. Compared to the national accounting standards and practical use of international standards in most countries, it increases the use of fair value in accounting for financial instruments significantly. It complies with the concept of fair value in a more comprehensive way than prescribed in IAS 32.

IAS 39 supplements the disclosure requirements of IAS 32 for financial instruments. Under IAS 39 all financial assets and financial liabilities are recognized on the balance sheet, including all derivatives. They are initially measured at cost, which is the fair value of whatever was paid or received to acquire the financial asset or liability. Purchases and sales of financial assets in the market place are recognized either at the trade date or settlement date. Croatian banks generally use the settlement date.

Transaction costs should be included in the initial measurement of all financial instruments. All financial assets are adjusted to fair value, except for the following, which should be carried at amortized cost: (a) loans and receivables not held for trading; (b) other fixed maturity investments such as debt securities; and (c) financial assets whose fair value cannot be reliably measured, e.g. some equity securities, forwards, and options on unquoted equity securities. There is consensus at the EU level that IAS 39 has to be introduced in the accounting systems of member states starting in 2005.[2]

Some financial instruments are not regulated by IAS 39, but by other international accounting standards. For example, IAS 27 – Consolidated financial statements – refers to parent and subsidiaries, IAS 28 – Investments in Associates – refers to equity instruments with significant influence, IAS 31 – Reporting of Interests in Joint Ventures, IAS 17 – Accounting for Leases – refers to instruments of finance leases, IAS 37 – Provisions, Contingent Liabilities and Contingent Assets – refers to future possible liabilities, such as financial guarantees, IAS 19 – Employee Benefits – refers to instruments connected with employees, and IAS 22 – Business Combinations – refers to instruments connected with unpredictable provisions.

According to IAS 39 all financial instruments can be categorized as being held for trading, available for sale, held to maturity and loans that an enterprise has originated. Instruments held for trading and available for sale are accounted for at fair value. Held to maturity assets and originated loans are carried at amortized cost. Banks have an option for the instruments available for sale to recognize unrealized profits or losses not only through the profit or loss account, but through principal correction until the moment of realization.

IAS 39 prescribes strong guidelines for the instruments being held to maturity. If a bank decides to sell the instrument from that category or to move it into another category, it must move all instruments from that category into the category of the instruments being held for trading or available for sale and use the fair value method for these instruments. After that, it must not in the current year or the following 2 years put the existing or new instruments into the held to maturity category. Such strong limitation prevents possible manipulation with financial result from unrealized profit or losses by moving instruments from one category to another and by changing the valuation method.

IAS 39 also emphasizes the need to revalue instruments at least once a year to make sure the current value is reflected. Such revaluation affects the profit and loss account too. IAS 39 establishes conditions for determining when control over a financial asset or liability has been transferred to another party. For financial assets a transfer normally would be recognized if (a) the transferee has the right to sell or pledge the asset and (b) the transferor does not have the right to reacquire the transferred assets. With respect to derecognition of liabilities, the debtor must be legally released from primary responsibility for the liability either judicially or by the

---

[2] Euronext, stock-market of Amsterdam, Brussels and Paris, requires IAS using for all companies included in indexes Next Economy and Next Prime.

creditor. If part of a financial asset or liability is sold or extinguished, the carrying amount is split based on relative fair values.

IAS 39 for the first time defines accounting for derivatives.[3] Derivatives have to be measured according to fair value until they are used as hedging instruments. Then they are accounted for in the same manner as the item hedged. Earlier, derivatives were part of complex agreements, not disclosed as separate financial instruments and with hidden risk. Hedge accounting is also defined by IAS 39, but its application in practice requires coordination between accountants, treasurers, and tax experts.

Hedging, for accounting purposes, means designating a derivative or (only for hedges of foreign currency risks) a nonderivative financial instrument as an offset in net profit or loss, in whole or in part, to the change in fair value or cash flows of a hedged item. Hedge accounting is permitted under IAS 39 in certain circumstances, provided the hedging relationship is clearly defined, measurable, and actually effective. Hedge accounting is permitted only if an enterprise designates a specific hedging instrument as a hedge of a change in value or cash flow of a specific hedged item, rather than as a hedge of an overall net balance sheet position.

In order to avoid some incompatibilities between IAS 39 and legal rules in Croatia, the Central Bank made the decision to use International Accounting Standards in every case when there is discordance between rules and standards.

The correlation between IAS and Croatian accounting practice in the area of securities is shown in Fig. 4.1.

IAS 39 eliminates the profit and loss effect of internal transactions in a bank's published financial statements. This follows normal consolidation practice where a group preparing financial statements is treated as a single entity and should not be able to generate apparent profits or losses through internal transactions. General accounting practice is for the financial statements only to reflect the effects of transactions with third parties. It requires the ability to distinguish those from internal transactions through their accounting systems.

4.5 Accounting Aspects of the Corporate Income Tax System

IAS 12 regulates accounting procedure with the corporate income tax. It deals with current and deferred tax liabilities and asset recognition, presentation, and reporting. While taxable income is defined by tax authority rules, accounting income is defined by accounting standards and policies, and it is the value before the tax expense deduction. The difference between accounting and tax income is caused by two reasons. The first reason is the fact that some kinds of costs are not

---

[3] USA has in the frame of US GAAP (US Generally Accepted Accounting Principles) FAS 133 (Financial Accounting Standards) – Accounting for derivatives and hedging activities – it establishes similar principles like IAS 39.

Fig. 4.1 Correlation between IAS and Croatian accounting practice for securities

Croatian accounting practice		International Accounting Standards		IAS No.
Trade portfolio of equity and debt securities	Fair value method	Assets being held for trading (trading book)	Fair value method	39
Investment portfolio of equity securities	LOCOM method	Assets available for sale	Fair value method (or historical cost if there is no market price and testing for mitigation)	39
Investment portfolio of debt securities	Amortized cost method	Assets held to maturity (banking book) Assets available for sale Originated loans (purchased debt securities from issuer directly)	Amortized cost method Fair value method (or historical costs if there is no market price and testing for mitigation) Amortized cost method	39
Shares with significant influence (more than 20%)	Equity method	Shares with significant influence (more than 20%)	Equity method	28

recognized for tax purposes and some kinds of revenues are not taxable. That produces so-called permanent differences. The second reason is the consequence of accounting policies that dictate different accounting periods for some items compared with periods recognized by tax authorities. These are so-called temporary differences.

Expenses not recognized for tax purposes are regulated by tax rules of a particular country and they increase the real tax rate compared with the nominal rate. There are two kinds of such expenses. The first kind is expenses that increase accounting income in order to tax base forming, and the second kind are expenses that are included in the tax base, but are treated as personal income for the recipient with a withholding tax. The second kind does not cause a difference between accounting and tax income in corporations, but has a nature of tax nonrecognized expenses.

The most important items from the first group of tax nonrecognized expenses are the 70% of representation costs, penalties, 30% of costs of personal motor vehicle usage, value of gifts higher than 2% of last year's revenues, stock higher than the permitted prescribed value, hidden profit payments, and expenses based on a value adjustment relating to participating interests and shares. Hidden profit payments are all given to shareholders (owners) at more favorable than market price or compensation. Expenses based on a value adjustment relating to participating interests and shares are deducted from expenses only if the company uses the share method of value adjustment. It is the only item that is not directly connected to cash or other asset outflow.

The most important items from the second group of tax nonrecognized expenses are: some staff costs, abnormally low creditor's interest and overvalued debtor's interest. Costs of employees and staff above prescribed values (traveling allowances and expenses, other allowances and reimbursements) are treated as personal income with accounted withholding tax. Abnormally low creditor's interest relating to shareholders, owners, or employees – lower than 6% – are taxed as personal income of the debtor too.

All accounting revenues are taxable except those from value adjustments relating to participating interests and shares in group companies. Nontaxable revenues are dividends and participating interests that were taxed in the issued company. These are deductible items from tax-recognized revenues.

The permanent differences between accounting and tax income appear not only because of tax nonrecognized items that are included in accounting. There are some items that are tax relevant and are not included in accounting, like opportunity costs or omitted benefits, for example, abnormally low creditor's interest. Revaluation of long-term assets due to increases in capital value is taxable income, but not accounting recognized revenue or cost. Also, there are some items that are recognized in either income, but their value is permanently different.

That is the case in some provisions for charges and risks, and value adjustments of receivables from trade and other receivables. In those cases the tax authority prescribes specific conditions that are not covered in IAS. For example, value adjustments of receivables from trade and other receivables are tax recognized only if they are in law-court proceedings or if it passes more than 4 months after the unpaid receivable maturity in the current period. If such receivable is not law-court proceeded in the next period, a value adjustment has to be included in tax revenues. Provisions for charges are tax recognized under prescribed conditions, but for risks are not recognized for tax purposes, with the exception of financial institutions.

Temporary differences on the basis of revenues, according to IAS 12, appear when the accounting rules defer some revenue recognition, that under the tax rules has to be included in tax revenues, or contrarily, when tax rules defer some revenue recognition that is included in accounting revenues. According to the Croatian tax prescription, temporary differences on the basis on revenues appear only in the first situation, when some revenue has to be included in tax revenues, without regard to its accounting recognition, and the second situation is not permitted.

Examples are: (a) interests that are related to current periods and included in tax revenues, but will be recognized for accounting purposes when settled according to accounting policy, (b) income of stocks and shares sale that has to be included in tax revenues in the period of sale, but can be recognized for accounting purposes after payment, and (c) reservation cancellation according to tax rules that are tax revenues, but must not be accounting revenues of the current period. Finally, in cases where items can be included in accounting revenues that were included in tax revenues of a previous period and the value of those items is the decreasing sum from taxable income of the current period.

Temporary differences on the basis of costs, according to IAS 12, appear: (a) when some costs can be capitalized and amortized according to accounting policy, but have to be recognized for tax purposes in the period of emergence, (b) when tax and accounting depreciation methods are different and (c) in some other cases connected with revaluation, business combinations, and goodwill.

Depreciation is the most important source of temporary differences. In the periods when tax depreciation is higher than accounting depreciation, a deferred tax liability appears, because the current tax liability is less than the tax expense. Contrarily, when accounting depreciation is higher than tax depreciation, a deferred tax asset appears. During amortization periods, those temporary differences will be liquidated, according to IAS 12. Croatian practice differs from that order in two ways:

1. Depreciation taken for tax purposes is conditioned by the same value stated in accounting, for the purpose of business income assessment. There are several reasons for such rules. Amortization rates and prescribed assets lifetime are very high; for example, for production inventory 10% or 10 years, for office machines, hardware, software, telecommunications equipment, and motor vehicles 25% or 4 years, furniture in trade, tourist trade, and catering industry 20% or 5 years.[4] Additionally, it is possible to completely depreciate a long-term asset in the year of purchase or building, and to use double rates. The intent of such high tax credits and postponement of tax payments is to stimulate a higher degree of self-financing and investment by enterprises. On condition that the depreciable value has to be recognized in accounting, at the same time, is an incentive that the enterprise would not take such high depreciation to avoid payment of tax, but would show a high net income and distribute it as dividends. That would be abasement of the tax credit. On the other hand, such rules distort reality of the financial statements and expressly underestimate assets values and financial results. Despite high amortization rates for tax purposes, the share of depreciation in business costs is less than 5% in the last 10 years, and the financial loss is higher than profits of Croatian enterprises.[5]

2. Depreciation value for accounting purposes can be lower than allowable for tax purposes, but cannot be higher. In other words, positive temporary differences between accounting and tax-recognized depreciation are recognized, but negative differences are not recognized. The consequence is that Croatian enterprises use the straight-line depreciation method permitted by tax rules and do not create their own amortization accounting policy, which would be harmonized with real lifetime and exploitation of long-term assets. That means that

---

[4] Amortization regulations, Official Gazette of the Republic of Croatia, 54/2001.

[5] Statistical information of Fina (Croatian national financial agency) – different years of publishing.

Croatian enterprises do not use IAS in this area and that rules derogate their proclaimed use.

The described regulation of depreciation results in temporary financial benefits in the form of free of cost tax credits, but it is a hidden benefit because it is not reported in accounting and financial statements.

According to IAS 12, tax losses and unused tax incentives can be carried forward and back. In that way, an enterprise realizes a tax benefit, because it decreases its tax in periods when it realizes positive taxable income or it returns taxes paid in previous periods. It is believed that it is not opportune to tax enterprises in successful business years without the possibility of carrying losses of bad business years. It is opportune that enterprises pay tax on the sum of incomes and losses during the longer business cycle. Many legislatures take this into consideration in their corporate tax rules.

According to Croatian tax rules, the tax loss is the negative difference between tax revenues and costs and can be carried only forward for up to 5 years. If an enterprise does not realize positive taxable income in that period, tax losses remain unused. This means that a tax benefit can be realized in the value accounted according to realized taxable income. Tax incentives and exemptions are prescribed for enterprises in the areas that were destroyed in the war, in free zones, and for new investments and employment. Only incentives for employment can increase a tax loss and can be carried forward as an ordinary tax loss. Other incentives can be used only if an enterprise realizes taxable income.

4.6 Cost and Managerial Accounting

Traditional product costing systems that rely on simplistic methods to allocate overheads to products have two basic limitations: they overvalue high volume-produced products and they make the financial result dependent on fluctuation of inventories, not only on goods and services sold. The first limitation is caused by allocating overheads to products on volume-related bases. Retaining fixed costs in the value of inventory causes the second limitation.

Traditional costing systems are appropriate for allocating the manufacturing costs incurred during a period between cost of goods sold and inventories and for external financial reporting requirements. However, they are not suitable for decision-making purposes. They report distorted product costs whenever an organization produces a diverse range of low-volume and high-volume products. Traditional systems work under the following circumstances: few very similar products, low overhead, homogeneous producing processes, homogeneous customers and markets, low administrative costs and very high margins.

Throughout the mid-1980s the most prominent critic of management accounting was Robert Kaplan. He claimed that management accounting lost its relevance and does not provide the information that is required for today's manufacturing and competitive enterprises. Recently, activity-based costing (ABC) has been advocated by Cooper and Kaplan as an alternative method for assigning overheads to products. It is claimed that ABC provides a more reliable basis for assigning nonmanufacturing overheads to products.

ABC defines categories of activity in overhead departments, which on the one hand are recognizable to overhead department managers but, on the other hand, are driven by factors (cost drivers) that are characteristic of products and other cost objects. This has allowed a much higher proportion of total company cost to be allocated to products more strictly according to causation.

Target costing is a price-based system. It offers an improvement over cost-based pricing. Target costing begins with the assumption of the customer's ability to pay. Since earning a profit is considered as given, then a target cost becomes a calculated number that cannot be exceeded. Target cost is the difference between market-priced sales and target profit. According to Berliner and Brimson,[6] companies operating in an advanced manufacturing environment are finding that about 90% of a product's life-cycle cost is determined by decisions made early in the cycle. In many industries a large fraction of the life-cycle cost consists of costs incurred on product design, prototyping, programming, process design, and equipment acquisition.

Focusing on costs after the product or service enters production results in only a small proportion of life-cycle costs being manageable. Target costs should be established throughout the life cycle of new products before entering production. Product costs are computed based on design specifications and compared with the target cost. If the projected cost is above the target cost, then product designers focus on modifying the design so that it becomes cheaper to produce. A team of designers, engineers, marketing, and production personnel and management accountant should concentrate on production that meets the target cost requirement. The term life-cycle costing is used to describe a system that tracks and accumulates the actual costs and revenues attributable to each product from inception to abandonment.

Modern costing systems such as activity-based system and target costing have many advantages compared with traditional systems:

- They trace costs to products according to the product's demands for activities
- They attribute the true costs to products and services taking into account volume and set-up variety, size and complexity variety, process complexity, and customer variety
- They reveal the cost consequence of every form of diversity
- They make a link between costs and activities and assess costs to the phases of the life cycle
- They are models of resource consumption, not spending
- They attempt to measure the total organizational resources required to produce a product

[6] Berliner, C., Brimson, J. A, (1988): *Cost Management for Today's Advanced Manufacturing*, Harvard Business School Press, Boston, pp. 26.

- They are designed to identify priorities for managerial attention
- They involve an external oriented approach and highlight the relative competitive positioning of the organization
- They are enabled to support appropriate pricing decisions based on good cost information, appropriate product mix decisions based on good profitability information and cost management by focusing on activities and cost drivers

Success of implementation of the costing system depends on an adequate conception of the problems involved and the factors that should have been considered. Successful system implementation is 5% software with its interfaces and 95% a combination of model design and behavioral change management.

Enterprises in Croatia have many difficulties in implementing and sustaining modern costing systems. They can be summarized as: personal, organizational, and financial difficulties.

Personal difficulties are the widest and the most important. Enterprises do not have enough experience in making and implementing the organization chart, building an activity dictionary, and looking for problems and opportunities. Experience gives us the tests first and the lessons afterwards. This is the point of view of the modern flexible management team. Such teams are not built or are in the building process in Croatian enterprises.

The environment of transition business is very unstable supporting static and short-time-oriented behavior. It is necessary to prevail over some common misconceptions that cause a fear of modern costing systems. These are the attitude that modern costing systems require a massive amount of data and tremendous maintenance; that it creates a separate set of financial books, which leads to confusion; that it cannot do without special and expensive software; and that a project of implementing a modern costing system is a competing improvement program rather than aid to existing improvement programs.

Frequently, management is not prepared to face the facts discovered by modern costing systems. Personnel do not know how to react or take appropriate actions once they are confronted with the new winners and losers of profitability, whether they are products, services, or customers. The data can lead to reorganizing people and restructuring their work in different ways that may eliminate or replace some existing people and equipment.

Enterprises in Croatia have a traditional organizational structure that is not suitable for modern costing systems. Modern costing systems need modern organization with a flexible and transparent structure and flowing information. It is a prerequisite for defining responsibility of cost and profit centers.

In the case of Croatia the dominant organizational structure is a mix of functional and divisional structure or functional structure territorially diversified. The development of managerial accounting is not at the desired level because of financial, personal, and organizational limitations. A modern costing system is rarely used.

Recent research shows that 50% of enterprises in the hotel industry use the Uniform System of Accounts for Hotels (UsoAfH), but few of them use information in the proper way. Numerous enterprises in other fields of the economy use a full costing system and some of them use a direct-costing system.

But it has to be kept in mind that enterprises in Croatia with some exceptions work with a loss and that the main problem is inefficiency and illiquidity. Traditional organizations make a modern costing system a parallel and off-line information system that competes with the official regulatory accounting system. It causes employee resistance to change and disbelief with the new costs. Also, in traditional organizations many relevant or detailed data are unavailable and it is hardly enough to make a link between activities and costs or define cost drivers. Enterprises have difficulties in determining objectives, issues, and end-users of data.

Finally, enterprises have financial difficulties in implementing modern costing systems. Although they must not be too expensive, they require financial resources for necessary reorganization, education, training, software installation, and introduction. In circumstances where there is a lack of financial resources, enterprises will not consider modern costing techniques to be a priority.

4.7   Concluding Remarks

It can be concluded that the accounting practice in Croatia is far from IAS (IFRS) despite their legal introduction and despite the accounting profession's efforts to implement them in practice. Accounting harmonization is not only the thing of someone's will and attention, but also more than anything the thing of entire circumstances in the area of law, capital and financial markets, and the accounting profession. Researched difficulties described in this paper show that the issued accounting harmonization process in transition countries, particularly in Croatia, is very complex, long-term, and uncertain.

The most important IASs for the banking sector, IAS 39 (*Financial instruments – recognition and measurement*) and IAS 32 (*Financial instruments – disclosure and presentation*) are partly used, because: (1) there is no condition for fair concept measurement, (2) Croatian accounting practice classifies financial instruments in a different way, not according to IAS 39 (3) transaction costs are not included in initial measurement. In the absence of active markets, like in Croatia, there are difficulties in obtaining or calculating reliable fair values.

Analyzing and describing accounting practice in the area of income tax and its comparison with IAS 12 leads to the following conclusions: (1) Despite a valid balance sheet liability method, proclaimed by IAS 12, Croatian enterprises use the income statement liability method, because of its simplicity. (2) Permanent differences between accounting and taxable income are numerous and significant, and can be divided into ordinary differences, and tax non-recognized items, that are treated as personal income. (3) Temporary differences differ from IAS 12 in the areas of: some revenue items recognition, depreciation, and tax losses and incentive treatment. It is needed to make better conditions and possibilities for consistent application of IAS 12 in order to enable proper accounting policies to be formed.

There are many difficulties in implementing and sustaining modern costing systems in enterprises in transition. They can be summarized as personal, organizational and financial. That's why the process of implementation has to be slower and more gradual in Croatia than it is in developing a market environment.

References

Basel Committee on Banking Supervision, (2000), Report to G7 Finance Ministers and Central Bank Governors on International Accounting Standards. Basel.

Basel Committee on Banking Supervision, (2001), The Relationship Between Banking Supervisors and Banks' External Auditors. Basel.

Basel Committee on Banking Supervision, (2002), The Third Quantitative Impact Study. Basel.

Basel Committee on Banking Supervision, (2003), Third Consultative Paper. Basel.

Basel Committee on Banking Supervision, (2003), Sound Practices for the Management and Supervision of Operational Risk. Basel.

Basel Committee on Banking Supervision, (2003), The New Capital Accord. Basel.

Basel Committee on Banking Supervision, (2003), Overview of the New Basel Capital Accord. Basel.

Basel Committee on Banking Supervision, (2003), Quantitative Impact Study – Overview of Global Results. Basel.

Basel Committee on Banking Supervision, (2004), Principles for the home-host recognition of AMA operational risk capital. Basel.

Basel Committee on Banking Supervision, (2004), Modifications to the Capital Treatment for Expected and Unexpected Capital Losses in the New Basel Accord. Basel.

Berliner, C., Brimson, J. A., (1988), Cost Management for Today's Advanced Manufacturing, Harvard Business School Press, Boston.

Bhattacharya, S., Boot, A. W. A., Thakor, A. V., (1998), The Economics of Bank Regulation. Journal of Money, Credit, and Banking, 30(4), 1998, 745–769.

Burch, J. G., (1994), Cost and Management Accounting. A Modern Approach, West Publishing, St. Paul.

Caouette, J., Altman, E., Narayanan, P., (1998), Managing Credit Risk: The Next Great Financial Challenge, Wiley, New York.

Chorafas, D. N., (2001), Managing Operational Risk. Risk Reduction Strategies for Investment and Commercial Banks. Euromoney Books, London.

Cokins, G., (1996), Activity Based Cost Management, Irwin, Chicago.

Combarros, L. L., Accounting and Financial Audit Harmonisation in the European Union, EAR 4/00., London, 2000.

Coyle, G. A. B. (2000), Framework for Credit Risk Management, Glenlake Publishing Company, Chicago.

Croatian legislative, (1992, 2002, and 2003), National Gazettes, Zagreb:

- Accounting Act, National Gazette 90/1992.
- Amortization regulations, Official Gazette of the Republic of Croatia, 54/2001.
- Audit Act, Official Gazette of the Republic of Croatia, 90/1992.
- Banking Act, National Gazette 84/2002.
- Bank Rehabilitation and Restructure Act, National Gazette 44/1994.
- Corporate Income Tax Law, Official Gazette of the Republic of Croatia, 127/2000.
- Decision on consolidated financial statements of banking group, National Gazette 17/2003.
- Decision on credits and potential liabilities classification, National Gazette 17/2003.
- Decision on capital adequacy, National Gazette 17/2003.
- Decision on currency risk exposure of banks, National Gazette 17/2003.

- Decision on banks' financial statements and business activities audit, National Gazette 17/2003.

Croatian statistical information and data: different sources

Drury, C., (1997), Management Accounting for Business Decisions, International Thomson Business Press, London.

EU Council Directives, Luxembourg:

- 89/646/EEC: Second directive on the coordination of the laws, regulations and administrative provisions relating to the taking up and pursuit of the business of credit institutions and amending Directive 77/780/EEC
- 86/635/EEC: Directive on the annual accounts of banks and other financial institutions
- 77/780/EEC: Directive on the coordination of the laws, regulations and administrative provisions relating to the taking up and pursuit of the business of credit institutions
- 89/647/EEC: Directive on a solvency ratio for credit institutions
- 83/349/EEC: Seventh Directive on consolidated accounts
- 92/121/EEC: Directive on the monitoring and control of large exposures of credit institutions
- 93/6/EEC: Directive on the capital adequacy of investments firms and credit institutions
- 92/30/EEC: Directive on the supervision of credit institutions on a consolidated basis

Freixas, X., Santomero, A. M., (2002), An Overall Perspective on Banking Regulation, Federal Reserve Bank of Philadelphia, Working Paper No. 02–01, February 2002.

Greenbaum, S. I., Thakor, A. V., (1995), Contemporary Financial Intermediation, The Dryden Press, Chicago.

IMF Country Report No. 02/180, (2004), Republic of Croatia: Financial System Stability Assessment, Including Reports on the Observance of Standards and Codes on the Following Topics: Banking Supervision, Payments System, Security Regulation, Insurance Regulation, and Monetary and Financial Policy Transparency.

International Accounting Standards Committee, (2003), International Accounting Standards. London.

Mann, F., Michael, I., (2002), Dynamic provisioning: issues and application. Financial Stability Review, Bank of England, December 2002, pp. 128–136.

Power, M., (2003), The Invention of the Operational Risk, London School of Economics and Political Science, Centre for Analysis of Risk and Regulation, Discussion Paper No.: 16.

Chapter 5
Accounting Reform in the Czech Republic

Marcela Žárová

5.1 Introduction

The Czech accounting system demonstrates how global capital market demands impact national accounting systems, as well as the consequences of the European Commission's decision to apply the IAS/IFRS at the national level. This section concentrates upon Czech accounting from the early 1990s to the present time.

The first Accounting Act (hereafter the Act) was approved by the Czech Parliament in 1991, commencing the process of transition from a centrally planned economy to a market economy. In May, 2004, the Czech Republic joined the European Union (EU). The general character of the Czech accounting system is a continental European approach with a strong influence from taxes. Becoming a member of the EU has been crucial to speeding up reform of the Czech accounting system. As a member, the Czech Republic is committed to requiring its listed companies to comply with international financial reporting standards in their consolidated financial statements. But what is unclear is how to deal with the July 2002 Regulation of the European Union on the application of IFRS and to what extent this requirement will be extended to other companies.

The period from the first Act in 1991 to the present day can be divided into three stages. Sequential steps of accounting reform can be illustrated in the Czech Republic using an historical overview of the legal framework of accounting development during this timeframe.

5.2 Period 1: 1991–2002

Prior to fundamental political change in 1989, accounting and financial reporting were subordinated to the requirements of the central planning system and reflected the diminished scope of financial management in a centrally planned economy. The

M. Žárová
University of Economics, Prague

R. W. McGee (ed.), *Accounting Reform in Transition and Developing Economies,*
© Springer Science + Business Media LLC 2008

principal function of accounting became the provision of factual data to assess plan fulfilment and to generate statistics for other planning-related purposes. Accounting generally required adherence to a prescribed chart of accounts and did not involve taking a view on the financial position of an enterprise, since it was not answerable for its financial performance. Therefore financial reporting, providing a true and fair view on financial performance of enterprises to the general public, did not exist in the former Czechoslovakia before 1989.

State enterprises were obliged to produce financial statements for tax and statistical authorities, which treated the statements as private information. This situation began to change after 1989 as the change to a market economy and privatization of enterprises proceeded. The dissolution of the Czech-Slovak Federation on December 31, 1992 and the successful completion of the first wave of "voucher" privatization were the most significant political and economic events in Czechoslovakia during 1992.

A complete reform of Czechoslovak accounting was undertaken, through the Accounting Act that came into effect on January 1, 1992 (although certain provisions were delayed until January 1, 1993). The Chart of Accounts and Accounting Procedures for Business also came into force on January 1, 1993. This delay was related to delays in the tax reform, which also became effective on January 1, 1993.

Accounting practices were reformed in the context of the wider reforms adopted to create the institutions of market economies. In common with other areas of institutional reforms, government was seeking, as far as possible, to ensure that new laws were consistent with those of the European Community (EC), so as to facilitate transition to full membership. New legislation was therefore influenced by EC accounting practices, particularly the Fourth and Seventh Directives on Company Law.

The accounting law was a curious amalgam reflecting the variety of international influences plus residual practices from the previous regime (Zarova et al., 1997). Corporate taxation had an effect on company financial reporting and rules relating to financial statements, but accounting income differed from taxable income. The remaining Chart of Accounts increased effort in separation from taxation, and the increased scope for interpretation and judgment created both difficulties and opportunities for practitioners.

While the Accounting Act that set out the general principles to be applied remained unchanged since July 1, 1994, the Chart of Accounts and the detailed guidance notes on the Accounting Procedures for Business were subject to many minor amendments that went into effect at various times from 1994 to 2002. Despite the amendments, obstacles in changing the primary purpose of the financial statements still existed in the new accounting environment (e.g., from tax-oriented accounting to the means by which owners and management measure the financial position and performance of the business).

The EC adopted a communication in June 2000, which proposed that all listed companies prepare their consolidated financial statements in accordance with IASB standards by 2005 at the latest. Adoption of the 2002 EU Regulation on the application of IFRS also had fundamental effects on further development of accounting in the Czech Republic.

The Czech National Accounting Council, an independent national accounting body, was established by the initiative of Czech accountants, the Chamber of Auditors, academics from the University of Economics in Prague, and the Chamber of Tax Advisors in 2001. The main aim of this body is to support the development of accounting toward an independent respected profession in the Czech Republic, to establish a chamber of accountants, and to participate in the process of issuing national accounting standards.

The main characteristic of this period is accounting regulation that could be best described as regulation without hierarchy, a "legal level," or one-level accounting. From a legal point of view, accounting regulation consisted of the Act only. The Ministry of Finance issued detailed regulatory guidance for accounting, which consisted of a chart of accounts and accounting procedures. Even though Regulatory guidance for accounting was not part of the Act, it became obligatory as it was strictly required by tax authorities.

One-level accounting regulation
Accounting Act
• Regulatory guidance for accounting
• Chart of Accounts
• Accounting Procedures
• Financial Statements, Notes to Accounts

5.3 Accounting Act

The Act covered all accounting entities, including general business enterprises, banks, insurance companies, public (budgetary) entities, nonprofit organizations, municipalities, national property funds, and even small entities using cash-based accounting. The Act was divided into seven parts.

Parts one and two, General provisions and Accounting systems respectively, specified two forms of accounting: cash-based accounting, used by sole traders and various nonprofit organizations, and accrual accounting, used by all other entities, including any sole trader who is registered in the Commercial Register. The accounting unit was required to fulfil conditions of completeness, supporting documentation, and consistency of the accounting records included under the Act. For example, the Act required consistency: an accounting unit could not change its method of valuation or depreciation or of preparing financial statements during an accounting period. Changes could only be effected between accounting periods, and the reasons for any changes, and their financial effects, were required to be disclosed in the financial statements. In addition, accounting records were to be maintained in the Czech language, in conformity with the provisions of the Act, and the fiscal year was required to be a calendar year.

Part three specified the financial statements to be prepared. For most business entities, these were the balance sheet, income statement, and explanatory notes.

The format of the balance sheet and income statement, as well as the content of the notes, which include a cash flow statement, were described in detail in regulatory guidance for accounting. Accounting units that were not obliged to have their financial statements audited could prepare abbreviated financial statements and notes.

Accounting units regulated by special legislative acts, such as joint stock companies, banks, and insurance companies had to have their financial statements audited, and they were required to publish certain information from their financial statements. Other business companies and cooperatives had their financial statements audited only if in the year prior to the year subject to audit, their net turnover exceeded CZK 40 million or their net assets exceed CZK 20 million (the exchange rate was approximately 1 USD = 34 CZK in 2002). All business companies (partnerships or cooperatives) that had at least a 20% ownership interest in another company prepared consolidated financial statements, and all companies being consolidated were obliged to be audited.

Information from audited financial statements, including the auditor's opinion, had to be published within 1 month of being approved by the annual general meeting. Audited accounting units published an annual report too. As the principle of materiality was not included in the Act, detailed requirements concerning financial statements, and a commentary on the results and the future expected development of the accounting unit, were included in the regulatory guidance for accounting.

Part four set out the valuation methods for all assets and liabilities in the accounting records and financial statements. The accrual concept was required for accounting units using the double-entry bookkeeping system. Thus, all revenues and expenses relating to an accounting period were included in the income statement regardless of the date of payments.

The prudence concept required that the valuation of assets and liabilities should reflect the risks, losses, and deterioration in assets and liabilities known to the accounting unit. Events happening after the balance sheet date were ignored by the Act. The Act stipulated that all assets and liabilities denominated in foreign currency should be translated in the financial statements according to the appropriate official rates ruling at the balance sheet date. The Ministry of Finance subsequently clarified that fixed rates determined by the accounting unit could be used during the accounting period.

Assets were generally valued at their historic cost, subject to the recognition of any diminution in value. Identical items of inventory or securities could be valued using a weighted average or a FIFO basis. The use of LIFO or the base-cost method was not permitted, nor was replacement cost other than for livestock (breeding animals).

An accounting entity could determine its own depreciation policy, although intangible assets had to be written off within 5 years of their acquisition (excluding "goodwill" arising on the acquisition of assets, in the course of privatization, or on the purchase of an enterprise, which were written off over 15 years).

Part five of the Act concerned inventory taking of assets and liabilities. The concept of inventory taking applied to all assets and liabilities, not just to physical verification of stocks. Inventory-taking differences were required to be recorded in the period to which the inventory taking related. Part six of the Act concerned accounting documents and their maintenance. Common, temporary, and closing provisions were stated in part seven.

The last amendment of the Act before 2003, effective as of January 1, 2002, brought important, but not fundamental changes in the regulatory framework. They were as follows:

1. The accounting period for all entities was changed from a mandatory calendar year to any 12 successive months
2. A definition of true and fair view was included
3. The voluntary compliance with IAS for consolidated financial statements only was allowed
4. Fair value for financial instruments and their derivatives was introduced

5.4   Regulatory Guidance for Accounting

Detailed obligatory guidance for accounting was issued by the Ministry of Finance. Although these were not part of the Act, they were strictly required for taxation, so essentially they were followed for all purposes. This regulatory guidance consisted of:

(a) Chart of accounts
(b) Accounting procedures
(c) Financial statements, notes to accounts

5.4.1   Chart of Accounts

There were separate charts of accounts for different types of entities, e.g., for business enterprises, banks, insurance companies, public (budgetary) entities, nonprofit organizations, municipalities, and national property funds. The main aims of the Chart of Accounts were (1) to standardize the organization of the individual enterprise accounting system, at the level of major categories of financial transactions and their effects on financial position, and (2) to standardize presentation by the enterprise of its profit or loss and financial position.

The first objective was pursued in the code through its standardized chart of accounts for classifying data entries in the accounting system and through standardized terminology for identifying or describing financial transactions and their effects. The second objective was pursued in the code through a set of model financial statements and schedules, to be used by enterprises in drawing up financial statements periodically.

The Chart of Accounts was organized in a rigid set of control accounts as for the content and numbering. The chart of account for general business entities was classified into the following account classes:

Class 0 – Intangible and tangible assets and investments
Class 1 – Inventory
Class 2 – Financial accounts
Class 3 – Clearing
Class 4 – Capital accounts and long-term liabilities
Class 5 – Expenses
Class 6 – Revenues
Class 7 – Closing balance sheet accounts and off-balance sheet accounts
Class 8 – Management accounts
Class 9 – Management accounts

Within each account class, there was a hierarchy of accounts:

I   Group accounts
II   Nominal accounts
III   Subsidiary accounts

Numbering of group accounts and nominal accounts was obligatory in compliance with the rigid chart. All accounting units that did not require a statutory audit could use simplified rules and use group accounts only (except in certain specified cases), or a combination of one or more nominal accounts and the group account for the rest of the account group. Only subsidiary accounts were allowed to be created in accordance with managerial purposes. On the other hand, there were various accounts for which subsidiary accounts were obligatory, including the following items:

- Short-term and long-term assets and liabilities
- Assets or liabilities denoted in different currencies
- For tax purposes, in particular where a nominal account contains items that were either deductible or nondeductible for tax purposes

Classes 8 and 9, entitled Management accounts, have not included the rigid list of accounts centrally determined by the Ministry of Finance. These two classes were used by the accounting unit for creation of their own management accounting system.

5.4.2   Accounting Procedures

This second part of the regulatory guidance consisted of detailed double-entry bookkeeping rules and detailed instruction on using the chart of accounts.

5.4.3   Financial Statements and Explanatory Notes

This third part of regulatory guidance set out the fundamental rules for:

1. *Conditions for preparation and presentation of financial statements, data to be published from financial statements.*

In compliance with the Act, full or abridged statements were prepared. This part stated a minimum extent of published data from financial statements, balance sheet, and income statement.

2. *Forms and explanations for the preparation of balance sheet and income statement.*

There was a rigid layout of the balance sheet and income statement identical to the EC 4th Directive. The Ministry of Finance chose only the horizontal layout for the balance sheet and one vertical layout for the income statement, with classification using the nature of expenses. Classification using the function of expense method was not allowed. Aspects of materiality and aggregation in statements were not respected. Line items of statements were required to have direct relations to the accounts prescribed by the Ministry of Finance. The income statement has three parts: operating, financial, and extraordinary. Gains and losses were not expressed exclusively. Unusual and infrequent transactions were included under extraordinary items.

3. *The contents of the notes to the financial statements.*

The notes contained general explanations, fundamental data of the firm (company), information on accounting methods, accounting principles and methods of valuation. Besides supplementary information, a cash flow statement with separate parts for operating activities, investment activities, and financing activities was required.

5.5   Period 2 – 2003

The structure of accounting regulation for the year 2003 was temporary, as regulatory guidance for accounting described above had to be replaced by National Accounting Standards by the end of 2003. The main reasons for this fundamental change of accounting regulation were preparation for membership in the EU and the influence of the Czech National Accounting Council. In compliance with the EU assumption and the influence of the National Accounting Council, accounting reform started to be realized. The result was another sequent step in rebuilding the regulatory system. Decrees issued by the Ministry of Finance became part of the regulatory system.

The structure of accounting regulation for the year 2003 differed from the previous year and consisted of two levels of accounting regulations:

Two-level accounting regulation
1. Accounting Act

2. Decrees
   • Regulatory guidance for accounting
   • Accounting Procedures

5.5.1   Accounting Act

The Accounting Act as amended, effective as of January 1, 2003 differed from the prior amended Act in few requirements. There was no change in using IAS under the amended Act.

5.5.2   Decrees

Seven new accounting decrees covering different sectors of the economy were issued (general business entities, banks, insurance companies, etc.). The substance of these decrees was expressly stated by the Act and involved charts of accounts and the layout of the financial statements. As the other Decrees covered accounting methods only, there was a need for leaving the regulatory guidance for accounting in effect until the end of 2003. Regulatory guidance for accounting procedures gave detailed bookkeeping rules. This arrangement existed until the end of 2003.

Layouts of the balance sheet and income statement became part of the decrees from 2003. An option for accounting entities was provided as to the layout of the income statement. Entities could prepare income statements with classification by the nature of expenses or the function of expenses. There were still no options for the balance sheet layout. On the other hand, important changes were implemented to the chart of accounts, which became mandatory, but have been more flexible since 2003.

5.5.3   Regulatory Guidance for Accounting

Regulatory guidance for accounting was used during the year 2003 for the purpose of bookkeeping rules and other provisions not included either in the Act or Decrees. The contents of the notes to the financial statements and data to be published from financial statements were regulated temporarily by regulatory guidance for accounting until the end of 2003.

5.6   Period 3 after 2003

Changes to the regulatory framework were completed as of January 1, 2004. Regulatory guidance for accounting was replaced by a new phenomenon in Czech accounting, National Accounting Standards, which are written and issued by the Ministry of Finance exclusively. Three levels of accounting regulations have been in force since the beginning of 2004.

Three-level accounting regulation
1.   Accounting Act
2.   Decrees
3.   National Accounting Standards

5.6.1   Accounting Act

The Act as amended, effective as of January 1, 2004, includes fundamental changes. The amended Act incorporates implementation of IAS/IFRS as required under European Union regulation. Use of IAS/IFRS has become obligatory for consolidated accounts of publicly traded companies since May 1, 2004. Requirements of the 2002 Regulation on the application of IFRS has been extended to annual accounts of publicly traded companies if their securities are admitted to trading on an EC-regulated market in the Czech Republic.

Cash-based accounting for general business enterprises was eliminated from the Act and became part of tax evidence under the tax law. An obligatory simplified accounting approach has been introduced for small entities (under specified conditions).

5.6.2   Decrees

Decrees are separate for different accounting entities. Amended decrees set out the accounting procedures with primary emphasis on the substance of transactions. The mandatory but flexible chart of accounts from 2003 remains in effect. Amended decrees demand higher qualifications for accountants. The balance sheet and income statement finally consider aspects of materiality and aggregation, and the income statement continues to allow classification by nature or function of expenses.

5.6.3   National Accounting Standards

National accounting standards are an integral part of the three levels of accounting regulation. Standards are issued by the Ministry of Finance. They are not developed under due process, where organizations or individuals submit their suggestions. Standards are issued separately for different accounting entities and determine admissible accounting method or procedures. A list of standards in effect as of January 1, 2004 is listed in Table 5.1.

Standards in effect as of January 1, 2004 were revised. Minor editorial amendments were incorporated. Conflicts and redundancies were eliminated. Amended standards are in effect as of January 1, 2005.

5.7   Tax Accounting

Accounting reform started when the first steps towards changing a tax-oriented accounting system into an investor-oriented system were introduced. Separate accounting for tax purposes under the tax law was first introduced for the period starting in 2004. This point is a crucial one and a necessary condition for the implementation of IAS into local practice.

Table 5.1 Standards as of January 1, 2004

Standard 1	Accounts and procedures for making entries in account
Standard 2	Opening and closing of books of account
Standard 3	Deferred tax
Standard 4	Provisions
Standard 5	Adjustments, allowances
Standard 6	Foreign exchange gains and losses
Standard 7	Inventory-taking differences and natural diminutions within limits
Standard 8	Marketable securities and ownership interests
Standard 9	Derivatives
Standard 10	Receivables – special operations
Standard 11	Business combinations
Standard 12	Changes in equity
Standard 13	Intangible and tangible fixed assets
Standard 14	Long-term financial assets
Standard 15	Inventories
Standard 16	Short-term investment and short-term bank loans
Standard 17	Receivables and payables
Standard 18	Capital account and long-term liabilities
Standard 19	Expenses and revenues
Standard 20	Consolidated financial statements
Standard 21	Settlement, compulsory settlement, bankruptcy and liquidation
Standard 22	Inventory- taking of assets and liabilities on transfers of state-owned property to other parties
Standard 23	Cash flow statement

Emerging issues in the national accounting system have become changing rule-based legislation towards principle-based legislation, which is in compliance with the Directive 2003/51/EC amending accounting EC directives on the annual and consolidated accounts of certain types of companies. A natural consequence of changing rule-based legislation towards principle-based legislation is harmonization of National Accounting Standards with IAS/IFRS.

In the Czech Republic, where accounting has been traditionally influenced by taxation requirements, there seem to be obstacles in determining the tax base independently from accounting income. As a move to IFRS reporting could have a substantial impact on the tax base, the necessary step in harmonization of National Accounting Standards with IAS/IFRS is the determination of tax base independently of accounting income.

5.8   Conclusion

The Czech Republic has proposed a regulatory system for different categories of enterprises, solving the fundamental problem of tax influence on accounting:

- Listed companies – full version of IAS/IFRS for consolidated and individual accounts
- Non-listed entities with outside interest – choice of IAS/IFRS or National Accounting Standards (NAS)
- SME – choice of IAS/IFRS or NAS
- Smaller entities – simplified version of NAS

The main advantage of the proposed system is fluent change of categorization of entities and the ability to comply with demanding requirements without changes of accounting principles. Realization of the proposal is planned for the period starting in 2006.

References

Czech legislation:
Accounting Act No 563/1991 Coll. as amended by Act No 437/2003 Col.
Decree on Accounting for Business No 500/2002 Col. as amended by Decree No. 472/2003Col.
Czech Accounting Standards 1–23 in effect as of January 1, 2005, issued by the Ministry of Finance in compliance with article 36 of Accounting Act No 563/1991 Coll. as amended by Act No 437/2003 Col.
Congress papers:
Comparison study "Comparison of IAS and Czech accounting principles", IAS Conference Prague 1998, 1999, 2000.
Implementation of IAS as emerging Issue of Czech Accounting system, International conference, Niagara University, USA 2000.
Emerging Issues in Czech Accounting System and Proposal for Solution, EAA Congress, Athens, Greece 2001.

Implementation of the IAS/IFRS – Czech accounting system, Warsaw conference for SME, 2003.

Harmonisation of the Czech accounting system with IAS/IFRS, EAA Congress, Prague 2004.

Critical review of IAS/IFRS implementation into the Czech accounting regulatory system, International conference in Göttingen University, 2003.

Zarova M., Zelenka, I., Seal, W., Sucher, P. (1997) Accounting and Societal Transition: The Bohemian Accountant and the Velvet Revolution, Centre for Research into Post-Communist Economies. Communist Economies and Economic Transformation, Vol. 9, No 3, 1997.

Zarova, M., Moizer, P., Sucher, P. (1999) The Images of the Big Six audit firms in the Czech Republic, The European Accounting Review, Vol. 8, number 3.

Zarova, M. (1999) International Accounting from the Perspective of European Development, Acta Oeconomica Pragensia, pp. 213–224.

Zarova, M. (2000) EU Accounting Directives and Proposal to the Valuation Amendments. Bulletin to the international conference "Accounting in the worldwide process", 2000, pp. 236–240.

Chapter 6
Development of Accounting and Implementation of International Financial Reporting Standards in Estonia

Jaan Alver and Lehte Alver

6.1 Introduction

Estonia is a small European country. It covers an area of 45,200 km². The population is about 1.3 million. The official language (state language) is Estonian. The monetary unit is the *kroon* (crown), which is denoted by the symbol *EEK*. The *Kroon* is made up of 100 *sents*.

The first time independence was recognized internationally for Estonia was in 1920. It was lost in 1940 and recovered in 1991. In 1940 and following the German occupation in 1941–1944, Estonia was incorporated into the USSR (Soviet Union).

In the context of accounting in Europe, Estonia is one of the less-known countries. Estonian accounting regulation has only a relatively brief history compared to those of some other European countries. Until the beginning of the 20th century, there was very little information about accounting in Estonia. At the same time Estonia is one of the first European countries, which allows International Financial Reporting Standards (IFRSs) also in stand-alone financial statements for statutory purposes.

6.2 Accounting in Estonia 1918–1940

Estonia is a quite new country. It was independent the first time between 1918 and 1940. All elements of the market economy were known during this period.

6.2.1 Russian Commercial Law

During the above-mentioned period the czarist *Russian Commercial Law* regulated all areas of business activities in the independent Republic of Estonia, including accounting and taxation. This Law was in force since 1834. The law established

J. Alver and L. Alver
Tallinn University of Technology

R. W. McGee (ed.), *Accounting Reform in Transition and Developing Economies,*
© Springer Science+Business Media LLC 2008

the classification of enterprises, the books of accounting records, which each enterprise had to keep, and the general accounting requirements. According to the law all enterprises were classified as big, medium, and small. The number of obligatory books were established and named by the law. The law also described how to document and record business transactions, how to make corrections, and retain the books. Accounting for doubtful accounts was known from the Russian Commercial Law. All doubtful accounts must be shown in the balance in the amount of 1 cent.

Correct keeping of accounting records (books) was very important. If any illegal transaction was found it was possible to declare the bankruptcy of the enterprise and big penalties could be assessed without any explanations.

The owner of an enterprise was responsible for bookkeeping. All books had to be saved for 10 years. Some of the main shortcomings of the Russian Commercial Law were:

1. Due to its longevity the Russian Commercial Law was outdated. The bookkeeping requirements were set up for trading companies, but not for industrial enterprises.
2. The requirement for physical inventory was missing.
3. Many of the obligatory accounting books mentioned in the law were not used in real life.

Law of Golden Balances On January 1, 1926 the *Law of Golden Balances* came into force. The importance of the law was to unify different currency units because before enforcement of the *Law of Golden Balances* Russian gold and paper rubles and Estonian marks were used simultaneously.

Law of Language for Business Enterprises Before 1935 it was possible to keep books in all languages, except Hebrew. From 1935 it became obligatory to keep books in Estonian.

Auditing was not conducted on a good professional level. Only firms that raised capital abroad used international auditors. The main problem in Estonia was to find good auditors. So, in 1932 in cooperation with English Chartered Accountants and German Treuhand & Büchherrevisoren the Association of Auditors (Arveasjanduse Revidentide Ühing) was established in Tallinn. The best accounting specialists were members of that organization. The aim was to provide auditing on a very high professional level.

Education During the period 1918–1940 commercial colleges were quite popular in Estonia. It was possible to take accounting courses at several commercial colleges all over Estonia. Short and also long time courses mostly in South-Estonia – in Tartu, Viljandi, and Valga, and also at Tartu University. In 1920 the Law Faculty of Tartu University opened the Institute[1] of Commercial Studies. In 1936 the Accounting Department was established at Tartu University.

---

[1] Department.

6.3   The Regulation on Accounting

For half a century accounting in Estonia was a part of the Soviet accounting system. The Soviet accounting system applied in Estonia was an integral part of the centralized administrative institutional structures for the direction and control of the command economic system. The first step on the way to change the situation was made in 1990, while Estonia remained, albeit reluctantly, a constituent republic of the USSR. On July 6, 1990, the Regulation of Accounting was adopted by the National Government and came into force on January 1, 1991. It is of special interest because it was the first measure adopted in any of the constituent republics of the USSR to mark a departure from the path of the Soviet accounting evolution. It was really an "accounting step" on the transition from a command economy to a market economy. Although, legally, the measure was a regulation and not a statute (i.e., not approved by a legislative assembly but adopted by the executive action of the government) it was comparable to a fundamental, or basic, accounting law.

When examining the *Regulation on Accounting*, it should be borne in mind that it was framed when Estonia was still part of the USSR and the outcome of any transitional process for the Estonian economy was neither assured or certain. The declared purpose of the *Regulation* was to bring about the organization of accounting in the conditions of a market economy. Real accounting continued to be perceived as properly subject to centralized prescription and its primary purpose the meeting of the needs of the central authorities, i.e., the central authorities of Estonia (Statistics Bureau, Tax Department) and not, as hitherto, those of the USSR.

This document introduced a number of new accounting concepts and principles, new terms, and a new set of annual statements (including the balance sheet, the income statement and the statement of changes in financial position and notes). The main characteristic of that period is that it was mixed with the past (some elements of the former Soviet accounting system remained in force), present (real usage of new methods, principles and financial statements), and future (usage of many new terms of the market economy that really were not represented in the Estonian economy).

In the creation of a market economy state enterprises were transformed into privately owned enterprises. By the special legal act the responsibility for organizing of accounting in enterprises was laid upon the chief executive (director). For fulfillment of this responsibility the director of the enterprise might have an accounting department, use services of accounting firms or use the services of accountants.

According to the Regulation each enterprise was required to prepare a chart of accounts. In 1991 the accounting system was based on a chart of accounts published by the Ministry of Finance USSR. The former Soviet standard chart of accounts was officially used in Estonia until December 31, 1992. Since January 1, 1993 there is no standard chart of accounts in Estonia. Every company can introduce its own chart of accounts.

The annual report included the balance sheet, income statement, statement of changes in financial position, and footnotes. The financial year was generally the same as the calendar year. The Regulation was in force until 1995.

6.4 The First Accounting Act

The second step started with the introduction of the first *Estonian Accounting Act*, which was passed by Parliament on June 8, 1994 and came into force on January 1, 1995. It was supported by the introduction of the Estonian *Commercial Code*, which was passed by Parliament on February 15, 1995 and came into force on September 1, 1995. *The Commercial Code* was corrected several times but still remains in force.

In the Commercial Code the following legal forms of business organization were (and are) defined:

- Public limited liability company (*aktsiaselts, AS*)
- Private limited liability company (*osaühing, OÜ*)
- Limited partnership (*usaldusühing*)
- General partnership (*täisühing*)
- Commercial association (*tulundusühistu*)
- Sole proprietor (*füüsilisest isikust ettevõtja, FIE*)

The two most common types of companies in Estonia are the public limited company (*Aktsiaselts*, or *AS*) and the private limited company (*Osaühing*, or *OÜ*). From September 1, 1997 public limited companies must have a share capital of at least EEK 400,000, while a private limited company must have company capital of at least EEK 40,000.

If a foreign company wants to permanently offer goods or services in its own name in Estonia, it shall enter a branch (*filiaal*) in the commercial register. A branch is not a legal person. In the cases provided by law, a company shall obtain a license in order to found a branch in Estonia.

The *Accounting Act* did not contain a detailed set of rules and can best be characterized as constituting a legal framework. The legal framework was general and applied to all legal entities and physical persons registered as businesses in Estonia (referred to as accounting entities in the *Act*) with the exception of the Bank of Estonia.

The *Accounting Act* was supplemented by a number of methodological recommendations (guidelines) on accounting matters issued by the National Accounting Board. These recommendations related to such accounting areas as accounting principles, preparation of financial statements, revenue recognition, business combinations, and others. All together there were 16 so-called Estonian accounting standards, which set up a conceptual framework of generally accepted accounting principles, revenue recognition, business combinations, leases, government grants, earning per share and long-term construction contracts. The only problem was these standards were not for obligatory use. They were only recommendations and in the case of contradictions with the *Accounting Act*, requirements of the *Accounting Act* have to be followed. Estonian *good accounting practice* (Estonian GAAP) was introduced. It was declared to be based on internationally recognized accounting principles, which were established with the *Accounting Act* and Estonian accounting guidelines. The true and fair view (*TFV*) override was declared.

The first *Accounting Act* was in force for 8 years (from 1995 to 2002) and was changed several times. Unfortunately, these changes were mostly cosmetic.

In Estonia no attempt was made to enlist the support of the accounting community for changes in accounting practices. There was no publication of drafts of the *Regulation on Accounting* and the *Accounting Act* prior to their enactment. There has been no general discussion of the purpose or the proper understanding of the required accounting changes or the manner of their implementation.

6.5   The Second Accounting Act

The first *Accounting Act* of Estonia (with an effective date of January 1, 1995) had recognized as valid international accounting requirements, as well as the majority of the requirements of the 4th Directive of the EU. Meanwhile the *IFRS*s had been amended and a number of requirements had become contradictory to those of the new *IFRS*s.

The third step started with the introduction of the new Estonian *Accounting Act*, which was passed by Parliament on November 20, 2002 and came into force on January 1, 2003. The requirements of the *Act* are applicable to annual reports for reporting periods that began on January 1, 2003 or later. The goal of the *Act* is declared to create the legal basis and establish general requirements for organizing accounting and financial reporting pursuant to internationally recognized principles. The new *Accounting Act* is applied to the Republic of Estonia as a legal entity in public law, local governments, all legal entities in private or public law registered in Estonia, sole proprietors, and branches of registered foreign companies that are accounting entities. The new *Accounting Act* also modified the status of the National Accounting Board, which became an independent commission.

Instead of the former two basic statements (the balance sheet and the income statement) the annual report now includes four statements: the balance sheet, the income statement, the cash flow statement, and the statement of changes in owner's equity.

The *Accounting Act* is supplemented by a number of guidelines (standards) of the *National Accounting Board*, which can be characterized as "mini versions" of *IFRS*s. All accounting entities must choose one of the following accounting frameworks:

1. Estonian *good accounting practice* (*Estonian GAAP*)
2. *International Financial Reporting Standards* (*IFRS*s)

Since 2003 *IFRS*s are permitted for all companies instead of the local accounting guidelines. All listed companies as well as credit and financial institutions
and insurance companies will be required to apply *IFRS*s in their consolidated
and separate accounts from January 1, 2005.

The new *Accounting Act* allows all companies to apply *International Financial
Reporting Standards* (*IFRS*s) instead of the local accounting guidelines (standards)
in both consolidated and the parent's financial statements. Thus, the companies that
choose the requirements of *IFRS*s are no longer obligated to prepare double
reports.

Following the proposal of the European Commission, the *IFRS* requirements are
compulsory for companies registered with the stock markets of Estonia or other EU
member countries as well as to credit and financial institutions and insurance companies from January 1, 2005 (most of them did it already before that requirement).
All other Estonian companies are free to decide whether to choose to follow the
IFRS or the *Estonian GAAP*. Large companies are expected to choose the full
*IFRS*s option (from 2005 the translated text of international standards is also available). Small- and medium-sized companies are likely to use the revised Estonian
GAAP as their accounting framework.

It should be taken into account that the only official language (state language) in
Estonia is Estonian. The Estonian language is mandatory for financial statements.
Listed companies often publish their annual reports in English as well.

6.6   Estonian Gaap

Since 1993, the overall strategy has been to align *Estonian GAAP* with *IAS/IFRS*.
The *Estonian GAAP* (Estonian *good accounting practice*) is based on the
Accounting Act and the local guidelines (*Raamatupidamise Toimkonna Juhendid* =
RTJ). Together with the new *Accounting Act*, 17 new guidelines (RTJs), covering
all the major fields in accounting, were effective on October 1, 2004. The content
of RTJs is mostly summaries of the respective International Financial Reporting
Standards, meant in most cases for the entities that do not have to follow the full
set of *IFRS* requirements. The new *Accounting Act* requires the local accounting
guidelines to be harmonized with *IFRS*s and cross-referenced to the applicable
paragraphs of *IFRS*s. Any differences in the local guidelines compared to *IFRS*s
must be explained and justified. In areas that are not covered by the local guidelines, the *IFRS*s treatment is recommended, but not mandatory.

Estonia was the first nation in Europe to align national GAAP with international
accounting standards by law. The *Accounting Act of 1995* stated that *Estonian*

GAAP was based on the standards interpretations and guidelines promulgated by the *IASC*.

Estonian GAAP should be preferred by small- and medium-sized companies due to better availability, for the shorter texts and that of being written in the local language. Table 6.1 compares Estonian GAAP and IAS/IFRS

Table 6.1 Comparison of accounting and reporting methods **Estonian GAAP versus IAS/IFRS**

Methods	Estonian GAAP	IAS/IFRS
Methods allowed for inventory valuation	Specific identification, FIFO, weighted average method.	Specific identification, FIFO, weighted average method.
Methods allowed for depreciation of tangible fixed assets	The straight line method should be used. The use of other methods should also be considered if they reflect more objectively the allocation of expected future economic benefits.	Straight line, reducing (or diminishing) balance, units of production.
Methods allowed for amortization of intangible fixed assets	The straight line method should be used, except in cases when another method provides a more objective view of the allocation of future economic benefits. In the last case only such methods are acceptable under which the accumulated amortization expense at each given time period is not lower than calculated under the straight line method.	The straight line method should be used unless the time pattern of consumption the asset's economic benefits can be determined reliably and clearly indicates that one of the other methods (straight line, diminishing balance, units of production) is more suitable.

6.7   Some Critical Remarks

6.7.1   *Terminology*

The draft of the *Accounting Act* was prepared by the National Accounting Board and approved by all ministries of Estonia. Then it was passed by Parliament. Unfortunately the government employees as well as members of Parliament who are not specialists in accounting expressed their imaginations and as a result a couple of special accounting terms and definitions were replaced by other (incorrect) definitions and legal terms.

Section 3 of the *Accounting Act* contains definitions of 12 terms, which are important in the process of the preparation of financial statements. Let us compare definitions of five basic accounting terms (original wordings have been preserved).

6.7.1.1   Asset

IASB Framework: A resource controlled by the enterprise as a result of past events and from which future economic benefits are expected to flow to the enterprise.

Estonian Accounting Act (original version): A monetarily measurable object or right belonging to an accounting entity (NB! Instead of asset wealth is defined!).

Estonian Accounting Act (English version): A monetarily measurable object or right belonging to an accounting entity.

6.7.1.2   Liability

IASB Framework: A present obligation of the enterprise arising from past events, the settlement of which is expected to result in an outflow from the enterprise of resources embodying economic benefits.

Estonian Accounting Act (original version): A monetarily measurable debt of an accounting entity (NB! Instead of liability the term "obligation" is defined and used everywhere!).

Estonian Accounting Act (English version): A monetarily measurable obligation of an accounting entity.

6.7.1.3   Income

IASB Framework: Increases in economic benefits during the accounting period in the form of inflows or enhancements of assets or decreases of liabilities that result in increases in equity, or other than those relating to contributions from equity participants.

Estonian Accounting Act (original version): Inflows of an accounting period that are accompanied by an increase of assets or decrease of obligations and that increase the owner's equity of the accounting entity, except payments made by owners to owner's equity.

Estonian Accounting Act (English version): An increase in economic benefits, except contributions to owner's equity made by owners, during an accounting period which take the form of an increase in assets or a reduction in liabilities and which increase the owner's equity of the accounting entity.

6.7.1.4   Expenses

IASB Framework: Decreases in economic benefits during an accounting period in the form of outflows or depletions of assets or incurrences of liabilities that result in decreases in equity, other than those relating to distributions to equity participants.

Estonian Accounting Act (original version): Outflows of an accounting period that are accompanied by a decrease of assets or increase of obligations and that decrease the owner's equity of the accounting entity, except payments made to owners from owner's equity.

Estonian Accounting Act (English version): a reduction in economic benefits, except payments made to owners from owner's equity, during an accounting period which takes the form of a reduction in assets or an increase in liabilities and which reduce the owner's equity of the accounting entity.

Comment: According to the definition in the *Accounting Act* depreciation, amortization, and depletion amounts are not expenses!!!

6.7.1.5 Equity

IASB Framework: The residual interest in the assets of the enterprise after deducting all its liabilities.

Estonian Accounting Act (original version): The difference between the assets and obligations of an accounting entity.

Estonian Accounting Act (English version): The difference between the assets and liabilities of an accounting entity.

It can be pointed out that the definitions of the studied terms in the *Accounting Act* contain misstatements and contradictions and sporadically differ materially from those given in the *IASB Framework*. In many cases Estonian definitions are not supported by recognition criteria. It should be mentioned that the definitions used in accounting guidelines are closer to the definitions set up in *IFRS*s and sporadically differ materially from those established by the *Accounting Act*.

The problem can arise from the fact that the *Accounting Act* has prevailing character and in case of contradiction between the *Accounting Act* and the guidelines the law will prevail. This means that the correct accounting terminology in the sense of the *Accounting Act* is really illegal in Estonia. By the way, it is worth mentioning that Estonian accounting terminology is underdeveloped and incorrect wordings and misstatements in original (Estonian) texts are very common. For that reason the translation of accounting literature is extremely difficult.

6.7.2 Assumptions, Qualitative Characteristics and Constraints

The basic principles for the preparation of annual accounts were and are presented in both *Accounting Acts* (13 in the old *Act* and 10 in the new one), but unfortunately practitioners have not paid any attention to these principles. The basic principles of the *Accounting Act* are not in line with the ones in the *IASB Framework*, and different from the *IASB Framework*. The *Accounting Act* does not differentiate underlying assumptions, qualitative characteristics, and constraints.

According to the *Accounting Act* the purpose of the annual accounts (annual report) is to give a *true and fair view* of the financial position, economic performance, and cash flows of the accounting entity. This is also an obligatory part of the

Management declaration. At the same time the management must declare that the accounting entity is carrying on its activities as a going concern. Unfortunately the true and fair view is not defined in the *Accounting Act*, guidelines or anywhere else. The *TFV* override was declared in the old *Accounting Act*, which was in force between 1995 and 2002, but this is not emphasized in the new *Accounting Act*.

In local guideline RTJ 1 the position that the true and fair view on presenting the financial position, performance, and changes in the financial position of an enterprise can still be followed by the management, despite the controversy of the requirements of the *Accounting Act* and the RTJs, is emphasized. The requirements of RTJs can be omitted if these procedures are recognized and explained in public in the notes to the annual accounts. Again, the problem can arise from the fact that the *Accounting Act* has a prevailing character and in case of contradiction between the *Accounting Act* and the guidelines the law will prevail. The *Accounting Act* does not clearly declare the *TFV* override. It should be mentioned that the importance of the *TFV* never has been an issue in the Estonian accounting theory as well as practice.

6.7.3   Some Contradictions – Estonian Accounting and IFRSs

The definitions of the basic terms (asset, liability, equity, income, expense) differ from each other. As the *Accounting Act* prevails over the RTJs, the *true and fair* recognition of the economic results cannot be guaranteed.

6.8   Summary

In this chapter the development of accounting and financial reporting as well as national characteristics of financial reporting in Estonia have been examined.

The study, focusing on the evolution of the development of accounting in Estonia, revealed that the development of accounting and the financial reporting system can be divided into three stages: (1) beginning of accounting reforms, (2) beginning of the system-building by implementation of internationally recognized accounting principles (*IAS*s), (3) improvement of the accounting system.

The Estonian accounting legislation includes the *Accounting Act* and a number of guidelines (standards) issued by the National Accounting Board, which can be characterized as "mini versions" of *IFRS*s. Guidelines are generally in line with the requirements of the *IFRS*s.

The Estonian accounting legislation allows all companies to apply *IFRS*s instead of the local accounting guidelines (standards) in both consolidated and the parent's financial statements. Thus, the companies that choose the requirements of *IFRS*s are no longer obligated to prepare double reports.

There are some shortcomings in the Estonian accounting legislation, which are worth mentioning:

1. The definitions of several basic terms differ materially from definitions included in the *IASB Framework*.
2. The *TFV* override is not emphasized in the *Accounting Act*. As the *Accounting Act* prevails over the RTJs, the true and fair recognition of the economic results cannot be guaranteed.
3. Some parts of the Estonian accounting guidelines are not in line with *IFRS*s.

Appendix

Some general data about business environment and financial reporting

Business background

The principal forms of business enterprise are private (closed) and public (open) limited liability companies, general and limited partnerships, and sole proprietorships. The two types of limited liability companies that have been mainly chosen for entrepreneurship in the Baltic States are the following:

- Private limited liability company
- Public limited liability company

Both are treated as separate legal entities with liability of the shareholders restricted to the value of the company's assets. The requirements of the minimum registered share capital:

Minimum required share capital of private limited liability company	2,555 EUR(EEK 40,000)
Minimum required share capital of public limited liability company	25,565 EUR (EEK 400,000)

For comparison it should be mentioned that the minimum required share capital of 120,000 EUR has been set up for a new type of European limited liability company – *Societas Europe (SE)*.

General requirements for preparation of consolidated statements

Net sales exceed	639,400 EUR (EEK 10,000,000)
Total assets exceed	319,700 EUR (EEK 5,000,000)
The average number of employees	10

The management board shall submit the approved annual report to the commercial register not later than 6 months after the end of the financial year.

General requirements for auditing of financial statements

The annual financial statements shall be audited if at least two of the three following criteria are met:

Net sales exceed   639,400 EUR (EEK 10,000,000)
Total assets   319,700 EUR (EEK 5,000,000)
The average number of employees   10

Taxation

Tax rates and tax applications:

Corporate income tax   23%*
VAT (generally)   18%
Social security tax:

• Employer   33%
• Employee   –

Individual income tax   23%
Real Estate Tax   0

Financial Statements

Balance Sheet

In Estonia the so-called North-American type of balance sheet is used. According to the layout of the balance sheet presented in the annex to the *Accounting Act*, assets should be presented in order from most to least liquid ("decreasing liquidity") and liabilities with shorter term first and longer term last (decreasing degree

---

*As of January 1, 2000, legal entities registered in Estonia and foreign entities with continuous operations in Estonia do not pay taxes on profits that are redirected into investments. The corporate income tax applies to an actual distribution of profits by companies, mainly to dividends or to gifts and benefits that have been distributed. In 2006 the tax payable is at the rate of 23/77 of the actual payment (23% of the gross dividend). In 2005 and 2004 the tax payable was at the rate of 24/76 and 26/74 of the actual payment respectively.

of maturity). The Estonian *Accounting Act* allows companies to use vertical presentation of items in the balance sheet (report format). The layout was changed at the end of 2005. From 2006 it is shorter and all items should be shown in net amounts. It means that the importance of notes to the accounts has increased substantially. At the same time it is notable that the main difference between Estonian accounting guidelines (*Estonian GAAP*) and *IAS/IFRS* (*International GAAP*) lies in the sphere of disclosure.

Income Statement

The Estonian *Accounting Act* allows companies to choose one of two formats of income statement whose layouts are presented in the annex to the *Accounting Act*:

- Vertical income statement by nature
- Vertical income statement by function

Chapter 7
Accounting Reform in Lithuania

Vaclovas Lakis and Laimute Kazlauskiene

7.1   Inception of the Accounting Reform

The reform of accounting started in 1992 when the Supreme Council of the Republic of Lithuania passed the Law on the Principles of Accounting. In the period between 1990, as the year of the declaration Lithuanian's independence, and 1992, accounting used to be performed pursuant to instructions in operation under the administrative command system. However, certain slight changes resulting mainly from economic reforms and privatization initiated at that time were undertaken in the area of accountancy.

The Law on the Principles of Accounting obligated enterprises to organize their accounting procedures so that tax-counting offices, statisticians, creditors, and commercial partners could receive faithful and timely information. For the first time *in* the history of Lithuanian accountancy the Law demanded that accounting should be carried out in conformity with the provisions of International Accounting Standards and the European Union (formerly European Economic Community) Directives.

The Law prescribed three main principles of accounting: going concern, accrual basis, and comparability. The Law provided the procedure for the formalization and signing of documents confirming the execution of economic operations, the composition and the procedure for the authorization of financial statements, the methods of assets valuation, and the necessity of a stocktaking procedure.

Later in October 1993, the Government of the Republic of Lithuania approved the Order for the drawing up of financial statements. It came into force in 1994. The following structure of above-mentioned financial statements was approved: Balance Sheet, Income Statement, Profit (Losses) Allocation Statement, Cash Flow Statement, and Explanatory Notes. The financial statements were to be submitted by enterprises having the status of a legal entity if their indices exceeded the ones specified in the least two positions set forth below:

V. Lakis
Vilnius University

L. Kazlauskiene
Institute of Accountants, Vilnius

R. W. McGee (ed.), *Accounting Reform in Transition and Developing Economies,*
© Springer Science+Business Media LLC 2008

- The amount on the Balance Sheet is 5 million Litas (1.45 million Euro)
- Revenue from sales through the reporting year amounts to 10 million Litas (2.9 million Euro)
- 6,000 minimum wages were paid for hired workers through a year

Smaller entities were allowed to render short-form financial statements consisting of a short-form Balance Sheet, Income Statement, Profit (Losses) Allocation Statement, and Explanatory Notes.

Explanatory Notes had to include information concerned with the activity of enterprise yet not presented in the financial statements. All enterprises had to submit general data about the enterprise, and explanations of large amounts provided in the financial statements, if the said amounts had influenced the evaluation of the enterprise's position.

Furthermore, the Explanatory Notes of large and middle-sized enterprises were required to indicate the position of intangible assets and their change over the reporting period, the position of long-term tangible assets according to their key classes, the acquisition value of financial assets and their change over reporting period, the composition of enterprise capital, lease liabilities, the provisions for large amounts, the results of the enterprise by each type of activity, the average number of hired workers, the revenue from financial activity, and the costs under every large amount.

The Ministry of Finance approved a model chart of accounts to be followed by enterprises when rendering their own charts of accounts.

The approval of the Law on the Principles of Accounting and related standard acts was a substantial step toward the reorganization of accounting in Lithuania. Although the implementation of the International Accounting Standards and European Union Directives was not yet started then, this indicated clearly that accounting in Lithuania should be fully harmonized with the accounting in other market economics. Key principles of accounting provided by the Law formed a beneficial basis for further reorganization.

The Institute of Audit and Accounting was established in 1995. It purposed to participate in the preparation of standard acts governing area of accounting, and projects for audit, as well as to control the development of accounting and auditing in Lithuania.

7.2   Accounting Reorganization, EU Directives and IAS

Another important stage of the reorganization and development of accounting started in 2001 following the approval, by Seimas of the Republic of Lithuania, of three new laws: the Law on Accounting, the Law on Financial Accountability of Companies, and the Law on Consolidated Financial Accountability of Companies.

The Law on Accounting regulates the arrangement of accounting. It also defines general requirements for the handling of accounting, the legalization and keeping of accounting documents and accounting registers, and the responsibility for the arrangement of accounting and safekeeping of documents. This Law provides only the general procedures for the handling of accounting. The Law specifies that profit-seeking limited civil liability legal persons are to handle accounting in pursuance of the Business Accounting Standards. The standards are to be announced by the Institute of Accounting while general methodological guidance is to be performed by the Ministry of Finance.

Economic entities whose securities are traded on a regulated market are to handle their accounting in accordance with the International Accounting Standards. The Law on Financial Accountability of Companies prescribes the general accounting principles, the requirements for the preparation of financial statements, the composition of financial statements, and the evaluation of assets and liabilities.

The Law on Consolidated Financial Accountability of Companies specifies the conditions for the consolidation of financial statements, the order for the preparation and audit of consolidated financial statements.

An enterprise having one or more subsidiaries is to draw up consolidated financial statements. Consolidated financial statements comprise:

1. Consolidated balance sheet
2. Consolidated income statement
3. Consolidated cash flow statement
4. Consolidated Statement of Changes in Equity
5. Explanatory notes

Consolidated financial reporting includes all assets, liabilities, and equity as of the balance sheet date of enterprise being consolidated, also its income and expenses related with the reporting period.

7.3   The Institute of Accounting

In order to reorganize accounting more rapidly and to harmonize it with the International Accounting Standards and European Union Directives, the Institute of Audit and Accounting was reorganized as the Institute of Accounting in 2002. It carries out the following functions:

1. To draw up business accounting standards
2. To prepare methodical recommendations for the financial accounting issues
3. To give suggestions for the preparation of new legal acts, the augmentation of existing ones and for corresponding amendments in the area of accounting and financial accountability
4. To issue periodical, methodical, and another literature on accounting
5. To arrange courses, seminars, conferences, and other professional events

The Board of Standards, the Commission of Experts, and The Committee of Consultation function under the Institute of Accounting. The Board of Standards consists of five members. Specialists in accounting and audit are appointed Board members for 3 years. The Board of Standards confirms and announces Business Accounting Standards and methodical recommendations.

The Commission of Experts consists of nine members nominated for a 3-year period. Commission takes part in the preparation exposure drafts of Business accounting standards and methodical recommendations, discusses them and submits to the Board of Standards.

The Committee of Consulting, consisting of 17 members, is created for 3 years. It submits to the Board of Standards its opinion on the drafts of Business Accounting Standards according and methodical recommendations as well as its suggestions for drafts' improvement.

Exposure drafts of the Business Accounting Standards are prepared according to the plan approved by the Board of Standards. The Board of Standards also approves the structure of standard in preparation. Up to 3 months are given for the preparation of the standard. In some cases this period may be longer. The members of the Committee of Consulting and of the Commission of Experts analyze the exposure draft for 15 working days. Their comments and proposals are submitted to the Institute of Accounting.

The Institute sorts comments received by groups and directs them to the Board of Standards. Subsequently the exposure draft is discussed at the meeting of the Board of Standards attended also by the members of the Committee of Consulting and of the Commission of Experts. The Board of Standards confirms the exposure draft or organizes a working group for its improvement. Not later than within 3 months after the announcement of an exposure draft, all concerned persons may state their opinion on the contents of the standard. Afterwards the Board of Standards confirms and announces the particular Business Accounting Standard. The Board of Standards has confirmed the following 20 Business Accounting Standards so far:

BAS 1 "Financial statement"
BAS 2 "Balance sheet"
BAS 3 "Income statement"
BAS 4 "Statement of Changes in Equity"
BAS 5 "Cash flow statement"
BAS 6 "Explanatory notes"
BAS 7 "Changes in accounting policies, accounting estimates and correction of errors"
BAS 8 "Equity"
BAS 9 "Inventory"
BAS 10 "Revenue from sales"
BAS 11 "Cost of sales and operating costs"
BAS 12 "Noncurrent tangible assets"
BAS 13 " Intangible assets"
BAS 14 "Joint venture"
BAS 15 "Investments in associates"

BAS 16 "Consolidated financial statements and investments in subsidiaries"

BAS 19 "Provisions, contingent liabilities and assets and events after the balance sheet date"

BAS 20 "Operating lease, financial lease and loan-for-use"

BAS 21 "Grants and subsidies"

BAS 22 "Changes in foreign exchange rates"

7.4 General Accounting Principles

The Law on Financial Accountability of Companies provides the following ten general accounting principles:

1. Entity concept
2. Going concern
3. Periodicity
4. Consistency
5. Monetary measure
6. Accrual basis
7. Comparability
8. Prudence
9. Neutrality
10. Substance over form

The Entity Concept means that every enterprise preparing financial statements is considered a separate accounting unit and the financial statements should reflect only its assets, equity, liabilities, income, expenses, and cash flows.

The Going Concern Principle means that the financial statements are prepared on the assumption that the time of enterprise's activity is unlimited and that enterprise is not going to be liquidated. If while preparing financial statements the management of the enterprise becomes aware of material uncertainties that may cast doubt upon the enterprise's ability to continue as a going concern, those uncertainties should be disclosed in the explanatory notes. If due to certain reasons a going concern principle is disregarded all assets and liabilities of the enterprise become current assets or liabilities. Assets should be carried at possible net realizable value, and liabilities – at the estimated amounts of final settlement.

The Periodicity Principle means that financial statements must be prepared on the basis of data on the last day of the financial year. The financial years of a stock company or a closed stock company are artificial years. The financial year and close dates terms other than 12 months may be set out in its statute. However, under certain circumstances, such as the enterprise's start up, reorganization, liquidation, or changing the beginning of financial year, the duration of one financial year may be other than 12 months. It may be shorter than 12 months, but no longer than 18 months. Reasons for that should be explained in the explanatory notes to the financial statements. In addition, a note, saying that data in income statement, statement of changes in shareholders' equity, and the cash flow statement is not comparable with the data contained in the financial statements of the previous reporting period should be included.

The Consistency Principle means that an enterprise should apply the selected accounting method continuously or for sufficiently long time, unless some material events or circumstances result in the need to change the accounting policy. Classification of financial statement items or the way of presentation of information can be changed only when it becomes clear that the applied accounting methods prevent from fairly reflecting the enterprise's performance and financial position.

The Monetary Measure Principle means that all assets, equity, and liabilities of the enterprise are expressed in cash in financial statements.

The Accrual Basis Principle means that under this basis, the effects of transactions and other events are recognized when they occur and they are recorded in the accounting records and reported in the financial statements of the periods to which they relate irrespective to whether cash or its equivalent is received or paid.

The Comparability Principle means that income earned during the reporting period is related to expenses incurred when earning such income. Financial statements should include the information of the reporting year and at least of one previous financial year.

The Prudence Principle means that when preparing financial statements all subjective estimations should be checked, such as the possibility to collect doubtful receivables, miscellaneous provisions, and reserves.

The Neutrality Principle means that information contained in financial statements must be objective and free from bias.

The Substance over Form Principle means that registering transactions and other events should be carried out, firstly, taking into consideration their substance and economic reality, and not only the formal presentation requirements. Transactions and other events have to be included into accounting and presented in financial statements according to their substance and economic reality even when the presentation differs from the legal form.

7.5   Chart of Accounts

A new chart of accounts was confirmed in 2004. The applicable chart of accounts is divided into six classes:

1. Noncurrent assets
2. Current assets
3. Equity
4. Amounts payable and liabilities
5. Revenue
6. Expenses

Every class is divided into subclasses; subclasses are divided into related groups of accounts, which combine a few or more accounts that reflect current assets, equity, liabilities, revenue, and expenses. For example, a group of current assets is divided into four subclasses:

1. Inventory, prepayments, and contracts in progress
2. Amounts receivable in 1 year
3. Other current assets
4. Cash and cash equivalents

The subclass of amounts receivable in 1 year is divided into three groups of accounts: trade receivables, receivables from subsidiaries and associates, and other receivables. The group of accounts of other receivables combines seven accounts. These are VAT receivable, budget debt for enterprise, social insurance agency debt for enterprise, other amounts receivable, responsible persons, compound revenue receivable, and bad debts. Other classes of chart of accounts are divided similarly.

7.6 Financial Statements

7.6.1 Structure and Key Requirements

The structure, forms, and preparation principals of financial statements are given in the first five business accounting standards.

Financial statements of an enterprise include the following components:

1. Balance Sheet
2. Income Statement
3. Statement of Changes in Equity
4. Cash Flow Statement
5. Explanatory Notes

Model statements are set out in the Business Accounting Standards. Financial statements may include full, shortened, and short forms of Balance Sheet, Income Statement, and Cash Flow Statement.

If amounts of any two criteria on the accounting day are more or less than those specified below and if they have not been changed for 2 years running the enterprise prepares shortened annual financial reporting, which consists of a Balance Sheet, Income Statement, and Cash Flow Statement:

1. Net sales revenue during the accounting year amounts to 10 million Litas (2.9 million Euro);
2. The amount of assets in the Balance Sheet is 5 million Litas (1.45 million Euro);
3. The average schedule hired workers number during the accounting year is 250 people.

If amounts of any two criteria on the accounting day are more or less than those specified below and if they have not been changed for 2 years running the enterprise prepares a short form of annual financial reporting which consists of the Balance Sheet, Income Statement, and Cash Flow Statement:

1. Revenue from sales during the accounting year amounts to 1 million Litas (0.29 million Euro)
2. The amount of assets in the Balance Sheet is 500,000 Litas (0.145 million Euro)
3. The average schedule hired workers number during the accounting year is 50 people

When preparing financial statements enterprises follow the general accounting principles and the Business Accounting Standards for the evaluation of assets, equity, and liabilities. An enterprise should choose and apply accounting policy so that financial statements could reflect the financial position of enterprise, the results of activity and cash flows fairly.

If Business Accounting Standards do not prescribe any procedure for the registration and presentation of economic transaction or event the enterprise should follow accounting policy ensuring that information disclosed in financial statements:

(a) Would be useful for users
(b) Position, results from activity and cash flows of entity would be indicated fairly
(c) Would reflect the subject and the economic meaning of economic transactions and events, not only the formal requirements for presentation
(d) Would be independent and neutral
(e) Would be prepared in conformity with general accounting standards
(f) Would be comprehensive in all significant cases

Data presented in financial statements should be arranged in reference to accounting policy and general accounting principles.

7.6.2 Balance Sheet

Information in the Balance Sheet is presented as follows:

A. NONCURRENT ASSETS

    I. Intangible assets
    II. Tangible assets
    III. Financial assets

B. CURRENT ASSETS

    I. Inventories, advance payments, and contracts in progress
    II. Amounts receivable within a year

III. Other current assets
IV. Cash and cash equivalents

C. EQUITY

I. Capital
II. Revaluation reserve (results)
III. Reserves
IV. Retained earnings (losses)

D. GRANTS, SUBSIDIES
E. AMOUNTS PAYABLE AND LIABILITIES

I. Amounts payable after 1 year and long-term liabilities
II. Amounts payable within 1 year and current liabilities

Data within all enterprises, the Balance Sheets should be grouped and presented according to the items indicated above. Items of the enterprise presenting the full form of the Balance Sheet should be more detailed.

Noncurrent intangible assets are to be detailed as follows: development works, goodwill, licences and patents, computer software, and other intangible assets. Noncurrent tangible assets detailed as follows: land, buildings and construction, plant and equipment, vehicles, other property, plant and equipment, construction in progress, and other tangible assets. Noncurrent financial assets: investments in subsidiaries and associates, loans to subsidiaries and associates, amounts receivable after 1 year, and other financial assets.

Inventories: raw materials and completing products, work in progress, finished products, goods for resale. Prepayments and contracts in progress are not detailed. Amounts receivable within 1 year: trade amounts receivable, receivables from subsidiaries and associates, and other amounts receivable. Other currents assets: Current investments, time deposits, and other current assets.

Capital: authorised (subscribed), subscribed uncalled share capital (–); share premium; own Shares (–).

Reserves: legal reserve, reserve for acquiring own shares, and other reserves.

Retained earnings (losses): profit (loss) of the reporting year and profit (loss) of the previous year.

Noncurrent amounts payable and liabilities: financial debts (leases and similar obligations, to credit institutions, other financial debts), trade amounts payable, amounts received in advance, provisions (for covering liabilities and demands, for pensions and similar obligations, other provisions), deferred taxes, other amounts payable, and noncurrent liabilities.

Current amounts payable and liabilities: current portion of noncurrent debts, financial debts (to credit institutions, other financial debts), trade amounts payable, amounts received in advance, profit tax liabilities, liabilities related with labor relations, provisions, other amounts payable, and current liabilities.

7.6.3 Income Statement

Information about enterprise activities during the reporting period is grouped into ordinary and extraordinary activity items for the Income Statement purposes. Normal activities of the enterprise cover repeat business transactions, related to all enterprise activities. Data on normal operation are also grouped into normal operation and atypical activity items. Data on normal activities of the enterprise comprise sales income, cost of sales, and operating expenses. Data on extraordinary activities of the enterprise comprise other, financial and investing activities.

Extraordinary items comprise the results of occasional business events, which cannot be included into ordinary activities. Whether or not an event is attributable to normal activities of the enterprise, ordinary activities is determined according to its nature, compared with normal business of the enterprise, other than according to the frequency of such event. Frequency is only one of the criteria used when designating an item as extraordinary.

Information on the face of the Income Statement should be presented according to the following items:

   I. Sales income
  II. Cost of sales
 III. Gross profit (loss)
  IV. Operating costs
   V. Operating profit (loss)
  VI. Other activities
 VII. Financing and investing activities
VIII. Profit (loss) from ordinary activities
  IX. Gains
   X. Losses
  XI. Profit (loss) before taxation
 XII. Profit tax
XIII. Net profit (loss)

Sales income item covers net income from sales, and cost of sales item includes the net cost of sales. Operating costs item includes sales as well as general and administrative costs. Other activities item includes the result of extraordinary activities (except for financing and investing activities). Income from other activities includes: income from extraordinary activities' output, income from goods held for sale and rendering of services, income from use of enterprise's noncurrent assets, royalties, for example, patents, trademarks, copyrights, computer software, etc., profit from transfer of noncurrent assets (except for financial assets), etc. The item of other activities costs comprises costs and losses related to income from other activities. Other activities costs include: cost of sold products of extraordinary activities, cost of goods held for sale or services, losses from transfer of noncurrent assets (except for financial assets), etc.

Item of income from financing and investing activities consists of income from financing and investing activities earned within the reporting period. This income includes: interest on loans granted to clients or enterprise employees, interest on cash deposited in the bank, foreign currency exchange gain, recognized fines and penalties for late settlements, dividend income, noncurrent investment transfer, and revaluation profit. Item of financing and investing activities' expenses includes: foreign currency exchange losses, fines and penalties imposed for delayed settlements, losses from transfer and revaluation of noncurrent investments, interest calculated on assets acquired on lease, loan interest expenses.

Gross profit (loss) ratio is calculated as the difference between sales income and cost of sales.

Gross profit (loss) = sales income − cost of sales

Operating profit (loss) ratio is calculated as the difference between gross profit and operating costs.

Operating profit (loss) = gross profit − operating costs

Profit (loss) from normal activities ratio shows the performance of enterprise normal (operating and extraordinary) activities during the reporting period.

Profit (loss) from normal activities = operating profit (losses)
+ other financing
+ investing activities performance

Profit (loss) before taxes ratio shows the result of normal activities and extraordinary items of the enterprise.

Profit (loss) before taxes = profit (loss) from normal activities
+ gains − losses

Net profit (loss) ratio shows the final result of the enterprise activities, i.e., the distributable profit remaining in the enterprise, or losses.

Net profit (loss) = profit (loss) before taxes − profit tax expenses

7.6.4   Statement of Changes in Equity

The Statement of Changes in Equity is used to disclose net increase or decrease during reporting period and other changes in equity excluded from income statement. The Statement of Changes in Equity should include:
1. Items of equity at the beginning and end of the reporting and a comparative periods
2. Result of a change in accounting policies
3. Result of correcting errors
4. Recalculated items of equity at the beginning of the reporting period (according to adjustments referred to in items 5.2 and 5.3 hereof)
5. Revaluation result of noncurrent tangible assets

6. Revaluation result of financial assets
7. Own shares
8. Other profit (loss) not recognized in the Income Statement
9. Net profit (loss) of the reporting period
10. Declared dividends and other payments related with the distribution of profit
11. Increase/decrease in authorized capital and balance at the beginning and end of the reporting period
12. Changes in reserves and balance at the beginning and end of the reporting period

7.6.5 Cash Flow Statement

For the purposes of the Cash Flow Statement the cash flows of the reporting period should be classified into cash flows from operating, investing, and financing activities. Enterprise's cash flows from operating activities show principal (producing, commercial, service producing) enterprise activities' (except for investing and financing activities) capacity to generate cash flows. Such cash flows are the principal financing source for maintaining and developing enterprise activities, repaying loans, paying dividends, and making new investments. Enterprise's cash receipts from operating activities of the enterprise are:

1. Inflows from the sale of goods and the rendering of services
2. Inflows from commissions, fees and other revenues
3. Inflows from advance settlements from customers
4. Inflows from recovery of trade debts
5. Insurance benefits received
6. Inflows from sales of available-for-sale noncurrent assets
7. Inflows from sales of available-for-sale securities of other enterprises (e.g., shares, bonds), and other short-term investments
8. Dividends received from other enterprises (if these receipts are classified as operating activity according to the accounting policies)
9. Interest received (if these receipts are classified as operating activity according to the accounting policies)

Enterprise's cash payments arising from operating activities are:

1. Outflows to suppliers for raw materials, goods, and services
2. Outflows to enterprise employees
3. Taxes paid
4. Outflows to acquire short-term investments
5. Insurance payments paid
6. Outflows to acquire available-for-sale noncurrent assets
7. Outflows to acquire available-for-sale-securities of other enterprises

8. Dividends paid (if these payments are classified as operating activity according to the accounting policies)
9. Interest paid (if these payments are classified as operating activity according to the accounting policies)

Enterprise cash flows from operating activities can be disclosed using a direct or an indirect method. To disclose cash flows from operating activities using the direct method, data on cash inflows and outflows are presented in addition with value added tax (VAT).

To disclose cash flows from operating activities using the indirect method, net profit (loss) of the reporting period is evaluated in the amount of cash inflows and outflows in enterprise operating activities.

Cash flows from investing activities show cash amounts spent for assets purchase, which will render future economic benefits and cash receipts from transfer of such assets.

Enterprise's inflows from investing activities:

1. Inflows from transfers of long-term assets (except for available-for-sale assets)
2. Inflows from loans recovered from third parties
3. Inflows from transfers of not-available-for-sale securities of other enterprises
4. Dividends received from other enterprises (if these receipts are classified as investing activity according to the accounting policies)
5. Interest received for loans granted (if these receipts are classified as investing activity according to the accounting policies)
6. Interest received for cash held in finance institutions (if these receipts are classified as investing activity according to the accounting policies)

Enterprise's outflows arising from investing activities:

1. Outflows to acquire noncurrent assets (except for available-for-sale assets)
2. Outflows to build, reconstruct or repair noncurrent tangible assets, disposed by enterprise, and being increased in value
3. Outflows upon lending to third parties
4. Outflows to acquire securities

Cash flows from enterprise financing activity show how enterprise used external financing sources during the period.

Enterprise's inflows from enterprise financing activities:

1. Inflows from issuing shares of all kinds
2. Inflows from issuing bonds, bills and other securities
3. Inflows from borrowing (irrespective of maturity) from third parties (including credit institutions)

Enterprise's outflows arising from enterprise financing activities:

1. Outflows for purchasing own shares
2. Dividends paid (if these payments are classified as financing activity according to the accounting policies)

3. Outflows for redeeming enterprise bonds, bills and other previously issued securities
4. Recovery of loans
5. Interest paid on loans (if these payments are classified as financing activity according to the accounting policies)
6. Outflows for lease (finance lease)

Cash inflows and outflows of the reporting period arising from investing and financing activities are disclosed in the statement separately. Reporting such cash flows in the Cash Flow Statement under the direct or indirect method does not differ, because these parts of the Cash Flow Statement are reported exclusively according to the direct method.

Cash flows arising from acquisition or transfer of subsidiaries and other business entities must be reported separately, as cash flows from investing activities.

Extraordinary cash flows as well as exchange differences should be disclosed within separate lines.

7.6.6 Explanatory Notes

Explanatory Notes consist of three parts: general, accounting policy, and notes.

At the beginning of the general part of the Explanatory Notes the general data about the enterprise should be presented:

1. Enterprise registration date
2. Number of branches and representative offices of the enterprise, names and head offices of subsidiaries and associates
3. Brief description of enterprise activities
4. Material conditions under which the enterprise is operating and which are likely to influence its development
5. Enterprise activities in the sphere of research and development, if such activities are important
6. Changes in the authorized capital, where appropriate, and root causes of such changes
7. Average number of employees on establishment of the enterprise during the reporting and previous financial years, or average staff numbers at the end of the reporting and previous financial years

Accounting policy covers information that is likely to influence decision-making of the users of information provided in financial statements. For example:

1. Legal acts and accounting standards used as a basis for preparing financial accountability
2. If accounting policies change in the course of the financial year, the effects of such change on the enterprise's performance should be indicated and discussed, specifying indices calculated applying old and new methods

3. Asset valuation methods applied for the purpose of preparing financial statements (purchasing cost, net realizable value, fair value, etc.)
4. Noncurrent tangible and intangible assets' accounting policies
5. Investment, biological assets, borrowing and other similar expenses, business combinations, construction and long-term contracts, lease, research and development costs, grants, subsidies, foreign currency transactions assets received gratis and offsetting of financial instruments accounting methods
6. Asset revaluation methods
7. Revenue and expense recognition methods
8. Definition of business and geographical segments and the basis for allocation of income and costs between segments
9. Definition of cash and cash equivalents (explaining what is attributed to cash and cash equivalents)
10. Financial risk management policies
11. Provision formation principles
12. Enterprise policies and programs in the fields of environmental protection, energy saving, use of ecological materials and waste utilization, water pollution, and reduction of emissions

Comments of the Explanatory Notes disclose detailed significant amounts; also, information required by the Business Accounting Standards that is not presented elsewhere and also the information, which is necessary for achieving a more precise depiction of circumstances that are likely to influence the enterprise's activities, financial condition, performance results, and cash flows. For example, condition of the enterprise's intangible assets and its development during the reporting period, periodicity and reasons of revaluation by groups of such noncurrent tangible assets, pledge of noncurrent tangible assets and other restrictions of ownership rights, depreciation rates. Presenting information about inventories carrying amount, value by kinds of inventories, carrying amount of inventories pledged, inventories held by third parties. Name of another enterprise, in which the enterprise has significant influence or control is prescribed. Structure of the enterprise's capital is explained specifying the number of shares and their nominal value, as well as distribution of profit, payable amounts, material amounts recorded in off-balance sheet accounts are explained, and off-balance events are prescribed.

7.7 Audit

Annual audit of financial statements should be performed in all stock companies. Audit of financial statements of close stock companies is performed only if amounts of any two criteria on the accounting day are more or less than specified below:

1. Net sales revenue during the accounting year amounts to 5 million Litas (1.45 million Euro)

2. The amount of assets in the Balance Sheet is 2.5 million Litas (0.725 million Euro)
3. The average schedule hired workers number during the accounting year is 50 people

Audit of consolidated financial statements should be exercised over enterprises preparing consolidated financial statements.

Audit enterprise is selected by the general meeting of shareholders. Every shareholder or group of shareholders of the enterprise has the right to enter into contract with a selected audit enterprise to examine the activity and accounting documents of the enterprise, to determine any insolvency or features of deliberate bankrupty, as well as to determine whether assets of the enterprise are not overspent, onerous contracts are not negotiated, rights of shareholders are not violated, including invalid payments for workers or applied discounts and exemptions that cause decrease in profit of enterprise or incurrence of losses. Expenses of such examination are paid by shareholders who enter into contract with audit enterprises. If the auditor confirms the facts of signed application of shareholders, the entity must repay examination expenses for shareholders, but not more than one fourth of the damage made by the enterprise or its shareholders.

Chapter 8
Accounting Systems and Structures in Poland

Navchaa Lamjav

8.1 Introduction

This chapter contains an analysis of the changes of the accounting systems and structures for Poland. The focus will be on the changes in systems and structures that have taken place after the political system of Poland was changed from being a centrally planned economy into being a market-based economy in 1989. The aim is to evaluate how Poland has been able to adapt its accounting systems to the new political, economic, and cultural situation. This chapter also aims to define a link between the development of a transparent and international accounting system to the speed of economic development.

When analyzing the changes in the accounting systems I will base the analysis on the Gray's model presented in Annex I.

Annex I: International pressures for accounting change

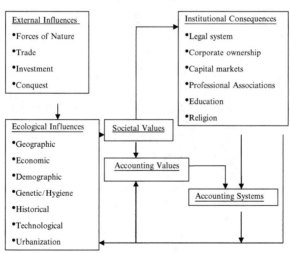

Annex I: International Pressures for Accounting Change
(Gray's Model)

N. Lamjav
Copenhagen Business School

R. W. McGee (ed.), *Accounting Reform in Transition and Developing Economies,*
© Springer Science+Business Media LLC 2008

8.2   Overview of the Change of Accounting Systems During the 20th Century

A national accounting chart for Poland did not exist before the 1930s although an accountants' Association was already established in the year 1907. The period up to the Second World War was strongly influenced by the German system at that time. And the rules of the uniform German General Plan of accounts were in force. This system was, however, changed after the Russian occupation and a centrally planned economy was introduced. Since 1989 when Poland moved away from Russian dominance, the accounting system was also changed. This change was undertaken gradually because already at this stage it was recognized that the process of change and the guiding principle of legislation would stretch over a considerable time span needing numerous changes, corrections, and adaptations (Alicja, 1993).

The new systems were market-driven and more in the direction of the accounting systems practiced in Western Europe. Since Poland joined the OECD in 1996 and the EU in 2004 the accounting system and structure were to be transformed into systems that could comply with the EU standards. Poland is consequently committed to require listed companies to comply with International Financial Reporting Standards (IFRS).

Within the period from the beginning of the 20th century the accounting systems and standards in Poland were changed completely at times where the political situation was changed in a dramatic manner. The Polish example is thus a good example of how the national accounting system is determined by changes in the socioeconomic and political structures of the country.

8.3   From Planned Economy to Market Economy – Effects on the Accounting System

The accounting history of Poland is linked to dramatic changes in the political and socioeconomic and cultural situation. Under the command economy of communism the foremost objective of the accounting system was the provision of financial statistics for use in higher level budgets. There was very little emphasis on accountability, which is a crucial element in accounting in a market economy (Katarzuna et al., 2004).

In the transition from a planned to a market economy, accounting principles form an active instrument for calculation of economic performance as well as an instrument for communication on the international level between markets, which enabled Poland to be a member of the international community, enhancing economic growth (Alicja Jaruga et al., 1993).

After 1989 the Polish Ministry of Finance developed a framework for regulating the accounting system. In this process the Ministry revived the commercial code of 1934 as the framework developed by the plan economy was useless in the new situation. Because of lack of professionals the state acquired a dominant position in defining the process to reform the new system. The Ministry used the accounting system that was previously seen as an instrument of administrative control over state enterprises to become a tool for control and monitoring of the privatization process (Katarzuna et al., 2004).

In the transition period from planned economy to market economy, the accounting system was under strong pressure to change according to the new political and economic reality. In Gray's model for international pressures (see Annex 1) many factors (external as well as ecological) required an adoption of the accounting principles. Such factors included:

- Foreign investments and Capital inflow
- Change of ownership of the production plants (privatization and commercialization)
- Influence of the EU system
- Closer cultural contacts with Western Europe
- Pressures from IBRD (International Bank for Reconstruction and Development/ World Bank) and IMF for introduction of international accounting principles for investment evaluation

Through these pressures the need for changes in the social and accounting values evolved and new laws and regulations were introduced. Also the importance of the professional associations as well as the training of the members of the associations increased.

The new accounting systems introduced were planned to adapt to the new realities. In addition, Poland introduced an accounting system in line with the accounting systems used in the EU, maybe in an early expectation to join the EU at a later stage.

Annex II lists some of the key new legislation and regulations introduced during the period.

Annex II: Governmental acts regulating accounting in Poland (Alicja Jaruga, 1993)

Year	Name of Act/Regulation
June 1934	The Commercial Code
July 1990	Privatization of State Enterprises
January 1991	Principle of Accounting
March 1991	Public Exchange of Securities and Trustee Funds
June 1991	Companies with Foreign Shareholding
July 1991	Stock Exchange Listing
October 1991	Examination and Disclosure of Financial Reports and Auditors and their Self Government
1991	Detailed Requirements for Listed Securities Projects
February 1992	Taxation of Legal Entities
March 1992	Fixed Assets, Intangibles and Assets. Principles and Rates of Depreciation and Revaluation of Fixed Assets
September 1994	Amendment to the Accounting Act
October 1994	Auditors and their Self-governing Body (Amended in year 2000)
1994	Privatization Law
November 2000	New Accounting Act

Thus the vicinity of the EU has determined the development focus as well as the process aiming at structural integration at the continental level (e.g., the direction of foreign trade and EU integration) (UN/ ECE, 2001; WB, 2000).

The production plant was run down and outdated by 1989 and Poland was lacking the necessary capital in order to modernize and restructure the national enterprises on competitive bases. Attracting foreign investors was crucial at this juncture. Potential foreign investors are concerned with the accuracy and readability of accounting reports, transparency of information regarding capital flows and the application of familiar (standard) accounting principles (Dutia, 1995). Consequently, the application of International Accounting Standards (hereafter IAS) could form the platform for increased foreign investment and foreign trade (King et al., 2001).

8.4   Polish Accounting Principles and the EU

As a candidate for EU membership, Poland has prepared itself by developing new accounting systems. One of the key instruments is harmonization of the financial reporting systems with the European Directives and with the International IAS (The British Know How Fund, 1999).

The EU is trying to harmonize company laws and accounting principles through a set of directives and regulations. The directives should be adapted by the membership countries by national legislation. Regulations (three) are automatically valid throughout the EU and do not need to be adopted through national legislation.

The 14 Directives of relevance for corporate accounting go back to 1964. Of these in particular the 4th Directive (Formats and Rules of Accounting), 7th (Consolidated Accounting), and 8th (Qualifications and work of Auditors) are of particular importance.

Already in 1991 the Accounting Law (see Annex II) introduced changes that attempted to comply with the 4th Directive, thus bringing the Polish Accounting System closer to the EU system. The law that was amended in 2000 followed in the same direction bringing the Polish Accounting System close to the EU. This law copes with new categories (e.g., intangible assets), new transitions (e.g., hedging), and complexities of the market economy (real value vs. historic cost valuation methods).

The 7th Directive, which is considered more difficult, was not dealt with in the 1991 law but became part of the year 2000 legislation.

The 8th Directive was dealt with in the laws of October 1991 and October 1994 and the amendment of the year 2000. The Act of 1991, unlike the directive, only allows people with a higher education to undertake auditing. The Act of 1994 requires auditors to be full-time professionals.

Poland has through this new legislation provided a good base for being a member of the EU, which also happened in 2004.

8.5 Auditing

The Accountants Association in Poland (AAP) was created in 1907. However, the Association was weak with limited influence during the initial years of existence. During the years of the planned economy from 1944 to 1998 there was limited need for professional accountants and by 1998 when Poland got into a transition period from a planned economy to a market economy, the shortage of professional accountants formed a major bottleneck for the transition. Since 1998 the situation has changed, spearheaded by the AAP and a National Council of Statutory Auditors (NCSA) established through an Act of October 1994 (law on Auditors and their self-governing body).

The NCSA has an obligation to continuously improve the standard and qualifications of the auditors. The law was amended and enhanced in the year 2000.

The NCSA jointly with AAP has undertaken training and development of auditor standards through undertaking a number of training courses. From 2000 up to and including planned courses for 2006, 25 courses in accounting and auditing respectively took place.

In addition, a high number of training organizations have been nominated to undertake continuing professional development of Statutory Auditors.

8.6 Case Study: Grupa Lotus SA

To illustrate the changes in the accounting principles a case study of Grupa Lotus SA has been selected. This company is well-known in Poland with 3,365 employees with sales in 2004 of 11.2 billion PLN. It is an integrated company within the oil sector. The company has a number of subsidiaries. It is listed on the Warsaw Stock Exchange. The analysis of the financial statements of 2001 and 2004 is shown in the following table.

Comparison of the Accounting Policies of Grupa LOTOS SA from the financial statements as per 31 December 2001 and 31 December 2004

List of principles	Financial year-end 31 Dec 2001	Financial year-end 31 Dec 2004
Goodwill	No information available	Goodwill of subordinated entities is the surplus of the purchase price over the adequate part of net assets fair valued. Negative goodwill is the surplus of the adequate part of net assets fair valued over their purchase price.
R&D	No information available on R&D.	There is no information available on measurement of R & D. However, the development expenses have been listed without any figure in balance sheet.

(continued)

(continued)

List of principles	Financial year-end 31 Dec 2001	Financial year-end 31 Dec 2004
Property, plant and equipment	Property, plant and equipment are recoded at cost (or revalued cost) or the cost incurred in their manufacture, extension or modernization Depreciation- on straight-line or declining balance basis	Depreciation over useful life Plant and machinery 2–40 years Building 10–40 years
Inventories (stock)	Stocks are stated at the lower of cost and net realizable value Net realizable value is based on the possible selling price less costs to prepare the assets for sale and cost to execute the sale	Stated at the lower of acquisition cost or cost of production and net realizable value Purchase cost calculated on weighted average basis

The table compares the financial statements of December 31, 2001 and 2004 (the only 2 years available on the net in English).

As can be seen from the table, the presentation of the four-key accounting principles has changed considerably from 2001 to 2004. The statement of the year 2001 is prepared as an unconsolidated financial statement complying with the Polish Accounting Standard of 1994. The statement of the year 2004 was prepared according to the accounting decree of 2004 as a group consolidated financial statement prepared on the basis that the group is a going concern. This difference between the 2 years is because Poland joined the EU in 2004 and listed companies were obliged to present consolidated financial statements according to EU requirements and requirements of the Warsaw stock exchange.

8.7 Expected Future Trends and Developments in the Accounting Systems and Structures

Poland has aimed at establishing an international accounting system and the Ministry of Finance has for instance established an Accounting Standards Committee. The Committee, which has a wide range of key stakeholders, has as an aim to improve the Accounting Act of 1994 to develop national accounting standards in line with international practices.

Considering the complexity of accounting rules and practices, the accounting system reform can only be a gradual process, starting from the most general principles and then developing more detailed instructions and regulations. Poland has followed such a process step by step.

Transformation processes need to be supported with specific measures, including the development of an appropriate institutional framework, education of accounting professionals, legal enforcement, as well as the development of professional best practices. These steps have all been taken as shown in Section 5.

The reforms of the accounting systems will need to incorporate legal and educational changes as shown in Gray's model.

Development of business reporting and emphasizing the importance of transparency, accountability, and comparability in disclosure, the national accounting system may influence the speed of sociopolitical transition and economic reforms. It also may have a significant impact upon the process of attracting foreign investment. At present there is a tendency for a substantial number of EU companies to move to Poland to enjoy the cheap labor, the stable political situation, and the lower tax system.

8.8 Findings and Conclusions

During the 15 years of transition from 1989, the Polish economy has changed considerably. Although Poland still has a high unemployment rate, its GDP has had a considerably higher growth rate than the average of the 15 "old" EU member countries.

The economic success has been made possible through adaptation of the accounting system to the new reality following the principles outlined in "Gray's Model." In 1989 Poland had to change its regulations and the legal basis of the accounting system. Its historical basis for this change was the Commercial Code going back to 1934 when Poland had a market economy. In spite of the difficult base situation Poland has been able to introduce most of the changes required to ensure that the accounting system would not be a barrier to economic growth although some of the measures can be considered as being of a temporary/interim nature (Alcja, 1993).

Poland still has some way to go but with the focus on the development of professionalism within accountants and auditors and the legal flexibility outlined, it is likely that Poland will in the near future have an accounting system that is fully in line with the OECD and EU requirements as outlined in the IFRS.

It is difficult to define the direct impact of the accounting system reform on the economic transformation, as there are many other conditions that have influence on the transition process. However, with the central position of financial reporting and control in the economic system of a market-based economy, it is logical to assume that countries that are more effective in reforming the accounting system (adapting to the requirement of the market based economy) would move faster toward economic transformation.

Poland has changed its political, socioeconomic and cultural situation over a very short time span. These changes have been reflected in the accounting systems and the laws and regulations providing the frame for the systems. Also the professional standard of accountants and auditors have adapted quickly to the changes.

At present there is still room for improvement compared to the international standards and an analysis of the status of the Polish accounting system compared to the IFRS undertaken in 2003[1] point at a number of areas of non-compliance with the international rules.

However, with the speed and professionalism of the main forces behind developing a uniform system there is no doubt that Poland will succeed in developing its own national accounting system that will be in strong compliance with the IFRS.

The Report indicates that the anticipated link between economic growth and the accounting system has proven to be correct at least in the case of Poland.

References

Alicja Jaruga, *Changing rules of accounting in Poland*, European Accounting Review 1993, 1, 115–126

British Know How Fund (1999), Foreword, *Romanian Accounting Law*

Dutia, T. (1995), The restructuring of the system of accounting in Romania, *The European Accounting Review*, 4(4):739–748

Grupa LOTOS, Polish company's website: http://www.ir.lotos.pl/en/term_reports.html

Katarzuna Kosmala, MacLullich, and Calin Gurau, *The Relationship between Economic Performance and Accounting System Reform in the CEE Region: The Cases of Poland and Romania*, October 2004, Discussion Paper. Available at: http://www.sml.hw.ac.uk/cert

King, N., Beatie, A., Cistecu A. M. and Weetman, P. (2001), Developing accounting and audit in a transition economy: the Romanian experience, *The European Accounitng Review*, 10(1): 149–171

KMPG Poland, *New Polish Accounting Act*, November 2001, Newsletter. Available at: http://www.kpmg.pl/dbfetch/52616e646f6d49565d7edcb03590dda6d4bbdfafee4e8a11/npaa.pdf

National Chamber of Statutory Auditors website: http://kibr.org.pl/en/index3_10.phtml

Nobes C. and Parker R. *Comparative International Accounting* 8th edition, 2004, Prentice Hall, New Jersey

UN/ECE (2001), *Economic Survey of Europe*, Geneva: United Nations

World Bank (2000), *Process Toward the Unification of Europe*, Washington: The World Bank

---

[1] Refer to Table 14.1 Areas on which there are IFRSs but not Polish rules and Table 14.2 Polish practices that differ from IFRS rules page 343, 344. *Comparative International Accounting,* 8th ed. Nobes C and Parker R.

Chapter 9
Accounting Reform and the Role of Cultural and Historical Paradigms in Transitional Economies of Eastern Europe: The Case of Russia

Arsen M. Djatej, Robert H. S. Sarikas, and David L. Senteney

9.1 Introduction

Accounting is the communication of financial or other management information for the purpose of decision-making by investors, creditors, or managers. Accounting information is created in a cultural context and is transmitted to the receiver and processed in a manner according to certain cultural norms which have been influenced by history and other social realities. This paper will examine certain prior work that combines culture, history, and accounting. The primary contribution will be a discussion of how Hofestede's theory can provide insight into Russian culture and the relationship between accounting, culture, and history in Russia.

9.2 Accounting, History and Culture in Russia

In recent years, institutional and evolutionary economists have become increasingly aware that culture and history play an important role in the development of accounting. The development of accounting in a multicultural society like Russia is always shaped by historical and cultural factors. Due to Russia's historical and cultural specifics, historical case studies can contribute to the understanding of the links between culture and accounting. More specifically, studies of history can provide a better understanding of how the evolution of accounting ideas is dependent on cultural paradigms. Culture and history have been identified within the international accounting literature as important factors influencing the development of accounting systems in different countries.

Dr. Shraddha Verma of the University of London brilliantly summarized the influence of cultural attributes on the process of accounting change and develop-

A. M. Djatej
Eastern Washington University

R. H. S. Sarikas and D. L. Senteney
Ohio University

R. W. McGee (ed.), *Accounting Reform in Transition and Developing Economies,*
© Springer Science+Business Media LLC 2008

ment (Verma, 1998, p. 3). Verma extensively investigated past research of the most prominent authorities on this subject including Belkaoui, Choi, Mueller, Violet, and Jaggi (Verma, 1998, p. 3). Bikki Jaggi identified and compared (Jaggi, 1973, pp. 75–84; Verma, 1998, p. 3) the cultural aspects of developed and less-developed states and concluded that due to deep cultural differences, more advanced accounting principles might not be suitable for the economic systems of less-developed countries. Jaggi analyzed the connection between management cultural predispositions and the reliability of financial statements and concluded that due to different value systems, financial statements generated in developed countries were more reliable than those produced in the developing world (Jaggi, 1973, pp. 75–84).

Choi and Mueller presented (Choi and Mueller, 1992; Verma, 1998) accounting as a technical tool identified with unique institutional, cultural, and religious systems of values. According to their arguments, accountings performed a service function, and, since accounting systems were different, accounting had to be dissimilar among countries. In addition, institutional, cultural, and political factors were important in understanding differences in accounting systems and financial statements of different countries (Choi and Mueller, 1992).

Bloom and Naciri provided an analysis (Bloom and Naciri, 1989, pp. 70–97; Verma, 1998) of the similarities and differences in accounting standard-setting process using examples of the United States, Canada, England, Germany, Australia, New Zealand, Sweden, Japan, and Switzerland. By separating cultural differences in these countries, they concluded that accounting standard-setting in a country was strongly dependant on economic, political, and cultural factors of each country.

According to Belkaoui (1989, pp. 93–101), culture plays an important role in organizations. Accounting knowledge is organized in a culturally standardized format, which tells individuals how to react to a particular accounting phenomenon. Violet (1983, pp. 1–12) reviewed the development of International Accounting Standards through the prism of anthropological perspective and concluded that the adoption of the standards is strongly influenced by a variety of cultural variables. According to Violet, culture is recognized as the system, which encompasses and determines the evolution of social institutions. Accounting is a social institution and, as such, reflects the attributes of its culture (Verma, 1998, pp. 4–5). Violet concluded that each unique culture produces a unique accounting structure shaped by cultural constraints and other variables (Verma, 1998, pp. 4–5).

With the fall of the "Iron Curtain," the formerly closed societies of the former Soviet Union and Eastern Europe are open again. Russia, like many other former communist states, is undertaking a painful transformation from a planned system to a free market economy. Therefore, like many times in its history, Russia needs to acquire overseas expertise and knowledge related to professional science.

Sustainable economic growth in Russia requires both direct and indirect capital investments. The adoption of a new accounting system is an important qualification for Russia's participation in world financial markets and a key determinant of Russia's ability to attract a greater share of world capital. The current accounting system was designed to satisfy the needs of a planned economy and was generally unsuited to decision making in a market economy.

Before the October Revolution Russia had one of the most sophisticated accounting systems in the world. The origins of this system were based on a combination of various factors. The most important factor is attributed to the openness of Russian society under the tsars and susceptibility of its national culture to the adaptation of foreign scientific ideas penetrating through intercultural communication. Today, once again, this phenomenon is becoming a central point of economic transition in Russia. The economic transition ongoing today in Russia is similar to the reforms that took place during the 18–19th centuries when a new progressive accounting system was adopted.

There are multiple kinds of cultures; however, this research employs the notion of a "national culture." Samovar and Porter (2003, p. 8) have defined the culture of a nation as "the deposit of knowledge, experiences, beliefs, values, attitudes, meanings, social hierarchies, religion, notions of time, roles, spatial relationships, concepts of the universe, and material objects and possessions acquired by a group of people in the course of generations through individual and group striving." Samovar and Porter go on to list six characteristics of culture including their assertions that culture: is learned, is transmitted from generation to generation, is based on symbols, is subject to change, is selective, and is ethnocentric (Samovar and Porter, 2003, pp. 5–26). Hall's differentiation of nations by their cultures is conceptualized in his works *The Hidden Dimension* and *The Silent Language*.

In *The Hidden Dimension* Hall analyses (Hall, 1959, p. 159; Hall, 1966, pp. 159–160) cultural dimensions and behavioral patterns of Arabs and in *The Silent Language* his focus is on the Latin Americans. The contribution of these works is to show how culture redefines the behavior of individual members, outlines rules, habits, and expectations from the others and, eventually, unifies them in one entity (Hall, 1959). Hall categorizes the thinking and the decision-making process for the members. Hall's definition is also important because "it sets the gestures, space, and timing of interactions (Hall, 1976, p. 17).

In addition, the collaboration of Geertz's model of culture would significantly supplement the context of this research (Geertz, 1973). Geertz (1973, p. 89) sees culture as a "historically transmitted pattern of meanings embodied in symbols, a system of inherited conceptions expressed in symbolic form by means of which men communicate, perpetuate and develop their knowledge about and attitudes towards life." Even though cross-cultural communication has experienced some problematic dimensions in the past, the relevance of past research is significant. Therefore, as an improvement to prior research, this paper will add LeVine's ethnographic viewpoint of collective and organized nature of culture.

From LeVine's collective perspective (LeVine, 1984, pp. 68, 69) "culture represents a consensus on a wide variety of meanings among members of an interacting community" where "every human community functions with a group consensus about the meanings of the symbols used in communications that constitute their social life, however variable their behavior and attitudes in other respects, because such a consensus is as necessary for encoding and decoding messages in social communication in general as agreement about speech rules is to encoding and decoding in the linguistic mode." Individual culture is based on "an organized set of contexts from which customary beliefs and practices derive their meaning" (LeVine, 1984, p. 72). Since the historical perspectives of Russian accounting are strongly correlated with other academic subjects including economics, international relations, trade, and entrepreneurship, this paper will utilize a business administration framework for analyzing cultural differences in historical and business processes.

French doctor Andre Laurent described (Laurent, 1983, pp. 75–96) relevant cultural paradigms using different levels of task variations influencing relationships among participants in social and organizational structures. He identified organizations as political systems. In his model, cultural variations are influenced by authority systems and organizational communication and intercultural relationships are identified as role formulation systems. According to Laurent (1983, pp. 75–96), organizational culture is a system of hierarchical relationship. Understanding "culture" in the global context by definition is related to the understanding of national cultures. Even though there are multiple kinds of cultures, and every one of them can make a valuable contribution to the studies of intercultural communication, the contextual limitations of the chosen subject motivates me to narrow the focus of this research to only the "national culture."

This inquiry focuses on the process of adoption and development of the accounting discipline in Russia. Cross-cultural communication and knowledge transfer between Russia and European countries have heavily influenced this adoption. Understanding differences between cultures can provide the tools to understand the extent to which Russian culture differs from the cultures of those countries that made a substantial contribution to the accounting system in Russia.

Identifying how differences affect cross-cultural communication, allows for the development of a better societal picture. Since Russia and Russian history is the broad context of this research, this paper focuses only on the understanding of Russian culture and the outline of its unique traits and characteristics. To diagnose and understand these traits and characteristics this paper will apply Geert Hofstede's "Cultural Dimensions Model of Differences in National Cultures" (Hofstede, 1994a). The application of Hofstede's theory will provide a unique insight into Russian culture and will make it possible to understand the essential patterns of thinking, feeling, and acting. This research will also differentiate Russian culture using Edward T. Hall's "Model of Culture." The characteristics that describe high/low context cultures result from collectively held assumptions about the way Russian society has related to other societies.

9.3   Power Distance

In his work "Management Scientists Are Human", Hofstede defines dimension of power distance "as the degree of inequality among people which the population of a country considers as normal" (Hofstede, 1994b, p. 5). The conceptual outline of this dimension focuses on the degree of equality, or inequality, between people in the society. "A country's population can consist of various ethnographic groups, or been mono-ethnic, however it will be divided according to their status and social class" (Vladimirsky-Budanov, 1995, p. 27).

Throughout Russia's long and violent history, successive governments have allowed, and in some instances encouraged, and stimulated, inequalities of power and wealth. The czars successively maintained a social system that did not allow significant upward mobility of its citizens; a system called "estates" (*sosloviya* [сосповия), or social classes or social groups. According to the Merriam-Webster Online dictionary (October 17, 2005), the meaning of the word estate is "a social or political class; specifically: one of the great classes (as the nobility, the clergy, and the commons) formerly vested with distinct political powers."

The traditional view of Russia's social structure identified four primary categories of estates: nobility, clergy, townspeople, and peasantry – a model not unlike the formal structure of medieval Europe (Freeze, 1986, p. 11). Other accounts of medieval Russia record over 500 separate social categories of societal differentiation (Kochin, 1937, pp. 435–440). Therefore, the composition of the social system was quite complicated because it regulated the actions and behavior of individuals depending on their estate ranking in the Russian Empire.

Each estate had various lower subgroups and strict rules regulated the moving either up or down on the social ladder. These estates were primarily hereditary. In the pre-reform Russia of the 19th century, there existed numerous *sosloviyas* (estates), *klassys* (social classes), and *sostoyaniyas* (socioeconomic differentiation) among the people of Russia (Pestel', 2001). The *soslovie* system existed until the Bolshevik takeover in 1917 (Freeze, 1986, p. 35).

The October Revolution abolished the Russian monarchy and the old social infrastructure (Dekrety Sovetskoi Vlasti, 1957, p. 72). A new form of social differentiation replaced the hereditary system of estates. This new social structure of the Soviet Union was also characterized by limited opportunities for political and social advancement (Russia. Social Stratification, 1996).

For the majority of the population access to higher education was limited and restricted. Workers lived in cramped apartments shared with other families while members of the ruling elite resided in lavish houses furnished with expensive Finnish furnishings and full amenities (Voslenskii, 1991, pp. 112–116, 267–351; Russia. Social Stratification, 1996). Ordinary Soviet citizens had limited access to food and other necessities including poor medical care.

The living conditions of peasants and farmers in rural areas were appalling because they resided at the bottom of the Russian social ladder (Russia. Social Stratification, 1996). Limited access to education and medical care, restricted opportunities for social advancement, and meager pay also characterized the existence of ethnic minorities during the Soviet years. In Soviet villages amenities such as autos, washing machines, running water, gas heating, indoor latrines, and televisions were considered rare and luxury items. On the top of the Soviet social pyramid resided the upper class called the *nomenklatura* (nomenclatura) (Voslenskii, 1991, pp. 109–173). The *nomenklatura* itself was a rigidly centralized class system and the make-up of this class consisted of a small fraction of Communist Party members. After the Communist takeover in 1920 the "nomenclature system was institutionalized" (Hanley et al., 1995, p. 641).

This class "was widely seen (and resented) by ordinary citizens as a bureaucratic élite that had simply supplanted the earlier wealthy capitalist élites. Members of the *nomenklatura* enjoyed special privileges such as shopping at well-stocked stores and being allowed to travel abroad" (Wikipedia, the Free Encyclopedia, 2005). Within its structure, the *nomenklatura* had several layers of party groups of different status and positions (Voslenskii, 1991, pp. 174–264).

Members of the Politburo and the Central Committee were at the top of this hierarchy. The next level constituted the regional leaders. This system continued down to the local party bosses situated at the bottom (Voslenskii, 1991, pp. 174–264). By the time of the Soviet collapse, the growing economic problems widened the gap between social groups in Russia. After the dissolution of the Soviet Union, "there was more continuity than discontinuity between the *nomenklatura* that dominated the Soviet Union in 1988 and the elite that rule over Russian society today" (Hanley et al., 1995, p. 641).

According to Vladimir Shlapentokh, "contemporary Russian presents a peculiar society (in political sense) for which the best parallel (albeit limited, as the case with any historical comparison) is early West European feudalism as it existed between the ninth and twelfth centuries" (Shlapentokh, 1996, p. 393). Moreover, "just as it was one thousand years ago, property and power are closely intertwined, and it is often impossible to separate them from each other. Just as royal emissaries turned their districts into private fiefdoms instead of using them to serve the king, Russian officials have tended do the same with their positions in the hierarchy" (Shlapentokh, 1996, p. 394).

In the business world of today's Russia, "the main source of power" is "not personal traits but position in hierarchical structure. Only the head takes all decisions" (Akperov and Maslikova, 2002, p. 7). In addition, in Russia "an organization functions in accordance with system of rules, procedures and standards. There is a strict administrative hierarchy between employees in Russian companies; each person of which bears certain labor responsibilities (Akperov and Maslikova, 2002, pp. 5–8).

9.4   Collectivism /Individualism

The next dimension identified by Hofstede is Collectivism/Individualism. Hofstede defines this dimension as "individualism pertains to societies in which the ties between individuals are loose: everyone is expected to look after himself or herself and his or her immediate family. Collectivism as its opposite pertains to societies in which people from birth onwards are integrated into strong, cohesive in-groups, which throughout people's lifetime continue to protect them in exchange for unquestioning loyalty" (Hofstede, 1994a, p. 5).

This concept is the most popular and the most applied in fundamental research in marketing and intercultural communication. An individualistic culture implies a social framework where people take care of themselves; each member is the most important unit in the society; and a high degree of independence in political, economic, and social life is strongly emphasized (Hofstede, 1980, p. 45). Individualism is the cultural belief that the person comes first with a high degree of self-respect and independence. People in individualistic cultures often put their own success over the good of the group they belong to. In workplaces and "organizations, individualism is manifested as autonomy, individual responsibility for results, and individual-level results" (Newman, 1996, p. 758).

In collectivistic cultures, a more rigid social framework with well-defined networks of extended families, tribes and coworkers usually defines these cultures (Hofstede, 1980, p. 45). In these tight social structures, individual members expect others to look after them (Hofstede, 1980, p. 45). In collectivism, each individual member puts a greater emphasis on the views, needs, and goals of the group. Personal freedoms, interests, and success are expected to be sacrificed for the benefit of the society as a whole. In these cultures, personal responsibility for the failure of the society as whole is related to each individual member. "Collective management practices emphasize work unit solidarity and team-based rewards" (Newman, 1996, p. 758).

Even though Russian territory spans over 11 time zones, it offers only a very small amount of land capable of providing economically successful agriculture. The CIA's annual World Factbook describes the climate of Russia as the "largest country in the world in terms of area but unfavorably located in relation to major sea lanes of the world; despite its size, much of the country lacks proper soils and climates (either too cold or too dry) for agriculture" (The World Factbook, 2001).

This geographic positioning predisposed Russians to operate in groups and adapt a collective mentality as the way to survive. Therefore, "the origins of Russian collectivism can be seen even from prehistoric times (Chapman, 1998, p. 12). The *zadruga* – a clan or extended family commune – formed the basis for Slavic tribal society. This then evolved into the *mir*, (Chapman, 1998, p. 12) an agricultural village commune." "A second main thread of cultural continuity in the Russian countryside (Wegren, 1994, p. 222) can be discerned by looking at rural equalitarianism." The great Russian philosopher Nikolai Berdyaev described (Berdyaev, 1990, p. 278) the structure of Russian society when he wrote, "the person is dissolved always and drowned in the natural collectivism, which is mistaken as being a spiritual *Sobornost*-Communality."

"By the time Gorbachev came to power there were two main characteristics that defined Soviet culture in the countryside: collectivism and the existence of welfare state egalitarianism" (Wegren, 1994, p. 216). The collapse of the Soviet Union and its newly found democratic and economic freedoms did little to fundamentally change Russian collective mentality. Today like centuries ago, Russians remain broadly attached to the culture of egalitarianism and collectivism. "According to the results of research done between the years 1996 and 2000 by the Laboratory of Ethnic Sociology and Psychology of St. Petersburg State University (Russian Mentality: Uncertainty and Fatalism, 2002), the basic values of the Russian people include the following: egalitarianism, collectivism as a preference for group as opposed to individual self-identification, paternalism and the Russian version of etatism, which is, adherence to strong consolidating state."

9.5 Uncertainty Avoidance

Hofstede defined (Hofstede, 1994b, p. 5) uncertainty avoidance "as the degree to which people in a country prefer structured over unstructured situations." He refers to reaction of individual cultures to situations when a culture feels threatened by ambiguity and uncertainty. Cultures with a high avoidance index develop many rules to control social behaviors and establish more structure. In these cultures, there is also a low tolerance for ambiguity. "In organizations, uncertainty avoidance is manifested by the clarity of plans, policies, procedures, and systems. Reliance on clear procedures, well-known strategies, and well-understood rules" help to "reduce uncertainty and cope with their discomfort with unknown situations" (Newman, 1996, p. 756). Russian culture has been characterized as being high in uncertainty avoidance (Elenkov, 1998, pp. 133–156).

Russians have been always suspicious of their rulers and they are usually not enthusiastic about radical changes. The absolute power of Russian czars, and 70 years of the rule-oriented and ideology-influenced society of the Soviet Union, created a culture that rejected dissent as a cultural value. Consensus was still a preferred principle of Russian people. As a result, the breakup of the USSR and economic chaos and political instability caused higher anxiety in the Russian society.

"Since Russian employees are accustomed to a high level of certainty" Russians require certain levels of assurances before they proceed with any changes (Michailova, 2000, p. 108). They also "are more comfortable with following a vision or plan that is laid out for them" (Tolstikova-Mast and Keyton, 2002, p. 127). This shows that in Russia "psychologically people take the transformation of their lives rather hard. This is the reason for the constantly growing psychological uneasiness and uncertainty as to what may follow" Russian Mentality: Uncertainty and Fatalism, 2002). The modern Russian state, unlike those cultures that developed and functioned in rather stable and modernized political and economic systems, is in the midst of fundamental economic and political changes. Therefore, individuals living in the Russian culture tend to be uncomfortable with unknowns and not eager to take risks or try new things.

9.6 Masculinity

The next dimension is called masculinity. Masculinity is "the degree to which values like assertiveness, performance, success, and competition, which in nearly all societies are associated with the role of men, prevail over tender values like the quality of life, maintaining warm personal relationships, service, care for the weak, and solidarity, which in nearly all societies are more associated with roles of women. Women's roles differ from men's roles in all countries; but in tough societies, the differences are larger than in tender ones" (Hofstede, 1994b, p. 6).

In organizations, masculinity "is reflected in merit-based opportunities for high earnings, recognition, advancement, and rewards, characteristics" (Newman, 1996, p. 759). Femininity emphasizes the quality of interpersonal relations and quality of working life issues (Newman, 1996, p. 759). In strong masculine cultures the role of males and females are strictly regulated and differentiated. Hall considers a predetermined masculinity throughout human history when he wrote that "…nothing was said about women; and world history was the history of war, primarily a male pursuit" (Hall, 1994, p. 172).

The constitution of the Soviet Union officially declared gender equality however, males dominated a significant portion of the society and power structure. Males "had an at once more limited and higher status role to play (Hall, 1994, p. 172). They were to serve as leaders, managers, soldiers, and workers" (Ashwin and Lytkina, 2004, p. 193). Males also dominated within the family while women were responsible for reproduction and performed household duties. "Women were also underrepresented in the CPSU and its leadership. In 1983 women constituted only 27.6 percent of the membership of the party and only 4.2 percent of the Central Committee; in 1986 they were totally absent from the Politburo. Historically, Russian culture has reinforced the traditional masculine achievement, control, and power" (*Soviet Union, Country Data*, 2001).

After the dissolution of the Soviet Union, Russian society underwent tremendous changes. The ideological and doctrinal influence on culture has been abolished, a new economic system has been introduced, and political freedoms have taken roots. Yet, gender equality has failed to materialize or, advance. According to the Canadian International Development Agency (Schalkwyk and Woroniuk, 1999, p. 1) "the marginalization of women is occurring in politics as well as the economy – there has been a sharp fall in the number of women in Parliament (from about 1/3 in the Soviet period to about 10 percent in 1995)." In addition, women are underrepresented in decision-making positions in government ministries and other institutions that are now presiding over major changes that will shape the society of the future. Therefore, Russia continues to be affiliated with the category of the high masculinity nations indicating that it experiences a high degree of gender differentiation.

9.7 Long-Term Orientation

According to Hofstede (2001, p. 359), "long Term Orientation stands for the fostering of virtues oriented towards future rewards. Its opposite pole, Short Term Orientation, stands for the fostering of virtues related to the past and present." This dimension focuses on the abilities of individual cultures to maintain long-term orientation to its values and traditions, respect for elders and ancestors, and a strong sense of duty and obedience (Hofstede, 1991, pp. 159–174).

It indicates the ability of individual members of the culture to identify and support long-term commitments. This ability relates to long-term rewards expected from today's input. This dimension also indicates the extent to which a society exhibits a pragmatic future-oriented perspective rather than a short-term point of view. In the workplace, long-term orientation is associated with "long-term employment and solving problems for the long term rather than making quick fixes" (Newman, 1996, p. 759). In cultures with a short-term orientation individuals express strong political and economic desires for stability. They expect quick results from their business and other projects and a "spending for today" attitude prevails over long-term savings.

The great Russian philosopher and writer of 19th century, Alexander Herzen, defined the Russian national culture during his lifetime: "Caring for the future is not our way; by word of mouth we are willing to bear the burden of the whole world, to become Socialists or Democrats, to speculate upon high principles with blood in our eyes. In practice, though, we are afraid of any work, any thought.

We live by the present moment; our bureaucrats pilfer in order to booze, or to bribe other bureaucrats and promote their sons. Peasants work in order to get dead drunk. Very few put anything aside for a rainy day; whoever cares for the future becomes an object of ridicule, contempt, and intense dislike (Herzen, 1859, pp. 122, 123). The importance of this quote is its understanding of how Russian culture in the 19th century was focused on short-term objectives. In 2003 only 17% of Russia's total population admitted having a long-term plan, 35% said that they were planning "something" for the short-term and 44% did not have any plans for future (Rossiyane Zhivut "Odnim Dnem", 2003). "Living today, not caring about long term consequences" is the dominant trend in the lives of ordinary Russian people (Kolodnyi, 2004).

9.8   High- and Low-Context Cultures

Edward T. Hall developed a theoretical framework in cross-cultural communication dividing individual cultures in categories of "high context" cultures or "low context" cultures. The argumentation for this division was presented in several books such as *The Silent Language (1959), The Hidden Dimension (1969), Beyond Culture (1976), and The Dance of Life, The Other Dimension of Time (1983).* According to Hall (1976, p. 101), "high context transactions feature pre-programmed information that is in the receiver and in the setting, with only minimal information in the transmitted message. Low context transactions are the reverse. Most of the information must be in the transmitted message in order to make up for what is missing in the context" In his concept of culture segmentation Hall separated individual cultures according to the size and the amount of contextual information being transmitted.

Communication in low-context cultures is clear, detailed, explanatory and precise, and is supported by plenty of facts and evidence. Verbal communication is the primary source of information, and channels of information are clear and relevant information is easily accessed. Cross-cultural communication variables, such as transmitter, recipient, and context do not matter. In low-context cultures what matters most are results and the outcome of the communication process. The interests of the individual member of the society outweigh the collective interests of the society as a whole.

In high-context cultures, variables such as recipient, transmitter, origin, ethnicity, customs, gender, history, traditions, organizational structure, religion, age, and geography strongly influence cross-cultural communication. In these cultures, strict rules, and norms of communication are clearly defined and enforced in order not to generate an unpleasant outcome or to damage a well-established web of personal relationships. Verbal communication is not the primary code of communication in this category of cultures. In traditional high-context cultures, the context of communication is strongly influenced by variables such as power, status, customs, traditions, hierarchy, etc. In contemporary Russia, "personal relationships are more important than relations based on the formal roles in political, social and economic structures.

This means that the most powerful people in the country are not elected officials but close friends of the President (Shlapentokh, 1996, p. 394). In Russia "the head has position of the first among equals, all the decisions being taken collectively. Ordinary employees take part in this process personally and are always aware of the plans of the heads" (Akperov and Maslikova, 2002, pp. 5–8). The most "powerful people in the country are not elected officials but close friends of the President". In Russia, "personal trust in each other is more important in economic relations than is trust in the judicial institutions" and collective interests far outweigh individual ones (Shlapentokh, 1996, p. 394).

9.9 Monochronic Culture vs. Polychronic Culture

Edward T. Hall developed a concept that deals with time management and time orientation by individual cultures. This concept is identified as "polychronic versus monochronic time orientation." According to Hall (Hall and Reed, 1990, p. 179), "time is one of the fundamental bases on which all cultures rest and around which all activities revolve. Understanding the difference between monochronic time and polychronic time is essential to success...." Hall presents monochronic culture as a culture of individuals, which is low-context and require detailed supplemental information to conduct communication.

The monochronic time concept follows the pattern of "one thing at a time," and everything is meticulously planned and organized. In these cultures people concentrate on doing one thing at a time and a commitment to the job and time is extremely serious. In these cultures, members follow rules of privacy and prefer not to disturb others unless it is totally necessary; show great respect for private property; and seldom borrow or lend. A short-term commitment in personal relationship is preferred over life-time friendships. Monochronic tendencies are common in individualistic, low-context cultures, such as in United States, Holland, and Germany, and prioritize individual needs over group needs (Hall, 1983).

Polychronic views predominate in collectivistic cultures that are high-context and more personal relationship-oriented. In this cultural environment multiple tasks are handled at one time. However, distractions and interruptions in these cultures are common and plans can be scrapped and changed easily. The context of communication in polychronic cultures is predisposed by the hierarchical and traditional structures where little information is needed.

Time dimensions of polychronic variables are another set of cultural differences affecting communication in Russia. Events in Russia can happen spontaneously and randomly and chronological order is not important. Russians do not consider strict adherence to schedules to be important. The Russian focus is on people and on completing transactions rather than adherence to specific time schedules. For example, just like in Russia, it is often expected that a Cuban therapist will periodically pause to converse with the client about non-therapy-related topics, or that a client's daughter may bring coffee for an anticipated break during the therapy session (Brice, 2000).

Polychronic cultures are more conscious of past and present than future. One would think that after centuries of brutal ruling by the Czars, and decades of communism, Russians would disdain an authoritarian model of governance. However, "recent studies show that despite some changes in traditional attitudes, the authoritarian beliefs of Russian citizens remain relatively high" (McFarland et al., 1992, pp. 1004–1010). This attitude toward its past echoes Edward Hall's observations in *West of the Thirties* that when "one cannot change the past, we can only put the past in a wider frame." Polychronic cultures include Latin American (e.g., Cuban), Middle Eastern, Asian, French, and Greek (Hall, 1983).

9.10   The Benefit of Hofstede and Hall's Models

The application of Hofstede's and Hall's models of cultural differentiation to the Russian state helps to understand the possible transformation of native culture after it undergoes an intense process of cross-cultural consolidation and communication. This is especially true for the knowledge adaptation and knowledge transfer from more developed cultures to less developed ones.

Through the usage of historical sources and documents it is possible to redefine cultural differences at any period of recorded history and to understand the basic patterns and characteristics of individual societies. However, it is important to mention that the application of these models does not and cannot provide a clear picture of an individual culture. Hofstede and Hall created a conceptual framework, which only provides a summary based on the statistically predominant patterns of cross-cultural communication. This means that even though Russians are considered to be monochronical, follow low uncertainty avoidance and is high context culture, there are probably many Russians who do not fit in this scheme. A good example illustrating the complexity of cultural variables in a multiethnic country like Russia is the following story.

According to a Russian story (Peacock, 1971, p. 137), a worker in a certain factory pushed a wheelbarrow through the exit gate every afternoon at quitting time. Every time he pushed the wheelbarrow through the gate, the guards inspected the wheelbarrow. The wheelbarrow was always empty so the worker always got through. Then after many months it was discovered that the worker had been stealing wheelbarrows."

This story presents dangers of narrowing and codifying dimensions of national cultures based on human behavior of millions of individual members of these societies. Therefore, Hofstede's and Hall's concepts do not represent absolute and unconditional facts. They should be considered as tendencies. According to Littleton, with accounting history, as with general history, interdependence of events runs throughout the story and change is a permanent feature. In this special field of accounting the need for perspective is not as great as in affairs of state, perhaps, but accountancy is still evolving (Littleton, 1966, p. 361).

It may be even now in the midst of its greatest movement-and we are poorly equipped to understand its trend if our historical perspective is weak (Littleton, 1966, p. 361). We are badly poised to assist the wider movements of the development if the trend is too dimly perceived. Even in the busy present, therefore, we need some knowledge of the interesting past of bookkeeping and accounting (Littleton, 1966, p. 361). In Russia's transition economy, culture and history have been identified as important factors influencing accounting systems and the process of accounting change. Culture is recognized as the system, encompassing the evolution of social institutions and social phenomena, which enables mankind to interpret his environment and the social phenomena he faces. Culture is learned or acquired behavior resulting from man's response to his environment, which, once acquired, then conditions man's response to his social environment. The values of a culture determine a systematic choice by a society for explaining and rationalizing social phenomena and based on these values, customs are created and adopted.

These customs themselves develop into or exist as social institutions. Accounting is argued to be one such social institution and, as such, must reflect the values of its culture. Russia's history and country's rich culture are seen to be an important influence on accounting and has been defined as the influence of country's past on accounting, the influence of historical trends on accounting. Historical studies of accounting change in Russia have been identified as an important addition to the literature on culture and history on accounting systems. A suitable framework is needed in order to investigate the influence of culture and politics on accounting in single countries and on the process of accounting change. The framework based on models developed by Hofstede and Hall is expected to provide the cultural and historical analysis necessary to implement accounting change and development in Russia.

References

Akperov, Imran G. & Maslikova, Zhana V. (2002). Peculiarities of Forming Organizational Culture in Russia. *Theory of Communication and Applied Communication*, 1, 5–8.

Ashwin, S. & Lytkina, T. (2004). Men in Crisis in Russia: The Role of Domestic Marginalization. *Gender and Society*, 18(2), 189–206.

Belkaoui, Ahmed R. (1989). Cultural Determinism and Professional Self-regulation in Accounting: A Comparative Ranking. *Research in Accounting Regulation*, 3, 93–101.

Berdyaev, Nikolai A. (1990). *Dukhovnye Osnovy Russkoy Revolyutsii. Philosophia Neravenstva.* Paris: YMCA-Press.

Bloom, R. & Naciri, M.A.R. (1989). Accounting Standard Setting and Culture: A Comparative Analysis of United States, Canada, England, West Germany, Australia, New Zealand, Sweden, Japan and Switzerland. *International Journal of Accounting Education and Research*, 24, 70–97.

Brice, Alejandro. (2000). *An Introduction to Cuban Culture for Rehabilitation Service Providers*, Retrieved January 18, 2006 from http://cirrie.buffalo.edu/cuba.html

Chapman, Steven R. (1998). Collectivism in the Russian World View and its Implications for Christian Ministry. *East-West Church & Ministry Report*, 6(4), 12–14.

Choi, Frederick, & Mueller, Gerhard G. (1992). *International Accounting*. Second Addition, Englewood Cliffs, NJ: Prentice Hall.

Dekrety Sovetskoi Vlasti. (1957). T.1. Moscow: Gosudarstvennoe Izdatel'stvo Politicheskoi Literatury.

Elenkov, Detelin S. (1998). Can American Management Concepts Work in Russia? A Cross-Cultural Comparative Study. *California Management Review*, 40(4), 133–156.

Freeze, Gregory L. (1986). The Soslovie (Estate) Paradigm and Russian Social History. *The American Historical Review*, 91(1), 11–36.

Geertz, Clifford. (1973). *Interpretation of Cultures*. New York: Basic Books, 1973.

Hall, Edward T. (1959). *The Silent Language*. Garden City, NY: Doubleday.

Hall, Edward T. (1966). *The Hidden Dimension*. Garden City, NY: Doubleday.

Hall, Edward T. (1976). *Beyond Culture*. Garden City, NY: Doubleday.

Hall, Edward T. (1983). *The Dance of Life*. New York: Doubleday.

Hall, Edward T. (1994). *West of the Thirties: Discoveries Among the Navajo and Hopi*. New York: Doubleday.

Hall, Edward T. & Reed Hall, Mildred. (1990). *Understanding Cultural Differences*. Yarmouth: Intercultural Press.

Hall, Edward T. & Reed Hall M. (1990). *Understanding Cultural Differences*. Yarmouth: Intercultural Press.

Hanley, E., Yershova, N. & Anderson, R. (1995) Russia – Old Wine in a New Bottle? The Circulation and Reproduction of Russian Elites, 1983–1993. *Theory and Society*, 24(5), 639–668.

Herzen, Aleksander I. (1859). *Voices From Russia*. Book VI. London.

Hofstede, Geert. (1980). Motivation, leadership, and organizational: Do American theories apply abroad? *Organizational Dynamics*, 10(1), 42–63.

Hofstede, Geert. (1991). *Cultures and Organizations: Software of the Mind*. New York: McGraw-Hill.

Hofstede, Geert. (1994a). *Cultures and Organizations, Software of the Mind: Intercultural Cooperation and Its Importance for Survival*. London: McGraw-Hill.

Hofstede, Geert. (1994b). Management Scientists Are Human. *Management Science*, 40(1), 4–13.

Hofstede, Geert. (2001). *Culture's Consequence. Comparing Values, Behaviors, Institutions and Organizations across Nations*. Thousand Oaks CA: Sage.

Jaggi, Bikki L. (1973). The Impact of the Cultural Environment on Financial Disclosures. *The International Journal of Accounting*, Spring, 75–84.

Kochin, G.E. (1937). *Materialy dlia Terminologicheskogo Slovaria Drevnei Rossii*. Moskva/Leningrad: Izdatel'stvo Akademii nauk SSSR.

Kolodnyi, Aleksandr. (2004). Rossiiskaya Tragediya. My zhivem odnim dnem. *Rodnaya Gazeta* 14(83), 14 May 2004, editorial, final edition.

Laurent, Andre. (1983). The Cultural Diversity of Western Conceptions of Management. *International Studies of Management and Organization*, 13, 75–96.

LeVine, Robert A. (1984). *Properties of Culture. An Ethnographic View*. New York: Basic Books.

Littleton, Ananias C. (1966). *Accounting Evolution to 1900*. New York: Russell & Russell.

McFarland, Sam G., Ageyev, Vladimir S., & Abalakina-Paap, Marina (1992). Authoritarianism in the Former Soviet Union. *Journal of Personality and Social Psychology*, 63(6), 1004–1010.

Merriam-Webster Online Dictionary, Retrieved October 17, 2005, from http://www.m-w.com/

Michailova, Snejina. (2000). Contrasts in Culture: Russian and Western Perspectives on Organizational Change. *Academy of Management Executive*, 14(4), 99–112.

Newman, Karen L. (1996). Culture and Congruence: the Fit between Management Practices and National Culture. *Journal of International Business Studies*, 27(4), 753–779.

Peacock, James L. (1971). The Silent Language. *College Composition and Communication*, 22(2), 137–140.

Pestel', Pavel I. (2001). *Russkaya Pravda ili Zapovednaya Gosudarstvennaya Gramota Velikogo Naroda Rossiiskogo sluzhaschaya Zavetom dlya Usovershenstvovaniya Gosudarstvennogo Ustroistva Rossii i Soderzhaschaya Vernyi Nakaz kak dlya Naroda tak i dlya Vremennogo Verkhovnogo Pravleniya. Glava Tret'ya. O Sosloviyakh v Rossii Obretayuschikhsya. § 1 Izchislenie Soslovii v Rossii obretayuschikhsya*. Retrieved February 15, 2005, from http://vivovoco.nns.ru/VV/LAW/VV_PES_W.HTM

Rossiyane Zhivut "Odnim Dnem". (2003). Retrieved January 18, 2006 from http://www.utro.ru/news/2003/08/12/222449.shtml

Russia. Social Stratification. (1996) Retrieved February 10, 2006, from http://www.country-data.com/cgi-bin/query/r-11420.html

Russian Mentality: Uncertainty and Fatalism. (2002). *Pravda*, 26 March, final edition.

Samovar, Larry A. & Porter, Richard. (2003). *Intercultural Communication: A Reader*. (14th ed.). Belmont, CA: Wadsworth.

Schalkwyk, J. & Woroniuk, B. (1999). Russia: Gender Equality Issues and Resources in Brief. *Canadian International Development Agency, Report Prepared for the Central and Eastern Branch*.

Shlapentokh, Vladimir. (1996). Early Feudalism-the Best Parallel for contemporary Russia. *Europe-Asia Studies*, 48(3), 393–411.

Soviet Union, Country Data. (2001). Retrieved November 29, 2005, from http://www.country-data.com/cgi-bin/query/r-12550.html

The World Fact book. (2001). Retrieved November 29, 2004, from n.d., http://www.cia.gov/cia/publications/factbook/geos/rs.html

Tolstikova-Mast, Y. & Keyton, J. (2002). Communicating about Communication: Fostering the Development of the Communication Discipline in Russia. *Theory of Communication and Applied Communication. Bulletin of Russian Communication Association*, 1, 119–134.

Verma, Shraddha. (1998). *Culture and Politics in International Accounting: An Exploratory Framework*. [Electronic version]. Birkbeck, University of London: School of Management and Organizational Psychology.

Violet, William J. (1983). The Development of International Accounting Standards: An Anthropological Perspective. *The International Journal of Accounting Education and Research*, Spring, 1–12.

Vladimirsky-Budanov, Mikhail F. (1995). *Historical Review of Russian Legal System*. Rostov-on-Don: Fenix Press, 1995.

Voslenskii, Mikhail S. (1991). *Nomenklatura. Gospodstvuyuschii klass Sovetskogo Soyuza*. Moscow: Sovetskaya Rossiya/MP Octyabr'.

Wegren, Stephen K. (1994). Rural Reform and Political Culture in Russia. *Europe-Asia Studies*, 46(2), 215–241.

Wikipedia, the Free Encyclopedia, 2005, Retrieved November 29, 2005, from http://en.wikipedia.org/wiki/Main_Page

Chapter 10
Prospects of Transition of the Russian Banking Sector to International Accounting Standards

Vladimir V. Kachalin

10.1 Introduction

The issue of financial transparency (in the internationally recognized understanding of the term) receives a growing importance in the overall market-oriented reform of the present day Russian society and attracts increasing attention from policymakers. The national banking system plays a pivotal role in insuring the financial transparency of the entire national economy and, therefore, the reform of accounting in the banking sector, along with achieving transparency in the stock market and accounting in production and trade, became a political issue and a matter of special concern for the Russian establishment. The transition of the Russian banking sector and the economy in general to International Accounting Standards (IAS) is one of the important conditions for Russia to enter the World Trade Organization (WTO), as well.

The international community also does not play the role of an indifferent observer of the developments in the Russian banking sector criticizing the Russian authorities for delays in introducing internationally acceptable accounting principles on one hand and facilitating the transition by a variety of international donor programs on the other hand (Galuzina & Pupshis, 2005).

Thus, the transition process was enforced by a set of the relevant policy decisions made by the Russian authorities involved and facilitated by the EU and US technical assistance. Both sides managed to find workable coordination mechanisms for their activities referring to each other in practical issues. The "big four" and numerous other international accounting and auditing consultancies were also involved finding the transformation process to be a growing market for their services.

10.2 Prospects of Transition

At present the rules of accounting and reporting in Russian credit institutions are determined by the Russian legislation, normative documents of the Bank of Russia, the Ministry of Finance (MoF), and other legislation and regulations. A complete

V. V. Kachalin
Adviser to the Head of Antimonopoly Service of Russia

R. W. McGee (ed.), *Accounting Reform in Transition and Developing Economies,*
© Springer Science+Business Media LLC 2008

transition to IAS can be performed only under the conditions of improvement of civil and tax legislation of the RF that form the basis for performing banking transactions. A number of normative documents prepared by the Bank of Russia provides for applying IAS provisions. The absence of a legally approved right to use IAS-compliant financial statements hinders the implementation of these standards and their use in supervision practice (Giliarovskaya, 2003).

The strategy of the development of the banking sector of the RF was adopted by the Government of the RF and the Bank of Russia on December 30, 2001 and provided for transferring the Russian banking sector to International Accounting Standards (further – IAS) from January 1, 2004 (Nechitailo, 2005). The transition issue is being broadly discussed among the government bodies involved, the professional community, and the bankers.

Currently IAS proliferate in the Russian accounting system (both in the banks and nonbanking companies) primarily due to the introduction of IAS-oriented changes in the Russian accounting regulations. When issuing new regulations the Bank of Russia and the Ministry of Finance tend not to fall into controversy with IAS and seek to avoid issuing accounting rules and instructions that would contradict international accounting principles.

Meanwhile, at the grassroots level of the accounting system, i.e., in enterprises and banks, accountants have to learn newly issued regulations and follow them in their job. Thus, in case a specific accounting issue at the enterprise is simple enough and can be easily addressed by reference to a specific regulation, this top-to-the-bottom process of IAS proliferation works more or less efficiently. However, when a more sophisticated assessment or choice of accounting treatment is required the skills of rank and file banking and accounting personnel may not suffice. Large companies and banks that encounter this situation more frequently used to apply to professional consultants and auditors in these cases.

It is hard to assess the timing of completion of Russia's transition to IAS in terms like "the country's transition to IAS accounting both in the banking and non-banking sectors will be finished by … (specific date)." Some enterprises dealing with international investors and other stakeholders have already introduced IAS accounting into their practice. Others (mainly small and working in isolation from international commodity and financial markets) may continue to maintain more familiar accounting and their approximation to IAS foes via following IAS compatible novelties in accounting regulations (Adamov & Rogulenko, 2004).

Within the framework of the International Coordination Committee on Development of Banking Business in Russia in 1999 a Working Group (WG) on improving accounting and reporting in the banking system of the RF was created and continues its activities. The WG develops methodology and ways of its implementation in practice within a framework of the Technical Aid to the Commonwealth of Independent States (TACIS) program. The Russian national bank – the Bank of Russia – is considered as a major agent in reforming the national banking system and a gravity point for focusing the international efforts on facilitating it. Therefore, the Bank of Russia became subject to intensive international assistance in the matter of preparing banking regulations eventually aimed at introducing IAS-compatible accounting into the Russian banking sector in general. Several EU project initiatives should be mentioned in this respect.

Among them there is the European Community-financed Project on "Assistance to the reform of accounting and reporting in the banking system of the Russian Federation" performed within a framework of the TACIS Program. The project was started in June 2000 and was completed in July 2002. It involved PWC as a consultant that was selected by TACIS as a contractor for this project as the result of a tender. Among the project results the review of differences in accounting and financial reporting between the Russian rules of bank accounting and reporting and international standards can be specifically mentioned. A comprehensive work was performed on defining and analyzing of the substantial differences between the rules of accounting and reporting for the Russian banks and international systems of standards, including IAS. Specifically, the Project pursued the following goals:

- Training of different groups of providers and users of IAS statements
- Consulting on creating management reporting systems in the Russian credit institutions
- Consulting on improving internal control in the Russian credit institutions
- Consulting on improving work of departments of internal audit in the Russian credit institutions.

The results of the Project were:

- Preparation of 16 sections of most important instructions of the Bank of Russia on IAS-based accounting and reporting in the Russian credit institutions
- Six credit institutions were selected as pilot banks for transition to IAS. In these banks consulting projects on transferring to IAS were performed and financial statements that would comply with both IAS and the Russian according rules were prepared on a pilot basis
- A considerable number of providers and users of IAS statements were trained (mainly chosen from CBR staff members)

Upon the completion of the Project the EU experts performed certification of the instructors prepared by the Bank of Russia as a result of it within the succeeding TACIS project on "Supporting the Adoption of the International Accounting Standards in the Russian Banking Sector" finished in April 2003. For the moment the Bank of Russia received another EU 3-year long project on improving banking supervision techniques used by the Bank of Russia in compliance with recommendations of the Basel Committee on banking supervision.

As a TA project it included not only preparation of recommendations but a series of training programs as well. The training was delivered by the professional accounting and auditing companies working under the relevant contracts with the EC on rendering TA. The trainees were selected for courses by the management of the Bank of Russia based on their involvement in the introduction of IAS-related changes in the Russian accounting norms and regulatory practices.

The professional accounting companies normally have a kind of standard training courses that they can adapt to the needs of a specific audience (beginners, advanced, practitioners, academicians, etc.) and the time they have for delivering the training. In the case of the Bank of Russia these were about 70–100h courses tailored for advanced banking professionals and intended to acquaint them with the differences between IAS and Russian accounting rather than to teach them accounting basics (Nechitailo, 2004).

The EU assistance combined with the Bank of Russia's own effort to introduce IAS into the Russian banking system. In September 2002, upon completion of the first TACIS Project, the Committee of the Bank of Russia on Transition to IAS was created. The Committee was headed by the First Deputy of the Chairman of the Bank of Russia. The Committee primarily intended to plan and implement IAS in the Russian banking sector. Its activities were focused on preparing suggestions on implementing the Bank of Russia's policy on introducing IAS into accounting and reporting in the Russian banking sector.

The main tasks of the Committee included ongoing management and coordination of transferring to IAS and monitoring implementation of the plan of transferring to IAS. The Committee included the directors of major departments of the Bank of Russia such as: banking regulation and supervision, accounting and reporting, economic, legal, currency regulation and control, currency operations, payment systems and settlements, information systems, licensing, and financial rehabilitation of credit institutions, open market operations, as well as representatives of the Council of Federation and State Duma of the Federal Assembly of the RF and auditing and public institutions.

Thus, as a result of both Russian national and international efforts the Bank of Russia created a task-oriented Committee aimed at implementing IAS in the Russian banking sector. It enjoys support from both the Bank and top authorities, as well as from the international standard setting community and the European Commission. The Committee's goal is to implement IAS-compatible accounting in the Russian banking sector by the year 2006 and it has to reach it under the conditions of changing IAS and the Russian domestic legislation.

The IAS itself is not static. It passes through permanent changes and in its effort to comply with IAS the Bank of Russia and other Russian authorities involved have to take these changes into account.

IAS has been translated into Russian periodically by private companies since 2001 but these are not official translations endorsed by the IASB. The official translation has not been issued yet and the unofficial translations are made in the form of comments to IAS with lengthy quoted citations from the IAS themselves in order to avoid a copyright problem. Accounting practitioners can learn IAS accounting from numerous books dedicated to IAS in general or to IAS compliant treatment-specific accounting issues widely sold in bookstores. Therefore, translation of IAS into Russian is not a technical problem but that of copyright and official recognition of the Russian version of IAS by the IASB.

The International Accounting Standards Board (IASB) is an independent institution intended to unify accounting principles used by companies and other institutions for preparing and presenting financial statements worldwide. The Committee (its former name was the International Accounting Standards Committee) was founded in 1973 as a result of an agreement between professional accounting organizations of Austria, Canada, France, Germany, Japan, Mexico, the Netherlands, UK, Ireland, and the USA. In 1983 all the members of professional accounting organizations participating in the International Federation of Accountants became the members of the IASB as well. At present many other institutions from many countries that are not IASB members but that apply IAS are involved in the IASB's work, as well. EU member states made a decision to adopt IAS starting January 1, 2005 for institutions quoted on a stock exchange. The requirements of accounting standards effective in most of the European countries are generally in line with IAS requirements, as a rule (Galuzina & Pupshis, 2005).

It is important to mention that IAS is a "living document" that is permanently added to and upgraded in accordance with trends in business practices and conduct. IAS are reedited annually. However, a requirement of applying changes in IAS or new standards of preparation of financial statements becomes effective not earlier than the first reporting date of a financial year succeeding the year of publishing these changes.

According to the IASB, at present IAS are being substantially elaborated upon and this work will result in changes in the existing standards and preparation of new ones. The IASB plans to complete the elaboration of IAS by January 1, 2004 and then introduce a "moratorium" on introducing further changes in IAS for several years in order to insure gradual transition of different countries to IAS.

Substantial differences between the Russian accounting and reporting rules for credit institutions and real sector companies and IAS complicate the process of transition of IAS and require the introduction of changes in currently effective legislation as well as considerable time and resources (Galuzina & Pupshis, 2005). According to the Russian Minister of Finance Igor Kudrin, the Russian accounting standards mostly comply with IAS. Noncompliance and deviations from IAS may occur in accounting issues requiring IAS-based accounting opinion or evaluation, in our opinion. Generally, the more sophisticated the accounting issue is, the greater is the possibility of noncompliance.

As a first step, the Bank of Russia plans to arrange for publishing a certified official text of IAS in Russian that would be performed by the IASB. For the moment IAS is published in most European languages but not in Russian. The preparation of an official translation recognized by the IASB is now being negotiated between the Bank of Russia and the Ministry of Finance from one side and the IASB from the other. For the moment there are several translations of IAS circulating in Russia. However, none of them is recognized as official by the IASB and therefore cannot be referred to in the course of preparation of the financial statements by the Russian banks.

Regardless of the translation issue, the Russian banking community in cooperation with the Bank of Russia plans to make a transition of the Russian Banking sector to IAS that would include the following two aspects:

1. Insure preparation of financial reports by the Russian banks in accordance with IAS basing on the Russian financial statements prepared in accordance with

currently effective Russian accounting rules by means of applying a transformation method (i.e., by introducing necessary corrections in the financial statements prepared in accordance with the Russian accounting standards)
2. Performing supervision of activities of the Russian credit institutions based on IAS compliant financial statements prepared by means of introducing corrections.

It is important to mention that this "transition plan" has not been officially published. However, this approach received recognition by the major stakeholders, including both the authorities and the professional banking community.

The Russian banks are passing to preparation of financial statements in accordance with IAS starting January 1, 2004. Their IAS compliant financial statements will be prepared by introducing corrections to the Russian accounting data with IAS specifics taken into account. Meanwhile, the demand for the Russian banks to present a mandatory package of Russian financial statements and other reporting forms to territorial branches of the Bank of Russia will be effective January 1, 2006 with introduced changes taken into account. The Bank of Russia will work on optimizing and reducing the reporting forms to be provided by the credit institutions.

The simultaneous transition to IAS accounting is mandatory for both the banking and production sectors of the Russian economy in order to insure adequacy of the accounting principles used and presenting results of activities in the financial statements of both banking and production sector companies. The banking and the production sectors of the Russian economy will simultaneously take actions to introduce IAS compliant accounting principles in order to start their application from January 1, 2006.

In order to make IAS statements prepared by the Russian banking sector by means of transformation legally valid, the adoption of the relevant law of the Russian Federation is foreseen, in addition to issuing the relevant acts of the Bank of Russia. The transformations of the banking and production sectors of the Russian economy to be accounting compliant with IAS principles are linked to each other and correspond to the dates of introducing the relevant regulatory changes by the Ministry of Finance of the RF in cooperation with the Bank of Russia.

An important element of the foreseen transformation is an official recognition of the legal validity of the financial statements prepared in compliance with IAS by the Russian banks. For the moment IAS-compatible statements are mostly prepared by the Russian banks for use by their foreign shareholders, creditors, and banks cooperating with them. But these statements are not officially recognized by the Russian authorities as legally valid financial statements. The official statements are still prepared in accordance with the Russian national accounting standards.

Therefore, in order to make the statements compliant with both IAS and national standards, the Bank of Russia gradually introduced changes in the Russian standards intended to approximate them to the extent possible to IAS. However, in many cases these changes can contradict to other currently effective Russian accounting regulations, primarily to the national Taxation Code (Nechitailo, 2005). The financial and tax accounting are presented in the same set of books and reports in Russia and the reference to the Taxation Code presents a considerable obstacle for introducing IAS compatible representation of deferred taxes and some other issues, though accrual-based accounting (as opposite to that of cash-based) is now officially allowed in Russia.

The situation with banking supervision requirements is similar. The supervision is based on the accounting data prepared by the banks in accordance with the Russian national accounting standards. According to the Bank of Russia's unofficial estimate the gradual approximation of the Russian bank accounting rules to IAS will allow regular supervision of activities of the Russian banks based on IAS compliant statements starting from January 1, 2006.

The transition of the Russian banks to mandatory preparation of IAS-compliant financial statements is planned starting from January 1, 2004. The preparation of IAS-compliant statements will be made by means of introducing corrections in financial statements prepared in accordance with the Russian national accounting standards and adding supplementary financial information required by IAS. The Bank of Russia will publish the recommended procedure of making these corrections and calculations based on professional judgment in accordance with IAS principles.

The IAS compliant statements will be prepared for the periods ending June 30, 2004, September 30, 2004 and December 31, 2004. All the Russian banks will pass to preparation of IAS statements from January 1, 2004 without any exclusion, i.e., all the of them would submit their IAS statements for the reporting period to the Bank of Russia starting from this date. The Bank of Russia will specify the same composition of the financial statements to be mandatory presented by the Russian banks as IAS, i.e., balance sheet, income (profit and loss) statement, cash flow statement, statement on movement of own capital and notes to financial statements. It will also introduce a requirement that the annual financial statements should be confirmed by an independent auditor having the right to audit IAS-compliant statements.

In the course of planning the transformation to IAS the Russian authorities and banking community ran into a problem of comparability of accounting data presented in "pre-transitional" and "post-transitional" reports. IAS 1 "Presentation of financial statements," paragraph 38 requires the provision of comparable data for the preceding reporting period. The Russian banks can comply with this requirement only starting from financial statements for 2005 (monthly, quarterly statements, statements for 6 months, annual statements).

The auditor's statements prepared as a result of the mandatory audit of the banks' statements for 2004 will contain a clause on non-compliance with the IAS 1 requirement to provide comparable data. This non-compliance will not be an obstacle for an auditor to express his opinion on the reliability of Russian banks' statements for 2004 because this non-compliance will be explained by the fact that most of the Russian banks will prepare their IAS-compliant financial statements for 2004 for the first time. However, it will enable the Russian banks to present fully valuable IAS statements for 2005 with comparable data for 2004.

The procedure of the presentation of IAS compliant statements by banks with subsidiaries remains an open question for the moment since it is still to be decided on whether the subsidiaries should submit their statements to relevant territorial agencies of the Bank of Russia or a Russian bank would submit only its consolidated IAS statements to the territorial agency of the Bank of Russia in place of registration of the reporting bank's headquarters (Nechitailo, 2005).

In any case the transition should insure compliance of the Russian banks reporting with IAS 27 "Consolidated financial statements and accounting for investment in affiliated companies" and 28 "Accounting for investments in associated companies." IAS 27 and 28 provides for preparation of consolidated financial statements by the Russian banks in case the latter have subsidiary or associated companies. Meanwhile, IAS 27 and 28 allow for preparation of nonconsolidated financial statements by banks, if necessary. However, in this case IAS 27 and 28 do not recommend providing nonconsolidated and consolidated IAS financial statements together in the same document.

In case nonconsolidated and consolidated IAS statements are presented in separate documents, nonconsolidated IAS statements (supplemented with the auditor's statement) must contain an indication that the same institution also presents consolidated IAS statements and discloses information on major indicators of consolidated statements. They should also have a reference to a source of information available to the general public where the consolidated IAS financial statements of this institution can be obtained. The major indicators mentioned include:

- Currency of consolidated balance sheet for the last and previous reporting date
- Consolidated financial result for the last and previous reporting periods
- The amount of consolidated resources for the last and previous reporting dates

During 2004 and 2005, the IAS-compliant financial statements provided by the Russian banks will not be used for their supervision. IAS-compliant statements prepared by the Russian banks for different periods of 2004 will be used by the Bank of Russia and management of the Russian banks for analysis, comparison, and revealing problem areas in activities of each of the Russian banks.

Based on the comprehensive analysis the Bank of Russia will determine a periodicity of mandatory preparation of IAS statements by Russian banks for supervision purposes starting from January 1, 2006, i.e., from the planned date of introducing banking supervision based on IAS statements in Russia. The periodicity of preparation and presenting Russian banks' IAS statements to the Bank of Russia starting from January 1, 2005 will be additionally determined by the Bank of Russia.

The preparation of the IAS compliant statements will be supplemented with necessary training that will involve representatives of the Bank of Russia from supervision bodies, accounting departments, inspection service monitoring activities of the Russian Banks, and specialists from other interested units of the Bank of Russia. The staff of the Russian banks, tax bodies, Ministry of Finance, and auditing companies presenting auditing services to the Russian banks will pass this training, as well.

Training for the personnel of the Russian banks will include both theoretical foundations of IAS and practical skills of applying IAS in the course of preparation of IAS statements. The training will be performed in a centralized manner by the Bank of Russia or its contractor (or jointly) and in credit institutions separately.

The Russian banks involved in transactions with international stakeholders mostly undertook training programs fitting their needs. Training was delivered commercially by accounting consultants (mainly the "Big-4") and the contents and scope mostly depended on the requests of the banks. Moreover, banks recruited personnel who were familiar with IAS for positions requiring this type of skills.

In conjunction with the transition of Russian bank accounting to IAS a requirement of mandatory certification of the auditors of the Russian banks by internationally recognized and licensed institutions also will be introduced. The only organization of this type in the European Union is the International Association of Certified Accountants (IACA) that performs its activities practically in all the countries of Western and Eastern Europe, RF, and CIS. The official representative office of this institution has worked in the RF since 2000. The certification process will be coordinated and facilitated by the Ministry of Finance.

The transition of the Russian banks and production sector companies to accounting in accordance with IAS principles will be performed by the Ministry of Finance in coordination with the Bank of Russia in cooperation with Ministry of Taxation and Duties of the RF, State Duma (the lower chamber of the Russian Parliament), and other federal agencies involved. The transition to IAS accounting and reporting requires introduction of the necessary changes in the currently effective legislation (Civil Code, Tax Code, number of Federal Laws, etc.) that would create conditions for implementing IAS principles (e.g., prevalence of substance of a transaction over its form). Most probably a joint working group on introducing the relevant changes in the legislation will be created. These activities are intended to create a legal and bylaw basis for issuing a set of Bank of Russia's guidelines to the Russian banks providing for:

- Principles, rules, and procedures of transition of the Russian banking sector to preparation of IAS-compliant financial statements starting January 1, 2004
- Rules and procedures of transition of the Russian banking sector to performing regular supervision of activities of the Russian Banks based on IAS-compliant financial statements starting from January 1, 2006
- Principles, rules, and procedures of transition of the Russian banking sector simultaneously with the real sector to performing accounting based on IAS principles in order to insure the application of these principles starting January 1, 2006
- Guidelines to auditors prescribing the basic principles of auditing the banks' financial statements prepared in accordance with IAS that would comply with internationally recognized auditing principles

The transition to IAS will also require joint practical efforts by the Bank of Russia and the Russian banks that can be briefly specified as follows:

- Efforts to be undertaken by the Bank of Russia:

    Publication of the normative documents regulating preparation of IAS statements by the Russian banks

Publication of the recommended algorithm of making corrections to the Russian statements in order to achieve their compliance with IAS and the order of calculating the corrections with application of the professional judgment in accordance with IAS

- Efforts to be undertaken by the Russian banks:

Development of accounting policy for preparing IAS statements

Development of forms of reporting of the affiliations to the headquarters (and possibly to the relevant territorial agencies of the Bank of Russia) for the purposes of preparing consolidated IAS statements

Development of forms of reporting of the daughter (subsidiary) and associated companies to the mother company for the purposes of preparing consolidated IAS statements of the group of banks

Development of methodology of implementing accounting policy of the credit institution on IAS as well as software for preparing IAS statements

Transition of the Russian bank accounting to IAS will be naturally supplemented with the necessary changes in bank auditing. The audit should be performed in compliance with IAS, International Auditing Standards, and effective Russian legislation. It will require the auditors to comply with three regulations at the same time that would tend to complement each other or at least not contradict each other. Specifically, the auditors will have to observe the requirements of IAS regarding the compliance with IAS 27 and 28 and requirements of the International Standards on Auditing regarding the date of signing consolidated and nonconsolidated financial statements of the banks.

The audit of the IAS-compliant statements prepared by the Russian banks will be mandatory and performed on a regular basis, i.e., all Russian banks would present their annual IAS statements to the Bank of Russia with the requirements of IAS 27 and 28 taken into account and certified by the auditor. This requirement will be valid in case of normal regular activities of the credit institution. Apart from that the Russian banks will need to present their audited IAS statements to the Bank of Russia in cases provided for by currently effective Russian legislation, specifically upon the registration of securities issued, in case of reorganization of banks in the form of merger, acquisition, restructuring, separation, dividing, etc. (the relevant documents certifying these events should be presented to the registering body of the Bank of Russia by the banks, as well).

According to currently effective requirements of the Instruction of the Bank of Russia of June 22, 2002 No. 102 – "On the rules of emission and registration of securities by credit institutions in the territory of the Russian Federation" the Russian banks have to present financial statements for the last 3 years before submission of the emission prospect, application for registering merger, acquisition, etc. This requirement is in line with the standard requirement of the Generally Accepted Accounting Principles of the USA (US GAAP) that provide for presenting comparable data in the financial statements for 3 years and for the number of key indicators – for 5 years. Applicable to IAS statements this requirement will become obligatory for all the Russian banks tentatively starting January 1, 2007, i.e., when every Russian bank will have its IAS statements for 2004, 2005, and 2006.

The expected requirement to the Russian banks to provide their audited IAS-compliant statements to the Bank of Russia presents both a challenge and an opportunity for the auditing profession in Russia. Of course large Russian banks can refer to "big four" subsidiaries in Russia and other international auditors as they already use to do in order to get their IAS and/or US GAAP-compliant statements audited. However, for smaller banks "big four" services can be too costly and less efficient and they would need to turn to domestic auditors who should be skilled enough to perform this type of service. Therefore, there is a growing need for professional training and retraining of auditors of the Russian banks in theory and practice of IAS. It is very likely that the Bank of Russia will apply to international donors to perform this training and coordinate the dissemination of knowledge received and best practices.

The Russian auditors trained in IAS and International Auditing Standards will have to pass through the mandatory professional certification by internationally recognized and licensed institutions. The Ministry of Finance will also be involved in the certification. In Russia accountants working internationally seek to receive the relevant certification by a recognized international body. Moreover, domestic certification institutions are currently being created.

Summing up this brief survey of plans and activities of various stakeholders involved in the transition of the Russian banking accounting to IAS, we can mention that the transition is an ambitious task, of course, complicated by imperfections in banking regulation, changes in IAS, and insufficient skills in international accounting. However, the Russian accounting community has substantially increased its awareness in principles and techniques of international accounting, specifically in the banking sector. The transition process has moved from declaratory phase to practical and reasonable steps that provide grounds to argue its successful completion, although delays in timing might be possible.

References

Adamov, N. & Rogulenko, T. (2004). Basics of Accounting. Piter Publishing, St. Petersburg.
Belikova, T. (2005). Accounting and Reporting: From Zero to Balance Sheet. Piter Publishers, St. Petersburg.
Galuzina, S. & Pupshis T. (2005). International Accounting and Auditing. Piter Publishers, St. Petersburg.
Giliarovskaya, L. (2003). Accounting for Financial Reserves of a Company. Piter Publishing, St. Petersburg.
Nechitailo, A. (2004). Accounting for Financial Results and Distribution of Profits. Piter Publishers, St. Petersburg.
Nechitailo, A. (2005). Theory of Accounting. Piter Publishers, St. Petersburg.

Chapter 11
A Reemerging Professional in an Emerging Market: The Story of the Modern Serbian Accountancy Profession[*]

Željko Šević

11.1 Introduction

In the market economy the state is primarily interested in protecting the social order and ensuring that the basic rules of the game are observed. In order for market institutions to function, it is necessary to ensure that there is a high level of trust in the structure of social organisations. Therefore, the certification of those who perform various functions for the public has been a tradition in leading Anglo-American market economies. Continental European countries, however, placed their emphasis on formal education, rather than acquired competencies gained through professionally supervised practice and skill-focused examinations. In Continental European countries, accounting was primarily regulated by law, while in Anglo-Saxon countries self-regulation flourished. This was the case of affairs for more than 100 years (see Barber, 1963; Ben-David, 1963–64; Larson, 1977; Millerson, 1964; Perkin, 1989, 1996; Smith, 1992; Wirt, 1981).

However, with a number of recent scandals where accounting and/or auditing companies badly failed to discharge their public duties and companies that were regarded as sound for years went bankrupt, then even in Anglo-Saxon countries

---

[*] This research has been supported by the Institute of Chartered Accountants of Scotland (ICAS). The remit of the approved project was to analyze the trends and recent developments in the accountancy profession in at the time Yugoslavia. In the meantime the country changed the name into Serbia and Montenegro and the focus shifted onto the larger republic that constitutes 96% of the country. In 2006 Montenegro declared its independence and the State Union collapsed. The results of this research present the situation which was in place in Serbia, in 2004. In 2005 the Serbian Association of Accountants and Auditors fully endorsed the ACCA programme of professional training, which is delivered in a locally spoken language. Professor Vivien Beattie, at the time the ICAS Director of Research, gave some initial invaluable comments on the directions of this research, which have been largely endorsed. Dues are also to Robert W. McGee, editor, anonymous referees, and Nicholas G. Hand for their comments on earlier versions of this paper. The Secretary-General of the Association of Accountants and Auditors of Serbia Mr Pero Škobić was always ready for discussion and made access to the Association's archives available, which very much facilitated this research. However, the usual disclaimer remains. All errors are the sole responsibility of the author.

Ž. Šević
University of Greenwich

R. W. McGee (ed.), *Accounting Reform in Transition and Developing Economies,*
© Springer Science + Business Media LLC 2008

there emerged an issue of what was to be done with the accounting profession. Many in the USA would like to see accounting more tightly regulated, and professional bodies stripped of their self-regulatory powers. Recent statements by many leading government officials and leading figures in the business world certainly point in the direction of a legislator deciding to introduce new laws. These would change the face of the profession that we know in the USA and Britain, as the leading countries of the Anglo-Saxon world (see Liesman et al., 2002; Economist, 2002).

It is difficult to speculate as to future developments in the regulation of the accounting profession. At present American regulation is more interested in delineating conflicting interests and preventing situations where accountancy services may lead to more 'inter-twined' relations and lucrative nonaccounting contracts provided by the professional accounting firms. Certainly, the American legal system gives the rights to the Security and Exchange Commission to regulate more tightly the accounting profession and to intervene in its developments. Whether this will really happen is very difficult to say.

Interestingly, whilst the Anglo-Saxon countries are opting for a more direct legislative approach to accounting regulation, the Continental European, and especially European transitional countries, are working towards a more independent accounting profession and delegated self-regulation. This is generally in line with the overall trends of delegation of certain public duties to non-core civil service organisations and agencies. It is believed that the professional can deliver services better than a 'multi-skilled' civil servant, who has general but not highly specialised professional knowledge.

In this paper we will focus on the main aspects of development of the accounting profession in Serbia, primarily in the last decade. As Serbia was a republic in the former Yugoslav federation, the story over there is significantly different than for other Central and East European countries (CEECs), which closely followed the Soviet socialist blueprint. In the case of the former Yugoslavia, the reforms initiated in the 1950s and especially the 1960s led to a specific hybrid planned market economy underlined by workers' self-management as a dominant model of economic governance. Accountants were gathered together in a professional association, but accountancy as such did not have the 'guild' respect that was given to lawyers and doctors.

The reason why these two latter professions preserved their prestige was that aspiring lawyers and medical doctors were required to undergo a serious and complex state examination in order to be allowed to practice. Accountants in turn, remained unregulated. In other words, anybody could become an accountant without any constraint. This is why people often say that there was no profession with more members trained in a different profession than the accounting one.

11.2   Building a Professional Association
in Socialist and Post-Socialist Contexts

Yugoslavia was for a long time an example of a country that tried to develop a hybrid economic and political model. The Yugoslav aim was to develop a *plan-market economy* that would combine the advantages of both main models and avoid their shortcomings. It was believed that a plan can steer the economy in the proper direction and through proactive industrial policies could avoid the duplication of production and waste of social capital.

A supplementary (or rather a corrective) role of the markets was to give proper information to the planning model, and disclose the needs of the population and abilities of the real sector to meet those needs. In general, the model was theoretically feasible, but in practice it did not work. This was mainly because of the predominant role reserved for a strong political factor, expressed through the overall supremacy of the Communist party (the Union of Communists). Being moderate, the Yugoslav communists did not destroy completely the foundations of 'free professions' that existed prior to the 'socialist revolution', i.e. before World War II.

To a large extent, the development of the modern Yugoslav accounting profession was heavily influenced by the political development and changes of directions in Yugoslav social development. Immediately after the war the profession was not regulated, and one may say that it was treated just as a handicraft. Everyone was able to become an accountant, as particular education and training was not, formally, required. However, in practice, firms looked for a number of years of practical experience.

For a number of years, no (good) university graduate would pursue a career in accounting. During the years of the first Five Year Social Plan (1945–1950), which was prepared following a Soviet blueprint, accounting's role was to record the changes and to report on the physical output. The obsession with physical production, rather than efficiency and effectiveness, which already dominated the Soviet economy, was to be introduced in the Yugoslav economy. The strong waves of agricultural collectivisation meant that agricultural co-operatives were treated as regular enterprises and an accountant had to record transactions and ensure that there were enough resources to fulfil the allocated plan. Due to a soft-budget constraint (see Kornai, 1986), when resources were needed for the fulfilment of the plan, they were given without a question.

The formal role of the Chief Accountant was pretty much a charade, as in fact that person did not have any power, and was simply a senior bookkeeper. Entry to the profession was mainly by allocation, rather than choice. Usually a trainee would be allocated arbitrarily to different departments within the organisation, and they (trainees) were able to do very little to change what seemed to be destiny (Poland, Krzywda, et al. 1995).

A prospective accountant was put into an accounting department and usually started with handling so-called material accounting (accounting of supplies and material reserves), which was followed by training in the ledger-book division. Occasionally, this may have been accompanied by some general accounting training, but very rarely. The main focus was put on the accuracy of work carried out and the experience that a trainee obtained performing the *routine* operations. There was no need for the use of analytical financial information, due to the neutrality of money (i.e. the use of money just as a unit of account; see Šević, 1997, 1999c). In the very early post-revolutionary years (1945–1950) the main criteria for entry into accounting was that the person be regarded honest and with respectable integrity (Sorensen & Sorensen, 1970).

The situation began to change, although very slowly, after 1948 and the break-up with the other socialist countries (at the time called the 'peoples' democracies') and the USSR. Yugoslavia looked for an alternative model of socialism that would be more worker-centred. In 1950 the Workers' Councils were introduced, primarily in the industrial enterprises.

This was followed, in 1953, by the introduction of *social self-management*, which became a social model and the basis for the emerging political regime. Workers (formally) got the powers to make necessary decisions, and the classical rigid Soviet blueprint became a thing of the past. Rapprochement with the USA, which began in the early 1950s, meant a wider opening of the country and additional financial injections, which initiated accelerated growth.

The financial resources were also accompanied by people's enthusiasm, which remained high after World War II. It was necessary to introduce larger changes in the processes and procedures and realign business functions in enterprises to support formal and *de facto* independence of enterprises. From the very late 1940s, the Administrative-Management Units (AOR), which tightly controlled all branches of the economy were gradually abandoned and none of them survived the early 1950s.

Enterprises were not forced to meet their production targets at any cost, and they were, more or less, free to choose what to produce and how the process of production be organised. This was facilitated through the pretty comprehensive liberalisation of prices, and a return to money with all its functions. The central bank abandoned a 'cash plan' instrument of monetary policy (if one agrees that a classical socialist central bank led any monetary policy), which eliminated administrative ceilings imposed on companies when handling cash (see Šević, 1996a).

When the process of deregulation and liberalisation accelerated, the Association of Bookkeepers of Serbia was established in 1955. The Federal Yugoslav Association followed later the same year. It is argued that it was the first case of self-organising of bookkeepers in Serbia (Milošević, 2000) and indicated a realisation that in the new market-plan conditions the profession would become more important. Initially the Association was regarded as a so-called 'social organisation', that is a society whose goals, aims, and objectives were beneficial to the society as a whole.

The Association did not have any self-regulatory powers. It tried to promote the profession and professional behaviour, and to work on the organisation of continuous professional development (CPD) of its members. There were no formal membership criteria set. Anyone who worked in accounting was eligible to be a member, or in fact anyone who was interested, as it was against the law for social organisations to deny membership to an interested party. The freedom of self-organisation of citizens was guaranteed by the Constitution, and the norm was literally interpreted that no one, except the court, can deny the right to any citizen. As in all socialist countries, the Association and its social position were heavily influenced by political shifts in society.

With the introduction of an advanced concept of 'workers' self-management' named *associated labour*, the Association renamed itself, using at the time popular political jargon. From 1972 to 1991 the Association operated under the name the

Association of Accounting and Finance Workers. The legal status did not change much although the Association was required to re-register with the Ministry of the Interior a few times. The favourable status of a 'social organisation' was kept, which meant that the organisation was not a subject to direct taxation, and enjoyed many financial advantages.

In organisational terms, it spread widely and all people working on accounting and bookkeeping posts were encouraged to become members. The practice of organising seminars and other forms of CPD was strengthened and it became the norm to organise an Annual Congress of Accountants in the last week of May; with a selection of chosen professional and academic papers addressing many burning issues facing accounting theory and practice, and with a large number of delegates/ participants in attendance.

The Association discharged its functions through extensive publication activities, development of a very strong pool of lecturers who delivered courses across the country and through joint ventures with other interested parties. For instance, the Association was one of the co-founders of the College of Economics and Commerce in 1956. It is today an independent College of Business, an integral part of the Yugoslav system of higher education.

The College initially offered associate degrees in Economics, Finance, Insurance, and Accounting. Recruited staff were very good, and many of the professors were prominent researchers, although they taught at a 2-year College. The study in the College lasted for four, and later five semesters. All students were asked to take a compulsory dissertation unit and to prepare and defend a *viva voce* dissertation at the end of semester five. Also, each of the students had to undergo a semester-long work placement (as a part of a separate course called 'Professional Practice'). This practice has remained until now, and the College is the major national provider of non-degree economists (of which over a half specialised in accounting and related disciplines).

The moves to seriously reform (more like abandon) the socialist system were made first in 1988, with the introduction of a set of reform laws. However, the laws were not very far-reaching, but anyway set the stage for further changes. The Association perceived opportunities and took an active role in supporting the changes. Luckily, the Association had a well-established material base and in the early 1990s began the work on the re-establishment of the profession.

The Federal Law on Accounting introduced in 1993 laid good foundations for the creation of the accounting profession. For the first time since the end of the World War II, the Law explicitly stipulated that keeping the books and the preparation of financial statements must be done by a professional (Art. 6/1). A professional has to be a Yugoslav national with a professional qualification who was not sentenced for a criminal offence which made him or her unfit to practice accounting.

The law classified these professionals into three *classes*: (1) accountant (*računovodja*), (2) autonomous accountant (*samostalni računovodja*), and (3) certified accountant (*ovlašćeni računovodja*). The accountant in the Yugoslav classification would be an equivalent of 'accounting technician' in the UK accounting terminology. Namely, a person who can sit an examination in order to get a professional title of an accountant must have a secondary school leaving certificate where the programme of study had a significant element of economics and accounting, and substantial professional experience (minimum 3 years).

A candidate for an independent accountant must have an associate degree in economics and have 3 years professional experience in accounting. In order to get the professional title of a certified accountant a graduate with an economics degree has to sit a fairly complex professional examination, after 3 years of experience in accounting. The candidates for all three professional titles have to gain at least 3 years of supervised professional experience. There is no specific regulatory requirement regarding the professional experience.

However, it is assumed in practice that all candidates will be given an opportunity to work on all the aspects of accounting work covered by the programme of study. The idea is that the successful candidate will possess the capacity to keep the books and prepare financial statements alone, and to practice the profession without any formal supervision. As the professional examination focuses on a list of competencies that a prospective professional accountant must have, those competencies must be achieved through individual study, attendance of lectures organised by the Association, and finally through professional experience.

The Law explicitly requires that a company internally decides the requirements for their accountants. However, large firms can entrust their accounts only to a certified or independent accountant. Also, there is a provision for a company to contract-out accounting services, either to a company registered for accounting services or to an individual with an appropriate professional qualification. However, large firms, insurance companies, banks and other financial institutions cannot contract an outsider to keep their books. They have to organise their own accounting departments or to sign a contract with an accounting firm. However, in practice only small and medium enterprises (SMEs) contract-out their accounting function, and in most cases they have an individual taking care of their books.

The Law entrusted 'public authorisation' to the Association of Accountants and Auditors. In fact, the Law authorised the Federal Association to set accounting standards, to prepare a programme for professional qualifications and to fix the examination fee, to establish a Commission for the recognition of professionals titles, to issue a certificate to professional accountants and to produce and maintain a list of professional accountants. The Law requires an accountant to be a Yugoslav citizen, in the first instance.

Foreign nationals can practice accountancy in Serbia under the condition of reciprocity; that is, if a Serbian accountant is allowed to practice in that particular country. Therefore, the Association's Commission for Professional Training should be in a position to license a foreign accountant and allow him or her to practice the profession in Serbia. The Law also gave the powers to the Federal Ministry of Finance to supervise the Association in performing these duties, and if necessary, to inform the Federal Government of all shortcomings detected during inspection visits.

The Federal Ministry usually performs its duties through occasional administrative inspections, and, following the visit, all eventual shortcomings are to be addressed within a given period of time. Of interest to us is, also, the transitional provision in Law that all people who had the required educational qualifications and more than

15 years of professional experience in accounting were to be given a professional qualification, without needing to sit an examination. However, this was not done automatically, as a prospective professional accountant was required to prepare a portfolio confirming that he or she met the standards and had to apply personally to the Association to have the qualification bestowed. Also, the Law fixed a cut-off date of 6 months from the day of his enactment. The process of granting initial professional qualifications based on prior extensive experience ended on June 30, 1997.

Nowadays, prospective accountants are usually 'produced' by a number of secondary economics schools, a few Colleges offering only associate degrees and six economics faculties in the country (Belgrade, Kragujevac, Niš, Subotica,[1] Priština[2] and Podgorica, Montenegro). The entry quotas for pupils in the secondary schools and students in Colleges and Universities are set by the Government.

Basically, it is assumed that the Government will take into consideration different criteria in deciding on a number, but research has shown that there is very little rational behaviour in setting entry targets for educational institutions (Sećibović et al., 1993). Therefore, a large number of students will study in the field of social sciences, business and law, as these academic disciplines require relatively low investment per student.

The government is usually fairly reluctant to increase entry quotas for medicine, technical disciplines and basic sciences, but many of these disciplines had problems anyway in recruiting in recent years. Only in the case of medicine high interest was shown by students and their parents, and, after frequent demonstrations by parents, in June/July the Government increased the quota 'for the last time'. However, the government-imposed quota is not the biggest problem.

The Serbian universities are still run in a traditional Humboldtian style,[3] with the focus on research and scholarship, and collegial management. There is very little, if any, contact with future employers, professional organisations, associations of businesses and so on. In other words, the Universities are still the 'Ivory towers' that do not consult with their stakeholders.

Students are heard, but usually the student organisations are interested in themselves and professors have an almost exclusive authority in the class. There are, of course, exceptions, but those are few. Not having a close contact with all these

---

[1] That is, 'Szabadka' in Hungarian. Subotica is a major city in Serbia with predominantly Hungarian population that played a prominent role in economic developments of Vojvodina (Northern Serbian Province) in the late 19th and very early 20th century. This is still an important border town on the border with Hungary.

[2] There are currently two Universities of Priština, one Albanian speaking in Priština itself, and another relocated to northern part of Kosovska Mitrovica, which is the only remaining significant Serbian enclave in Kosovo. The Serbian authorities technically recognise both 'universities', although it is clear that they do not have any control over the Albanian speaking one. The sad part is that the UN authorities have also seriously failed to resume control over the education in Kosovo, and are more interested in privatising public enterprises, especially public utilities.

[3] It has been reported in Serbian mass-media that the Rector of the University of Belgrade clearly favours the Humboldtian-type university, which put off some major donors like USAID, which decided to support provincial universities, rather than the national university.

social stakeholders tempers the quality of programmes and their modernity. Our recent look at the literature listed for accounting and finance courses in a few universities in Yugoslavia disclosed that many courses are taught in an old-fashioned manner with very little practical element. In fact, most courses have a complicated theoretical content which is of very little use for a modern accountant.

The Association does not have any input in the process of designing and revalidating programmes. Usually programmes are reviewed every 10 years, although minor changes can be made at any time. However, the latter possibility has been exercised only rarely, and, if done, it was usually to meet the wishes of a professor who would like to teach a course in the area of his or her specialism. In most cases the course syllabi remained unchanged for a number of years, list of readings included.

As a consequence of a highly theoretical approach to teaching, graduates are well-read and educated, but with very little ability to fit into day-to-day business practices. This is a problem that the Association has been trying to address in recent years since the professional examinations were introduced. Preparation for professional examinations is more *competence-based*, and it is expected that a successful candidate be able to keep the books autonomously and competently.

11.3   Sitting Examination and Being Certified

After being employed as an accountant for at least 3 years, a person can apply to sit for a professional examination. The application is to be lodged with the Association with supporting documents. After the supporting documents are examined the candidate will be officially registered and will be sent an examination schedule.

The Association offers a preparation programme of 120 h for all those interested, and the programme is free for all members of the association. It is usually expected (at least after 1993) that all people working in the accounting profession are members of the Association. As on December 31, 2001, the Association had 13,564 members who are professionally qualified as 'accountants', 7,265 who qualified as 'independent accountants' and 6,855 who qualified as 'certified accountants'. Under the previous Law on Auditing, 143 people acquired a professional qualification as auditors and 42 as 'certified auditors'.[4]

The candidates are required to sit for a number of papers depending on the type of professional qualification sought. All papers have to be completed in one day, but if the candidate fails one of the papers he or she can retake it in the next examination period. Usually exams are sat in April and October, in a few major cities across the country.

There is no flexibility in the examination arrangements. The examination is organised by the Association in compliance with JRS 31. The Standard clearly spells out what the programme of study is that a candidate for each of the profes-

---

[4] This information was provided by Ms Rada Stojanović, Head of Training at the Association of the Accountants and Auditors of Serbia in February 2002.

sional qualifications should follow. Although the programme takes into consideration the developments in theory, it is very practical and competence-based. All
prospective candidates are required to complete a case study and to hand it in before
taking the examination. The case study will be defended *viva voce* before the
examination commission.

The purpose of an oral examination is to establish whether a candidate did the
work himself and whether he or she is capable of communicating effectively about
accounting and finance matters with outsiders. The ability to communicate effectively and present accounting information in a useful manner has become a very
important issue that the Association has been trying to address.

As we have already said, the Association promotes competence-based training
and it is the first time that a professional organisation in Yugoslavia has endorsed
this methodological approach. The Bar and medical associations are more focused
on assessing candidates' overall (mainly theoretical) knowledge, whilst the
accountants are required to perform their duties in an effective and efficient manner
satisfying both the legal requirements and their customers.

In order to promote competence-based training the Association, in JRS 31,
clearly stipulated the outcomes of the training programme, and what a successful
candidate must demonstrate. It seems that the Association applied *educational
benchmarking* in setting the standards for a successful candidate, which is, again, a
novel approach for Central and Eastern European Countries (CEECs).

First of all, a prospective candidate has to pass a certain number of papers where
he or she has to demonstrate overall theoretical and practical competencies. A candidate for an 'accountant' professional title (equivalent to the British Accounting
Technician) is required to sit papers in:

1. The Organisation of Accounting and Finance Functions
2. Financial and Management Accounting
3. Tax System
4. Business Law I
5. Information Technology in Accounting
6. Principles of Audit

In order to be successful, the candidate must demonstrate that he has the *basic
knowledge* of the position of accounting and finance functions in a firm; accounting
information systems; professional accounting ethics; the roles and content of the
Yugoslav and International accounting standards; legislation on accounting and
finance; tax system and enforcement of tax laws and regulation, and financing
business endeavours. The *basic knowledge* must be accompanied by the candidate's
ability for independent work on: the preparation of basic financial statements (JRS
19)*, keeping the ledger book and other related documents (JRS 22); interpreting
financial statements applying JRS 1 to 19; preparing internal accounting documents

---

*Yugoslav Accounting Standards have been superceded by the Serbian Accounting Standards,
where the text remained, more or less the same. Serbian Accounting Standards are now applied to
small and micro-enterprises, whilst IFRS are applied to listed, large and medium business entities.

for internal use; communication with the management; and preparation of accounting documents in accordance with JRS.

The minimum level of competence will be tested in the examination through checking whether a candidate has achieved the required level of professional and practical skills necessary for independent accounting work (keeping the books, preparing financial statements, supporting company's management, etc.). A person with an 'accountant' qualification in practice will mainly support the holders of the other two professional titles, who will in the majority of cases be their superior. To a large extent, the Association pays attention to collective work and development of a collegial relationship in discharging the accounting duties. It is strongly encouraged that every prospective candidate has a development mentor who will guide him or her until they are fully qualified.

A candidate with an associate degree for a number of years in the Yugoslav practice was a typical representative of the profession. A network of Colleges of Economics (and/or Business) educated a large number of economists who spent entire careers in accounting. In the Yugoslav higher education system, there are titles economist (*ekonomista*) and graduated economist (*diplomirani ekonomista*). While the former has completed a College economics programme that lasted 2 or 2½ years, the latter completed 4 years of study, or often 4½ years as he or she was expected to complete a dissertation. However, as we mentioned above, it was not popular for graduates to start or finish their career in accounting. University graduates traditionally preferred operational departments.

An 'independent accountant' is defined as a professionally qualified person who possess a defined level of professional and practical knowledge and experience for independent keeping of the books, preparation of accounting statements, organisation of accounting department (function) and internal audit in a company. All these competencies have to be assessed in a professional examination, especially through a case study.

A candidate with an associate degree wishing to qualify as 'an independent accountant' will take the following papers:

1. The Organisation of Accounting and Finance Functions
2. Financial Accounting I
3. Management Accounting I
4. Tax
5. Business Finance I
6. Business Law II
7. Information Technology in Accounting
8. Principles of Audit

An 'independent accountant' must have the *knowledge* of principles of accounting in a complex business system, accounting for not-for-profit organisations, internal control and internal audit (JRS 28); commercial and contract law; advanced management accounting and financial management in complex corporations. This knowledge has to be demonstrated through the ability for independent discharge of the following duties: preparation of Profit and Loss account, financial plan and other accounting statements as set out by the JRS 20, analysis of actual (nominal) values and competent comparison between actual and planned values, preparations of the respective accounts in the situation of hyperinflationary environment (JRS 29), and competent preparation of the consolidated accounting statements.

A prospective candidate for a 'certified accountant' title will be examined in all the papers as for an independent accountant, plus a number of revised and broadened papers specially designed for this title, such as the following:

1. The Organisation of Accounting and Finance Functions
2. Financial Accounting II
3. Management Accounting II
4. Tax
5. Business Finance II
6. Business Law III
7. Business Information Systems
8. Audit

A 'certified accountant' is defined as a professionally qualified person who possesses the necessary level of professional and practical knowledge and experience for independent keeping of the 'business books', preparation of accounting statements, general organisation of the accounting function, internal control (audit), organisation of accounting function in a multicultural environment such as joint ventures, foreign direct investments and organisation of the accounting function in parts of a company or separate legal entities owned by the mother company abroad. For a certified accountant, it is clearly stated that he or she must have *advanced knowledge* of the principles of accounting in different types of business systems (corporations, holdings, groups, etc.), theory and policy of capital structure, financial analysis and methods of business organisation, complex asset valuation and portfolio theory and practice.

The candidate's competence for independent work will be primarily assessed through his or her ability to apply, in practice, methods of company and share valuation, to prepare and defend the capital investment decision and prepare accounting information necessary for management decision-making. A 'certified accountant' has a legal right to sign all types of accounting and financial statements, and therefore he or she performs an important public function. They guarantee with their signatures that the law and the Yugoslav accounting standards were respected and that information contained in the statements is true and fair, giving a correct picture of the financial situation of a particular legal entity.

Initially JRS 31 stipulated that candidates for auditing professional titles have to sit a professional examination. Two professional titles were mentioned: auditor and certified auditor. Candidates for both auditors' titles had to demonstrate the competencies envisaged for the accounting professionals, plus advanced knowledge of the economic environment and processes and procedures of auditing in different business environments. JRS 31 which came into force in 1994, was later (1996) amended when the examinations for all auditing professional qualifications were taken over by the Federal Ministry of Finance, which organised an Examination Commission. The Association was of the general view that there should not be special examinations for potential auditing candidates, following the practice adopted in most developed economies.

JRS 31 and the Rules for Acquiring an Accounting Professional Qualification were endorsed by the Annual General Meeting of the Association in 1995, stipulating that a candidate must achieve at least 70 out of 100 marks in order to pass the paper. This is a pretty high threshold and many professional accountants complained that the minimum requirement is set very high and that many candidates fail the examination in the first attempt.

The Association is generally interested in keeping standards high, and does not keep statistics on the number of candidates passing the exam on their first attempt. According to interviews with professional accountants, not many of them passed on their first attempt.

The response of the Association to the high failure rates was a strengthening of their professional programme and an increase in the number of hours taught on the preparatory programme run by the Association. It seems that this policy action has started paying off as in the recent examinations a larger proportion of candidates was successful.

The professional examination is, at the moment, highly competence-based (as recommended by IFAC), but the Association's strict interpretation of competence-based learning means that the examination is overwhelmingly focused on the book-keeping capabilities of candidates, with a very strong bias towards Financial Accounting. Although, papers like financial decision-making and accounting/finance information systems were introduced there is very little evidence that serious strategic considerations are given to the classic accounting issues.

Certainly, a more strategic and transferable skills focused examination format would be welcome. At the moment, the programme demonstrates a strong technical bias, and, in our opinion, the focus should be moved onto the development of interpretative skills.

11.4 Remaining Certified: Continuous Professional Development

The Law on Accounting is primarily interested in professional accountants being properly educated and trained when they get a license to practice the profession. There are no specific, either implicit or explicit, requirements to regularly update the knowledge of already registered accountants. However, the Association sets and controls the standards of entry and is also empowered to re-examine the ability to act as an accountant. The Law implicitly acknowledged that practising the accounting profession is a 'quasi-public service' and therefore has to be executed in the interest of the public. Therefore, monitoring of accountants' behaviour and practices is in the remit of the Association, on behalf of the Federal Ministry of Finance which is responsible to the Federal Government for the implementation of the Law on Accounting and related by-laws.

In order to maintain its position as a leading professional accounting organisation in Yugoslavia/Serbia the Association is re-focusing on the organisation of different programmes for professional development of accountants. The CPD activities are grouped into a few clusters: (1) professional publishing; (2) annual congress and symposium; (3) conferences and seminars and (4) professional consulting. The publication of professional material can be divided into six groups: (a) publication of the compulsory and optional material for the professional qualification examinations; (b) publication of advanced professional material, dealing with recent developments in national and international accounting, (c) publication of research studies, (d) publication of comments on the recent Law and by-laws related to accounting, (e) publication of the templates of the accounting statements, and (f) publication of academic and professional journals.

The Association is authorised to define the programme and organise the examinations for the professional accounting qualifications, and to commission and publish the compulsory and support material for all professional examinations. At the moment, they produce a single textbook for the examinations at all three levels. However, in order to eliminate duplication, the higher-level professional examination comprises also the material examined at the previous examination. That is, the material solely examined at a previous level will be necessary for solving problems at the next one. Therefore, the Association has consistently applied the principle of *continuity in education and training*.

The books are regularly updated, especially those that are closely related to current legislation. They are produced with a very good layout and to a large extent they are unified, which makes the preparation for the various examinations easier. However, this activity is not particularly profitable as the main idea is to cover the costs incurred and make a reasonable margin to be used for regular updating of the materials.

Occasionally, but increasingly, the Association publishes books and monographs that deal with important issues of practice. These publications are more of a doctrinal and professional nature. In our view, this activity can be used to indirectly introduce strategic perspectives on the classical accounting functions.

As we have already pointed out, the current curriculum is fairly classical in its nature, and there is a need to introduce more strategic considerations in the programme. Since this material is mainly used by professionally qualified accountants and postgraduate students, it seems that its use can mitigate our criticism of the professional examinations for their rigidity.

The advanced professional studies are also complemented by a number of solicited and unsolicited research books and monographs that address the major theoretical issues in accounting and related fields. They are mainly written by university professors or practising accountants as a result of their work on a higher degree. These studies are fairly refreshing and have the particular advantage that they are released relatively quickly, so they are usually published in a timely fashion. A number of recent studies focused on the issues of privatisation and the role of accounting in the privatisation process. Also, under the auspices of this programme, the Association translated IAS/IFRS, and published annotated comments for the use of Yugoslav accountants.

The Association regularly publishes comments on the recent Laws and by-laws, as well as opinions of the respective ministries of finance. This is an important activity, as laws are amended fairly often in Serbia, and sometimes opinions issued by the Ministry of Finance can limit the reach of law, although *stricto lege* this should not be possible.

There are also a few serious systemic problems. For instance, until recently opinions issued by the Ministry of Finance were not applied by the Republican Public Revenue Administration (which until recently operated as an independent government agency), requiring so-called authentic interpretation of law, which can only be given by the legislator. This created a lot of problems in consistency of application of the law.

Since the Association focuses on all sources of law related to accounting it can be said that their commentaries are the most comprehensive in the country. Also, in this field there is a lot of competition from the private consultancy firms. There are at least two other companies that regularly publish commentaries on the changes in accounting and financial legislation. As one of them was doing this before the Association, it still has a fair share of the market, although it seems that the Association may takeover the primacy in the years to come.

With aggressive advertising campaigns and personal calls to companies, the Association is succeeding in attracting more subscribers. This is an important activity, as it can be the main source of revenue for the Association, with membership fees accounting for a fairly small portion of the Association's annual revenue.

The Association is trying to entwine this activity with the organisation of regular seminars and conferences devoted to the current issues in accounting and financial legislation. Connected with this activity is the publication of templates of financial statements and other reporting forms that are required by the authorities. However, this is not the primary activity of the association as many publishing companies are authorised to publish and retail those forms, including the government-owned Stationary Office that publishes the Official Gazette[5] and other documents for and on behalf of the Government. Also, many forms are published by the Payment System Administration, which is a Directorate of the National Bank of Serbia (Škobić, 2000).

The role of the Association in maintaining the professional standards is paramount. As the legislator regulates only the basics with regard to the accounting profession, the Association, in executing entrusted functions, can and does set the minimum requirements for professional development of practising accountants. However, due to the ongoing lack of capacity of local chapters, the main duty rests with the Association headquarters, which in turn cannot really effectively serve the entire country.

---

[5] *Službeni list* is published at confederal level (The State Union of Serbia and Montenegro, which is a subject of International Law), by the fully state-owned enterprise bearing the same name as publication and *Službeni glasnik* at the republican level in Serbia, again published by the whole republican government-owned enterprise with the same name as the respective publication. However, both companies are also major publishers of professional and other literature, and more recently they entered into publishing fiction and other books for the classical book market.

There have recently been some actions undertaken to improve the ability of local chapters and to delegate CPD duties to them. This has yielded some results, but the main CPD activities are still carried out by the Association's headquarters through regular 'travelling seminars' and long lecture tours (see Škobić, 2000).

11.5   Conclusion

The accounting profession in Serbia is slowly gaining in social prestige, and it seems that the society recognises its importance. This is certainly the result of the good work done by the Association, but also thanks to the Government in deciding to firmly establish a professional accounting qualification framework as an important requirement for the practising of 'free professions'. Full recognition of the accounting profession was late compared to lawyers' and medical profession, but nonetheless it is now fully respected and is getting its rightful social position.

The accounting profession in Serbia dates back to the late 19th century, although professional organisations have not always been highly empowered, as their existence and rights were regulated by law, and the law was more or less directly executed by the public bodies. Between the two world wars, some steps were undertaken to develop a more independent accounting profession, and mainly through Chambers of Commerce and Industry this has been done, although the main emphasis was given to the auditing profession rather than accounting.

The socialist revolution represented a setback, but in contrast to other 'socialist countries' the former socialist Yugoslavia followed, from the late 1940s, its own, fairly specific socialist development path. The professional organisations were encouraged to be formed again in the mid-1950s, and the national association of accountants was reborn, but with no power to regulate the classical professional issues (primarily, entry to and exit from the profession).

Right up to the 1990s the accounting profession was perceived as offering different forms of education and ensuring that those without proper academic qualification for performing accounting duties acquire one through approved degree programmes or through non-degree courses offered by the Association or some of the institutions of higher education. This particular role was played by Colleges of Economics/Business, which offered accounting-focussed economics degrees emphasising the role of bookkeeping. Therefore, to a large extent, the accounting profession prior to the 1990s was essentially a bookkeeping profession.

With the changes in the political system and emphasis on building a market-oriented economy, an independent accounting profession gained currency, and accounting laws introduced at the time emphasised the role of certifying those undertaking accounting work, and ensuring that they had the necessary professional and other qualifications. Following the introduction of Yugoslav (later Serbian) Accounting Standard No. 31, the minimum criteria for entry into the accounting profession has been set.

The entry is still largely based on the education of potential entrants, and the membership grade depends on their highest level of education. However, the professional examination is highly dependent on the initial entry criteria. There are different examination settings for those who enter with secondary school, associate degree or a full degree. Further, the competency level that a prospective candidate has to demonstrate differs based on their level of education. There have been moves to equalise the entry of those with associate and full degree, and this has been passed in the new accounting law, in force from 2003.

The development of the accounting profession in Serbia has been initiated by two different forces. First, the strength of the Association itself played an important role in steering the desired changes, but also the entry of foreign investors and funding agencies triggered the speed in development of the profession. The initiation of the South East European Programme for Accounting Development (SEEPAD) played an important role in bringing the accounting professions in different countries in the region together to consider mutual recognition of certificates, enabling the members to practice in different national jurisdictions.

Taking into consideration that many countries in the region share the same language (which now has a number of various names), common legal experience, and finally were interconnected for many years, emphasises further the practicality of such action. Certainly, the Serbian Association is at the forefront of developments facilitating such moves for mutual collaboration and recognition.

Nevertheless, it is fairly difficult to say firmly what future developments will be. However, it is certain that the accounting profession is there to stay and survive, contributing significantly to changes in the national economies and facilitating professional communication with other countries.

References

Abrahamson, M. (1967), *The Professional in the Organisation*, Chicago: Rand McNally

Association of Accountants and Auditors of Serbia (1996), *Informator o uslovima za sticanje profesionalnih zvanja u računovodstvu prema JRS 31* [Handbook on the Conditions for Getting a Professional Title in Accounting Pursuant Yugoslav Accounting Standard 31], 3rd amended and updated edition, Belgrade: The Association of Accountants and Auditors of Serbia (referred to in the text as 'Informator')

Barber, B. (1963), Some problems in the sociology of the professions, *Daedalus*, 92, 668–688

Ben-David, J. (1963–64), Professions in the class system of present-day societies: a trend report and bibliography, *Current Sociology*, 12(3), 247–330

Economist (2002), When the numbers don't add up, Special report: The Trouble with Accounting, *The Economist*, February 9, 67–70

Kornai, J. (1986), Soft Budget Constraint, *Kyklos*, 39(1), 3–30

Krzywda, D., D. Bailey and M. Schroeder. (1995), A Theory of European Accounting Development Applied to Accounting Change in Contemporary Poland, *The European Accounting Review*, 4(2), 625–657

Larson, M. S. (1977), *The Rise of Professionalism*, Berkeley: University of California Press

Liesman, S., J. Weil and M. Schroeder (2002), Accounting Woes Spark Calls for Change, *The Wall Street Journal Europe*, Thursday, February 7, 3

Luck, W. (1984), Public Accounting in West Germany, in H. P. Holzer, et al., eds. *International Accounting*, New York: Harper & Row

Millerson, G. (1964), *The Qualifying Associations: A Study in Professionalisation*, London: Routledge & Kegan Paul

Milošević, K. (2000), 45 godina postojanja i rada Saveza računovodja i revizora Srbije [Forty five years of the existence and activities of the Association of Accountants and Auditors of Serbia], *Glas računovodja*, 1(1), 7–9

Perkin, H. (1989), *The Rise of Professional Society*, London: Routledge

Perkin, H. (1996), *The Third Revolution; Professional Elites in the Modern World*, London: Routledge

Šećibović, R., M. Arandarenko, Ž. Šević, R. Vesković and R. Eleković (1993), *Atlas nezaposlenih Srbije* [Atlas of Unemployed in Serbia], Belgrade; Ministry for Youth and Sports of the Republic of Serbia (Youth Department)

Šević, Ž. (1996a), *Centralna banka: Položaj – Organizacija – Funkcije* [Central Bank: Position – Organisation – Functions], Belgrade: Balkan Center for Public Policy and Cigoja štampa

Šević, Ž. (1996b), *Political Economy, Economics and Art of Negotiation and Reconciliation: A Production of Law in a Polycentric Federation of a Yugoslav Type*, paper presented at the 9th Maastricht Seminar in Law and Economics, University of Limburg, Maastricht, April, 2–4

Šević, Ž. (1996c), *Financial Reform in a Transitional Economy: Some Conceptual Issues*, Tokyo-Belgrade: SYLFF-YASF

Šević, Ž. (1997), "*The Notion of 'Money' in the Soviet Economic Thought Prior to 1924*", mimeo, Dundee: University of Dundee, Department of Economic Studies

Šević, Ž. (1999a), Financial Innovations, in P. A. O'Hara, ed. *Encyclopaedia of Political Economy*, London: Routledge, pp. 392–394

Šević, Ž. (1999b), *Accounting for Institutional and Structural Reform(s): The Changing Framework and Accounting Change*, paper presented at the Conference on Management Accounting Change, Manchester: The University of Manchester, March 14–19

Šević, Ž. (1999c), Banking Reform in Central and Eastern European Countires as a Part of Macroeconomic Changes toward Market-Oriented Economics, Belgrade: Balkan Center for Public Policy and Related Studies and Čigoja štampa

Škobić, P. (2000), Association of Accountants and Auditors, Today, *Glas računovodja*, 1(1), 10–18

Smith, B. (1992), The Role and Organisation of the Accounting Profession, in OECD, *Accounting Reform in Central and Eastern Europe*, Paris: OECD

Soresen, J. E. and T. L. Soresen. (1970), The conflict of professionals in bureaucratic organisations, *Administrative Science Quarterly*, 15, 417–426

Wirt, F. (1981), Professionalism and political conflict: a developmental model, *Journal of Public Policy*, 1(1), 61–93

Zakon o računovodstvu [Law on Accounting], *Službeni list Savezne Republike Jugoslavije* [Official Gazette of the Federal Republic of Yugoslavia], Nos. 46/96 and 60/96

Zakon o reviziji [Law on Auditing], *Službeni list Savezne Republike Jugoslavije* [Official Gazette of the Federal Republic of Yugoslavia], No. 30/96

Chapter 12
Reform of Slovak Accounting

Alberta Suhanyiova and Marian Gal

12.1   Introduction

A change of the economic and the political conditions in Middle and Eastern
Europe after 1989 initiated a change in the economy – from central planning to
a market economy. The state was not the single owner of businesses anymore
and private owners and entrepreneurs became a part of the economy. The reconstruction of the economic mechanism was inspired by former soviet "perestro-
jka." It was necessary to privatize the national sector and secure a private free
trade economy.

This transformation also required a change in the character and a role for the
accounting system in Slovakia. These facts became a part of a new accounting
system that was based on the Act no.563/1991 on Accounting, effective January 1,
1993. This Act has been amended five times since. The goal of these revisions was
to harmonize the basic accounting system with that of the European Union, specifically its fourth, seventh, and eighth Directives.
The basic juridical norms concerning accounting are:

- Commercial Code – states the obligation for entrepreneurs to keep books, to
  generate accounting reports and in certain instances to certify the correctness of
  the accounting report by an auditor.
- Act on Accounting – as a general juridical norm
- Decrees of the Ministry of Finance of the Slovak Republic – define the accounting methods and procedures within a single-entry bookkeeping, as well as within
  double-entry bookkeeping system. Decrees also classify a form, a structure, and
  a content of individual and consolidated accounting reports for different types of
  entrepreneurial and non-entrepreneurial units.

A. Suhanyiova and M. Gal
Technical University of Kosice

R. W. McGee (ed.), *Accounting Reform in Transition and Developing Economies,*
© Springer Science+Business Media LLC 2008

12.2   Reform of Slovak Accounting

In the process of joining the European Union, it was important to harmonize the accounting system of Slovakia with that used in the member states of the European Union. The European Parliament and the European Council came up with Regulation No.1606/2002, according to which all companies that hold their shares on regulated markets in the member states of the EU will have to create their consolidated accounting reports according to International Accounting Standards/International Financial Reporting Standards (IAS/IFRS), starting in 2005 (in special cases in 2007).

The Slovak Republic prepared a new act – Act No.431/2003 on Accounting, which harmonized Slovak accounting with the directives of the EU and allowed the use of IAS/IFRS in given cases. This Act has been effective since January 1, 2003 and cancelled previous Act No.563/1991 on Accounting.

Act No.431/2003 on Accounting still remains a general juridical norm and is used by every accounting unit. The basic philosophy of the act "a truthful and an accurate representation" has not changed. The Ministry of Finance issued Decrees for different types of accounting units, concerning the accounting methods and procedures for both the single-entry as well as the double-entry bookkeeping systems, also the form, the structure, and the content of the individual and the consolidated accounting report. These Decrees have been effective since January 1, 2003.

The Act on Accounting defines all subjects that have to keep accounts and generate accounting reports. For the purposes of this Act, persons listed below shall be considered as accounting units:

1. Legal entities – legal persons
2. Foreign individuals and legal persons
3. Individual (natural) persons, who are engaged in business or other profit-making activities, if reporting their expenses necessary to generate, assure, and maintain their income for purposes of determining the income tax base

Accounting units use the:

- Double-entry bookkeeping system
- Single-entry bookkeeping system

The double-entry bookkeeping system is a basic accounting system and every accounting unit is required to keep its accounting records using this system, although the act states an exemption that specifies which accounting units can use a single-entry bookkeeping system.

The accounting unit shall account for events that are the subject of accounting within the period to which these events relate, taking into consideration their nature and timing. This period is called the accounting period and it can be:

- A calendar year (from 01/01 to 12/31 of a relevant year)
- A financial year (a period of 12 consecutive calendar months not identical with the calendar year)

The accounting unit shall keep books and construct accounting reports in the monetary units of Slovak currency and in the state language. An accounting document issued in a language other than the state language must be easily comprehensible. The accounting units shall keep their accounting records correctly, completely, provably, comprehensibly, and by methods guaranteeing permanency of their accounting documents.

The accounting unit accounting in the double-entry bookkeeping system shall keep the following books of account:

(a) *A journal* – the accounting entries are in chronological sequence
(b) *A general ledger* – the accounting entries are in systematic sequence

The Act on Accounting defines the valuation of assets and liabilities used for bookkeeping and generating accounting reports. Assets and liabilities are valued either at the date of the accounting transaction, at the date of generating the accounting report or at another date during the accounting period if it is required by a special directive (e.g., Act on Banks).

The assets and liabilities are valued at:

1. Acquisition cost
2. The entity's own costs (costs incurred)
3. Nominal value
4. Replacement costs

The accounting unit should adjust the value of assets and liabilities by appropriate amounts expressing risks, losses, and deterioration at the date of preparation of the accounting report. All anticipated risks, losses, and deteriorations are expressed in the accounting report through reserves and depreciation.

A parameter for valuation, called real value, was taken from IAS and has been used since 2003. The real value for the purposes of the Act on Accounting is:

(a) Market price – a price at a domestic or foreign stock market or other kind of market
(b) Qualified estimation or expert's testimony – in a case that market price is not accessible or if market price does not express a real value
(c) Valuation according to special directives – if it is impossible to use above-mentioned points, then the Act on Collective Investment is used

Real value is only used for valuation of: market shares, securities, reserves, assets, and liabilities of accounting units cancelled without liquidation.

The accounting report shall reflect truthful and accurate representation of unit's assets, liabilities, expenses, revenues, and financial results. This principle of truthful and accurate representation is major and all other principles (e.g., principle of not changing methods used) are subordinate.

There are three kinds of the accounting report:

(a) Ordinary accounting report – generated on the last date of accounting period
(b) Extraordinary accounting period – generated in other cases when books of accounts are closed during an accounting period (e.g., liquidation of business)
(c) Interim accounting report – generated if it is required by separate legislation

Individual accounting reports shall be audited, if the accounting unit:

1. Is a joint-stock company
2. Is a cooperative or a trading company with compulsory registered capital, if at least two of the following conditions were met in the year preceding the year of auditing the accounting reports:

    (a) The total asset value exceeded SKK 20,000,000
    (b) The net turnover exceeded SKK 40,000,000
    (c) The average number of employees exceeded 20

3. Has this obligation prescribed under separate legislation
4. Is a legal entity whose sum of annual accepted tax ratio exceeds SKK 1,000,000

The accounting report shall be audited from the end of the accounting period following the relevant accounting period.

Under the double-entry bookkeeping system, the accounting reports consist of:

(a) Balance sheet
(b) Income statement (or profit and loss statement)
(c) Notes (here are attached other statements, if necessary, e.g., cash-flow statement in case the accounting report has to be audited)

The accounting report shall be constructed within 6 months from the due date of the accounting report. All facts in the accounting report have to be useful, significant, comprehensive, comparable, and reliable.

The accounting units, that are required to have their accounting reports audited, also generate an annual report. This annual report shall be audited as well.

The amendment of the Act on Accounting has been effective in the Slovak Republic since January 1, 2005. This amendment harmonizes accounting terminology and Slovak accounting legislation with the legislation of the European Union, specifically in the area of generating the accounting report and annual report.

Starting on January 1, 2006, the accounting units such as banks, subsidiaries of foreign banks, the Export-Import Bank of the Slovak Republic, insurance companies, subsidiaries of foreign insurance companies, Slovak Stock Exchange, etc., will be required to generate individual accounting reports compatible with the requirements of IAS/IFRS.

The same requirement applies also for a trading company, if at least two of the following conditions were met in at least two consecutive accounting periods:

(a) The total asset value exceeded SKK 5,000,000,000
(b) The net turnover exceeded SKK 5,000,000,000
(c) The average number of employees exceeded 2,000

In this case the accounting report will have to be audited.

The publishing of the data from the accounting report and the creation of the consolidated accounting report will use the new rules starting in 2005.

The accounting units, which are registered in the Commercial Register, are required to submit their accounting report and annual report to the Documents Collection of the Commercial Register within 30 days from the approval of the accounting report. The accounting report can be a part of the annual report.

The consolidated annual report and the consolidated accounting report (which is a part of the consolidated annual report) are submitted to the Documents Collection of the Commercial Register within 1 year from the end of the accounting period. The consolidated Balance Sheet and the consolidated Income Statement are submitted to the Commercial Publication within 1 year as well.

The accounting units that generate the accounting report in accordance with IAS/IFRS are also required to put their accounting reports on the Internet at the same time and to the same extent as they were submitted for commercial publication.

The consolidated accounting report and the consolidated annual report are generated by the parent (mother) accounting unit. The parent accounting unit (a trade company, a cooperative, etc.) is an accounting unit that:

- Has a majority of votes or
- Has a right to appoint and to impeach a majority of statutory board members or supervisory board members and is a partner or a shareholder at the same time or
- Has a right to manage the accounting unit or
- Is a partner or a shareholder of the accounting unit and a majority of statutory board members and supervisory board members were appointed by this partner or shareholder or
- Is a partner or a shareholder of the accounting unit and has a majority of votes based on the agreement with other partners or shareholders.

The parent accounting unit that is a subsidiary (daughter accounting unit) at the same time, does not have to generate the consolidated accounting report and the consolidated annual report if its parent company is under the EU regulations, owns all the subsidiary's (daughter's) shares or at least 90% of the subsidiary's (daughter accounting unit's) shares and other shareholders and partners of the accounting unit agreed with this exemption.

The parent accounting unit generates the consolidated accounting report and the consolidated annual report, if at least two of the following conditions were met on all levels of the consolidation in their individual accounting reports in two consecutive accounting periods:

(a) The total asset value of parent and subsidiaries exceeded SKK 350,000,000
(b) The net turnover of the parent and subsidiaries exceeded SKK 700,000,000
(c) The average number of employees in the parent and subsidiaries exceeded 250.

The consolidated accounting report generated in accordance with IAS/IFRS will be generated for the first time for the accounting period starting on January 1, 2005. The criteria for the consolidated accounting report were adopted from the Seventh Directive of the EU.

The accounting system of large accounting units in the Slovak Republic as well as in the other countries of the EU is very clearly defined and governed by IAS/

IFRS. But the development of the accounting system of small- and medium-sized units is still questionable and the most discussed problem. The International Accounting Standard Board (IASB) agreed on the document about small- and medium-sized companies in April 2004. In this document, IASB recommends applying general accounting standards, which means to generate the accounting reports to the same extent as it is in the case of large accounting units.

In the first phase, all accounting standards will be adapted for the accounting needs of small- and medium-sized units and they will be published as an item. Later, every proposal of an accounting standard will have a clause specifically prepared for small and medium units. The small and medium units are a significant part of the accounting units in the Slovak Republic and if the European Committee approves this clause for the small and medium units, it will play an important role in accounting legislation and in the accounting profession. The application of these norms will require the strong support of the European Committee or an agreement between the member states.

Chapter 13
Spain and the Transition to IFRS[*]

Ana Zorio

13.1 Introduction

The aim of this paper is to look into the current regulation of accounting in Spain and the main lines of its future reform towards a high-quality reporting framework based on International Financial Reporting Standards (IFRS), as a result of the EU Regulation 1606/2002. A critical analysis is provided on the perspectives and reactions triggered by this process, which will surely open up new and exciting avenues for future accounting research to explore.

Even though Spain is a country that has substantially improved its accounting model in the past 2 decades, it now envisages a process of transition towards a high-quality reporting framework based on IFRS as a result of the EU Regulation 1606/2002 (EU, 2002a). Also, as we show along this paper the quality of Spanish accounting research has greatly increased and played an important role in the promotion of how accounting is now regarded not only in Spain (e.g., in education, regulation, or the professional realm) but also overseas. Indeed, hopefully, research can provide interesting insights and shed some light on the debate on the would-be reform on the Spanish accounting model.

Hence, the aim of this paper is to look into the current regulation of accounting in Spain, and the main lines of its future reform, as well as to provide a critical analysis of its implications. It should be borne in mind that precisely the origin of this reform lies in the need to keep pace with the international accounting harmonization developments.

Indeed, the increasing globalization of capital markets and the subsequent need of multinational companies to access the most developed capital markets in the world have put great pressure to support the use of just one set of accounting standards in the international arena. In this sense, the International Organization of Securities Commissions (IOSCO) encouraged its members to allow incoming multinational companies to use the standards issued by the International Accounting

[*] Proyecto de investigación BEC 2003-05952 del Ministerio de Ciencia y Tecnología.

A. Zorio
Universidad de Valencia

Standards Committee (IASC, now renamed Board, IASB), for cross-border offerings and listings, in a Resolution issued in 2000. Shortly afterwards, the European Commission issued a Communication on a strategy for future financial reporting in Europe to introduce the International Accounting Standards (IAS, now also renamed International Financial Reporting Standards, IFRS) requirement for the consolidated accounts of the EC companies listed on regulated markets.

Regulation 1606/2002 was passed and the IAS requirement will come into force in 2005 at the latest. The global support for the IASB standards has gathered momentum with the "Norwalk Agreement" signed by the US Financial Accounting Standards Board and the IASB in 2002 with the purpose to increase convergence of their accounting standards, as well as with the pronouncements to follow IAS/IFRS made by the standard-setters from many other countries, such as Russia, Nicaragua, New Zealand, Philippines, Bulgaria, or Colombia, for instance.

Since all companies compete for resources in the goods, service, and capital markets, as a result of the globalization of the economy, the European Union justifies this important change in the field of financial reporting to ensure comparability of financial information prepared by companies in different countries. The European Commission aims to promote the preparation of useful and high-quality financial reporting, to keep in line with the changes of a globalized business environment. In this context, the standards set by the International Accounting Standards Board seem to be the best point of reference. Moreover, according to EU Regulation 1606/2002, they are to be followed in the preparation of consolidated information by European-listed companies, from 2005 at the latest.

As we analyze in other sections of this paper, the European Union is not only concerned about the use of just one set of accounting standards. It has also published other documents with a view to designing a high-quality financial reporting system, where the enforcement of standards, the auditing of financial information and corporate governance issues are also adequately addressed.

After this brief introduction, the rest of the paper is organized as follows. Section 13.2 provides a general overview of the financial reporting system in Spain as it is nowadays, i.e., before the reform comes into effect. Section 13.3 looks into the evolution of accounting research in Spain, because in a sense, it also reflects how Spain is in the process of converging with international trends not only in the standard setting field but also in research. Section 13.4 is devoted to the future reform, and has been divided into several subsections. Firstly, it explains how the strategy to converge with IFRS has been designed. Secondly, it presents some general recommendations regarding the Spanish accounting reform, according to the Experts' Commission White Paper published in this regard by the Spanish accounting standard setter. Thirdly, it looks into the timing and scope of the accounting reform. Lastly, it presents some initiatives other than in the accounting standard-setting field, so as to support the creation of a high-quality financial reporting model in Spain. Finally, Section 13.5 concludes the paper with a critical view of the reactions and perspectives of the would-be reform.

13.2   The Spanish Accounting and Auditing Model at the Turn of the Millennium

The French Napoleonic tradition based on Codes early influenced the development of accounting in Spain, which highlighted the importance of legal factors such as bookkeeping and the presentation of accounts.

Today, Spanish Company Law is mainly regulated by the Commercial Code of 1885, which has been modified several times in order to provide a better response to a changing economic environment. Indeed, as a consequence of the entrance of Spain in the European Community in 1986, the Commercial Code had to be substantially changed. Thus, the Commercial Reform Act 19/1989[1] was issued so as to adapt the Spanish mercantile regulation to the IV European Directive. The Legislative Royal Decree 1564/1989 was also issued as part of this reform. This document includes the Companies Act of 1989[2] and sets substantial control of accounting practices, as well as further guidance and regulations for the preparation and presentation of financial reporting.

In addition to the above-mentioned legal documents, this reform process was culminated with the issuance in December 1990 of the General Accounting Plan of 1990 (PGC-90) by Royal Decree 1643/1990. As Martínez and Zorio (2003) put it, the importance of the PGC-90 is that "it means a new understanding of accounting practices in Spain." The main aims of the PGC-90 were to improve transparency and achieve comparability of the accounts, as well as to adapt Spanish accounting practice to international trends. The PGC-90 sets compulsory accounting principles, valuation rules, and information to be disclosed in the annual report according to formalized models of the annual statements (which comprise the balance sheet, the profit and loss account, and the notes), so as to fulfil the legal obligation to give a true and fair view of the net worth and financial position of the companies.

The Royal Decree 1815/1991 should also be regarded as an important piece of regulation since it sets the procedures for the Consolidation of Annual Accounts as a development of the Commercial Reform Act of 1989, in transposition of the VII European Directive (Mora and Rees, 1998).

In the auditing realm, the Auditing Act 19/1988 meant the transposition of the VIII European Directive to Spanish law. This Act established a standard setting body in the area of accounting and auditing, i.e., the *Instituto de Contabilidad y Auditoría de Cuentas* (ICAC), to watch over the auditing function in Spain. The ICAC has issued several documents to regulate auditing practice, which are mandatory for all auditors.

The Auditing Act 19/1988 also established an official registry of auditors, the *Registro Oficial de Auditores de Cuentas* (ROAC), where all auditors are to be registered, once they are allowed to do so by the ICAC. To get such permission,

---

[1] *Ley 19/1989 de Reforma Mercantil y Adaptación a las Directivas de la CEE.*

[2] *Texto Refundido de la Ley de Sociedades Anónimas.*

individual auditors must pass an exam and fulfil some requirements regarding academic qualifications and personal skills. Every auditor must also register with any one of the three existing professional auditing institutes, i.e., the *Instituto de Auditores-Censores Jurados de Cuentas* (IACJC), the *Colegio de Economistas* (REA), or the *Colegio de Titulados Mercantiles* (REGA).

When the Auditing Law was issued in 1988, auditors were to be appointed for a minimum of 3 years and a maximum of 9 years. The same auditor could not be appointed by the company again unless 3 years later. This requirement was changed in 1995 so that once the 9-year period had expired companies could appoint any auditors annually, even the current auditor. This implied that the auditor rotation requirement was never really enforced (Arruñada and Paz-Ares, 1997).

The Auditing Act 19/1988 established compulsory audits for:

1. Listed companies
2. Companies with public issues of debentures
3. Banks and credit or financial institutions
4. Insurance companies
5. Companies receiving government grants or undertaking contracts with the State
6. Any other companies within the limits determined by the government. According to the Commercial Reform Act of 1989, the audit is compulsory for all companies, except for those that qualify for an abridged balance sheet

Within the scope of the audit, the auditor must review as well if the financial data included in the director's report agrees with the annual accounts of the company. Also, auditors are required by the Companies Act of 1989 to carry out special reviews of certain situations with regard to the companies' legal operations. Such reviews are regulated by the ICAC, which has issued several standards to be complied within these cases.

As already mentioned, the Auditing Act issued in 1988 created the *Instituto de Contabilidad y Auditoría de Cuentas* (ICAC). This regulatory body is responsible not only for the control and regulation of auditing, but also for the development of accounting practice, the issuance of interpretations of accounting rules, and the approval of any new regulation needed for those purposes. To fulfil this end, the ICAC has issued several resolutions covering a wide range of issues.

The industrial group adaptations of the accounting plan issued by the ICAC extend and customize the contents of the PGC-90 to the different sectors of the economy in order to assure that the annual accounts properly present the true and fair view of the company. Industrially adapted accounting plans have already been issued for the following sectors: building and construction, sports federations, building promoters, sports companies, health assistance companies, insurance companies, electricity companies, nonprofit organizations, motorways concessionaire companies, water concessionaire companies, sports companies – revision, electricity companies – revision, wine producers companies, and finally, aircraft transportation. The ICAC issued a draft on joint ventures and on cooperative accounting, which are still under study.

Nonetheless, apart from the ICAC, in Spain there are other public institutions that develop a standard-setting activity as regards accounting by insurance companies (*Dirección General de Seguros y Fondos de Pensiones*, the Insurance Regulatory Authority), banks and credit institutions (*Banco de España*, Bank of Spain), capital markets agencies (*Comisión Nacional del Mercado de Valores*, Securities Exchange Commission), and public administrations (*Intervención General de la Administración del Estado*, the State Intervention Office).[3]

Apart from the public initiative, which is of utmost importance in the Spanish regulatory framework, it should be highlighted that a private association of professionals representing the different sectors of the accounting and business community, i.e., academics, preparers of accounting information, auditors, and standard-setters, was created in 1979, the *Asociación Española de Contabilidad y Administración de Empresas* (AECA). This association issues pronouncements on accounting matters, which are considered as further guidance and many times have been used by the ICAC to develop compulsory accounting regulation.

13.3 Evolution of Spanish Accounting Research

In this section, we review the evolution of accounting research in Spain, from a very normative approach at its beginnings to a high level of quality covering a wide range of areas at present. Surely this fact can be of great use to promote the future reform of accounting in Spain, and will provide a good follow-up of the changes that are finally undertaken.

During the 1950s and 1960s, the most prestigious Spanish authors in the field of accounting were strongly influenced by Italian thought, whereas the German doctrine had an important impact in the area of cost accounting. Later on, the most influential countries in the Spanish accounting evolution were France, Germany, and the United States given their scientific leadership as well as their commercial and cultural ties with Spain. Indeed, the 1957 *Plan Comptable* in France was regarded as a benchmark by practitioners and academics in Spain, who were highly influenced by the leading French authors of the time (see Montesinos, 1998).

In the early 1970s, an important step was taken towards the modernization of the financial reporting of Spanish companies since the PGC-1973 (General Accounting Plan) encouraged financial reporting according to accounting principles rather than just tax rules. Compliance with this PGC was voluntary, though. Also by this time, and in line with the ASOBAT study published by the American Accounting Association in 1966, some Spanish academics began to be concerned with the objectives of accounting information and its usefulness for decision-making (Montesinos, 1975, 1978; Cañibano, 1979). This led to the development of a deductive theoretical line of thought as regards accounting in Spain. This new

---

[3] *Ley 13/1992.*

approach was based on a set of agreed general principles to be fully developed through standards, more in line with the advances of research in the most developed accounting models. Nonetheless, the Spanish contribution to the accounting debate of that time seems mainly restricted to importing the international trends to the national arena.

As mentioned in the section above, since Spain reformed its accounting system subsequent to its entrance in the European Community, accounting practice has changed in many ways as a result of compulsory application of the PGC-1990, obligatory auditing, and preparation of group accounts for certain companies. This fact together with easier access to accounting data, as well as a more valued status of research as regards promotion in the academic career has meant an increase in quantity and quality of accounting research by the Spanish faculty. Indeed, this research has been increasingly acknowledged in the international realm, through participation in international conferences and accounting events, and publication of articles in high-impact double-blind refereed journals authored by Spanish researchers. This higher visibility of Spanish authors in the international scenario has favored an increasing number of coauthorships with researchers from foreign universities (mainly from the United Kingdom and the United States).

At the time of the accounting reform in the last decade, normative research was most widespread, mainly because of the interest in the changes of the accounting model and its harmonization with the European Community through the transposition of accounting Directives or the accounting standardization that the PGC-90 itself implied (García-Ayuso and Sierra, 1994). The initial optimism in this regard turned into a concern for the impact of the changes on relevance and reliability of financial reporting (Tua, 1990; Condor, 1991). In this sense, many Spanish researchers have looked into the need to improve accounting information, for instance, as regards the area of intangibles (Cañibano et al., 2000a, b; Ballester et al., 2003; García-Ayuso, 2003a, b).

Shortly after the last accounting reform was enforced, research proved that there was no expectations gap between auditors and users of financial information (García-Benau et al., 1993). Nonetheless, as financial scandals turned up an emerging expectations gap was detected (see, e.g., García-Benau et al., 1998, 1999). The more recent scandals in the international arena such as Enron, Worldcom, Adecco, or Parmalat that put the auditor under the spotlight, have also attracted the attention of Spanish researchers (see for instance, de Fuentes and Pucheta, 2003). In addition, other fields of research as regards rotation of auditors (Arruñada and Paz-Ares, 1997) and their dismissal to avoid a qualified report (Gómez and Ruiz, 2003) are also looked into by researchers, as well as the need to improve business ethics (Espinosa, 1999).

The interest of academics and practitioners as regards accounting research also seems to have diverged with time. In this sense, the pioneer study in this area concluded that there was no gap between accounting theory and practice (Martínez-Churiaque, 1992), whereas later on conflicting evidence was obtained to this end (García-Benau et al., 1996).

The delay to adopt a positive approach in Spanish research can be explained by the fact that statistical information and databases were very scarce until the mid-1990s. By this time, more uniform data series were available for researchers as the requirement that audited accounts from large- and medium-limited liability companies should be filed in the Mercantile Registry came into force. As a result, a growing trend of research has come about to study the capital market reaction to accounting figures (see for instance, Giner and Rees, 1999; Arcas and Rees, 1999; Giner and Reverte, 2001; Arce and Mora, 2002).

As a result of the publication in 1994 of a Public Accounting Plan (Plan General de Contabilidad Pública), both normative and positive approaches on public accounting research in Spain have gained momentum (e.g., Vela, 1994; Pina and Torres, 1992; Montesinos and Vela, 1994, 1996, 2000; Torres and Pina, 2001, 2003).

Another important area for academic research in accounting has been financial reporting comparability in the EU, as regards accounting systems classifications and the measurement of European harmonization (see for instance, Condor, 1991; García-Benau, 1995; Jarne, 1996; Laínez et al., 1996; Cañibano and Mora, 2000; Laínez and Callao, 2000; Garrido et al., 2002; García-Benau and Zorio, 2002, 2004).

Other areas of interest explored by Spanish researchers include the accounting implications of the agency theory and environmental accounting (e.g., Carmona et al., 1993; Céspedes, 1993, Moneva and Llena, 2000; Larrinaga et al., 2001, 2002; Larrinaga and Bebbington, 2001) and the analysis of accounting in organizations and the influence that social, technological, and cultural changes have on this field of research (e.g., Amat, 1991; Carmona, 1993; Ruiz, 1995). Indeed, new insights into the history of accounting can also contribute to this perspective by means of providing a better understanding of the present situation through the analysis of social, political, and economic factors in the past (see Hernández, 1981; Donoso and García-Ayuso, 1993; Macías, 2002; Nuñez, 2002; Álvarez et al., 2002; Carmona and Gómez, 2002; Boyns and Carmona, 2002).

Whereas other methodologies have had significant impact in Spanish accounting research, the critical approach is rarely undertaken by Spanish researchers (see for instance Ruiz, 1995; Carrera et al., 2001).

Research in management accounting has concentrated mainly on the study of AECA's documents relating to the general framework of management accounting, cost accounting, budgets, cost classification, or specific industry documents on management accounting (e.g., Amat et al., 1994; Carmona et al., 1997, 2002; Purdey and Gago, 2002).

As it has also happened in the international realm, Spanish researchers have also made contributions to accounting literature as regards the use of the Internet for financial reporting purposes and the challenges that advances in information technology might bring about for the accounting profession (see for instance Gowthorpe and Amat, 1999; Bonsón and Escobar, 2002; Larrán and Giner, 2002).

In conclusion, Spanish accounting research has increased its quality and visibility from an international perspective, covering a wide range of fields of interest.

This fact is widely acknowledged by the international accounting community, which confirms the *rapid emergence of Spanish accounting research at an international level from a starting position of limited English-language competence for this purpose and little interest in research themes of international significance* (Standish, 2003, p. 201). As stated in the last section of the paper, the accounting reform ahead opens up new avenues that future research will surely explore, not only in a local setting but also by comparison to other countries also moving to IAS/IFRS.

13.4 Insight into Financial Reporting Reform

13.4.1 Convergence with IFRS as a Result of the European Union Financial Reporting Strategy

Being an EU member state, Spain is to be bound by the EU Regulation 1606/2002 and therefore has started to plan the necessary changes to create a coherent accounting and auditing legal framework. In March 2001, the ICAC (*Instituto de Contabilidad y Auditoría de Cuentas*) set up an Experts Commission to publish a White Paper on how to design this reform. More specifically, the Experts Commission was asked to address the current Spanish accounting model, the regulation of specific operations, and the quantity and format of the financial information that is to be disclosed by the companies.

Shortly afterwards, several subcommissions were also created so as to deal with specific aspects such as (i) the study of IAS alternative treatments; (ii) practical aspects of IAS use; (iii) comparative accounting regulation; (iv) the study of the economic agents' opinions on the accounting reform; (v) the links between accounting and taxation; (vi) financial entities supervision and accounting by credit institutions; and finally (vii) company law implications.

Hence, the White Paper is a general reference for the accounting reform in Spain, aimed at achieving an efficient transition to accounting normalisation in line with the IFRS (ICAC, 2002). The White Paper was finally published in July 2002 and it suggests important changes to be made in the Spanish mercantile and accounting regulations.

13.4.2 General Recommendations Regarding the Spanish Accounting Reform

In this section, the most relevant aspects of the conclusions and recommendations in the White Paper are looked into, so as to provide a broad overview of the transition that the accounting model in Spain is expected to undertake in the near future.

The main conclusion of this report highlights the need to promote a gradual process of reform of the Spanish accounting system to adapt the Spanish generally accepted accounting principles (GAAP) to IASB GAAP.

In this sense, it recommends the introduction of "fair value accounting," which is regarded as a very important change since in Spain the principle of prudence is of paramount importance and the historical cost convention is mostly used for valuation purposes. As regards fair value accounting, the Experts Commission thinks that the conditions to identify the fair value should be clearly stated, for instance as regards the decision on whether there is an active market for the element and a clarification of the alternative valuation methods allowed.

The Commission holds the view that changes in value should be included in an equity account (which should be treated as non-distributable profit until realization) except for financial instruments held for trading, whose changes in value should be reported as a component of results. The Experts Commission believes that a clear distinction should be made between the financial instruments that are to be included in the different portfolios (i.e., held for trading, held to maturity, and available for sale investments), in order to avoid accounts manipulation because of reclassifications of financial instruments among those portfolios.

Regarding fair value accounting of other balance-sheet components, the Experts Commission is in favor of this valuation treatment for investment properties (as in IAS 40.27–28) or for the exchange of dissimilar assets (IAS 16.21) or business combinations with payment in kind (IAS 22.36). Nonetheless, it is contrary to fair value accounting with regard to agricultural and biological assets (IAS 41.12–13), property, plant and equipment (IAS 16.29), as well as intangible assets (IAS 38). The Commission feels that fair value information regarding these elements could be provided in the notes. Regarding hedge accounting, the Commission highlights the need to develop a regulation to this end in Spain.

With regard to the IAS/IFRS adaptation to Spanish GAAP, the Experts Commission holds the view that if several alternatives are allowed by international standards, the Spanish standard-setter should sometimes make a choice bearing in mind the Spanish accounting tradition as well as the user-relevance perspective. More importantly yet maybe arguably, the Commission pinpoints that this way the Spanish view might be further considered in the European and even international realm in future standard-setting activity.

The Commission feels that the Statement of Equity Changes and the Cash Flow Statement (which would replace the present funds flow statement) is required in the new Spanish accounting model, in addition to the existing compulsory annual accounts (i.e., the balance sheet, income statement, and notes to the accounts, the latter having to include further required disclosures, for instance as regards segmental information, which is nowadays hardly ever presented).

It recommends following IAS 27, and hence not excluding from full consolidation subsidiaries with different activities. With regard to the identification of the entities to be considered in the preparation of group accounts, the Experts Commission highlights the difference that the IAS/IFRS imply as opposed to existing Spanish GAAP. According to IAS 27.11 all subsidiaries must be included in the consolidated information, unless control (i.e., power to govern the financial and operating policies of an enterprise so as to obtain benefits from its activities, IAS 27.6) is temporary or if there are severe long-term restrictions on the transfer of funds from the subsidiary to the parent (IAS 27.13).

On the other hand, current Spanish GAAP in accordance with the VII EU Directive excludes the companies with different activities from the consolidation perimeter. The Experts Commission supports the use of the equity method and proportional consolidation for investments in associates, instead of the current method of accounting at cost. Also, it encourages disclosure of information about the business risks and the companies' policies and actions taken to cover, mitigate, and manage those risks.

The Commission recommends issuing of regulations to assure the reliability and transparency of any information published in the Internet and also suggests the issue of a digital format of financial reporting. The need to create efficient and reliable services to certify financial reporting in digital format is also pointed out.

It is required that all half-yearly information of listed companies include all financial statements required by IAS 34 and it considers the convenience to submit these financial statements to a limited review by the statutory auditors. By the way, the White Paper highlights that the external control to verify compliance with accounting standards corresponds to the statutory auditors, even though it suggests that the Spanish Stock Exchange Commission should establish an effective control on public financial information with regard to compliance with accounting regulation.

In this sense, it is recommended that the Spanish and the rest of European exchange commissions develop common institutional control to improve the quality of financial information of listed companies. Thus, the Experts Commission recommends increasing surveillance on disclosures and on the quality of information provided by companies, and more especially by listed companies. Nowadays, no penalties are imposed on non-compliance, unless a private claim is filed for personal damages being derived from the decisions made on fraudulent financial reporting. The Experts Commission suggests not only letting the general public know about the claims for non-compliance, but also enforcing the penalties regime laid out in legislation, which is very rarely applied nowadays.

The White Paper highlights the need to issue a Spanish standard on business combinations, which nowadays are normally accounted for in Spain using the acquisition method. Regarding the treatment of goodwill, the Experts Commission prefers the systematic amortization system, although it points out that this matter is now under discussion in the IASB agenda. A majority of the Experts Commission agrees on how goodwill should be treated, i.e., they are in favor of systematic depreciation, even though there are also those who support an annual impairment test in line with the IASB agenda project and the US SFAS 142, issued in 2001. With regard to business combinations, the Commission is in favor of the acquisition method currently used in Spain, even though it has not made any official statement with regard to the pooling of interest method for uniting of interests, whose elimination the IASB seems to be considering.

Several recommendations and suggestions are put forward to simplify the obligations in accounting reporting for small companies. Also, the Commission considers that the existing hierarchy established in the Spanish accounting rules (Commercial Code, Companies Acts, PGC, sector adaptations of PGC, Resolutions of ICAC y Consultations to ICAC) should be kept, so that the fundamental pronouncements should establish the basic principles, whereas secondary legal sources should deal with aspects that may need a more flexible approach. A Conceptual Framework should be included in accounting regulation as a source of doctrine for future accounting developments. The Commission suggests the incorporation of certain references about the economic sense with retroactive accounting effects as regards certain mergers and spin-off operations. The current tax accounting approach should be kept except for the inclusion of certain minor changes. However, it is recognized that the accounting standards on business combinations and other operations, which may potentially produce differences between the tax value and accounting value for assets and liabilities, must include the obligation to account for the corresponding deferred tax assets or liabilities.

As regards standard-setting in the field of accounting, the Experts Commission recommends:

- Setting up just one regulatory body instead of the several public institutions that are nowadays involved with accounting standard-setting. Definitely, a new process will be needed to issue new accounting standards and interpretations in a more flexible and timely fashion
- A formal split between the accounting standard-setter and the controller of the auditing activities
- The establishment of a chartered body as a permanent Accounting Regulation Committee and a Finance Activities Commission as a mechanism to facilitate collaboration between the financial supervising bodies and the standard-setter and to enforce the effectiveness of accounting regulation
- Considering how to adapt the new accounting standards for each industry sector. The Experts Commission is in favor of maintaining the specific economy sector adaptations of the PGC as specific regulatory texts for the companies involved in the corresponding sectors, as it is currently in Spain
- Proactive participation in the international standard-setting process

Some recommendations are made as regards accounting for Public entities and not-for-profit organizations. The current restrictions regarding capitalization of intangible assets should be reduced in line with the IASB framework. Guidance should be developed as regards the accounting treatment of financial instruments. The Management Report should be standardized and include the procedures followed by the companies so as to manage the business risks as well as the policies undertaken regarding corporate governance.

A standard should be issued on voluntary or pro-forma information, in order to avoid potential misunderstandings among users. It is recommended that rules should be established to assure the coherence and feasibility of review and comparability of any information that companies could publish about prospective activities or trends. A minimum set of financial ratios should be clearly defined and disclosed in the financial report of the companies.

The Experts Commission backs the idea that a PGC (Plan General de Contabilidad) should be kept even though Spanish GAAP increasingly adopts the IFRS solutions. The current structure, contents, and objectives of the Commercial Code will have to be changed in order to create a new Spanish accounting model more in line with international trends. For instance, it seems that a Conceptual Framework should be incorporated to the Commercial Code, instead of the current list of accounting principles. In this sense, the Experts Commission feels that the Spanish Commercial Code should also be modified to include the objectives of the annual accounts (i.e., fulfil users' needs), the qualitative characteristics of the financial information (namely relevance and reliability) and the basic principles of financial reporting.

The main features of the Conceptual Framework should therefore be considered within the Commercial Code, whereas the detailed presentation of the Conceptual Framework should be provided in Part I of the PGC, as stated above. On the other hand, Parts II (list of coded accounts) and III (definitions and relationship among the coded accounts) of the PGC should be kept as they are very user friendly and highly clarifying. Part IV (on the annual accounts) should be thoroughly modified, including mainly the following changes:

- A statement of changes in equity should be presented on a compulsory basis.
- The statement of cash flows should be prepared by all the companies that do not use the abridged balance-sheet format.
- The profit and loss account should be presented using a "list format" of income and expenditure classification by nature and not an "account format" as is required nowadays.
- The notes to the accounts should be modified to include additional disclosure requirements set by the IAS/IFRS.
- Use of abridged formats should be prohibited for listed companies.

The Experts Commission puts forward the creation of an Accounting Committee depending on the ICAC's Consultative Board to develop the would-be Spanish accounting standards adapting the IFRS to the local context. A discussion paper should then follow a due process, so that the Spanish PGC developments fit the most convenient legal form and a swift modification might be undertaken if circumstances change in the future.

The Commission is aware of the legal difficulties that the concept of equity according to IAS/IFRS may imply, so it suggests that a clear definition of equity be provided (the problem could arise because accounting for hybrid instruments and treasury shares is very different between IAS/IFRS and current Spanish GAAP).

As regards performance reporting, the Experts Commission has expressed two main concerns. Firstly, it points out that realized profits should be distinguished from a category of total gains and losses that, for instance, should include non-realized changes in fair value. Hence the Commission makes the following proposals: (i) Realized profit should be reported as an explicit category within the income statement or as a supplementary statement showing the reconciliation between the total profit or loss and the realized (and distributable) result for the period. (ii) All the changes in equity should be clearly disclosed in the statement of changes in equity.

Secondly, the Commission has pointed out that important changes should be implemented in the Spanish model so as to adapt the distinction between ordinary and extraordinary results to the IASB standards. Indeed, IAS 8 restricts substantially the items that are to be considered extraordinary by comparison to Spanish GAAP. Moreover, the Commission thinks that discontinuing operations should be defined in local GAAP and the subsequent results should be disclosed under a separate caption. Lastly, the Commission is in favor of maintaining the current distinction between the result from operations and the financial results as separate subcomponents of the result from ordinary activities.

13.4.3   Timing and Scope of the Accounting Reform

Up to now there is just one single accounting model in Spain. Nonetheless, the new Regulation 1606/2002 could impose an accounting dichotomy between the consolidated information prepared by listed companies and the rest, because it requires that listed companies prepare their consolidated accounts according to IAS from 2005 onwards, yet as regards other kind of financial reporting member countries are given the choice to permit or require IAS application (article 5). Member countries are also given the chance to delay the deadline until 2007 under some circumstances (article 9)

Article 5: Options in respect of annual accounts and of non publicly-traded companies. Member States may permit or require:

(a) nonlisted companies to prepare their annual accounts,
(b) companies other than those bound by the 1606/2002 Regulation to prepare their consolidated accounts and/or their annual accounts, in conformity with the international accounting standards adopted in accordance with the procedure laid down in Article 6(2).

Article 9: Member States may delay the IAS requirement for each financial year starting on or after January 2007 to those companies:

(a) whose debt securities only are admitted on a regulated market of any member state within the meaning of Article 1(13) of Directive 93/22/EEC; or
(c) whose securities are admitted to public trading in a non-member state and which, for that purpose, have been using internationally accepted standards since a financial year that started prior to the publication of this Regulation in the Official Journal of the European Communities.

As a result, the international and European accounting developments could have a different effect on the Spanish companies depending on certain corporate characteristics (listed/not listed; consolidated/annual accounts) at a different pace (2005/2007/ ever?). Bearing in mind the conclusions drawn by the Experts Commission on how the different kind of companies should be tackled by the reform and the views that the ICAC itself has provided as regards the would-be changes (López Combarros, 2003), we present next the main lines of the accounting reform in Spain as regards its timing and scope.

The Experts Commission holds the view that the IASB model should be the best reference for financial reporting of all kinds of companies, no matter if they are listed or not, in both consolidated and individual accounts, with a view to achieving the highest degree of comparability. The process of change should start as soon as possible so as to be finished by the time the EU Regulation requires that listed companies prepare their consolidated information according to IAS. More specifically, as regards the scope of the reform, i.e., the different kind of companies bound by the changes and the timing, the following groupings can be made.

- With regard to the consolidated accounts of listed companies, the Experts Commission recommends not to use the possibility to require/allow the preparation of consolidated information according to the IFRS before 2005. Otherwise, comparability would be jeopardized even before the EU Regulation comes into force. In any case, if there is no conflict with Spanish GAAP, it could be promoted that additional disclosures in line with IAS/IFRS are provided on a voluntary basis, before the 2005 deadline.
- Regarding the consolidated information prepared by non-listed companies, the Experts Commission also suggests direct IAS/IFRS application from the EU Regulation deadline onwards. Therefore, the knowledge to understand consolidated accounts will be consistent, no matter the listing status of the group of companies. This will lead to a higher degree of comparability. In this sense, according to the President of the ICAC (López Combarros, 2003), group accounts of non-listed companies might be prepared according to IAS from 2005, yet if this choice is made, compliance with IAS will have to be kept in the future (no possibility to go back to Spanish GAAP).
- Regarding the annual accounts of listed companies, the Experts Commission puts forward the IFRS requirement from 2005 onward. Before then, financial reporting according to IAS/IFRS should be promoted as long as Spanish GAAP is always complied with, i.e., by choosing IAS/IFRS alternatives in line with local standards. This way, the Commission argues that the listed companies that belong to a group of companies will use the same basis of financial reporting for the individual accounts as for the consolidated accounts, which will make the consolidation process easier. The other advantage of this approach is that the multiplicity of accounting regulators will be reduced as IAS/IFRS would be enforced as the IASB itself develops its own accounting model, no delays resulting from special local adaptations for listed companies. Nevertheless, the Experts Commission highlights some drawbacks with regard to this point, such as the legal and fiscal implications that it may have, as for the pay-out policy of the company (the concept of distributable profit will no longer be in place), the calculation of taxes on income and specific legalistic implications derived from the role played by the equity and result figures in order to waive or be subject to

certain legal rights or commitments. Probably these drawbacks are the reasons why López Combarros (2003) has stated that the annual accounts of listed companies will have to be prepared according to Spanish GAAP, even though they might present an IAS balance sheet and profit and loss account as an annex, on a voluntary basis.

- As regards annual accounts of non-listed companies, the Experts Commission holds the view that different solutions should be taken depending on the size of the company, i.e., large companies should also apply IAS/IFRS directly (without adaptation to local GAAP); small- and medium-sized companies should prepare their financial information according to Spanish GAAP, which should be progressively developed to adopt IAS/IFRS dispositions and finally the smallest companies for which financial reporting requirements should be simplified. In spite of the Expert Commission views on this matter, it seems that the ICAC will require compliance with Spanish GAAP by all non-listed companies, whatever their size (López Combarros, 2003).

In conclusion, the Spanish accounting standard-setter will only delay the 2005 deadline to 2007, as permitted by the 1606/2002 Regulation, for companies other than banks and credit institutions which have only debt securities listed on stock exchanges (EU, 2004a). Hence, the remaining listed companies will have to prepare their consolidated accounts according to IAS on a compulsory basis from 2005 onwards. Non-listed companies will have the chance to apply IAS in the preparation of their consolidated accounts from 2005 onwards yet they will not be allowed to change their reporting framework back to Spanish GAAP, again.

The ICAC has expressed its intention to change the whole accounting system (the PGC-1990, the consolidation standards and other accounting dispositions) so as to transpose the IASB model into the Spanish legal system. Indeed, according to López Combarros (2003) a new PGC in line with IAS/IFRS should be enforced in 2007.

13.4.4   Other Reforms Underway in Order to Support a High-Quality Financial Reporting Model in Spain

In line with the arguments developed by SEC (2000) and discussed by Zorio et al. (2004), the Spanish standard-setter is aware that in order to set a high-quality accounting model, all the components of the accounting model must be of high quality (the auditing profession, the accounting standard-setter, as well as the securities commissions watching over the adequate compliance of the companies with accounting standards). This is also a consequence of being a member of the European Union. In this sense, the European Commission asked a High-Level Group of Company Law Experts to suggest new proposals so as to create "A Modern Regulatory Framework for Company Law in Europe" and has published a "Plan to Move Forward" (see European Union, 2002b, 2003), with special relevance as regards Corporate Governance issues.

Regarding the enforcement issue, for instance, the Committee of European Securities Regulators (CESR) has issued a consultation paper on a Proposed Statement of Principles (SOP) of Enforcement of Accounting Standards in Europe (see CESR, 2002). It points out that competent independent administrative authorities set up by member states should have the ultimate responsibility for enforcement of compliance of the financial information provided by the listed companies (and those applying for listing) with the reporting framework. This seems to support the creation of oversight boards in EU member states similar to the Public Company Accounting Oversight Board (PCAOB) set up in the United States by the Sarbanes-Oxley Act of 2002 (indeed, this is one of the proposals included in a EU Draft Directive on Auditing recently published, see EU, 2004b). Last March 2003, the CESR published its Standard No. 1, Enforcement of Standards on Financial Information in Europe, which is aimed at creating a common approach to the enforcement of International Accounting Standards (IAS) throughout the EU (see CESR, 2003).

In December 2003, the Committee of European Securities Regulators (CESR) published several recommendations on how listed European companies can communicate the financial impact of the move to IFRS in 2005:

1. In the 2003 annual report companies should explain (a) how they intend to carry out the transition to IAS/IFRS (plans and degree of achievement for the transition) and (b) the key differences between their present accounting policies and the ones they know with sufficient certainty they will have to apply under IAS/IFRS
2. As soon as a company can quantify the impact of the change to IAS/IFRS on its 2004 financial statements in a sufficiently reliable manner, it should disclose the relevant quantified information
3. In interim financial reports for 2005 (half-yearly and quarterly financial reports), listed companies should start applying as of January 1, 2005 either IAS 34, Interim Financial Reporting, or, if this is not possible, at least the IAS/IFRS recognition and measurement principles that will be applicable at year end and
4. CESR proposes a format ("the bridge approach") for presenting comparative figures if the national standard-setter requires/permits three successive periods of comparative information but the company has not restated under IAS/IFRS the earliest period presented (2003) Along these lines, in January 2004, the Committee of European Securities Regulators (CESR) has submitted to the European Commission its Recommendations on the content of prospectuses.

With regard to auditing, the EU Committee on Auditing (established by the Commission Communication "The Statutory Audit in the European Union: The Way Forward" of May 1998) has among its objectives to carry out an examination of the external quality assurance systems for statutory audit, as well as an examination of a set of core principles on audit independence and objectivity developed by the Fédération des Experts Comptables Européens (FEE). The Commission Recommendation 2002/590/EC of May 16, 2002 – "Statutory Auditors' Independence in the EU: A Set of Fundamental Principles" puts forward several proposals to enhance auditor independence.

The above-mentioned Committee on Auditing was also set up to undertake a review of the International Standards on Auditing (ISAs) developed by the International Federation of Accountants (IFAC), as a benchmark for EU audit requirements. In May 2003, the Commission issued a Communication titled "Reinforcing the Statutory audit in the European Union" (COM /2003/286), where an action plan is established as to improve quality and protect investors against scandals like Enron and Worldcom. The plan announces future proposals for new EU laws to provide a comprehensive set of EU rules on how audits should be conducted and on the audit infrastructure needed to safeguard audit quality.

Among the short-term priorities of the plan are strengthening public oversight of auditors at member state and EU level, requiring ISAs (International Standards on Auditing) for all EU statutory audits from 2005 and the creation of an EU Regulatory Committee on Audit, to complement the revised legislation and allow the speedy adoption of more detailed binding measures. Along these lines, in March 2004 issued a Draft Directive on Auditing to replace the current 8th Directive and amend the 4th and 7th Directives, which as the Sarbanes-Oxley Act in the US, focus as well in auditor oversight and corporate governance issues (EU, 2004b).

Bearing in mind all these concerns raised at a European level, the Spanish standard-setter has taken the legislative initiative in some regards to enhance the domestic financial reporting environment.

In fact, a new act on the Financial System in Spain passed in 2002 [4] has important implications in the auditing field and on corporate governance. This law is a step in the right direction according to the above-mentioned EU Recommendations and Communications in this realm. In this sense, this new law states that auditors must be "and seem" independent. As a guarantee of independence, this law prohibits auditors from: (i) fulfilling some positions in the audited firm, (ii) keeping a financial interest in the audited firm, (iii) keep family and affinity ties, (iv) providing services under certain characteristics, (v) keeping business relationships, and (vi) concentration of emoluments.

Other important features of the new law related to auditing are (i) the compulsory publication of the fees paid by companies to their auditors for auditing and additional services; (ii) the compulsory creation of audit committees in companies with listed securities; (iii) the compulsory rotation of the audit team responsible for the audit of a listed company or with net sales over 30 million euros; (iv) sanctions are strengthened.

As regards corporate governance and the establishment of audit committees in listed companies, the Aldama Report published in January 2003 by the Spanish Stock Exchange Commission (*Comisión Nacional del Mercado de Valores,* CNMV) looks into the audit committee composition among other issues, including financial reporting in the Internet by listed companies. An act passed in July 2003[5] addresses the transparency of information by listed companies and reforms the laws

---

[4] *Ley 44/2002; de 22 de noviembre, de Medidas de Reforma del Sistema Financiero.*
[5] *Ley 26/2003 de 17 julio 2003.*

on public companies and capital markets. It sets some requirements as regards loyalty by executive and non-executive members of the Board of Directors. A ministerial order passed in December 2003 looks into further details on the annual corporate governance report that listed companies must publish and other sources of communication that companies might use.[6]

Another important change that the Spanish standard-setter envisages is to simplify the accounting requirements and procedures for newly created and small-sized companies. An Exposure Draft of this new Law states that the accounting treatment of tax and leasing will be simplified following a cash basis approach. Also, the ledger will follow a matrix presentation so that the financial statements of the companies will be easily derived from it. In addition, the line items of the annual accounts will be reduced.

The ICAC will surely have to follow the international debate in the auditing field, and most probably start designing the adoption of the latest trends in this area (mainly the use of ISA) and their incorporation into the Spanish financial reporting system, even though apparently there are no significant differences between Spanish auditing standards and ISA (Martínez and Zorio, 2003).

13.5   Reactions and Perspectives on the Reform

In November 2003, Mazars published a survey on the views of European companies regarding the transition to IFRS (Mazars, 2003). This study highlights that listed Spanish companies perceive the change to IAS-IFRS as a great opportunity to improve transparency and create a single financial market. Nonetheless, very few of them have started preparing the move to IAS-IFRS, since they feel it is a very costly and complex process.

Unlike in other countries, listed companies in Spain will surely hire the aid from external consultants to undertake the change in a way that is not restricted to financial matters, yet under a broader approach, paying special attention to other issues such as information systems or staff training. The non-listed companies surveyed mostly expressed the view that they see the move to IAS-IFRS as a very long and difficult process, which discourages them from following the IASB standards on a voluntary basis.

Another study focused only on Spain has surveyed 360 Spanish companies, with a total turnover of 990,000 million euros and more than a million employees (Deloitte, 2003). According to its results, 81.2% of the companies in the sample reckon that the change to IAS is positive or very positive, whereas only 5.2% feel it is a negative or very negative move. Spanish companies' main concerns as regards the change to IAS/IFRS highlight the increased level of disclosure required, fair value accounting, lack of practical guidance for certain issues, and the feeling

---

[6] *ORDEN ECO/3722/2003 de 26 de diciembre.*

that sector adaptation of standards might be needed for certain industries. One out of three companies in the sample states that has already assessed the impact of the change to IAS, and nearly the same proportion of companies do not plan to assess the changes before 2005 (10.9%) or do not answer this question (17%).

As regards the reactions of the auditing profession to the new requirements imposed by the above-mentioned Financial Act (Ley 44/2002), García-Benau et al. (2003) find that the auditors welcome the new restrictions except for the partner rotation requirement. Indeed, the authors suggest that it may trigger a process of mergers and acquisitions of small- and medium-sized audit firms, which could lose clients as a result of the new law being enforced.

In our opinion, the IASB standards are so different from Spanish GAAP that the reluctance to follow IAS-IFRS can be easily understood. It should be stressed that up until 2003 no Spanish textbook or practical guide on IAS application with numerical examples and business-like exercises has been published, to explain how to apply the IASB standards in a straightforward manner, easy to understand by a Spanish reader educated within the Spanish accounting system. Therefore, it is very difficult for someone brought up within our highly codified local reporting framework to understand many of the changes that the IAS move implies, not only because of the use of valuation methods or recognition criteria that Spanish readers are not familiar with, but also and very importantly because the terminology used in the IASB standards and the way they are written are completely different from their Spanish equivalents. Nonetheless, this should be just a question of time. As IAS-IFRS textbooks with numerical examples start being published in Spanish in the near future adapted to the local accounting mentality, domestic users and preparers of accounts will gain confidence in this new scenario.

Also, researchers should start to look into this area and provide evidence that can be valuable in the standard-setting process. For instance, by means of analyzing how listed companies plan their transition to IAS and finally prepare to consolidate their accounts according to IAS from 2005. Research should also try and draw conclusions of interest towards the development of a new PGC that the ICAC plans to issue by 2007, especially if some IAS/IFRS options are to be prohibited in the local realm as it seems that the ICAC is considering doing (López Combarros, 2003).

One might think that Spanish researchers could have already made some kind of contribution in this regard, given the importance of the changes ahead with the 2005 IAS target. Nonetheless, the lack of research in this field can easily be explained by the absence of sufficient data from a Spanish setting to obtain significant empirical results.

To illustrate this point, it should be mentioned that just one Spanish company applies IFRS in the preparation of financial statements nowadays, even though it also has to present a dual set of financial statements according to Spanish GAAP to fulfil Spanish legal requirements: Amadeus is an information technology company, publicly listed since 1999 in Spain, and later on in Paris and Frankfurt, which provides worldwide marketing and distribution services to the travel industry. Table 13.1 shows Amadeus reconciliations of income and shareholders equity from Spanish GAAP to IAS for the year ended 2003.

Table 13.1 Amadeus reconciliations of net income and shareholders equity from Spanish GAAP to IFRS

		For the years ended December 31,	
Reconciliation of Net Income	Note	2003 (Unaudited)	2002
Net Income-Spanish GAAP		**150,127**	**84,820**
Adjustments for IFRS purposes:			
Acquisition of Amadeus Operations KG	1	23,309	23,826
Treasury shares and other similar equity instruments	2	(13,179)	30,628
Public Offering expenses	3	3,194	3,194
Unrealised exchange gains	4	2,277	(580)
Accounting for financial Instruments	5	(1,467)	(670)
Equity related Instruments	6	(4,147)	5,869
Net Income-IFRS		**160,114**	**147,087**
		For the years ended December 31,	
Reconciliation of Shareholders' Equity	Note	2003 (Unaudited)	2002
Shareholders' equity Spanish GAAP		**903,141**	**791,868**
Adjustments for IFRS purposes:			
Acquisition of Amadeus Operations KG	1	(94,973)	(115,163)
Treasury shares and other similar equity instruments	2	(107,316)	(96,308)
Public Offering expenses	3	(2,512)	(5,706)
Unrealised exchange gains	4	7,172	4,895
Accounting for financial instruments	5	18,815	6,101
Equity related Instruments	6	33,386	36,653
Shareholders' equity-IFRS		**757,713**	**622,340**

Unlike other countries in the European Union where companies tend to comply with IASB standards given a more flexible legal approach to IAS use (see for instance García-Benau and Zorio, 2002, where determining factors for IAS-use are explored among European companies), the legal framework of accounting in Spain does not allow companies to depart from Spanish GAAP (as explained in Section 13.2 above).

This has surely put off Spanish researchers from exploring the comparison between Spanish GAAP vs. IFRS from a more empirical point of view. Given that in 1987, two Spanish companies got listed in the NYSE, and in the following years a few more companies have also been quoted in US capital markets, empirical data using 20-F income and shareholders reconciliations from Spanish GAAP to USGAAP have been examined by Spanish researchers. The impact of differences between these two sets of standards have been looked into, even though results cannot be really extrapolated given the reduced sample size (a maximum of eight observations per year, see Ucieda, 2003).

However, as the accounting reform is gradually enforced, numerical data will be available and surely researchers will look into the consequences of the changes from a positive perspective, and also try to contribute to the standard-setting process with evidence that can shed some light in the normative process in a Spanish setting, and hopefully in the European or even international realm.

References

Álvarez, M.J., Gutiérrez, F., Romero, D. (2002) "Accounting and quality control in the Royal Tobacco Factory of Seville, 1744–90: an historical perspective," *Accounting Business and Financial History*, 12(2): 253.

Amat, J., Carmona, S., Roberts, H. (1994) Context and change in management accounting systems: A Spanish case study," *Management Accounting Research*, 5(2): 107–122.

Amat, J.M. (1991) *Los Sistemas de Control en las Empresas de Alta tecnología*. Madrid: ICAC.

Arcas Pellicer, M.A., Rees, W. (1999) "Regularities in the equity price response to earnings announcements in Spain," *European Accounting Review*, 8(4): 585–607.

Arce, M., Mora, A. (2002) "Empirical evidence of the effect of European accounting differences on the stock market valuation of earnings and book value," *European Accounting Review*, 11(3): 573–601.

Arruñada, B., Paz-Ares, C. (1997) "Mandatory rotation of company auditors: A critical examination," *International Review of Law and Economics*, 17: 31–61.

Ballester, M., Garcia-Ayuso, M., Livnat, J. (2003) "The economic value of the R&D intangible asset," *European Accounting Review*, 12(4): 605–635.

Bonsón, E., Escobar, T. (2002) "A Survey on Voluntary Disclosure on the Internet. Empirical Evidence from 300 European Union Companies," *The International Journal of Digital Accounting Research*, 2(3): 27–52.

Boyns, T., Carmona, S. (2002) "Accounting history research in Spain, 1996–2001: An introduction," *Accounting Business and Financial History*, 12(2): 149–157.

Cañibano, L. (1979) *Teoría Actual de la Contabilidad*. Madrid: ICE.

Cañibano, L., Mora, A. (2000) "Evaluating the statistical significance of the facto accounting harmonization: A study of European global players," *The European Accounting Review*, 9(3): 349–369.

Cañibano, L., Garcia-Ayuso, M., Sanchez, Paloma (2000a) "Accounting for Intangibles: A Literature Review," *Journal of Accounting Literature*, 19: 102–131.

Cañibano, L., Garcia-Ayuso, M., Sanchez, Paloma (2000b) "Shortcomings in the Measurement of Innovation: Implications for Accounting Standard Setting", *Journal of Management and Governance*, 4(4): 319–343.

Carmona Moreno, S. (1993) *Cambios Tecnológicos y Contabilidad de Gestión*. Madrid: ICAC.

Carmona, S., Ezzamel, M., Gutiérrez, F. (1997) "Control and cost accounting practices in the Spanish Royal Tobacco Factory," *Accounting, Organizations and Society*, 22(5): 411–446.

Carmona, S., Ezzamel, M., Gutiérrez, F. (2002) "The relationship between accounting and spatial practices in the factory," *Accounting, Organizations and Society*, 27(3): 239–274.

Carmona, S., Carrasco, F., Fernández, L. (1993) "Un enfoque interdisciplinar de la contabilidad del medio ambiente," *Revista Española de Financiación y Contabilidad*, vol. XXIII, Núm. 75: 277–305.

Carmona, E., Gómez, D. (2002) "Early cost management practices, state ownership and market competition: the case of the Royal Textile Mill of Guadalajara, 1717–44," *Accounting Business and Financial History*, 12(2): 231–253.

Carrera, N., Gutiérrez, I., Carmona, S. (2001) "Gender, the state and the audit profession: evidence from Spain (1942–88)," *European Accounting Review*, 10(4): 803–817.

Céspedes, J. (1993) "Ecología y principios contables," *Revista Española de Financiación y Contabilidad*, vol. XXIII, Núm. 75: 307–315.

Committee of European Securities Regulators, CESR (2002) *Consultation paper on a Proposed Statement of Principles (SOP) of Enforcement of Accounting Standards in Europe* European Union. Ref: CESR/02-188b.

Committee of European Securities Regulators, CESR (2003) *Standard No. 1 On Financial Information: Enforcement Of Standards On Financial Information In Europe*. Date: 12 March 2003. Ref.: CESR/03-073.

Condor, V. (1991) "The impact of EC Directives on Spanish accounting law, with special reference to group accounts," *European Accounting*, 33–39.

De Fuentes, C., Pucheta, C. (2003) "Estudio empírico de la reacción del mercado de capitales español ante el fraude Arthur Andersen-Enron". Paper presented at the XII AECA conference, held in Cádiz.

Deloitte (2003) *Barómetro de empresas No 18*. Madrid, 23 de diciembre de 2003.

Donoso Anez, R., García-Ayuso Covarsi, M. (1993) "La historia de la Contabilidad a debate: una encuesta a los académicos españoles," *Revista Española de Financiación y Contabilidad*, 22: 737–756.

Espinosa-Pike, M. (1999) "Business Ethics and Accounting Information. An Analysis of the Spanish Code of Best Practice," *Journal of Business Ethics*, 22(3): 249–260.

EU (2002a) *Regulation (EC) No 1606/2002 of the European Parliament and of the Council of 19 July 2002 on the application of international accounting standards*. Official Journal L 243, 11/09/2002.

EU (2002b) *Report of High Level Group of Company Law Experts on a Modern Regulatory Framework for Company Law in Europe*. Brussels, 4/11/2002.

EU (2002c) *A first EU response to Enron related policy issues*. Note for the informal Ecofin Council, Oviedo, 12 and 13 April, 2002, Brussels.

EU (2003a) *Modernising Company Law and Enhancing Corporate Governance in the European Union* – A Plan to Move Forward COM (2003) 284 final of 21 May 2003.

EU (2003b) *Reinforcing the statutory audit in the EU (Text with EEA relevance).Communication From The Commission To The Council And The European Parliament*. Document No: 03/10826 rev3. Date: May 2003. Brussels.

EU (2004a) *Table providing information on the intentions/decisions of Member States and EEA Countries concerning the use of options in the IAS Regulation*. Brussels, Date 8/03/04.

EU (2004b) *Proposal for a DIRECTIVE OF THE EUROPEAN PARLIAMENT AND OF THE COUNCIL on statutory audit of annual accounts and consolidated accounts and amending Council Directives 78/660/EEC and 83/349/EEC*. Brussels, March, 2004.

García-Ayuso, M. (2003a) "Factors explaining the inefficient valuation of intangibles," *Accounting Auditing and Accountability Journal*, 16(1): 57–69.

García-Ayuso, M. (2003b) "Intangibles: Lessons from the past and a look into the future," *Journal of Intellectual Capital*, 4(4): 597–604.

García-Ayuso, M., Sierra, G. (1994) "La relación entre investigación y práctica en contabilidad," *Revista Española de Financiación y Contabilidad*, 24: 235–87.

García-Benau, M.A. (1995) *Armonización de la Información Financiera en Europa*. Madrid: ICAC.

García-Benau, M.A., Humphrey, C., Moizer, P., Turley, S. (1993) "Accounting expectations and performance in Spain and Britain: a comparative analysis," *The International Journal of Accounting*, 28: 281–307.

García-Benau, M.A., Gandía, J.L., Vico, A. (1996) *Relación entre Teoría y Práctica Contable: Un Análisis de la Situación en España*. Madrid: AECA.

García-Benau, M.A., Ruiz Barbadillo, E., Vico, A. (1998) *Análisis de la estructura del mercado de servicios de auditoría en España*. Madrid: ICAC.

García-Benau, M.A., Ruiz Barbadillo, E., Humphrey, C., Al Husaini, W. (1999) "Success in failure? Reflections on the changing Spanish audit environment," *European Accounting Review*, 8(4): 701–730.

García-Benau, M.A., Vico, A., Zorio, A. (2003) "La opinión de los auditores sobre la regulación de la independencia," *Partida Doble*, 146: 32–48.

García-Benau, M.A., Zorio, A. (2004) "Audit Reports on Financial Statements Prepared According to IASB Standards: Empirical Evidence from the European Union," *International Journal of Auditing*, 8(3): 237–252.

García-Benau, M.A., Zorio, A. (2002) "Características de las empresas europeas que aplican las normas del IASC: evidencia empírica de cara al debate regulador en la nueva fase de armonización contable," *Revista Española de Financiación y Contabilidad*, 31(111): 75–110.

Garrido, P., León, A., Zorio, A. (2002) "Measurement of formal harmonization progress: – The IASC experience," *The International Journal of Accounting*, 37(1): 1–26.

Giner, B., Rees, W. (1999) "A Valuation Based Analysis of the Spanish Accounting Reforms," *Journal of Management and Governance*, 3(1): 31–48.

Giner, B., Reverte, C. (2001) "Valuation implications of capital structure: a contextual approach," *European Accounting Review*, 10(2): 291–314.

Gómez Aguilar, N., Ruiz Barbadillo, E. (2003) "Do Spanish Firms Change Auditor to Avoid a Qualified Audit Report?" *International Journal of Auditing*, 7(1): 37–54.

Gowthorpe, C., Amat, O. (1999) "External reporting of accounting and financial information via the Internet in Spain," *European Accounting Review*, 8(2): 365–372.

Hernández Esteve, E. (1981) *Contribución al Estudio de la Historiografía Contable en España*. Madrid: Banco de España.

Instituto de Contabilidad y Auditoría de Cuentas (2002) *Informe sobre la situación actual de la contabilidad en España y líneas básicas para abordar su reforma (Libro Blanco para la Reforma de la Contabilidad en España)*. Informe de la Comisión de Expertos. ICAC:Madrid.

Jarne Jarne, J.I. (1996) *Clasificación, evolución y armonización de los sistemas contables. Un análisis conceptual y empírico*. AECA.

Laínez, J.A., Callao, S. (2000) "The effect of accounting diversity on international financial analysis: empirical evidence," *The International Journal of Accounting*, 35(1): 65–83.

Laínez Gadea, J.A., Callao Gastón, S., Jarne Jarne, J.I. (1996) "International Harmonization of Reporting Required by Stock Markets," *The International Journal of Accounting*, 31(4): 405–418.

Larrán, M., Giner, B. (2002) "The Use of the Internet for Corporate Reporting by Spanish Companies," *The International Journal of Digital Accounting Research*, 2(3): 53–82.

Larrinaga, C., Bebbington, J. (2001) "Accounting change or institutional appropriation?—A case study of the implementation of environmental accounting," *Critical Perspectives on Accounting*, 12(3): 269–292.

Larrinaga, C., Carrasco, F., Caro, F.J., Correa, C., Páez, J.M. (2001) "The role of environmental accounting in organizational change -An exploration of Spanish companies," *Accounting Auditing and Accountability Journal*, 14(2): 213–239.

Larrinaga, C., Carrasco, F., Correa, C., Llena, F., Moneva, J. (2002) "Accountability and accounting regulation: the case of the Spanish environmental disclosure standard," *European Accounting Review*, 11(4): 723–741.

López Combarros (2003) "Principales aspectos de la reforma legal de la contabilidad en España," *Revista AECA*, No 64: 4–5.

Macías, M. (2002) "Ownership structure and accountability: the case of the privatization of the Spanish tobacco monopoly, 1887–96," *Accounting Business and Financial History*, 12(2): 317–346.

Martínez Churiaque, J.I. (1992) "University accounting education, present and future," in J.A. Gonzalo Angulo (ed.) *Accounting in Spain 1992*. Madrid: AECA, pp. 391–403.

Martínez, F., Zorio, A. (2003) "Spain". Included in *The Miller European Accounting Guide*. 5th Edition: Editors Alexander, D & Archer, S. Aspen Law & Business. New York.

Mazars (2003) The impact that changing to IAS-IFRS will have on European companies: somewhere in between opportunities and complexity. Paris, November.

Moneva, M., Llena, F. (2000) "Environmental disclosures in the annual reports of large companies in Spain," *European Accounting Review*, 9(1): 7–30.

Montesinos Julve, V. (1975) "La Contabilidad en la formación y manifestación de las expectativas empresariales," *Seguros*, 259–287.

Montesinos Julve, V. (1978) "Formación histórica, corrientes doctrinales y programas de investigación en Contabilidad," *Revista Técnica Contable*, 81, 135, 171, 219, 253, 285, 351, 373 *et seq.*

Montesinos Julve, V., Vela Bargues, J.M. (1994) "Performance measurement in the public sector: some implications of Spanish accounting regulation," in E. Buschor and K. Schedler (eds.) *Perspectives on Performance Measurement and Public Sector Accounting*. Berne: Haupt, pp. 397–416.

Montesinos Julve, V., Vela Bargues, J.M. (1996) "Governmental accounting in Spain: evolution and reforms," in J.L. Chan, R.H. Jones, and K.G. Luder (eds.) *Research in Governmental and Nonprofit Accounting*, Vol. 9. Greenwich, CT: JAI Press, pp. 219–238.

Montesinos, V. (1998) "Accounting and Business in Spain," *European Accounting Review*, 7(3): 357–380.

Montesinos, V., Vela, J.M. (2000) "Governmental Accounting in Spain and the European Monetary Union: A Critical Perspective," *Financial Accountability and Management*, 16(2): 129–150.

Mora, A., Rees, W. (1998) "The early adoption of consolidated accounting in Spain," *The European Accounting Review*, 7(4): 675–696.

Núñez, M. (2002) "Organizational change and accounting: the gunpowder monopoly in New Spain, 1757–87," *Accounting Business and Financial History*, 12(2): 275–316.

Pina, V., Torres, L. (1992) "Evaluating the efficiency of nonprofit organizations: an application of data envelopment analysis to the public health service," *Financial Accountability and Management*, 8(3): 213–224.

Purdey, D.E., Gago, S. (2002) "Public Sector Managers Handling Accounting Data: A UK Framework Validated in Spain," *Financial Accountability and Management*, 18(3): 233–260.

Ruiz Barbadillo, E. (1995) "Determinantes sociopolíticos en la emisión de la norma referida a las provisiones para pensiones," *Revista Española de Financiación y Contabilidad*, 25(85):1061–1115.

Securities and Exchange Commission, SEC (2000) *Concept Release on International Accounting Standards*. (Available at http://www.sec.gov/rules/concept/34-42430.htm, accessed in February 2004).

Standish, P. (2003) "Evaluating national capacity for direct participation in International Accounting harmonization: France as a test case," *Abacus*, 39(2): 186–210.

Torres, L., Pina, V. (2001) "Public-private partnership and private finance initiatives in the EU and Spanish local governments," *European Accounting Review*, 10(3): 601–620.

Torres, L., Pina, V. (2003) "Accounting for Accountability and Management in NPOs. A Comparative Study of Four Countries: Canada, the United Kingdom, the USA and Spain," *Financial Accountability and Management*, 19(3): 265–286.

Tua Pereda, J. (1990) "La reforma del ordenamiento jurídico mercantil en materia de información financiera," *Revista Técnica del Instituto de Auditores-Censores Jurados de Cuentas de España*, 12–34.

Ucieda, J.L. (2003) "A decade of reconciliation to USGAAP. What have we learned?". *Revista Española de Financiación y Contabilidad*, 115(special issue for the 26th annual Congress of the EAA (Seville)): 69–115.

Vela Bargues, J.M. (1994) "La comptabilité locale en Espagne," *Revue Française de Finances Publiques*, 105–114.

Zorio, A., García-Benau, M.A., Pucheta, C. (2004) "Calidad, un nuevo concepto clave en el desenlace del proceso de armonización contable internacional," *Revista Española de Financiación y Contabilidad*, 121: 313–348.

Chapter 14
The Changing Financial System in Taiwan

Doris H. Chuang and Jens Hölscher

14.1 Introduction

Over the past 5 decades, Taiwan has achieved rapid economic growth and has successfully transformed from an agricultural society to a technology-oriented industrialised society. Correspondingly, its financial system has been through a transformation in the process of economic development and the government's efforts have focused on implementing policies conducive to financial liberalisation and internalisation for the past 20 years. Taiwan's financial system has been transformed from a controlled system to a liberalised system and from a state banking to a private banking system. The financial liberalisation process in Taiwan has followed the order suggested by McKinnon (1993) to transfer the economy from a financially controlled to a market-oriented economy.

As Taiwan today is in a phase of transformation in political and economic affairs, having and maintaining a sound, efficient financial system has become significant in satisfying the needs of industry and promoting economic development. Appropriate financial reforms at the right moment can help ensure the operation of a sound financial system and equip Taiwan's financial institutions with the ability to cope with the increasing competitiveness of the financial environment. Taiwan's financial reform took place in 2001 and was aimed at maintaining the integrity of the financial market and facilitating the sound development of financial services.

This paper will start by introducing the general background of Taiwan to obtain a better understanding of its financial development. The structure and evolution of financial development in Taiwan will then be presented in sections three and four. In the fifth section, the pressures that drove Taiwan to undertake financial reform will be discussed, followed by the financial reforms since 2001. The paper is then summed up in the conclusion.

D. H. Chuang and J. Hölscher
Brighton Business School

R. W. McGee (ed.), *Accounting Reform in Transition and Developing Economies*,
© Springer Science + Business Media LLC 2008

14.2   General Background of Taiwan

Taiwan is an island off the south-eastern coast of China with a total area of about 36,000 km² and a population of about 23 million. It was colonised by the Netherlands in 1624–1662 and Japan in 1895–1943, and was returned to the governance of Republic of China (ROC) in 1945.

In 1949, the central government of the Republic of China, on the Chinese mainland, lost its battle against the Chinese Communist and relocated to Taiwan. Since then, Taiwan's economy has developed uninterruptedly, from the policy of 'using agriculture to support industry' to the export processing of the 1960s, the liberalisation and internationalisation of the 1980s, and the burgeoning IT industry of the

Table 14.1   Major Economic Indicators

Item	Unit	2000	2001	2002	2003
Economic growth rate (real GDP) increase)	%	5.86	−2.18	3.59	3.31
Gross national product (GNP)	US$ billion	313.9	286.8	289.3	296.5
Per capita GNP	US$	14188	12876	12916	13156
Changes in consumer price index (CPI)	%	1.26	−0.01	−0.02	0.03
Exchange rate (average)	NT$ per US$	31.23	33.8	34.58	33.97
Unemployment rate	%	3	4.06	5.17	4.99
Foreign exchange reserves (year end)	US$ billion	106.7	122.2	161.7	206.6

Source: Directorate-General of Budget, Accounting, and Statistics Executive Yuan, Taiwan

Table 14.2   Indicators for Financial Development

Yearly	GDP(Millions of NT dollars)	Domestic credit (Millions of NT dollars)	Total assets of domestic banks (Millions of NT dollars)	Domestic credit/GDP	Banks' assets/ GDP
1992	5,338,952	7,960,500	8,891,700	149.10%	166.54%
1993	5,918,376	9,511,000	10,440,400	160.70%	176.41%
1994	6,463,600	10,955,600	12,101,700	169.50%	187.23%
1995	7,017,933	12,100,300	13,206,000	172.42%	188.18%
1996	7,678,126	13,051,700	14,412,700	169.99%	187.71%
1997	8,305,267	14,307,500	15,502,800	172.27%	186.66%
1998	8,899,290	15,408,300	17,547,900	173.14%	197.18%
1999	9,244,438	15,952,300	19,260,100	172.56%	208.34%
2000	9,612,491	16,525,900	20,775,100	171.92%	216.13%
2001	9,447,649	16,367,700	21,740,800	173.25%	230.12%
2002	9,735,364	15,925,700	22,097,100	163.59%	226.98%
2003	9,844,203	16,358,900	23,740,800	166.18%	241.17%

Source: Directorate-General of Budget, Accounting, and Statistics Executive Yuan, Taiwan

1990s. During the past 2 decades, Taiwan has enjoyed rapid and sustained economic growth. The average economic growth rate was 7.24% from 1979 to 2000. In the year 2001, Taiwan had its first negative economic growth rate, −2.18%, when it experienced an economic downturn due to cyclical and structural phenomena. The growth rate recovered slightly to 3.59% in 2002 and to 3.31% in 2003 (see Table 14.1). From 1979 to 2003, the real GNP increased about nine times and the per capita GNP soared from US$1,920 to US$13,156.

According to the official statistical figures from the Government Information Office Taiwan, in 2002, trade volume totalled US$243.2 billion, ranking Taiwan 15th among the trading nations of the world. At year-end, Taiwan's foreign exchange reserves stood at US$161.7 billion, the third highest in the world.

Table 14.2 shows the indicators for financial development in Taiwan for the past 10 years. The banking sector is considered as generally stable and the level of financial intermediation remains quite high. The financial intermediation ratio, measured by total domestic credit as a percentage of GDP, steadily increased from 149.10% in 1992 to the peak of 173.25% in 2001. However, the bank credit growth rates substantially exceeded GDP growth for several years also imply an excessive bank lending presaging future credit-quality problems. In addition, Table 14.2 provides the evidence that the scale of Taiwan's banking sector has kept on expanding as the ratio of the national banks' assets to GDP has been continually growing since 1992.

These figures indicate that the financial system in Taiwan is more advanced even when compared with other transition countries that have more developed financial markets in Central Europe. For instance, the ratios of domestic credit to GDP in 2000 in Hungry and Poland are 42% and 39% while the ratios of banks' assets to GDP are 61% and 66%. It shows that these two figures in Hungry and Poland are only about one quarter of that in Taiwan.

14.3   The Structure of Taiwan's Financial System

14.3.1   Supervisory Authorities

Before financial reform took place, Taiwan used to manage financial institutions using the traditional concept: different regulation and different authorities manage different markets and different financial institutions.

1. Ministry of Finance

The Ministry of Finance (MOF) includes three major subordinate agencies, namely the Bureau of Monetary Affairs, the Department of Insurance and the Securities and Futures Commission. The MOF is responsible for financial administration and the supervision of the financial market and relevant institutions. It is obligated to formulate policies to facilitate the development of the financial industry.

2. Central Bank of China

The Central Bank of China (CBC) conducts monetary and foreign exchange policies and is responsible for a considerable amount of financial supervision. It issues the nation's currency, and serves as the bank of banks and the government's bank. Before 1979, the CBC came under presidential authority. Since 1979, the CBC has been under the control of the Executive Yuan (the highest administrative institution in the government), and is thus not as politically and economically independent as before.

3. Central Deposited Insurance Corporation

The authority of the Central Deposited Insurance Corporation (CDIC) is conferred by the Ministry of Finance: it was established in an attempt to safeguard the assets of depositors in financial institutions and encourage saving.

14.3.2 Financial Institutions

14.3.2.1 Deposit Money Banks

Except local branches of foreign banks in Taiwan, domestic deposit money banks can be divided into three groups. (1) Commercial banks and savings banks: the former focus on short-term deposits and loans while the latter focus on medium- or long-term deposits and loans. (2) Specialised banks: the purpose of these banks is to provide specialised lending for small and medium enterprises in order to promote economic development and industrial upgrading. (3) Credit Cooperatives: banking services in regional communities. It is noted that the Credit Department of Farmer's Associations and the Credit Department of Fishermen's Associations, as the most grass-roots financial institutions, are unique financial institutions in Taiwan. They provide encouragement for rural and small town residents. Their main function is to promote economic development among farmers and fishermen in residential areas.

Other Financial Institutions: Insurance Institutions, the Postal Saving System, Credit Card Institutions, Investment and Trust Companies, Offshore Banking Units, the Credit Guarantee Fund and Financial Market Professional Institutions.

14.3.2.2 Financial Holding Company

The financial holding company is a newly formed financial institution in Taiwan. Fourteen financial holding companies were established in 2001 and their investments in subsidiary institutions were engaged in different kinds of financial services such as banking, insurance, securities, bills financing and venture capi-

Table 14.3 Financial Institutions

	1995	1999	2001	2003
Domestic banks	34	47	48	45
Branches	1,361	2,288	2,712	2884
Medium business banks	8	5	5	5
Taiwan branches of foreign banks	38	41	38	36
Credit cooperatives	73	50	39	35
Credit departments of farmers' Associations	+285	287	260	253
Credit departments of fishermen's associations	27	27	25	25
Postal savings system	1	1	1	1
Branches	1,515	1,547	1,567	1,445
Investment and trust companies	5	3	3	3
Life insurance companies	29	31	28	29
Insurance institutions	22	27	27	24
Bills finance companies	10	16	15	14
Securities finance companies	4	4	4	4
Financial holding companies	–	–	14	14

Source: Directorate-General of Budget, Accounting, and Statistics Executive Yuan, Taiwan

tal. Cross-selling of financial products is partially allowed under the holding company structure and information and equipment may also be shared under one roof.

14.3.3   The Informal Financial System

Like many other developing countries, Taiwan has a dual financial system, i.e. a formal financial system and an informal financial system. The informal financial system includes the markets and mechanisms where borrowing and lending activities by businesses and households occur without the government's approval. Until the abolition of restrictions on financial institution establishment, many of the formal institutions in Taiwan were either state-owned or state-dominated and their interest rates were highly restricted by the government.

As a result, they rationed credit by serving primarily large private and government enterprises, leaving other businesses (mostly small businesses and medium-sized enterprises) to the informal financial agents. It is believed that the more backward a country's financial system, the more developed is its underground financial system. Therefore, since Taiwan's financial liberalisation, the composition of business sector financing sources provided by informal financial sectors is continuously reducing. According to Shea, Kuo and Huang (1995), informal financing accounted for around 50% of the total financing by private enterprises in the 1960s. This ratio declined to between 35% and 45% in the mid-1980s and to 25% in the early 1990s.

14.3.4   Financial Market

There are three main financial markets in Taiwan: Money Market, Capital Market and Foreign Exchange Market. The Money Market and Capital Market are classified according to the maturity of the financial instruments they handle.

Money market: This includes the short-term bills market and the interbank call loan market. Currently, the major instruments traded in the short-term (less than 1 year) money market include: treasury bills, commercial paper, banker's acceptances, negotiable certificates of deposits and so on.

Capital market: The capital market is composed of the bond market, which includes listed and over-the-counter, the stock market which includes listed and over-the-counter, and the futures market, which was set up in 1998. Instruments in the market include equity securities and debt securities with maturities of more than 1 year.

Foreign Exchange Market: The foreign exchange market in Taiwan can be characterised as a two-tier trading system which includes the bank customer foreign trading market and the interbank foreign transaction market. The main participants of the first tier foreign exchange market are the authorised foreign exchange banks and their customers. The CBC, the authorised foreign exchange banks and the foreign exchange brokerage firms play the leading roles in the interbank foreign transaction market, namely, the second tier of the trading system.

14.4   Evolution of Taiwan's Financial System

14.4.1   Review of Taiwanese Financial Repression History 1960s–1970s

In the 1960s, the Taiwanese government used contractions policies for growth promotion and economy stabilisation, which created a comparative advantage for Taiwan. During this time, the Taiwanese authorities frequently intervened in the financial system, either formally or informally. Shea (1994) listed the four interventionist policies adopted by Taiwan's government during this time, which were:

1. Government ownership of banks
2. Strict entry regulations
3. Interest rate control
4. Selective credit rationing policies

This system therefore gave the government the ability to efficiently direct domestic savings to banks and productive investment projects in the presence of financial market failure. By correcting market failure problems, financial repression helped Taiwan to improve the efficiency of its financial system and to increase economic growth. McKinnon (1993) commented on the success of Taiwanese financial repression, stating that a high real interest rate is the key to improve the efficiency of capital markets. However, it was also the stability of price levels that kept Taiwan from any major financial collapse and hence promoted Taiwan's financial development and output growth.

14.4.2   Financial Modernisation Process 1980s–1990s

In the late 1970s, the authorities gradually removed the controls on the financial market in order to enhance and strengthen Taiwan's financial system through competition to meet the trend of global financial liberalisation. The process of Taiwan's financial market modernisation was undertaken in an orderly and progressive manner from the 1980s. As far as the Ministry of Finance is concerned, this process covered two parts, namely, liberalisation and internationalisation.

14.4.2.1   Deregulation of Interest Rate and Foreign Exchange Rate

Liberalisation of Interest Rate. Before 1975, the interest rate was wholly determined by the Central Bank. All banks were either owned or partially owned by the government and had to accept the designed rate. As the banking system became more mature, direct control over the interest rate was no longer necessary. Therefore, since 1980, the Central Bank has adopted a series of measures to gradually remove the controls over the interest rate and the liberalisation of the interest rate was completed when the Banking Law was revised in July 1989. The upper and lower limits on all kinds of loan and deposit interest rates that had to be approved by the Central Bank were abolished and the banks are allowed to price their own interest rate. To date, the interest rate totally depends on the demand and supply of the market.

Liberalisation of Foreign Exchange Rate. From 1949 through 1978, the exchange rate of the New Taiwan dollar was pegged to the US dollar and controlled by the Central Bank to help Taiwan's trade deficit and foreign exchange shortage. In 1979, the foreign exchange system moved from a fixed rate system to a managed flexible rate system, while the Taipei foreign exchange market was also established in this year. Under this new system, banks and their customers were able to trade foreign exchange within a small range which was defined by the weighted average of the exchange rates on transactions among banks on the previous day. This was designed to prevent drastic fluctuations in the foreign exchange market.

During the 1980s, Taiwan's trade surplus increased substantially and foreign exchange was no longer a scare resource. In April 1989, a new exchange rate system on the basis of free negotiation with bank customers was put in place, as the government was confident enough to release the foreign exchange rate from its control. By 1990, the Central Bank allowed the exchange rate for all transactions to be determined by market forces.

Liberalisation of Capital Movement. Before 1978, capital movement was strictly controlled by the government. During the 1980s, the trade surplus started to increase and foreign exchange reserves began to accumulate. The government gradually removed capital control, such as removing the restrictions on trade-related capital transactions and the inward remittance of foreign exchange. However, both outward and inward direct investments were subjected to approval by the government and there was still a strict ceiling for non-traded-related outward remittance by local residents.

Until the late 1980s, rapid economic growth caused a huge increase in both the current account surplus and short-term capital inflow. The government took steps towards liberalisation but the capital account has not yet been fully deregulated in the sense that the amount of foreign investment permitted in the stock market is still restricted.

Liberalisation of the Establishment of Financial Institutions. Before the 1990s, 77% of banks were owned by the government (see Table 14.4) and undertook the responsibility for helping economic growth. In the central government, three large commercial banks played a significant role in promoting industrial development, and many local financial institutions assisted farmers and small businesses a great deal.

In 1991, the Private Bank Act was promulgated and 15 new private banks were established in the same year. For the past 10 years, the transformation of Taiwan's banks can be divided into three stages. Due to liberalisation, banks have tended to improve their competitive advantage in the market by setting up branches.

In the second stage, the profit of banks has decreased because of over-banking and over-competition. In addition, the standard of service required by the customers has become higher. Those banks that are not strong enough will be eliminated through this competition. State-owned banks were forced to privatise and restructure (see Table 14.4). In the third stage, over-banking led to a worsening of performance that forced banks to integrate with other financial institutions.

14.4.2.2 Deregulation of Securities Market

The deregulation of the securities market started in 1988 when the securities and exchange law were revised to lift the restrictions on the establishment of new

Table 14.4 Change in the number of stated owned banks and private banks

	Number of banks Before 1991	Number of banks By the end of 2003
State-owned	13	8
Banks owned by central government	4	4
Banks owned by provincial government	7	3
Banks owned by municipal government	2	1
Private banks	4	42
Total	17	50

Source: Directorate-General of Budget, Accounting, and Statistics

securities companies. The number of securities companies rose dramatically from 28 in 1988 to 381 at the end of 1990. In the following year, over-the-counter trades were embarked upon. Furthermore, permission was granted to domestic companies to issue equity abroad in 1991. The government also made a great effort to open up the stock market for foreign investors and thus the participation of foreign investors in Taiwan's market was allowed to increase gradually. Such a slow increase led to Taiwan's domestic market not completely separating from the global financial market. It is also this conservative liberalisation policy and partial deregulation of capital movement that allowed Taiwan's economy to be secure from the speculative attacks of the foreign hedge and mutual funds.

14.4.2.3   Internationalisation of Financial Institutions

During the past decade, some concrete measures have been undertaken by the government to promote financial internationalisation; for example, the establishment of an institutional framework for offshore banking business and the encouragement of both public and private local banks to establish branches overseas. On the other hand, restrictions were also relaxed and foreign banks were given incentives to establish branches in Taiwan. By 2004, 16 Taiwanese banks had set up a total of 80 branches overseas and 35 foreign banks had established 67 branches in Taiwan.

14.5   Pressures for Financial Reform

14.5.1   External Pressures

Since the East Asian financial crisis began in Thailand on July 2, 1997, none of the countries in the region have been able completely to avoid its impact. At the end of 1998, the Asia Financial Crisis began to influence the economy of Taiwan, with the banking sector among the first to be affected. The added weight of a global economic downturn made things even worse for domestic enterprises and left asset quality deteriorating.

14.5.2   Internal Pressures

14.5.2.1   The Quality of Banks' Assets

After the Bank Privatisation Law was enacted in 1991, the excessive number of new entrants and the rapid expansion of existing institutions led to the deterioration of their operational environment. The number of head offices of domestic banks increased from 16 before 1991 to 50 in the end of 2003 and the number of their

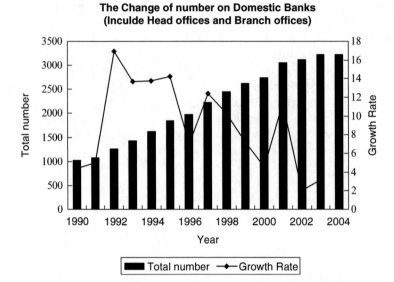

Fig. 14.1 The change of number on domestic banks (include Head offices and Branch offices)
Source: Directorate General of Budget, Accounting, and Statistics

branch offices displayed about a fourfold growth (see Fig. 14.1). Taiwan, a nation of 23 million people, is crowded with 52 domestic banks, 36 foreign banks and more than 300 other types of financial institutions. Cutthroat competition has led to deterioration in the profitability of banks and the quality of their assets.

In addition, the capital liquidity of Taiwan's financial institutions is going down because there has been an undue reliance on real estate and stock as collaterals for banks loans. Therefore, when the real estate and stock market experience a downturn, the banks have to liquidate the collateral and thus drive both markets further downward. During the past few years, Taiwan has experienced two economic downturns: one started in 1998 and the other one in the fourth quarter of 2000, and both caused a depression in real estate and stock market. This became a vicious cycle which led not only to an increase in the non-performing loan ratio but also to bank capital being frozen in, which caused difficulties for some financial institutions.

As a result of this, Taiwan's overall non-performing loan ratio for domestic financial institutions climbed from 2.85% at the end of 1995 to a record high of 7.48% at the end of 2002, an increase of NT$351.5 billion to $1.4 trillion (US$10.2 billion to $40.7 billion) in bad debt (see Fig. 14.2). Among the worst offenders were the grass-roots banking organisations, which had an NPL ratio registering at 18.5% in June 2001. Both the return on assets (ROA) and return on equities (ROE) declined from 7.99% and 0.59% in 1998 to −5.11% and −0.49 in 2002, respectively. At the same time, the capital adequacy ratio decreased and the net profit margin worsened (see Fig. 14.3).

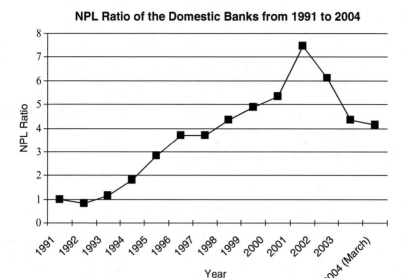

Fig. 14.2 NPL ratio of the domestic banks from 1991 to 2004
Source: Central Bank of China, Taiwan

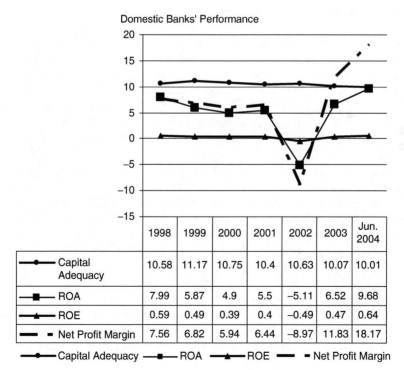

	1998	1999	2000	2001	2002	2003	Jun. 2004
Capital Adequacy	10.58	11.17	10.75	10.4	10.63	10.07	10.01
ROA	7.99	5.87	4.9	5.5	−5.11	6.52	9.68
ROE	0.59	0.49	0.39	0.4	−0.49	0.47	0.64
Net Profit Margin	7.56	6.82	5.94	6.44	−8.97	11.83	18.17

Fig. 14.3 Domestic banks' performance
Source: Central Bank of China, Taiwan

14.5.2.2 The Rotation of Political Parties

From 1949 to 2000, Taiwan remained under the governance of one party, the Chinese Nationalist Party (KMT, KuoMingTang). During this period, banks were often used as political machines and the collusion between political and financial business has always been an issue. Due to political intervention, some inappropriate missions were imposed on banks, especially those that were state owned. In 2001, Chen Shue-Bian of the Democratic Progressive Party (DPP) was elected president, ending 50 years of KMT rule. Some hidden problems, such as non-performing loans, over political lending and bad debts then surfaced.

14.5.2.3 Lack of Comprehensive Regulatory Framework

The lack of a comprehensive regulatory framework and efficient financial examination to meet the trend of financial consolidation and the rapid development of bigger, full service, global financial corporations was another reason to push financial reform in Taiwan.

14.5.2.4 The Pressure of WTO Entry

Taiwan finally joined the World Trade Organisation (WTO) in 2001: financial institutions will consequently encounter increased competition and threats from their counterparts abroad. This has also raised the issue of cross-strait financial affairs, as both China and Taiwan joined the WTO in 2001 and will have to fulfil WTO commitments, such as the most-favoured-nation (MFN) treatment and non-discriminatory principles. This means that both Taiwan and China will have to progressively remove the cross-strait restrictions set up between them over the past 30 years due to political barriers.

In addition, cross-strait economic trade has become an irresistible trend as Taiwanese investors have poured US$60 billion of investment into more than 40,000 businesses on the mainland. However, they are facing difficulties regarding cross-strait financial transactions; for example, the investors had to make remittances and account settlements through third parties, mostly banks in Hong Kong or the United States. This also drove financial reform in Taiwan for developing efficient cross-strait financial access.

Indeed, the drastic changes in the domestic and international financial environment have brought severe challenges to Taiwan's financial institutions. In order to help these institutions cope with the adverse impact, the government has endeavoured to expand the scope of their businesses on the one hand, and to carry out financial reforms to solve the root cause of financial problems on the other.

14.6   Financial Reform since 2001

Due to these pressures, the government was determined and committed to restructure Taiwan's financial industry so as to match up with those of more advanced countries. Many important financial laws and regulations were enacted or amended from November 2000 onwards to create a solid foundation for the reform. These laws include the Six Financial Regulations – 'Enacting Statute for the Establishment and Administration of the Financial Reconstructing Fund of the Executive Yuan', 'reversing the Deposit Insurance Act', 'reversing the Business Tax Law', 'enacting the Financial Holding Company Law', 'enacting the Law Governing Bills Finance Business', 'reversing Insurance Law' – revisions to the Banking Law, the Financial Institutions Merger Law and so on. As the Six Financial Regulations that are considered to be the most important rules for financial reform became effective in 2001, this year was announced by the government as the first year of Taiwan's financial reform.

Under the blueprint of the relevant laws and regulations concerning financial reform, the Executive Yuan set up a Financial Reform Task Force in July 2002. The Task Force has five sub-committees, each of which is responsible for the reform of banking, insurance, the capital market, community financial institutions and combating financial crime, respectively. The aim of the financial reform is to make financial institutions stronger and healthier through expansion by mergers and acquisitions, universal banking and globalisation, thereby enhancing their international competitiveness.

14.6.1   Encourage Mergers and Acquisitions

In line with raising the efficiency and economic scale of Taiwan's financial institutions, the Financial Institutions Merger Law and Financial Holding Company Act offer both tax and non-tax incentives to encourage voluntary mergers among financial institutions. At the same time, those small-scale financial institutions such as farmers' and fishermen's associations are strongly encouraged to upgrade from a cooperative structure to one limited by shares so as to merge with other financial institutions through favourable tax laws.

Furthermore, the enactment of the Financial Holding Company Act allows banks, insurers and brokerage clusters to operate under a single corporate structure and hence facilitate a holding company to enlarge its business scale, increase its volume of customers, diversify its service, disperse its risk and reduce its operation cost. In this way, the international competitiveness and profitability of Taiwan's financial industry is expected to increase through an economy of scale, multifaceted marketing and cost saving. The Financial Institutions Merger Law also provides an appropriate market exit mechanism with legal grounds to break through the barriers of resolving the problem of insolvent community financial institutions.

Since the Financial Holding Company Act was enacted in 2001, 14 financial holding companies have been added and different financial institutions have merged with each other or formulated financial holding companies. During the past 3 years, they have completed mergers and acquisitions with 68 financial institutions, with 51 of the transactions taking place between banking institutions.

14.6.2   Enhance the Quality of the Assets

14.6.2.1   Deal with Non-Performing Loans (NPL)

In line with dealing with the bad debts of financial institutions, revision of the Business Tax Law reduced the value-added tax (VAT) for the financial sector from 2% to 0%o to help with the reduction of financial institutions' bad debts.

According to the Financial Institutions Merger Law, asset management companies (AMC) are to be set up to facilitate the process of handling the bad debts and associated collateral of financial institutions. Accordingly, the government has suggested to all members of the Taiwan Banks Association to formally establish an asset management company to help deal with banks' non-performing assets or collateral securities. The Taiwan Banks Association responded to the government's policy by inviting 30 banks and 3 bill finance companies to set up Taiwan's first asset management company in November 2001, named Taiwan's Asset Management Corporation (TAMCO).

At the same time, a NT$140 billion (US$4 billion) Financial Reconstruction Fund was set up by the government in 2001, aimed at cleaning up the bad loans troubling the grass roots financial organisations within three years. The government entrusted The Central Deposit Insurance Corporation (CDIC) to take charge of the Financial Restructuring Fund's Management Committee. This committee is responsible for deliberating the use and operation of the fund and also providing public disclosure in relation to the fund.

From 2002 to 2003, domestic banks wrote off NT$650.7 billions (US$18.98 billions) and by May 2003, asset management companies had purchased bad assets worth around NT$161.2 billion (US$4.7 billion) from domestic banks. Compared with the peak amount of non-performing loans of NT$1,147.6 billions in March 2002, the total amount had reduced by NT$517 billions to NT$ 630.6 billions by the end of 2003. The NPL ratio also steadily backed down from a peak of 8.04% in March 2002 to 6.12% at the end of the year. It steadily reduced from 5% in 2003 to 4.45% in April 2004.

14.6.2.2   Financial Asset Securitisation

In line with promoting the securitisation of a bank's assets to increase its capital liquidity, the 'Financial Asset Securitisation Act' and the 'Real Estate Securitisation Act' were enacted on July 24, 2002 and July 23, 2003 respectively. According to these Acts, assets with predictable cash flows such as housing loans, business loans and automobile loans, rights under credit cards, account receivables and real estate are allowed to be securitised.

In this way, the banks will be able to utilise their long-term collateral more efficiently with the high turnover rates of funds and hence enhance the banks' capital liquidity. By the end of 2003, six issuances of such securities had been approved, including the first overseas issuance, totalling NT$37.6 billion or about US$1.1billion.

14.6.3   Financial Supervisory Reform and Increased Transparency

In line with the integration trend in the financial markets, financial management should be function-oriented, not institution-oriented. In July 2003, the 'Organic Act of the Financial Supervisory Commission, Executive Yu' was promulgated to serve as the guidelines for consolidating financial supervision in a single agency. According to this Act, the Financial Supervisory Commission, Executive Yuan (FSC) was set up in July 2004. It promotes uniformity in the supervision of financial institutions and thus can eliminate the blind spots that occur in separate examinations of function. Moreover, the Financial Supervisory Commission (FSC) is independent of the Ministry of Finance and directly under the Executive Yuan. It can therefore exercise its powers independently, which not only avoids various organisations trying to benefit from the financial policy but also combats the collusion between political and financial business.

In addition, The Ministry of Finance's regulatory philosophy is shifting from merit-based regulation to disclosure-based regulation. According to the newly-amended Banking Law, all publicly listed banks are required to use their web site to make quarterly disclosures of their Certified Public Accountants CPA – reviewed financial information. At the same time, the MOF is tightening the screws on banks to achieve greater transparency of their lending information and make statistics better reflect reality.

14.6.4   Encourage Foreign Capital Inflow to Invest in the Domestic Financial Market

The Qualified Foreign Institutional Investor (QFII) system was introduced to Taiwan in 1991 to act as a buffer to prevent rapid flows of currency in and out of the island. In line with Taiwan's internationalised capital market, regulations governing foreign investment were revised, in large part lifting restrictions formerly placed on foreign investors investing in the securities market. The longstanding Qualified Foreign Institutional Investor (or QFII) system was abolished on October 2, 2003, reducing application approvals to a one-step process, and simplifying other related procedures. Deregulation was aimed at lowering the operational costs for foreign investment and attracting foreign capital. At the same, it was hoped that it would stimulate Taiwan's economy and provides better international access for local companies and improve their competitiveness.

Due to the concerted efforts of the government, there have been some promising preliminary results of this implementation. By the end of 2003, net inflow of foreign investment reached US$66.4 billion, reflecting a substantial increase of nearly US$23½ billion over the year before. The shareholdings of foreign investment have represented around 15% of the total market capitalisation of Taiwan's stock market.

14.6.5 Create a Flexible Mechanism for Cross-Strait Financial Transactions

Since 2001, a series of amendments were made to the 'Guidelines for Conducting Remittance to Mainland China by Financial Institutions in the Taiwan District' and 'Guidelines for Conducting Foreign Exchange Businesses relating to Export and Import from Mainland China by Banks in the Taiwan District'. In June 2001, the government permitted the establishment of mainland representative offices by Taiwan banks. However, the banks that establish representative offices will only be able to collect business information and provide consulting services; they will not be able to handle deposit and loan operations.

Later, in November 2001, the government announced the authorisation of direct cross-strait remittances by offshore banking units (OBUs), with the scope of the business including the remittance of deposits, the remittance of funds, and trade financing, meaning that funds no longer have to be transferred through banks in a third country. In this way, the island's residents will be able to save between 20% and 30% in service fees when they remit money to the mainland, and the remittance time will be cut by half. In August 2002, the government moved further to allow the overseas branches and offshore banking units (OBUs) of banks in the Taiwan District to provide credits to and to purchase accounts receivables from Taiwanese businessmen on the mainland.

Since 2002, seven representative offices of Taiwan banks were permitted to be established in Shanghai Mainland China, as well as 17 securities firms, seven insurers and one insurance brokering company. From January to May 2004, the total amount of cross-strait financial transactions has been pushed to NT$42 billions.

14.7 Conclusion

For the past 50 years, Taiwan has experienced massive financial development, from a controlled system to a capitalised market system. Several external and internal challenges occurred during the liberalisation process and hence pushed the government to undertake the financial reform in 2001. For the past 3 years, some improvements have started to become apparent, but the speed of the reform is rather slow.

This paper concludes with few things to bear in mind for further financial reform in Taiwan.

After 3 years of effort, the average NPL ratio for domestic banks has been pushed down to a tolerable level of just over 3.5%. However, reducing the NPL ratio and easing the burden of non-performing collateral assets is only one aspect of financial reform. The longer-range and more fundamental objective is the effective enhancement of the competitiveness of Taiwan banks in both domestic and global markets.

From the angle of competitiveness, the basic problem is the proliferation of too many economically small-scale banks. Taiwan has the most fragmented banking market in East Asia and even the market share accounted for by 'large' Taiwanese banks is not great. Until 2004, none of the subsidiary banking units of the nation's 14 financial holding companies had a market share above 10%; their degree of international competitiveness remains inadequate. Moreover, the three biggest banks – the Bank of Taiwan, the Taiwan Cooperative Bank and the Land Bank of Taiwan – of the nation's 51 banks had a combined market share of 26%. This figure is much lower than in other Asian countries. Therefore, the local banking sector should continue to consolidate.

However, even though mergers and acquisitions can benefit financial institutions with economies of scale, they will not necessarily work for their efficiency of operation and profitability. For instance, a diversified financial service is required by the customers for a well-presented financial company. However, Taiwan's financial institutions lack an innovation culture and employees who are good at financial innovation. In addition, some measures which the Taiwanese government adopted for financial reform are from Western countries.

These regulations, which work in other countries, might not necessarily work in Taiwan due to cultural differences. For example, the Credit Department of the Farmer's Associations and the Credit Department of the Fishermen's Associations, as the most grass-roots financial institutions, even now play an important role for the small groups of farming and fishing populations. However, the trend for large-scale, internationalised, diversified financial services makes it difficult for these grass-roots financial institutions to survive. In the process of financial consolidation, the government should also take minority groups' welfare into consideration, and not only aim to improve efficiency but also to do it with justice.

In addition, high non-performing loans are considered to be the most serious problem in Taiwan's financial institutions and, as mentioned earlier, in Taiwan's case, movement in the real-estate market and stock market have a great impact on non-performing loans. Therefore, it is necessary to carry out industrial policy along with financial reform in order to strengthen these two markets and boost Taiwan's economy. In this way, the root of the problem associated with non-performing loans is more likely to be solved.

Finally, a stable political environment will be vital for the performance of further financial reform. Since the presidential election in March 2004, there has been political deadlock between Kuomintang and the Democratic Progressive Party. However, at a time when many rival economies are rapidly improving their attractiveness to foreign investors, political deadlock or a lack of attention to economic exigencies are luxuries that Taiwan can hardly afford. Both parties should appreciate how vital it is for Taiwan to push forward with further financial reform and, for the good of Taiwan's prosperity and economic security, partisan infighting should not be allowed to interfere with its implementation.

References

Anon (2002) Cross-Strait direct remittance. *Dajiyan Newspaper*, 15 February. In Chinese [online] Available from: http://www.epochtimes.com/b5/2/2/15/n170667.htm

Anon (2003) MOF to take new measures to attract foreign capital. *Taiwan Headlines*, 25 August. [online] Available from: http://www.taiwanheadlines.gov.tw/20030825/20030825b5.html

Bureau of Monetary Affairs, Financial Supervisory Commission, Executive Yuan, Republic of China (2003a) *The Modernisation of ROC Financial system*. [online] Available from: http://www.boma.gov.tw/modules/ensection/article.php?articleid = 102

Bureau of Monetary Affairs, Financial Supervisory Commission, Executive Yuan, Republic of China (2003b) *The Financial system in ROC*. [online] Available from: http://www.boma.gov.tw/modules/ensection/article.php?articleid = 103

Bureau of Monetary Affairs, Financial Supervisory Commission, Executive Yuan, Republic of China (2003c) *Recent Financial Reform in Chinese Taipei*. [online] Available from: http://www.boma.gov.tw/modules/ensection/index.php?category = 31

Bureau of Monetary Affairs, Financial Supervisory Commission, Executive Yuan, Republic of China (2003d) *The Report of Financial Reform in R.O.C.* In Chinese [online] Available from: http://www.boma.gov.tw/modules/basection/index.php?category = 114

Bureau of Monetary Affairs, Financial Supervisory Commission, Executive Yuan, Republic of China (2004a) *Overview of Banking Sector*. [online] Available from: http://www.boma.gov.tw/modules/ensection/index.php?category = 26

Bureau of Monetary Affairs, Financial Supervisory Commission, Executive Yuan, Republic of China (2004b) *Annual Report 2003*. [online] Available from: http://www.boma.gov.tw/modules/ensection/article.php?articleid = 154

Central Bank of China, Republic of China (2004) *Condition and Performance of Domestic Banks*. [online] Available from: http://www.cbc.gov.tw/EngHome/publications.asp

Central Deposit Insurance Cooperation, Taiwan, R.O.C (2004) *The Executive Yuan's Financial Restructuring Fund*. [online] Available from: http://www.cdic.gov.tw/eng/rtc_e.jsp

Chan, V. L. and Hu, S. C. (2002) Financial Liberalisation in Taiwan. *Review of Pacific Basin Financial Markets and Policies*, Vol.3, No. 3

Directorate-General of Budget Accounting and Statistics Executive Yuan, Republic of China (2004) *Statistical Yearbook of the Republic of China 2004*. Taipei: The Chinese Statistical Association

European Central Bank (2002): *The Eurosystem's dialogue with EU accession countries*. In: Monthly Bulletin, July Government Information office, Republic of China (2004) *Taiwan Yearbook 2004*. [online] Available from: http://www.gio.gov.tw/taiwan-website/5-gp/yearbook/P155.htm

The International Commercial Bank of China, Economic Review (2001) *Central Banking Policies in Taiwan*. Taipei, (No. 319)

The International Commercial Bank of China, Economic Review (2001) *Challenges of Financial Reforms*. Taipei, (No. 320)

Mckinnon, R. (1993) *The Order of Economic Liberalization: Financial Control in the Transition to a Market Economy*, 2nd ed. Baltimore: Johns Hopkins University Press

National Policy Foundation, R.O.C. (2001a) *Financial Supervisory and Financial Reform*. In Chinese [online] Available from: http://www.npf.org.tw/English/Publication/FM/FM-R-090-059.htm

National Policy Foundation, R.O.C. (2001b) *How could Taiwan have been insulated from the 1997 Financial Crisis*. [online] Available from: http://www.npf.org.tw/English/Publication/FM/FM-R-090-043.htm

National Policy Foundation, R.O.C. (2003) *The Role of Financial Development in Economic Growth: The Experiences of Taiwan, Korea, and Singapore*. [online] Available from: http://www.npf.org.tw/PUBLICATION/FM/092/FM-R-092-001.htm

National Policy Foundation, R.O.C. (2004a) *Six Financial Regulations and Financial Reform*. In Chinese [online] Available from: http://www.npf.org.tw/PUBLICATION/FM/090/FM-R-090-060.htm

National Policy Foundation, R.O.C. (2004b) *The Establishment of Financial Restructuring Fund*. In Chinese [online] Available from: http://www.npf.org.tw/PUBLICATION/FM/090/FM-R-090-034.htm

Shea, J. D. (1994) Taiwan: Development and Structural Change of the Financial System. In *Financial Development of Japan, Korea, and Taiwan: Growth, Repression, and Liberalization*, edited by Hugh T. Patrick and Yung Chul Park. New York: Oxford University Press

Shea, J. D., Kuo, P. S. and Huang, C. T. (1995) The Share of Informal Financing of Private Enterprises. *Academia Economic Papers*, 23: 265–297

The Bankers Association of the Republic of China (2004) *Financial Development*. [online] Available from: http://www.ba.org.tw/english04.asp

Wade, R. (1985) East Asian Financial Systems as a Challenge to Economics: Lessons from Taiwan. *California Management Review*, 27: 106–129

Wang, J. F. (2001) *Development and Innovation of Taiwan Banking Industry at Current Predicament*. Kaohsiung: Liu Kuai Chih Foundation

Wieman, E. (2002) Promote Cross-Strait Financial Relation Through Vigorous, translated from the Chinese Language Economic Daily, 5 March [online] Available from: http://sir.cyivs.cy.edu.tw/~hchung/promotefinance.htm

Yang, Y. H. (1994) Taiwan: Development and Structural Change of the Banking System. In *Financial Development of Japan, Korea, and Taiwan: Growth, Repression, and Liberalization*, edited by Hugh T. Patrick and Yung Chul Park. New York: Oxford University Press

Yu, T. S. (1999) The evolution of commercial banking and financial markets in Taiwan. *Journal of Asian Economics*, Vol.10, pp.291–307

Part II
Accounting Education

Chapter 15
Reforming Accounting Education in a Transition Economy: A Case Study of Armenia

Robert W. McGee

15.1 Introduction

Armenia was one of the first countries to join the Soviet Union after the communist revolution of 1917. Historically, Armenia had been on friendly terms with Russia, which furnished Armenia with military protection up through the 19th century (Bournoutian, 2001; Sunny, 1993). As a Christian country, it was often in danger of invasion by the Turks, who tried to kill the population or convert them to Islam. Such a massacre actually occurred in 1915, which resulted in the deaths of a substantial portion of the Armenian population (Miller and Miller, 1999; Melson et al., 1992; Graber, 1996; Hovannisian, 1986; Dadrian, 1995), with many more fleeing to other countries. Interestingly enough, one of the young girls who was taken prisoner and sold into slavery to a Bedouin later found sanctuary with a young accountant (Derdarian, 1998). After the breakup of the Soviet Union, Armenia went to war with Azerbaijan, another former Soviet republic over Karabagh, an Armenian enclave located within the borders of Azerbaijan (Walker, 1991). It is now struggling to convert its accounting and legal systems into a Western, market model (World Bank, 2002; Libaridian, 1999).

It is probably fair to say that there are now more Armenians living outside of Armenia than within. Many of them settled in Beirut, Venice, Jerusalem, California, France, and Australia, although there are Armenian communities in many other countries as well (Marsden, 1993). Mount Ararat, where the remains of Noah's Ark is supposed to have been found, used to be in Armenia, but is now in Turkey as the result of a change in borders after the Turk invasion.

While the fact that so many Armenians had to leave their own country is sad, in a way it also provides Armenia with some economic advantages that some of the other former Soviet republics do not have, because a large percentage of the Armenian ex-pat community is engaged in business in whatever country they are living in. They have accumulated capital, and some Armenian business people are favorably inclined to invest in their former homeland, partly out of a sense of patriotism or ethnic pride more

R. W. McGee
Florida International University

R. W. McGee (ed.), *Accounting Reform in Transition and Developing Economies,*
© Springer Science + Business Media LLC 2008

than potential profit. Also, because the ex-pat community has relatives in Armenia, they have a network of contacts, which makes it easier to establish business ties.

That is especially important in a country like Armenia, which does not yet have a strong rule of law. It is a well-known fact of international business that personal contacts are invaluable in countries that do not have a strong rule of law, so the fact that there are such unofficial networks connecting Armenia to sources of foreign capital is extremely important. However, the Armenian ex-pat community has limited capital for investment in Armenia, and patriotism goes only so far when it affects the pocketbook. Armenia needs an infusion of more capital than can be provided by the ex-pat community alone. That is where accounting reform comes in. Once Armenia adopts a system of financial transparency, non-Armenian foreign investors will seriously consider it as a possible place to invest.

Armenia is a small country in the Caucasus. It is bordered by Georgia to the north, Iran to the south, Azerbaijan to the east, and Turkey to the west (Hewsen, 2001). It is in Asia geographically, although most Armenians insist that they are European. Its population is between 3 and 3.5 million, although it is impossible to say how many Armenians actually live in Armenia at any given time because so many of them emigrate for short or long periods to work in other countries.

The favorite destinations for Armenian workers are Russia and Ukraine, which are perceived to have more economic and job opportunities than Armenia. Also, since Armenians are fluent in the Russian language, it is easier for them to obtain employment in Russia and Ukraine, since Russian is spoken in both these countries.

Many Armenians would prefer to work outside the country, either temporarily or permanently because of the perception that there is no future for them in Armenia. Although they would prefer to work in Western Europe, the United States or Australia, it is difficult for them to obtain visas and working papers for these countries, so countries like Russia and Ukraine are really their fallback choices. One attraction that the United States Agency for International Development (USAID) accounting reform program offered was the possibility to obtain a credential that would make them marketable in more than 100 countries, which we shall discuss in more detail below. Many of the younger students saw the programs offered by USAID as a one-way ticket out of the country, which greatly increased demand for the programs.

When the Soviet Union broke up, Armenia declared its independence (Libaridian, 1991), but it retained the Russian administrative system, including its system of accounting. The Russian accounting system was, and is still highly centralized. The various Soviet republics got their chart of accounts from Moscow and they had to stick to it. What the Soviets called accounting, accountants who live in market economies would call bookkeeping. In fact, there was not even a word in the Armenian language for accountant in the Western sense of the term, a fact that sometimes caused translation problems.

There was no analysis of balance sheet or income statement ratios because they did not have any balance sheets or income statements. Mostly they had journal entries and some kind of statement that looked quite similar to a funds statement.

Cost accounting was nonexistent, which made it impossible to calculate costs or determine whether they were making a profit or loss. As a result, there was a massive misallocation of resources. In fact, at least one economist predicted as far back as the 1920s and 1930s that their lack of a cost accounting system would eventually lead to the demise of their system (Mises, 1990, 1981; Kirzner, 2001). Thus, there was a need to adopt an accounting and financial reporting system that would allow the former Soviet republics to participate and compete in the market economy after the collapse of the Soviet Union.

The United States Agency for International Development (USAID), the World Bank, EU-TACIS, and other organizations have established programs to assist economies in transition to make the necessary changes to their accounting systems. Some accounting reform programs started shortly after the fall of the Berlin Wall in 1989. After the Soviet Union collapsed, additional accounting reform programs were undertaken in various Eastern European countries and several former Soviet republics. Armenia was one such republic that received USAID assistance. This paper summarizes the phase of that program that aimed at upgrading accounting education to international standards.

One of the factors that attract foreign investment is financial transparency. Investors have to know what they are investing in, and that requires financial statements that are based on some kind of recognized accounting principles. There are various ways that a country can gain the confidence of foreign investors. It can adopt International Accounting Standards (IAS), since such standards are accepted in dozens of countries. It can adopt the system used in the United States, which is highly regarded throughout the world but is not used in nearly as many countries as is International Accounting Standards. Or it can adopt some other system that has a high recognition factor.

Adopting some kind of recognized accounting standards is only the first step. If companies start using some such standard and there are other impediments to investment, such as the lack of a rule of law, corruption or too many regulations, investors will bypass the country and invest where the investment climate is more to their liking.

15.2 Economic Freedom

Although Armenia has adopted International Accounting Standards, it is still not an extremely attractive place to invest (McGee, 1999a), although it is getting better. The *1999 Index of Economic Freedom* ranked it 106 out of 161 countries (Johnson et al., 1998), which means there were 105 countries that provided a better investment climate than Armenia. Its rank has improved markedly in recent years (perhaps because of accounting reform and the resulting transparency in financial reporting). The *2002 Index of Economic Freedom* ranked it 45 out of 161 countries, which placed it in a tie with France and Poland (O'Driscoll et al., 2001). It was ranked 32 as of 2007. It is possible to purchase an investment guide to Armenia

(International Business Publications, 2002), which is an encouraging sign, since it indicates there is now a market for such information.

Its overall score, which is a composite of a number of variables, has also been improving. On a scale of 0 to 100, where 100 is the most free, its scores according to the *Index of Economic Freedom* (2007) in recent years have been as follows:

1996 – 38.9
1997 – 43.0
1998 – 48.7
1999 – 55.7
2000 – 62.4
2001 – 65.7
2002 – 67.0
2003 – 67.0
2004 – 67.7
2005 – 67.7
2006 – 74.6
2007 – 69.4

Chart 15.1 illustrates the degree of improvement.

Chart 1 Freedom Score

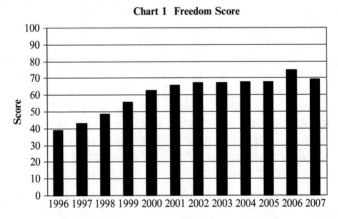

Chart 15.1   Freedom Score

That is a remarkable improvement, considering the limited human resources that Armenia has to work with. Until a few years ago, practically no one in Armenia had studied market economics to the same extent that students in Western Europe and the United States have. There were no texts in the Armenian language that students could refer to. Before the early 1990s, few people knew English. They studied Armenian and Russian.

After the fall of the Berlin Wall and the dissolution of the Soviet Union, a number of changes occurred. Students shifted their study efforts away from Russian and into English, so much so that, in some countries, a large percentage of Russian language instructors became unemployed. Another big change was that textbooks started becoming available in the local language, not so much in Armenian but in a number of other languages. However, Armenian students could use any text that was translated into Russian because they were fluent in Russian. Much of the credit for these translations can be attributed to George Soros and the various foundations he funds. The Soros Foundations poured a great deal of money into the translation of Western texts into the languages of Eastern Europe and the former Soviet Union. USAID did the same thing for accounting textbooks, as we shall discuss below.

15.3   The Impetus for Change

After the dissolution of the Soviet Union, the various Soviet republics retained their old Soviet accounting system, which consisted almost entirely of the chart of accounts that Russia had been using for the past 70 years. That system worked well enough for a centrally planned economy, at least as far as recordkeeping was concerned. However, the old Soviet system was not adequate for the other functions that a good accounting system must perform. Accounting should be used not only for recordkeeping but also for decision making, and the old Soviet system was not up to the task. Thus, there was an impetus for change. However, having an impetus for change is not always enough to actually make a change.

It is a general rule of any bureaucracy that the best way to do something is precisely the way it is presently being done. There is tremendous inertia against making change, especially when the system is not driven by the profit motive (Friedman and Friedman, 1984). Somehow, that inertia had to be overcome. In the case of accounting in former centrally planned economies, there are actually two inertias that must be overcome, the change to a new, market-oriented accounting system and a change in the education provided to future and existing accountants.

The Finance Ministry realized that Armenia would have to adopt some sort of modern, market-oriented accounting system. It briefly considered the French system, mostly because Armenia had historic ties with France, but adopted International Accounting Standards and International Standards on Auditing (ISA) because of the belief that these standards were more internationally recognized. The USAID accounting reform project helped the Finance Ministry adopt IAS and ISA, not only by paying for and supervising the translation of these documents into the Armenian language, but also by providing technical assistance and answering questions as they developed.

Adopting IAS and ISA triggered an instantaneous demand for a change in accounting education throughout the whole country, both in the universities and institutes and in the training of existing practitioners. When the new rules were adopted and made mandatory, they were adopted into law just a few months before accountants had to start using them. However, practically none of the practicing accountants and auditors in Armenia knew anything about IAS or ISA. Courses in these subjects were not part of the university curriculum and, until they were translated into Armenian, the standards were not available to the local accounting population. Armenian accountants and students were not even able to get a Russian translation of the standards because the people working on the Russian translation in Moscow had not yet completed their work. Thus, there was immediate and strong demand to learn the new rules that they would have to use, and limited opportunities for learning what they needed to know. In economic terms, one might say that the demand curve for accounting education had shifted swiftly and sharply to the right.

As is true whenever the demand curve shifts sharply to the right while supply remains constant (almost nonexistent in this case), the price of the product or service goes up. This fact created another problem because Armenian accountants and students were not able to pay the market price for the materials and training they needed. This problem was solved by having USAID subsidize accounting education throughout the country.

15.4 Accounting Education Under the Soviet System

Universities in the old Soviet system did not offer a degree in accounting. Accounting education consisted of a course or two that students took as part of their economics study. One course consisted basically of learning the chart of accounts and learning how to make journal entries. Another course consisted of some kind of auditing (Enthoven et al., 1998), although it is difficult for a Westerner to imagine what might be included in such a course, since there were no financial statements to audit. Footnotes and other disclosures did not exist in the old Soviet system.

Accounting education in Armenia was modeled on the Soviet system. The only innovation was that some of the textbooks had been translated into Armenian. Russian texts were used for some courses as well. After the USAID Accounting Reform Project came to Armenia, some minor changes were made to the Armenian chart of accounts, but most of the Soviet chart of accounts remained intact.

When one of the USAID consultants suggested to the Finance Ministry that the Soviet chart of accounts be scrapped and that each company be allowed to make its own chart of accounts, the Finance Ministry person at first thought that the USAID consultant was joking. To him, it was inconceivable that the Soviet chart of accounts could be replaced. When it was explained to him that American companies are completely free to make their own chart of accounts, and that companies in many other countries also have this freedom, he could not understand how it could be possible to make your own chart of accounts and still comply with International Accounting Standards. So the matter was dropped and USAID decided to assist Armenia convert to a market-oriented accounting system within the parameters that were feasible, which meant that the old Soviet chart of accounts would only be tweaked, not scrapped.

15.5 The USAID Approach to Accounting Education Reform

USAID's approach to accounting education reform was as comprehensive as possible, given the constraints that existed in the present system, including the inertia that had to somehow be overcome. There were also some cost constraints that had to be faced.

There were a number of different audiences or target markets that had to be educated. The immediate need was to educate existing accountants and auditors, since they would be the ones who had to work with and implement the new rules within a matter of months. This group consisted of both public accountants and auditors and also enterprise accountants. Tax inspectors also had to be educated at some point, since they would have to understand the new rules when they visited companies to perform their audits. Or at least that was USAID's opinion when it initiated accounting training.

As an adjunct to the accounting education phase of the USAID project, there was also a need to upgrade certification requirements to meet international standards. Another large part of the resources that USAID had available had to be devoted to the training of future accountants and auditors. That meant that at least some of the universities and institutes in Armenia had to adopt a completely new accounting curriculum.

When USAID agrees to go into a country to reform its accounting, economic, or legal system, it generally deals with people at the top – the prime minister, the finance minister, the justice ministry, etc. The agreement that is hammered out is hammered out at the highest levels of government. But implementation is done by the people who work at the third tier. In the case of the USAID Accounting Reform Project in Armenia, the person at the finance ministry who was in charge of seeing that the reforms were successful reported to the assistant finance minister. In other words, he was a third-tier employee of the finance ministry. No one consulted with him before the agreement was finalized. He had no input into the process until after the deal was made. Luckily for the project, and for Armenia in general, he fully supported the reform effort and the agreement that was entered into did not have any major flaws. However, such is not always the case.

Often, when USAID or some other government agency makes a deal with some government to reform something in the target country, the fact that people on the third level are not consulted can lead to major problems, especially if the people on tier one do not know what is going on below them, which is often the case if they are political appointees. Another reason why some reform projects fail is because the people who have to implement the reforms have something to lose if the reform is successful. Luckily, that was not the case here, but it has been the case in other reform projects in other countries.

15.6 The University Curriculum

There was general agreement that the accounting curriculum at the university level had to be drastically changed if future accountants and auditors were to be competently trained in market-oriented accounting. The question was how shall the reform be accomplished and where should the reform start? There were a number of different approaches that were considered in the early planning phase of the project, before the deal was finalized between USAID and the finance ministry. The present curriculum could be replaced with one that is modeled on the American system, with about ten accounting courses plus some other business courses in economics, management, etc. Another option was to implement a curriculum that followed international accounting standards. A third option was to adopt a syllabus that paralleled that used for the Canadian Certified General Accountant (CGA) designation.

One might think that the American model would have been chosen, since USAID is an American organization, part of the US State Department. But such was not the case. It was thought that Armenian accountants would benefit more if they learned international accounting standards and rules, since most of the countries they would be dealing with had adopted at least some of the international accounting rules. Whether the Canadian system should be adopted was debated briefly, since the Canadian system was adopted by some former Soviet republics in Central Asia. But the international approach was deemed to be the best in this case, mostly because its curriculum was more generally recognized on a worldwide basis.

One positive aspect of the international approach was that the course materials were readily available, although not in the local language. The Association of Chartered Certified Accountants (ACCA) is a British organization that provides certification testing at three different levels for accountants on a worldwide basis. At the time the accounting reform program started in Armenia, ACCA certification was recognized in 150 countries. That number has since increased to 160. With such widespread acceptability, it was easy to sell the program to the university administrators, especially after the finance ministry told them they had to accept the changes being suggested by USAID.

Another decision that had to be made was which universities and institutes should be approached first with the revised curriculum, because not all institutions that offered accounting programs could be approached at the same time. The private consulting firm that won the USAID Accounting Reform contract had only one ex-pat assigned for reforming the university curriculum, so decisions had to be made about how the curriculum reform would spread throughout the country.

The USAID Accounting Reform Project was headquartered in Yerevan, the capital of Armenia, and there were several institutions that offered accounting training, so the initial decision was made to start by contacting the largest institutions in Yerevan, which also happened to be the largest institutions in the country. One institution was generally considered to be number one, because most of the country's finance ministers had graduated from there, so that was the first institution targeted for the new program.

Once the word got out that the premier institution for accounting education in Armenia was going to replace its existing curriculum with the help of USAID, there was no need to contact the other institutions. They contacted USAID and asked for assistance in reforming their accounting curriculums as well. Their eagerness to adopt the new curriculum was not so much because they were concerned for the quality of the education their students were receiving, but because of the perception that if they did not adopt the new curriculum, they would not have any accounting students in a few years. Their decision was mostly or perhaps completely based on competitive forces. The fact that the transformation could be made at absolutely no cost to them did not hurt either, since USAID was subsidizing the whole program.

The new curriculum consisted of adopting the ACCA syllabus in toto. That curriculum consisted of 14 courses, most of which were accounting but some of which were other business-related courses. It was thought that adopting the ACCA syllabus would kill two birds with one stone, since not only would the accounting curriculum meet international standards, but also the students would be well on their way toward passing the national certification exams, which would also be based on the ACCA syllabus. Those students who were fluent in English would also have the opportunity to take the ACCA exams, which were offered only in English, so some segment of the student population would qualify for a certification that was internationally recognized. More information on the new certification requirements is given below.

Once the decision to adopt the ACCA syllabus was made, the choice of which texts to translate had to be decided. Several publishing companies publish texts to prepare students for the ACCA exams. The two choices given the most consideration were Foulkes Lynch and BPP Publishing, both British companies. Foulkes Lynch was chosen because it was the official supplier of texts for ACCA and because the person who made the decision thought that the Foulkes Lynch books were marginally better in quality than the BPP texts. Interestingly enough, that same person chose to use the BPP books for the USAID Accounting Reform Project in Bosnia shortly thereafter.

The texts published by both companies are quite similar in terms of layout and content. The texts are designed to prepare students for the ACCA exams and cover the ACCA syllabus completely. It might also be mentioned that the ACCA syllabus complies with International Federation of Accountants (IFAC) and United Nations Conference on Trade and Development (UNCTAD) guidelines. There are two texts for each exam. One book consists of textual materials with plenty of examples. The other book, somewhat smaller, consists of prior examination questions and answers. Those who are familiar with the Gleim and Wiley books that are used to prepare American students for the CPA, CMA, and other professional certification exams would find much in common with these texts, although there are practically no multiple choice questions.

After the texts were chosen, the next step was to determine which language they should be translated into, since many of the students were not sufficiently fluent in English to use the English language versions, and even if they were fluent enough, some of their professors were not. One might think that such a decision would be easy, since the program was being implemented in Armenia, where Armenian is spoken. However, Armenian was not the language chosen, which caused a bit of a problem.

Russian was selected because the Armenians were also fluent in Russian and because USAID did not want to pay to have the texts translated into more than one language. There were other USAID accounting reform projects going on in several other countries where Russian was one of the languages spoken, and USAID wanted to use the books in several of these other former Soviet republics. It did not want to have to translate them into Georgian, Azeri, Kazak, etc. and it felt that there was no need to do so. This decision upset some of the Armenians in both the finance ministry and universities as well as in the local accounting association, but they did not complain too loudly because the books they were getting were practically free. Besides, they did not have the resources to do their own translations into Armenian even after they had the Russian version to refer to.

The next step was to assemble a translation team to do the translations. That task might not seem difficult. One might just go to the local yellow pages of the telephone directory or call the local Berlitz for names. If that failed, surely there were people in the local universities who could do the job. Unfortunately, that approach did not work. The people needed for the task had to be fluent in both English and Russian and should also be familiar with accounting terminology. It was impossible to find individuals who met all of those qualifications. Not even the university professors were familiar with the accounting terminology. Furthermore, the Russian language did not even have terms for some of the concepts that had to be translated.

The solution was found by trial and error. Positions for translators were advertised in all the obvious places, translators were interviewed, and those who passed the first hurdle were given a short assignment, which they were paid to translate no matter how bad the final product was. If they did a good job, they were given more and longer assignments. Those who did not do a good job were not called in for further assignments. After a few months, the best individuals were identified and given more permanent offers of employment. There was a core staff that worked full-time on company premises. They were supplemented by a cadre of part-timers who completed the work whenever and wherever they could.

The core staff consisted of physicists, geologists, English literature majors, and a few people who had an economics background. Since they were unfamiliar with the terminology, they asked one of the ex-pats, who was also a certified public accountant, to explain what the term meant. Then the translators had discussions among themselves to decide how they would translate this term that had no Russian equivalent.

There were some coordination problems, especially in the early stages, since each translator seemed to use different words to express the same thought. This created problems for the editor, who had to go through each translation meticulously and try to conform the different vocabularies and styles to be more uniform. In the early stages, it took the editor as much time to edit the work as it would have taken for him to translate the material from scratch. A partial solution was found by creating a glossary of terms, which expanded on a daily basis at first. This glossary was distributed to both the full-time and part-time staff. As new terms were added, new versions were distributed.

The same trial and error method that was used to select the full-time translators was used to select the part-timers. But in the case of the part-timers, another complication set in. If there were too many part-timers turning in materials, the editor was not able to coordinate the submissions. He had his own work to do in addition to coordinating and merging the translations that the part-timers were doing, and if the project had more than about six part-timers submitting manuscripts, the system broke down. The solution, which was arrived at only after several breakdowns occurred, was to cut back on the number of part-timers by retaining only the best ones.

There was another problem that developed with the translation portion of the project. Although the texts were (nearly) all translated into Russian, some materials, such as the International Accounting Standards and International Standards on Auditing, had to be translated into Armenian, because those documents were to be used by the finance ministry and practicing accountants and had to go through Parliament. Also, there was somewhat of a nationalist sentiment that had to be reckoned with. USAID could get away with translating textbooks into Russian, but not documents that would be enacted into law.

So another group of translators had to be found who could translate from English into Armenian. One might think that the same group of translators who were translating books into Russian could be used for this task, but such was not the case. Although they were all fluent in Armenian as well as Russian, some of them were not sufficiently fluent to translate technical accounting materials into Armenian (for which there were no terms in any event).

During the Soviet era, Armenia had two different school systems. Some schools taught primarily in Armenian and also taught enough Russian so that the students could be fluent in Russian as well. Other schools taught mostly in Russian, and taught enough Armenian so that the students could function in that language, too. The Russian schools were considered to be the better choice to send children to, since the language needed for advancement within the system was Russian. As a result, many Armenians, although fluent in the Armenian language, were better in Russian.

Fortunately, the project was eventually able to find individuals who could translate the standards into Armenian to the satisfaction of the finance ministry. One of the translators, the one who translated most of the International Standards on Auditing, was also an auditor. He was later retained to teach the auditing course, the text for which was in Russian.

As the translations for the first-year texts were nearing completion, some decisions had to be made about how to introduce the new courses into the system. Although the universities had agreed to accept and implement the new syllabus, none of the professors were qualified to teach the courses. There was no such thing as cost accounting in the old Soviet system, and there was not much financial accounting either. Even the professors who had been educated in Moscow did not get any exposure to Western style accounting. Something had to be done to bring at least a few of the professors up to speed.

Two remedies were implemented. The first stage consisted of giving a pilot course in financial accounting to professors and practicing accountants. This course was held in the training facility of the Armenian Association of Accountants and Auditors (AAAA). The fees for practicing accountants were subsidized, since they could not afford the course otherwise. Tuition fee of $100 was charged, which is a lot of money in a country where a family of four can be raised for $80 a month. Professors could take this initial course for free.

The only person who could teach this initial course was the American CPA who was working with the USAID contractor firm, but he could not speak Armenian. So an interpreter was hired to assist. He lectured in English. The interpreter translated into Armenian. The textbooks the students used were in Russian. So the translator had to know both the Russian and Armenian terms. Using an interpreter slowed everything down by 50%, but there was no alternative.

At the end of the course, participants were given a written examination. Those who had the highest scores were offered jobs as part-time instructors. Luckily, some of the professors who took the course also received some of the highest grades. This pilot course, which also served as a train the trainer course, had to be given in an accelerated format, since practically all of Armenia wanted to take these new courses and trainers were desperately needed to conduct the courses.

After some trainers had been selected to teach the first course, a second course, on management accounting was offered. The same process was used for that course. The American CPA did not have to teach the auditing course, which came later in the sequence, because the Armenian auditor who translated the International Standards on Auditing into Armenian was able to teach that course. However, a problem developed as soon as he stepped into the classroom. A large percentage of the class did not want him to be their instructor. There was a widespread perception that the foreigner – the American CPA – would do a better job. But the American did not want to teach the course and was not available in any event because he had to coordinate a large chunk of the accounting reform project in addition to teaching multiple sections of the lower level courses.

The Armenian auditor was a good choice for several reasons. For one thing, he knew all the terms in both Russian and Armenian. He was one of the few people in the whole country who had read the International Standards on Auditing in any language, since the ISA had not yet been published and distributed to the Armenian auditing community. And since he could speak Armenian, there would be no need for an interpreter, which would speed up the presentation by 100%. When all his advantages were explained to the class, and when they were told that they had no alternative, they grudgingly accepted their plight. However, that class had a high absentee rate because many of the students decided to study on their own at home.

The second phase of preparing professors to teach the courses consisted of sending some of the better English-speaking students to the United States for a year to earn a master's degree in accounting. Most of the applicants who applied for this opportunity had taken one or two of the courses offered by USAID but a few applicants were new to the program. Forty-three people applied for the five openings. The five people who were chosen were the cream of the crop. They were selected by USAID to prevent any politics or nepotism from entering the process. Several universities were considered. The University of Texas at Dallas was selected, partly because of its reputation for international accounting and partly because it had experience with foreign students.

The program was a success. All five students completed the program and all five returned to Armenia, although one of the five later returned to the University of Texas to work on a second master's degree, this time in information systems.

15.7   Continuing Education for Existing Accountants

Although reforming the accounting curriculum in the universities was part of the task that USAID had set for itself, the more urgent goal was to educate existing accountants and auditors, since they had only a few months to learn the rules that they would soon have to apply. The Finance Ministry deliberately did not have any phase-in rules when it adopted IAS and ISA. It wanted accountants and auditors to start implementing the new rules immediately.

The local accounting association (AAAA) was chosen as one of the sites for training. However, it had just one training room. Once the training got into full swing, this room would be used most week nights as well as weekends, and even that would not be enough, since multiple sections of several courses were being offered by the end of the first year of the program, which soon moved into other cities in Armenia.

As training moved into other cities, another problem had to be faced. The first train-the-trainers course, which was held at the AAAA facility in Yerevan, gave full scholarships to three individuals who lived in Gyumri, the second largest city in Armenia, with the understanding that they would be the lead trainers for Gyumri when the training facility in that city was opened. The problem was that the accountants from Gyumri did not want the local trainers to conduct the courses there. There was a perception that a trainer from Yerevan, the capital, was somehow better than a local trainer. So those three individuals were trained but could not be trainers in Gyumri. People from Yerevan had to be hired and had to travel to Gyumri to conduct the training.

The training that USAID conducted and supported at the headquarters of the AAAA and at the regional branches became part of the AAAA's continuing professional education program. Although the AAAA had offered some seminars in the past, the seminars it offered were nothing like the courses that they offered as part of the accounting reform program.

In addition to offering the full range of Russian/Armenian language ACCA courses, the AAAA also offered the English version of those courses. The ACCA exams are given only in English and some of the English speakers expressed a strong desire to take the courses in English so that they could prepare for the ACCA exams. Because of the strong demand, several English language ACCA courses were offered. The ACCA was contacted and Yerevan was chosen as an examination center. The first English language ACCA exam was given in Yerevan less than 3 months after the USAID Accounting Reform Project came to Armenia. That is how fast things moved.

The pass rate was quite low for that first battery of exams, mostly because the students only had a few weeks to prepare, and they had to take at least two exams in order to gain admittance to the examination in the first place. USAID was noticeably upset when the exam results were released, which led to a change in approach. For the first ACCA English language exams, the policy was that anyone who wanted to take the exams would be allowed to take the training needed to prepare for the exams. The reason for that policy was to increase the number of trained accountants as quickly as possible. After the poor exam results were released, USAID decided that the goal should be to increase the pass rate, which meant ending the open admission policy.

The results for the next exam were much better. Screening potential applicants was partly responsible for the better scores, but so was the fact that they had more time to prepare for the exams. In the first round, the classes started less than 2 months before the exams, and students had to prepare for two exams. On the second round, classes started more than 3 months before the next battery of exams, which gave the students much more time to prepare.

In addition to holding Russian/Armenian language accounting classes at the AAAA headquarters, some classes were held at the Central Bank facilities. The Central Bank classes actually started before the classes at the AAAA because of the persistence of some of the accounting personnel at the Central Bank. Central Bank administrators had contacted more than 20 banks that were doing business in Yerevan and asked them to nominate students for the courses. They signed them up, processed all the paperwork, then presented their case to USAID, saying that they already had the facilities and the students; all they needed were texts and someone to teach the class. Since the only person who could teach the class that early in the program was the American CPA, he was nominated to be the instructor. The interpreter he used was one of the accounting department managers. Again, the instructor spoke in English, which was translated into Armenian to the students, who were using Russian texts.

15.8   The New Certification Model

Part of the accounting reform program included upgrading accounting and auditing certification to international standards. In the past, the exam consisted of a few essays and a few multiple choice questions, some of which were used year after year. Exam takers wrote their names on the exam, which meant that the person grading the exam knew whose exam was being graded. This system provided the opportunity for corruption.

The AAAA scrapped this system and replaced it with one that closely paralleled the ACCA examination system. Rather than have one exam, there were 15, which included the same 14 topics as the ACCA exams plus an exam on the Armenian chart of accounts. Certification was three-tiered, just like the ACCA scheme. Exams were just like ACCA exams. In fact, questions from former ACCA exams were translated into Armenian and given as questions on the first exam offered under the new scheme. Students were assigned numbers, which they put on their exam papers. Their names no longer appeared, so the person grading the exam did not know whose exam was being graded.

The only difference was that the Armenian exams were four hours in length whereas the ACCA exams are three hours long. Under the old Soviet system, students could take as long as they wanted to complete an exam. The AAAA committee that was coordinating the exams thought that adopting a three-hour requirement would be too much for the Armenian students' emotional systems to bear, at least on the first exam.

Students who passed the English language ACCA exams did not have to also take the Armenian language exams. There was reciprocity, which enhanced the desirability of taking the English version even more. It also enhanced the perception of the quality of Armenian certification, since it was modeled on the ACCA syllabus. Unfortunately, the AAAA later changed the reciprocity. Those who pass the English language version of the ACCA exams no longer get credit if they want to get credit for those exams for their Armenian accounting or auditing license.

The 15 exams included the subjects listed in Table 15.1.

The ACCA changed its syllabus after this plan was adopted. It is likely that the AAAA will change its certification exam requirements to mirror the ACCA changes. As anyone familiar with the ACCA syllabus will notice, the AAAA exam contents are not quite identical to those of the ACCA. The ACCA, for example, requires two exams in the British tax system. The AAA thought that there was no need for Armenian accountants to learn the British tax system, so that requirement was replaced with two exams on the Armenian tax system. The ACCA syllabus includes a course in British business law. Again, the AAAA saw no need for this subject, so it substituted an exam in Armenian business law. The 15th exam is on the Armenian Chart of Accounts. The ACCA syllabus has no similar exam.

Some of the exams included questions on Armenian accounting standards, Armenian auditing standards, and Armenian ethics. The uninformed reader might easily conclude that Armenian accounting, auditing, and ethics standards must therefore be somewhat different from international standards. However, such is not the case. Armenian accounting standards are identical to IAS. Armenian auditing

Table 15.1 Exam topics

Exam	
1	Financial Accounting I
2	Armenian Business Law
3	Management Accounting
4	Organizational Framework (a management exam)
5	Information Analysis (an exam on information systems)
6	Auditing I (based on the ACCA syllabus plus Armenian auditing standards and ethics)
7	The Armenian Tax System
8	Managerial Finance
9	Information for Control and Decision Making
10	Financial Accounting II & Auditing II (based on the ACCA syllabus plus Armenian accounting and auditing standards)
11	Tax Planning
12	Management and Strategy
13	Financial Reporting Environment
14	Financial Strategy
15	The Armenian Chart of Accounts

standards are identical to ISA. The code of ethics adopted by the AAAA is a direct translation of the IFAC Code of Ethics. The AAAA insisted on making the distinction in terminology – Armenian instead of International – for strictly nationalistic reasons. Armenia was almost always under the domination of some other country. Prior to the breakup of the Soviet Union, the only time it was ever an independent republic was for a few months after World War I. Insisting that the standards be referred to as Armenian was a way of asserting national independence.

15.9   Training Enterprise Accountants and Managers

Some of the training for enterprise accountants was already discussed above. The ACCA Russian/Armenian courses held at the AAAA headquarters and Central Bank included enterprise accountants, as did the courses held in other Armenian cities. So did the ACCA English language courses. But the training of enterprise accountants was not limited to the ACCA courses. There was also another, more basic course, which was aimed at providing basic training for individuals who worked at enterprises and who were not accountants but who needed to know some basic accounting.

Accounting for Nonaccountants was the name of the course and the name of the text as well (McGee, 1999b). This book was used in the United States as the main text for a 2-day seminar aimed at individuals who had little or no accounting background but who needed some knowledge of accounting. The book was translated into both Armenian and Russian and used in a series of 2-day seminars throughout Armenia. About 1,000 individuals attended these seminars.

Because the cost of translating the book was relatively low, it was thought that translating it into both Armenian and Russian would be a good idea, since there was some sensitivity about using Russian language texts. This potential problem was eliminated by translating the book into both languages. Since the book was available in Russian, it could also be used in the accounting reform projects of several other former Soviet republics and East European countries. The book has since been translated into Bosnian and Serbian as well, for use in the accounting reform project in Bosnia and Herzegovina, where language is a much more sensitive issue than it was in Armenia.

15.10   Educating Tax Inspectors

The original USAID plan called for educating tax inspectors as well as certified accountants, auditors, and enterprise accountants. It was thought that tax inspectors would have to be trained in the new financial reporting rules so that they would understand the books they were auditing. However, this part of the plan ran into some difficulty. One of the top tax inspectors in the country indignantly announced at a meeting that tax inspectors do not need to be educated and that the present (meaning the old Soviet) system works just fine and does not need to be replaced.

One who is familiar with the way taxes are sometimes collected in Armenia and some other former Soviet republics can understand such a mentality. Tax inspectors in Armenia do not always go into a firm and ask to look at the books, pouring over every detail and every journal entry. Tax inspectors have a reputation for sitting in the back room of their tax office, dressed in long black coats, smoking cigarettes and drinking coffee. When they are finished drinking and smoking and want a change of scenery, they pick a target company, pay it a visit and "collect." Firms that cannot pay are closed down. One rather large firm in Armenia was closed down just this way because it could not afford to pay the $30,000 demanded by the tax inspectors. Not much education is needed to perform the tax collection function using this approach.

15.11   Converting Enterprise Accounting Systems

Another phase of the USAID Accounting Reform Project in Armenia involved enterprise conversions. What this entailed was going into enterprises and assisting them to convert their present accounting system to comply with IAS. Several hundred of the largest enterprises in Armenia had their accounting systems converted using this approach.

The conversion team consisted of nine Armenians, all women and under the direction of a female American CPA. All were excellent English speakers. Many had MBAs from the American University of Armenia. They started each conversion with a seminar for the accountants at the enterprise, followed by an examination of the enterprise's books. They made suggestions and answered questions. Not all nine Armenians visited the same enterprise. They worked in teams of two or three, which made it possible to cover many more enterprises. Some of the accountants who worked for these enterprises also enrolled in the courses offered at the AAAA, so they were able to receive several different kinds of training.

15.12   Concluding Comments

The USAID Accounting Reform Project in Armenia had some unique features, but the basic model has been used in every country where USAID has an accounting reform project. Accounting education is a big part of an accounting reform program, but a comprehensive accounting reform program includes other activities as well, such as helping a country to adopt IAS and ISA, which was not discussed in the present paper. Another task of most USAID accounting reform programs includes forming a national accounting association or strengthening an existing association. That aspect of the reform project in Armenia was also not discussed.

Upgrading the certification requirements of the target country includes many aspects that were not included in the present paper. There are some interesting synergies and problems that take place when all phases of an accounting reform program are started at the same time rather than undertaken sequentially, but space does not permit a discussion of these synergies and problems.

USAID now has completed several accounting reform programs. Other programs are still in process. They all have some common elements but also some differences. Although USAID is far up the learning curve, accounting reform projects do not lend themselves to a cookie cutter approach. Each must be customized to the needs, conditions, and circumstances of the target country. While the education segment of the USAID Armenian accounting reform program was successful, using an identical approach in another country might not prove to be so successful because the fact situation and the culture may be different.

References

Bournoutian, George A. (2001) Armenians and Russia, 1626–1796: A Documentary Record. Mazda Publishers.

Dadrian, Vahakn N. (1995) The History of the Armenian Genocide: Ethnic Conflict from the Balkans to the Caucasus. Berghahn Books.

Derdarian, Mae (1998) Vergeen: A Survivor of the Armenian Genocide. Los Angeles: ATMUS Press Publications.

Enthoven, A.J.H., Sokolov, Y.V., Bychkova, S.M., Kovalev, V.V. and Semenova, M.V. (1998). Accounting, Auditing and Taxation in the Russian Federation. The IMA Foundation for Applied Research and the Center for International Accounting, University of Texas at Dallas.

Friedman, Milton and Friedman, Rose (1984). The Tyranny of the Status Quo. New York: Harcourt Brace.

Graber, G.S. (1996). Caravans to Oblivion: The Armenian Genocide, 1915. New York: Wiley.

Hewsen, Robert H. (2001) Armenia: A Historical Atlas. Chicago: University of Chicago Press.

Hovannisian, Richard G. (1986) The Armenian Genocide in Perspective. New Brunswick, NJ: Transaction Publishers.

Index of Economic Freedom (2007). Washington, DC/New York: The Heritage Foundation/*The Wall Street Journal*. www.heritage.org.

International Business Publications (2002). Armenia Investment & Business Guide. Washington, DC: International Business Publications.

Johnson, Bryan T., Holmes, Kim R. and Kirkpatrick, Melanie (1998). 1999 Index of Economic Freedom. Published jointed by the Heritage Foundation and *The Wall Street Journal*.

Kirzner, Israel M. (2001) Ludwig von Mises: The Man and His Economics. Intercollegiate Studies Institute.

Libaridian, Gerard J. (1999). The Challenge of Statehood: Armenian Political Thinking since Independence. Blue Crane Books.

Libaridian, Gerard J., (Ed.) (1991). Armenia at the Crossroads: Democracy and Nationhood in the Post-Soviet Era. Blue Crane Books.

Marsden, Philip (1993). The Crossing Place: A Journey among the Armenians. London: Harper Collins.

McGee, Robert W. (1999a). The Investment Climate in Armenia: Some Legal, Economic and Ethical Issues. Journal of Accounting, Ethics & Public Policy 2(2) Spring: 310–317.

McGee, Robert W. (1999b). Accounting for Nonaccountants, third edition. Dumont, NJ: McGee Seminars.

Melson, Robert, Kuper, Leo and Nelson, Robert (1992) Revolution and Genocide: On the Origins of the Armenian Genocide and the Holocaust. Chicago: University of Chicago Press.

Miller, Lorna Touryan and Miller, Donald Eugene (1999) Survivors: An Oral History of the Armenian Genocide. Berkeley: University of California Press.

Mises, Ludwig von (1981). Economic Calculation in the Socialist Commonwealth. Auburn, AL: Ludwig von Mises Institute.

Mises, Ludwig von (1981). Socialism: An Economic and Sociological Analysis. Indianapolis: Liberty Fund, Inc.

O'Driscoll, Gerald P., Jr., Holmes, Kim. R., and O'Grady, Mary Anastasia (2001). 2002 Index of Economic Freedom. Published jointly by the Heritage Foundation and *The Wall Street Journal*.

Sunny, Ronald Grigor (1993). Looking Toward Ararat: Armenia in Modern History. Indiana University Press.

Walker, Christopher J., (Ed.) (1991) Armenia and Karabagh: The Struggle for Unity. Paul & Company Publishing Consortium.

World Bank (2002). Growth Challenges and Government Policies in Armenia. Washington, DC: World Bank.

Chapter 16
Accounting and Business Education in China

Guo Zhiwen

16.1 Introduction

Past 25 years has seen the rapid development of Chinese higher education in which accounting and business education plays an important role in providing managerial talents to support and ensure the economic reform, state sector restructuring, and the prosperous economy. Facing globalization and employment pressure, Chinese business schools are taking actions to reform the old-fashioned instructional pattern to enhance graduates' employability and adapt themselves to environmental change such as China's accession to the World Trade Organization (WTO) and international accounting norms.

This paper provides an introduction to the current reform of Chinese accounting and business education, analyzes the labor market for graduates and graduates' employability, and sets forth a framework of accounting and business educational reform, with a case study of accounting education at the author's university.

Since the reform and opening launched in the late 1970s, the demand for Chinese higher education has tremendously exceeded its supply. In the past 2 decades, only a few high-school leavers could have opportunities to be admitted into colleges and universities. It was very easy for graduates to be assigned or find jobs. Entering universities was considered as a great event that could bring honor to one's ancestors.

Universities and colleges produced graduates in batches without pondering their quality, individualistic needs, and employability. Since the late 1990s, however, it has been another story. The expansion of university recruitment started in 1999, competitive pressure from foreign counterparts, graduates employment pressure, criticism from labor the market, students' complaints, among others, have been triggering reform and readjustment.

The Ministry of Education and higher educational institutions at all levels are taking great efforts to implement reform in order to adapt to the new environment in higher education. As the most commonly operated specialty in colleges and univer-

G. Zhiwen
Hubei University

R. W. McGee (ed.), *Accounting Reform in Transition and Developing Economies,*
© Springer Science + Business Media LLC 2008

sities, accounting and business education[1] at the undergraduate stage in particular catches the eye. There is an extreme shortage of qualified accountants and managers for businesses including state-owned enterprises, private companies, and multinationals as well. Despite deepening of the Chinese social and economic reform in the past 25 years, accounting and business education still uses the old model without much change. Experts in both education and the business world criticize its lag behind the need of rapid economic development in Mainland China. Change is inevitable and reform is absolutely necessary.

Based on a brief review of business education in China, this paper analyzes the main challenges from globalization after China's accession to the WTO, and gives an introduction of the current labor market for university graduates. It particularly focuses on introducing the strategic reform directed by higher education authorities, an analysis of accounting and business graduates' employability and rise up the career ladder, and a notional framework of accounting and business educational reform. Lastly, the case of accounting education at Hubei University is provided.

16.2   Challenges from Globalization and Employment

China's present higher education system was established in the early 1950s with the deliberate intention of training higher-level personnel as effectively as possible for service in all sectors of the new socialist state. Based on a planned economic system, the higher education in which the model was copied directly from the Soviet Union comprised few business-related specialties (Duan, 2003). Since the reform and opening in the late 1970s, almost every college or university has launched accounting and business education to meet the demand for managerial talents and rapid economic growth.

At this time, Chinese higher education draws close to the advanced western world, especially in the field of accounting and business education. Most accounting and business concepts and ideas in university classrooms come from American or European publications, in spite of the different business practices such as Chinese accounting norms at the early period.

---

[1] Undergraduate students in accounting and business administration account for the largest group in business education in China. According to *The Undergraduate Specialty Catalog of Common College and University* issued by China's Ministry of Education in 1998, business (or business administration) education in the undergraduate stage is referred to a wider specialty mix, including sub-specialties such as business administration (or business in short), accounting, human resource management, financial management, tourism and hotel management, logistics management, marketing, and international business management, etc. Many universities are presently trying to widen students' knowledge base by providing students with general business curricula in the first 2 years and sub-specialty curricula in the second 2 years. As such, students can choose their favorite sub-specialty after 2 years of study rather than being assigned to a fixed sub-specialty at the time of enrollment.

With the continuous social and economic change, Chinese higher education has achieved the transition from elitist to mass higher education with a gross enrollment ratio of 17% in 2003, compared with that of 1% in 1980 and 3.4% in 1990 (Jiang, 2004). The higher education expansion of recruitment in 1999 is the critical turning point. In 2002, there were 1,396 regular institutions of higher education for undergraduates, with 9.03 million undergraduate students and 1.33 million graduate students.[2] Business undergraduate students (including those in the accounting specialty) accounted for 14.7% of the total enrollment in 2000, which was the largest segment of all specialties students (Zhao, 2003).

Obviously, like higher education in other fields of specialty, accounting and business education is on the way to produce graduates in batches. Lack of teaching staff and material resources in most business schools, out-of-date teaching patterns, and neglect of training students' skills and abilities have received criticism from stakeholders. Students complain about teacher-centered and exam-oriented learning. The rote memorization instructional model makes students always busy coping with doctrine and dogma in textbooks rather than learning how to learn.

Employers are generally dissatisfied with the performance of graduates and feel that the current graduates have high exam scores but low ability. Many students have no idea of how to even express and present themselves in a job interview. Some of them who have difficulty finding jobs choose to pursue further studies in higher education institutions. Some poor students suffer from employment pressure, resulting in mental problems. Since 1997, the policy of guaranteed job assignment has been cancelled (Plafker, 1997). But most educators have not awakened to this new environment.

In fact, on the one hand companies have a huge demand for accounting and business graduates, whereas an average of 20% of business graduates cannot find jobs within 6 months after graduation. The paradox is attributed to the big gap between employers' requirements and students' ability (Guo, 2004a). Some multinationals and Chinese enterprises have to seek and hunt for professional accountants and managers from Hong Kong or those who have overseas education background.

After China's accession to the WTO in 2001, Chinese business higher education is facing and will face more challenges than before. Firstly, globalization and internationalization bring forward new requirements for both the business world and the business education sector. The environment of business education has changed a lot. One of those changes is the standardization and internationalization of the Chinese accounting norms and system.

Accounting and business educators should rethink their fundamental goals from a global perspective. Secondly, multinational enterprises rolling in China as before to seek a gold mine need local accountants and managers who have global thinking while local companies need talents who can do business with foreign counterparts. Thirdly, foreign higher education institutions intensively compete for Chinese

---

[2] See *Education Statistics Report of Year 2002*, Department of Development and Programming of Ministry of Education (27/2/2003). The statistics exclude data on vocational higher education.

students. As of the end of 2003, there are 527,400 students studying in foreign higher education institutions.[3] Many students who are going to study in foreign colleges and universities see a business specialty as their first choice, which is attractive to both multinationals and Chinese businesses.

The traditional career path is disappearing. Life-long employment does not exist any more. Accounting and business graduates, who used to be called unusually lucky persons, need to transfer their careers when required. Unlike some technical work, business work needs more generic skills than specific skills. Employability is a matter of motivation and generic skills. An employable graduate will be keen to work and possess the qualities that recur in all studies of what employers seek in graduates – initiative, critical thinking, problem solving, data handling, communication, team working, etc. These qualities can be developed in many ways, but above all they are learned in a context (McNair, 2003). It is not enough for a business school to provide only a diploma for graduates. Rather, the core skills and abilities that can make students employable should be instructed.

16.3   The Labor Market for University Graduates

According to the white paper of *China's Employment Situation and Policies* issued by the Information Office of the State Council (IOSC, 2004), the total population of China in 2003 reached 1.292 billion (excluding the Hong Kong Special Administrative Region, the Macau Special Administrative Region and Taiwan Province). The population over the age of 16 was 998.89 million, of which the urban population was 423.75 million and the rural population 575.14 million; the economically active population was 760.75 million and the workforce participation rate was 76.2%.

Among the population over the age of 16, the population with junior middle school education level and above was 61.7% and that with junior college education level and above, 6.6%. Among the population of technical workers, those of the elementary grade took up 61.5%, those of the intermediate grade, 35%, and those of the advanced grade, 3.5%.

In 2003, the total urban and rural employed population reached 744.32 million, of which the urban employed population was 256.39 million, accounting for 34.4%, and the rural employed population was 487.93 million, accounting for 65.6%. From 1990 to 2003, the employed population increased by 96.83 million, an average increase of 7.45 million per annum.

Despite high economic growth of averaging 10% in the past 2 decades, China has been facing big pressure to provide jobs for the rural surplus workforce, the laid-off workers from state-owned enterprises (SOEs) due to reform and restructur-

---

[3] The data includes students in all stages, some researchers and visiting scholars. See the website of *China Education and Research Network*: http://www.edu.cn/20040216/3099048.shtml.

ing in the state sector, and annually added working age population such as university graduates in particular. The large working-age population with a low average educational level results in a very prominent problem of unemployment. This is primarily manifested in the coexistence of the contradiction of the total volume of workforce supply and demand and the contradiction of employment structure, in the simultaneous appearance of increasing pressure on urban employment and acceleration of the shift of surplus rural laborers to nonagricultural sectors, and in the intertwining of the employment problem for new entrants to the workforce and that of the reemployment for laid-off workers.

The reform and opening in the late 1970s started in villages and towns. Farmers could enjoy the benefit from land reform characterized by family-contracted land use with high productivity. At the same time, the bulk of farmers were employed in village enterprises, which evolved quickly to meet a pent-up demand for consumer goods and take advantage of a pool of cheap rural labor. From the mid-1990s, however, falling prices for crops, the overload of local government regulations on farmers, the downsizing of village enterprises and land loss owing to industrialization and urbanization, made most rural workforces leave their homes and land for the developed coastal urban areas to make a living. Estimates of the migrant population vary, ranging between 80 million and 150 million since 1990.

Urban registered unemployment has risen since the mid-1990s owing to job losses in the state sector. The SOE's reform and restructuring in the past decade generated a huge number of laid-off workers in the Northeastern old industrial base. The registered unemployment rate was relatively constant at around 2½–3% in the 1990s, but rose to 4.3% by the end of 2003 (IOSC, 2004). Alternative measures show higher unemployment in coming years because of the effects of China's entry into WTO and deepened adjustment of the economic structure.

For university graduates who used to be assigned jobs or who could find satisfying jobs easily a few years ago, the labor market is really grim. As more and more young high school graduates enter into universities and colleges, finding jobs for university graduates has become a big concern in China today. In 2003, there were totally around 2.4 million college students who graduated, up by 40% compared with the previous year (Zhang, 2004). There will be 2.8 million graduates in 2004 as well as 600,000 unemployed graduates from previous years.

Competition in the job market is fierce. Female graduates have the disadvantage over their male counterparts with sex discrimination seen at most recruiters, and outsiders over local residents due to the immobility-based residence system (*Hukou*), which limit the graduates' choice.

Even appearance matters in applying for jobs for some, as in the case of a very short candidate. The new graduates have therefore seen the hardest time in finding jobs. According to the Ministry of Education, only 83% of graduates got job contracts within 6 months of graduation in 2003. Some criticize the oversupply of university graduates. In terms of either the rate of college enrollment or average years of schooling of the labor force, however, China is still falling far behind the developed countries.

Then, is the problem due to a shortage of demand for the graduates? In fact, almost all employers in China would complain of a shortage of talent when they are asked about what they need the most. Therefore, it seems that the problem is neither of oversupply, nor that of shortage of demand. In particular, many employers say it is difficult for them to recruit qualified accounting and business talent from business schools.

In fact, the problem lies in the mismatch between the supply and the demand. China's education system has indeed made a good number of college graduates every year, but what the market needs is nothing else but real talent who really deserve their value. Are the college graduates all talented? The graduates themselves might think they certainly are, and so do the old criteria for talent formulated in China's planning system in 1982, which states that anyone who has an educational attainment above technical secondary school or at least has a primary professional title can be regarded as a talent.

Obviously, such criteria worked in the planned economic system in which everyone needs to be assigned a job by the plan. But in a market economy, the market has the say on whether you are talented. To solve the problem of graduates' employment, the priority is not to reduce the number of college students, but to reform the rigid educational system, which was designed for the command economy and remained almost unchanged during China's economic reform. With a market-oriented education system, higher education institutions should focus on students' competence-based employability and training students' skills for their future careers, which has been neglected or not drawn adequate attention by educators before, rather than only provide them with diplomas.

Additionally, the mismatch between graduates' supply and demand can be reflected on graduates' viewpoints of employment. Most students still regard jobs in the state sector, permanent jobs. and working in big cities such as Beijing and Shanghai, as respectful. Since the mid-1990s, the employment contribution has mostly come from the non-state sector while SOEs have downsized to enhance profitability and competitiveness through kicking out workers (Brooks and Tao, 2003). The employment capability of big cities, government organizations, institutions. and foreign companies has neared saturation. So graduates are encouraged to seek jobs in the West of China and small cities where there is a large demand of qualified workers.

16.4   Enhancing the Marketability of Graduates

The challenges and pressures mentioned above have drawn attention from the Ministry of Education. In 2001, the Ministry issued an instructional document for improving the quality of undergraduate teaching.[4] The document calls for actions

---

[4] See the full document: http://www.gsau.edu.cn/jiaowuchu/jxwj/jxwj6.htm.

to enhance teaching quality in colleges and universities, most of which are controlled by the Ministry of Education and local governments.

One of the requested actions is for bilingual teaching in some WTO-related specialties such as biological technology, information technology (IT), business and law, etc., in order to absorb the state-of-the-art knowledge from the developed education. Within 3 years, the proportion of bilingual courses should reach 5–10%. This policy urges higher education institutions to take advantage of first-rank foreign textbooks (most in English) and resources to teach students advanced knowledge. Teachers can first use English to explain key academic terms and concepts in class, and then use Chinese to give most lectures in detail. Complete English teaching is certainly encouraged. The Ministry of Education is hoping higher education can foster talents with global thinking through bilingual education, as a way to promote internationalization of Chinese universities. Another requirement is to intensify practical instruction and pay attention to students' initiatives and practical ability. The goal lies obviously at students' need of future career and employability.

On March 3, 2004, the State Council approved and disseminated *The 2003–2007 Action Plan for Invigorating Education*[5] (hereinafter called the Action Plan) prepared by the Ministry of Education. This Plan is the fundamental blueprint for all parties involved in education to further implement the strategies of Rejuvenating China through science and education and reinvigorating China through human resource development and to speed up educational reform and development in the years to come. The Action Plan points out that in the 21st century and with the context of economic globalization and the knowledge economy, the competition in economy, science, and technology lies its root in the competition of education and the advantage in human resources.

The Action Plan has 14 parts with 50 articles and over 13,000 words, including two major strategic priorities, six priority projects, and six important measures. With regard to higher education, the first project is the 'Project for Quality-oriented Education in the New Century.' It aims at promoting quality-oriented education, strengthening moral education, deepening curriculum reform, and the reform of the evaluation system.

The third project of the Action Plan refers to the 'Project on Teaching Quality and Teaching Reform in Higher Education Institutions.' It emphasizes the overwhelming importance for higher education to strengthen and improve its quality. This new Action Plan puts more emphasis and efforts on the teaching reform and the establishment of an evaluation and quality assurance system.

A once-every-5-year evaluation mechanism for regular universities has been launched and demonstrated satisfactory primary results. The fourth project of the Action Plan is the 'Project on Employment Promotion for University Graduates'. Employment is the basis of people's livelihood. With emphasis attached by the central government, improvements have been witnessed in the graduates' employment.

---

[5] See the full text of the Action Plan in English: http://www.moe.edu.cn/news/2004_03/19_1. htm.

For the institutionalization and systemization of this issue, this Action Plan will further strengthen the construction of the leadership system, operation mechanism, policy framework, and service system for the employment of university graduates, and will deepen reforms both inside and outside the domain of education orientated by the labor market.

As a whole, the central government cares about the quality of higher education which influences the employment of graduates, or takes actions to enhance the employability of graduates. Universities are under increasing pressure to take account of what they are doing. Students, their parents, and central and local governments all want evidence of value for money, in terms of career prospects and lifetime earnings. Performance indicators linked to graduate employment rate, and to graduate careers are increasingly important in governmental funding decisions.

Employability enhancement becomes a priority of higher education goals. Colleges and universities can no longer neglect the cultivation of students' skills, qualities, and core competences that consist of employability. In particular, accounting and business education should focus on fostering students' core skills from curricula, assessment, and teaching activities. More students' participation and classroom involvement, rather than teaching what the textbooks say, must be added.

16.5 Employability of Chinese Graduates

Employability has not previously been of such strategic importance to business schools in China, so most of business schools do not have a coherent approach to it. Employability is as much an issue for higher education institutions as central services. Good higher education teaching should develop precisely the kind of skills that make a graduate employable, but if the relevance is not pointed out, it is often missed. Furthermore, unless it is embedded in the curriculum, the students who most need support are least likely to get it. Delivering employability therefore needs to be a partnership between academic departments and central specialists, especially in career services.

But what are accounting and business graduates' employability and how to enhance it? As a difficultly defined concept, employability itself is infrequently explicitly and clearly defined. In all cases the core notion relates to the propensity of students to obtain a job. Most definitions overlay this notion in major ways such as job types, timing of getting a job, attributes on recruitment, further learning, and employability skills (Harvey, 2001). Employability skills for business graduates imply generic skills or attributes to the most extent (Zhao, 2003). Knight and Yorke (2003) provided a USEM theory to illustrate what makes up employability. USEM is an acronym for understanding of subject knowledge, skills (subject-specific and generic), efficacy beliefs (and self-theories generally), and Meta-cognition (including reflection).

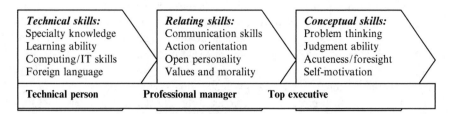

Technical skills:	Relating skills:	Conceptual skills:
Specialty knowledge	Communication skills	Problem thinking
Learning ability	Action orientation	Judgment ability
Computing/IT skills	Open personality	Acuteness/foresight
Foreign language	Values and morality	Self-motivation
Technical person	**Professional manager**	**Top executive**

Fig. 16.1 Career ladder of prospective accountant and manager (accounting and business graduates) with skills in three stages

Commonly, a manager plays three kinds of roles, e.g., an interpersonal role, an informational role, and a decisional role (Mintzberg, 1973). So communication skills of business and accounting graduates must be emphasized. Especially in China, personal relationships and personal networks, or *guanxi* in Chinese, are very powerful. This is because in China the rules may be fixed, but people can be flexible. You cannot do anything without *guanxi*, even in the business world. Good communication skill is critical for a prospective manager to build *guanxi* with people internally and externally.

From the viewpoint of career development, accounting and business graduates will experience a three-stage career ladder (Fig. 16.1): technical person (or lower level manager), professional manager (or middle manager), and top executive (or top manager), where he or she should have technical skills, relating or human skills, and conceptual skills, respectively although a mix of these skills can be depended on at any stage (Katz, 1974). Generally, when successful at the first stage, a technical person with potential relating skills may step up to the position of professional manager, and then top executive if doing well as a middle manager. It must be noted here that an accountant belongs to one of the managerial roles, which include, for example, marketing manager, personnel manager, and logistics manager.

In order to perform the functions of management and to assume multiple roles, managers must be skilled. Robert Katz (1974) identified three managerial skills that are essential to successful management: technical, human or relational, and conceptual. Technical skills involve process or technique knowledge and proficiency. Managers use the processes, techniques, and tools of a specific area.

Human skills involve the ability to interact effectively with people. Managers interact and cooperate with employees. Conceptual skills involve the formulation of ideas. Managers understand abstract relationships, develop ideas, and solve problems creatively. Thus, technical skill deals with things, human skill concerns people, and conceptual skill has to do with ideas.

A manager's level in the organization determines the relative importance of possessing technical, human, and conceptual skills. Top-level managers or executives need conceptual skills in order to view the organization as a whole. Conceptual skills are used in planning and dealing with ideas and abstractions. Supervisors need technical skills to manage their area of specialty.

All levels of management need human skills in order to interact and communicate with other people successfully. But relatively, for example, technical skills shown in Fig. 16.1 have significance for a newcomer's success. In other words, a business graduate will benefit more from his or her technical skills than from conceptual skills. It is worthwhile to note that on recruitment a company definitely values potential content of a business graduate's conceptual skills. But what really matters for successful employment of accounting and business graduates at the beginning are technical skills and relationship skills. It must be pointed out that the skills used here implicate all related factors of employability skills, abilities, competences, qualities, attributes etc., which are often used in literature.

As shown in the figure, each kind of skill comprises four different sub-skills. They are technical skills: accounting and business knowledge, learning ability, computing and IT skills, and foreign language; relating skills: communication skills, action orientation, open personality, values, and morality; conceptual skills: problem thinking, judgment ability, acuteness/foresight, and self-motivation.

In past accounting and business education activities, students could only learn stiff accounting and business knowledge rather than learn it in a context. Most of the skills mentioned above are neglected due to job assignment practice before 1997 and full employment of graduates a few years ago. Learning skills, for instance, is about how, why, and what to learn, and has high relevance with life-long learning.

Learning strategies for mastering new expertise and the transferability of these are seen as important in the context of continuing to be a valuable employee (Van Der Heijden, 1998). Another example of a neglected skill is communication skill. Classroom teaching was previously the lecturer's monodrama without students' participation and involvement. Spoon-fed instruction in business schools impairs prospective accountants and managers' independent thinking, resulting in their lack of skills and abilities.

16.6   Accounting and Business Education Reform

As Chinese accounting and business education fails to cultivate students' employability in a wider skills mix, it is absolutely necessary to reform and change the present educational model as a whole. Business schools should transform their current educational system characterized by exam-oriented and teacher-centered teaching, into employability-directed education. All education activities should encompass development of students' skills that can enhance their employability.

The most pressing reform is to redesign curricular modules, structure and system with employability enhancement embodied to promote employability for accounting and business students. The curriculum for a business school should be flexible enough to provide a major and a minor program, with the major program providing focused in-depth training in a specialized area; and the minor providing training in multi-disciplinary areas (Gill and Lashine, 2003).

The flexibility and granulation of the modules is of central importance. Owing to a rapid change in technology, it is imperative to update the curriculum to keep pace with the advancements. An effective strategy would be to develop a change-driven curriculum where the curriculum design and learning paths should be reviewed periodically according to market needs.

Some vocational courses such as career management, entrepreneurship and management communication, and some courses related to global and international business, or those reflecting up-to-date development in the business world, should be added into the curriculum. It is helpful for business graduates to adapt to globalization and labor markets. Case studies in a global and local context should be emphasized to simulate the real-life environment and develop skills and approaches to solve accounting and business problems.

Complementary teaching materials are particularly important for accounting education due to new developments such as updated accounting norms or newly revised business laws and regulations. By introducing bilingual teaching into business schools, students can absorb existing knowledge from developed countries so that they will be more employable when seeking jobs with multinationals or large organizations. Those accounting and business graduates who have a good command of English or other foreign languages can often gain good jobs (Guo, 2004b). In addition, lectures should give opportunities for students to participate and involve themselves in classrooms, by which they can develop their communication skills and problem-thinking skills. Accounting and business teachers should be good at guiding students to debate upon booklore in a practical context instead of being anxious to give them a conclusion.

The academic staff in business schools plays a core role in enhancing students' employability. However, many academic staff enter university early in their careers and have limited work experience, and their knowledge and awareness of the world of work as experienced by their graduates is therefore necessarily limited. Moreover, many academics see employability as a marginal concern, far from the core business of academic life.

In a research-led institution in particular, giving substantial time to graduate employability may be seen at best as eccentric, and at worst as not being a serious academic activity. That is why in recent years the Ministry of Education has continuously stressed the importance of teaching quality in higher education. This can be reinforced by systems of promotion, which recognize teaching, research, and employability work as three core academic tasks (McNair, 2003). Additionally, it is valuable for business schools to engage accountants, managers, and foreign teachers to give lectures for their students.

Enforcing graduates' career guidance by the student affairs department is often effective for graduates' employability. The service is often the focus of relationships with the employer community, and has a great deal of experience working with students to manage their career planning and job applications. Currently, this is being done in many universities although there is no integrated tool coordinated within the normal educational system. At the same time, student unions and consortiums should take an interest in supporting students' employability enhancement.

In many higher education institutions, student unions and different consortiums have initiatives and programs designed to help its members to develop their employability. Examples of initiatives run by student unions include: contests such as speech games to develop generic and transferable skills, and volunteering schemes, which provide students with the opportunity to develop a wider range of skills.

Strengthening employability can be embedded in a tutorial system, which requires students to discuss critically their progress, developments, and future career direction with a member of the academic staff. According to students' individual traits, the tutor can create a tailored personal career planning program for the student. Unlike the past practice where staff is only concerned about a student's academic achievements, the whole development of a student should be considered.

16.7 Accounting Education at Hubei University

Hubei University (HUBU) is a provincial university, located in Wuhan, the capital of Central China's Hubei Province. Its 7-decade development turns HUBU into a key comprehensive university covering arts, history, philosophy, science, engineering, economics, management, law, education, and medicine. HUBU offers at its main campus 48 undergraduate (bachelor degree) and 42 postgraduate (master degree and doctorate degree) courses in ten faculties: Humanities, Business, Law, Mathematics and Computer Science, Life Science, Physics and Electronic Engineering, Chemistry and Material Science, Education, and Foreign Studies. The main campus also includes an Adult Education College and an International School. There are 23 research institutes and centers, plus two national centers: the Centre for Chinese Language and Literature and the Centre for Biochemistry. Fifteen key disciplines and one laboratory are qualified as reaching the top standard at the provincial level.

HUBU launched accounting education in 1993, mainly providing a 3-year certificate training at the Department of Economics and Management between 1993–1995 and a 4-year undergraduate program at the Department of Accounting of the Business School since 1995. Currently, there are 21 accounting teachers and more than 400 full-time undergraduates at the main campus. After many years of experimentation and adjustment, accounting education at HUBU has developed and structured a dynamic curricula, which can make accounting graduates adaptable and employable in the labor market.

An accounting undergraduate should finish 2,700 teaching hours or 150 credit hours of compulsory courses (Table 16.1) and 252 teaching hours or 14 credit hours of optional courses (Table 16.2) within a 4-year or 8-semester accounting undergraduate education. As shown at Table 16.1, A1–A12 courses are compulsory courses that students in any specialty at HUBU should finish.

B1–B10 courses are compulsory courses that students in business administration subjects should finish. That means students in accounting, business administration, human resource management and marketing, and so on should finish these courses.

Table 16.1 Curricula for accounting undergraduates at HUBU: Compulsory courses

No.	Course title	Teaching hours	Credit hours	Semester
A1	Marxist Political Economics	36	2	1st
A2	Marxist Philosophy Theory	54	3	2nd
A3	Generality of Maoism	54	3	3rd
A4	Dengism and Three Representatives	72	4	4th
A5	Military Skills Training	54	3	1st
A6	Morality and Ethics	54	3	1st
A7	Basic Computer	54	3	1st
A8	Law Fundamentals	36	2	2nd
A9	Commonweal Labor	18	1	2nd
A10	College English	72*4	16	1–4th
A11	Physical Training	36*4	8	1–4th
A12	World Economy and Politics	36	2	4th
B1	Calculus	72*2	8	1–2nd
B2	Linear Algebra	54	3	3rd
B3	Applied Computer	54*2	6	2–3rd
B4	Database Techniques	54	3	3rd
B5	Probability and Quantitative Statistics	72	4	4th
B6	Microeconomics	54	3	3rd
B7	Macroeconomics	54	3	4th
B8	Management Fundamentals	54	3	4th
B9	Statistics	54	3	5th
B10	Principles of Accounting	72	4	2nd
C1	Financial Accounting	72*2	8	3–4th
C2	Cost Accounting	72	4	4th
C3	Management Accounting	72	4	5th
C4	Auditing	72	4	5th
C5	Accounting Information System	72	4	5th
C6	Financial Management	72	4	6th
C7	Practice of Accounting Process	36	2	6th
C8	Advanced Financial Accounting	72	4	7th
D1	Research Paper (about 5,000 words)	36	2	5th
D2	Accounting Practice	108/36	8	7–8th
D3	Thesis (about 18,000 words)	108/180	16	7–8th
	Total	2700	150	

C1–C8 courses are accounting specific compulsory courses. D1–D3 part is of practice in accounting education. E1–E5 courses, as shown in Table 16.2, are optional for all non-natural science students. F1–F15 courses are optional courses that accounting students can choose to finish.

They should finish the required 14 credit hour or 252 teaching hour optional courses. Currently, B8, C3, C8, F13, and F15 are bilingual courses provided to enhance students' global thinking. The accounting curricula are of the 2003-revised edition and evolved from the 1999 edition. The Department of Accounting can submit curricular redesign, based on the demand of the labor market and accounting development, to the Department of Teaching Affairs to evaluate and ratify each

Table 16.2 Curricula for accounting undergraduates at HUBU: Optional courses

No.	Course title	Teaching hours	Credit hour	Semester
E1	College Chinese	54	3	1st
E2	Audiovisual English	36	2	1st
E3	Introduction of Natural Science	36	2	3rd
E4	Computer Language	54	3	4th
E5	Economic and Business Laws	54	3	5th
F1	Public Finance	54	3	4th
F2	Accounting English	54*2	6	5–6th
F3	Securities Investment Analysis	36	2	5th
F4	Accounting Software Application	54	3	6th
F5	Taxation Laws	54	3	6th
F6	Computer Network System	54	3	6th
F7	Accounting Theory	54	3	6th
F8	Budget Accounting	36	2	6th
F9	Marketing	36	2	6th
F10	Construction Accounting	36	2	7th
F11	Accounting Report Analysis	36	2	7th
F12	History of Accounting	36	2	7th
F13	International Accounting	54	3	7th
F14	Accounting System Design	36	2	7th
F15	Advanced Financial Management	36	2	7th
	Required Total	252	14	

year at HUBU, thereby heightening the curricula flexibility and making graduates' skills more adaptable to the labor market.

In 2003, there were 151 accounting graduates from HUBU entering the labor market, 8 pursuing masters degree and 15 unemployed or staying at home ready for further study abroad. The employment rate (excluding the graduates who pursue master study) within 6 months after graduation reaches 87%, slightly higher than the national average level of 83%. Of those employed, 57%of the graduates have accounting related jobs, 21% have marketing related jobs, 13% entered government units to work in the non-business field, and 9% fall into other categories. This fact highlights that it is reasonable to widen students' knowledge base and enhance their employability from a wider perspective.

16.8 Conclusion

Facing globalization and employment pressure, it is highly suggestive for Chinese business schools to foster their graduates' employability skills with educational authorities seeing employability enhancement as a priority. The mismatch between supply and demand of graduates in the labor market shows the need of higher education reform based on competencies demanded by the market. For Chinese accounting and business students there are three kinds of skill clusters: technical, relating and conceptual with each having four sub-skills. Career ladder coined in this paper tries to illuminate the prospective business student's career stages with differently needed skills. The employability enhancement is not a separate task for business schools but an integrated activity. Its success and effectiveness depend on employability-embedded curricula with periodic evaluation, staff's intention to promote it, a tutorial system to help students develop a personal career plan, and student union involvement as well. There are still some critical research topics not mentioned in this paper. For instance, how to heighten entrepreneurship through business education in China is an interesting subject for probing. In addition, the framework of employability skills shown in Fig. 16.1 does not have enough empirical support.

References

Brooks, R. and Tao, R. (2003). China's Labor Market Performance and Challenges. IMF Working Paper, WP/03/210.

Duan, X. (2003). Chinese Higher Education Enters a New Era. Academe, Nov/Dec, Vol. 89, 22–27.

Gill, A. and Lashine, S. (2003). Business Education: A Strategic Market-Oriented Focus. International Journal of Educational Management, 17/5, 188–194.

Guo, Z. (2004a). A Reform Notion for Business Instructional Pattern. Journal of Chinese Education (Hong Kong), April 112–115.

Guo, Z. (2004b). Exploration of Bilingual Teaching in Curricula of Business Administration Specialty. Journal of Modern Education Research (Hong Kong), March 31–35.

Harvey, L. (2001). Defining and Measuring Employability, Quality in Higher Education, 7(2), 97–109.

IOSC: The Information Office of the State Council of China (2004). China's Employment Situation and Policies, http://english.peopledaily.com.cn/200404/26/eng20040426_141553. shtml

Jiang, N. (2004) College and University Recruitment in Year 2004: An Interview with Official of Ministry of Education. China's Education Daily, 11/2(5).

Katz, R. (1974). Skills of an Effective Administrator. Harvard Business Review, Sept/Oct, 90–101.

Knight, T. & Yorke, M. (2003). Learning, curriculum and employability in higher education, London: Routledge Falmer.

McNair, S. (2003). Employability in Higher Education: Developing Institutional Strategy, http:// www.ltsn.ac.uk/genericcentre/index.asp?id=19312

Mintzberg, H. (1973). The Nature of Managerial Work, New York: Harper Row.

Plafker, T. (1997). China to Stop Assigning Jobs to Graduates, Chronicle of Higher Education, 2/14/97, 43(23), A45, 1/6p.

Van Der Heijden, B. (1998). The Measurement and Development of Professional Expertise through the Career. Netherlands: Print Partners Ipskamp, 213.

Zhang, J. (2004). Employment of College Graduates and Talents – The Sunday Column, China Business Inforcenter, http://www.cbiz.cn/NEWS/showarticle.asp?id=2018

Zhao, C. (2003). A Report of Business Education in China, Peking: Tsinghua University Publishing Company.

Chapter 17
Accounting Education in the Republic of Croatia

Katarina Zager

17.1 Introduction

Accounting education in the Republic of Croatia is part of the general education system. Secondary schools of economics generate lower-level bookkeepers, while universities generate professionals hierarchically higher in view of rights, responsibilities, and benefits, i.e., accountants. The basic types and characteristics of the accounting profession depend on the accounting education system and the actual accounting system as well.

The most significant changes in the accounting system in the Republic of Croatia occurred in 1993 when the Accounting Act was passed, introducing the compulsory implementation of International Accounting Standards. On the other hand, the Croatian education system implements the latest international solutions and prepares accountants for practical work.

The most significant qualitative changes occurred in 2005 with the implementation of the Bologna Declaration when higher education institutions were harmonised with EU standards. All faculties in the Republic of Croatia adjusted their teaching plans and programmes with European and other known study programmes. Smaller faculties chose the 3 + 2 + 3 model, while the biggest and most well-known faculties chose the 4 + 1 + 3 model (bachelor + master + Ph.D.).

New teaching plans and programmes introduced lots of news, such as – all courses are taught in one semester, a larger number of elective courses, a smaller number of teaching hours in a lecture room, and a larger share of individual student work. It is necessary to notice that all suggested programmes were subjected to domestic and international evaluation. That kind of approach generates good assumptions for comparison of our programmes with study programmes of other universities and for stronger mutual cooperation, as well as student mobility.

In the process of financial reporting in the Republic of Croatia the application of International Accounting Standards (now called International Financial Reporting Standards) is obligatory. All companies that are obliged to make financial statements, accordingly to the Accounting Act, are put in three groups: small, medium,

K. Zager
University of Zagreb

R. W. McGee (ed.), *Accounting Reform in Transition and Developing Economies,*
© Springer Science+Business Media LLC 2008

and large. All large companies and medium-sized companies organised as joint stock companies are obliged to publish their financial statements once a year, together with an auditor's opinion.

According to the Accounting Act, which has been applied since 1993, basic financial statements include the Balance Sheet, Profit and Loss Statement, Statement of Changes of Owner's Equity, Cash Flow Statement, and Notes to the Financial Statements. After presentation to owners, financial statements should be delivered to the Court Register of Companies. These financial statements that are presented to the public, to owners, and delivered to the Court Register of Companies are annual financial statements.

As a rule, the business, i.e., accounting year is identical to the calendar year. However, there is the possibility of making financial statements for the business year different than the calendar year. The Minister of Finance makes a decision about that on request of the company with the seasonal character of activities taken into account.

The Accounting Act prescribes the minimal number of items in financial statements for certain companies depending on their size. In defining the structure of the financial statements, provisions of IV European Union Directives are respected. For medium-sized and large companies detailed classification of certain positions in financial statements has been defined. Only the forms of the Balance Sheet and the Profit and Loss Account have been recommended, while the Cash Flow Statement is prepared on the basis of IAS 7. In application of IAS the government of the Republic of Croatia appointed members of the Croatian Committee for Accounting and Accounting Standards, whose task is to follow, harmonise, and explain the application of IAS in the Croatian environment.

The Accounting Act required the audit of financial statements for every business year, for all large- and medium-sized companies organised as joint stock companies. The Auditing Act was passed at the same time as the Accounting Act.

The Law on Audit that has been applied since 1993 includes a procedure of questioning and evaluating financial statements, data, and methodologies used for their preparation. The goal of that questioning and evaluation is to express an opinion on the reality and objectivity of the financial position and business results. In the Republic of Croatia the basic criteria upon which financial statements are judged as realistic and objective are included in accounting principles, International Accounting Standards, law, and accepted accounting policies. The procedure of evaluating the reality and objectivity of financial statements is based upon International Auditing Standards; the Code of Professional Ethics approved by the Croatian Association of Auditors, and the Law on Audit.

According to the existing regulation, only audit firms that fulfill certain common and specific requirements prescribed by the Law on Audit can conduct audits. Among others, it is understood that an audit company must employ at least one authorised (chartered) auditor and that at least 75% of its capital must be owned by authorised (chartered) auditors or other authorised audit company. Confirmation on fulfilment of these conditions as well as the license to work is given by the Ministry of Finance, according to the Law on Audit. The legal obligation of a client audited by an audit company is to provide auditors with all statements, evidences, and documents, as well as all relevant information necessary for the audit and preparation of the auditor's statement. In addition, the client must choose the audit company before the business year-end. If these obligations are not fulfilled, sanctions are generally imposed. The Law on Audit prescribes certain sanctions for the auditing company, too, in the following cases:

- If the audit is not conducted according to the Law on Audit and International Auditing Standards
- If the audit is conducted without a license given by the Ministry of Finance
- If the audit company conducts an audit of a client (company) with which it has a capital interest
- If the audit company does not insure itself against liability and
- If the audit company does not provide a statement on the results of the audit to the legal representatives of the entrepreneur

So, we could say that the audit has a very important role in providing reliable financial statements for different users.

17.2 Accounting Education System

Generally speaking, the accounting profession is generated from the existing education system. The following needs to be distinguished:

- The secondary school level
- The university education level

Secondary schools of business generate lower-level bookkeepers, while colleges generate professionals hierarchically higher in view of rights, responsibilities, and benefits, that being accountants. These two tracks represent the basic accounting profession.

Accounting education is part of the general business education system. The most important role belongs to the university education system, which generates high-level professionals called accountants. In the Republic of Croatia there are several universities that educate accountants. Although many private business schools and private faculties have come into existence recently, most students still study at state institutions. The reason for that is not only the lower price of university fees, but also a higher level of work quality, supervision, and eminent world-known professionals and professors who work at state faculties.

In addition, the labour market prefers economists from state faculties. The Faculty of Economics in Zagreb is the largest university, not only in Croatia, with more than 12,000 students, but is also the oldest faculty of this kind in South East Europe and has a tradition of 85 years of providing economic education. These facts contain sufficient elements for a conclusion that the Faculty of Economics in Zagreb has the tradition and experience in this kind of education. All of the above-mentioned facts are the reason for taking it as a representative education institution for this research.

During the Bologna process (which took place mostly during 2004 and 2005) the Faculty of Economics in Zagreb has so far compared its programmes with more than 200 foreign universities and business schools. The frequent analysis of the universities whose courses were used for comparison in the ECTS project showed that, of 211 universities and business schools that were analysed, the study programmes of the Faculty of Economics in Zagreb are most similar to the universities of the United Kingdom, Germany, Spain, Portugal, Sweden, Slovenia, and Italy.

17.2.1 Study Model in Higher Education

According to the Bologna Declaration and according to the Croatian Law on Higher Education, universities could choose two models: 3 + 2 or 4 + 1. Both models have equal status. That is the reason why there is a dual system of higher education in economics. It is important to stress that models 3 + 2 and 4 + 1 provide 5-year higher education.

The 3-year model of undergraduate studies gives students an opportunity to acquire certain knowledge and an academic title at an earlier stage and thus get into the labour market sooner, which also represents a lower cost for the state. The model is thus acceptable for schools that are younger, insufficiently known on the education market and exposed to more fierce competition from private business schools. A digression should be made in order to point out that business and economics schools in Croatia (traditionally called "faculties of economics") are the only schools facing increasing competition on the part of private faculties and business schools.

The Faculty of Economics in Zagreb as the oldest and the largest faculty has decided upon the 4 + 1 study model because the 4-year study offers students more comprehensive education of better quality both in methodological and specialist disciplines. Since economic theory and practice are themselves developing, the shortening of the undergraduate study impoverishes students' readiness to identify, understand, and make an impact on economic events and processes. Also, practice has shown that in 90 of cases students who have completed a 3-year study programme in schools that have adopted the 3 + 2 model continue their studies upon graduation.

One of the major reasons for choosing the 4 + 1 + 3 model refers to our business strategy in the market of higher education, and is related to the necessity to achieve differentiation in comparison with other faculties of economics and business schools. It is therefore necessary to have more products that are specific and recognizable on the market. The scheme of this model is shown in the appendix in Chart 17.1.

All the study programmes (undergraduate and graduate) are as open as possible to student mobility, both horizontally and vertically. It should be pointed out that mobility of students from other faculties of economics in Croatia has been made possible as a result of cooperation and agreements reached in the last 2 years. A series of meetings of deans, vice-deans, and course coordinators has been held in order to discuss compatibility of courses taught in Croatian faculties of economics.

The high compatibility of the programmes is particularly present in the first 2 years of study with the predominance of methodological and fundamental

Academic study programmes at the Faculty of Economics in Zagreb

ACADEMIC STUDY PROGRAMMES		
UNDERGRADUATE STUDIES (BACHELOR)		
1st year	60 ECTS	
2nd year	60 ECTS	
3rd year	60 ECTS	
4th year	60 ECTS	
Total	**240 ECTS**	
GRADUATE STUDIES (MASTER)		
1st year	60 ECTS	
Total	**60 ECTS**	
POSTGRADUES STUDIES		

Chart 17.1 Academic study programmes at the Faculty of Economics in Zagreb

economic disciplines. Such preparation has created pre-conditions for student mobility. This has been achieved in spite of the fact that other faculties of economics in Croatia have opted for the 3 + 2 model. This is the application of one of the essential principles of the Bologna Declaration, which stresses the need to acknowledge diverse study models and specific position of certain faculties, but also to implement student mobility among different programmes. The credit system based on student workload will efficiently resolve all the problems that may arise.

Student mobility within the programmes also is pointed out. A high percentage of elective disciplines, which practically cannot be compared to the past study programmes, enable students to have a lot of freedom in the independent creation of their own education. In the third and fourth year of study, students can choose among a total of 12 elective courses (six courses of their major, and six belonging to other majors). Additionally, over these 2 years of study, students can choose six more courses from other faculties and universities. The level of the openness of the programmes and student mobility has thus reached an unprecedented level.

17.2.2   Study Programmes in Accounting

The Faculty of Economics, University of Zagreb, organises and delivers two basic academic study programmes with appropriate majors at the undergraduate and graduate levels, these being:

BUSINESS STUDY PROGRAMME with the following majors:

- Finance
- Accounting and Audit
- Marketing
- Management
- Informatics for managers
- Trade
- Tourism
- Analysis and business planning

17.3   Economics Study Programme (Major in Economics)

Chart 17.2 presents the types of study programmes and their majors in greater detail. The charts show all types of the Business and Economics study programmes organised as undergraduate and graduate academic studies.

Undergraduate study in Accounting and Auditing lasts 4 years, and graduate study 1 year. Students obtain 60 ECTS credits for each completed year of study. After the completion of the undergraduate study with the acquired 240 ECTS, students can continue their education in a graduate study programme.

The requirement for undergraduate study is the completion of a 4-year high school and/or exams towards a state high school graduation certificate. It is important to emphasise that the Faculty of Economics in Zagreb accept only the best students. This is proved by high selection criteria and a ratio between the number of candidates and quotas approved for enrollment. Usually 2/3 of all candidates are excellent students. Probably, this is one of the reasons why most of them continue their education and professional development after finishing their studies.

The requirement for the graduate study programme is the completion of the undergraduate study programme (4 years). Requirements for students who will have completed their 3-year undergraduate studies in other faculties providing education in economics or related fields is set as a special case. The Study ordinance defines how to obtain the remaining number of ECTS credits (ECTS differentials) necessary for enrolment. After completion of the graduate study students can continue their education in postgraduate studies: 1-year specialisation in the major or 3 years in a doctoral programme.

Upon completion of the undergraduate study, a certificate is issued to a student confirming the completion of the studies and the acquisition of the academic title:

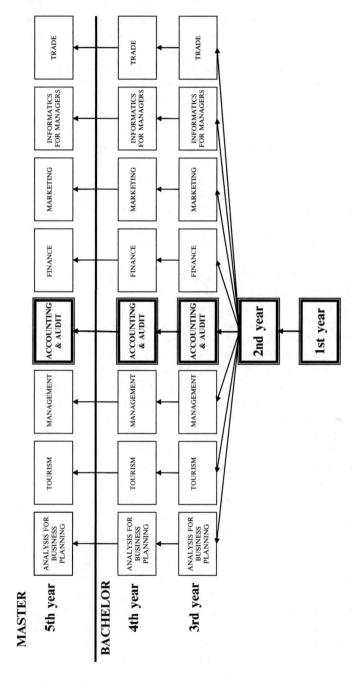

Chart 17.2 Scheme for the Majors of the Undergraduate and Graduate Study Programmes

«*prvostupnik*» (*baccalaureus* – Bachelor) for men or «*prvostupnica*» (baccalaurea – Bachelor) for women, together with the specification of the qualifications (Business, Economics) and the respective major, as stipulated by the law and the Statute of the University of Zagreb. After the completion of graduate study, a diploma is issued to a student confirming the completion of the studies and the acquisition of the academic title («*magistar*» – Master of Business), as stipulated by the Law. Table 17.1 shows general information about the major «Accounting and Auditing» and Tables 17.2–17.10 (in the appendix) the study programme for this major (bachelor and master).

As is shown in Chart 17.2, 2 years relate on the completion of general economic and methodological courses that are obligatory for all majors. In the third year students choose one of eight possible majors. New teaching plans and programmes are coordinated with European and world-known university programmes.

In the accounting module there are courses that are recognised in the world by their name and by their content. The proof for this is the fact that students of the Faculty of Economics can find a job, not only in Croatian, but also in international companies that have branches in Croatia, as well as in companies located in other countries.

Knowledge acquired within the major is based on course curriculum, accessible domestic and foreign literature, and on professors who are continually developing their knowledge and pass it on the new generations. Usually, every year at least one professor from the Department of Accounting spends some time abroad for profes- sional development. Also many professors from this department participate in inter- national conferences – so this has become a part of our tradition. The reason for that is a positive attitude and financial support of the Faculty management to all profes- sors, but especially to younger teaching staff willing to improve their knowledge.

The proof of module quality is an increasing number of students who choose this major every year. With the modules finance and marketing, the accounting module is the most popular one at the Faculty. It is necessary to emphasise that the account- ing major enrolls the best students. From the major title and all courses (accounting and other economic) contents it is noted that accounting students acquire wide economic knowledge and because of that they are easily integrated into the labor market and they easily take over executive positions in their companies.

The organisation of teaching classes is done according to lecture, a schedule that is prepared in advance. The winter semester lasts from October until January, and the summer semester lasts from March until the middle of June. Regular exam terms are held during February, June, July, and September.

One school hour lasts 45 min, followed by a 15-min break. New teaching plans and programmes reduced the number of teaching hours in the lecture room (on average by 40%) and increased participation of individual student work. Table 17.8 show the estimated time needed for an individual student to prepare for an exam based on the professor's estimation and goes from 1 to 1.5 h on behalf of additional student work. Also it is necessary to notice that the biggest news in new plans and programmes is that all courses are taught in one semester. A detailed overview of undergraduate and graduate study programmes is shown in from Tables 17.1 to 17.10.

Table 17.1 Academic undergraduate and graduate – study major (Accounting and Audit) – general information

Name of study programme/major	Undergraduate study of business-accounting and audit	Graduate study programme of business-accounting and audit
Length of study:	4 years of study; 8 semesters	1 year of study; 2 semesters
Requirements for enrolment:	Completed 4 years of high school, exams towards the state high school graduation certificate and/or entrance exam results	Completion of undergraduate studies of Business or Economics (min. 240 ECTS) in line with the rules of the studies
Competences acquired by graduates:	Adopting scientific disciplines that enable students to understand a broader field of accounting and audit. Acquiring theoretical and practical knowledge in the broader field of accounting and audit that enables students to understand and apply the accounting and auditing methods, techniques and procedures in business practice. Accounting and Audit majors acquire knowledge in the fields of financial reporting, accounting systems, cost accounting methods and cost management techniques, accounting methods for business combinations, consolidation methods, accounting aspects of tax calculation, financial statement analysis, business planning techniques, evaluation of performance effectiveness, auditing methods and procedures, and internal control systems. Additionally, the students are also provided with an opportunity to expand their knowledge of specific accounting systems, such as trade, tourism, banking, investment and pension fund or insurance company accounts, and to learn about the accounting systems of the EU countries.	Adopting new and developing the existing scientific methods, analytical skills, problem-solving skills in business decision-making, information and communication skills, and other skills necessary for the students to take leading roles in entrepreneurial operations that are becoming increasingly demanding. This study programme provides the students with additional insight and opportunity to improve their existing scientific knowledge in the broader field of accounting and audit, enabling them to familiarise themselves with and understand current scientific methods and procedures and their application in business practice.
Academic title	*Baccalaureus/baccalaurea-Bachelor* of Business, major in Accounting and Audit	Master of Business, major in Accounting and Audit

Table 17.2 Compulsory courses for the first year of the undergraduate study programme

FIRST YEAR OF STUDY – Compulsory courses of the study programme					
1st semester	ECTS	Hours	2nd semester	ECTS	Hours
1. Principles of Economics	8	90	1. Microeconomics	8	90
2. Mathematics	8	90	2. Statistics	8	90
3. Informatics	7	75	3. Organisation	6	75
4. Commercial Law	7	75	4. Entrepreneurship	6	60
5. Physical Education	–	30	5. Business Foreign Language I	2	45
			6. Physical Education	–	30
Total	30	360	Total	30	390

Table 17.3 Compulsory courses for the second year of the undergraduate study programme

SECOND YEAR OF STUDY – Compulsory courses of the study programme					
3rd semester	ECTS	Hours	4th semester	ECTS	Hours
1. Accounting	8	90	1. Croatian Economy	7	90
2. Macroeconomics	8	90	2. Business Finance	7	90
3. Financial Institutions and Markets	6	75	3. Marketing	7	90
4. Management Basics	6	60	4. International Economics	7	90
5. Business Foreign Language II	2	45	5. Extended essay	2	20
6. Physical Education	–	30	6. Physical education	–	30
Total	30	390	Total	30	410

The Accounting and Audit major acquires knowledge in the fields of financial reporting, accounting systems, cost accounting methods and cost management techniques, accounting methods for business combinations, consolidation methods, accounting aspects of tax calculation, financial statement analysis, business planning techniques, evaluation of performance effectiveness, auditing methods and procedures, and internal control systems. Additionally, the students are also provided with an opportunity to expand their knowledge of specific accounting systems, such as trade, tourism, banking, investment and pension fund or insurance company accounts, and to learn about the accounting systems of the EU countries.

A labor market analysis has identified a large demand for highly educated employees of this profile. All business entities from all sectors of the economy contribute to the demand for highly educated experts in accounting and audit. This demand is generated both by complex business systems and the government and self-government units, as well as small entrepreneurs.

The issue of business accounting and financial reporting in conformity with law represents the priority interest of all business entities. However, since in the contemporary business conditions the accounting system is recognised as a quality and necessary source of information for business decision-makers, there is an ever-increasing demand for internal reporting to the governance bodies of business entities. In view of this fact, there is a growing demand for accounting experts oriented to internal reporting, an area with parallel links to the broad field of internal audit as the extended arm of governance structures in business entities.

Table 17.4 Compulsory and elective courses for the third year of the undergraduate study programme – major accounting and audit

THIRD YEAR OF STUDY – Accounting and Auditing major					
5th Semester	ECTS	Hours	6th Semester	ECTS	Hours
1. Public Finance	6	60	1. Monetary Policy	6	60
2. Accounting Information Systems	6	60	2. Financial Accounting	6	60
3. Cost Accounting	6	60	3. Tax Accounting	6	60
4. and 5. Elective courses of the major – student chooses 2 out of 4 offered	4 + 4	60 + 60	4. and 5. Elective courses of the major – student chooses 2 out of 4 offered	4 + 4(6)	60 + 60
(a) Accounting of Financial Institutions	(4)	(60)	(a) Accounting of Non-Profit Organisations	(4)	(60)
(b) International Accounting	(4)	(60)	(b) Accounting of SMEs	(4)	(60)
(c) Financial Mathematics	(4)	(60)	(c) Document Management in Business	(4)	(60)
(d) English for Accounting	(4)	(60)	(d) Business Decision Making	(6)	(60)
6. Elective course – other majors/ faculties*	4	60	6. Elective course – other majors/faculties	4	60
Total	30	360	Total	30(32)	360

Table 17.5 Compulsory and elective courses for the fourth year of the undergraduate study programme – major accounting and audit

FOURTH YEAR OF STUDY – Accounting and Auditing major					
7th semester	ECTS	Hours	8th semester	ECTS	Hours
1. Economic Policy	6	60	1. International Business	6	60
2. Management Accounting	6	60	2. Analysis of Financial Statements	6	60
3. Auditing	6	60	3. Internal Audit	6	60
4. and 5. Compulsory course of the major – student chooses 1 out of 2 offered	4 + 4(6)	60 + 60	4. and 5. Compulsory course of the major – student chooses 1 out of 2 offered	4 + 4(6)	60 + 60
(a) Accounting in Trade and Tourism	(4)	(60)	(a) Government Audit	(4)	(60)
(b) Fiscal policy in the EU	(6)	(60)	(b) Information System Audit	(6)	(60)
5. Elective course of other major/faculty	4	60	5. Elective course of other major/faculty	4	60
6. Elective course of other major/faculty	4	60	6. Elective course of other major/faculty	4	60
Total	30(32)	360	Total	30(32)	360

---

* The intention of suggested elective courses from other majors and Departments is merely to assist students inmaking decision in tje right decision when it comes to choosing the compatible couses which they cnnot asses properly in advance. Apart from this list student can choose any other elective course from other majors or faculties, accordin to the Study Ordinance.

Table 17.6 Elective courses of other majors and departments of the undergraduate study programme

Semester	Course title	ECTS	Hours
5th	Preferential Trade Liberalisation	4	60
	Economic Sociology	4	60
6th	Operations Research	4	60
	European Market Law	4	60
	Statistical Methods for Economic Analysis	4	60
7th	Regional Economic Integrations	4	60
	Demographic Methods and Models	4	60
	Competition Law	4	60
8th	Mathematical Economics	4	60
	Business English III	4	60
	Sampling Methods	4	60

Apart from this list a student can choose any other course from other majors or faculties, according to the study ordinance.

Table 17.7 Compulsory and elective courses of the graduate study programme – major accounting and audit (Master in Accounting)

FIFTH YEAR OF STUDY – Master in Accounting					
9th semester	1 ECTS	Hours	10th semester	2 ECTS	Hours
1. Responsibility Accounting	5	30	1. Research Methodology	4	30
2. Financial Reporting and Auditing	5	30	2. Extended Essay I	2	20
3. Strategic Accountant	5	30	3. Extended Essay II	2	20
4. and 5. Elective course of the major – student chooses 2 out of 4 offered			4. Critical Review	1	10
(a) Internal Control System	4	30	5. Graduation Thesis	20	220
(b) Professional Ethics of Accountants and Auditors	4	30			
(c) Corporate Governance	4	30			
(d) Liquidity Management	4	30			
6. Elective course – other majors/faculties	4	30			
7. Elective course – other majors/faculties	4	30			
Total	31	210	Total	29	300

Table 17.8 Elective courses of other majors and departments of the graduate study programme (5th year)

Semester	Course title	ECTS	Hours
9th semester	Economic Analysis of European Union	4	30
	Time Series Analysis and Forecasting	4	30
	Nonlinear Programming	4	30
	Actuarial Mathematics	4	30

Apart from this list a student can choose any other course from other majors or faculties, according to the study ordinance.

Table 17.9 Breakdown of Curriculum by Category Four-Year Bachelors Degree, Faculty of Economics in Zagreb

	Lecture hours	Seminar hours	Total hours in class	Study hours	Total hours	% of Total
Accounting						
Accounting Principle	45	45	90	120	210	
Financial Accounting	30	30	60	80	140	
Cost Accounting	30	30	60	80	140	
Accounting Information Systems	30	30	60	80	140	
Management Accounting	30	30	60	80	140	
Tax Accounting	30	30	60	80	140	
International Accounting	30	30	60	80	140	
Accounting of Financial Institutions	30	30	60	80	140	
Accounting of Non-Profit Organisations	30	30	60	80	140	
Accounting of SMEs	30	30	60	80	140	
Accounting in Trade and Tourism	30	30	60	80	140	
Auditing	30	30	60	80	140	
Government Audit	30	30	60	80	140	
Information System Audit	30	30	60	80	140	
Analysis of Financial Statements	30	30	60	80	140	
Total Accounting	465	465	930	1,240	2,170	30.65
Other Business						
Principles of Economics	45	45	90	140	230	
Mathematics	45	45	90	185	275	
Statistics	45	45	90	160	250	
Informatics	45	30	75	125	200	
Commercial law	45	30	75	110	185	
Microeconomics	75	15	90	120	210	
Macroeconomics	60	30	90	110	200	
Organisation	45	30	75	85	160	
Entrepreneurship	30	30	60	110	170	
Business Foreign Language I	15	30	45	45	90	
Financial Institutions and Markets	60	15	75	125	200	
Management Basics	30	30	60	80	140	
Business Foreign Language II	15	30	45	45	90	
Croatian Economy	45	45	90	130	220	
Business Finance	45	45	90	110	200	
Marketing	60	30	90	180	270	
International Economics	60	30	90	110	200	
Public Finance	40	20	60	120	180	
Financial Mathematics	30	30	60	80	140	
English for Accounting	20	40	60	120	180	
Monetary Policy	30	30	60	120	180	
Document Management in Business	30	30	60	80	140	
Business Decision Making	30	30	60	120	180	
Economic Policy	30	30	60	120	180	
Fiscal policy in the EU	40	20	60	80	140	
International Business	30	30	60	120	180	
Total Other Business	1,045	815	1,860	2,930	4,790	67.66
Nonbusiness – Physical Education	120	0	120	0	120	1.69
TOTALS	1,630	1,280	2,910	4,170	7,080	100

Table 17.10 Breakdown of Curriculum by Category 4-Year Bachelors Degree, Faculty of Economics in Zagreb – Summary

	Hours in class	% of Total	Total hours	% of Total hours
Accounting Courses	930	31.96	2,170	30.65
Other Business Courses	1,860	63.92	4,790	67.66
Nonbusiness Courses	120	4.12	120	1.69
Totals	2,910	100	7,080	100.00

17.4 Basic Characteristics and Segments of the Accounting Profession

17.4.1 The Basic Segments of the Accounting Profession – Specialisation after Academic Degree

The accounting profession is one of the basic professions without which there would not be relevant and reliable information on corporate operations. It is, therefore, very important that its members are properly educated and organised. In that respect, there are opportunities for further education and additional occupations in the Republic of Croatia. The education programme and certification is carried out by authorised institutions that keep pace with modern international trends and have applied them in Croatia. This has created the basic prerequisites for the good performance of Croatian employees working in accounting. Generally speaking, the accounting profession is generated from the existing education system

- The secondary school level or
- The university education level

Secondary schools of economics generate lower-level bookkeepers, while universities generate professionals hierarchically higher in view of rights, responsibilities, and benefits, i.e., accountants. These two professions represent the basic accounting professions.

In addition to this basic education, bookkeepers and accountants were offered further education after 1993. Persons who have completed a secondary school of economics can become "independent accountants," while persons who have graduated from a faculty of economics (minimum bachelor or master) can continue their education for one of the following occupations:

- Certified accountant
- Certified internal auditor
- Certified external auditor
- Certified government auditor
- Tax adviser
- Certified business valuator

The education is provided by certified professional organisations as defined by the law or professional authority.

17.4.2 The Basic Conditions for the Individual Specialties

The scope of education and the curricula differ depending on the chosen occupation. For example, the education for a "certified auditor" lasts 120h, covering the following areas:

- Accounting and Financial Statements
- Auditing
- Law for Auditors
- Financial Management
- Enterprise and Management
- Information Technology for Auditors

In addition, there are some basic conditions for a person to receive a certificate. The basic conditions for the individual professions are shown in Table 17.11.

As can be seen from the table, the conditions to be met in order to receive the title for a particular occupation are basically the same. They all require a university degree, a particular number of years of work experience (with professional jobs for which one wishes to become Certified) and that the exam for the occupation be passed. In addition to this, one is required to have certain moral qualities and accept and comply with the Code of Professional Ethics. It must be mentioned that according to the existing regulations, for now, there is no subsequent licensing; once received, the certificate is permanent. Recently, the need to "check" or licence particular occupations, especially within the auditing profession, has been discussed more and more.

Therefore it could be expected that this practice, common throughout the world, will also be common in Croatia. All these occupations started to appear in the Republic of Croatia after 1993, after the Accounting Act and the Auditing Act had been passed. It can be expected that special fields will require new specialisations and new knowledge, especially in the field of auditing.

The additional and continuous education of accountants became necessary. In addition to learning how to apply the International Accounting Standards, a need and desire to learn more and earn particular certificates slowly started to emerge among members of the profession. It introduced the obligatory audit of all companies and defined the conditions for the person performing the audit. This laid the modern foundations of the auditing profession in Croatia. Also, a number of different tax regulations and the enactment of the Tax Counselling Act in 2000 brought about the emergence of a new profession in Croatian terms, that of the tax adviser. Though closely connected to the accounting profession, it was very specific with respect to it.

On the basis of the above mentioned, it can be concluded that the desire to join the developed Western world directly or indirectly imposed the emergence of some new knowledge and professions that have contributed to the quality of work and increased dignity of accountants. In this context, the enactment of some laws, primarily the Accounting Act, the Auditing Act, and the Tax Counselling Act, played an important role.

Table 17.11 Conditions necessary for specific certificates

Certificate	Conditions
Certified Accountant	Degree from the Faculty of Economics (min. bachelor)
	3 years work experience
	Exam passed
	No criminal record
	Membership in the Association of Accountants
Certified Internal Auditor	Faculty Degree (bachelor)
	3 years work experience
	Exam passed
	No criminal record
	Citizen of the Republic of Croatia
Certified Public Accountant	Faculty Degree (bachelor)
	3 years work experience
	Exam passed
	No criminal record
	Citizen of the Republic of Croatia
	Must meet conditions set out in the Auditors Code of Professional Ethics
Certified Government Auditor	Degree of the Faculty of Economics or Law (bachelor)
	3 years of work experience
	Exam passed
	No criminal record
	Citizen of the Republic of Croatia
	Meets other conditions set out in the Code of Professional Ethics
Certified Tax Advisers *(Certified Tax Experts)*	Degree from either the Faculty of Economics or Law (bachelor)
	5 years of work experience
	Exam passed
	No criminal record
	good health and capacity for work
	Resident of the Republic of Croatia
	Knowledge of the Croatian language
Certified Business Valuators	Degree from the Faculty of Economics or a technical degree (bachelor)
	3 years work experience
	Exam passed
	No criminal record
	Complies with the Valuators Code of Professional Ethics

The need and demands for the continuous education of business people, especially accountants, will probably contribute to certification for other types of knowledge and skills. This primarily refers to information technology; it can thus be expected that one relatively new profession, that of information technology auditors, will start developing in the Republic of Croatia.

Table 17.12 Structure of people
employed in accounting by gender

Gender	Percentage
Female	86.50%
Male	13.50%

All the above mentioned occupations represent additions to the basic accounting profession. Although they are not obligatory, recently more and more people have decided to take the exams and take up an occupation that will provide some other business opportunities. This is especially the case as the number of people working in accounting is decreasing due to the computer data processing that is dominant nowadays.

On the other hand, the data about the characteristics of accountants working in companies are interesting. According to the results of the empirical research[1] carried out, the accounting profession is still "reserved" for women (Table 17.12).

Women make up a majority in the total number of people employed in accounting. As for the level of education, the most significant share belongs to the secondary school education (65%), while the 2- and 4-year university education accounts for 35%. The fact that the accounting job is rather demanding is confirmed by the data that mostly young and middle-aged people work in accounting (26% of people surveyed were younger than 30, 57% of people surveyed were younger than 40).

17.5   Professional Associations

Different professions have joined together to form various professional associations in order to protect their interests and improve the profession. The same is the case in accounting. Generally speaking, there is a separate association for each certified occupation in the Republic of Croatia. However, the following associations have the most important roles and the longest traditions:

- The Croatian Association of Auditors (certified public accountants, i.e., external auditors)
- The Association of Internal Auditors (certified internal auditors)
- The Croatian Accountant (certified accountants)

In addition to protecting the interests of their members, these professional associations have established Codes of Professional Ethics and have participated in the

---

[1] K. Zager: "Influence of Accounting Policies on the Financial Position and Successful Operations of a Company", doctoral dissertation, Faculty of Economics, Zagreb, 1997.

preparation of legislation. Apart from them, there exist other forms of association for promoting mutual interests (for example, the Croatian Union of Accountants and Financial Employees, the Association of Bookkeeping Services, and so on), but those previously mentioned are the most important.

Many consultant houses publish professional magazines with the aim of sharing professional knowledge among their members. Some of the most important ones are "Racˇunovodstvo i financije" ("Accounting and Finances" – 50 years old), "Racˇunovodstvo, revizija i financije" ("Accounting, Auditing and Finances"), "Slobodno poduzetništvo" ("Free Enterprise"), "Pravo i porezi" ("Law and Taxes"), etc. Furthermore, news from the field is presented to the interested public at different seminars and symposiums. There is no doubt that the above-mentioned organisations contribute to the quality of work and activities within the accounting profession in Croatia. In other words, Croatian accountants possess all the prerequisites necessary for quality work.

17.6   Conclusion

Based on a research report it is possible to conclude that the accounting profession in the Republic of Croatia is well developed. A significant contribution is made with the change in the accounting system and coordination between the normative frameworks in the Republic of Croatia with those in the European Union. The most significant changes occurred in 1993 when the Accounting Act was passed, introducing the compulsory application of International Accounting Standards.

The Auditing Act was passed at the same time. The Auditing Act regulates obligatory audits of financial statements for all companies, especially all large companies organised as joint stock companies. Obligatory application of these Acts and International Accounting Standards generated the need for additional accounting training and created positive surroundings for the development of the accounting profession. Specialisation for specific occupations began in such surroundings without any formal or legal obligation. The biggest interest today is for the following occupations: certified public accountant and certified internal auditor.

On the other hand, the Croatian education system generated the required profile and specialised staff, especially in the accounting field – a field that was the most exposed and difficult because of continual changes in the statutory system. Although the basic knowledge that students obtained is recognizable in the world, still the biggest and the most significant reform of the higher education system was acceptance and implementation of the Bologna Declaration.

Particularly, the most significant qualitative changes occurred in 2005 with the implementation of the Bologna Declaration when higher education institutions were harmonised with EU standards. All faculties in the Republic of Croatia adjusted their teaching plans and programmes to the European and world-known university programmes. Smaller faculties chose the 3 + 2 + 3 model, while the biggest and well-known faculties chose the 4 + 1 + 3 model (bachelor + master + Ph.D.).

New teaching plans and programmes introduced lots of news, such as – all courses are taught in one semester, a larger number of elective courses, a smaller number of teaching hours in the lecture room and larger participation in individual student work. It is necessary to notice that all suggested programmes passed through domestic and international evaluation. That kind of approach generates excellent assumptions for the comparison of our programmes with other universities' programmes and for stronger mutual cooperation, as well as student mobility.

After getting the Bachelor degree students can enter the labor market or continue their education (master, postgraduate study). Becoming a part of the labor market they become active members of the accounting profession, which is organised according to individual specialisation (accountants, auditors, tax consultant, etc.).

In order to protect their interest accountants are organised in different professional associations. Those associations publish professional magazines, follow international changes in the field of European Union Directives and International Financial Reporting Standards, as well as changes in domestic legislation; they organise professional seminars and issue a licence for specific occupations. In one word they protect the dignity of the accounting profession.

Based on the above, we can conclude that the institutional framework of financial reporting based on International Accounting Standards and the new educational model adjusted to the Bologna Declaration principles generated excellent foundations for accounting profession development in the Republic of Croatia. The proof for that is the fact that there are no unemployed accounting professionals and most of the students take over executive positions in their companies very easily.

References

1. K. Zager: Experiences in the Implementation of International Accounting Standards in Republic of Croatia, Eighth International Scientific Conference, Bratislava, 2002.
2. K. Zager: The Accounting Profession in the Republic of Croatia, International Scientific Conference, MicroCAD 2003, University of Miskolc, Hungary, 2003.
3. D. Gulin, V. Vasicek, K. Zager: Accounting Regulation in the Europe and its Effects on the Accounting Regulation in Croatia, Ninth International Scientific Conference. Quantitative Methods in Economy – Compatibility of Methodology and Practice with the EU Conditions», Bratislava, 2003.
4. K. Zager, B. Tusek: The Accounting and Auditing Profession in Transition Period – Craotian Experience, Tenth Anniversary Congress, University of Lodz, Faculty of Management –Lodz, Poland, 2004.
5. Academic study programmes, undergraduate and graduate studies, Book I, University of Zagreb, Faculty of Economics, March 2005.
6. www.efzg.hr

Chapter 18
Accounting Education in the Czech Republic: A Case Study

Eva Holínská

18.1 Introduction

Accounting Education on economically specialized high schools and universities in the Czech Republic has a very long tradition. Current accounting education may be divided into four fundamental categories:

1. Accounting education in secondary (high) school
2. Accounting education in higher economy school
3. Accounting education in economically specialized universities (University of Economics in Prague)
4. Adult accounting education (postgraduate education programs, education training agencies, professional chambers, and unions)

Accounting education in secondary (high) school is intended to prepare graduates in business, accounting and practical bookkeeping. That is why accounting tutorials are centered on practical accounting techniques and the legislative rules of the Czech Republic.

Accounting education in higher economic schools and in economic faculties at various universities often varies regarding what constitutes universal accounting knowledge and what is required to prepare them for the profession in the real world, but preparation is mostly concerned with identification of accounts and legislative acts. Solutions to problems depend on departmental notions and approaches and are thus not uniform throughout the country.

18.2 Accounting Education at Specialized Economic Universities

In contrast to accounting education in secondary (high) schools, where the emphasis is on lead bookkeeping in accordance with national laws, accounting education at the University of Economics in Prague (which offers the best academic economics

E. Holínská
University of Economics, Prague

R. W. McGee (ed.), *Accounting Reform in Transition and Developing Economies,*
© Springer Science+Business Media LLC 2008

education in the Czech Republic) specializes in general accounting education for all students at the university. That education includes:

- Fundamental accounting theory from the very beginning
- Bases of accounting (bookkeeping) methods
- Fundamental principles of economic enterprises as displayed in financial accounting
- For undergraduates in Accounting and Enterprise Financial Management there are further lectures on special topics, namely:

  Accounting according to IAS/IFRS
  Auditing
  Accounting specifics for various company types and industries (only one of many of the courses is accounting according to national law and it focuses on accounting harmonization with international standards)
  Managerial accounting and management information systems

These courses in University of Economics in Prague are offered in a separate department of Managerial Accounting. This department was partitioned from the Department of Accounting in 1990. The university now has two departments, the Department of Financial Accounting and the Department of Managerial Accounting. Some of the courses taught in these departments include:

1. Financial Accounting – which teaches how to provide information required by external users such as potential and current owners, banks, business partners, stock exchanges, and other financial and capital market participants
2. Managerial Accounting – which provides information that is useful for managers and other entity employees, including tools for successful enterprise control, management information systems, etc.

There is also what might be classified as a third area, Tax Accounting, which focuses on providing information that is useful in establishing tax liability. Most accounting courses at the university focus on either financial or managerial accounting. Tax accounting problems are addressed only secondarily in the Department of Financial Accounting, mostly by short courses or seminars. In some other economics schools tax accounting plays a more prominent part of the curriculum.

Although both accounting departments are separate, they cooperate and are involved in many joint research and educational projects (e.g., official translation of International Financial Reporting Standards, research involving US GAAP, post-graduate study projects).

18.3 Accounting Education in the Department of Managerial Accounting

The Department of Managerial Accounting deals with accounting information that is used by managers at different levels. The information is used to control the entrepreneurial process and concerns decision making for both the present and the future.

Managerial-oriented accounting usually also includes other valuable information, such as planning and budget systems, output costing, the intradepartmental price system, and also information about natural entrepreneurial processes. These aspects of the total system are all integrated into a single information system.

Courses taught in the Department of Managerial Accounting include two main courses and several supplementary courses. The two main courses are cost accounting and managerial accounting. These courses are designed for both undergraduate and other students. The separation of the contextual themes (information about process control where decisions have already been made and decisions that affect the future) is very difficult and is done mostly for pedagogical reasons.

Other courses present information and information systems (for control and decision making). These courses deal with general theory. The Enterprise Information Systems course aims to solve conceptual problems related to accounting information as part of the Enterprise Information System. The course on Computer Integrated Management focuses on how to utilize software as part of the information system. The Department of Managerial Accounting offers several other courses as well, such as Cost Accounting – PC Workshop, Strategic Management Accounting, Bank Controllership, and a series of various seminars that address managerial accounting problems.

The Cost Accounting and Managerial Accounting courses are relatively straightforward and are not controversial but such cannot be said about some of the other courses. These two courses are stable and do not change much from year to year. The Enterprise Information Systems courses are a bit controversial, partly because of the conceptual approach chosen and the fact that their content changes more frequently.

The Enterprise Information Systems courses should be viewed as traditional courses for accounting undergraduates but the rapid changes in computer and software technology make the content of these courses more volatile. Computer and software technology is growing in importance for enterprises and because of that these courses have taken on increased significance.

18.4 The Enterprise Information Systems Course

One of the essential courses with diffused accounting themes is the Enterprise Information Systems. Earlier (approximately from 1960), this course contained only two lectures weekly, and since 2002 it has expanded to include a weekly lecture about practice. The objective of this course is to expose students to both the theory and the practice of functional Enterprise Information Systems from a user's perspective, emphasizing vertical communications systems within an enterprise. The course progresses from a knowledge of general systems theory to more advanced concepts.

One aim of the course is to point out the differences between the users' criteria for business management and that of the owners or external users. The state of current business practices is discussed as well as recent developments, especially in the areas of accounting, costing, and budgeting. It is a synthetic, conceptual course oriented toward information coverage of various decision making tasks of entrepreneurial managers. The course takes a user's perspective rather than a process approach.

18.4.1   Content and Structure of the Course

The content and structure of the course might be summarized as follows:

1. The approach to conception of an Enterprise Information System.
2. The systems approach to an Enterprise Information System.
3. The enterprise as an object, user and initiator of the information system.
4. The specifics of intradepartmental control and the use of information between departments for decision making.
5. Information content in an Enterprise Information System.
6. Information as a process and the communication of information.
7. Content and structure of the Enterprise Information System.
8. The management information system from a user's perspective.
9. Information tools for value management and aspects of the reproduction process.
10. Accounting as an unsubstitutable component of the Enterprise Information System.
11. Valuation as a basic accounting principle.
12. Costing as a tool for control; a prime cost company.
13. Budgeting as a tool for intradepartmental control and intradepartmental responsibility accounting.
14. Systems problems.

18.4.1.1   Detailed Structure of the Course

1. The approach to conception of an Enterprise Information System

The aim of this topic is to understand the working concepts of an Enterprise Information System, the differences from other approaches and concepts of Enterprise Information Systems, the importance of basic system knowledge for the understanding of economic activity and the importance and limitations of a system's capabilities.

2. The basic systems approach to an Enterprise Information System

The aim of this topic is to determine the different possibilities for conceptualizing systems, which is a basic branch of universal systems theory.

3. The enterprise as an object, user and initiator of the information system

The aim of this topic is to clarify the importance of a systems approach to an enterprise, discuss the enterprise position and behavior in an external environment, specific attributes of the enterprise's internal environment, and the interface of the enterprise as a whole and the enterprise's internal environment.

4. The specifics of intradepartmental control and the use of information between departments for decision making

The aim of this topic is to determine intradepartmental control principles and methods and identify specific intradepartmental control requirements for an enterprise's information system.

5. Information content in an Enterprise Information System

The aim of this topic is to determine the information base, information attributes, information structure, and the possibilities and limitations of the enterprise's conceptual information system.

6. Information as a process and the communication of information

The aim of this topic is to determine the reasons for the communication of information, the elements of a communication process, the structure of a communication channel and management system and its importance for the conceptualization of an enterprise's information system.

7. Content and structure of the Enterprise Information System

The aim of this topic is to determine the content and structure of the Enterprise Information System.

8. The management information system from a user's perspective

The aim of this topic is to explain the different concepts of the management information system (MIS), taking a user's approach and also becoming familiar with the basic information tools for intradepartmental control.

9. Information tools for value management and aspects of the reproduction process

The aim of this topic is to clarify the basic concepts and utilization of value control, especially economic costs, fixed costs, variable costs, and standard costs.

10. Accounting as an unsubstitutable component of the Enterprise Information System

The aim of this topic is to clarify the accounting content, the objectives of accounting and accounting methods.

11. Valuation as a basic accounting principle

The aim of this topic is to clarify basic valuation concepts and examine alternatives.

12. Costing as a tool for control; a prime cost company

The aim of this topic is to clarify the cost function and examine some specifics of costing as a tool for control.

13. Budgeting as a tool for intradepartmental control and intradepartmental responsibility accounting

The aim of this topic is to determine the importance of intradepartmental unit budgets, the contents of various intradepartmental budgets and the various kids of budgets under changing conditions.

14. Systems problems

The aim of this topic is to clarify the nature of systems problems and identify the various kinds of systems problems that may be encountered.

18.4.2   Training Content and Structure

Students complete a case study exercise solving a concrete problem encountered in real business practice. The exercise may be prepared at home. The practical exercise case study includes the following themes:

- Value engineering, namely functional cost analysis and managerial utilization
- Information system design for quality management
- A team project involving the control and information system of a small construction company
- Using standards costs for value control, using a company from the USA as a case study

18.5   Company Computer Integrated Management

The teaching aim is to introduce undergraduate students to principles they can use to integrate a management information system in a computerized atmosphere so that they will be able to:

- Cooperate on the generation of IS/IT concepts
- Judge the efficiency of these systems
- Generate a background for successful implementation and development of IS/IT in terms of life cycle

18.5.1   Summary

1. Computerized support development influence on managerial processes:

   - Fundamental term definition (information, information system, etc.)
   - Development trends IS/IT
   - Managerial action informative resource

2. Entrepreneurial atmosphere influence upon production and implementation IS/ICT:

- Changes in entrepreneurial atmosphere
- Development procedural management
- Conceptual information like company strategic expansion

3. Information systems architecture:

- Information systems architecture definition
- Management IS/ICT in a company's management system
- Information systems implementation

4. Enterprise Resource Planning – ERP system:

- Fundamental principles ERP system
- ERP implementation according to type of logistical actions in a company
- ERP systems risks

5. Fundamental method used in terms of ERP systems:

- Just in Time, Total Quality Management, Master Production Schedule
- Manufacturing Resource Planing MRP II
- Implementation of MRP II

6. Customer Relationship Management:

- Relations with customers management computerized support – Customer Relationship Management – CRM
- Company communications with consumer
- CRM like fundamental premise for company development
- Software applications for CRM developmental in practice

7. Supply Chain Management – SCM:

- Supplier and customer interconnection upon base ICT
- Supply chain optimalization
- SCM, CRM, and MRP II Integrity

8. MFG/PRO, QAD Inc.:

- Software product MFG/PRO modularity
- System integrity
- Software upgrade (CAD, CAP, CRM, SCM)
- System implementation

9. Management information systém:

- Management information system concepts
- Software superstructure above ERP
- Managerial decision-making actions for software support
- Business intelligence (MIS Alea Minerva, Business Navigation)

10. Business Process Reengineering – BRP:

- Business process concept
- Process quality management (PQM) method
- Process analysis
- Process perfection

11. IS/IT production and implementation:

- Making by order
- Complete software purchase
- Outsourcing and its forms

12. IS/ICT developmental tendency utilization in management:

- Computer and communication technical integration
- Process approach in management development
- Knowledge management
- Expert systems and decision support systems development

18.5.1.1 Practice Content and Structure

Global sample elaboration: Order running by production to utilize software products MFG/PRO, QAD Inc., its license provides MINERVA CR.

18.6 Conclusion

The decision as to whether the information systems course for undergraduate accounting students at the University of Economics in Prague should be conceptual and theoretical or practical and technical was a significant problem to be overcome. It seems that the traditional conceptual and theoretical approach could not be overcome by the advent of computers. Many computer themes have been theoretically answered a long time ago.

Although it seems that at present computer techniques and the rapid development of information technology preclude other than technological approaches to company information systems, it need not be the optimal method of accounting education. Excessive reliance on computer applications can cause one to lose sight of the basic process. The search for an optimal approach to accounting education involving information technology has not yet been found.

Chapter 19
The Development of Accounting Higher Education in the Czech Republic

Miloslav Janhuba

19.1 Introduction

Emperor Charles IV of Luxembourg (1316–1378) introduced the first known regular bookkeeping into Bohemia. He required keeping records about royal and manorial funds. At that time Czech accounting followed the older German patterns and corresponded slightly to the fragmentary single-entry bookkeeping system (cash, receivables, property, and debts).

Charles IV sent for Italian experts in order to manage finance and accounting in Bohemia. One of them, named Ceroni, settled in the town of Ceske Budejovice and, in addition to his duties as scribe, established the oldest school of accounting in Bohemia. In his accounting system Ceroni perhaps included some features of a single-entry cameral system of bookkeeping, based on the evidence of obligatory payments (debts), cash receipts, and cash expenditures. Some historical discoveries of accounting records were found in Bohemia that proved that this system was applied not only to royal but also to manorial administration, e.g., the Accounts of Monastery in the town of Trebon of 1367/68 and Municipal Accounts of the town of Nove Hrady Land from 1390/91 both kept in Latin by Roman numerals.

Emperor Ferdinand II of Habsburg introduced a complex system of double-entry accounting within his Middle-European empire (including Bohemian lands) in 1628. Accounting training of mercantile guilds was organized by the end of the 18th century. So-called "continual commercial schools" were founded to promote mercantile activity where there was instruction in various commerce areas, including accounting. Within the Hapsburg monarchy in the town of Senec (nowadays Slovak Republic) the oldest college, Collegium Oeconomicum was founded, where bookkeeping was taught.

M. Janhuba
University of Economics, Prague

R. W. McGee (ed.), *Accounting Reform in Transition and Developing Economies*,
© Springer Science+Business Media LLC 2008

19.2   Some History

The first regular lectures on accounting had been in German (for the first time as an integral part of one of the following subjects: mathematics, architecture, economy, and the teaching of wood craft) at the Prague Polytechnic Institute (a part of the Charles-Ferdinand University, Faculty of Arts) in 1806. The lectures were oriented toward graduates who should have become surveyors, engineers, state officials, forest engineers, teachers, professors, etc.

The Department of Public Accounting (Prague University, Faculty of Law) was established in 1830 and was managed by Professor Johann Christian Ammann until 1849. His lessons were based on his own lecture notes and later also on his textbook that contained a concise German-Czech accounting and economic dictionary.[1] Education had only a supplementary character.

Technical literature consisted of only practical textbooks. The main task of these textbooks was to present the mechanism of an accounting system and bookkeeping methods. These textbooks also helped to support Czech accounting terminology and created the fundamentals for scientific work.

Dr. Dominik Ullmann, who taught in German, and Dr. Antonin, Knight of the Meznik, who taught in Czech, achieved the first private associate professorship for accounting in Prague in 1864. Antonín Sk ivan and Karl Petr Kheil (Jr.) wrote very important textbooks during this period. Antonín Sk ivan is often called "the father of the Czech accounting terminology."

Charles Peter Kheil, Jr., was born into the family of a businessman and commercial school teacher in 1843. He attended the lower gymnasium, and was educated in his father's business as well. He finished evening studies and passed leaving exams. At the same time he continued his studies at the commercial school owned by A. Skrivan. In 1870 he taught in the Prague Gremial Commercial School. He passed qualification exams and after 1875 he opened his private commercial school in Prague.

His habilitation in 1877 was not certified and until 1887 he was a private senior lecturer on accounting at the Czech Technical University in Prague. His work at the university should have been rewarded by a professorship for the first time in 1900, next in 1906; but in both cases the reward was turned down by the government.

In addition to lecturing at the University he was a trustee and chief officer of the bank "Slavia" in Prague and an authorized expert in accounting at the penal court in Prague. His major works were historical books and he wrote historical studies, which were issued in German in Prague and in Vienna.[2] He died of pneumonia in

---

[1] Verrechnungskunde, theoretisch und praktisch dargestellt, Prag 1845.

[2] These works include Uber Einige Altere Bearbeitungen des Buchhaltungs-Tractates von Luca Pacioli (1896), Valentin Mennher und Antich Rocha 1550–1565 (1898), Benedetto Cotrugli Raugeo (1906, also in Czech), Uber Amerikanische' Buchfuhrung ein Beitrag zur Geschichte der Franzosischen Buchhaltungsliteratur des XIX Jahrhunderts (1908).

the spring of 1908. Two days after his death the confirmation of an appointment as a governmental counselor was delivered.

The contribution of K. P. Kheil Jr. has been recognized on an international scale. He gained an international reputation for the Czech accounting science in the second half of the 19th century. Kheil also published a very extensive writing about accounting history.

His accounting-history research is admirable even today. He was the first (and maybe the only one) who translated *Summa Arithmetica* (written by Luca Pacioli in 1494) into Czech and who also compared the original and the second edition of this famous book. The translation of Luca Pacioli was his last effort.

Responsibility for lectures on accounting was undertaken by JUDr. Josef Pazourek in 1907 and by JUDr. Karel Chlum in 1911. Mr. Chlum lectured on *Double-entry bookkeeping and the balance of commercial cooperatives, especially of agricultural cooperatives* and on *The balance sheets of joint-stock and limited companies according to the Act No.58, from 6th March 1906.* He died in 1913 at the age of 40 and his publications were forgotten.

Professor JUDr. Josef Pazourek was born into the family of a businessman in 1843 and attended secondary school for future teachers and became a teacher at a primary school. He kept on studying in the higher secondary school by distance study. In 1883 he began studying at the Faculty of Law in Prague and after a year continued his studies at the Faculty of Law in Vienna where he successfully graduated.

He acquired a teaching qualification for commercial sciences in Prague in 1894 with a main interest in accounting. He published two textbooks: *Double-entry bookkeeping and different ways of double-entry bookkeeping* and *Accounting for secondary schools.* In 1900 he began publishing, at his own expense, the first Czech professional journal on accounting, *Accounting Papers*, and was editing the journal for 15 years until 1915.

He continued his law studies from 1902 and got a Ph.D. degree in 1905. His Ph.D. thesis on "Balance sheet of share companies" was published the following year and he became associate professor for accounting at the Czech Technical University and professor of commercial science and accounting in 1909. He prepared a four-semester teaching program for secondary schools preparing teaches of accounting. He played an important role in the foundation of the Commercial University in Prague and was a rector for the period 1929–1932 until he retired. He died in 1933.

The lectures on accounting were targeted for future teachers at the business schools until 1919. Studies of accounting had been scheduled to be taken over a 2-year period. The first degree was focused on problems like double-entry bookkeeping, single-entry and cameral bookkeeping, legal framework of accounting, depreciation, reserve funds, stockholder's equity, share premium, balance sheet value, balance sheet studies, organization of an accounting system, and business correspondence. The higher degree concentrated on bonds, mergers, bankruptcy, liquidation, etc.

In 1919 the Commercial College was founded and it started a new era – an era of systematic development of the accounting discipline. In the first place, it was to the credit of Professor Pazourek, who was appointed dean of the College (in those days the Faculty of Technical University with a master-degree "engineer", since 1934 Doctor of Commercial Science).

In 1920 the Czech academic textbook of accounting at the Commercial College was (for the first time) published – *Theory and practices of accounting systems*-written by Professor JUDr. J. Pazourek.

There were two degrees of education at the Commercial College. Both of them contained problems of accounting and related economic issues (accounting terms, principles, kinds of accounting, accounting theories, history of accounting, legal framework, bookkeeping, stabilization and mergers, components of the financial statements, depreciation, reserve funds, secret accounting, accounting in banks, factories and agricultural companies, tax rules, monetary questions in accounting, special export/import bookkeeping). Professors J. Šlemr, F. Koštál, and others also taught there.

After World War II, Professor K. Žlábek started to lecture and also RCDr. Ing. Josef Blecha. Professor F. Salavec provided exercises. Lectures on accounting were supplemented by other subjects like controls and revisions, property administration, economic and accounting consultancy. Other universities (especially agricultural, forestry, electro technical, and civil engineering) provided lectures on accounting as well – Professors Fiala, Dr. Hauptmann, Ing. Pelikán, and Ing. Batrla were among the pedagogues.

A gradual decline occurred after February 1948. The volume of accounting problem lectures was systematically reduced and at the end it was only a part of so called "enterprises accountancy." "The Commercial College was liquidated (1949 – The University of Political and Economic Sciences)."

The University of Economics was established in 1953 and consisted of four faculties (General Economics, Finance, and Credit; Statistics; Production Economics; Commerce). According to the Soviet Union model – lectures on accounting varied from four to eight lectures per week except in the faculty of "accountancy." In 1981 Professor Ji í Klozar assessed this period in the following way:

> During this period various departments focused on national-economy topics and the lectures on accounting had many opportunities to explain issues in business. Some of these aspects (business finance, costs and expenses, economic result, price, price-costing, income distribution etc.) were later solved in other subjects and thus suggestions to reduce the scope of accounting lectures and to concentrate on how to transform economic reality into the accounts appeared as well.

The volume of lectures remained unchanged during the 1960s. The content was mainly practically oriented – basic methodology of bookkeeping, bookkeeping of simple economic transactions, and a detailed survey of current practice. Thanks to several individuals there were also lectures on *theories of accounts and balances* and about *the financial statements in the so-called Western countries.*

During the 1970s the content of lectures on accounting at the University of Economics changed because of changes in focus of individual faculties. The Ministry of Education controlled changes.

Accounting themes lectured at the particular faculties were, e.g.,

- Faculty of Production Economics – accounting practice, theory of costs, costing in agriculture (doc. Br ák), costing in industry (Professor Janout), costing in transport, and communication (Professor Svoboda)
- Faculty of Commerce – specific tasks of accounting in domestic and foreign trade (Professor Klozar and Professor Pilný)
- Faculty of National Economy – accounting theory and experience in both domestic and foreign countries including nonprofit organizations (Professor Bá a, Professor Fireš, doc. Janovský, Professor Schroll, Ing. T etina, doc.Vihan, doc. Zavadil)

In the 1970s the department of accounting was merged with the Faculty of Statistics and provided education primarily for students of this faculty, who were majors in accounting under the study program "economic information and control."

Accounting topics at the other universities were lectured in a very fundamental form (in compliance with the legislation rules only) at the Czech Technical University in Prague (Professor Vysušil), The University of Agriculture in Prague, VŠB – Technical University in Ostrava and the University of Technology in Brno.

Education in accounting was transformed and reinforced after the Velvet revolution in 1989. The Faculty of Finance and Accounting at the University of Economics in Prague was established in 1991. The department of accounting was split into two departments – the Financial Accounting Department and the Management Accounting Department. These departments provide the education of accounting and financial management for students who are major in accounting.

The content of education is continuously more and more focused on both Czech and standard aspects of accounting (IASIFRS) as well as on auditing of the financial statements.

Chapter 20
Quality and Effectiveness of PreQualification Education of Professional Accountants in the Czech Republic

Bohumil Král and Libuše Müllerová

20.1 Introduction

The increasing pressure on all-round professional accountants' competence is reflected also in the harmonization of the requirements on their prequalification education. The most recent example of this effort has been the IFAC initiative to implement International Education Standards (IES). Consequently, this pressure influences national prequalification systems including the education and exam systems of both professional bodies that operate in the Czech Republic – the Union of Accountants (UA) and Chamber of Auditors of the Czech Republic.

20.2 The Union of Accountants

The system was introduced in 1997 as the result of the Project of Certification and Education of Accountants in the Czech Republic. It was developed under the supervision of the Czech Ministry of Finance, EU PHARE and in cooperation with the British ACCA, but also with the Netherlands Royal NIVRA. Despite the international context it was adapted especially with regard to the special needs required to enhance the Czech accountancy profession as a whole – from the lowest to the highest level. The system, therefore, is structured – it gives the opportunity to gain three levels of qualification: technician, executive accountant, and chartered accountant. Candidates may either complete all three stages or they may finish their studies at a lower first or second level.

The basic design of the project that included – besides others – a system of examinations and preparation of first versions of 15 textbooks for all three stages was developed from August 1996 to November 1997. To achieve a high quality of the textbooks, their syllabi were prepared under the supervision of experts from ACCA and PHARE. Also, concrete parts of the textbooks were translated and veri-

B. Král and L. Müllerová
University of Economics, Prague

R. W. McGee (ed.), *Accounting Reform in Transition and Developing Economies,*
© Springer Science+Business Media LLC 2008

fied by leading experts in the respective disciplines – ACCA authors. Each textbook contains a "teaching guide" in order to guarantee a high standard of instruction and glossary, which gives harmonized definitions of terms. The textbooks were developed with regard to situations that participants could meet at work and they contain many case studies and examples from practice.

20.2.1 Contents and Characteristics of Qualification Levels and Modules

A. Accounting technician

The graduate is qualified for accounting practice in manufacturing companies, in commerce or nonmanufacturing branches. He or she is able to process usual accounting transactions and has a basic knowledge of their tax consequences and associated disciplines.

Requirements for certificate issuance are stated in Table 20.1.

B. Executive accountant

The graduate is able to work as an accountant in medium-size entities individually or manage a particular accounting unit of big entities. He or she is able to process all important accounting transactions up to the level of financial statements, including the solution of tax consequences and their expression in management accounting and evaluation, their influence on the return on capital, the financial position, and the company's ability to generate and invest cash. To a certain extent the executive accountant is able to think in international circumstances, especially when disclosure is different according to Czech accounting legislative and IAS/IFRS.

Requirements for certificate issuance are stated in Table 20.2.

C. Chartered accountant

A graduate is able to work individually at the position of chief accountant even in big entities including multinational companies. He or she acquires a full set of theoretical and practical knowledge for positions of a chief financial officer, treasurer,

Table 20.1 Accounting technician requirements

Required entry education	• Complete secondary education or
	• Complete secondary vocational education
Required work experience	• Minimum of 1 year and
	• Compliance with competencies determined for this level
Passing examinations in subjects	• Economics
	• Accounting – Part I
	• Legal System of the Czech Republic – Part I
	• Taxes – Part I
	• Quantitative Methods and Information Technology

Table 20.2 Executive accountant requirements

Required entry education	• Complete secondary education or
	• Complete secondary vocational education
	• Passing or recognition of the first level of examinations
Required work experience	• One more year, e.g. 2 years in total and
	• Fulfilment of competencies determined for the first and second level
Passing examinations in subjects	• Accounting – Part II
	• Legal System of the Czech Republic – Part II
	• Taxes – Part II
	• Management Finance
	• Quantitative Methods and Management
	• Management Accounting

Table 20.3 Chartered accountant requirements

Required entry education	• University degree, including Bachelor's degree and
	• Passing the examinations determined for the first and second stage
Required work experience	• One more year, e.g., 3 years in total and
	• Fulfilment of competencies determined for all three levels
Passing examinations in subjects	• International Accounting Standards and Consolidated Accounts
	• Financial Strategy
	• Financial Analysis
	• Auditing[1]

[1] All four examinations must be passed in four consecutive days.

controller, or any other high position in companies whose execution is based on perfect understanding of all accounting circumstances. But he or she is also provided with the qualification prerequisites and pieces of knowledge for a number of economic positions in the field of external (statutory) audit and taxes including positions of statutory auditor and tax advisor.[1] The chartered accountant is fully able to think in international circumstances of transactions expression, including different kinds of business combinations and consolidated accounts.

Requirements for certificate issuance are stated in Table 20.3.

20.2.2   Examinations

The scheme of examinations is fully consistent with the principles and procedures used by ACCA in order to guarantee their utmost compatibility.

---

[1] Nevertheless – it is necessary to stress that chartered accountants – graduates of the system are not allowed to work as statutory auditors or statutory tax advisors as the Act of Auditors and Act of Tax Advisors give the authority to verify their knowledge and experience to different professional bodies – to the Chamber of Auditors of the Czech Republic and to the Chamber of Tax Advisors.

Examination sessions take place twice a year at all three stages at one time, namely the third week of June and the second week of December. Examinations at a higher stage cannot be taken until the lower stage examinations were completed successfully (or exemptions granted – see later). The candidate at his own discretion sets the pace and number of papers.

The principal aim of the examinations is to guarantee an objective assessment of professional knowledge and skills to apply theoretical learning to solving practical problems in line with the structure of knowledge required at different levels of accountancy qualifications. Examinations should also verify the student's professional attributes such as coping with stress and concentration on solving an assignment in a limited period of time.

20.2.3   Recognition of Previous Education

Unlike the system of the Czech Chamber of Auditors the system of the Union of Accountants is based on a broad system of recognition of previous education. Its main principles are the following:

- At the first and second stage all examinations may be recognized. At the third stage, only the auditing examination may be recognized for auditors registered by the Chamber of Auditors of the Czech Republic.
- At the first or second stage, exemptions may be granted for individual as well as for all examinations.
- Exemptions are granted only in case where the adept has passed a concrete exam as a part of business secondary or university studies examinations and if the syllabus of the subject matter covered by the respective examination is equivalent to a professional exam.
- The candidate is a graduate of a business secondary school or university. Thus, examinations passed by the candidate without full completion of the respective education degree are not recognized.
- Examinations of the first stage can be recognized for the graduates of state business secondary schools who passed their secondary school-leaving examination in the last 5 years.
- Examinations for the first and second stages are fully recognized for the graduates of the specialization "Accounting and the Company Financial Management" of Finance and Accounting of the University of Economics, Prague who completed a masters or doctoral degree program in the last 5 years.
- Both Law and Tax examinations are fully recognized for the candidates working as tax advisors and registered by the Chamber of Tax Advisors of the Czech Republic.
- All examinations for the first and second stage are recognized for the candidates working as auditors and registered by the Chamber of Auditors of the Czech Republic. They also have exemption for an auditing pass for the third stage (see the first point).

The system was introduced without any support by law, which makes it mandatory for the performance of accountancy profession. Despite this fact, from 1997 (when the system was started) to the end of 2003 more than 6,500 accountants entered the system and 2,500 of them are certified in one of three levels of the system. Also in this year (2004) we expect the increase by 900 new participants. It seems to be proof that the system meets the need of differentiating the quality of services and competence of accountants on the market.

Apart from this project, the Union of Accountants organizes a large number of non-obligatory courses on its own making it possible for candidates to choose the best way to prepare for examinations.

20.3   Chamber of Auditors of the Czech Republic

The Chamber of Auditors of the Czech Republic (CACR) system was introduced in 1992 and partly updated in 2000 – in connection with the requirements of substantial amendment of the Act on Auditors (effective from January 2001). For applicants to serve as statutory auditors the amendment states obligations of

- Preceding 5 years of postgraduate studies
- Three years work experience as assistant auditor
- Passing the maximum of ten written and a final oral exam in a period of 3 years

In compliance with the Act the Chamber states the obligation to pass eight written exams, taking from 4–6 h, and a final 90-min oral exam.

Written exams cover the following problem areas:

- Accounting
- Business Combinations and Consolidated Accounts
- Corporate Finance
- Business Law
- Taxation
- Quantitative Methods and Information Technology
- Economics
- Auditing

Each of the written exams takes place twice a year. Consequently, the Chamber of Auditors organizes annually 16 written exams that are – with the exception of July and August – regularly spread over the year.

The content of the final oral exam consists of 100 questions; the participants lot four of them. The questions are conceived in the cross-sectional way; which means that each of them includes five important aspects that professional accountants can encounter in their activities: general economic, accounting, legal (including tax), information (including technology), and auditing topics.

Traditionally, Czech business, accounting, and tax legislative (including Czech audit, legal, and professional standard requirements) have been the principal subject of oral examinations. However, the stress on the substance of the examined area requires the adept to be able to understand and explain alternative solutions applied in the developed world. Moreover, this tendency is strongly supported by the increasing stress on the Czech financial accounting to be in compliance with IAS and by the accession of the Czech Republic to the EU.

It is possible to classify oral questions according to the following viewpoints:

- According to the generally accepted accounting principles that are applied in the information ability assurance of financial, tax, and management accounting (those questions include for example such areas as valuation, the application of the generally accepted accounting principles in practice, the elements of the accounting method, and the areas of costing, budgeting, and transfer pricing)
- According to their relation to the subject of accounting (those questions include for example the areas of tangible and intangible fixed assets, investments, inventory, receivables, equity, provisions etc.)
- According to their way of presentation in documents that are the subject of audit (the structure and content of financial statements and the annual report of a company or consolidated entity)
- According to the branch of undertaking or the area of operation of an audited entity (the specifics of banks, insurance companies, pension funds, companies oriented toward production, commercial, agricultural activities, but also not-for-profit organizations and municipalities are the subject of examinations)
- According to the legal form of undertaking (the specifics of public limited companies, limited companies, and state companies are the subject of examinations)
- According to substantial changes in the operations of companies (transactions connected with company liquidation, with its sale or with its bankruptcy are the subject of examinations)

20.4   Comparison of the Systems

In comparison with the system of the Union of Accountants the following features characterize the Prequalification Education and Examination system of the Chamber of Auditors:

- While the extent of knowledge required by the Union of Accountants system is included in textbooks and (with the exception of examinations of taxes and law where – additionally – the recent Czech legislative solution is one part of the exams) generally there are no additional requirements above the extent of textbooks. The CA CR system is based on the set of requirements stated in the printed "Summary of knowledge"; it also includes references to literature; it is the fact that the references are also to corresponding textbooks of the UA system in some problem areas
- Besides the examination of Accounting, other exams are similar in structure and content with the corresponding examinations of the UA system; the CA CR

Accounting exam contents test not only general knowledge of financial, tax, and management accounting but also the most important specialties of accounting of banks, not-for-profit organizations, municipalities, investment funds, and entities in the public sector[2]

- As it has been mentioned, unlike at the UA the CA CR examination sessions are not held at one time but they are regularly spread over the year; the main reason of that is the legal requirement to pass all exams (including a final oral exam) in a period of 3 years starting with the date of the first attempt.

20.5 Systems Analysis in Light of Less Requirements

There is no doubt that the future development of prequalification education of professional accountants as well as auditors is substantially influenced by the development of the IFAC International Education Standards.

What inspiration does their implementation bring to the development of professional education in the Czech Republic?

- We believe that the most important conclusion is positive. The education and examination systems of both bodies was arranged in order to follow the original International Education Guideline 9 (IEG 9). This Guideline – together with other documents arranging qualification requirements, especially with the 8th Directive of the European Union and the UNCTAD Qualification Guideline – has been taken into account while forming education and examination systems both in the CACR and the UA. We can say that both systems are in compliance with the IEG 9 requirements.[3]
- On the other side it is true that since IEG 9 adoption a long time has passed. Thus, the Standards are newly shaping, or stressing, tendencies that have influenced accounting in the last decade. These tendencies, for example more emphasis on professional ethics, values and attitudes, development of communication abilities, and IT usage, are in our opinion built in our systems on the level of "traditional" IEG requirements only. Consequently, their correspondence with the

---

[2] Extremely broad content and structure of the exam seems to be one of the most important problems for the future. Adepts complain about the broad spectrum of knowledge that is not possible – in their opinion – to absorb. It can lead to decreasing requirements for the exam. This is one of the reasons why the Common Body of Knowledge, recently developing for both institutions comes from the Union of Accountants system, meaning from the separation of financial and management accounting exams and from the conception to narrow the content of written exams to general requirements that – consequently – would lead to the transfer of the branches' specifics to Continuing Professional Education and Development.

[3] This fact has been confirmed by comparative analysis initiated by UA and prepared by a team of experts headed by Alain Burlaud who is the French representative in the IFAC Education Committee.

Standards is now the subject of a more detailed analysis than the traditional requirements based on "the triumvirate" of accounting – taxes – law.

- To enhance the accountants' competence worldwide the effort is visible not only to specify problem areas and references to literature sources but also to develop the system of textbooks and other educational instruments (including computer applications) that are worked out with respect to the profile of professional accountants. These measures are not explicitly required by Standards but they are considered to be more effective, timesaving, and more friendly to applicants. It would be, therefore, more suitable to go this way.

- Unfortunately, this way is also more expensive and more demanding for experts who prepare textbooks, examination papers, and take care of program development. In this regard we realize that the Czech Republic is too small to be able to attain reasonable costs and sufficient number of experts for the separate operation of two systems.

- Therefore, it has been decided that the principal aims of both professional bodies in the field of accountant education are

  o To co-ordinate efforts of both institutions in order to meet the requirements of the International Education Standards and

  o To prepare – in connection with the secondary and university education – the common education and examination system. Such system should respect differences in the preparation of professional accountants and auditors, but at the same time should be founded on a common knowledge base.

  o The development of "the common body of knowledge" was started in 2003. The project that is being developed in mutual collaboration of both professional bodies is at the stage when

  o The system structure and content and the mutual recognition conditions are being discussed in the Education Committees of both bodies

  o At the same time the legal preconditions that should be implemented into the updated Act on Auditors have been discussed with the Ministry of Finance representatives

- The common body of knowledge follows two main targets:

  o To update the content and structure of the prequalification systems of education and exams so that they are in compliance with recent global trends

  o To recognize the general as well as specific requirements for the education of future auditors and professional accountants in practice and to make it possible for them to learn and pass exams on a common basis. This concept would also lead to savings of start-up and operating costs

- A new integrated system of education and exams should become effective from January 2005. The draft comes from the new IES, but also from IEG 9 and 11, the UNCTAD prequalification guidelines and from the present education systems of both bodies. It respects the following principles:

  o Harmonization of the systems will be based on the three-level structure of the present Certification and Education System of the Union of Accountants;

- ○ The common body of knowledge will be created by the second and third level of the system;
- ○ To gain the qualification of a Chartered Accountant is obligatory but not a sufficient precondition for gaining the auditor qualification; the "super-structure" for auditors should include the final oral exam (based on the same conditions as the present one) and an extensive written exam in auditing.

- The aim to minimize the costs of educational instruments and textbooks; text-books "Certification and Education System of the Accountant", issued by the UA in the Czech Republic should be implemented as much as possible in the preparation of new textbooks or revision of the old ones. In this regard all new textbooks that were published in 2003 and early 2004 had been already developed with the intention of their common usage.
- The "personal union" also supports the whole process – many experts preparing textbooks, developing exam papers, and teaching in the prequalification education system are involved in both systems.

20.6   Conclusion

The above-described challenges are not simple but can be solved. We are convinced that the new integrated system will not only save costs and human effort but also enhance the quality of professional education of accountants in the Czech Republic.

Chapter 21
Accounting Education in Russia and the USA: A Comparative Study

Robert W. McGee and Galina G. Preobragenskaya

21.1 Introduction

This study compares and contrasts the accounting education provided by Russian universities with that given at American universities. Two typical universities were chosen for comparison purposes, one Russian and one American. Their curricula were compared and evaluated. Accounting educators at five Russian universities were also interviewed. The information gathered during the course of those interviews is also discussed. It was found that Russian accounting students spend a significantly longer amount of time studying both accounting and other subjects during the course of their university attendance. Part of the reason is because the average Russian accounting program is 5 years, compared to 4 years in the American system. However, Russian accounting students also spend more time at their studies each year.

Before the collapse of the Soviet Union, Russia and the other Soviet republics had a more or less uniform accounting educational program in the universities. Accounting actually formed a very minor part of the university curriculum. Students studied accounting as part of the economics major. The main emphasis was on the chart of accounts. There was also something about cost accounting, although cost accounting in Soviet times did not involve prices, since all prices were arbitrarily determined and were not used to allocate resources or measure profits. Financial statements consisted mostly of what would be called a funds flow statement in the West. There were no audit courses until the early 1990s.

Since Russia became an independent nation that is making the transition from a centrally planned economy to a market economy, it has had to adopt an accounting system that is more in tune with a market economy (Cheney, 1990; Enthoven, 1999; Verrue, 1995). Perestroika has caused major changes in the economy and those changes have filtered through to the Russian accounting system (Enthoven, 1992;

R. W. McGee
Florida International University

G. G. Preobragenskaya
KIMEP, Kazakhstan

R. W. McGee (ed.), *Accounting Reform in Transition and Developing Economies*,
© Springer Science+Business Media LLC 2008

Shama and McMahan, 1990; Sherry and Vinning, 1995). Even before perestroika, Russian managers realized that there was a need to change the way things are accounted for in the former Soviet Union (Chastain, 1982). The Russian Finance Minister has declared that all Russian banks and many Russian businesses must start using International Financial Reporting Standards by January 1, 2004. No one who is knowledgeable about the state of Russian accounting expected that to happen, and in fact it has not, but the mere fact that the Finance Ministry wants to push Russian accounting practices in that direction so fast – a year ahead of a similar requirement to be adopted by the EU – indicates that there is strong support for upgrading accounting in Russia.

One of the major impediments to converting from the accounting system Russia had under central planning to the system they need for their emerging market economy is that there is an insufficient number of accountants in Russia who are trained in the new system. Before 1998 International Accounting Standards (IAS), which are promulgated in the UK and used in dozens of countries worldwide, were not available in the Russian language. The translation that is now available has several flaws. For one, it does not incorporate any of the numerous changes that have been made to IAS since 1998, although some of the more recent international standards have been translated into Russian since then. Another criticism of the Russian version of IAS is that the translation of certain passages leaves a reader wondering what the standards say. Some passages contain major translation errors. At least one sentence leaves out the word "not," leading the reader to believe that something must be done when it fact it must not be done (Preobragenskaya and McGee, 2004).

There is also a lack of recent, high-quality texts and other learning material. Although some western accounting texts have been translated into Russian, many of the texts that are available are two or more editions behind what is available in western universities. A US text dated 2003 in the 11th edition might be available in Russian only in the 8th edition, published in 1994 (Preobragenskaya and McGee, 2003). Another problem with using US texts in Russian universities is that they are based on US GAAP, not IAS. If Russian students need to learn IAS, they must find another way to do it, since the US texts they are using say little or nothing about IAS.

Another impediment to fully adopting and implementing IAS is the lack of professors who are familiar with the subject. It is difficult to teach IAS and western audit techniques to the new generation of Russian accounting students if the professors themselves are not familiar with these subjects. Professors who graduated from a Russian university before 1990 or so had little or no exposure to the accounting concepts they are being called upon to teach. Many of the Russian professors who graduated after 1990 also have not had sufficient exposure to IAS and the International Standards on Auditing (ISA) to give adequate lectures, unless they learned IAS and ISA on their own. The situation is even worse outside the major cities of Moscow and St. Petersburg, since the demand to learn the new accounting is much less outside of Russia's two capitals. One reason for the lack of demand is because only Russia's largest companies need to use IAS, and the main reason they need to use IAS is to attract foreign capital. Otherwise, there would be no need, since the Russian tax authorities demand information that is compiled using Russian

Accounting Standards (RAS). Where there is no demand, there is also no supply. So the situation outside of Russia's largest cities will not change any time soon.

That being the case, the authors wanted to learn what Russian universities are doing in the area of accounting education. Specifically, they wanted to learn what is being taught to accounting students in Russian universities. A comparison was then made to the accounting curriculum offered by the average US university.

21.2   Review of the Literature

A wealth of literature exists on accounting education in the United States. However, most of this literature is irrelevant for purposes of the present study, which focuses on accounting education in Russia.

A second category of literature pertaining to accounting education addresses accounting education in transition economies. The International Federation of Accountants (IFAC) provides some guidelines that are being adopted in several transition economies (IFAC, 2003a–h).

The third category of literature addresses accounting education in Russia (Anon., 2001, 1994; Coyle and Platonov, 1998; Enthoven et al., 1998; Kobrak, 1991; Smirnova et al., 1995). There is also some literature that discusses accounting education in other former Soviet republics (McGee, 2003). This literature was also examined, since the accounting education in other Soviet republics was more or less the same as the accounting education received by Russian accounting students, although accounting education has been evolving in different directions in the various former Soviet republics since the demise of the Soviet Union. Unfortunately, most of the literature on accounting education in Russia and other former Soviet republics has become dated, since it was published before the recent changes.

21.3   Methodology

After reviewing the literature on accounting education in Eastern Europe and the former Soviet republics, the authors developed a tentative list of questions to ask Russian accounting educators. A sample of accounting educators representing state universities was then selected and contacted. Interviews were scheduled and held during the summer and fall of 2003 in Moscow, St. Petersburg, Omsk, and Kazan. Interviews were held at the following universities:

St. Petersburg State Polytechnic University [www.spbstu.ru]
St. Petersburg State Railway University (a.k.a. Petersburg State Transport University) [www.pgups.ru]
Timiryazev Agricultural Academy, Moscow [www.timacad.ru]
State University of Omsk [www.omsu.omskreg.ru]
Kazan State Finance Economic Institute [www.kfei.kcn.ru]

Interviews were held with deans, accounting department chairs, and other accounting professors. Materials describing their accounting programs were gathered as well.

21.4   Accounting Education in Russia

Russian universities do not necessarily offer their accounting programs over the same period as American universities. Whereas American universities offer the bachelor's degree over 4 years, the vast majority of Russian universities have a 5-year program. Less than 10% of all Russian universities offer a 4-year bachelor's degree in accounting. The vast majority offer a 5-year specialist designation. One reason for the popularity of the 5-year program is because most Russian employers think that a bachelor's degree holder does not offer much value to their company. They prefer to hire someone who has the specialist designation because of the perception that specialists have more to offer.

St. Petersburg State Polytechnic University was chosen for comparison purposes. It was chosen because its accounting curriculum is relatively innovative and modern by Russian standards. Its curriculum represents the trend in Russian accounting education, with the result that the comparison of its curriculum to that of the average American AACSB school will stand the test of time longer than the curriculum of some other Russian universities that have not progressed to the same point as St. Petersburg State Polytechnic University.

This university offers a 4-year bachelor's degree, a 5-year specialist designation and a sixth year master's degree. However, only about 20% of the students who complete the specialist designation go on for the sixth year master's degree. There are a number of reasons for not getting the master's. For one, the government will not subsidize the sixth year of study, so the university has to pay the expenses for the sixth year out of its own budget. However, the interview in Kazan revealed that the university there does receive funding for the sixth year, so the policy regarding the sixth year of accounting education does not seem to be uniform throughout Russia. Also, people who earn the master's degree are not able to command a higher salary than students who left school after earning just the specialist designation, so there is little incentive to go the extra year for the master's degree. Students who decide to go for the master's anyway often do so because it will make them more marketable in the West.

Table 21.1 shows how hours are allocated among the various disciplines for students enrolled in the 5-year specialist program. The 5-year program was chosen for analysis because the 5-year program is the most popular and frequently offered program, not just at St. Petersburg State Polytechnic University but throughout Russia. If a comparison is to be made between accounting education in Russia and that in the United States, it was thought that the program chosen should be the one that most Russian accounting students actually take. That is why the bachelor's degree program was not selected, even though the Russian 4-year bachelor's degree

Table 21.1 Allocation of hours among subject categories 5-year specialist designation Russian Government Recommendation

Disciplines (including practice)	Total hours	% of Total
General Humanities and Social Economics Disciplines	1,800	19.4
General Mathematics and Natural Science Disciplines	1,400	15.1
General Professional Disciplines	2,200	23.7
Special Disciplines	2,790	30.1
Additional Courses	1,090	11.7
Totals	9,280	100

program covers the same period of time as the American bachelor's degree program.

The number of hours spent in the various categories seems large, and it is. However, these numbers may be inflated. Heyd, in another chapter of the present volume, points out that the official number of hours required for a degree in a Ukrainian university is highly inflated. There is no way to tell with any degree of accuracy what the actual hours are. Since the Russian and Ukrainian educational systems are about the same, one may reasonably conclude that the Russian figures are also inflated. However, in the absence of better data, we will go with the official data, keeping in mind that the data is likely inflated.

Russian students who study accounting spend a significant amount of time studying other subjects, many of which have nothing to do with accounting. In this respect, they are much like their American counterparts. Much time is spent by all students, regardless of major, studying social sciences, humanities, mathematics, and natural sciences. Table 21.1 shows the standard accounting curriculum recommended by the Russian government. A total of 9,280 h are required to earn the accounting specialist designation.

Table 21.2 gives a detailed breakdown of subjects studied for accounting majors at St. Petersburg State Polytechnic University. Its curriculum varies slightly from the Russian government's recommended curriculum, which is permitted under the Russian Education Ministry regulations. There are separate columns for lectures, class study, laboratory study, and self study. This table was compiled from official university documents. Hours for class study, self study, etc. are not the authors' estimates. They are the actual hours programmed into the university's curriculum.

Table 21.3 shows the breakdown of the curriculum by category. There are separate categories for accounting, other business, and nonbusiness. Some arbitrariness was involved in making these three categories. For example, statistics and probability theory were classified as business courses, when in fact they could be either business or mathematics. Some US universities teach statistics in the business school, whereas other schools teach it in the mathematics department. Jurisprudence was classified as other business, since some of the content of that course includes business law. Information science was classified as other business, since this topic is often taught in US business schools, although some US schools teach it in arts and sciences.

Table 21.2 Curriculum for Specialty "Accounting, Analysis and Audit" St. Petersburg State Polytechnic University 5-year specialist designation

		Number of hours				Total	
Subjects	Lectures	Class study	Laboratory study	Total classhours	Self study	Hours	% of Total (8,208 = 100%)
General Humanities and Social Economic Disciplines	**272**	**969**		**1,241**	**561**	**1,802**	**22.0**
Federal Component	*170*	*901*		*1,071*	*391*	*1,462*	
Foreign Languages		340		340	170	510	6.2
Physical Training		408		408		408	5.0
Russian History	34	17		51	34	85	1.0
Philosophy	34	34		68	34	102	1.3
Economic Theory	102	102		204	153	357	4.3
Regional (university) component	*102*	*34*		*136*	*102*	*238*	
Social Science	34			34	34	68	2.4
Jurisprudence	68	34		102	68	170	2.1
Electives		*34*		*34*	*68*	*102*	
Culture Science		34		34	68	102	1.3
General Mathematics and Natural Sciences	**440**	**187**	**355**	**982**	**560**	**1,542**	**18.8**
Federal Component	*338*	*119*	*321*	*778*	*492*	*1270*	
Mathematics	119	119		238	153	391	4.8
Information Science	85		204	289	170	459	5.6
Information Systems in Economics	66		66	132	33	165	2.0
Concepts of Modern Natural Science (Ecology)	68		51	119	136	255	3.1
Regional (University) Component	*68*	*34*	*34*	*136*	*34*	*170*	
Econometrics	68	34	34	136	34	170	2.1
Electives	34	34		68	34	102	
Probability Theory	34	34		68	34	102	1.2
General Professional Disciplines	**758**	**369**	**153**	**1,280**	**942**	**2,222**	**27.1**
Federal Component	*656*	*301*	*153*	*1,110*	*721*	*1,831*	
Economics of Enterprises	85		68	153	51	204	2.5
Management	51	34		85	136	221	2.7
Marketing	34	34		68	34	102	1.2
Statistics	68		68	136	34	170	2.1
World Economics	34	34		68	51	119	1.4
Financial Management	68	17	17	102	34	136	1.8

(continued)

Table 21.2 (continued)

Subjects	Number of hours					Total	
	Lectures	Class study	Laboratory study	Total classhours	Self study	Hours	% of Total (8,208 = 100%)
Finance	34	17		51	51	102	1.2
Insurance	51	17		68	34	102	1.2
Cash, Loan, Banks	48	32		80	48	128	1.6
Stock Exchange Market	48	32		80	96	176	2.1
Taxes	51	34		85	51	136	1.8
The Theory of Accounting	34	17		51	51	102	1.2
International Accounting Standards	34	17		51	34	85	1.0
International Standards of Audit	16	16		32	16	48	0.6
Regional (University) Component	*34*	*34*		*68*	*153*	*221*	
Business Communications (Contracts)	34	34		68	153	221	2.7
Electives	*68*	*34*		*102*	*68*	*170*	
Pricing	34	17		51	51	102	1.2
Vital Functions "Safety & Protection of Labor	34	17		51	17	68	0.8
Special Disciplines	*539*	*269*	*201*	*1,009*	*1,157*	*2,166*	*26.4*
Financial Accounting	85	34	34	153	153	306	3.7
Management Accounting	51	34		85	51	136	1.7
Financial Statement Analysis	34	17		51	51	102	1.3
Complex Economic Analysis of Enterprise Activity	68	34	34	136	102	238	2.9
Audit	68	51		119	119	238	2.9
Class Training (A case study of accounting of an enterprise activity)			82	82	182	264	3.2
Electives	*48*	*16*		*64*	*96*	*160*	
Investment Analysis/ Real Estate Economics	48	16		64	96	160	1.9

(continued)

Table 21.2 (continued)

Subjects	Lectures	Class study	Laboratory study	Total classhours	Self study	Hours	% of Total (8,208 = 100%)
		Number of hours				Total	
Specialization Discipline	*185*	*83*	*51*	*319*	*403*	*722*	
Cost Accounting, Budgeting for Different Industries	66	66		132	165	297	3.6
Accounting, Analysis and Audit of Foreign Economic Activity	34	17		51	68	119	1.5
Logistics	85		51	136	170	306	3.7
Practical Training							
Additional Courses		**476**		**476**		**476**	**5.7**
TOTAL (hours)	2,009	2,270	709	4,988	3,220	8,208	100
Army Course		476		476		476	
TOTAL	2,009	2,746	709	5,464	3,220	8,684	

21.5   Accounting Education in the United States

Accounting education in the United States is not identical from university to university, although there is not much variation, especially at the undergraduate level. One reason for the relative uniformity is because the Association to Advance Collegiate Schools of Business (AACSB), the agency that accredits some business schools in the United States, has rather rigid requirements regarding what must be taught to gain accreditation (www.aacsb.edu). Although the AACSB accredits less than half of the business schools in the United States, it is very influential because the schools that are AACSB accredited tend to be the larger schools. Nearly all of the universities that offer a Ph.D. in accounting are AACSB accredited.

That being the case, the authors decided to use the curriculum requirements of an AACSB accredited school for comparison purposes. Barry University was chosen because it is a small university, with slightly fewer than 9,000 students, and it received AACSB accreditation in April 2003, so, presumably, its accounting curriculum meets the current AACSB standards (although some AACSB standards are in the process of changing, but those standards do not relate to curriculum). Barry University is representative of the schools that most recently became AACSB accredited. When the AACSB first began accrediting schools, it was mostly the larger schools that applied for accreditation. Now it is mostly the smaller schools that apply for AACSB accreditation.

Table 21.4 shows the breakdown of curriculum for the 4-year bachelor's degree in accounting. There are separate categories for accounting, other business, and

Table 21.3 Breakdown of curriculum by category 5-year specialist designation St. Petersburg State Polytechnic University

	Hours	Subtotals	% of Total
Accounting			
Taxes	136		
The Theory of Accounting	102		
International Accounting Standards	85		
International Standards of Audit	48		
Financial Accounting	306		
Managerial Accounting	136		
Financial Statement Analysis	102		
Complex Economic Analysis of Enterprise Activity	238		
Audit	238		
Class Training (A case study of enterprise accounting)	264		
Electives	160		
Cost Accounting, Budgeting for Different Industries	297		
Accounting, Analysis and Audit of Foreign Economic Activity	119		
Practical Training	476	2,707	31.2
Other Business			
Economic Theory	357		
Jurisprudence	170		
Information Science	459		
Information Systems in Economics	165		
Econometrics	170		
Probability Theory	102		
Economics of Enterprises	204		
Management	221		
Marketing	102		
Statistics	170		
World Economics	119		
Financial Management	136		
Finance	102		
Insurance	102		
Cash, Loan, Banks	128		
Stock Exchange Market	176		
Business Communications (contracts)	221		
Electives	170		
Pricing	102		
Vital Functions Safety and Protection of Labor	68		
Investment Analysis/Real Estate Economics	160		
Logistics	306	3,910	45.0
Nonbusiness		2,067	23.8
Total		8,684	100

nonbusiness. Barry University uses the semester hour system. Each semester hour represents 15 academic hours of class meetings. One academic hour consists of 50 min. However, for purposes of simplicity, we have defined one academic hour as 60 min. For comparison purposes, we have estimated that 1.5 h is spent in study for each hour spent in class.

There was some arbitrariness in the categorization of some subjects. For example, Barry University lists macroeconomics as a social science but we have listed it as a business course. Barry University classifies precalculus for business and elementary probability and statistics as mathematics courses. We listed them as business courses. Barry lists basic computer applications as a nonbusiness course. We classified it as a business course.

Table 21.4 Breakdown of curriculum by category 4-year Bachelor's degree Barry University

	Semester Hours	Hours in class	Study hours	Total hours	% of Total
Accounting					
Financial Accounting	3	45			
Managerial Accounting	3	45			
Intermediate Accounting I	3	45			
Intermediate Accounting II	3	45			
Intermediate Accounting III	3	45			
Cost Accounting	3	45			
Federal Income Taxation	3	45			
Accounting Information Systems	3	45			
Advanced Accounting	3	45			
Auditing	3	45			
Total Accounting	30	450	675	1,125	23.8
Other Business					
Introduction to Business	3	45			
Microeconomics	3	45			
Macroeconomics	3	45			
Applications of Statistics in Business	3	45			
Introduction to Information Systems	3	45			
Organization Behavior and Management	3	45			
Operations Management	3	45			
Marketing Concepts and Applications	3	45			
Business Law I	3	45			
International Business	3	45			
Financial Management I	3	45			
Strategic Management	3	45			
Business Electives	3	45			
Basic Computer Applications	3	45			
Precalculus Mathematics for Business	3	45			
Elementary Probability & Statistics	3	45			
Social & Ethical Issues in Business	3	45			
Total Other Business	51	765	1,148	1,913	40.5
Nonbusiness	45	675	1,013	1,688	35.7
Totals	126	1,890	2,836	4,726	100

21.6 Comparisons

It is difficult to make a strict comparison between the university curriculum that a Russian accounting student would follow and the curriculum an American student would follow. For one thing, the courses they take are much different. Their entry level backgrounds are also different. Various international standardized exams that allow student achievement to be compared between and among students in different countries uniformly show that American students are at or near the bottom of the scale in terms of math and science skills. Russian students, on the other hand, have a reputation for having strong math and science skills. Thus, one might conclude that the average first year student at a Russian university is better prepared for academic work than is the average American student. If true, Russian universities would be able to demand more from their first-year students than would be the case for American universities.

This initial view was confirmed by interviews one of the present authors has had with a variety of students from East European countries over the years. They generally felt that American universities did not challenge them as much and that some of the courses they took at American schools consisted mostly of material they had already learned when they were high school students. However, that general view did not extend to some of the accounting courses they took at American universities. Intermediate accounting seemed especially demanding, although none of the students interviewed said that intermediate accounting was any more rigorous than some of the courses they took at their East European university.

But that is not the only difference between the attributes of first-year students in Russian and American universities. A higher percentage of high school graduates enter universities in the United States than in Russia, so even if the average Russian high school student were the rough equivalent of the average American high school student, the average Russian first-year university student would be superior to the average American first-year student because Russian universities tend to accept only the best high school graduates, whereas some American universities will accept almost anyone who graduates from high school. Some American universities will even accept high school dropouts who are over the age of 23, the rationale being that they have acquired some work experience and maturity by then. Taking all these factors into account would take us too far afield from the main area of investigation, which is a comparison of the university accounting curriculum of Russian and American universities, so we will leave discussion of these other items for another day.

There are other reasons why comparing the accounting curriculum at a Russian university to the accounting curriculum at an American university may be difficult. For one thing, the period of study may be different. At American schools, the total curriculum consists of between 120 and 128 semester hours, with each semester hour being the equivalent to 15 h spent in class. But each class hour consists of just 50 min. The curriculum can be completed over 4 years by a full-time student.

The time period for Russian universities is not so uniform. Some Russian universities have a curriculum that stretches over 4 years, while others have a 5-year program. Some Russian universities also have a sixth year, which often results in a master's degree. Also, in Russian universities, study is not measured only in terms of hours spent in class. Other factors are included, such as study time, laboratory time, and time spent working as an intern or practicing accountant. Also, some lectures are given in big lecture halls by full-time professors, whereas other sessions are given in smaller groups and are conducted by assistant professors, so there may be some qualitative differences between the lectures received in small universities and large universities, if one believes that the quality of instruction declines as class size increases. There is the perception that smaller classes result in a better educational experience than large classes held in lecture halls. Students tend to pay more attention, do not talk to each other as much and can hear the professor's lecture better in a small classroom. This same format is used in some of the larger American universities, at least in the first year or two of instruction, but it is not used in the smaller universities.

In an attempt to equalize these differences, we have made some assumptions regarding the American system. For comparison purposes, we have assumed that the average American student spends 1.5 h studying outside of class for each hour in class, and we have treated each hour as if it consisted of 60 min, for simplification purposes, although an academic hour consists of just 50 min.

For comparison purposes, we decided to compare the Russian 5-year program to the American 4-year bachelor's degree program. While such a choice might seem odd, the reason for it can be justified. As was previously mentioned, less than 10% of the Russian universities that offer accounting programs offer the 4-year bachelor's degree. The vast majority of them offer the 5-year specialist degree. Thus, if the goal is to compare the accounting offered by the "average" Russian university to that offered by the average American school, the decision to compare the 5-year Russian specialist program to the 4-year American bachelor's degree program seems most appropriate.

Table 21.5 compares the accounting curriculum of the Russian and American universities selected for comparison purposes. As one might expect, Russian accounting majors spend more time studying all three categories of subjects than their American counterparts. One reason for the extra study hours is because the Russian program is 5 years, whereas the American program is 4 years. The comparison could be tightened up a bit if the numbers were annualized. If one divides the Russian total (8,684 h) by 5 and the American total (4,726 h) by 4, the annual

Table 21.5 Comparison on Russian and American accounting curricula

| | Russian University (Table 21.3) | | American University (Table 21.4) | |
	Hours	% of Total	Hours	% of Total
Accounting Courses	2,707	31.2	1,125	23.8
Other Business Courses	3,910	45.0	1,913	40.5
Nonbusiness Courses	2,067	23.8	1,688	35.7
Totals	8,684	100	4,726	100
Hours per year	1,737		1,182	

study times are 1,737 and 1,182, respectively. If these numbers are reliable estimates of time spent studying, that means that the average Russian accounting student spends an additional 555 h a year (47%) studying.

If one compares the total study times, the results are even more remarkably different. Russian students spend 8,684 h earning their diploma, compared to 4,726 for the average American accounting student, a difference of 3,958 h. That is an extra 84%.

The evidence seems overwhelming, on the surface at least, that the average Russian accounting graduate is better prepared than the average American accounting graduate. Russian universities are more selective regarding whom they allow into their programs and Russian students study many more hours in total as well as in accounting. Russian students spend 31.2% of their time studying accounting, compared to 23.8% for American students. Russian students spend 2,707 h studying accounting, compared to 1,125 h for American students. That's an extra 1,582 h, or 141%.

However, there are other factors to consider. For example, the quality of Russian textbooks and other study materials may not be as good as those used by American students. Russian accounting texts do not have nearly as many examples as American textbooks. There are no Russian texts that are closely comparable to an American intermediate accounting book in terms of depth or breadth of coverage. Although some American texts have been translated into Russian, the Russian translation may be 8 or 10 years old and the quality of the translation may be less than perfect.

Furthermore, many Russian students, perhaps the great majority, do not own many (or any) accounting textbooks. They are too expensive for the average Russian student. They compensate for this factor by going to the library and reading the books the library has. This approach to study is quite common in Russian universities. The problem is that Russian university libraries sometimes do not have enough books for all the students who want to read them. This is especially true outside of Moscow and St. Petersburg. Or at least that is what one professor told us, although information we received elsewhere seems to dispute this general claim. Other people interviewed also thought that the libraries had a sufficient number of books for the students, so perhaps it cannot be said that there is any widespread shortage of textbooks.

Another solution that was discovered during the course of the interviews was that some student book purchases are subsidized. For example, the Agriculture Ministry, which has a great deal of control over Timiryazev Agricultural Academy, subsidizes book purchases so that the average book costs students about $2, which is a sufficiently low price that students are able to afford to purchase their own copies of the books they need for class. However, this practice was not present at the other universities that were interviewed.

Subsidizing the cost of textbooks was also done in the accounting reform projects carried out by the United States Agency for International Development (USAID) in Armenia and Bosnia. In those countries, USAID gave books to the university libraries or subsidized the cost of translating and publishing accounting books so that the local accounting association could sell the books at an affordable price. However, the interviews conducted as part of the present study did not find much evidence of text subsidization in Russia, with the exception of Timiryazev Agricultural Academy.

It could also be mentioned that some accounting texts only cost about $3 without the subsidy, making it possible for Russian students to purchase books if they want to. However, there is another reason why many Russian students do not buy texts even if they can afford them. Why pay $3 to own a book on econometrics when you can read it in the library for free? The Russian thought process here is that it does not make sense to spend money on a book that has no value after graduation, either because, like econometrics, it will never be read again or, in the case of accounting, because the text will become outdated by the time one graduates.

Another factor that needs to be discussed regarding the relative "raw material" and "finished goods" that the universities produce, if one thinks of accounting students as products and the universities as manufacturers, involves the processing of the raw material into the finished product. Although the raw material (first-year student) that goes into Russian universities may be of higher quality, it cannot be said categorically that the end product is better, because the processing is different, not only because of the difference in the quality of textbooks but also because of the gauntlet that students must successfully pass through to get their diploma at the other end of the production line.

It is a well-known fact in American universities that the first financial accounting course acts as a screen. It is part of the weeding-out process. There is a high failure rate in that class because many students who take that course do not belong in the business school, or perhaps in any part of the university. Low admission standards at many American universities allow many students in who do not really belong in a university, but they do not protect them once they are admitted and start taking classes. They have to demonstrate a certain amount of intellectual ability to remain, survive, and prosper.

Students who pass the financial accounting course must also pass the managerial accounting course, which also acts as a screen to prevent the least able students from progressing to the next level. These courses are not intended to weed out a certain percentage of students. However, they do have that effect, since they are somewhat more rigorous than what some students can take.

The first financial and managerial accounting courses are the only accounting courses that business majors have to take, unless they are accounting majors. The next phase in the screening process is intermediate accounting, which is required only for accounting majors. A certain percentage of accounting majors who managed to survive financial and managerial accounting are unable to pass the first or second intermediate accounting courses. The vast majority of students who are able to pass the first two intermediate accounting courses are able to complete the other accounting courses and graduate.

The bottom line is that the average American accounting graduate may not be so inferior to the average Russian accounting graduate because only the best American accounting students can survive the gauntlet of accounting courses. The dropout rate is higher in American schools, which serves to narrow the differences between the finished product in American and Russian accounting programs.

Another factor to be considered is opportunity cost. If one were to make a comparison of Russian and American accounting graduates 5 years after they enter the university, it would be necessary to include all of their educational-related experiences over those 5 years. The analysis above did not do that. It compared the 5-year Russian educational experience to the 4-year American educational experience. A better comparison would be to compare what both groups did in the 5 years after entering their respective universities.

If we assume that the American accounting students who graduated after 4 years entered the workforce and worked 2,000 h in some accounting capacity, those hours of practical work experience could be added to the American statistics, just like the practical training that the Russian accounting students received as part of their training was included in the statistics of their educational programs. However, adding the full 2,000 h to the amount of time spent in educational activities might distort the amount of actual education that took place, since much of what a first-year accountant does is repetitious. Table 21.6 shows what the relative statistics would look like if half of the 2,000 postgraduate hours were added to the hours spent in a 4-year bachelor degree program.

Table 21.6 shows that, if half of the first year of work experience were included in the American statistics, the American accounting graduates would have 2,125 h of accounting, compared to 2,707 for the Russians, lessening the disparity to 582 h. Of course, it could be argued that such a comparison is not appropriate if the goal were to compare the Russian university accounting program to the American university accounting program, since the fifth year is not spent studying accounting, but practicing it. Such a criticism has some validity. But so does the analysis of total hours spent in accounting over the 5-year period, since this methodology compares both groups over the same time period rather than using 5 years of data for the Russian students and 4 years of data for the American students. However, even if 5 years of data are used, the Russian accounting graduates still have more total hours than their American counterparts, 8,684 compared to 5,726. That is an additional 2,958 h, or 52%. That's more than a full year of additional educational experience, if one defines a year as 2,000 h.

Table 21.6 Five-year comparison

| | Russian accounting majors | | American accounting majors | |
	Hours	% of Total	Hours	% of Total
Accounting courses & Practical experience	2,707	31.2	2,125	37.1
Other business courses	3,910	45.0	1,913	33.4
Nonbusiness courses	2,067	23.8	1,688	29.5
Totals	8,684	100	5,726	100
Hours per year	1,737		1,145	

We believe that the most valid comparison of American accounting programs to Russian accounting programs is to compare the 4-year American bachelor's degree to the 5-year accounting specialist diploma that Russian universities award. As we mentioned above, the rationale for this comparison is because the vast majority of Russian universities offer the 5-year specialist program. Very few Russian students opt for the 4-year bachelor's degree. Thus, if one were to compare the program the average American student takes to that of the average Russian student, the choice is clearly to compare the 4-year American bachelor's degree program to the 5-year Russian specialist diploma program.

However, one of the referees who commented on the first draft of this article criticized us for making this comparison. In spite of our explanation for comparing the 4-year American program to the 5-year Russian program, he/she insisted that it would be better to compare the American 150-h program to the Russian 5-year specialist program. While we think that making such a comparison has some merit, in theory at least, we also think that such a comparison suffers from several weaknesses.

For one, there is really no such thing as an American 150 semester hour program. Although most states in the United States require students to take 150 semester hours of coursework in order to be eligible to sit for the CPA (certified public accountant) exam, most students who complete a 120-h or 128-h bachelor's degree do not merely keep taking classes until they reach the 150 semester hour mark. They take a master's degree, either in accounting or in business. An MS degree in accounting can be anywhere from 30 to 42 semester hours. An MBA can be anywhere from 36 to 60 semester hours. Thus, it is difficult to compare what an average American student would take to reach the 150 semester-hour level with what the average Russian student would take to earn the 5-year specialist diploma.

Perhaps a more valid comparison would be to compare what the American master's degree student would take to what a Russian master's degree student would take. But this comparison also suffers from some weaknesses, the most noticeable being that only about 20% of Russian students take a master's degree, which is the sixth year of education in Russian universities. Thus, such a comparison would be between a Russian student that is unusual (only 20% take such a degree program) and a usual American student who is preparing for the CPA exam, which is not actually the usual American student, since only a small minority of American students take and eventually pass the American CPA exam. Also, such a comparison would involve comparing a Russian student taking a 6-year program to an American student who takes either 5 or 6 years of university education, depending on whether the bachelor's degree was 120 or 128 h and whether the master's degree consisted of 30 or 60 h of coursework, or something in between 30 and 60 h.

Another problem with using an American master's degree for comparison purposes is that the amount of accounting that must be taken in such a program varies widely. For example, an MS in accounting might require a student to take only 12 or 15 h in accounting, with the remainder of the program being in other business areas, with the possibility of taking 3–9 h outside the field of business. An MBA with a concentration in accounting might require a student to take just

9–15 h in accounting out of a program that might consist of up to 60 semester hours of total coursework.

It might also be pointed out that the 150 semester-hour requirement in most states does not require students to take *any* accounting courses beyond the bachelor's degree. The 150 semester-hour requirement can be met by taking *any* university courses, at either the undergraduate or graduate level. Thus, an American student who has a bachelor's degree in accounting can qualify to take the CPA exam by taking all additional courses in Spanish or even basket weaving, provided such courses were at university level.

All things considered, we do not think that comparing an American 150 semester-hour program to the Russian 5-year specialist diploma provides as valid a comparison as that between the typical 4-year American accounting program and the Russian 5-year program that is taken by the vast majority of Russian accounting students.

21.7 Concluding Comments

Russian universities seemingly have a solid accounting program. Their students spend more time studying accounting and other subjects than do their American counterparts. The interviews the authors conducted at three of the Big-Four accounting firms in Moscow and St. Petersburg for another research project (Preobragenskaya and McGee, 2004) confirmed that recent graduates were adequately prepared for entry-level accounting positions.

However, it cannot be said with as much certainty whether students who study accounting at universities outside of Russia's major cities receive the same quality of instruction. The interviews indicated that the quality of educational materials outside of Russia's major cities might be lower and professors in the regions might not be as well-versed in International Accounting Standards, a factor that, if true, must have an adverse effect on the quality of the accounting education they provide.

The people interviewed who seemed to think that the quality of education provided outside of Russia's two capitals was at a lower level might have been exaggerating the point, at least to a certain extent. While it is probably true that the best universities in Moscow and St. Petersburg provide a better accounting education than universities in other Russian cities, it could also probably be said that many Russian universities outside of those two cities provide an accounting education that is roughly comparable to that offered by the second-tier universities in Moscow and St. Petersburg. At least that was the view of some of the other people interviewed as part of the present study.

The authors would be the first to admit that the comparisons made in this study are not the only comparisons that could be made. Choosing different American and Russian universities would produce slightly different results. Choosing a non-AACSB American school would perhaps produce somewhat different results as well. Choosing a Russian university that has a longer (or shorter) accounting program would produce different results. Choosing a Russian university that is not located in one of Russia's two capitals also might produce different results. Thus, there is room for further research, which could either replicate the present study or differentiate itself from the present study.

Studies could also be made comparing some American university to a university either in some other former Soviet republic (there are 15 of them) or to some university in the former satellite countries such as Poland, Hungary, the Czech Republic, etc. Other studies could be made that compare the accounting curriculum in a Russian university to that of one of the other former Soviet republics. It would be interesting to see how curricula have evolved in these former Soviet republics since the dissolution of the Soviet Union, and to speculate as to why the accounting curricula in the different countries are evolving in different directions. Or maybe they are evolving in the same direction, which is a distinct possibility, given the increased influence and spread of International Accounting Standards throughout both the EU and transition economies. Only additional research would reveal in which direction these universities are evolving.

Another possibility would be to replicate the present study in 2 or 3 years. Examining the curriculum at the same universities in a few years might produce different results, since the curriculum in Russian universities is in a state of change. Although the general movement is toward IAS, it is a movement with a Russian flavor. Russian accounting standards are not going to disappear overnight. Indeed, they are likely to be around for a long time. The Russian tax authorities are not interested in looking at financial statements or footnotes prepared using IAS or GAAP. The tax law requires tax liability to be computed using RAS and it is unlikely that this rule will change in the near future. So some Russian companies will have to use two sets of accounting standards in the normal course of business.

References

Anon. 1994. Tanya Bondarenko Seeks American Education. Baylor Business Review 12(1): 12ff.

Anon. 2001. Accountants in Russia Gain International Skills. Financial Management, p. 44 (April).

Chastain, C. E. 1982. Soviet Accounting Lags Behind the Needs of Enterprise Managers. Management International Review 22(4): 12–18.

Cheney, G. A. 1990. Western Accounting Arrives in Eastern Europe. Journal of Accountancy (September): 40–43.

Coyle, W. H. and V. V. Platonov. 1998. Insights Gained from International Exchange and Educational Initiatives between Universities: The Challenges of Analyzing Russian Financial Statements. Issues in Accounting Education 13(1): 223–233 (February).

Enthoven, A. J. H. 1999. Russia's Accounting Moves West. Strategic Finance 81(1): 32–37.

Enthoven, A. J. H. 1992. Accounting in Russia: From Perestroika to Profits. Management Accounting 74(4): 27–31 (October).

Enthoven, A. J. H., Y. V. Sokolov, S. M. Bychkova, V. V. Kovalev and M. V. Semenova. 1998. Accounting, Auditing and Taxation in the Russian Federation. A joint publication of the IMA Foundation for Applied Research, Montvale, New Jersey/The Center for International Accounting Development, University of Texas at Dallas.

IFAC. 2003a. Introduction to International Education Standards. New York: International Federation of Accountants, October. www.ifac.org.

IFAC. 2003b. Framework for International Education Standards. New York: International Federation of Accountants, October. www.ifac.org.

IFAC. 2003c. IES1: Entry Requirements to a Program of Professional Accounting Education. New York: International Federation of Accountants, October. www.ifac.org.

IFAC. 2003d. IES2: Content of Professional Accounting Educational Programs. New York: International Federation of Accountants, October. www.ifac.org.

IFAC. 2003e. IES3: Professional Skills. New York: International Federation of Accountants, October. www.ifac.org.

IFAC. 2003f. IES4: Professional Values Ethics and Attitudes. New York: International Federation of Accountants, October. www.ifac.org.

IFAC. 2003g. IES5: Practical Experience Requirements. New York: International Federation of Accountants, October. www.ifac.org.

IFAC. 2003h. IES6: Assessment of Professional Capabilities and Competence. New York: International Federation of Accountants, October. www.ifac.org.

Kobrak, F. 1991. Is There an Accounting Textbook Market in the New Soviet Union? Publishers Weekly, September 20, pp. 43–44.

McGee, R. W. 2003. Reforming Accounting Education in a Transition Economy: A Case Study of Armenia. Presented at the Twelfth Annual Business Congress of the International Management Development Association (IMDA), Vancouver, British Columbia, Canada, June 24–29, 2003. Reprinted on the Social Science Research Network website at http://papers.ssrn.com/sol3/papers.cfm?abstract_id = 408980.

Preobragenskaya, G. G. and R. W. McGee. 2003. Accounting Education in a Transition Economy: A Case Study of Russian Universities. Presented at the Academy of International Business – Southeast Annual Conference, Clearwater, Florida, November 13–14. Reprinted on the Social Science Research Network website at www.ssrn.com.

Preobragenskaya, G. G. and R. W. McGee. 2004. Problems of Implementing International Accounting Standards in a Transition Economy: A Case Study of Russia. Presented at the 8th International Conference on Global Business and Economic Development, Guadalajara, Mexico, January 7–10. Reprinted on the Social Science Research Network website at www.ssrn.com.

Shama, A. and C. G. McMahan. 1990. Perestroika and Soviet Accounting: From a Planned to a Market Economy. The International Journal of Accounting 25: 155–169.

Sherry, G. and R. Vinning. 1995. Accounting for Perestroika. Management Accounting 76(10): 42ff.

Smirnova, I. A., J. V. Sokolov and C. R. Emmanuel. 1995. Accounting Education in Russia Today. The European Accounting Review 4(4): 833–846.

Verrue, R. 1995. Economic Transition in Eastern Europe. Management Accounting (London) 73(6): 6ff.

Chapter 22
Accounting Education in the Slovak Republic

Radoslav Tusan and Lenka Stasova

22.1 Introduction

Changes in accounting education in the Slovak Republic are connected with the social and the economic conditions after 1989. The adoption of the Commercial Code in 1991 enabled the establishment and development of business in its various forms. The former accounting legislation did not accomplish its basic functions: documentation, information provision, control, and support for the decision-making process. Because of these facts, it was necessary to initiate the accounting reform. This radical reform was made by publishing the Accounting Procedures (National Accounting Standards) on January 1, 1991.

22.2 Accounting Education

The legal framework of accounting and the accounting report did not classify terms such as assets, liabilities, registered capital, profit, expenses, or revenues, even though these terms were used in the accounting directives. A new Act on Accounting, effective since January 1, 2001 was the first legal document that defined all these terms.

All changes in accounting education were made in connection with the changes in accounting legislation. Since 1993, accounting has became an executive and a decision-making instrument. At the same time universities started to teach a Business Accounting.

University education has three levels in the Slovak Republic. The first level is the bachelor degree and it takes 3 years to get this degree. The second level is the engineer degree (equivalent of American master's degree); it takes 2 years and this level is more specialized in the chosen field of study. Graduates of the third level – a doctorate degree – use the title Ph.D.

R. Tusan and L. Stasova
Technical University of Kosice

R. W. McGee (ed.), *Accounting Reform in Transition and Developing Economies,*
© Springer Science+Business Media LLC 2008

Accounting is a compulsory course at all universities in the Slovak Republic with an economic orientation. The goal of this course is to teach students to create and to use accounting data in the financial management of profit as well as non-profit businesses in the market economy.

Accounting is a compulsory course on the first level of university education and is usually divided into two semesters. The first semester of the accounting course aims at imparting knowledge of accounting and an understanding of the double-entry bookkeeping system. The main topics explain accounting legislation, the methodical resources, common accounting terms, and accounting policies. In connection with these basics of accounting theory, a student at the end of this semester must be able to keep accounts of assets, liabilities, expenses, and revenues. Also, through the understanding of the basic financial accounting, a student should be able to analyze and interpret the main financial relations (internal and external) of the company.

The accounting course continues in the second semester. It specializes in definitions and the accounting recording of long-term assets, the accounting for the financial accounts, the inventory accounts, the owners' equity, and long-term payables. A special area of the accounting course is concerned with classification and bookkeeping of expenses and revenues. Another part of the accounting course is the accounting report – methods used for calculation of income and income taxes. The last part of this course specializes in the formation of the ordinary accounting report and the accounting documents, in the verification of the accounting report by the auditor and its disclosure.

Curriculum of the accounting course includes:

- Accounting methods and accounting procedures valid since January 1, 2003
- Classification, structure, and valuation of the long-term tangible and intangible assets
- Purchase of long-term tangible assets with advance payments
- Purchase of long-term intangible assets with advance payments
- Acquisition of long-term tangible assets
- Financial investments from the corporation's own resources of the accounting unit
- Depreciation
- Liquidation of long-term tangible assets – accumulated depreciation and adjustments to profit of the accounting unit
- Revenues from sold long-term tangible and intangible assets
- Shortages, damages, and surplus of long-term tangible and intangible assets
- Donation of long-term tangible and intangible assets
- Long-term capital investments – definition, valuation, accounts
- Long-term capital investments – loans, deposits
- Long-term capital investments – shares and bonds
- Purchase of merchandise in the Slovak Republic with advance payments
- Purchase of merchandise in foreign countries – exchange rate differences
- Utilization of merchandise and revenues from sold merchandise

- Activation and donation of merchandise, merchandise for marketing purposes
- Inventory created by the accounting unit
- Shortages, damages, and surplus of the inventory
- Products of the accounting unit – production, utilization, and sale
- Products – shortages, damages, surplus, donation
- Purchase and sale of goods
- Current asset accounts: cash, bank accounts, and receivables
- Short-term investments – purchase and sale of shares
- Short-term and long-term bonds
- Paid and received advance payments
- Receivables and payables from commercial relations
- Bills of exchange
- Travel expenses
- Wages and salaries
- Social security accounts
- Individual income tax – advance payments
- Revenues and costs of future accounting periods
- Income and expenses of future accounting periods
- Definition and structure of owners' equity
- Registered capital
- Classification of costs and revenues and calculation of profit at the end of the accounting period
- Profit distribution
- Off-balance sheet accounts

The accounting courses at the higher levels of the university education are more specialized in the chosen field of study. Each study specialization has different requirements in its accounting system. Students can choose from these courses:

- Accounting for insurance companies
- Accounting for banks
- Accounting for non-profit companies and state funds accounting
- Managerial accounting
- Cost accounting and controlling
- Accounting reports

Future changes in the accounting courses will concern themselves not only with the content of the course and the teachers' approach, but also about new forms of education. Modern information and communication technologies bring crucial changes into the educational system and of course, also into the accounting courses. These technologies enable students to obtain knowledge using more means and without the presence of a teacher. Slovak universities (not only those with an economic orientation) offer long-distance education through self-instructive materials, educational technologies, the Internet, and a tutor's help.

Authors of educational textbook scripts present an electronic version as well. The textbooks have a compact style. They separate crucial information from secondary data, and they specify entry-level knowledge necessary for the study of different chapters. Methodical instructions and a system of tests and accounting examples are important components of the textbooks and they allow verification of accounting knowledge and skills. The new technologies change the entire educational process and they offer an education for a larger number of students. The important aspect of these changes is especially fast and easy access to information and motivating environment.

Some Slovak universities teach accounting course in English (as an optional course), because many Slovak students stay abroad and study at foreign universities through different exchange programs.

Accounting education follows the national legislation on accounting. Content of the accounts is defined by the mandatory accounting chart of accounts and Slovak accounting procedures. The aggregation of the accounts into the accounting statements is mechanical, because accounting legislation specifies a stable and unified form of these statements for all accounting units. Accounting education is therefore focused on the obtaining of bookkeeping skills and knowledge. This way of studying tempted students to habitual matching of the accounts with the accounting transactions. Students did not think deeply about the business transaction and its final impact on the financial situation of the accounting unit. This is a reason why it was important to modify the system of accounting education at Slovak universities and start to teach accounting instead of bookkeeping.

The World Bank offered an international grant and a grantee-McGill University in Montreal- prepared a new teaching plan and a curriculum for the financial accounting courses, which should be the basis for a new trend in accounting education at Slovak universities. The purpose of this grant was to provide help to the Slovak Republic in the implementation of the World Bank's recommendations, norms, and acts. The goal of this grant is to improve the accounting curriculum at institutions of higher education, introduce courses with a practical application of the International Accounting Standards (IAS), International Financial Reporting Standards (IFRS), International Standards on Auditing (ISA), and courses in the auditor's professional work ethic. It is also necessary to increase the number of professors and other professionals from the accounting and auditing area and to provide high-quality training in international accounting and auditing courses at the Slovak universities.

Technical aid by the World Bank was provided for these purposes:

1. To reform the accounting curriculum at all institutions of higher education, to support a practical application of IAS/IFRS/ISA and to increase auditors' professional work ethic
2. To organize retraining programs for accounting and auditing instructors of the institutions of higher education by international experts
3. To prepare textbooks and study material in accordance with IAS/IFRS and ISA
4. To arrange special training programs for the officials of the tax administration and other departments of the Ministry of Finance
5. To organize the training programs for entrepreneurs, corporate management, government officials, and others interested in the international dimensions of accounting

Therefore, a goal of accounting education is to teach students the content and methods of accounting. Also, students should be able to understand the accounting data and their structure. At the same time it is necessary to respect general accounting principles of the accounting reports, the billing, the valuation, and the disclosure of information according to the international instruments of the accounting regulations.

Proposed structure of accounting education at the Slovak universities includes:

- Generally accepted international accounting principles
- Financial accounting information users
- Content and scope of the accounting report
- Financial statements and their analysis
- Consolidated accounting statements

Chapter 23
Comments from a Fly on the Wall: An Outsider's Inside View of Ukrainian Education

Jeffrey D. Heyd

23.1 Introduction

Why is adaptation and change in post-Soviet higher education so challenging? An American professor living and teaching in Ukraine offers some practical observations and advice. An insider's viewpoint of the current condition of Ukrainian higher education, along with possible causes of mediocrity, is offered. The author suggests helpful rules of thumb and tips for successful policy making, research, and change programs.

Ask any American or Western European who's spent some time in former Soviet countries and most of them will tell you that it takes some time to understand the way things really are here. The real truth is that most of us who either visit or spend a short time as a temporary resident in these places only get a glimpse of the surface features of this complex cultural terrain. It takes much longer than most westerners realize to understand the inner workings of modern Slavic society.

For those whose business it is to understand the hows and whys of post-Soviet transitional economies and institutions, an accurate understanding is crucial to successful policy making, research, development projects, investments, and the like. I, by no means, can claim to understand the Slavic mind or the mysterious processes that make transition and development characteristically difficult here. What I *do* have is a unique placement on the inside of an educational establishment in a very typical post-Soviet university. I don't have the status of a visiting scholar funded by some external program, I don't have a time-limit on my commitment here, and I earn (and live on) the same salary as my Ukrainian colleagues. I am becoming as close to being an "insider" as an outsider can get.

For, the last year I have been teaching as a professor of International Management and Economics at a University in Poltava, Ukraine. Prior to this I spent a short time working with the management program at a State university in Sevastopol, Ukraine. My knowledge about the higher educational system in Ukraine comes both from my official capacities and from countless hours of conversations with students and ordinary instructors at various universities throughout Ukraine who have become very close friends.

J. D. Heyd
Poltava University of Consumer Cooperatives in Ukraine

R. W. McGee (ed.), *Accounting Reform in Transition and Developing Economies,*   343
© Springer Science + Business Media LLC 2008

I don't think anyone fully understands the inner workings of the bureaucratic monstrosity these institutions have become, nor does anyone completely understand how to steer this stubborn behemoth in a new direction. I simply offer some insights that may be helpful in guiding those who are attempting to gain such understanding.

23.2   The Situation

Now that the layers of secrecy, propaganda, and wishful thinking have been removed and the results of the Soviet educational system have been exposed, it's amazing to discover that there are many who are still singing its praises. I continue to encounter this attitude, especially among older colleagues as well as younger people who don't speak English and haven't been exposed to the outside world. Svitlana Malnyk, an assistant professor at Kyiv National Taras Shevchenko University (one of the top universities in Ukraine), was quoted in the Kyiv Post as saying, "My students were very surprised when they did not find our university among the top 100 universities of the world" (as quoted in Marone, 2007). In fact, according to the 2007 THES – QS World University Rankings, the highest former soviet university is Moscow State University ranked at number 231 (THES-QS World University Rankings, 2007).

Contrary to what some of the remaining holdouts believe, it's well known at this point in history that the famed Soviet educational system was good at certain aspects but was most definitely lacking in others. Its failings today are most evident when the need for adaptation, critical thinking, and creative problem solving becomes necessary. During a large-scale economic and institutional transition, these three abilities are essential; hence the failings of the Soviet educational system account for much of the lack of these core abilities in today's leaders and adult citizens in former Soviet States.

Imagine generations of people whose innovators, critics, and creative persons have literally been culled from the gene pool. How can we expect the kind of innovation, adhocracy, embracing of change, and the other traits necessary to recreate an entire society? As is true in nearly every sphere, change in the education system here has certainly been slowed because of the general lack of these essential qualities.

In light of this, I find it actually quite amazing what progress has been made thus far. There are several cases where certain institutions in Ukraine have been very open and willing to adopt new standards and methods, especially in the business, economics, and accounting areas. At my university, for example, we have developed an English language-based program teaching International Management and International Economics using the latest textbooks and concepts from the western world. Creating innovative programs means facing bureaucratic roadblocks at every turn and makes the process of change much more difficult than it ought to be. Even so, much progress is being made.

Ukraine is facing the possibility of a shortage of qualified professionals in various sectors of the job market. "Ukraine's troubled education system is struggling to keep up with the country's growing need for a professional workforce" (Marone, 2007). "Ukraine's colleges and universities have still not changed to meet the times by revamping their courses and faculty" (Oleksander Samolyuk as quoted in Marone, 2007). My personal observations concur with these comments. I have observed a definite lack of ability in the graduates here when it comes to practical application of theoretical knowledge and creative problem solving. Admittedly, these qualities are difficult to measure, but I am confident in my assessment that there is a significant lack of performance ability of graduates caused by systemic problems.

Further, I have observed a general lack of concern for these problems from among my colleagues or university administration. The times I've questioned people about these issues I am faced with an argument about how my observations are not accurate (denial) and I am accused of bias, or I am given the standard response (apathy), "That's just the way things are and it's impossible to change them." Based on my observation and conversations, this denial and apathy is common to most Ukrainian institutions of higher education. Again the lingering belief that "our system is the best in the world" dies hard.

23.3   Striving for Mediocrity

So why is mediocrity in university graduates so common here? Here are some observations of systemic problems that contribute to lower educational performance:

As in most former Soviet States, the education system is highly subject to corruption. In Ukraine, "...today's education system is considered one of the most corrupt spheres in the entire country" (Bondarchuk, 2007). This is no surprise in a country were 50% of the population admits to paying bribes, with bribes to teachers being the second highest form of bribery reported (Aksyonova, 2007). Bribes and under-the-table payments for nearly every aspect of the educational process is so common and widely accepted that it has diluted the value of the resulting degrees... almost to the point where degrees are meaningless when it comes to finding a job. Degrees have basically become nothing more than a prerequisite and no longer a qualification. The good students who study and perform well end up with the same degree diplomas as those who rarely come to class and skip exams.

As for myself, I have yet to personally witness or even hear a first-hand account of outright bribery in the institutions I've been involved with. What I have seen, however, is questionable students being given diplomas and I've heard abundant rumors about the money that was needed to make it happen. I have also observed cases where students were absent from classes... sometimes more than an entire semester, and then be accepted into the Magisters program (Ukrainian version of the Masters Degree), which has limited competitive slots available.

While outright bribery is, necessarily, hidden from view, its existence does provide some explanation of how grossly underperforming and unqualified students continue to graduate.

Another contributor to the gravitational force of mediocrity is the difficulty of failing. Although it is possible for a student to perform poorly and eventually be dropped from the university entirely, it is rare. Ukrainian education is still based on the Soviet-style group concept. Students are assigned to a group as freshmen and remain with this group taking all the same classes together for their entire term of study.

There are a limited number of spaces for each program granted by the Ministry in each university. To garner the maximum revenue, universities must fill as many of these slots as possible and keep them filled throughout the 4- or 5-year course of study. Dropping students usually means lost revenue because, due to the group concept, there are really no students to fill the vacated slots. Thus, there is a strong financial disincentive to fail students.

Because of the group system, if one student fails a course, he/she can't just simply repeat the course because their schedule must always be the same as the other students in the group. So what happens is that poorly performing students are given extra work and must repeat exams and assignments until they achieve a successful outcome (or the professor has "punished" them enough to pass them along). If handled strictly by the instructors, this system could work well enough to produce quality graduates. Unfortunately, knowing that if you don't pass an exam on the first try you will get another chance, work can be turned in late without significant penalty, and knowing you will get your degree no matter how you perform... well, it all adds up to a severe lack of incentive for peak performance. How else can one explain the reason that, in our international program for example, after 4 to 5 years of English language study less than 50% of the students can adequately use the English language?

On the instructor side, there is also a severe lack of incentive to perform optimally. The very low salaries (below living wages for most instructors) certainly don't provide incentive. The system of not being able to fail students serves to "punish" the instructors more than the students. The extra work and make-up exams for the students creates even more extra work for the instructors. Because of this, there is a very strong incentive to make the courses very easy for everyone to pass.

I must admit I've experienced this myself already. For example, I created a fair exam for one of my classes. I knew all of the students (100%) actively participate or benefit from cheating... really, cheating is a norm here. So I created several variants of the exam to make cheating more difficult... and obvious. The moment the exam started, I quickly began to realize that if the students really took the exam on their own, with no possibility of cheating; I would have a group of 40 students who would need extra work and perhaps another make-up exam in order to get their grades up to where they needed to be. Believe me, you won't be hard-nosed about individual performance after you go through the process of almost failing an entire class. ...and the students know it. (...and yes, I did suggest the theoretical concept of actually *studying* to the students as a possible alternative to cheating.)

What most instructors do here, instead of paper exams, is to ask each student questions individually. This decreases the cheating possibility. It also reduces the quality of assessment (they are only asked 3 to 5 questions covering a whole semester's material). The problems with this method are obvious; the instructors can (consciously or subconsciously) aid the students in answering the questions, there is no record of what answers the students gave the professor, and the private nature of assessment opens the door for corruption. Consequently, real assessment is a big problem here in general. The lack of assessment again reduces incentive to perform and covers up the whole mess with good grades.

The unspoken, and perhaps subconscious, underlying principal belief is something like, "So what if our students aren't learning anything? Who will ever know? They have assigned jobs after graduation anyway (Soviet era). There are no jobs for them anyway (today's situation)."

23.4   Two Important Observations

Keeping two basic rules in mind are important when undertaking any analysis in this region of the world. First and foremost is that things are not always as they seem. The second is that you can't teach an old dog new tricks. These two bits of old country wisdom have practical applications everywhere... but nowhere more so than in post-Soviet transitional economies. It is imperative that anyone attempting research, policy making, or development anywhere in this part of the world remember what these two rules really mean.

23.5   Things are Never as they Seem

While there is always some difference between plans and practice, ideals and reality in every organization, institution, and country... it is difficult to imagine a generalized example that would be more endemic and extreme than what I constantly find in the higher education system in Ukraine.

The educational system here, when viewed by outside observers at face value, looks quite rigorous. The Educational Plans for each group of students has an impressive array of courses, lectures, loads of practical discussion class hours, and high expectations of the many hours of individualized study spent on huge lists of required reading. In fact, many international institutions do recognize these educational plans (something like transcripts) and award transfer hours or (as in the case of immigration in Canada) acceptance of equivalent educational qualifications. What's more, the European Union and the Bologna Process aims to make these educational qualifications more easily recognizable and transferable.

If these educational plans were ever followed exactly and if the students performed all the duties required of them and then had their knowledge retention properly assessed in the past is difficult to say. Unfortunately, now, plans and reality are quite some distance apart. Lectures do not always occur nor is attendance strictly enforced. Practical discussion classes rarely contain anything practical and not much of what westerners would consider real discussion. Usually these "Seminar" classes, as they are called, are just students answering some general topic questions by reading from their notes or texts. Individual study? This is the biggest joke in the whole system. Most of the academic hours in the Educational Plan are allotted for individual study. If you know a student or former student well enough to get an honest answer… you will discover that only 20–40% of the individual study time is used.

Consequently, if you factor out the missing reality from the plans, you will discover that, in many (but not all) programs and institutions only about 50–60% of the Educational Plan takes place. Combine this fact with the lack of quality of assessment, lack of practical application of knowledge, lack of performance incentives, etc. and you get a clear understanding of why graduates of former Soviet institutions cannot perform adequately in the global (or local) job markets.

In addition, much of the written coursework is often plagiarized, done by paid third parties, recycled from previous semesters/other students, or worse. Yes, I know this occurs everywhere, but here it is endemic and quietly accepted. As an example: fourth-year students are required in the management (and most other) programs to participate in some practical experience and create a large document reporting on it. Most of these experiences are completely fictitious and result in a large creative writing effort. As long as the typographical format is followed, the content is somewhat believable, and the student can answer some basic questions, the reports are accepted year after year. (Of course some of the more ambitious students do actually go out and find, usually through family contacts, a real practical mini-internship, but this seems to be the exception). The results of this and other systemic issues is that graduates rarely have any practical aspect to their education… almost none whatsoever.

It has taken me a long time to finally figure out the simple idea that words and concepts don't always translate. Here's what I mean: When I first came here I assumed the word "exam" meant something similar to what I knew in the United States… i.e., an individualized assessment of retained or applied knowledge. What it means here, in all practicality, is a feigned, miniscule, verbal assessment in order to create a plausible reason to give a good grade. This is one of many examples that could be given, but it suffices to make my point; always be aware that things are not what they seem, insist on objective direct observation and exact details.

In much the same way it is prudent to be cautious of *reported* reality. There is a Slavic tendency to have a different reality when it comes to reporting potentially negative information to outsiders (Dalton, 2001). To get real information that somewhat resembles reality takes time, digging for hard evidence, and verbal confrontation. To get to that point you need to develop close, long-term relationships with people on the inside to the point that they will confess these embarrassing issues to you. The typical questionnaire approach to research will not always produce accurate or useful information.

Further complicating the picture is the phenomena that, despite a plethora of evidence to the contrary, many here in Ukraine continue to think the system is working. These well-intentioned individuals have been conditioned to believe that the Soviet system was the best in the world. Most of them have never had the opportunity to personally experience working in a world-class educational institution. Therefore, having no basis for comparison, they can't see the failings of the current system. Why should research or policy be based on information obtained from these people?

23.6 The Futility of Teaching Old Dogs

Although I have never tried, I suppose it's true that you really can't teach an old dog new tricks. This old saying is often invoked when resistance to change is encountered. Fortunately, people (especially Ukrainians) are *not* dogs and always have the capacity to learn. My colleagues here in Ukraine, for the most part, are intelligent, honest, and are as hard-working as their counterparts anywhere. On the other hand, institutions in general and especially old, entrenched bureaucracies are very much like old dogs that are quite content to do no tricks at all... let alone learn anything new.

I suppose if one tried to teach an old dog some new trick the result would be wasted time, useless expenditure of energy and resources, complete frustration, and perhaps being bitten by the dog. Those familiar with the change process in transition economies are chuckling to themselves as they read this because they understand this implied analogy all too well. The system here is an intricate web developed over a long period of time within a particular system for very legitimate self-protective reasons. It's not something to be trifled with haphazardly by outsiders.

I don't claim to understand this system, but I know enough now to say that if one were to attempt to change only one part of it without understanding the implications for the rest of the system, you would cause much more damage and problems than you might solve. Again using the example of assessment; if you create a real assessment method, you would potentially disrupt the whole group system (because accurate assessment is useless without the possibility of failure) or completely overload the instructors' time and information tracking capacities. It would also cause an unpredictable chain of events that could, in theory, bring the whole system crashing down like a stack of cards. This is why little is done by those within the system; everyone knows it is such a giant can of worms that no one is foolhardy enough to open it.

This may be one reason why the Ministry of Science and Education of Ukraine is rather resistant to certain changes. To a western mind-set, this centralized control may seem arcane and heavy-handed, but I am beginning to learn that there are some good reasons for this approach. If the Ministry was to implement a hands-off approach, several universities (the ones that are ready to innovate) would implement various novel programs such as distance learning and online programs, new curricula, specialized degrees, etc. The problem, as I am now beginning to understand it, is that it would cause a degree of chaos and the mid-term result would be a reduction in educational capacity in the country. Ukrainian educational institutions are simply not ready to function independently (ICPS, 2007).

Those institutions that are ready to innovate, market, and sustain novel programs would have the most advantage and the students would begin to gravitate toward those universities. This would leave the other universities with a lack of students and funds. Survival of the fittest is well and good, but in this case at this time, it would most likely concentrate the educational ability in regions already at an advantage (Kiev, Odessa, Kharkov, etc.) and would leave the cities and entire regions that need it most... devoid of institutions. After some time passes and these "lesser" universities are prepared to manage themselves independently (be able to make sound financial plans and decisions, effectively market themselves, and maintain some ethical standards internally) then some differentiation could serve the greater good.

23.7   Working Within the Existing System

In regard to quality, the centralized control of curriculum content and methodology facilitates the State control process. How can the state develop standardized testing for its quality control program if the university system isn't homogeneous? Certain course subjects in the system have the same basic required elements that make it possible for the State to give standardized exams in order to determine the educational outcomes. Yes, there are other ways to assure quality in education, yes this effectively squelches adaptation and innovation... but in this current condition of de-stabilized transition, one must admit that this current form of centralization is better than a wild-west style free-for-all.

Some universities have learned to adapt within this framework. Western style MBA programs have popped up in the major innovative universities. A few have begun English-language-based instruction. They have also developed quality curriculum within the Ministries guidelines that would compare well with courses in any other part of the world. (Just because the Ministry has required specific course content doesn't mean those requirements are not high quality elements within the curriculum.) All this is to say that, within the current Ukrainian system of higher education, it should still be possible to create quality educational programs.

23.8   Advice for Researchers and Policy Makers

For those doing research or making policy regarding the educational system in former soviet states I recommend a holistic approach. Remembering that everything relates to the other parts of the system is important when recommending any change program. It is impossible and foolhardy to approach institutional changes with a typical western mindset. Keep in mind that there are often good reasons for things being the way they are and those reasons are not always apparent. The underlying fundamental processes as well as the affects on the entire system must always be carefully considered before implementing any change.

The devil's in the details. Rule number 1 mentioned above is important when it comes to analysis of any current condition here. Without an accurate understanding of the way things really are (and why) that is based in reality (not *reported* reality), successful change programs are impossible. Don't assume people are able to report accurate detailed information. Don't assume the documentation means anything at all. Careful, direct, precise observation is the only way to be assured of anything. Some basic examples: Time spent in the classroom must be physically observed and recorded... not pulled from the Educational Plan. Assessments must be given in a heavily controlled, proctored environment or the results will certainly be a group effort, not an individual assessment.

"The first step to solving your problem is to admit you have one," ...so the old mantra goes. It's important for outsiders to remember that many here still don't agree that there's a problem to be solved. There's a part of the culture and mentality that continues to insist that "It ain't broke so stop trying to fix it!" A delicate and respectful approach toward these people (generally those who are in charge at present) will go a long way toward mutual understanding and cooperation.

Innovative change programs are quite possible here, but it will take a holistic approach. In order for The Ministry to approve programs, they need to be assured that control processes equal to the task are in place and that plans match reality. Believe me, they know about the difference between plans and reality better than anyone else and have a healthy suspicion of any new plan or program. You will also need to prove that your innovative program won't have unintended negative effects on the rest of the system (this is the difficult part). As I alluded to previously in this paper, what might be a great program in one place could potentially unravel the rest of the system. Although it might prove to be cumbersome and frustrating, working with The Ministry is entirely possible as well as beneficial for all concerned.

23.9   Another Perspective

In soliciting critique of this paper I received several endorsements from among my colleagues and other American educators with Ukrainian experience. Most thought my views were dead on or too mildly articulated while one thought I was being too judgmental. I received an excellent synopsis of another perspective on Ukrainian Higher Education from Dr. Myron P. Kuropas of Northern Illinois

University (personal communication, January 24, 2008). He has a great deal of experience with Ukrainian Higher Education and describes it thus:

Education in Ukraine: Reflections by Myron B. Kuropas, Ph.D.

During the 1980's my institution, Northern Illinois University, enrolled a number of students from China. Some majored in adult education and found themselves in my social foundations class. China had a need for this specialty because, during his cultural revolution, Mao had all but destroyed schools in China, especially at the university level. This left a population with many poorly educated adults. The Chinese government realized this and decided to address the problem. Chinese students at NIU, I discovered, were diligent and hard working. Some came to class with an English/Chinese dictionary to make sure they understood everything. It was my understanding that they were sponsored by the Chinese government and were guaranteed teaching positions when they returned. Other Chinese students majored in the physical sciences; they also returned to good paying jobs in a China which recognized the need for an educated populace able to compete with other countries. China, as we have seen, prospered tremendously.

The situation in Ukraine today is similar in many respects to what it was in a post-Mao China. The approach of Ukrainian educational leaders, however, is very different from that of the Chinese. When Ukraine became independent in 1991, the Ukrainian government was not interested in sponsoring students to the United States to improve Ukraine's intellectual base. There was no need to study abroad, it was believed, because Ukrainian education, inherited from the Soviets, was the best in the world. Nevertheless, a number of American institutions – the U.S. State Department, Fulbright, Eurasia, etc. – thought it would be helpful to Ukraine to offer opportunities for Ukrainian teachers and students to come to the United States to broaden their horizons. It was a wonderful idea but somewhat naïve, I suspect. My wife and I sponsored some of these teachers during a ten year period and, thanks to a grant from Eurasia and teaching assistantships from NIU, my departmental colleagues and I were able to bring five outstanding teachers from the National University of Ostroh Academy to our campus.

For a number of years professors from throughout the world would meet annually at the University of Illinois for a week-long summer conference on Ukrainian topics. Beginning in the 1990's, professors from Ukraine, sponsored by Ukrainian American organizations, would arrive and present papers. They read their papers in the most mundane, monotonous tone imaginable, totally avoiding eye contact. It should be noted that in the Ukrainian language, professors do not teach classes, they read lessons (chitayut leksiye). When the topic of higher degrees came up, their denial was breathtaking. They became incensed when it was demonstrated, that American degrees required class attendance and far more research. With rare exceptions, most argued that Ukrainian education was and remains the best in the world, even after learning that no Ukrainian university is ranked among the top 500 universities in the world.

When it was mentioned that the rector of a Catholic university in Lviv was not recognized by Ukraine's Ministry of Education even though he had a Ph.D. from Harvard, I was told that the rector needed to be certified in Ukraine. Examinations and official papers (read bribes) needed to be taken care of. The best that he could hope for even then was a Kandidat Nauk degree. When it was pointed out that many of the dissertations and doctorates in Ukraine were purchased, Ukrainian professors argued that the same was true of the United States. When some of the laughable titles of certain dissertations were read and the conclusions presented, Ukrainian educators became extremely angry.

Later, when I spoke with some of the younger professors on a one-to-one basis, they were willing to admit that I was correct but it was pointless to try to change anything. Since the Ministry of Education grants degrees (as in Soviet times when every degree had to be vetted for ideological purity), university professors are powerless to do anything, even if they want to. At the same time, however, they argued that if universities were allowed to grant degrees as they are throughout the world, corruption would be even greater in Ukraine than it is now.

23.9.1   Concluding Thoughts

There are excellent teachers at all levels of Ukrainian education. Ukrainian education itself, however, remains in thrall to a self-perpetuating, corrupt system that will not change until some of the members of the current, mediocre educational establishment are no longer in power. Before that happens, however, Ukrainian educational institutions need to adopt a transparent system of examinations and grading so that the best and the brightest can thrive.

A good beginning would be to make all university entrance exams anonymous and machine-scored. Some universities, such as the National University of Ostroh Academy and Kyiv-Mohyla University are already moving in this direction. Until this happens, and until teachers at all levels are paid a salary that will attract competent and dedicated practitioners, Ukraine will remain a third-world power.

According to the 2008 Heritage Foundation/Wall Street Journal Index of Economic Freedom, Ukraine ranks 133 out of 157 nations, behind Gabon, Ethiopia, Cambodia and Zambia (Heritage Foundation, 2008). In 12th place is Estonia, a former Soviet republic which adopted the three level degree program of higher education soon after regaining its independence. I believe there is a relationship.

23.10   Conclusion

Ukraine has inherited a load of problems and has created a few of its own over the course of its short recent history as an independent country. Much of Ukraine's future success will depend on how well it manages and corrects these problems within its educational system. While much of what I have observed relates to the negative aspects of this topic, I believe these problems can and will be solved. I am very optimistic about the future health of Ukrainian education. I believe Ukraine, one day, will be a model of how to transition to a more adaptive and useful system. I believe this because I know the people involved. There are thousands of good, honest, hard-working, intelligent people who are working toward a new future of educational excellence. In time, their efforts will culminate into a modern, world-class educational system... for now, they could really use some help and support.

References

THES-QS World University Rankings (2007). Retrieved January 16, 2008, from www.topuniver-
    sities.com Web site: http://www.topuniversities.com/worlduniversityrankings/results/2007/
    overall_rankings/top_400_universities/
Aksyonova, M. (2007, September 20). Study: half of citizens give bribes. *The Kyiv Post*, p. A1.
Bondarchuk, O. (2007, September 3). Degrees of corruption: Gaft in the education system.
    Business Ukraine, 1(23), 10–13.
Dalton, M. (2001). *Culture shock: A guide to customs and etiquette Ukraine*. Portland, OR:
    Graphic Arts Center Publishing, p. 98.
Heritage Foundation (2008). Country rankings. Retrieved January 25, 2008, from Index of
    Economic Freedom Web Site: http://www.heritage.org/research/features/index/countries.cfm
ICPS (2007, February 19). Ukraine needs a new educational policy. *ICPS Newsletter*, #6(353), 1
Marone, J. (2007, July 25). Education flunking on job market. *The Kyiv Post*, p. A1.

Chapter 24
Teaching and Training of International Accounting Standards in Former Soviet Republics and the Balkans 1994–2005

Laszlo J. Urmenyhazi

24.1 Introduction

My first exposure to overseas consulting work on accounting and financial reporting started when I was hired and sent to Kazakhstan on Labor Day of 1994 to join the first team of consultants of the Price Waterhouse (now PricewaterhouseCoopers) accounting and auditing firm.

I was told by the director who hired me that my assignment will be a short-term assignment and probably I will be back by Thanksgiving. In fact, I was back on Thanksgiving, but due to a very favorite tool used by consulting firms, namely "extensions," I did come back on Thanksgiving holiday of the following year!

The first 5 years of my consulting was as an employee of Price Waterhouse, the remaining 7 years I worked as an independent contractor in Accounting Reform Projects for various consulting firms.

24.2 Chart of Accounts

In 1994, my task was to support our team involved with the Accounting Reform in Kazakhstan, specifically, to develop a chart of accounts that will replace or modify (eventually eliminate) the "KORRESPONDENZIYA" used for decades, throughout the Soviet communism regime.[1]

L. J. Urmenyhazi
Consultant, Philadelphia

[1] KORRESPONDENZIYA is a small booklet originally issued by the Finance Ministry, Accounting Methodology Department (MINFIN). Usually it contained 100–150 pages, size 6 by 9 in. This booklet was the "Bible" for all bookkeepers in the former Soviet Union accounting system. It described the compatibility or the "correspondence" among accounts. For example, for a given "debit balance account," the corresponding "credit balance account or accounts" are listed. The acceptable choices are already prescribed. The accountant did not have the right to use a different credit account other than the one prescribed in the book. For all control accounts (approximately 300–350), the book gave at least one applicable corresponding control account.

R. W. McGee (ed.), *Accounting Reform in Transition and Developing Economies*,
© Springer Science+Business Media LLC 2008

It is very easy to understand the importance of a Chart of Accounts in a communist regime. It is the quintessential guide for all bookkeepers. The purpose to have only one Chart of Accounts is very much compatible with the communist regime in the former Soviet Union. From their perspective, it created a better financial control to measure the 5-year plans (centrally planned plans); it also facilitated tasks for bookkeepers or record keepers; whose main function was to insure that there is compliance with the tax law.

Generally, the accounting personnel consisted of women (90–95%), and they made up 10–15% of the total personnel of any company. It was the same all over the former Soviet Union, from Moldova to Kazakhstan, including all other countries in between such as Ukraine, Georgia, Armenia, Azerbaijan, Kazakhstan, and Kyrgyzstan.

In Western countries, accounting personnel are around 50% women and accounting personnel are not more than 3–4% of total personnel.

The Chart of Accounts in former Soviet Union/communist countries was copied from the Chart of Accounts developed in Moscow. Now, the directives originated from Moscow had to be replaced with a planned reform on accounting. Consultants in the accounting reform had to use the following methodology: proposals on the chart of accounts, then proposals on new standardized financial statements, followed by intensive training on the understanding and application of the International Accounting Standards (IASs).

The preliminary approach to the Chart of Accounts consisted of keeping as many "control" accounts as possible. Control accounts in former communist country accounting parlance are called "synthetic" accounts. My task was to insert additional control or "synthetic" accounts that were necessary primarily for the accrual method of accounting. It was obvious that their whole accounting system was based on the "Cash Basis" accounting system. All recordkeeping was geared towards cash transactions. The accrual system was not recognized or understood in the early 1990s.

Control accounts, or synthetic accounts, were accounts identified by three digits. There were usually between 300 and 350 control accounts. My goal was to reduce them to at least between 180 to 220 "active" control accounts.

After the first round of discussions of explaining the elementary and basic "accrual" control accounts, I was able to convince them to insert new control accounts while still keeping their own chart of accounts structure. Then, the discussions continued with additional sub-accounts. Again, in their jargon the sub-accounts were referred to as "analytical" accounts. Sub-accounts or analytical accounts were identified with accounts having at least four digits. The number of

---

By the middle of the 1990s the Accounting Associations in the Newly Independent countries undertook the task of issuing instructions on for example, what credit balance account should be used for a given debit balance account. I have seen an accounting clerk elevated to the Accounting Methodology Department head position in one of the Central Asian countries because she mastered the KORRESPONDENZIYA booklet. She knew by memory the answers as prescribed by the MINFIN of that country.

digits was regulated in most of the countries. I have seen up to 7-digit sub-accounts in some Newly Independent Countries.

I made sure that my proposed control accounts and sub-accounts would be required for the minimum information listed in "Disclosure" paragraphs of International Accounting Standards (IAS).[2]

Upon arrival in my assigned country, the first request was to have the latest local language chart of accounts with its translation. Then I counted the number of synthetic and analytical accounts they have in their Chart of Accounts.[3]

My second request was to prepare a list of "questionable accounts and questionable account titles." In most of the cases (over 30–40% of the time), fruitless discussions and misunderstandings resulted from poor translations. The American business terms were not our translators' forte. Usually translators were trained for non-accounting types of translations. The accrual concept of accounting and terms used only in a market or capitalist environment created additional reasons for endless discussions, frustrations, and finally to "refinements" that took over 50–60% of the consultants' time.[4]

I devised a "definition" of the Chart of Accounts. My proposed definition was totally out of place most of the time because I used the International Accounting Standard IAS 1, Presentation of Financial Statement Appendices as a guideline in countries where the IAS training of financial reporting had not yet begun. The definition becomes understood and acceptable when the local association members (as well as small business accountants) started to be interested in the training in various accounting standards, specifically the International Accounting Standard IAS 12, Income Taxes.

I worked in eight former Soviet Union countries. The first 3–4 years, the changes in their National Chart of Accounts were the most controversial and difficult to explain because of their lack of knowledge of accrual accounting

---

[2] Disclosure paragraphs in the IAS were the last paragraphs in each Financial Reporting Standard. These paragraphs were the minimum disclosure requirements necessary for transparency purposes, as perceived by the IAS Board. A careful review of disclosure requirements is the best method to supplement the proposed National Chart of Accounts.

There were about 32 International Accounting Standards (IAS) in the early 1990s. By 2003, there were 41 IASs. The 1,500 page IAS of 2001 has Standards numbered through 41; however, 7 Standards were superseded, and therefore the IAS book had only 34 "active" Standards.

The International Accounting Standards Board's annual publication for "2004" of all standards included extensive changes in its 2,250 pages. There were 5 "International Financial Reporting Standards" and only 32 "active International Accounting Standards," although they were still numbered through 41.

[3] I have never seen even one "accountant" to know exactly the number of synthetic accounts existing in their national –one fits all – Chart of Accounts. As mentioned earlier, they averaged between 300 and 350 synthetic accounts.

[4] In one of the Balkan countries, I found 53 questionable accounts out of 1,183 three-digit synthetic and four-digit analytical accounts immediately after the publication of their official and latest National Chart of Accounts accepted by their MINFIN Accounting Methodology Department.

and of IAS Disclosure requirements. Their general attitude was to have the Chart of Accounts modified before accepting any other changes, such as changing the financial statement format to agree with IAS 1 Financial Statement Presentation of 2002.[5]

The first couple of years I received very non-flattering comments from the local accounting officials. I was representing the "change" (or the challenge) to their system "that had worked fine for 70 years," meaning throughout the span of the communist regime in their country.

As the National Accounting Standards were developed or modeled according to the International Accounting Standards during the second half of the 1990s, it became obvious to local accounting officials and to local bookkeepers that accrual accounting had to replace their cash basis accounting, necessitating very special purpose synthetic accounts and analytical accounts.[6]

In some countries the acceptance of a new national chart of accounts "compliant" with International Accounting Standards required a new Business Law, or a Presidential decree, or in most cases Ministry of Finance and Revenue Ministry approval.[7]

Within a 12-year period, I have observed the introduction of a new national chart of accounts by the Ministry of Finance in most of the former Soviet Union countries. The depth of changes in their 70-year old "leftover Chart of Accounts" and the attitude towards accepting new control accounts and new analytical accounts were directly influenced by their acceptance of the International Accounting Standards – although reluctantly sometimes.[8]

---

[5] My counterparts were the MINFIN Accounting Methodology Department heads. The standard setting authority was gradually taken over by new accounting associations as they were organized. Setting by-laws for new accounting associations was also part of the Accounting Reform in each country. This task was taken over by other consultants. Towards the late 1990s my counterparts were all accounting association presidents.

[6] The most dramatic examples can be given on required new synthetic and new analytical accounts in order to comply with the disclosure requirements of the IAS 12 Income Taxes, 2002. Specifically "Deferred Tax Assets" and "Deferred Tax Liabilities" control (synthetic) accounts.

[7] Generally, the Revenue Ministry was in charge of tax collection matters.

[8] With the exception of Georgia, all remaining seven Newly Independent Countries I worked in decided to have a "simplified" IAS and then rename it as their National Accounting Standard. The simplification was justified, in my opinion. Usually the simplified version of the IAS amounted to the granting of fewer options for the accounting profession. A typical example would be to allow only one treatment in terms of recognition or measurement: "The Benchmark Treatment" as labeled by IAS.

The second treatment for recognition and measurement – acceptable by IAS was the "Allowed Alternative Treatment". This treatment generally was excluded from the national standards. There are less than six IAS's calling for both treatments as acceptable, among 41 standards. Another typical complaint that came from academe was the "flexibility" expressed or "too much room for interpretation" in some paragraphs of the IAS. This fact was against their traditional, centrally planned accounting and reporting system in force for decades.

Apparently economic reasons were behind the full adoption, without any changes, of the acceptance of International Accounting Standards as National Standards by Georgia in 1999.

24.3 Financial Statements

I conducted seminars and training sessions on all IAS as requested by the host country officials and as specified in the "Scope of Work" prepared by United States Agency for International Development (USAID) and the home office project administration personnel. As a second step in the westernization of the accounting system, financial statements also had to change drastically.

The change of financial statements, namely Balance Sheet and Income Statement, or in communist system jargon, Statement number 1 and Statement number 2, respectively, were revised quite often during the last 12-year period.

Before the introduction of "IAS 1, Presentation of Financial Statements," a "communist product Balance Sheet" (officially referred to as "Statement Number 1") on the average had over 180–220 lines and an Income Statement (officially called Statement Number 2) on the average had over 100–120 lines.

One can appreciate the shock created by the Accounting Reform consultant's proposal to have their Balance Sheet reduced to a minimum of 28 lines and their Income Statement reduced to a minimum of 17 lines. By the way, these numbers of lines are "recommended minimum" lines for respective financial statements by the IAS Board.

When I started my "Training of Trainers" on the first – and the most important – international accounting standard, the "IAS 1 Presentation of Financial Statements" (revised in 1997), I knew that I was conducting training in countries where the IAS was not officially accepted and it was a crime to criticize the shortcomings of the current locally accepted accounting system.[9]

24.3.1 Balance Sheet

If the chart of accounts represented the foundations of the accounting system, the balance sheet or Statement Number 1 in former Soviet Union countries represented the structure or the four walls built upon the foundations.

The Accounting Reform in a Newly Independent Country usually had at least three main areas of activity (excluding audit- and tax-related reforms):

1. Financial Reporting. It consisted of training via introduction of the International Accounting Standards to facilitate the preparation of the local financial statements.

---

[9] I was technically doing subversive work by teaching international accounting standards in a country where neither laws nor regulations existed for the practice of an accounting system other than the one imposed by Moscow for decades. One cannot keep admiring the efforts done by then Russian Federation president Yeltsin (1990–1997) in opening doors to Western capitalist reforms, specifically to Western accounting system as represented by the International Accounting Standards promulgated by the International Accounting Standards Board in London, UK.

2. Accounting Associations. Creation of a professional association that will be
   the standard-setter instead of the MINFIN Accounting Methodology
   Department officials. Included in this task was the preparation of by-laws for
   a National Accounting Association and for its committees.
3. Accounting education. Change in curriculum in higher education to include
   accounting courses.

Each activity was conducted by separate expatriate consultants. My involvement
was with the first sphere of activity in ten East European and Central Asian countries in the last 12-year period.

Several outside (international) factors existed to justify the need for preparing a
new accounting and financial reporting system in former Soviet Union countries:

1. Requirement from the World Bank. Almost all Newly Independent Countries
   requesting loans must first satisfy the financial reporting requirement. Since
   the World Bank is issuing its Financial Statements based on International
   Accounting Standards, it was natural to require from countries requesting a
   loan to accept the introduction of financial statements that will be compatible
   with International Accounting Standards.
2. Requirements from the International Monetary Fund. Same justification as
   given for the World Bank requirement.
3. International Organization of Stock Exchange requirements (IOSCO).
4. European Union Parliament requirements. Effective January 1, 2005 for
   listed companies that are member of any European Stock Exchange must use
   IAS when presenting their financial statements to Stock Exchanges.

It was like a marathon among Newly Independent Countries as well as in Balkan
countries to be "part of the action" by eliminating the remains of the centrally
planned economy accounting requirements and jump to the bandwagon of accounting reforms.

One of the first questions I used to face on my arrival in a new country was:
"How are we doing compared to other Newly Independent Countries in terms of
accounting reforms?" The same question came from MINFIN officials to local
accountants, regardless of the location from Moldova to Kazakhstan, and from all
others in between.

There is not an objective way to assess the progress done by each country.
Government, in principle, is in agreement with the World Bank to have international accounting standards adopted within an agreed period. The methodology to
be used also could be the same as far as the consultants are concerned, but the priority sequences mostly depend on local officials who are in charge of the
implementation.

I had to come up with some objective evaluation. One of my favorites is the
research and publication done by "Research International," a firm located in Berlin,
West Germany, founded in 1993.

Although I am not familiar with the criteria used in ranking 100 plus countries
in the world, I do know the published results through their web site. This company

measures the legal and administrative assistance – or lack of it – when doing business in any country. Their researchers rank all countries evaluating various business criteria. Without specifying any country name, I used to group countries by their geographical location (by continents) and divulge the ranking given by "Research International" (www.transparency.org).

Year after year, the first ten countries in the ranking were New Zealand and Australia followed by most of the Scandinavian countries. The USA usually is ranked between 9 and 13 positions followed by most of the Western European countries in the 15–25th positions. Almost all Newly Independent countries were between position 30 and 45. It is worth mentioning that the last two or three positions were made up of countries in oil rich Central Africa like Nigeria and neighboring countries.

I have also tried to point out that although each country may have the same methodology applied, in some countries, the Reform related to the new National Chart of Accounts was quicker than in another country, while the adoption of a new format Balance Sheet and a new format Income Statement was still being debated.

I used to conclude that the progress made since 1990 cannot be denied; however, the measurement among eight New Developing Countries should be based on "what else is left to be done," instead of "what was accomplished." One must admit the very remarkable and impressive progress done in some countries.

The progress, that is the adoption of the International Accounting Standards compliant Financial Statements requirements and their requirements in ten countries, was accomplished and understood easily by the people in the under-50 age group. A higher education also was another factor for the acceptance of the Western Market system. People between 50 and 65 represent the skeptics. People over 65, generally retired military men, retired school teachers, and retired civil servants are still thinking about the "good old days during the communist regime, when the job and the monthly salary were secure." This age bracket resented the term "professional judgment," a typical term used in Western accounting profession circles to show the independent thinking and decision making in financial reporting matters.

One needs to accept that the IAS must be used only as a model when creating the national accounting standards. The model unfortunately was not always as clear as black and white. We had to mention several times that "professional judgment" was necessary in solving some critical issues. The foundation of the Western accounting system can be said to be the proper exercise of professional judgment. On the other hand, how ironic it is that "professional judgment" is mentioned only once in the Standards book of 2003, in the "Framework of the IAS, paragraph 45." The use of "professional judgment" in the former Soviet Union was equated with crime against the State. It was a typical leftover of the communist attitude.

Another example that frustrated the Eastern European accountants was the following phrase: "International Accounting Standards are not intended to apply to *immaterial items*." This phrase is in the introductory paragraph of each accounting standard, 41 of which have been issued, plus several International Financial Reporting Standards (IFRS).[10]

The proposed Balance Sheet format and the Balance Sheet content were severely criticized without exception in each Newly Independent Country. The officials and the academy had difficulty in accepting a Balance Sheet format that was based on the "Liquidity" concept. I have to admit the indirect help I received from the most forward looking, progressive MINFIN Accounting Methodology Department among countries I worked was the MINFIN at the Russian Federation.

The Russians had the most translated accounting textbooks, the largest number of accounting professors, and an organization called the "International Center For Accounting Reform in Russia – www.ICAR.RU" whose objective was to "Russify" International Accounting Standards by working closely with the Russian Federation Ministry of Finance Accounting Methodology department head, among other officials.

Despite the fact that Moscow-controlled communism was over, each former Soviet Union country still communicated with Moscow, at least at the very highest level.[11]

If the Russian Federation accounting methodology officials accepted the modification of the format or content of Statement No. 1 and Statement No. 2 (i.e., the Balance Sheet and the Income Statement), I was almost sure that my proposals would be accepted sooner or later.

Since 1997, I have subscribed to the monthly accounting reform updates "Alerts" prepared by the Price Waterhouse Moscow office that enabled me to be abreast of the "Russification" efforts in the Russian Federation.[12]

New financial statements were a radical change that necessitated the Revenue Ministry's approval in each country. Quarterly estimated tax returns and year-end tax returns had to be prepared using the pre-reform tax returns. In most of

---

[10] IAS 1 lists the five components of a set of financial statements: the balance sheet, the income statement, the statement of changes in equity, the cash flow statement, and the explanatory notes or disclosures – starting with accounting policies. The skeptics are those who make the following remarks: "We have followed our Tsars, their system (one person rule for 10 centuries) turned out to be wrong, then we had the communist regime (one class rule for 70 years), they were also wrong. Now what makes us sure that the market economy ("free" for all) is the correct system for us?" By the way, this remark was made by a Russian official representing the biggest country and with the most educated and literate (percentagewise) among former Soviet Union countries.

[11] We need to emphasize that the Russian language is the "Lingua Franca" over at least 15 countries encompassing 11 time zones.

[12] Due to Yeltsin's decrees on imposed reforms, the Russian Federation was eager to satisfy the World Bank requirement in terms of adopting the IAS compliant financial reporting system. Russification generally consisted of accepting the IAS Board decisions, but with slight modifications, always. Some countries accepted the standards as they were translated into the local language. Moldova and Georgia are examples. Some preferred to follow the Russian approach: slightly modify IAS concepts. A typical follower was, who else, the "little brother," Ukraine. The source of slight modifications was the academics' conceptual objections who were accounting professors since the communist regime's hey-days.

the countries, the Tax Reform was not as advanced or synchronized with the Accounting Reform that I was working. In those instances as consultants, I had to propose a limited use of the new reporting formats. As example, we proposed mandatory short-form financial statements for the Balance Sheet and for the Income Statement for businesses that were members of the local stock exchange. These companies had to use IAS for financial reporting purposes and for stock exchange membership requirement purposes. Their pre-reform tax returns were used to satisfy Revenue/Tax officials. Unfortunately for the businesses, it was a very cumbersome but temporary situation.

Moldova was the only country, to my best recollection, that legislated a Tax Reform and an Accounting Reform at the same time in 1997.[13]

One of the typical examples of Moscow's influence was on the presentation in the Balance Sheet of the original, first issue company shares that subsequently were reacquired by the company. In the USA, company shares that are bought back from the market are called Treasury shares, or Treasury Stock.

It took months, in every county, for the officials to agree with my proposal that the value of reacquired shares should not be shown as an asset in their Balance Sheet, but should be shown as a deduction from the total shares from the equity section of the balance sheet.

In mid-1998, the news in the "Alerts" was that the Russian accounting authorities were siding with SIC-16 on this issue. Since then, it became so easy to have the local accounting officials agree on this proposal. Some officials now were supporting me on this issue.[14]

24.3.1.1 The Socialist System Inherently Inflates the Balance Sheet

Items that generally should be classified as expenses in the income statement were recorded as assets in their balance sheets. Consequently, assets were inflated. For example, current year or prior year losses, organization costs, research and development expenses, start-up costs and the above-mentioned treasury shares were all capitalized and recorded as assets in the balance sheet.

Another example of inflation of the balance sheet was the liability section. The pre-reform system allowed the misuse (or overuse) of Reserve accounts grouped in the equity section of the balance sheet. Consequently, the equity side of the balance sheet was inflated; as a result, the tax liability was minimized, to the tax authorities' great chagrin.

---

[13] The MINFIN officials and academicians of Moldova were the most eager and cooperative in this regard. Days long, weeks long discussions were the order. However, the outcome was a success coming from the smallest and poorest former Soviet Union country.

[14] The MINFIN officials and academicians of Moldova were the most eager and cooperative in this regard. Days long, weeks long discussions were the order. However, the outcome was a success coming from the smallest and poorest former Soviet Union country.

24.3.2 Income Statement

Expenses in income statements were always understated, because of the capitalized expenses, not to mention the application of IAS 36: Impairment of Assets.

The socialist system accounting as practiced in communist countries ignored period expenses in the income statement. The breakdown of expenses for "management" purposes was not necessary. The line items of the income statement were not a matter of management concern, only the bottom line was important.

Top managers in most of the Eastern countries were vehemently opposed to the accrual system based IAS income statement. Their livelihood was threatened with the accrual system imposed by the IAS. In many instances the accounting personnel or the chief accountant of the company was expressing their consent for the accrual method but they were quick to point out that the "general manager" of the state organization (the company CEO in charge since the communist era) had to be convinced first!

In my experience, when a local income statement was converted to the IAS-based income statement I have practically never seen a "net profit for the period." Almost all the time the conversion resulted in a "net loss for the period" because of the corrections to their inflated asset section of the balance sheet items (these items should have been recorded as losses). This was one of the reasons the accrual method was not considered as fully acceptable by the local accountants whose training was on cash basis reporting.

24.3.3 Statement of Changes in Equity

An explanation of the importance of this statement and the mechanics to be used in preparing it was very difficult to comprehend for an accountant from the socialist bloc.

This statement did not exist in a socialist regime. The proposed format was part of the illustrations in the "IAS 1 Presentation of Financial Statements."

Most of the time, the local Company Law Articles were in contradiction with the requirements of the IAS.

24.2.4 Cash Flow Statement

The only financial statement that did not require an effort in teaching and training was the cash flow statement. For most of the Eastern countries the "Cash Movements Statement" was already an established statement. It did not follow the logic as seen in the IAS 7 Cash Flow Statements Appendix. Their "Funds Statement" or "Statement Number 3" represented a 100 plus line accounting statement during the socialist period. (The "IAS 7 Cash Flow Statement" requires a minimum of 27 lines).

24.3.5   *Accounting Policies and Disclosures*

Another concept that was difficult to justify was accounting policies and disclosures. In the mid-1990s I did some surveys among "future members" of the Russian Federation Stock Exchange. Out of 51 respondents, only one had a list of accounting policies, which consisted of a one-page list with the minimum basic accounting policies information. The remaining companies' general managers thought that accounting policies should not be divulged by a "public" company.

Three to four years later the "International Center for Accounting Reform in Russia" with the Russian MINFIN Accounting Methodology Department head's blessing, issued a "Sample" 2-page sheet including the minimum and necessary accounting policies a public company must divulge. So much for the secrecy requested by companies.

For an eastern block accountant the logic in any international accounting standard was relatively easy to follow. The most difficult part always was the Disclosures paragraphs. In terms of essence and in format, Disclosures or Explanatory Notes was a difficult concept to implement because it required the state organization's general manager's approval.

24.4   Concluding Remarks

Thanks to the Internet, the accounting community in former Soviet Union countries is able to follow the latest accounting news. This was evident in comparatively pretty advanced countries such as Ukraine and the Russian Republic.

Some accounting officials tried to embarrass me with questions such as:

- Why is there not a [national] chart of accounts in the USA?
- Why are International Accounting Standards not accepted in the USA?
- If US generally accepted accounting principles (GAAP) is superior to IAS in terms of disclosures, why was there an ENRON case, etc.?

Generally, my answer was short enough. I made it clear to them that they were trained in International Accounting Standards, not in US GAAP. In all the comparisons they should first look and understand the World Bank and the European Community adopted accounting rules and regulations – i.e., IAS. Not any other GAAP. For example, not the US GAAP, not the French GAAP and not the German GAAP. Differences between IAS and US GAAP will be harmonized and eliminated over time.[15]

---

[15] It is accepted that there are differences between the IAS and US GAAP. However, they should be minimal. Out of approximately 2,500 paragraphs in 41 Standards, one can expect less than 4–5% difference as of 2004. Probably major differences will be in the financial reporting in the income taxes area. With almost 95% similarity in the financial reporting, a consultant can make use of the textbooks and professional publications published in the USA for IAS Training purposes without reservation.

It is worth mentioning questions and discussions I had concerning the vocabulary used in the Standards. Regardless of the country in the former Soviet Union, questions were the same: what is the "Fair Value." A term repeated at least in ten different standards with exactly the same wording! I have the impression that the tendency in the IAS Board is to have "Full Fair Value Accounting." A challenge for consultants and for trainees![16]

---

[16] Excluding the definitions used in some special Standards, such as in the "Income Taxes Standard", definitions that raise eyebrows during training are less than thirty specific accounting terms. A consultant will face the same questions on these definitions from Moldova through Kazakhstan and in all other former Soviet Union countries in between.

Part III
Accounting Certification

Chapter 25
International Accounting Certification in the CIS, Eastern and Central Europe

Robert W. McGee and Galina G. Preobragenskaya

25.1 Introduction

Although most countries have their own national accounting and auditing certifications, there are a number of internationally recognized accounting certifications. These certifications are especially valuable in transition and developing economies, where the quality of the national certification is low. The most popular international certification is offered by the Association of Chartered Certified Accountants (ACCA). Until a few years ago, this certification was the only truly international certification. However, in recent years a few other certifications have started to become internationally recognized. This paper discusses the reasons for the popularity of international certifications, the reasons why resistance to them has been encountered, and reports on the status of the various internationally recognized accounting certifications in the former Soviet Union (CIS), Eastern, and Central Europe.

The vast majority of countries have some kind of accounting certification. Some countries offer several different certifications. Some countries in the former Soviet bloc offer separate certification for accountants and auditors. Some countries offer several levels of certification (McGee, 1999a).

Most certifications are national in nature. Because of that, it is not always possible for accountants in one country to obtain employment in another country at an equal level. From an international trade perspective, one may say that there are barriers to the movement of human capital.

There are several reasons why one country may not fully recognize a certification from another country. One reason is because the accounting and tax rules vary from one country to another, so the material being tested by one certification body may be substantially different from that tested by certification bodies in other countries. Another reason for the hesitancy to recognize foreign accounting

R. W. McGee
Florida International University

G. G. Preobragenskaya
KIMEP, Kazakhstan

R. W. McGee (ed.), *Accounting Reform in Transition and Developing Economies,*
© Springer Science+Business Media LLC 2008

certifications is due to lack of familiarity with the certification content, rules, and requirements of the many countries that certify accountants and auditors. Lack of familiarity does not foster trust and confidence, even though the quality of the foreign certificate may be acceptable.

A third reason for resistance to the recognition of foreign certification is the perceived or real lack of quality or credibility of some of these certifications. The quality of some national certifications is suspect, especially in transition and developing economies. In Russia, for example, some of the local accounting associations go to the countryside selling their own certifications (McGee and Preobragenskaya, 2004).

The fourth reason for resistance to the acceptance of foreign certification credentials is inertia. Bureaucrats of any nation prefer the status quo (Friedman and Friedman, 1984). Change of any sort is automatically resisted. Resistance is perhaps stronger than average for accounting certification, since implementing changes in accounting certification require the local bureaucrats to learn something new.

The fifth reason for resistance to the acceptance of any new certifications is protectionism. The old guard accounting establishment feels threatened by the possible introduction of new certifications (Pitts, 2004), especially if practicing accountants would be required to take and pass the new certification exams. USAID accounting reform programs in several countries, as well as their EU TACIS counterpart projects, have encountered resistance from local accounting associations when new certification models are first introduced into a new country.

A sixth reason for the nonrecognition of accounting and auditing certification is distrust or even hatred for the individuals who hold such certifications. The authors are aware of only one country, i.e., Bosnia and Herzegovina, where this reason for nonrecognition exists, but there may be others.

As a result of the Dayton Peace Accord of 1995, which ended the war there, this former Yugoslav republic was divided into two entities (Burg and Shoup, 1999; Daalder, 2000; Holbrooke, 1998; Zimmerman, 1999). The Muslim-Croat Federation, which consists of Bosnian Muslims and Roman Catholic Bosnian Croats, was to possess 51% of the real estate of Bosnia and Herzegovina. The other 49% went to the Orthodox Christian Bosnian Serbs. Their state within a state is now called Republika Srpska. The country of Bosnia and Herzegovina now consists of these two entities, which have at times gone out of their way to establish different laws and rules.

For example, one of the entities (the Muslim-Croat Federation) adopted the indirect method of accounting for cash flows. When word got out that one entity adopted the indirect method, the other entity (Republika Srpska) decided that only the direct method of accounting for cash flows would be appropriate for enterprises operating within its borders (Preobragenskaya and McGee, 2004a). International Financial Reporting Standards (IFRS) allow both methods, and both entities within Bosnia and Herzegovina are in the process of adopting (IFRS) – at different speeds, incidentally.

This animosity carries over to many other areas of economic and social activity. Someone who graduates from one of the universities in the Muslim-Croat Federation part of the country is not recognized to be a university graduate in Republika Srpska. The certification process for accountants and auditors is somewhat different for accountants and auditors in Bosnia's two political entities and certifications from one entity are not automatically recognized by the other entity.

These six reasons that serve to impede the recognition of accountants beyond national (or regional) borders is a major impediment to the free movement of human capital. However, nonrecognition is not an insurmountable barrier. The market process is dealing with the nonrecognition problem, with some degree of success.

In Russia, for example, the government does not recognize *any* non-Russian certification. But the marketplace *does* recognize some non-Russian certifications. The fact that the Russian government does not recognize certifications like those offered by the ACCA, Institute of Management Accountants (IMA), and other private groups is almost irrelevant (Preobragenskaya and McGee, 2004b). Employers in Russia are eager to hire individuals who have managed to pass one or more of these international certification exams and they are not at all concerned that the Russian government does not recognize such certifications. All that matters to Russian employers – which includes the Big-4 accounting firms – is the quality of the individual who holds the international certification. These certificate holders are perceived as being of high caliber because they were able to pass a certification exam that is known to be rigorous.

25.2 ACCA Certifications

The oldest and most widely recognized international accounting certification is that offered by the Association of Chartered Certified Accountants (ACCA), which is headquartered in the UK. The exam is given each June and December at regular or special exam centers in more than 200 locations in more than 140 countries worldwide. It is offered only in English, which has both positive and negative aspects. From the positive side, offering the exam only in English means that the same exam can be offered all over the world, so there is no perception that the quality or content of the exam varies by country. Offering an English-only exam also makes it truly international. Not offering the exam in other languages also keeps the cost of administration lower than could otherwise be the case.

However, there are some negative aspects of offering the exam only in English. The spread of the exam, which tests on IFRS, is greatly impeded by not offering it in other languages, since the majority of potential candidates in many countries cannot read English well enough to take the exam. The spread of the principles tested by the ACCA exams could spread faster, wider, and deeper if the exam were made available in languages other than English. Various countries have asked the ACCA to offer its exams in other languages but those requests have been denied, with the minor exception of the Diploma in International Financial Reporting, which is now available in Russian. It will be interesting to see how popular this diploma program becomes, as word of its existence reaches the 15 former Soviet republics.

The number of candidates taking the exam is unknown. The ACCA declines to provide detailed information about enrollments for competitive reasons. However, correspondence with the ACCA was able to discover that there are well over 1,000 students registered for ACCA exams in Russia as of late 2003 and well over 7,000 registered in Central and Eastern Europe (Brown, 2003). It has nearly 300,000 members in 160 countries. The ACCA has either regular or special exam locations in several locations in former Soviet cities as well as several locations in Central and Eastern Europe. The ACCA web site lists exam locations in at least two different places and the lists are not identical. The exam locations in Table 25.1 include cities that were included in at least one of the lists.

Table 25.1 ACCA exam locations in the CIS, Eastern, and Central Europe

Country	City
Former Soviet Union (CIS)	
Armenia	Yerevan
Azerbaijan	Baku
Belarus	None
Estonia	Tallinn
Georgia	None
Kazakhstan	Almaty
Kyrgyzstan	None
Latvia	Riga
Lithuania	Vilnius
Moldova	None
Russia	Moscow
	Novocherkassk
	Saint Petersburg
	Vladivostok
Tajikistan	None
Turkmenistan	None
Ukraine	Kyiv
Uzbekistan	Tashkent
Central and Eastern Europe	
Albania	None
Bosnia and Herzegovina	None
Bulgaria	Sofia
Croatia	Zagreb
Czech Republic	Prague
Hungary	Budapest
Macedonia	None
Montenegro	None
Poland	Warsaw
Romania	Bucharest
Serbia	Belgrade
Slovakia	Bratislava
Slovenia	None

As can be seen from Table 25.1, the ACCA now has exam locations in all of the large countries of the CIS, Central and Eastern Europe, and several of the small ones as well. The only country that has more than one location is Russia. However, the fact that the ACCA does not have exam centers in every country does not necessarily act as an impediment for students in those countries who want to take the exams. For example, potential candidates from Bosnia and Slovenia can take the exam in Zagreb, Croatia, which is just a few hours away. Students in parts of Kyrgyzstan can take the exam in Almaty, Kazakhstan, which is close to the Kyrgyz border.

Although the pass rates on the ACCA exams for individual locations are not public information, informal conversations with ACCA officials over the years reveal that the pass rates vary widely, and for a number of reasons. One study (McGee, 1999b), disclosed eight reasons why the pass rates for the first ACCA exam offered in Armenia, in December 1998, were low. These were as follows:

1. The first exams were given starting on December 7 and the exam preparation courses did not start until mid- or late September. Furthermore, students had to register for at least two exams. The preparation course for the first exam was offered over 6 weeks and the preparation course for the second exam was offered over a period of 4–6 weeks, depending on location. The optimal length for such courses is 14 or 15 weeks. Thus, exam candidates did not have sufficient time to prepare for the exams.
2. The books for the preparation courses did not arrive until 1 or 2 weeks after the start of the course. The text for the second ACCA preparation course was held up in Customs and the course almost had to be cancelled because Customs officials refused to release the books at first.
3. Under normal conditions the preparation courses would have been review courses. However, the vast majority of the students taking the courses were totally unfamiliar with market-oriented accounting rules. Many of the students in the first classes were not even accountants and never had an accounting course of any kind. Thus, they had to learn new material rather than review material they had learned in the course of their university studies. The texts used in the review courses assumed that students already knew the material and therefore did not provide many examples to illustrate basic material.
4. The usual route for certification review courses is to take the preparation course after graduating from some university. However, in the case of the first Armenian ACCA exam, 25 of the candidates were still undergraduate students.
5. Even the accounting students who took the "review" courses never had a western-style accounting course because those courses were just being introduced into Armenia.
6. There was really no such thing as an accounting major in Armenian universities at the time the first exams were given. One or two accounting courses were offered within the economics department, but that was all. Thus, even students who were familiar with Armenian/Russian accounting concepts were not adequately prepared to take an exam that was based on International Accounting Standards.

7. English was the third language for the students taking the exams. All Armenian students were fluent in Russian and Armenian but their English language skills were almost never at the same level as their skills in these other two languages.
8. Time management was a problem. Armenian students were not accustomed to taking a timed exam. Under the Soviet system they could take as much time as they wanted, but the ACCA exams were strictly three hours in length. The short review courses were not able to change the mentality of the students, who showed anxiety about being constrained by the 3-hour limit.

The ACCA offers several certificate and diploma programs. Its various programs are described on its web site (www.accaglobal.com). Offerings include:

Professional scheme, which is the multilevel certification that is the most comprehensive
Certified Accounting technician scheme, which is an abbreviated version of the Professional scheme
Diploma in Financial Management
Diploma in International Financial Reporting (available in English and Russian)
Diploma in Corporate Governance
Certificate in International Auditing
Certificate in International Financial Reporting

25.2.1 Certified Accounting Technician

The Certified Accounting Technician (CAT) scheme has adopted a new syllabus, which will be implemented starting with the June 2004 exams. The new syllabus includes ten exams, of which students must take nine. There are three levels of certification. The specifics are summarized in Table 25.2.

25.2.2 Professional Scheme

The Professional Scheme is the most comprehensive certification program the ACCA offers. Certification is at three levels. Almost all exams are written at present, although there are plans to put more exams on computer. Exams are 3 h long. Some exams are optional. Sixteen exams are offered but only 14 exams need to be passed to achieve level 3 certification. If certain conditions are met, candidates can take tax and law exams based on their own country's rules rather than the ACCA exams in these subjects, which are based on British law. Table 25.3 summarizes the requirements for each level of certification.

Some exams from Parts 1 and 2 can be waived if certain conditions are met.

Pass rates for the Professional Scheme exams are published on the ACCA web site. Pass rates for the most recent exams are given in Table 25.4.

Table 25.2   Syllabus requirements – Certified Accounting Technician (ACCA)

Paper	Content	Assessment	Pass mark
	Introductory		
T1	Recording Financial Transactions	2 h computer-based or written exam	55
T2	Information for Management Control	2 h computer-based or written exam	55
	Intermediate		
T3	Maintaining Financial Records	2 h computer-based or written exam	50
T4	Accounting for Costs	2 h computer-based or written exam	50
	Advanced		
T5	Managing People and Systems	2 h written exam	40
T6	Drafting Financial Statements	3 h written exam	40
T7	Planning, Control and Performance Management	3 h written exam	40
	Two Options From		
T8	Implementing Audit Procedures	3 h written exam	40
T9	Preparing Taxation Computations	3 h written exam	40
T10	Managing Finances	3 h written exam	40

Table 25.3   Syllabus requirements professional scheme (ACCA)

Paper	Content
	Part 1
1.1	Preparing Financial Statements
1.2	Financial Information for Management
1.3	Managing People
	Part 2
2.1	Information Systems
2.2	Corporate and Business Law
2.3	Business Taxation
2.4	Financial Management and Control
2.5	Financial Reporting
2.6	Audit and Internal Review
	Part 3
	Any Two Papers from
3.1	Audit and Assurance Services
3.2	Advanced Taxation
3.3	Performance Management
3.4	Business Information Management
	All Three Papers
3.5	Strategic Business Planning and Development
3.6	Advanced Corporate Reporting
3.7	Strategic Financial Management

Table 25.4 Pass rates (%) ACCA professional scheme exams

Paper	Dec. 2003	June 2003	Dec. 2002	June 2002	Dec. 2001
Paper 1.1	44	48	47	55	52
Paper 1.2	57	46	47	46	45
Paper 1.3	48	59	41	42	39
Paper 2.1	63	50	50	49	52
Paper 2.2	52	50	52	49	48
Paper 2.3	48	47	50	57	54
Paper 2.4	39	39	56	39	41
Paper 2.5	50	48	51	44	53
Paper 2.6	42	52	53	47	58
Paper 3.1	44	40	40	44	38
Paper 3.2	42	39	38	42	38
Paper 3.3	45	41	47	47	40
Paper 3.4	54	54	53	50	52
Paper 3.5	55	53	53	51	54
Paper 3.6	53	53	55	56	53
Paper 3.7	49	44	43	49	45

25.3   CMA/CFM Certifications

The Institute of Management Accountants (IMA) in New Jersey, USA, offers the Certified Management Accountant (CMA) and Certified Financial Manager (CFM) exams. Originally aimed at accountants in the USA, the exams have spread worldwide, although the largest share of exam candidates still come from the United States.

The CMA exam is undergoing major changes as of July 1, 2004. Those who register for the exam before then will still be able to take the old format exam through December 31, 2007. Gleim Publications (www.gleim.com) seems to think the old exam format is easier to pass than the new one will be. Its web site provides the following comparison (Table 25.5).

Unlike the ACCA exams, which are mostly paper-based and are offered only in June and December, the CMA and CFM exams are offered on demand on computer and can be taken anywhere in the world where proper approved computer facilities are available. Parts 1, 3, and 4 of the CMA exam are identical to parts 1, 3, and 4 of the CFM exam. The only difference between the CMA and CFM exams is part 2. Whereas the CMA exam tests on financial reporting, the CFM part 2 tests on corporate financial management.

The CMA and CFM exams are becoming increasingly popular in the CIS, Eastern, and Central Europe, in spite of the IMA's lack of marketing for these exams. Conversations with IMA officials seemed to indicate that spreading the exam worldwide was not a top priority and other budgetary items took priority. Table 25.6 summarizes exam results for candidates who took one or more parts of the CMA and/of CFM exams in CIS, Eastern, or Central European countries between April 6, 2003 and April 6, 2004.

Table 25.5 Comparison of old and new CMA exam topics

Part	Old exam (3h, 110 multiple choice question each part)	New exam
1	**Economics, Finance and Management**	**Business Analysis** (3h, 110 multiple choice)
	Microeconomics	Business Economics
	Macroeconomics	Global Business
	International Business	Internal Controls
	Environment	Quantitative Methods
	US Business Environment	Financial Statement Analysis
	Corporate Financial Management	
	Organization Management and Communication	
2	**Financial Reporting Analysis**	**Management Accounting & Reporting** (4h, 140 multiple choice)
	Financial Accounting Environment	
	Preparation of Financial Statements	
	Analysis of Financial Statements	Budget Preparation
		Cost Management
		Information Management
		Performance Measurement
		External Financial Reporting
3	**Management Reporting, Analysis and Behavioral Issues**	**Strategic Management** (3h, 110 multiple choice)
	Cost Measurement	Strategic Planning
	Planning	Strategic Marketing
	Control and Performance	Corporate Finance
	Evaluation	Decision Analysis
	Behavioral Issues	Investment Decisions
4	**Decision Analysis, Information Systems, Management Controls**	**Business Applications** (3h, 4–7 essays)
	Decision Theory and Analysis	All topics from parts 1, 2 and 3, plus:
	Investment Decision Analysis	
	Quantitative Methods	Organization Management
	Information Systems	Organization Communication
	Management Controls	Behavioral Issues
		Ethical Considerations

The results from Table 25.6 clearly indicate that there is much room for growth. Russia is by far the largest taker of CMA and CFM exams, but only 342 exam parts were taken during the 1-year period under study. Since the exams have four parts, that means that fewer than 100 individual-equivalents took the exams. If one considers the fact that each exam part may be taken multiple times within a 12-month period, this individual-equivalent statistic shrinks even further.

It is interesting to note that Kazakhstan is the second largest consumer of CMA and CFM exams. Perhaps the reason for Kazakhstan's relative eagerness to take the CMA and CFM exams compared to much more populous countries like Ukraine is because Hock Accountancy Training, a privately owned entrepreneurial provider of CMA and CFM review courses has offices in Moscow and Almaty, the capital of

Table 25.6 CMA/CFM exam results for the CIS, Eastern, and Central Europe April 6, 2003–April 6, 2004

Country	Parts taken	Parts passed	Pass rate (%)
Former Soviet Union (CIS)			
Armenia			
Azerbaijan			
Belarus			
Estonia	1	1	100.00
Georgia			
Kazakhstan	87	46	52.87
Kyrgyzstan			
Latvia			
Lithuania			
Moldova			
Russia	342	172	50.29
Tajikistan			
Turkmenistan			
Ukraine	15	11	73.33
Uzbekistan			
Central and Eastern Europe			
Albania			
Bosnia & Herzegovina			
Bulgaria			
Croatia			
Czech Republic	1	0	0.00
Hungary			
Macedonia			
Montenegro			
Poland			
Romania			
Serbia (listed as Yugoslavia)	1	0	0.00
Slovakia			
Slovenia			
Totals	447	230	51.45

Kazakhstan. It has an aggressive and effective marketing program that announces to the local accounting community that such exams exist. It is thus creating demand for exam preparation courses. Hock recently opened an office in Kyiv. It will be interesting to see the exam statistics for Ukraine a year or two down the road, after Ukrainian accountants become aware that it is possible for them to take the CMA and CFM exams in their country. If the ACCA can have 1,000 students registered in Russia and more than 7,000 registered throughout Central and Eastern Europe, it is reasonable to expect that the statistics for the CMA and CFM exams will grow over time.

The CMA and CFM exams have several advantages over the ACCA exams, at least from a student's perspective. For one, students need to pass just four exams to earn the full certification, whereas one must pass 14 exams to earn the full ACCA designation. Pass rates between the two are basically the same, so presumably they have the same degree of difficulty. Another advantage of the CMA exam is that students who pass all four parts can earn a second certification (the CFM) by passing just one more exam. A third advantage is that the CMA and CFM are offered on demand, whereas the ACCA exams are offered just twice a year, making it possible for CMA and CFM students to complete all exam requirements much sooner, since they can retake the exams several times in 1 year. One advantage the ACCA designation has over the CMA and CFM is that the ACCA has been around for a long time, its certification is recognized worldwide, and it is prestigious. Another advantage of the ACCA exams is that the exams may be taken without the use of a computer. Although the skills required to take a computer exam are not all that great, it is a factor to consider.

The CMA and CFM credentials are relatively new to the CIS, Eastern, and Central Europe, and they are aimed more toward corporate accountants, whereas the ACCA exams are aimed more toward public accountants.

25.4 CAP and CIPA Certifications

25.4.1 Overview

The International Council of Certified Accountants and Auditors (ICCAA) was formed in late 2001 with the assistance of the United States Agency for International Development (USAID) and others to offer internationally recognized accounting certification exams. Its target market includes the countries of the former Soviet Union, although its main focus at the moment is on the five Central Asian republics of Kazakhstan, Kyrgyzstan, Tajikistan, Turkmenistan, and Uzbekistan. It also has a presence in Ukraine, Russia, and Moldova.

Several reasons were given for the need for these certifications. For one, none of the existing certifications in the Russian zone have much credibility. In some countries, certification can be sold outright. In other cases, the exams are not sufficiently challenging to foster much credibility. Foreign investors are not impressed to see financial statements that are certified by accountants or auditors who possess a local certification. Thus, there is a very real need for a certification that is perceived to be of high quality. The only truly international accounting certifications, such as the ACCA, CMA, and CFM, are only offered in the English language, which greatly limits their accessibility within the Russian zone. The ability to attract foreign capital could be enhanced if a credible certification existed within the Russian zone that was widely accepted across borders. Such certification would be more credible and more valuable than a conglomeration of national certifications of questionable value.

The CAP and CIPA exams are given in the Russian language and are modeled after the Canadian Certified General Accountant (CGA) designation (www.cga-canada.org). The content of the exams complies with the International Federation of Accountants (IFAC) International Education Guidelines and UNCTAD's Global

Curriculum for Professional Education of Professional Accountants, as do the ACCA exams. According to Sholpan Assangaliyeva, Executive Director of ICCAA and holder of the American CPA, the CIPA exam "is sufficiently high and not less difficult in some cases than the CPA exam." The content is different in some cases but in the case of the auditing exam the content is the same as the American CPA (Assangaliyeva, 2004a).

Certification is on two levels. The first level is designated Certified Accounting Practitioner (CAP). This designation is earned by passing three exams – Financial Accounting 1, Management Accounting 1, and Tax & Law. One must also have 1 year experience and computer literacy. CAP exams are offered quarterly. The second level certification is called Certified International Professional Accountant (CIPA) and is earned by passing four additional exams – in Financial Accounting 2, Management Accounting 2, Finance and Audit. CIPA exams are offered semi-annually. As of mid-April, 2004, more than 1,500 candidates have passed all parts of the CAP exam and have been awarded certificates; 104 individuals have passed all parts of the CIPA exam (Kenney, 2004a). Table 25.7 shows the number of CAP holders by country and Chart 25.1 shows the number of CAP holders by country.

The exam is growing in popularity. Attendance for the March 2004 exams was at record levels in Kyrgyzstan, Tajikistan, and Uzbekistan. In Uzbekistan 1,002 candidates took the March 2004 CAP exams, compared to 564 in June 2003. More than 30,000 candidates took one or more exams between May 2002 and March 2004. The first exams were offered for free. Exam fees and registration fees were introduced in Kazakhstan, Moldova, and Ukraine starting in August 2003. Turnout – the number registered for the exam versus the number actually taking the exam – increased significantly after fees were introduced, from 61.7% to 84.7%, in Kazakhstan, for example (Kenney, 2004b).

The CAP exam results for March 2004 are summarized in Table 25.8. As can be seen, the largest number of exam candidates came from Kazakhstan (1,386), followed by Uzbekistan (1,002), Ukraine (910), Kyrgyzstan (882), Tajikistan (464), Moldova (139), and Turkmenistan (64). Noticeably missing is Russia, which has the largest potential market for international certification exams offered in the Russian language. More on that later.

Table 25.7 Number of CAP holders by country April 2004 (www.cipaen.org)

Country	Number of CAPs
Kazakhstan	519
Kyrgyzstan	324
Russia	6
Tajikistan	71
Turkmenistan	20
Uzbekistan	158
Ukraine	440
Total	1,538

Chart 1 Freedom Score

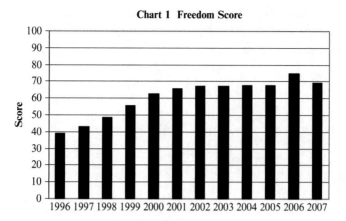

Chart 25.1 Number of CAP holders by country

Table 25.8 CAP passes for the March 12–14, 2004 exams (Kenney, 2004b)

Country	Financial Accounting 1	Tax & Law	Management Accounting 1	Total	% of Total
Kazakhstan	503	479	404	1,386	28.6
Kyrgyzstan	451	292	139	882	18.2
Moldova	39	67	33	139	2.9
Tajikistan	162	152	150	464	9.6
Turkmenistan	24	25	15	64	1.3
Ukraine	323	294	293	910	18.8
Uzbekistan	556	248	198	1,002	20.7
Totals	2,508	1,557	1,232	4,847	100.0

The number of individuals taking the CAP exams far exceeds those taking the CIPA exams, which might be expected, given that fact that the exams are relatively new and that the CAP exams must be passed before the CIPA exams may be attempted. Table 25.9 shows a comparison of the CAP and CIPA exams taken in the fourth quarter of 2002 and 2003 in all countries where the exams were given. The popularity of both exams has increased, by an average of 8.6%.

Table 25.10 shows the number of exams taken in the five Central Asian republics between September 2002 and August 2003. About 90% of the exams taken were the CAP exams. The pass rates for the lower level (CAP) exams were much higher (45.8%) than the pass rates for the higher level CIPA exams (8.4%). There seem to be at least two reasons for that. For one, the CAP exams test more basic material, which would make those exams easier to pass. The other reason is that candidates need to attain a grade of only 50% to pass the CAP exams, whereas the CIPA exams require a score of 75% (Kenney, 2004c).

Table 25.9 Comparison of CAP and CIPA exams taken Q4 – 2002 and 2003 (Kenney, 2004b)

Exam	2002 Q4	2003 Q4	Increase (%)
CAP	5598	6086	8.7
CIPA	659	711	7.9
Total	6257	6797	8.6

Table 25.10 Exams taken and pass rates of five Central Asian republics – September 2002 to August 2003 (Kenney, 2004b)

Exam	Exams written	Turnout ratio (%)	Pass rates (%)
CAP (90%)	13,880	63.1	45.8
CIPA (10%)	1,528	51.4	8.4
Total (100%)	15,408	61.7	42.4

Table 25.11 Exams by country – September 2002 to August 2003 (Kenney, 2004b)

Country	Exams taken	% of Total
Kazakhstan	8,049	42.1
Ukraine	3,707	19.4
Kyrgyzstan	3,119	16.3
Uzbekistan	2,734	14.3
Tajikistan	1,258	6.6
Turkmenistan	248	1.3
Total	19,115	100.0

Table 25.11 shows a breakdown by country of the CAP and CIPA exams taken between September 2002 and August 2003. As can be seen, the largest number of candidates taking the exam during the period under study came from Kazakhstan, with 42.1% of the total. Ukraine is a distant second with 19.4%. Turkmenistan was in last place, with 1.3%. Moldova is not included because exams did not start there until after August 2003. Russia is not included because regular exams did not start there until after August, 2003, although some potential trainers took a few exams as part of a pilot project. Chart 25.2 shows the number of exams taken by country graphically. As can be seen, the number of exams taken in Kazakhstan far surpasses the number of exams taken in any other country.

Pass rates have been increasing for both the CAP and CIPA exams, as shown in Table 25.12, which includes statistics for all countries where the exams were given. The CAP pass rates are comparable to the pass rates for other international exams, such as the CMA, CFM, and ACCA exams, although the CIPA pass rates are much lower.

25.4.2 Ukraine

Separate exam statistics are available for Ukraine, broken down by subject. Table 25.13 shows the number of candidates and pass rates for the CAP and CIPA exams from May 2002 to November 2003.

Table 25.12 Pass Rate Comparison CAP and CIPA Exams November 21–24, 2003 (Kenney 2004b)

	November Exams written	November Pass rate (%)	Comparison 2002–2003 1st year rates (%)
CAP (87%)	4,974	54.5	45.8
CIPA (13%)	711	14.2	8.4
Totals	5,685	50.9	42.1

Table 25.13 Level of activity and pass rates in CAP and CIPA exams Ukraine, May 2002–November 2003 (Mino, 2004)

	May 2002	Sept. 2002	Nov. 2002	March 2003	Aug. 2003	Nov. 2003
CAP Exams						
Examinees	435	551	1409	839	645	1034
Pass rate (%)	57	40	39	48	53	65
CIPA Exams						
Examinees	47		228		77	116
Pass rates (%)	34		0		19	16
Total All Exams						
Examinees	482	551	1637	839	722	1150
Pass rate (%)	55	40	33	48	50	60

As was true of pass rates in general, the CAP pass rates for Ukraine were higher than the pass rates for the CIPA exams. The 0% pass rate on the November 2002 CIPA exams could not get any lower.

Statistics for the individual exam parts for the Ukraine exams are also available. Table 25.14 provides a breakdown by exam and date. Some boxes are blank because not every exam was given in every examination period. Scores were remarkably low for some exams and for some exam dates. The November 2002 exams appear to be a disaster for Financial Accounting 2 and Audit, since not a single person passed either of those two exams. No one passed the next Financial Accounting 2 exam either. The low pass rates were attributed to poor preparation and training. The issue of poor training and preparation was addressed by giving a workshop for the trainers during summer 2003. Pass rates have since improved (Kenney, 2004c).

Table 25.14 also shows a major jump in the number of candidates appearing for the November 2002 exam. Two reasons were given for the jump in enrollment. For one, fall exams seem to be more popular than exams offered at other times of the year. But the more important reason for the jump is probably because the project announced that it would start charging fees for the exams beginning in 2003, which led many candidates to sign up for the November 2002 exam, which was free (Kenney, 2004c). A survey that was taken of potential exam candidates revealed that cost was a very important factor in determining whether to take the exams, so

Table 25.14 Level of activity and pass rates individual exam summary CAP and CIPA exams Ukraine, May 2002–November 2003 (Mino, 2004)

	May 2002	Sept. 2002	Nov. 2002	March 2003	Aug. 2003	Nov. 2003
Financial Accounting 1						
Examinees	102	194	525	263	219	362
Pass rate (%)	36	27	37	27	44	57
Tax & Law						
Examinees	238	263	561	396	236	326
Pass rates (%)	71	51	33	74	76	77
Management Accounting 1						
Examinees	95	94	323	180	190	346
Pass rate (%)	43	35	52	24	35	62
Financial Accounting 2						
Examinees	42		129		23	39
Pass rate (%)	29		0		0	21
Audit						
Examinees	5		99		15	21
Pass rates (%)	80		0		13	14
Management Accounting 2						
Examinees					27	32
Pass rate (%)					48	13
Finance						
Examinees					12	24
Pass rate (%)					0	13

free exams were much more attractive than exams that involved a fee, even if the fee were only a few dollars (Filshin and Karabekova, 2004).

25.4.3 Russia

The CAP and CIPA exams are the only truly international accounting certification exams offered in the Russian language. They test on International Financial Reporting Standards rather than national standards, which makes certificate holders more marketable, not only in every Russian speaking country but also to a certain extent in numerous other countries. The exam process is not corrupt, which also greatly enhances the credibility, acceptability, and prestige of the designations. But one glaring question seems to pop out when one examines the above statistics – Russia has the greatest population of any of the former Soviet republics, yet the statistics on the exam in Russia are practically nonexistent. Why is that?

The answer is quite simple. USAID intended to start the exams in Central Asia and Ukraine and work out the bugs in the system before exporting it to Russia (Kenney, 2004c). The CIPA program did not start in Russia until November, 2002, and even then it started only as a pilot program. Funded by USAID, the project had the following objectives:

- Identify potential trainers of accountancy courses (about 25 persons)
- Purchase complete sets of educational materials and distribute to potential trainers
- Conduct examinations of potential trainers
- Conduct pedagogical training of successful examinees and identify acceptable trainers
- Administer training of accountants through accepted trainers
- Conduct examinations of accountants

The first CIPA exam (actually CAP) was given in Moscow at the end of November 2002. Fifteen potential trainers took the Financial Accounting 1 exam and ten took the Management Accounting 1 exam. Two additional exams were given to potential trainers in March and June, 2003. As a result of these exams, ten candidates earned the CAP designation (Petrova, 2004).

Twelve individuals were selected to be trainers and the USAID project helped them organize and deliver some CIPA training courses in preparation for future exams. The first exams for non-trainers were given in November 2003. The results were as follows:

- Financial Accounting 1 – 42 candidates
- Management Accounting 1 – 27 candidates
- Tax & Law – 26 candidates
- Financial Accounting 2 – 5 candidates
- Management Accounting – 4 candidates
- Audit – 2 candidates
- Finance – 4 candidates

As a result of these exams, 13 additional individuals earned the CAP designation, raising the total number of CAPs in Russia to 23 by the end of 2003 (Petrova, 2004).

There are some additional reasons why the number of candidates in Russia taking the CAP and CIPA exams has been minimal. Russia has its own certification program based on Russian standards. More than 170,000 Russian accountants hold the Russian certification. Some members of the "old guard" believe the existing Russian certification exams should be taken rather than the new exams based on IFRS. The new ACCA Russian language diploma in IFRS is serving the needs of individuals who desire to be certified with a credential that verifies their IFRS competency, which reduces the need for another Russian language exam that tests IFRS (Assangaliyeva, 2004b). The fact that IFRS have not yet been fully and completely adopted by Russia also plays a role, since demand for IFRS specialists is not as high as would otherwise be the case.

The USAID pilot program is now completed. A new USAID accounting reform project has started in Russia with the objective of promoting the CIPA in Russia. However, it is too early to tell whether this new project will be successful or whether the market demand for the CAP and CIPA designations is sufficient to warrant continued marketing efforts. However, if the success of the program in

Central Asia is any indication, the Russian program can expect a groundswell of support, since there is no other international accounting certification available in the Russian language. Local accounting organizations are understandably hesitant to promote an unknown accounting certification, both because it is new and relatively unheard of and because any change in the status quo will chip away at the existing power base of the old guard.

25.4.4 Other Former Soviet Republics

There is evidence that interest in the CAP and CIPA exams is spreading to other former Soviet republics. Representatives from accounting associations in Armenia, Georgia, and Azerbaijan have expressed an interest in joining the ICCAA, the organization that sponsors the exams. Georgia requested that the exams be given in the Georgian language but their request was rejected (Assangaliyeva, 2004a). Some of the candidates who took the exam in Ukraine were from Moldova (Assangaliyeva, 2004b), since Moldova did not offer the exam until recently. Since Moldova is now part of the certification program, the number of people taking the exam in Moldova will likely increase.

Three former Soviet republics that do not seem to be at all interested in the new Russian language certifications are Estonia, Latvia, and Lithuania. There may be several reasons for this lack of interest. For one, only about half the population in these countries consists of ethnic Russians. When Stalin forcibly shipped trainloads of Russians to these countries in 1940 with the express aim of destroying the local cultures and "Sovietizing" these three republics, it caused a great deal of resentment that lingers to this day. As a result, a large percentage of the ethnic Estonians, Latvians, and Lithuanians view Russians and anything Russian in negative terms. Thus, the attraction of a Russian language certification is generally not very strong, even though the residents of these countries are fluent in the Russian language.

Another reason for the relative lack of interest in a Russian language certification may be because these republics are among the ten new members of the European Union (EU). They are facing West rather than East and Russian is not one of the official languages of the EU. If anyone in these republics is considering earning an accounting certification, it is more likely to be a certification in one of the EU languages than in Russian.

25.5   Certification Preparation Companies

Various USAID (United States Agency for International Development) and EU TACIS projects have provided exam preparation training in a number of countries since the 1970s, but these providers are not entrepreneurial, nor are these facilities sustainable. When USAID or TACIS closes a project, these training facilities also close down.

There has been an effort to turn over such training to various local accounting associations, but the results in this regard have been mixed. Turning over a training program to another bureaucratic organization is not the best way to carry on the work.

Interest in preparing for the various international certification exams has triggered a market response. Entrepreneurs have emerged to provide training courses for students who want help preparing for the exams. The largest entrepreneurial provider of English language accounting certification training in Russia is Hock Accountancy Training (www.hocktraining.com), which is headquartered in Moscow, with branch locations in Almaty (Kazakhstan), Kiev (Ukraine), and Hong Kong. It also offers classes in other locations, such as St. Petersburg, if demand warrants it. It offers classroom and distance learning instruction for the American CPA exam as well as the ACCA, CMA, CF,M and CIA exams. It also provides materials and instruction for the Russian language ACCA Diploma in International Financial Reporting (Hock, 2004).

Hock reports that 52% of Hock students who took the November 2003 CPA exam passed all four parts on their first attempt. This statistic is rather impressive when one considers that the exam has to be taken in English, which is the second or third language for the individuals taking the exams. But in the case of the American CPA exam there is also another factor to consider. The American CPA exam is not offered in Russia or Ukraine. It is only offered in the United States, which means that anyone in Russia, Ukraine, or elsewhere who wants to take the exam must arrange to fly to the United States to take the exam. Registering for the exam must be done through the mail, complete with money transfer, which is not always easy in some parts of the CIS. The expense is also more than many potential candidates from that part of the world can afford. The pressure to pass is also quite intense, since they may not be able to make more than one trip to the United States.

Hock's CMA/CFM pass rate is about 63%. Its CIA pass rate, based on a much smaller sample, is about 50%. The CMA exam is the one that has the largest number of candidates and it also has the fastest growth rate, in terms of students enrolling in the preparation courses.

Its CPA review program is composed mostly of Big-4 accounting firm employees, although there are a growing number of smaller accounting firms as well. The CMA, CFM, and CIA exam students are almost entirely industry accountants or finance people. They come from Russian companies (large and small) and multinational companies. Classes are taught by a combination of locals and expats. Almost all of their teachers are full-time Hock employees, with backgrounds in either academia or practice.

25.6 Concluding Comments

There is a definite need for internationally recognized certification in the CIS, Central, and Eastern Europe. The national certifications that presently exist are not very credible in the eyes of the international investing community. The requirements for national certification vary from country to country and international investors have neither the time nor the inclination to learn which national certifications are of sufficiently high quality to earn their trust and respect. Thus, companies in the former Soviet bloc that hire nationally certified auditors to audit their books are placing themselves at a competitive disadvantage in the worldwide capital market because of the perception that their financial statements are not credible. One way around this problem is to retain the services of a Big-4 accounting firm to conduct the audit, but this option can be expensive, since the Big-4 charge much higher fees than do national or local firms.

A high-quality certification credential is needed even in cases where the goal is not to attract foreign capital. Enterprises in transition economies need help and guidance in converting their accounting systems from the old Soviet model to one that is more in tune with a market economy. The present national certification models are not attuned to this new demand. Firms need accountants and financial managers who are educated in the new system. One way to identify who these people are is through international certification that is based on IFRS. The Russian language CAP and CIPA and the various English language accounting certifications are starting to make their mark in the financial reporting arena. However, the CAP and CIPA programs are just beginning and the English language programs are greatly constrained because only a minority of accountants know the language well enough to take and pass these exams.

References

Assangaliyeva, S. (2004a). Correspondence with Sholpan Assangaliyeva, Executive Director of ICCAA, 21 April.
Assangaliyeva, S. (2004b). Correspondence with Sholpan Assangaliyeva, Executive Director of ICCAA, 23 April.
Association of Chartered Certified Accountants (ACCA). www.accaglobal.com.
Brown, M. (2003). Correspondence with Muir Brown of ACCA, 5 November 2003.
Burg, S.L. and Shoup, P.S. (1999). *The War in Bosnia – Herzegovina: Ethnic Conflict and International Intervention*. Armonk, NY/London: M.E. Sharpe.
Daalder, I.H. (2000). *Getting to Dayton: The Making of America's Bosnia Policy*. Washington, DC: The Brookings Institution.
Filshin, S. & Karabekova, B. (2004). Market Survey Report, Performed by SIFE-AUCA. Bishkek, March.
Friedman, M. and Friedman, R. (1984). *Tyranny of the Status Quo*. San Diego, NY/London: Harcourt Brace Jovanovich.
Gleim Publications. www.gleim.com
Hock Accountancy Training. www.hocktraining.com
Hock, B. (2004). Correspondence with Brian Hock, 5 April 2004.
Holbrooke, R. (1998). *To End a War*. New York: The Modern Library.
Kenney, S. (2004a). Correspondence with Steve Kenney of the Central Asian Accounting Reform Project, 5 April 2004.
Kenney, S. (2004b). CIPA-EN Status Report. USAID/PRAGMA Enterprise Development Project, April.

Kenney, S. (2004c). Correspondence with Steve Kenney of the Central Asian Accounting Reform Project, 20 April 2004.

McGee, R.W. and Preobragenskaya, G.G. (2004). Problems of Implementing International Financial Reporting Standards in a Transition Economy: A Case Study of Russia. Presented at the Eighth International Conference on Global Business and Economic Development, Guadalajara, Mexico, January 7–10, 2004. Also published on the Social Science Research Network website at http://ssrn.com/abstract=459363.

McGee, R.W. (1999a). Certification of Accountants and Auditors in the CIS: A Case Study of Armenia. *Journal of Accounting, Ethics & Public Policy*, 2(2), 338–353. Also published on the Social Science Research Network website at http://ssrn.com/abstract=242552.

McGee, R.W. (1999b). International Certification of Accountants in the CIS: A Case Study of Armenia. *Journal of Accounting, Ethics & Public Policy*, 2(1), 70–75. Also published on the Social Science Research Network website at http://ssrn.com/abstract=251475.

Mino, R.J. (2004). Correspondence with Raymond J. Mino, Deputy Chief of Party, Ukraine Accounting Reform Project, 9 April.

Petrova, O. (2004). Correspondence with Olga Petrova of the USAID Accounting Reform Project in Russia, managed by Mag Consulting, 13 April.

Pitts, Barry. (2004). Interview with Barry Pitts, Chief of Party, Chemonics Ukraine Accounting Reform Project, 16 April.

Preobragenskaya, G.G. and McGee, R.W. (2004a). Reforming the Accounting Curriculum in Russia: Some Guidelines Based on the Armenian and Bosnian Experiences. *Research in Accounting in Emerging Economies, Supplement 2: Accounting and Accountability in Emerging and Transition Economies*, pp. 531–553. Also published on the Social Science Research Network website at http://ssrn.com/abstract=410766.

Preobragenskaya, G.G. and McGee, R.W. (2004b). International Accounting and Finance Certification in the Russian Federation. Presented at the 16th Annual Conference of the International Academy of Business Disciplines, San Antonio, TX, March 25–28, 2004. A revised, abbreviated version was published in C. Gardner., J. Biberman, and A. Alkhafaji, (Eds.) (2004). *Business Research Yearbook: Global Business Perspectives*, Volume XI (pp. 32–36), Saline, MI: McNaughton & Gunn.

Zimmerman, W. (1999). *Origins of a Catastrophe*. New York: Times Books/Random House.

Chapter 26
Accounting Certification in the Russian Language

Robert W. McGee

26.1 Introduction

The 15 former Soviet republics (CIS) all have their own national accounting and auditing certifications. They have been evolving in different directions since the break up of the Soviet Union. But they have at least one thing in common – their certifications are not held in high regard beyond their borders, and perhaps even within their own borders.

Several internationally recognized certification bodies have tried to fill the market need by offering their exams within the borders of the CIS, but these attempts have been only partially successful. Because these international certification exams are offered only in the English language, the majority of accountants in the CIS are not able to take advantage of these exams. Until recently, non-English speaking accountants within the CIS had no alternatives other than their national exams, which were not held in high regard even within their borders.

This situation is beginning to change. A few years ago a series of examinations based on the accounting principles used in the developed market economies was introduced in several former Soviet republics. These exams were offered in the Russian language, thus offering non-English speaking accountants an opportunity to earn a certification based on internationally recognized accounting principles. This chapter reports on this movement.

The old Soviet accounting system worked well for what it was called upon to do. Over a period of several generations a very elaborate system of bookkeeping evolved to keep track of accounting transactions. However, the old bookkeeping system did not collect and report on the information that is needed in a developed market economy. There was no calculation of profits and losses, which led to a massive misallocation of resources. This deficiency was pointed out by Ludwig von Mises as far back as the 1920s (Mises, 1920, 1923, 1935). Thus, when the Soviet Union collapsed and the former Soviet republics began their transition to a market economy, a new system of accounting was needed. Foreign experts from many

R. W. McGee
Florida International University

R. W. McGee (ed.), *Accounting Reform in Transition and Developing Economies,*
© Springer Science + Business Media LLC 2008

developed countries flooded into the Commonwealth of Independent States (CIS), Eastern, and Central Europe to provide advice and guidance during this transformation process. This advice included guidance on how to establish and use market-oriented accounting rules.

Although guidance was needed, one major impediment to the education process was the lack of accounting educational materials available in the local languages. This problem was partially solved by translating English language accounting texts into the local languages. However, these translations did not completely solve the problem. The early translations were often less than excellent (Preobragenskaya and McGee, 2004). Furthermore, some of the texts that were translated were already 5 or 10 years old, so the information the CIS accountants were getting was sometimes out of date. Also, many of the texts that were translated were American college texts, which were based on US generally accepted accounting principles (GAAP), whereas the rest of the world was using International Accounting Standards (IAS) as their guide.

The various former Soviet republics began to develop and adopt accounting and auditing certification programs that were based on Western models. However, it was the old guard that was in charge of this development process and they brought their old Soviet mindset with them. The corruption that was rampant under the old system did not evaporate as new, private accounting associations were created to provide the institutional framework for the new, private sector accounting profession.

Because of this lack of reform, the new accounting certification models that evolved lacked credibility in international capital markets, or even in the home country. In some republics accounting certifications could easily be purchased without the need of an exam. In other cases, the examination process was not sufficiently rigorous to screen out incompetent accountants (McGee, 1999a, b). The marketplace knew this and reacted accordingly by discounting the credentials of anyone who held a national certification.

Credible certified accountants were needed but none existed. The market rushed in to fill this vacuum. The UK-based Association of Chartered Certified Accountants (ACCA) already had a credible certification program that had been in place for nearly 100 years. ACCA certification was recognized in well over 100 countries. Its certification program was rigorous and had worldwide credibility.

The ACCA had somewhat of a monopoly on credible certification in the CIS for a few years. However, shortly after the transition process to a market economy began the US-based Institute of Management Accountants (IMA) began offering its Certified Management Accountant (CMA) and Certified Financial Manager (CFM) exams in some former Soviet and Eastern and Central European countries. Anyone who could pass these exams earned instant credibility. The problem with these exams was that they were offered only in the English language. Thus, the vast majority of accountants in these countries were not able to take advantage of this upgrade opportunity.

A few years ago an attempt to solve this problem was made by the United States Agency for International Development (USAID), which started supporting a Russian language certification model that was based on the Canadian Certified

General Accountant (CGA) exam. This certification model was tried first in five Central Asian republics and has now spread to Azerbaijan, Belarus, Moldova, Russia, and Ukraine.

26.2 CAP and CIPA Certifications

26.2.1 Overview

The International Council of Certified Accountants and Auditors (ICCAA) was formed in late 2001 with the assistance of the USAID and others to offer internationally recognized accounting certification exams. Its target market includes the countries of the former Soviet Union, although its main focus at the moment is on the five Central Asian republics of Kazakhstan, Kyrgyzstan, Tajikistan, Turkmenistan, and Uzbekistan. It also has a presence in Azerbaijan, Belarus, Moldova, Russia, and Ukraine.

Several reasons were given for the need for these certifications. For one, none of the existing certifications in the Russian zone have much credibility. In some countries, certification can be sold outright. In other cases, the exams are not sufficiently challenging to foster much credibility. Foreign investors are not impressed to see financial statements that are certified by accountants or auditors who possess a local certification. Thus, there is a very real need for a certification that is perceived to be of high quality.

The only truly international accounting certifications, such as the ACCA, CMA, and CFM,[1] are only offered in the English language, which greatly limits their accessibility within the Russian zone. The ability to attract foreign capital could be enhanced if a credible certification existed within the Russian zone that was widely accepted across borders. Such certification would be more credible and more valuable than a conglomeration of national certifications of questionable value.

The Certified Accounting Practitioner (CAP) and Certified International Public Accountant (CIPA) exams are given in the Russian language and are modeled after the Canadian Certified General Accountant (CGA) designation (www.cga-canada. org). The content of the exams complies with the International Federation of Accountants (IFAC) International Education Guidelines and UNCTAD's Global Curriculum for Professional Education of Professional Accountants, as do the ACCA exams.

Certification is on two levels. The first level is designated Certified Accounting Practitioner (CAP). This designation is earned by passing three exams – Financial Accounting 1, Management Accounting 1, and Tax & Law. One must also have 1 year experience and computer literacy. CAP exams are offered quarterly.

The second level certification is called Certified International Professional Accountant (CIPA) and is earned by passing four additional exams – Financial

---

[1] The CFM has been discontinued.

Accounting 2, Management Accounting 2, Finance, and Audit. CIPA exams are
offered semiannually.

26.2.2 Exam Data

Table 26.1 shows the number of participants tested between 2001 and 2007. As of the
end of 2007, exams have been offered in Kazakhstan, Kyrgyzstan, Uzbekistan,
Tajikistan, Turkmenistan, Russia, Ukraine, Moldova, and Belarus. Only four Central
Asian republics gave exams in 2001. Turkmenistan and Ukraine started giving exams
the following year. Belarus and Azerbaijan started giving exams more recently.

More participants have been tested in Kazakhstan than in any of the other former
Soviet republics. That is understandable, since the first headquarters for the examination program was in Kazakhstan. The headquarters has since shifted to Russia.

At some point it is reasonable to expect that Russia and Ukraine will have more
participants than any of the other countries offering exams, since they are the two
largest countries in terms of population. However, that has not yet happened. As of
the most recent year (2007), Kazakhstan had more than twice as many participants
as any other country. Ukraine and Uzbekistan each had more than 3,000 participants in 2007. Russia had only 568.

Chart 26.1 illustrates the number of participants tested annually by year. As can
be seen, the number of participants jumped dramatically in 2002, then jumped
again the following year, then declined the next few years before jumping to a new
all-time high in 2007.

Interviews with USAID representatives found that one reason why enrollments
dropped in 2004 is because the organizations offering the exams started to charge
fees in that year. Prior to 2004 some exam providers gave the exams for free.

The next few charts show the annual results for each country where the exams
have been given. The chart for Kazakhstan closely mirrors the chart for all the
countries combined in terms of ups and down if not numbers.

Table 26.1 Total participants tested

	2001	2002	2003	2004	2005	2006	2007	Totals
Kazak.	213	1,546	5,551	3,941	4,336	5,441	8,150	29,178
Kyrg.	222	1,856	2,711	2,362	1,389	1,117	1,267	10,924
Uzbek.	60	1,400	2,212	2,249	1,330	1,873	3,095	12,219
Tajik.	11	462	1,006	1,039	585	324	244	3,671
Turk.		88	184	224	262	506	314	1,578
Rus.			110	59	174	390	568	1,301
Ukr.		1658	2,211	2,454	2,812	3,081	3,852	16,068
Mold.			71	202	181	173	207	834
Bel.					213	721	142	1,076
Azer.							27	27
Totals	506	7,010	14,056	12,530	11,282	13,626	17,866	76,876

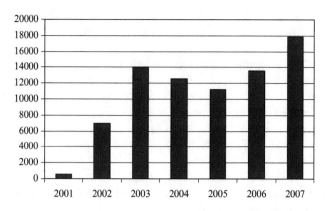

Chart 26.1 Total participants tested

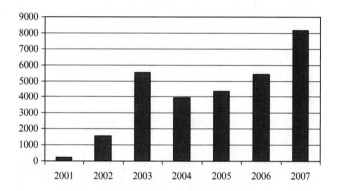

Chart 26.2 Kazakhstan. Total participants tested

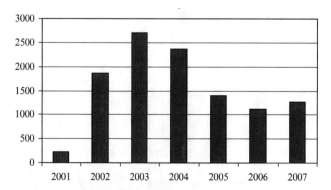

Chart 26.3 Kyrgyzistan. Total participants tested

Chart 26.3 shows the annual number of participants for Kyrgyzstan. Exams were first offered in 2001. Participation jumped in 2002 and increased again the following year before declining.

Chart 26.4 shows the figures for Uzbekistan. As was true with Kazakhstan and Kyrgyzstan, participation in Uzbekistan jumped at first, then declined before rising again.

The figures for Tajikistan are shown in Chart 26.5. Its pattern is somewhat different from that of the other Central Asian republics. Participation jumped in the first few years, as was the case with the other Central Asian republics, but in the case of Tajikistan the decline has been continuous whereas in the case of the other Central Asian republics the decline reversed.

Participation in Turkmenistan also jumped in the first few years, as is shown in Chart 26.6, but declined in 2007.

Chart 26.7 shows the figures for Russia. The first exams were given in Russia in 2003, a few years after they were first given in Central Asia. Participation dropped in 2004 but has risen every year since.

Chart 26.8 shows the results for Ukraine. Participation has increased each year since exams were first offered in 2002. The numbers are relatively large as well.

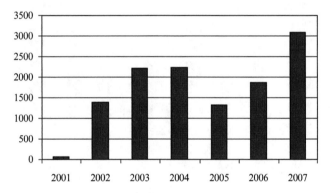

Chart 26.4 Uzbekistan. Total participants tested

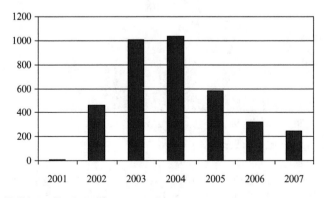

Chart 26.5 Tajikistan. Total participants tested

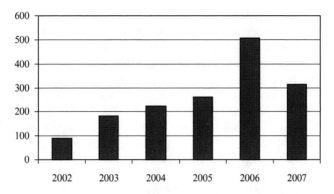

Chart 26.6 Turkmenistan. Total participants tested

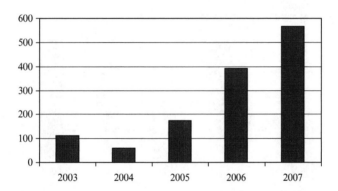

Chart 26.7 Russia. Total participants tested

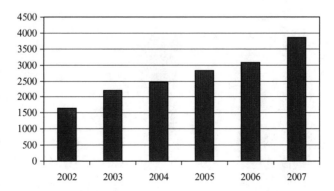

Chart 26.8 Ukraine. Total participants tested

Moldova's figures are shown in Chart 26.9. The numbers are small compared to most of the other countries where the exams have been offered and it appears that participation has leveled off, although it is too soon to say so definitively.

Chart 26.10 shows the results for Belarus. After only 3 years it is too soon to determine where there is a pattern. Participation is low compared to the other countries, but that is to be expected, since Belarus is a small country. Participation jumped in 2006, then fell to a level that was lower than the first year.

Chart 26.11 shows the pass rates from 2001 to 2007. One possible explanation for why pass rates dropped after the first year is because the pass rates for CAP exams are much higher than those for CIPA exams, and the CAP exams are taken before the CIPA exams.

Chart 26.12 shows total participants by country. Kazakhstan had the most participants, which is not a surprise given the fact that the exams were offered first in

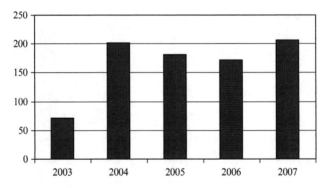

Chart 26.9 Moldova. Total participants tested

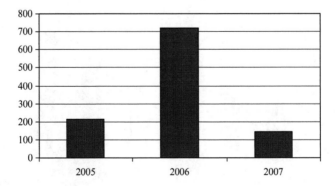

Chart 26.10 Belarus. Total participants tested

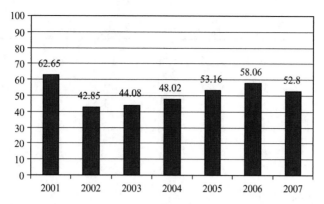

Chart 26.11 Pass rates

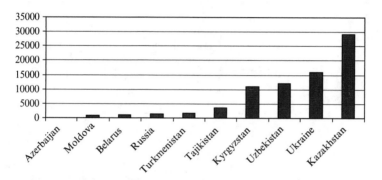

Chart 26.12 Total participants by country

that country. Kazakhstan was also the first headquarters for the exam program. Ukraine was in second place. Although it got started later in the process, the number of students taking the exams has expanded rapidly. As the second largest of the former Soviet republics in terms of population, its numbers will probably continue to expand as the program filters through the Ukrainian accounting community.

Uzbekistan and Kyrgyzstan also had more than 10,000 total participants. At the other end of the spectrum were Azerbaijan, Moldova, Belarus, Russia, Turkmenistan, and Tajikistan, all of which had less than 5,000 participants.

Table 26.2 shows the number of exam takers by gender. During the Soviet period accounting was among the lowest occupations in terms of prestige (Enthoven et al., 1998). The Russian language did not even have a word for accounting. They used the German word for bookkeeping. The vast majority of bookkeepers were women during the Soviet period.

The prestige of the accounting profession has increased markedly since the transition to a market economy and men are starting to enter the profession. However,

Table 26.2 Exams tested by gender

	2001	2002	2003	2004	2005	2006	2007	Total
CAP								
Female	306	3,938	9,220	8,614	8,270	9,692	12,896	52,936
Male	73	1,371	2,567	2,547	1,745	2,567	3,194	14,064
Total	379	5,309	11,787	11,161	10,015	12,259	16,090	67,000
% Female	80.7	74.2	78.2	77.2	82.6	79.1	80.1	79.0
CIPA								
Female	104	1,277	1,722	1,042	977	1,063	1,469	7,654
Male	23	422	545	327	276	280	301	2174
Total	127	1,699	2,267	1,369	1,253	1,343	1,770	9,828
% Female	81.9	75.2	76.0	76.1	78.0	79.2	83.0	77.9
TOTAL								
Female	410	5,215	10,942	9,656	9,247	10,755	14,365	60,590
Male	96	1,793	3,112	2,874	2,021	2,847	3,495	16,238
Total	506	7,008	14,054	12,530	11,268	13,602	17,860	76,828
% Female	81.0	74.4	77.9	77.1	82.1	79.1	80.4	78.9

Table 26.3 Percentage of women

	Mean (%)	Median (%)
CAP	78.9	79.1
CIPA	78.5	78.0
Total	78.9	79.1

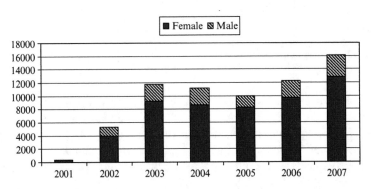

Chart 26.13 Exams taken by Gender – CAP

as the data show, the vast majority of participants in the certification programs continue to be women. The ratio of women fluctuated between the mid-70s and low 80s, but was never less than 74.2%.

Table 26.3 shows both the mean and median scores for women for both the CAP and CIPA exams. The ratios were consistently in the high 70s.

Charts 26.13 and 26.14 show the exams taken by gender graphically.

Chart 26.15 combines the results for the CAP and CIPA exams.

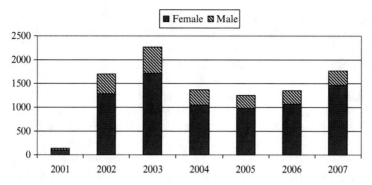

Chart 26.14   Exams taken by Gender – CIPA

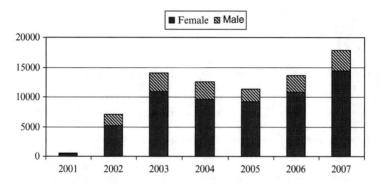

Chart 26.15   Exams taken by Gender – Total

26.3   Concluding Comments

The former Soviet republics have a problem of credibility as far as accounting and auditing are concerned. Financial statements audited by local or national firms lack credibility. There is also a basic lack of knowledge of International Financial Reporting Standards and International Standards on Auditing. The ACCA has been making some inroads in this area but their exams were, until recently at least,[2] only offered in the English language. Accountants who are not sufficiently versed in the English language were unable to take advantage of the ACCA exams.

USAID found a solution to the lack of IFRS and IAS knowledge by initiating a program to give accounting exams in the Russian language. It appears that the program is having a positive effect. More than 15,000 people took their exams in 2007 and the trend is likely to continue upward as the exams spread to Russia and Ukraine, the two largest of the 15 former Soviet republics.

---

[2] Some ACCA exams are now offered in Russian.

Offering uniform accounting exams across borders also helps labor to become more mobile. Accountants who pass the CAP and CIPA certification exams in one country have their credentials recognized in all the countries that offer the exams. The CAP and CIPA exams have become regional in nature and their recognition can only increase as they continue to spread.

Interestingly, some governments do not recognize the CAP and CIPA exams. They feel threatened by having a private sector certification program to compete with the official state certification systems. However, government approval is not needed, or even desired. The CAP and CIPA certification exams are recognized in the marketplace, which is the most important forum for capital markets. Some businesses require potential job candidates to pass one or more exams before being considered for promotion.

References

Enthoven, Adolf J.H., Yaroslav V. Sokolov, Svetlana M. Bychkova, Valery V. Kovalev and Maria V. Semenova (1998). Accounting, Auditing and Taxation in the Russian Federation. A joint publication of the IMA Foundation for Applied Research, an affiliate of the Institute of Management Accountants, Montvale, NJ/The Center for International Accounting Development at the University of Texas at Dallas.

McGee, Robert W. (1999a). Certification of Accountants and Auditors in the CIS: A Case Study of Armenia. *Journal of Accounting, Ethics & Public Policy*, 2(2), 338–353. Also published on the Social Science Research Network website at http://ssrn.com/abstract = 242552.

McGee, Robert W. (1999b). International Certification of A ccountants in the CIS: A Case Study of Armenia. *Journal of Accounting, Ethics & Public Policy*, 2(1), 70–75. Also published on the Social Science Research Network website at http://ssrn.com/abstract = 251475.

Mises, Ludwig von (1920). Die Wirtschaftsrechnung im Sozialistischen Gemeinwesen [Economic Calculation in the Socialist Commonwealth]. *Archiv fur Sozialwissenschaft und Sozialpolitik*, 47, 86–121.

Mises, Ludwig von (1923). Neue Beitrage zum Problem der sozialistischen Wirtschaftsrechnung [New Contributions to the Problem of Socialist Economic Calculation]. *Archiv fur Sozialwissenschaft und Sozialpolitik*, 51, 488–500.

Mises, Ludwig von (1935). Economic Calculation in the Socialist Commonwealth. In F.A. Hayek (Ed.), *Collectivist Economic Planning: Critical Studies on the Possibilities of Socialism* (pp. 87–130). London: Routledge & Kegan Paul.

Preobragenskaya, Galina G. & McGee Robert W. (2004). Reforming the Accounting Curriculum in Russia: Some Guidelines Based on the Armenian and Bosnian Experiences. *Research in Accounting in Emerging Economies, Supplement 2: Accounting and Accountability in Emerging and Transition Economies*, pp. 531–553. Also published on the Social Science Research Network website at http://ssrn.com/abstract = 410766.

Chapter 27
Accounting Certification in Central Asia

Robert W. McGee

27.1　Introduction

After the collapse of the Soviet Union, the 15 former Soviet republics all started converting their inherited Soviet bookkeeping system to a market-oriented accounting system. They encountered several problems along the way. No one knew what a market-oriented accounting system was all about. There were no books either in Russian or in any of the national languages on what might be termed western accounting, which made it difficult to learn the new system.

Terminology was often a problem. As books began to be translated into Russian it became apparent that there were terminology problems. Russian words simply did not exist for many English terms. Perhaps the most interesting word that does not exist in the Russian language is accountant. They use the German word for bookkeeper. The Soviet mentality also considered accounting to be no more than bookkeeping.

There was a certain logic for equating the two terms. In the Soviet era, accounting consisted mostly of bookkeeping. There was a chart of accounts that came out of Moscow in 1930 and it was adopted in all 15 Soviet republics. University students who studied bookkeeping took a course in bookkeeping that did not go beyond making journal entries. There was no such thing as financial statement analysis. Cost accounting was practically nonexistent. All prices are set centrally and have little or nothing to do with supply and demand. Calculating profit margins under such conditions becomes a meaningless exercise.

It eventually became apparent that the recently privatized businesses had to convert to some internationally recognized accounting system. In most cases that system was International Financial Reporting Standards (IFRS) and International Standards on Auditing (ISA). Any business that wanted to attract badly needed international capital had to be able to present financial statements that were based on an accounting system that could be understood and trusted internationally.

But the companies that wanted to attract foreign investment were mostly the large companies. Small companies saw no need to adopt IFRS, since the old Soviet bookkeeping

R. W. McGee
Florida International University

R. W. McGee (ed.), *Accounting Reform in Transition and Developing Economies,*
© Springer Science+Business Media LLC 2008

system seemed good enough for their purposes. Furthermore, national tax officials had no use for IFRS, since their tax systems were usually based on the cash method.

Where there is no demand, there will be no supply. So there was not much grassroots support for changing to a system that was internationally recognized.

Demand eventually began to increase as international investors and bankers demanded financial statements that used either IFRS or US GAAP and many of them demanded annual audits conducted by the Big-4 accounting firms.

During the 1990s, the United States Agency for International Development (USAID) launched a number of accounting reform programs in several of the former Soviet republics in an attempt to help them educate various segments of the accounting community in IFRS. Experts were hired to assist the various finance ministries understand and implement IFRS. Private sector accounting associations were formed; university accounting curricula had to be revised so that future generations of students could learn the market-oriented accounting system. But their professors could not teach the new system, since they were unfamiliar with it. So, USAID undertook a number of train-the-trainer courses so that professors would be able to teach the new curriculum.

Certification in the former Soviet countries was a joke. Accounting certification could be bought for a very reasonable price. Exams were easy to pass. Audit opinions could be bought. As a result, audit companies had no credibility.

USAID set out to change this situation by offering a series of certification exams that would have international credibility. Exams would be rigorous and the examination process would be secure. Students were not able to get advance copies of the exams. They could not purchase the certificates. They had to actually study quite hard for the exams and the pass rate was comparable to that of several accounting certification exams in the market-oriented countries. This chapter reviews the success of the certification program in Central Asia.

27.2 Accounting Certification in Central Asia

USAID initiated its accounting certification program in Central Asia. The pilot program was set up in Kazakhstan and spread to Kyrgyzstan, Uzbekistan, Tajikistan, and Turkmenistan. It later spread to a few other former Soviet republics and the headquarters moved to Moscow, but not for several years.

The exams tested subjects similar to those that were tested in Western accounting curriculums. Two certifications were established. Participants were awarded the Certified Accounting Practitioner (CAP) designation after passing exams in financial accounting, management accounting, and tax and law. The Certified International Public Accountant (CIPA) designation was awarded for passing four additional exams on more advanced topics. All exams were offered in the Russian language.

The next few tables show the data for the five Central Asian republics. Table 27.1 summarizes the data for Kazakhstan, the country where the exams started. Parts tested have had a healthy growth, from 213 in 2001 to 8,150 in 2007.

Table 27.1   Kazakhstan

	Pre-2001	2001	2002	2003	2004	2005	2006	2007	Total
Parts tested	554	213	1,546	5,551	3,941	4,336	5,441	8,150	29,732
Parts passed	405	166	974	2,826	1,991	2,223	3,082	3,787	15,454
Pass rate	73.1	77.9	63.0	50.9	50.5	51.3	56.6	46.5	52.0
Females	428	170	1370	4,930	3,595	4,005	5,075	7,676	27,249
Males	124	43	176	619	346	331	366	474	2,479
% Female	77.3	79.8	88.6	88.8	91.2	92.4	93.3	94.2	91.6
Exams									
FA1									15,561
MA1									12,909
T&L									13,278
FA2									1,313
MA2									559
AUDIT									1,048
FIN									505

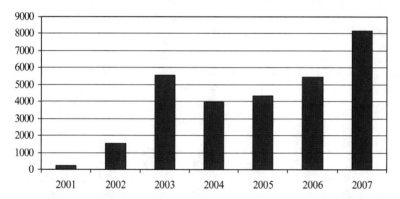

Chart 27.1   Parts tested – Kazakhstan

Pass rates are also shown. As students completed the three CAP exams – Financial Accounting 1 (FA1), Management Accounting 1 (MA1), and Tax & Law (T&L) – and moved on to the more difficult exams, pass rates declined. The number of exams taken for the CIPA exams – Financial Accounting 2 (FA2), Management Accounting 2 (MA2), Auditing and Finance – is far lower than the number of CAP exams taken. One reason for the decline is because students are still moving through the process. They must complete all the CAP exams before taking any CIPA exams. Another reason for the lower number of CIPA exams is because the CIPA exams are more difficult and many students decide to quit taking exams after they have taken the CAP exams.

Table 27.1 also provides information on exam by gender. Females account for between 77.3% and 94.2% of total exam takers. Furthermore, the percent of females taking the exam has gone up consistently over time.

Chart 27.1 shows the number of parts tested in Kazakhstan between 2001 and 2007. After dramatic jumps in the first 2 years there was a decline, followed by continued growth.

Chart 27.2 shows the pass rates for Kazakhstan, which have declined as the program has expanded. One reason for the declining pass rate is because the exams get more difficult as candidates progress from the CAP exams to the CIPA exams.

Chart 27.3 shows the rate of female participation in Kazakhstan. It started at a high level and rose from there, to the point where female participation is more than 90 percent.

Table 27.2 shows the data for Kyrgyzstan. The number of parts tested increased rapidly, then declined over time. One reason for the decline is because the organization giving the exams started charging a modest fee.

Pass rates have also declined, partly because the CIPA exams are more difficult and are taken only after the CAP exams have been passed. The CAP exams have much higher pass rates than the CIPA exams. The number of CAP exams taken (FA1, MA1 and T&L) is in the thousands, compared to CIPA exams taken, which is in the hundreds.

Gender comparisons were also made. Females as a percentage of the total have hovered around the 80–85 percent participation level.

Chart 27.4 shows the parts tested in Kyrgyzstan from 2001 to 2007. Parts tested jumped the first few years, then declined.

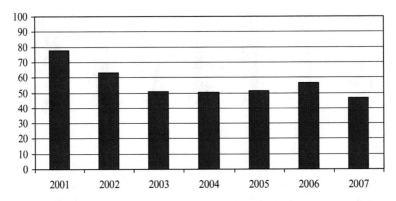

Chart 27.2 Pass rate – Kazakstan

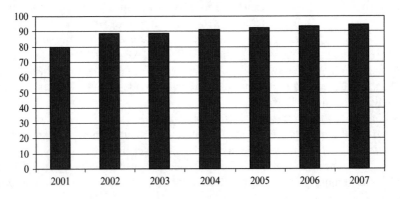

Chart 27.3 % female participation – Kazakhstan

Table 27.2   Kyrgyzstan

	Pre-2001	2001	2002	2003	2004	2005	2006	2007	Total
Parts tested	1,680	222	1,856	2,711	2,362	1,389	1,117	1,267	12,604
Parts passed	1,452	87	795	1,188	1,011	620	596	633	6,382
Pass rate	86.4	39.2	42.8	43.8	42.8	44.6	53.4	50.0	50.6
Females	1,399	190	1,497	2,253	1,909	1,154	922	1,047	10,371
Males	279	32	359	458	453	235	195	220	2,231
% Female	83.3	85.6	80.7	83.1	80.8	83.1	82.5	82.6	82.3
Exams									
FA1									6,880
MA1									3,047
T&L									3,438
FA2									463
MA2									147
AUDIT									346
FIN									224

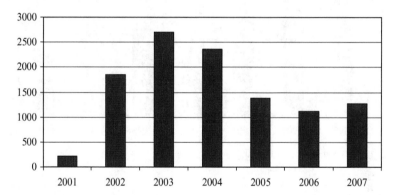

Chart 27.4   Part tested – Kyrgystan

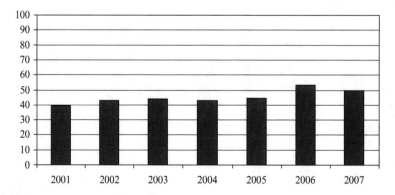

Chart 27.5   Pass rate – Kyrgyzstan

Chart 27.5 shows the pass rates for Kyrgyzstan. Unlike in some of the other Central Asian republics, pass rates have not declined in Kyrgyzstan over time, at least not yet.

Chart 27.6 shows the percentage female participation for Kyrgyzstan. It started out above 80 percent and has stayed there.

Tajikistan data is shown in Table 27.3. Parts tested did not reach an annual level of 1,000 until 2003 and have since dropped dramatically. Pass rates have also dropped dramatically. This drop may be partially explained by the fact that as students passed the relatively easy CAP exams they proceeded to take the relatively difficult CIPA exams.

One interesting finding in the Tajikistan data was that the percentage of female exam takers was substantially lower than was the case for the other Central Asian republics. The range was 29.4 percent to 53.8 percent, compared to the 70s and 80s for the other republics.

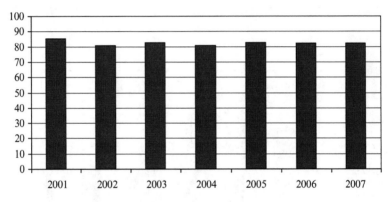

Chart 27.6 % female participation – Kyrgyzstan

Table 27.3 Tajikistan

	Pre-2001	2001	2002	2003	2004	2005	2006	2007	Total
Parts tested	34	11	462	1,006	1,039	585	324	244	3,705
Parts passed	34	11	201	330	314	145	118	73	1,226
Pass rate	100.0	100.0	43.5	32.8	30.2	24.8	36.4	29.9	33.1
Females	10	4	186	435	491	315	164	111	1,716
Males	24	7	276	571	548	270	160	133	1,989
% Female	29.4	36.4	40.3	43.2	47.3	53.8	50.6	45.5	46.3
Exams									
FA1									1,764
MA1									1,015
T&L									1,250
FA2									150
MA2									100
AUDIT									151
FIN									98

Chart 27.7 shows the trend in parts tested in Tajikistan. After increasing the first few years, parts tested have declined each year since the peak in 2004.

Chart 27.8 shows the pass rates for Tajikistan. After achieving a perfect 100 percent pass rate in the first year there was no place to go but down. The pass rate dropped dramatically in 2002, which might be expected, and have continued to decline most years since.

Chart 27.9 graphs the trend in female participation for Tajikistan. Starting from a low in the mid 30s, female participation increased for each of the next four years, then declined in each of the two most recent years.

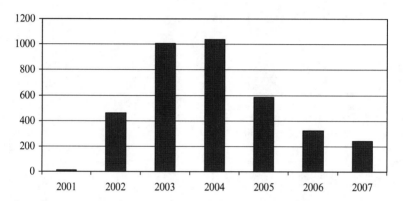

Chart 27.7 Parts tested – Tajikistan

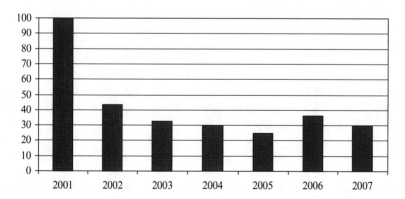

Chart 27.8 Pass rate – Tajikistan

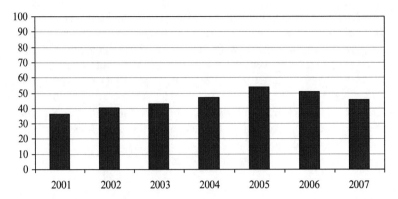

Chart 27.9 %female participation –Tajikistan

Table 27.4 Turkmenistan

	Pre-2001	2001	2002	2003	2004	2005	2006	2007	Total
Parts tested	1	0	88	184	224	262	506	314	1,579
Parts passed	1	0	44	90	112	120	229	141	737
Pass rate	100.0	0	50.0	48.9	50.0	45.8	45.3	44.9	46.7
Females	1	0	74	153	195	220	340	239	1,222
Males	0	0	14	31	29	42	166	75	357
% Female	100.0	0	84.1	83.2	87.1	84.0	67.2	76.1	77.4
Exams									
FA1									723
MA1									440
T&L									460
FA2									47
MA2									24
AUDIT									8
FIN									31

Table 27.4 shows the data for Turkmenistan. Parts taken annually have not yet exceeded 1,000. The peak year was 2006, when parts taken was 506. There was a substantial drop the following year.

The ratio of female exam takers was above 80 percent for four years, then dropped to as low as 67.2 percent in 2006 before rising to 76.1 percent the following year.

Chart 27.10 plots the changes in parts taken in Turkmenistan. After rising consistently in the early years there was a decline in the most recent year.

Chart 27.11 shows the pass rates for Turkmenistan. Although the pass rate has declined over time, the decline has been slight.

Chart 27.12 shows the trend in female participation for Turkmenistan. After starting strong in the first few years it has declined slightly in recent years.

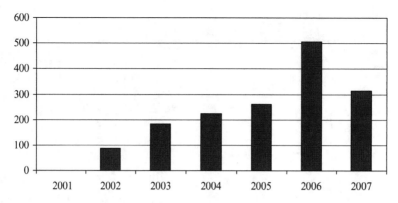

Chart 27.10   Pass tested – Turkmenistan

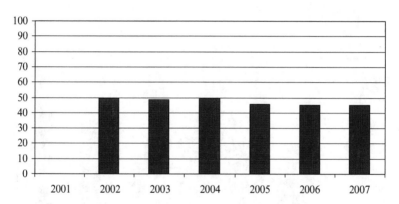

Chart 27.11   Pass rate – Turkmenistan

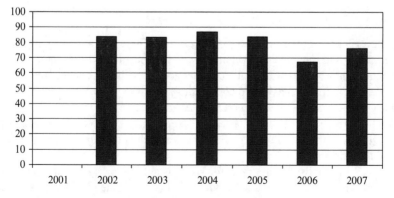

Chart 27.12   % female participation – Kyrgyzstan

Table 27.5 Uzbekistan

	Pre-2001	2001	2002	2003	2004	2005	2006	2007	Total
Parts tested	538	60	1,400	2,212	2,249	1,330	1,873	3,095	12,757
Parts passed	538	53	666	898	998	720	954	1,628	6,455
Pass rate	100.0	88.3	47.6	40.6	44.4	54.1	50.9	52.6	50.6
Females	407	46	730	1,217	1,281	865	707	1,271	6,524
Males	131	14	670	995	968	465	1166	1824	6,233
% Female	75.7	76.7	52.1	55.0	57.0	65.0	37.7	41.1	51.1
Exams									
FA1									6,981
MA1									3,207
T&L									3,254
FA2									448
MA2									338
AUDIT									569
FIN									259

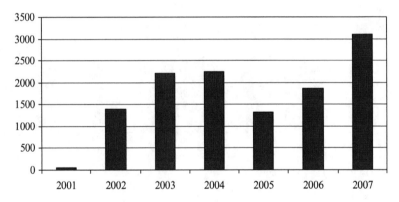

Chart 27.13 Parts tested – Uzbekistan

Table 27.5 shows the pass rates for Uzbekistan. There was a major jump in volume in 2002 and again in 2003. Parts taken leveled off in 2004, then dropped. Participation has increased dramatically for each of the last two years under study.

Female participation has varied considerably over the years, from the mid 70s in the early years to a low of 37.7 percent in 2006.

Chart 27.13 shows the parts tested in Uzbekistan. The trend has been rather erratic, jumping dramatically in the first two years, then leveling off before declining and then rising again.

Chart 27.14 graphs the pass rates for Uzbekistan. The pass rate was abnormally high in the first year, then declined predictably in each of the next two years before starting to rise again.

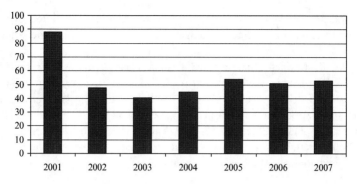

Chart 27.14 Pass rate – Uzbekistan

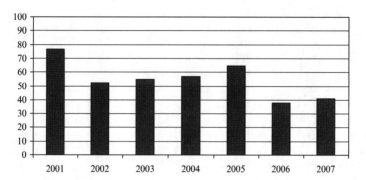

Chart 27.15 % female participation – Uzbekistan

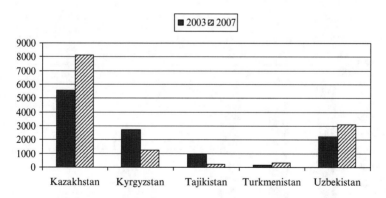

Chart 27.16 Parts taken

Chart 27.15 shows the female participation rates for Uzbekistan. The rate started rather strong, then declined in subsequent years. Female participation in the two most recent years has been less than 50 percent.

Chart 27.16 shows the parts taken in 2003 and 2007 for each of the five Central Asian republics. The chart shows the extent of the increase or decline for each republic and also makes it possible to compare the relative volume of activity between or among the republics. Kazakhstan has continued to have the largest volume of activity and its activity has risen substantially between 2003 and 2007.

Chart 27.17 shows the percentage of female participation in 2007 for each republic. Kazakhstan had the highest rate of female participation at more than 90%. Second highest was Kyrgyzstan, followed closely by Turkmenistan. Participation in Tajikistan and Uzbekistan was substantially lower than in the other republics.

The next five charts (Charts 27.18–27.22) show the volume of exams taken for each of the five republics. It is obvious that the three CAP exams have been taken far more frequently than the four CIPA exams.

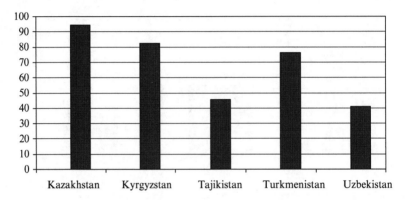

Chart 27.17   % female participation 2007

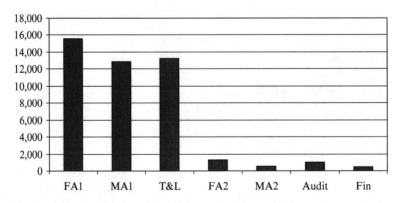

Chart 27.18   Exams – Kazakhstan

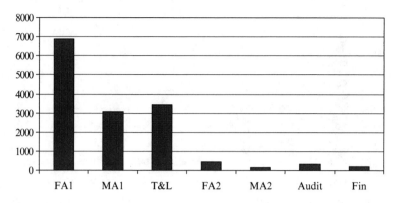

Chart 27.19 Exams – Kyrgystan

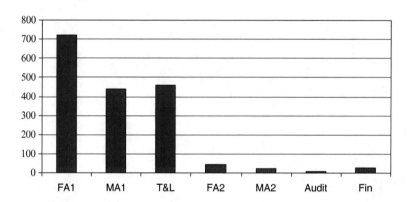

Chart 27.20 Exams – Tajikistan

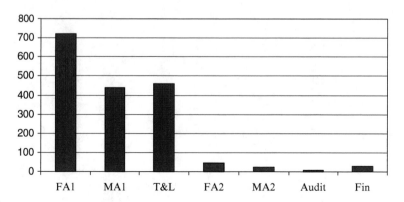

Chart 27.21 Exams – Turkmenistan

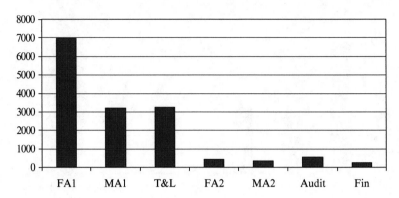

Chart 27.22 Exams – Uzbekistan

Chapter 28
Accounting Certification in Russia

Robert W. McGee

28.1   Introduction

The United States Agency for International Development (USAID) initiated a regional accounting certification program in the Russian language several years ago. It started in Central Asia and spread to Russia and a few other former Soviet republics several years later. Headquarters for the program later moved to Moscow. This chapter reports on the CAP/CIPA accounting certification program that has been going on in Russia.

28.2   Accounting Certification in Russia

Table 28.1 shows the data for Russia, including the number of participants tested, exams passed, and pass rates.

Chart 28.1 graphs the number of participants tested since the program in Russia began in 2003. There was a slight drop in the second year of the program but enrollments have increased every year since. Although participation has been far lower than that of some of the Central Asian republics, it is expected to rise as the program continues. The Russia program might eventually become the largest program, since Russia has far more population than any of the other former Soviet republics.

Chart 28.2 shows the pass rates. The pass rates are relatively high, and have remained relatively high, although they have declined somewhat.

Table 28.2 shows the participation rate by gender. Female participation varied between 69.1% and 86.1%.

Chart 28.3 graphs female participation, which has gone up practically every year.

R. W. McGee
Florida International University

R. W. McGee (ed.), *Accounting Reform in Transition and Developing Economies,*
© Springer Science + Business Media LLC 2008

Table 28.1 Participants and pass rates

Participants	2003	2004	2005	2006	2007	Total
Tested	110	59	174	390	568	1301
Passed	77	49	122	265	356	869
Pass rate	70.0	83.1	70.1	68.0	62.7	66.8

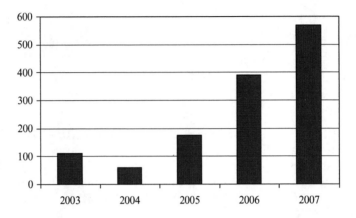

Chart 28.1 Participants tested

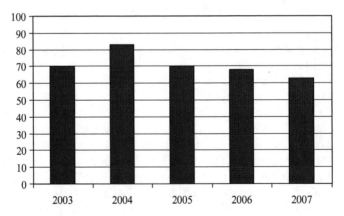

Chart 28.2 Pass rates

Table 28.2 Participants by gender

	2003	2004	2005	2006	2007	Total
Female	76	46	135	324	489	1070
Male	34	13	39	66	79	231
Total	110	59	174	390	568	1301
Percent female	69.1	78.0	77.6	83.1	86.1	82.2

Table 28.3 shows the number of people who took the three CAP exams in Russia between 2003 and 2007. The most frequently taken exam was Financial Accounting 1, followed by Managerial Accounting 1 and Tax & Law.

Chart 28.4 shows the total exams taken for all three CAP exams for each year. With the exception of a slight drop in 2004 the number of exams taken has increased each year.

Table 28.3 CAP exams

	2003	2004	2005	2006	2007	Total
FA 1	63	26	89	187	257	622
MA 1	52	28	74	132	282	568
T&L	46	30	85	142	162	465
Total	161	84	248	461	701	1655

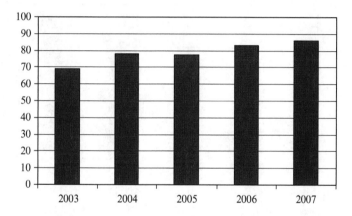

Chart 28.3 Percent female

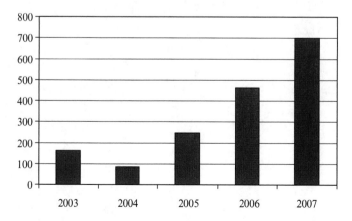

Chart 28.4 CAP exams

Table 28.4 shows the number of exams taken for each of the four CIPA exams for each year. Total exams taken were more or less stable until 2006.

Chart 28.5 shows the exams taken graphically.

Table 28.4 CIPA exams

	2003	2004	2005	2006	2007	Total
FA 2	15	5	7	46	38	111
MA 2	9	6	15	43	23	96
Audit	6	3	3	13	34	59
Finance	4	6	10	10	39	69
Total	34	20	35	112	134	335

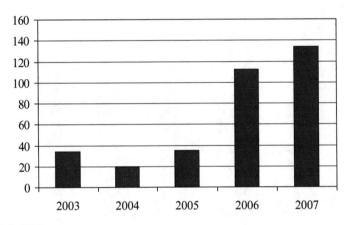

Chart 28.4 CIPA exams

Chapter 29
Accounting Certification in Ukraine

Robert W. McGee

29.1   Introduction

The United States Agency for International Development (USAID) initiated a regional accounting certification program in the Russian language several years ago. It started in Central Asia and spread to Ukraine and a few other former Soviet republics several years later. Headquarters for the program later moved to Moscow. This chapter reports on the CAP/CIPA accounting certification program that has been going on in Ukraine.

29.2   Accounting Certification in Ukraine

The next few tables and charts report on the CAP/CIPA program in Ukraine. Table 29.1 shows the results for all exams taken and passed in Ukraine between 2002 and 2007. Pass rates varied between 36.2% and 63.6%.

Chart 29.1 shows the changes in volume graphically. Volume increased each year. The jump was most dramatic in 2004.

Table 29.2 shows the numbers for the Financial Accounting 1 exams taken and passed for each year.

Chart 29.2 shows graphically the number of Financial Accounting 1 exams taken. The numbers increased almost every year.

Table 29.3 discloses the number of Managerial Accounting 1 exams taken and passed from 2002 to 2007. Although the number of exams taken increased every year, the pass rate fluctuated. Chart 29.3 shows the number of Managerial Accounting 1 exams taken graphically. The largest increase was between 2003 and 2004.

Table 29.4 shows the data for the number of tax and law exams taken and passed in Ukraine between 2002 and 2007. The number of exams taken and passed has gone up consistently over time.

R. W. McGee
Florida International University

R. W. McGee (ed.), *Accounting Reform in Transition and Developing Economies,*
© Springer Science+Business Media LLC 2008

Table 29.1 Ukraine all exams

Year	Taken	Passed	%
2002	619	224	36.2
2003	1,632	848	52.0
2004	4,099	1,938	47.3
2005	4,266	2,322	54.4
2006	4,345	2,645	60.9
2007	5,155	3,281	63.6

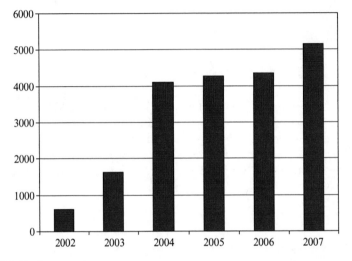

Chart 29.1 Total exams taken

Table 29.2 Ukraine Financial Accounting 1

Year	Taken	Passed	%
2002	616	222	36.0
2003	834	373	44.7
2004	1,120	627	56.0
2005	1,343	802	59.7
2006	1,270	894	70.4
2007	1,578	1,200	76.0

Table 29.3 Ukraine Managerial Accounting 1

Year	Taken	Passed	%
2002	1	1	100.0
2003	358	217	60.6
2004	979	479	48.9
2005	1,160	643	55.4
2006	1,215	826	68.0
2007	1,505	1,025	68.1

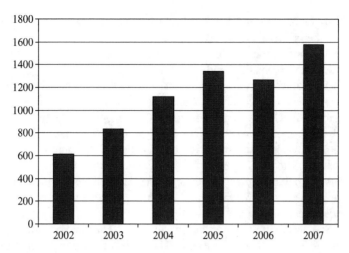

Chart 29.2 Exams taken financial accounting 1

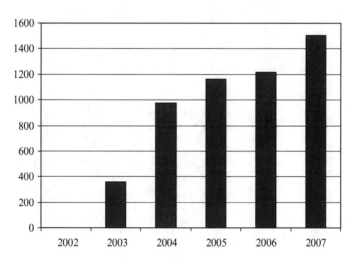

Chart 29.3 Exams taken managerial accounting 1

Table 29.4 Ukraine Tax & Law

Year	Taken	Passed	%
2002	2	1	50.0
2003	324	240	74.1
2004	906	669	73.8
2005	1,053	718	68.2
2006	1,081	732	67.7
2007	1,378	889	64.5

Chart 29.4 graphs the trend of tax & law exams taken. The trend is consistently upward, with the largest increase taking place in 2004.

Table 29.5 combines the data for the three CAP exams. The trend is consistently upward. Chart 29.5 graphs the trend.

The next few tables show the data for the four CIPA exams. Table 29.6 shows the number of Financial Accounting 2 exams taken and passed. The numbers are much smaller for the CIPA exams than for the CAP exams but the trend is more or less upward. Chart 29.6 shows the trend graphically.

Table 29.7 shows the statistics for the Managerial Accounting 2 exams in Ukraine from 2003 to 2007. The number of exams taken and the pass rates are lower for this exam than for the CAP exams. Chart 29.7 shows the numbers graphically. Although the figures for the most recent few years are up, it appears that the trend for recent years is down.

Table 29.8 shows the figures for the finance exam. The pattern is similar for the finance exam as for the other CIPA exams. There tends to be a large jump early on, followed by a downward trend in the most recent years. Chart 29.8 graphs the trend.

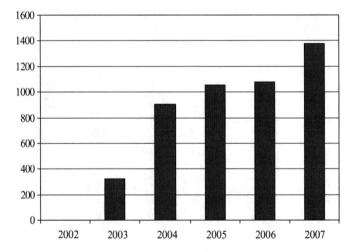

Chart 29.4 Exams taken tax & law

Table 29.5 Ukraine CAP Exams

Year	Taken	Passed	%
2002	619	224	36.2
2003	1,516	830	54.7
2004	3,005	1,775	59.1
2005	3,556	2,163	60.8
2006	3,566	2,452	68.8
2007	4,461	3,114	69.8

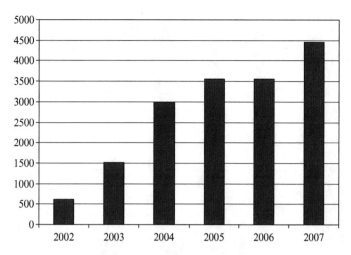

Chart 29.5 Exams taken all CAP

Table 29.6 Ukraine Financial Accounting 2

Year	Taken	Passed	%
2003	39	8	20.5
2004	322	40	12.4
2005	209	33	15.8
2006	240	36	15.0
2007	230	44	19.1

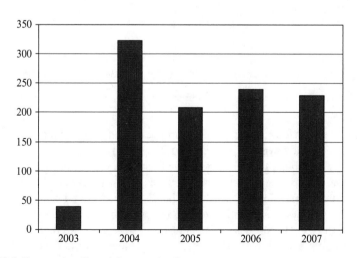

Chart 29.6 Exams taken financial accounting 2

Table 29.7 Ukraine Managerial Accounting 2

Year	Taken	Passed	%
2003	32	4	12.5
2004	273	47	17.2
2005	189	45	23.8
2006	200	88	44.0
2007	163	40	24.5

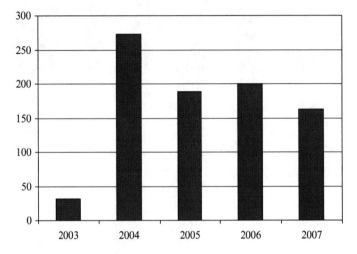

Chart 29.7 Exams taken managerial accounts 2

Table 29.8 Ukraine Finance

Year	Taken	Passed	%
2003	24	3	12.5
2004	245	34	13.9
2005	158	49	31.0
2006	177	38	21.5
2007	174	49	28.2

Table 29.9 shows the statistics for the auditing exam. There is a jump in the early years, followed by a downward trend. Chart 29.9 graphs the numbers.

Table 29.10 combines the numbers for the four CIPA exams. As was the case for the individual exams, the overall trend is up in the early years and down for the most recent few years. Chart 29.10 shows the CIPA trend graphically.

Chart 29.11 shows the pass rates for the seven exams. As can be seen, the pass rates for the three CAP exams are much higher than the pass rates for the four CIPA exams. This difference is understandable, given the fact that the three CAP exams are easier.

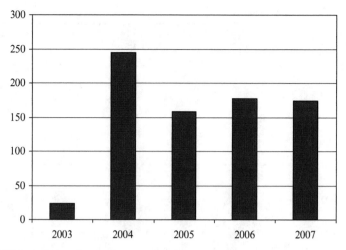

Chart 29.8 Exams taken finance

Table 29.9 Ukraine Auditing

Year	Taken	Passed	%
2003	21	3	14.3
2004	254	42	16.5
2005	154	32	20.8
2006	162	31	19.1
2007	127	34	26.8

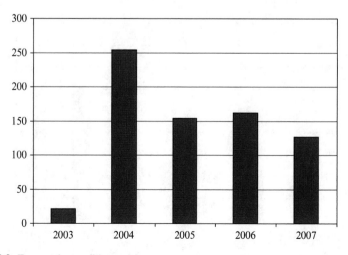

Chart 29.9 Exams taken auditing

Table 29.10 Ukraine CIPA Exams

Year	Taken	Passed	%
2003	116	18	15.5
2004	1,094	163	14.9
2005	710	159	22.4
2006	779	193	24.8
2007	694	167	24.1

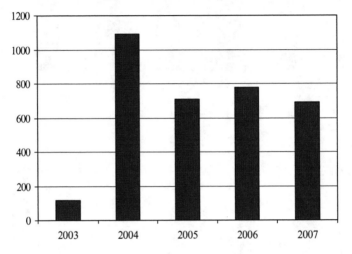

Chart 29.10 Exams taken all CIPA

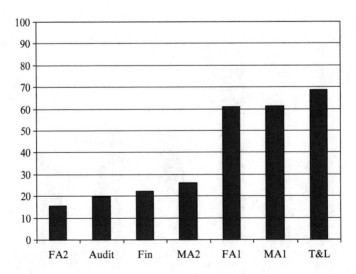

Chart 29.11 Pass rates

Chapter 30
Certification of Accountants in Georgia

Robert W. McGee

30.1 Introduction

Since the collapse of the Soviet Union each of the former Soviet republics has started the process of moving away from central planning and toward a market economy. Part of that process involves private sector institution building. One private sector institution that has generally experienced a degree of success and popularity is nongovernmental accounting associations. One task of such institutions is to provide certification for accountants and auditors. This paper provides a brief overview of private sector accounting certification in Georgia.

After the collapse of the Soviet Union the 15 former Soviet republics had to make a transition to a market economy. Part of that transition involved replacing the old Soviet accounting system with one that was more appropriate for a market economy. Each former Soviet republic has chosen a different path to achieve that goal, although there are some similarities.

The transformation process involved several aspects. Some kind of internationally recognized accounting standards had to be adopted. The options were International Accounting Standards (IAS), now called International Financial Reporting Standards (IFRS) and US Generally Accepted Accounting Principles (GAAP). As the old Soviet system began to be replaced by market-oriented systems, individual companies in the former Soviet Union that wanted to attract international capital chose either the US system or the international system, depending on where they wanted to raise capital. Companies that wanted to raise capital in the United States started using US GAAP for the financial statements they published in English whereas companies that wanted to raise capital outside the United States tended to use IFRS. Both systems provide instant credibility to financial statements. In some cases companies went forum shopping. They drafted tentative financial statements using both US GAAP and IFRS to see which set of standards gave them the better-looking financial statements (McGee and Preobragenskaya, 2006f).

R. W. McGee
Florida International University

R. W. McGee (ed.), *Accounting Reform in Transition and Developing Economies,*
© Springer Science+Business Media LLC 2008

However, adopting some kind of internationally recognized accounting standards was not sufficient. Several problems had to be overcome. In many cases neither US GAAP nor IFRS were available in Russian or any of the national languages, so translations had to be made. The first translations were criticized as being mediocre. Some passages contained outright mistakes (McGee and Preobragenskaya, 2005a).

Even with translations available, the national accounting profession in each country was almost totally unfamiliar with international accounting standards. They never studied it in school and they never used those standards in practice. There was absolutely no demand for them at the time of transition and there was very little demand for them even after transition, since the primary users of financial statements were tax officials and most post-Soviet tax systems were on the cash method. Tax officials saw no use for accrual-based accounting information. Where tax officials found no use for accrual-based accounting systems, it was difficult or impossible to persuade company officials that their financial statements should be prepared using an accrual-based system.

The one major exception was in cases where the company wanted to attract foreign capital. But problems remained because neither local practitioners nor company accountants knew anything about international accounting. This problem was partially alleviated by retaining the services of one of the Big-4 accounting firms to conduct the audits and do the consulting necessary to assist the companies convert their accounting systems to an internationally accepted accrual basis.

Training local accountants was a problem that had to be addressed in the early stages of the transition and remains somewhat of a problem even today. Although accounting materials had been translated, accountants had to read and understand them before changes could be made. But no one in the country could teach the new accounting because the local accountants and professors were unfamiliar with the rules and principles.

The United States Agency for International Development (USAID), TACIS, its European counterpart, the World Bank and some other organization assisted in the educational phase of the transition by supporting training programs and the restructuring of university accounting curriculums. They also provided funding to assist in the creation or expansion of accounting associations.

The Big-4 accounting firms were able to capture a monopolistic market share because they had no local competition. Although each former Soviet republic had some kind of accounting and/or auditing certification, their certificates had no credibility outside of their borders, and often inside their borders as well. Buying certification was a common practice in some countries and there was no credible structure in place to assure that the accountants who had certification were competent to conduct audits. Furthermore, audit opinions could often be purchased. Thus, financial statements that were audited by local accountants had no credibility in international capital markets, both because they were prepared using national rather than international standards and because they were audited by accountants whose qualifications were questionable.

As the lack of credibility became increasingly apparent, attempts were made to alleviate the credibility problem. USAID, with the assistance of various national accounting organizations, instituted a Russian language accounting certification program that tested on international accounting and auditing standards. The program started in the five Central Asian republics of Kazakhstan, Kyrgyzstan, Tajikistan, Turkmenistan, and Uzbekistan and later spread to Russia, Ukraine, Belarus, Moldova, and Azerbaijan (McGee, Preobragenskaya & Tyler 2004a). As of this writing, Armenia and Georgia have not become a part of this program, although they both have received USAID and/or TACIS assistance with accounting certification. The Baltic republics of Estonia, Latvia, and Lithuania expressed no interest in any kind of Russian language certification, mostly because of the animosity of these republics toward anything Russian and also because they were already starting to look west, toward membership in the European Union. This paper provides a brief overview of the approach to accounting certification taken by the former Soviet republic of Georgia. A telephone interview was conducted with Mr. Lavrenti Chumburidze, CEO of the Georgian Federation of Professional Accountants and Auditors (GFAA) to gather some of the information used in this paper.

30.2 Review of the Literature

A number of studies have been done on accounting reform in various transition economies. The earliest comprehensive study of accounting reform in Russia was done by Enthoven et al. in 1998. A more recent book length study of Russia was done by McGee and Preobragenskaya (2005a). Smaller studies of accounting reform in Russia have also been done (McGee and Preobragenskaya, 2006d; Preobragenskaya and McGee, 2004f).

Several studies have been done of accounting reform in Ukraine (McGee and Preobragenskaya, 2005b, 2006e). A book length manuscript that included studies of Ukraine and several other countries was done by McGee andPreobragenskaya (2006f). McGee did studies of accounting reform in Armenia (2006) and a more general study on adopting and implementing International Financial Reporting Standards in transition economies (McGee, 2006b).

A few studies have examined the relationship between foreign direct investment and financial reporting practices. Preobragenskaya and McGee (2004g) looked at accounting aspects of foreign direct investment in Russia. McGee and Preobragenskaya (2003) looked at problems of foreign direct investment in Russia. McGee (2006d) discussed attracting foreign direct investment with good financial reporting practices, using Russia as a case study. McGee (2006c) also examined foreign direct investment in South Eastern Europe.

Several studies have examined various aspects of accounting education in transition economies. Studies have been made of Armenia (McGee, 2003, 2005a, 2006a), Bosnia and Herzegovina (McGee 2005b; McGee and Preobragenskaya, 2006a), Russia (Preobragenskaya and McGee, 2003, 2004b, 2005a), and Ukraine (McGee and Preobragenskaya, 2006b). Studies have also been done on the segment of accounting education in Russia that is provided by the private sector

(Preobragenskaya and McGee, 2004c, d). A comparative study of accounting education in Russia and the United States was also done (Preobragenskaya and McGee, 2004a). McGee (2005c) conducted a study of educating accounting professors in Bosnia and Herzegovina.

Some studies have been made of accounting certification in various transition economies. McGee (2002) examined the role of the ACCA certification exams as a tool of accounting reform in emerging economies. McGee, Preobragenskaya and Tyler (2004a) examined the introduction of English language certification exams in the CIS, Eastern, and Central Europe. McGee and Preobragenskaya (2006c) looked at accounting certification in Central Asia and the former Soviet Union.

Several studies have looked at accounting certification in Russia (Preobragenskaya and McGee, 2004e; McGee, 2005c, 2008a). At least two studies have examined accounting certification in Armenia (McGee, 1999a, b). A few studies have reported on the programs in former Soviet republics to offer international accounting certification in the Russian language (Enthoven, 2005; McGee et al., 2004a, b; McGee, 2005d, e, 2008b, c, d, e; McGee and Preobragenskaya, 2008a). However, no studies to date have examined accounting certification in the former Soviet republic of Georgia. The present study is intended to fill that gap.

30.3   Accounting Certification in Georgia

Several different kinds of accounting certification are available in Georgia. The Association of Chartered Certified Accountants (ACCA) gives their certification exams twice a year. The ACCA exams test on international accounting and auditing standards. These exams have international recognition. The main problem from the Georgian perspective is that they are given only in the English language, which precludes the vast majority of Georgian accountants from participating in the ACCA program.

In recent years the Georgian Federation of Professional Accountants and Auditors has started offering parallel exams in the Georgian language. The program started independently in 1999. USAID started providing support in 2001. Although the Georgian exams are quite similar to those offered by the ACCA in English, they are not identical. Table 30.1 compares the content of the two sets of exams.

As can be seen, there are more similarities than differences in terms of content. ACCA Paper 1.3 on managing people is not tested, which is not a big loss, since this paper has no accounting content. At level 2, Georgian corporate and business law replaces the ACCA's corporate and business law class and Georgian taxation is studied instead of the ACCA's business taxation course, which is based on British law. These differences make sense, since there is little need to know the British rules in Georgia.

Part 3 of the ACCA exam scheme allows candidates to choose any two of four papers from among the first four papers offered in part 3. The Georgian exam scheme requires the papers on performance management and business information management and does not test on audit and assurance services or advanced taxation. The other topics for part 3 are identical.

Table 30.1 Comparison and ACCA and Georgian Accounting Certification

ACCA Paper #	ACCA exam topic	Georgian exam topic
	PART 1	
1.1	Preparing Financial Statements	Preparing Financial Statements
1.2	Financial Information for Management	Financial Information for Management
1.3	Managing People	Not tested
	PART 2	
2.1	Information Systems	Information Systems
2.2	Corporate and Business Law	Georgian Corporate and Business Law
2.3	Business Taxation	Georgian Taxation
2.4	Financial Management and Control	Financial Management and Control
2.5	Financial Reporting	Financial Reporting
2.6	Audit and Internal Review	Audit and Internal Review
	PART 3	
	ANY TWO	
3.1	Audit and Assurance Services	Not tested
3.2	Advanced Taxation	Not tested
3.3	Performance Management	Performance Management
3.4	Business Information Management	Business Information Management
	ALL THREE	
3.5	Strategic Business Planning and Development	Strategic Business Planning and Development
3.6	Advanced Corporate Reporting	Advanced Corporate Reporting
3.7	Strategic Financial Management	Strategic Financial Management

The Board in charge of accounting certification was aware of the CAP and CIPA exams that were being offered in other former Soviet republics (McGee & Preobragenskaya, 2006f). That program consisted of eight papers. However, they preferred the 14-paper program offered by the ACCA. It was thought that offering a parallel program in the Georgian language would give the program more credibility and recognition.

Some problems were encountered in the early stages. Finding qualified people to translate the materials from English to Georgian was a problem, as was terminology. In some cases there was no equivalent Georgian word for some of the English language terms. Some of the translators were chosen from among the best ACCA students, since these people understood the content of the exams and were in a better position to perform the translations.

Finding people to teach the courses was another problem, since no one in Georgia had any familiarity with the course content in the beginning, with the exception of a few Big-4 accounting firm employees and the people who managed to pass the English language ACCA exams. In order to teach the exam preparation courses, potential lecturers first had to pass the relevant exams. Lecturers must also have had experience as a teacher. Some professors have now passed at least some of the exams, which partially alleviates the problem of finding qualified instructors. Since some professors are now qualified to teach the exam preparation courses, it is now possible to teach the exam subjects in Georgian universities.

30.4 Concluding Comments

Georgia is well on its way toward achieving a high-quality accounting certification program. Its exams are now based on the ACCA model, which has been highly recognized and respected for more than 100 years. Accountants and auditors are being trained in the new model and international accounting and auditing rules have started to creep into university curriculums. But much still needs to be done. There is still the problem of corruption in general, some of which is also present in the accounting profession. It is still possible to purchase an audit opinion in some cases, although doing so is not quite as prevalent as was once the case. As the new system spreads and as accountants become more aware of acceptable accounting ethics, this practice will likely decline in frequency.

References

Association of Accountants and Auditors of Armenia (AAAA) website www.aaaa.am.

Association of Chartered Certified Accountants (ACCA) website www.accaglobal.com.

Certified International Professional Accountant Examination Network (CIPA EN) website www. cipaen.org.

Enterprise Development Project website www.casme.net

Enthoven, Adolf J.H., Yaroslav V. Sokolov, Svetlana M. Bychkova, Valery V. Kovalev and Maria V. Semenova (1998). *Accounting, Auditing and Taxation in the Russian Federation.* A joint publication of the IMA Foundation for Applied Research, an affiliate of the Institute for Management Accountants, Montvale, NJ, USSA and the Center for International Accounting Development at The University of Texas at Dallas.

Enthoven, Adolf J.H. 2005. An International Accounting and Auditing Programme and Certification in the Russian Language. International Journal of Accounting, Auditing and Performance Evaluation 2(1/2): 6–18.

Georgian Federation of Professional Accountants and Auditors (GFPAA) website www.itic.org. ge/gfpaa.

McGee, Robert W. (1999a). Certification Exams in the USA: A Model for Armenia?" *Law and Economy*, 2: 15–22 (in Armenian).

McGee, Robert W. (1999b). The ACCA Comes to Armenia, *Law & Economy*, 2: 23–26 (in Armenian).

McGee, Robert W. (2002). The ACCA Certification Program as a Tool of Accounting Reform in Emerging Economies. Presented at the World Bank Eighth Financial Management Forum, Cavtat, Croatia, May 22–23.

McGee, Robert W. (2003). Reforming Accounting Education in a Transition Economy: A Case Study of Armenia, Twelfth Annual World Business Congress of The International Management

Development Association (IMDA), Vancouver, British Columbia, Canada, June 24–29, 2003. Published in Erdener Kaynak and Talha D. Harcar, editors, Succeeding in a Turbulent Global Marketplace: Changes, Developments, Challenges, and Creating Distinct Competencies (Hummelstown, PA: International Management Development Association, 2003), pp. 139–146. An updated version is being published in Robert W. McGee, Accounting Reform in Transition and Developing Economies, New York: Springer (2008).

McGee, Robert W. (2005a). Reforming Accounting Education in Armenia. In John R. McIntyre and Ilan Alon, editors, Business and Management Education in Transitioning and Developing Countries. Armonk, NY/London: M.E. Sharpe, pp. 178–190.

McGee, Robert W. (2005b). Educating Professors in a Transition Economy: A Case Study of Bosnia and Herzegovina. In John R. McIntyre and Ilan Alon, editors, Business and Management Education in Transitioning and Developing Countries. Armonk, NY/London: M.E. Sharpe, pp. 191–207.

McGee, Robert W. (2005c). Accounting Certification in the Former Soviet Union and Its Importance to the Energy Sector.. *Russian/CIS Energy and Mining Law Journal*, 3(2): 23–30.

McGee, Robert W. (2005d). Accounting Certification in Transition Economies: Recent Developments in Russia, Ukraine, Moldova and Central Asia. Marjorie G. Adams and Abbass Alkhafaji, editors, *Business Research Yearbook: Global Business Perspectives*, Volume XII, No. 1 (International Graphics: Beltsville, MD., 2005), pp. 40–44.

McGee, Robert W. (2005e). International Accounting Education and Certification in the Former Soviet Union. *International Journal of Accounting, Auditing and Performance Evaluation*, 2(1–2): 19–36.

McGee, Robert W. (2006a). Accounting Reform in Armenia, in Robert W. McGee and Galina G. Preobragenskaya, *Accounting and Financial System Reform in Eastern Europe and Asia*. New York: Springer, pp. 75–93.

McGee, Robert W. (2006b). Adopting and Implementing International Financial Reporting Standards in Transition Economies. In Greg N. Gregoriou and Mohamed Gaber, editors, International Accounting: Standards, Regulations, and Financial Reporting Amsterdam: Elsevier, pp. 199–223.

McGee, Robert W. (2006c). Foreign Direct Investment in South Eastern Europe. In Radmila Jovancevic and Zeljko Sevic, editors, Foreign Direct Investment Policies in South-East Europe. Greenwich University Press, University of Zagreb Faculty of Economics and Business, Political Culture, Publishing and Research Institute, Zagreb, pp. 17–40.

McGee, Robert W. (2006d). Attracting Foreign Direct Investment with Good Financial Reporting Practices: A Case Study of Russia. In Radmila Jovancevic and Zeljko Sevic, editors, Foreign Direct Investment Policies in South-East Europe. Greenwich University Press, University of Zagreb Faculty of Economics and Business, Political Culture, Publishing and Research Institute, Zagreb, pp. 269–287.

McGee, Robert W. (2008a). Accounting Certification in Russia, in Robert W. McGee, editor (2008), Accounting Reform in Transition and Developing Economies, New York: Springer (forthcoming).

McGee, Robert W. (2008b). Accounting Certification in the Russian Language, in Robert W. McGee, editor (2008), Accounting Reform in Transition and Developing Economies, New York: Springer (forthcoming).

McGee, Robert W. (2008c). Accounting Certification in Central Asia. Winter Conference of the International Academy of Business and Public Administration Disciplines, Orlando, Florida, January 3–6, 2008. Published in IABPAD Conference Proceedings 5(1): 1767–1778. Winner of the RESEARCH AWARD. Forthcoming in the *International Journal of Business, Accounting and Finance*.

McGee, Robert W. (2008d). Accounting Certification in Central Asia, in Robert W. McGee, editor (2008), Accounting Reform in Transition and Developing Economies, New York: Springer (forthcoming).

McGee, Robert W. (2008e). Accounting Certification in Ukraine, in Robert W. McGee, editor, *Accounting Reform in Transition and Developing Economies*, New York: Springer (forthcoming).

McGee, Robert W. and Galina G. Preobragenskaya (2003). Problems of Foreign Direct Investment in Russia, Thirteenth International Conference of the International Trade & Finance Association, Vaasa, Finland, May 28–31, reprinted in Robert W. McGee and Galina G. Preobragenskaya, *Accounting and Financial System Reform in a Transition Economy: A Case Study of Russia*, New York: Springer, 2005, pp. 79–97.

McGee, Robert W. and Galina G. Preobragenskaya (2005a). *Accounting and Financial System Reform in a Transition Economy: A Case Study of Russia*. New York: Springer.

McGee, Robert W. and Galina G. Preobragenskaya (2005b). Accounting Reform in Ukraine. *Corporate Ownership & Control* 3(1): 30–45.

McGee, Robert W. and Galina G. Preobragenskaya (2006a). Accounting Education in Bosnia & Herzegovina, in Robert W. McGee and Galina G. Preobragenskaya (2006). *Accounting and Financial System Reform in Eastern Europe and Asia*. New York: Springer, pp. 195–212.

McGee, Robert W. and Galina G. Preobragenskaya (2006b). Accounting Education in Ukraine, in Robert W. McGee and Galina G. Preobragenskaya (2006). *Accounting and Financial System Reform in Eastern Europe and Asia*. New York: Springer, pp. 175–194.

McGee, Robert W. and Galina G. Preobragenskaya (2006c). Accounting Certification in Central Asia and the Former Soviet Union, in Robert W. McGee and Galina G. Preobragenskaya (2006). *Accounting and Financial System Reform in Eastern Europe and Asia*. New York: Springer, pp. 213–235.

McGee, Robert W. and Galina G. Preobragenskaya (2006d). Accounting Reform in Russia, in Robert W. McGee and Galina G. Preobragenskaya, *Accounting and Financial System Reform in Eastern Europe and Asia*. New York: Springer, pp. 7–43.

McGee, Robert W. and Galina G. Preobragenskaya (2006e). Accounting Reform in Ukraine, in Robert W. McGee and Galina G. Preobragenskaya, Accounting *and Financial System Reform in Eastern Europe and Asia*. New York: Springer, pp. 45–73.

McGee, Robert W. and Galina G. Preobragenskaya (2006f). *Accounting and Financial System Reform in Eastern Europe and Asia*. New York: Springer.

McGee, Robert W. and Galina G. Preobragenskaya (2008a). International Accounting Certification in the CIS, Eastern and Central Europe, in Robert W. McGee, editor (2008), Accounting Reform in Transition and Developing Economies, New York: Springer (forthcoming).

McGee, Robert W., Galina G. Preobragenskaya and Michael Tyler (2004a). English Language International Accounting Certification in the CIS, Eastern and Central Europe. Published in the Proceedings of the International Academy of Business and Public Administration Disciplines (IABPAD) Conference, Tunica, Mississippi, May 24–26, 2004.

McGee, Robert W., Galina G. Preobragenskaya and Michael Tyler (2004b). International Accounting Certification in the Russian Language: A Case Study. *Global Perspectives on Accounting Education* 1: 59–74.

Preobragenskaya, Galina G. and Robert W. McGee (2003). Accounting Education in a Transition Economy: A Case Study of Russian Universities. Presented at the Academy of International Business - Southeast Annual Conference, Clearwater, Florida, November 13–14, 2003. Published in the Proceedings, pp. 108–119. Reprinted in Robert W. McGee and Galina G. Preobragenskaya, *Accounting and Financial System Reform in a Transition Economy: A Case Study of Russia*, New York: Springer, 2005, pp. 109–133. Also published on the Social Science Research Network website at http://ssrn.com/abstract = 459361.

Preobragenskaya, Galina G. and Robert W. McGee (2004a). Accounting Education in Russia and the USA: A Comparative Study, *Journal of Accounting, Ethics & Public Policy*, 4(1): 15–43.

Preobragenskaya, Galina G. and Robert W. McGee (2004b). Reforming the Accounting Curriculum in Russia: Some Guidelines Based on the Armenian and Bosnian Experiences. Research in Accounting in Emerging Economies, Supplement 2: Accounting and Accountability in Emerging and Transition Economies, pp. 531–553. An updated version is being published in Robert W. McGee, editor, Accounting Reform in Transition and Developing Economies, New York: Springer (2008).

Preobragenskaya, Galina G. and Robert W. McGee (2004c). Accounting System Reform in a Transition Economy: A Look at Private Sector Accounting Education in Russia. *Business Research Yearbook*: Global Business Perspectives (Carolyn Gardner, Jerry Biberman and Abbass Alkhafaji, editors), Volume XI, Saline, MI: McNaughton & Gunn, pp. 27–31.

Preobragenskaya, Galina G. and Robert W. McGee (2004d). Private Sector Accounting Education in Russia, *Accounting and Finance in Transition* 1: 41–90 (2004). Reprinted in Robert W. McGee and Galina G. Preobragenskaya, *Accounting and Financial System Reform in Eastern Europe and Asia*. New York: Springer, 2006, pp. 97–173.

Preobragenskaya, Galina G. and Robert W. McGee (2004e). International Accounting and Finance Certification in the Russian Federation. *Business Research Yearbook*: Global Business Perspectives (Carolyn Gardner, Jerry Biberman and Abbass Alkhafaji, editors), Volume XI, Saline, MI: McNaughton & Gunn, pp. 32–36. An expanded version was published in Robert W. McGee and Galina G. Preobragenskaya, *Accounting and Financial System Reform in a Transition Economy: A Case Study of Russia*, New York: Springer, 2005, pp. 135–149.

Preobragenskaya, Galina G. and Robert W. McGee (2004f). Converting the Accounting System of a Transition Economy: A Case Study of Russia. *International Journal of Accounting, Auditing and Performance Evaluation*, 1(4): 448–464 (2004).

Preobragenskaya, Galina G. and Robert W. McGee (2004g). Accounting Aspects of Foreign Direct Investment in Russia. *Journal of Accounting, Ethics & Public Policy*, 4(2): 115–140.

Preobragenskaya, Galina G. and Robert W. McGee (2005a). Recent Developments in Accounting Education in Russia. In John R. McIntyre and Ilan Alon, editors, Business and Management Education in Transitioning and Developing Countries. Armonk, NY/London: M.E. Sharpe, pp. 99–114.

Ukraine Accounting Reform Project website (UARP) website www.capcipa.biz.

Chapter 31
Accounting Certification in the Slovak Republic

Anna Banociova and Jozef Lescisin

31.1 Introduction

Reform of accountancy profession certification was conducted in connection with the transformation of the social and economic system and with the process of the Slovak Republic's integration into European structures. This process required not only adjustments in legislation but also the harmonization of Slovak accounting with the accounting of the European Union (EU). After the reforms the Slovak accounting system will be acceptable in every country of the European Union.

A goal of this certification project is to achieve EU standards for its accounting profession and to raise Slovak accountants to the same level as accountants in the other countries of the European Union. The accounting profession is valued as one of the most reputable and irreplaceable professions and it plays an important role in all business activities.

The Slovak Chamber of Certified Accountants was founded in 2002. The principal objective of this association is to create an educational system that is comparable to similar systems in Europe in order to guarantee the recognition of its certificates on a par with other European countries (see the Directive on Mutual Recognition of Professional Education in the EU).

The accounting profession requires not only knowledge of accounting and taxation, but also knowledge from other areas such as law, economics, statistics, managerial accounting, finance, financial strategy and controlling, financial analysis, auditing, and International Accounting Standards.

The system of certification has been designed for the accountancy profession at large, i.e., it offers education in disciplines indispensable for the practice of accounting from the lowest level of skills through to the top level of the accountancy profession.

The system of certification has not been supported yet by any national legislation that would require certificates for practice of the accounting profession, but this project certainly helps to increase the quality of accounting services. The

A. Banociova and J. Lescisin
Technical University of Kosice

R. W. McGee (ed.), *Accounting Reform in Transition and Developing Economies,*
© Springer Science+Business Media LLC 2008

Slovak Chamber of Certified Accountants is preparing legislative standards for this profession. The Ministry of Education of the Slovak Republic approved and accredited the system of certification and this project became a part of the educational system in the Slovak Republic.

The certification program offers certificates on three levels. Each level requires different work experience, previously completed education, and different courses to pass. All courses are compulsory and it is necessary to pass all exams at a certain level to be able to obtain the certificate.

31.1.1 First Level: Accounting Assistant

- Required entry education: high school diploma
- Required work experience: 1 year
- Compulsory courses to obtain the certificate: Accounting I., Economics, Legislative System of the Slovak Republic I., Taxes I., Quantitative Methods in Economics, Information Technologies

A graduate at this level is qualified to perform accounting in industrial and nonindustrial companies and in public administration. A graduate is able to deal with common accounting transactions and prepare accounting statements and tax documents.

31.1.2 Second Level: Balance Accountant

- Required entry education: high school diploma and the first level certificate
- Required work experience: 2 years
- Compulsory courses to obtain the certificate: Accounting II., Taxes II., Managerial Accounting, Managerial Finance, Legislative System of the Slovak Republic II., Quantitative Methods and Management.

A graduate of this level is qualified to perform accounting in medium-sized companies and supervise the accounting departments of big companies. A graduate is able to deal with most special accounting transactions, generate accounting reports, and use the instruments of managerial accounting, financial management, and auditing.

31.1.3 Third Level: Accounting Expert

- Required entry education: university degree or PhD., the first level and the second level certificates

- Required work experience: 4 years
- Compulsory courses to obtain the certificate: Financial Strategy, Financial Analysis, Auditing, International Accounting Standards and Consolidation

A graduate of this level is qualified to perform accounting as a chief accountant in both medium-sized and big companies. A holder of this certificate can apply for a license that qualifies him/her to perform the profession of a judicial expert of economic activities.

Part IV
Corporate Governance

Chapter 32
Corporate Governance in Russia: Concept and Reality

Andrei Kuznetsov and Olga Kuznetsova

32.1   Introduction

The national system of corporate governance as reflected in the norms and provisions required to raise external finance is a key component of the institutional set-up in any market economy. Such systems may have different configurations but they have one crucial commonality: the task of providing means that help to institutionalize, i.e., regulate according to certain established rules, economic conflict between investors in companies and managers, facilitate information flows, and procure a solid and cost-efficient foundation for the growth of publicly held corporations. In other words, corporate governance is responsible for reassuring individual investors that the money they invest in a public company will be handled with due care by the management of the company, so that the interests of investors are protected.

Seen in this perspective, corporate governance presents itself as one of the fundamental institutes of modern Western democracy, acting as a guarantor of sustainable economic growth (Sullivan, 2002). In countries with a long-lasting tradition of private corporate management, reliable and functional corporate governance is taken pretty much for granted, which is obvious from the degree of public outrage and concern when the system misfires, as the cases of ENRON and Parmalat vividly illustrate.

The situation is different in transition economies. In Russia there is a sizable gap between the real assets of the firms and capitalization.[1] This indicates that corporate governance is not a well-established institution and investors are preoccupied with the safeness of their money.

The importance of corporate governance, and market institutions in general, was not fully appreciated at the beginning of market reforms in Russia. Instead

---

A. Kuznetsov and O. Kuznetsova
Manchester Metropolitan University

[1] At its peak before the 1998 collapse, the total stock market capitalization of all Russian industry only reached about $130 billion – less than Intel Corp (Fox and Heller, 2000).

R. W. McGee (ed.), *Accounting Reform in Transition and Developing Economies,*
© Springer Science + Business Media LLC 2008

macroeconomic reforms, privatization in particular, were prioritized as a means to establish the superiority of the market mechanism of resources allocation over central planning. In reality improvements in overall economic efficiency have been slow to materialize on the scale originally anticipated. As a result, interest in institutional aspects of reforms had grown and corporate governance was identified as one of central elements responsible of the success of transition (Stiglitz, 2002) as academics and policy makers gradually came to the realization that privatization, stabilization, and liberalization would not guarantee successful transition in the absence of an appropriate institutional environment.

More than 10 years in the making, the Russian system of corporate governance remains a controversial construct as far as its conceptual foundations, features, efficiency, and future development are concerned. This chapter is an attempt to evaluate the strengths and weaknesses of the national system of corporate governance in Russia in the context of post-communist reforms and identify those crucial issues that needs to be addressed in order to increase the effectiveness of this system.

32.2   Corporate Governance and National Environment

When Russia started to establish the foundations of corporate governance in the early 1990s, it had no experience it could rely upon. This might appear as an insignificant complication considering the amount of experience accumulated by other industrialized countries of the world and available for adaptation. In reality the challenge of choosing the model has proven to be quite daunting.

To begin with, Western practice has to offer more than one proven model of corporate governance. Typically in literature we find references to at least two alternative models, American (also known as Anglo-Saxon or market-oriented system) and continental (also known as Germanic or network-oriented system), although it is becoming increasingly common to identify further models these days.[2] The important point to notice is that the multiplicity of national systems of corporate governance is not so much a result of deliberate premeditation but rather has evolved in the course of an evolutionary process in response to the requirements of a particular national environment.[3]

---

[2] De Jong (1997) writes about the Anglo-Saxon, the Germanic, and the Latinic types of corporations with the latter represented by firms in France, Italy, Spain, etc. Yoshimori (1995) conducts his discourse in terms of monistic, dualistic, and pluralistic concepts of corporation. The first exists in the US and the UK with a focus on shareholders; the second is characteristic of Germany and France and put a premium on the interests of both the shareholder and employees. Japan is the home for the third concept that assumes that the firm belongs to all stakeholders.

[3] For instance, Potthof (1996) brings forward the historical roots of dissimilarities between Anglo-Saxon and Germanic systems. In the 19th century, German banks were looking for ways to transform their short-term assets into long-term ones, but were not interested in managing firms.

The fact that national systems of corporate governance are products of historical circumstances, i.e., that they have been influenced by cultural, political and socio-economic factors specific to age and nation, has important consequences for countries like Russia. Whilst it is possible to try and import conceptual and statutory underpinnings of corporate governance wholesale from the West, it is not possible to recreate the circumstances under which they emerged. Attempts to transfer best practices inevitably creates a number of immediate and long-term problems related to adaptation and interpretation of utilizable concepts and the evaluation of the consequences of their implementation in Russia.

To consider just one aspect of this problem, in an ideal world we would expect the decision-maker to choose for imitation the best of available models. In reality, such a choice is hardly possible simply because no such model exists. The recent discussion on comparative advantages of various models (Hart, 1995; Milgrom and Roberts, 1992; DeJong, 1997; Williamson 1985; Yoshimori 1995) has nominated no clear winner. Every system has its pros and cons but, as Moerland (1995) infers, it is impossible to say that one system is better than the other on theoretical grounds as the optimization of economic organization leaves room for multiple configurations. This claim is echoed by Rozman (2000) who, having compared Anglo-Saxon and Germanic systems, reaches a conclusion that both systems are logical and in harmony within themselves despite being different.

The conclusion that the variety of national systems of corporate governance is rooted in the nation-specific circumstances under which they develop and, despite the process of globalization, the parallel existence of alternative concepts will continue in the foreseeable future to have practical and conceptual implication for Russia: whatever system is chosen as a prototype, it is likely to be a poor fit initially and, when set up, would require to go through a more or less protracted period of adaptation to local conditions to an extent that the imported system finally acquires individual characteristics turning it into a unique national system. Evidently, this adaptation will depend on how soon the local conditions become stable. Considering the depth and breadth of changes through which the Russian economy and political system have been going since the beginning of 1990s, it comes as no surprise that the system of corporate governance in Russia finds itself exposed to some extreme pressures.

Therefore, the German system emphasises supervision, but not management by banks of joint-stock companies. By contrast, in Britain and in the US, capital was scarce. Risk-taking individuals wanted more control over their assets and hence demanded extended authority in respect of managers. As a result, the system that developed in Britain and in the US put emphasis on the responsibility of managers before shareholders, while in Germany the emphasis was on their responsibility before the law. In turn, LaPorta et al (1997) give precedence to a legal framework as the cause of variation in corporate systems, establishing a link between market-oriented model of corporate governance and the dominance of common low in Britain and the US, on the one hand, and the network-oriented model and civil law in continental Europe, on the other.

32.3 The Makings of the System

The effectiveness of the corporate system ultimately depends on how well it copes with the specific demands of the environment. In the case of Russia these demands have been determined by a number of factors.

First, as public corporations emerged as a product of mass privatization, they inherited the operational profile, the structure of assets and employment from their predecessors, and state-owned enterprises. By contrast to proper buy-out, in Russia "buy-outs" were imposed on insiders by the government whether or not there were resources to make new firms viable. In fact, many companies were doomed from the outset. Commonly for the insiders becoming owners was not so much the issue of increasing efficiency and returns as preserving their very livelihood in a hostile and uncertain environment.

Second, in 1990s the Russian economy was going through a period of demonetization and barterization in response to government attempts to introduce tight budget constraints and the shortage of financial resources in the country. Businesses had accumulated an enormous burden of unpaid and delayed payments. Practically all industrial firms were involved in barter and for many of them barter represented as much as half or more of their entire turnover (Aukutsionek, 2001). As a result the strength of monetary signals and incentives became diluted. The debt crisis acted as a great equalizer in the sense it was difficult for potential investors to make a distinction between well-managed firms and badly managed firms on the basis of their financial accounts. Open market competition for financial resources was unfeasible and the investment markets were extremely depressed.

The third feature of the business environment was the tendency to substitute networking and other informal arrangements for the market. Managers had to rely on successful networking as they sought to compensate the poor performance of formal institutions with arrangements based on personal contacts. The proliferation of informal networks affects the character of market relations in the country. On the one hand, informal relations were looked upon as a means to create zones of trust within the general environment of distrust, thus reducing transaction costs. On the other hand, by their nature networks, in particular informal, seek to maintain exclusiveness.

In the Russian context, networking often did not mean getting better knowledge of business partners and their needs but rather pursued the goal of conspiring against outsiders and avoiding legal control over financial and other transactions (Radaev, 1998). Business networks strived to resolve any "problems" internally, which provided more flexibility and more chances to reach a mutually satisfactory solution than available formal methods but often at a considerable social cost, for example, poor disclosure of information, price fixing, etc.

The fourth feature was the criminalization of economy. According to theory, without proper institutional safeguards economic agents are not encouraged to behave fairly as self-interested behavior with its focus on cutting costs meets no limits (Barry, 1998; Nellis, 1999). This pushes managers and entrepreneurs to adopt a "one shot" business strategy which entice them to defect from agreements and defy cooperation.

The direct outcome of these ambiguous circumstances is that there is hardly any generally recognized and implemented set of behavioral rules to induce a collaborative conduct. Russian experience has been in agreement with this scenario. In the first decade of transition in particular, the atmosphere was charged with the sensation of abounding opportunities for quick enrichment caused by the ownership vacuum that was produced by the dismantling of the socialist state.

The moral standard of business suffered as a result. On the one hand, organized crime has developed interest in business and deeply penetrated its structures.[4] On the other hand, the weakness of institutions stimulated dishonest behavior on the part of top managers and major shareholders.

If we try to summarize the likely impact of these four factors on the system of corporate governance as it was establishing itself in Russia during this period, what we get is a picture of struggle of epic proportions for control over enormous material resources, which was shaped by few formal rules or institutional constraints but provided ample chances for opportunists and artful dodgers.

According to the definition accepted in this paper, corporate governance has its focus on facilitating relations between managers and investors in public corporations. From this point of view the situation in Russia during post-communist transition was quite unusual because the parties involved in relations of corporate governance were fundamentally different from those in Western market economies.

To begin with, shareholders were not necessarily the same as investors as property rights were mostly appropriated through a give-away distribution rather than bought or sold. The privatization process had some similarities with insiders buyouts, but in fact was radically different as the acquisition of property by insiders in the course of mandatory privatization represented an entirely peculiar type of action in terms of motivation, objectives, and rational and therefore was utterly unlike anything ever assumed by standard corporate governance models (Kuznetsov and Kuznetsova, 2003).

Corporate governance also had to account to the fact that barterization, weak financial markets, rampant inflation, criminalization of economy seriously undermined the impact of standard financial instruments of control whilst at the same time forcing both investors and managers to develop aversion to long-term financial and business commitments. Overall the specificities of post-privatization era signified that the newly created shareholders were lacking, in terms of accepted theory, some central characteristics that were necessary to regard them as the primary constituent of the firm (McAlister et al., 2003).

The view that shareholders should enjoy preference for their interests over the interests of other corporate stakeholders is generally based on the convictions held

---

[4] According to Shelley (1997), organized criminals are in control of nearly half the Russian economy.

by neoclassical economic theory regarding human behavior and economic optimization. Accordingly, shareholders are singled out as most likely to behave towards a corporation as "responsible owners" because of a combination of economic risk and remuneration associated with tying up certain assets in a particular type of investment that they experience.

This assumption, however, was hardly appropriate for the situation in Russia. The way privatization was framed favored one particular group of population, the employees and manager of state-owned enterprises. In 1992–1993 the objects of privatization were small- and medium-sized enterprises, which had been already leased out to their "work collectives." They were usually transformed into partnerships or closed-type joint-stock companies with the employees becoming exclusive owners of equal shares of equity.

Later the government put a ban on transforming larger enterprises into closed-type companies. Nonetheless, insiders were allowed to retain up to 51% of equity. All in all, privatization complete, only half of the firms had shareholders-outsiders who in total owned no more than 10% of all outstanding shares. Even now managers and workers remain the largest groups of shareholders: their combined share is about 46% of total stock.[5] Individually the majority of shareholders are in possession of only an insignificant block of shares.

By acquiring it they did not take any additional risk but equally the prospect of remuneration was quite illusory considering the economic situation in the country. The necessary prerequisites for "responsible" behavior were missing: small shareholders-insiders were motivated more by their interests as stakeholders-employees, i.e., maintaining the viability of their organizations, then as investors-shareholders. Shareholders-outsiders were involved even less because they soon found that post-privatization small blocks of shares were almost worthless (Kuznetsov and Kuznetsova, 2001; Atanasov, 2002).

32.4   The Lasting Impact of Mass Privatization

The fact that the bulk of shareholders in Russia obtained ownership rights without injecting any capital of their own and that generally, during this period, external investors were extremely inactive and loans and credits to corporations were almost nonexistent, created not only conceptual difficulties (the standard definition of corporate governance as the ways in which suppliers of finance to corporations assure themselves of getting a return on their investment was proved inadequate) but, more importantly, some serious practical implications.

---

[5] A feature of the Russian corporate scene is that ownership of the largest resources exporting firms is concentrated in the hands of the handful of so-called oligarchs who exploited their special relations with the top state bureaucracy. They came into possession of their original stakes through the loans-for-shares tenders held by the Russian government in mid-1990s. Later they consolidated their control through diluting shares of the state or minority owners.

Small shareholders showed little motivation to use their powers or fight for their shareholder rights. According to some estimates, nearly 70% of property has been left without effective ownership control by genuine owners.[6] The capital market as the backbone of the mechanism of ownership control was and still is quite weak. Of hundreds of tradable stocks, only about 30 large issues see some trading. With little or no activity in most issues the disciplinary function of the securities markets is next to paralyzed.

Without doubt, the general apathy of small shareholders cannot be attributed exclusively to the circumstances under which they acquired their shares. The awareness that there is no mechanism in place on which they could rely for defending their rights plays its role as well. As our analysis of the business environment demonstrated, the capital market would inevitably struggle in fulfilling most of its functions like being the judge of economic performance of firms or supporting shareholders' right of exit as a measure disciplining managers. Any campaign to restraint managers (e.g., a proxy fight) would require resources and persistence that most of shareholders cannot afford.

Despite this reality, Western advice and official policies based on it for a long time were very much based on different assumptions. The American model quickly established itself as an implicit benchmark. This was not so much an informed choice as a reflection of the politics of reforms. From the outset Russian reformers were under influence of the American-style IMF-sponsored ideal of liberal capitalism. References to the Anglo-Saxon concept initially appeared in analytical materials prepared on behalf of international agencies (e.g., Pohl and Claessens, 1994).

In this context insider corporate governance was persistently scrutinized within the framework of a well-established debate on the relevant merits of "insider-controlled" and "outsider-controlled" firms (Frydman et al., 1999; Filatochev and Swain, 1997). The former were usually criticized on the basis that insider shareholding may undermine firm restructuring if it threatened wages and employment, but most importantly, because insider-controlled companies will experience great difficulty in raising outside capital following the agency problem faced by lenders and minority investors (Earle and Estrin, 1996).

What this analysis failed to recognize was the discrepancy between the nominal distribution of ownership rights, geared towards stakeholders, and the actual allocation of control. This is a very significant difference because the majority of insiders in Russia have only very small blocks of shares and they do not represent a united and coherent group. In other words, work collectives may still be the largest group of shareholders in aggregate terms, but actual control may lie elsewhere. Within the group of insider shareholders there is a huge divide between senior manager, who consolidate the power of shareholding with the power of decision-making, and ordinary employees.

This brings us to an important result: in the Russian context it is imperative to make a conceptual distinction between the largest and dominant shareholders.

---

[6] "Investitsionnaya politika v Rossii", *Nezavisimaya Gazeta*, August 26, 1997, p. 2.

Presumably, in market economies with a mature and sophisticated institutional set-up this distinction is irrelevant because domination is based on exercising ownership rights according to the principle "one share-one vote" (DeMarzo, 1993). In Russia poor legal protection of shareholder rights, lack of disclosure about the business operations or finances of corporations, the underdeveloped state of the security market, and a weak shareholder culture signify that possession of large blocks of shares may result in little or no effective control over the firm. Same conditions favor people who are privy to the firm's management decisions. This category includes primarily senior managers. As a result domination can be achieved by simple if unscrupulous means exploiting the fact that outsiders cannot accurately monitor day-to-day performance of the firm.

32.5   The Role of Senior Managers

In the light of our analysis it becomes apparent that the main issue of the Russian system of corporate governance at its current stage of development is not so much the relationship between investors and managers regarding the supply of finance to corporations as the relationship between different categories of stakeholders around the allocation of existing assets of privatized enterprises. Privatization has put senior managers in an exceptionally strong position vis-à-vis employees and outsiders. From the outset their control of the firms was far in excess of their share of ownership due to advantages inherent in the system.

As pre-privatization incumbents they enjoyed privileged access to information, admission to important networks and, at least initially, support of the labor force.[7] Later they developed special tactics designed to maintain and reinforce their position. These include, for example, keeping share registries locked up in their offices; keeping more than one registry; changing entries into the registry at will; threatening to fire workers who sold shares to outsiders; misleading "undesirable" shareholders about dates and venues of the shareholders general meetings; refusing to register share purchases by outsiders; declining to recognize board directors properly elected by minority shareowners, etc. These tactics brings results thanks to a low level of corporate transparency as well as of effective law enforcement.

In the end of the day, however, it was control over the financial resources of the firms that solidified the domination of managers. In the economy stricken with shortage of financial resources institutional chaos has opened to them an unravel opportunity to use corporate resources for illegal personal enrichment. In big firms the most popular scheme of such enrichment involves the creation of a number of

---

[7] In the chaotic world of transition many workers had to rely on their enterprises as providers of social and welfare services, which firms ruled by market interests would not normally provide. This and similar considerations made them suspicious of outsiders and natural allies to the incumbent management (Clarke 1995).

small affiliated firms which are put in charge of the cash flows of the big firm. This makes the control of cash flows extremely complicated and allows the organizers of the scheme to transfer money into their personal accounts either directly or through off-shore companies and various sham firms. These resources could be used by senior managers for increasing own block of shares and preventing other parties from accumulating more shares. Eventually, the combination of give-away privatization and underdeveloped institutions has brought about the situation in which in the majority of public companies the function of manager and the function of dominant owner became united.

Statistics are not too helpful in validating this fact. The secretive nature of the Russian corporate world makes it very difficult to quantify the structure of ownership. Officially in 1999 "insiders" (read senior managers) controlled only 27% of all firms, outsiders 60%, and the state 13% (Kapelyushnikov, 2001). In fact, according to expert evaluation based on in-depth empirical studies, senior management is in control of no less than 50% of firms because many shareholders-outsiders are just a façade for managers (Dolgopiatova, 2001; Sizov, 2004). The standard problem of corporate governance, therefore, transforms: it is no longer a conflict between managers and owners but rather a conflict between different categories of owners of which one has advantages because of its position within the firm. Consequently, Russian corporations acquire many features of manager-owned firms.

32.6 Entrepreneurial System of Corporate Governance?

The dominance of managers makes some experts describe the Russian system of corporate governance as "entrepreneurial," in which there is no separation between ownership and management (Konstantinov et al., 2002). In this system controlling owners have to occupy senior management positions in the firm as well because this is the only way to protect their controlling rights and make a real impact on the running of the firm. The protection of ownership rights is a major issue in Russia.

The legal system is entirely inadequate in this respect and actually quite often the legalistic hitches and corruption in the judicial system are exploited as a means of hostile takeover.[8] Predatory takeovers that rely on the abuse of the rights of shareholders have established themselves as a specific type of business in its own right.

---

[8] One of the common tricks is to obtain a judicial decision that bans the current owners of the firm to use their right to vote in the shareholders general meeting or take a position on the board of directors. Another ploy is to make the court requisite the registry of shareholders, the only legal proof of ownership, and then replace it with an alternative registry with a different composition of shareholders (Sizov, 2004). One notorious incident involved Krasnoyarsk Aluminum, which deleted from its share register a 20% stake held by the British Trans World Group, effectively wiping out its holding (Mileusnic, 1996).

Its profitability rates are estimated to be between 200% and 300%, and occasionally may reach 1,000% (Sizov, 2004). What makes these rates possible is that the value of the firm as a going concern may be lower than the value of its assets, in particular the land. In certain big cities even successful industrial firms, leaders in their industry, may find themselves under attack because the construction boom turns their land property into a magnet for developers.

The current system of corporate governance based on the concentration of ownership in the hands of senior managers has its pros and cons as far as the efficiency of corporate governance is concerned. On the negative side, very high ownership stakes weaken incentives for managers to act in the interests of small shareholders.[9] This is usually the aspect that raises the greatest concern of foreign experts and advisers. They justly point out that the very rationale for public corporation, i.e., to provide business with new and vast investment resources, will be defeated if minority shareholders are neglected.

There has been pressure on the Russian government to introduce and promote the principles of good corporate governance developed by the Organization for Economic Cooperation and Development (OECD, 2002). In 2002 a government body, the Russian Federal Securities and Exchange Commission, introduced the voluntary Code of Corporate Behaviour founded on these principles. Field studies demonstrate that the larger firms were more inclined to implement the Code (Guriev et al., 2002). This may be attributed to the fact that large firms are more likely to be interested in tapping the open financial markets than smaller firms.

In particular, Russian corporations that seek attracting financial resources from foreign and international markets may be seen making an effort to comply with the Code and other international standards like the US Generally Accepted Accounting Principles (GAAP) or International Accounting Standards (IAS), depending on which financial markets they are targeting. Generally speaking, however, the majority of firms do not feel pressure to abide by the letter or spirit of the 2002 Code of Corporate Behaviour.

Conceptually, this and similar codes implicitly have the assumption of a liberal and efficient market at its core. As far as Russia is concerned there is little hope that some external to corporation forces may come to rescue as the degree of efficiency achieved by the market remains low in comparison to Western economies. Enough to mention that the 2005 Index of Economic Freedom by the *Wall Street Journal*, which may be construed as an indirect measure of the maturity and efficiency of the market in various countries of the world, positions Russia in the "mostly unfree" category (*The Wall Street Journal*, January 12, 2005).

There are also arguments in favor of encouraging managers to maintain an ownership stake in their company. Jensen and Meckling (1976) famously argue that the most important agency conflict could arise from the fact that as a manager's ownership stake falls, his incentive to search out new profitable investment opportunities

---

[9] A study identifies the critical level of ownership concentration at 50% for Russia (Guriev et al, 2003).

decreases. Russian conditions demand some modification of this approach. As was demonstrated earlier, weak performance of formal institutions increases the role of informal institutions. Investors cannot rely on published accounts to make an informed decision; the level of trust in business relations is very low (Fox and Heller, 1999). Under this circumstances involvement of managers as shareholders may be seen by financial investors as an assurance of long-term commitment on the part of managers and may make raising capital easier.

The Russian system of corporate governance in its present form bears all the signs of an ad hoc construct. It is logical to assume that in a pursue of wealth maximisation the current generation of directors-owners, as western managers-owners before them, will embrace eventually the necessity to delegate executive functions to more competent managers than themselves and focus on strategic ownership. This choice will be the choice of self-interest and self-preservation.

In the current environment though same instincts prevent managers to give up direct control over the firm and its assets. Therefore the progress of corporate governance towards a more conventional modern model is unrealistic without changes in the political, social and economic realities of Russia in the first place. Insiders routinely loot companies, dilute shares of outsiders, fail to pay dividends and mistreat shareholders in other ways because they feel threatened by the general instability and uncertainty regarding property rights, inheritance rights, contract law, judicial protection, personal safety, etc. In other words, the current system of corporate governance is a further manifestation of the poor state of institutional infrastructure in the country.

The paradox is that certain behavioral patterns and business arrangements in Russia bring rewards although they should be a ticket to failure in a market economy as contradicting its rules and institutions. It this context the idiosyncratic behavior of economic agents determined to by-pass the 'legal' market economy is in fact a rational reaction to the uncertainty and challenges caused by institutional distortions. The high perceived cost of acting legally is a fundamental impediment to the progress in corporate governance along the lines suggested by the OECD code of corporate governance.[10]

There is growing consensus that the shortage of market-type responses in Russia has the frailty of market-based incentives as its cause. Present institutional arrangements reflect the drawbacks and weaknesses associated with a period of systemic change such as domination of short-term interests, poor access to business information, lack of trust, collapse of traditional business ties, parallel existence of incompatible business cultures, etc. These features have made inevitable the introduction of makeshift solutions, in particular because the state as an active force in creating an institutional set-up had been weakened and reticent during this period. However,

---

[10] Interviews with managers of companies importing white goods into Russia, the sector where the presence of 'grey' practices is very noticeable, revealed in 2001 that the choice between 'grey,' semi-legal schemes and fully legal procedures was entirely determined by the consideration of comparative cost (Radaev, 2002).

it is evident that these arrangements have reached the limits of their efficiency and have become a barrier to further development as they fail to provide a solid and cost-effective foundation for market transactions. The path for the further modernization of corporate governance in Russia is the path of a comprehensive modernization of the institutional framework as a whole.

References

Atanasov, V. (2002) "Valuation of Large Blocks of Shares and the Private Benefits of Control," Tuck-JQFA Contemporary Corporate Governance Issues II Conference.

Aukutsionek, S. (2001) "Barter: New Data and Comments," *Journal of East West Business*, 6(4), 23–35.

Barry, N. (1998) *Business Ethics* – London: Macmillan Press.

Clarke, S. (1995) "Formal and Informal Relations in Soviet Industrial Production" in S. Clarke (ed.) *Management and Industry in Russia*, Cambridge: Edward Elgar.

DeJong, H.W. (1997) "The Governance Structure and Performance of Large European Corporations," *The Journal of Management and Governance*, 1(1), 5–27.

Dolgopiatova, T. (2001) "Modeli korporativnogo kontrolia na rossiiskikh predpriatiach." *Mir Rossii*, 10(3), 46–60.

DeMarzo Peter M. (1993) "Majority Voting and Corporate Control: The Rule of the Dominant Shareholder." *Review of Economic Studies*, 60(3), 713–734.

Earle, J. and S. Estrin (1996) "Employee Ownership in Transition" in *Corporate Governance in Central Europe and Russia* (R. Frydman, C. Gray and A. Rapaczynski, eds.), World Bank/CEI Press.

Guriev, S. O. Lazareva, A. Rachisky and S. Tsukhlo (2002) *Spros na sovremennye standarty korporativnogo upravlenia v chastnom sektore Rossii*. New Economic School, Moscow.

Guriev, S., O. Lazareva, A. Rachinsky, S. Tsukhlo (2003) Corporate Governance in Russian Industry. CEFIR Working Paper, Moscow.

Filatochev, I. and A. Swain (1997) "Problems of Restructuring of Former State-Owned Enterprises in Russia, Hungary and China: Case Studies of Car-Making Firms," *Russian and Euro-Asian Bulletin*, University of Melbourne.

Fox, Merritt B. and Michael A. Heller (1999) "Lessons from Fiascos in Russian Corporate Governance." University of Michigan Law School Working Paper 99–012.

Frydman, R., C. Gray, M. Hessel and A. Rapaczynski. (1999) "When Does Privatization Work? The Impact of Private Ownership on Corporate Performance in the Transition Economies," *Quarterly Journal of Economics*, 114(4), 1153–1191.

Hart, O. (1995): "Corporate Governance: Some Theory and Implications," *The Economic Journal*, 105(430), 678–689.

Jensen, M. and W. Meckling (1976) "Theory of the Firm: Management Behavior, Agency Costs and Ownership Structure," *Journal of Financial Economics*. 3(4), 305–360.

Kapelyushnikov, R. (2001): The Largest and Dominant Shareholders in the Russian Industry: Evidence of the Russian Economic Barometer Monitoring, *Journal of East-West Business*, 6(4), 63–88.

Konstantinov, G., I. Lipsits, S. Filonovich (2002). Kak vybrat'sia iz lovushki molodosti. Ekspert, No. 5. Available at www.expert.ru/rus_business/2002/02/08ex-lipsic/

Kuznetsova, O. and A. Kuznetsov (2001) "The Virtues and Weaknesses of Insider Shareholding," *Journal of East-West Business*, 6(4), 89–106.

Kuznetsov, A. and O. Kuznetsova (2003) "Corporate Governance: Does the Concept Work in Transition Countries?" *Journal for East European Management Studies*, 8(3), 244–262.

LaPorta, R., F. Lopez-de-Silanes, A. Shleifer, and Vishny, R. (1997) Legal determinants of external finance. Journal of Finance 52(3): 1131–1150.

McAlister, D. T., O. Ferrell and L. Ferrell (2003) *Business and Society: A Strategic Approach to Corporate Citizenship*, Houghton Mifflin, Boston, MA.

Index of Economic Freedom 2005 *The Wall Street Journal*, January 12, 2005. Available at www.heritage.org/research/features/index/countries.cfm?sortby=country.

Mileusnic, Natasha, (1996) "The Great Boardroom Revolution", *Moscow Times*, July 16.

Milgrom, P. and J. Roberts (1992) *Economics, Organisation and Management*, Englewood Cliffs, NJ: Prentice Hall.

Moerland P. (1995) "Alternative Disciplinary Mechanisms in Different Corporate Systems," *Journal of Economic Behavior & Organization*, 26(1), 17–34.

Nellis, J. (1999) "Time to Rethink Privatization in Transition Economies?" *Transition*, 10(1), 4–6.

OECD (Organisation for Economic Cooperation and Development). (2002) White Paper on Corporate Governance in Russia. Available at www.oecd.org/dataoecd/10/3/2789982.pdf.

Pohl, G. and S. Claessens (1994) "Banks, Capital Markets, and Corporate Governance. Lessons from Russia for Eastern Europe," Policy Research Working Paper 1326, Washington: World Bank.

Potthof, E. (1996) Board-System versus duales System der Unternehmungsverwaltung – Vor – und Nachteile, Betriebswirtschaftliche Forschung und Praxis 3/96: 253–268.

Radaev, V. (1998) *Formirovanie novykh Rossiiskikh rynkov: transaktsionnyje izderzhki, formy kontrolia i delovaia etika.* Moscow, CIPE/Tsentr politicheskikh tekhnologij.

Radaev V., (2002) "Rossijskij biznes: na puti k legalizatsii?" *Voprosy ekonomiki*, (1), 68–87.

Rozman, R. (2000) "The Organizational Function of Governance," *Management*, 5(2), 99–115.

Shelley, L. (1997) "The Price Tag of Russia's Organized Crime," *Transition: The Newsletter About Reforming Economies*, February 1997, Washington: World Bank.

Sizov, Y. (2004) Novyi vitok korporativnykh konfliktov. Aktsionernoe obshevstvo: voprosy korporativnogo upravleniia. November 2004. Available at www.soveknik.orc.ru/texts/sizov.htm

Stiglitz, Joseph E. (2002) *Globalization and its Discontents*. New York: W.W. Norton.

Sullivan, John D. (2002) "Democracy, Governance and the Market." Center for International Private Enterprise. Available at http://usinfo.state.gov/journals/ites/0901/ijee/sullivan.htm

Williamson, O. (1985) *The Economic Institutions of Capitalism*, New York: Free Press.

World Bank (2001): *World Development Report*, Washington DC.

Yoshimori, M. (1995) "Whose Company Is It? The Concept of the Corporation in Japan and the West," *Long Range Planning*, 286(4), 33–44.

Chapter 33
Timeliness of Financial Reporting in the Russian Energy Sector

Robert W. McGee

33.1 Introduction

Transparency is one of those terms that has many facets. It is used in different ways. It can refer to the openness of governmental functions. It can refer to a country's economy. Or it can refer to various aspects of corporate governance and financial reporting. The Organization for Economic Cooperation and Development (OECD, 1998) lists transparency as one element of good corporate governance. Kulzick (2004) and others (Blanchet, 2002; Prickett, 2002) view transparency from a user perspective. According to their view, transparency includes the following eight concepts:

- Accuracy
- Consistency
- Appropriateness
- Completeness
- Clarity
- Timeliness
- Convenience
- Governance and enforcement

This chapter focuses on just one aspect of transparency – timeliness.

The International Accounting Standards Board considers timeliness to be an essential aspect of financial reporting. In APB Statement No. 4, the Accounting Principles Board (1970) in the United States listed timeliness as one of the qualitative objectives of financial reporting disclosure. APB Statement No. 4 was later superseded but the Financial Accounting Standards Board continued to recognize the importance of timeliness in its Concepts Statement No. 2 (1980). The US Securities and Exchange Commission also recognizes the importance of timeliness and requires that listed companies file their annual 10-K reports by a certain deadline.

R. W. McGee
Florida International University

The issue of timeliness has several facets. There is an inverse relationship between the quality of financial information and the timeliness with which it is reported (Kenley and Staubus, 1974). Accounting information becomes less relevant with the passage of time (Atiase et al., 1989; Hendriksen and van Breeda, 1992; Lawrence and Glover, 1998).

Studies show mixed conclusions regarding the relationship of quickness of reporting and the nature of the information being reported. Some studies show that good news is reported before bad news whereas other studies show that bad news is reported before good news.

There is some evidence to suggest that it takes more time to report bad news than good news (Bates, 1968; Beaver, 1968), both because companies hesitate to report bad news and because companies take more time to massage the numbers or resort to creative accounting techniques when they have to report bad news (Givoli and Palmon, 1982; Chai and Tung, 2002; Trueman, 1990). Stated differently, there seems to be a tendency to rush good news to press, such as better than expected earnings, and delay the reporting of bad news or less than expected earnings (Chambers and Penman, 1984; Kross and Schroeder, 1984). Dwyer and Wilson (1989) found this relationship to hold true for municipalities. Haw, Qi and Wu (2000) found it to be the case with Chinese companies. Leventis and Weetman (2004) found it to be the case for Greek firms.

However, Annaert, DeCeuster, Polfliet, and Campenhout (2002) found that this was not the case for Belgian companies and Han and Wang (1998) found that this was not the case for petroleum refining companies, which delayed reporting extraordinarily high profits during the Gulf crisis of the 1990s, perhaps because political repercussions outweighed what would otherwise have been a good market reaction. Rees and Giner (2001) found that companies in France, Germany, and the UK tended to report bad news sooner than good news.

A study by Basu (1997) found that companies tend to report bad news quicker than good news, presumably because of conservatism. Gigler and Hemmer (2001) discuss this point in their study, which finds that firms with more conservative accounting systems are less likely to make timely voluntary disclosures than are firms with less conservative accounting systems.

Building upon the Basu study (1997), Pope and Walker (1997) found that there were cross-jurisdictional effects when extraordinary items were either included or excluded, using US and UK firms for comparison. Han and Wild (1997) examined the potential relationship between earnings timeliness and the share price reactions of competing firms. But Jindrichovska and Mcleay (2005) found that there was no evidence of conservatism in the Czech accounting system when it came to reporting bad news earlier than good news, presumably because the Czech tax system offers little incentive to do so. Ball, Kathari, and Robin (2000) found that companies in jurisdictions that have a strong shareholder orientation tend to disclose earnings information sooner than companies in countries operating under a legal code system.

There is also a relationship between the speed with which financial results are announced and the effect the announcement has on stock prices. If information is released sooner, the effect on stock prices is more pronounced. The longer the time lapse between year-end and the release of the financial information, the lesser is the effect on stock price, all other things being equal (Ball and Brown, 1968; Brown and Kennelly, 1972). This phenomenon can be explained by the fact that financial information seems to seep into the stock price over time, so the more time that elapses between year-end and the release of the financial reports, the more such information is already included in the stock price.

Some countries report financial results faster than other countries. DeCeuster and Trappers (1993) found that Belgian companies take longer to report their financial results than do Anglo-Saxon countries. Annaert, DeCeuster, Polfliet, and Campenhout (2002) found this to be the case for interim information as well. Companies can report financial results faster on the Internet and the information can be more widely disbursed, but posting 2-year-old annual reports does nothing to improve timeliness (Ashbaugh et al., 1999).

Atiase, Bamber, and Tse (1989) found that large companies report earnings faster than small companies and that the reporting of earnings has a more significant market reaction for small firms than for large firms. In a study of Australian firms, Davies and Whittred (1980) found that small firms and large firms made significantly more timely reports than medium-size firms and that profitability was not a significant variable.

Whittred (1980) found that the release of financial information for Australian companies is delayed the first time an audit firm issues a qualified report and that the extent of the delay is longer in cases where the qualification is more serious. Keller (1986) replicated that study for US companies and found the same to be true. Whittred and Zimmer (1984) found that it took Australian firms in financial distress a significantly longer time to publish their financial information. A study of more than 5,000 annual reports of French companies found that it took longer to release audit reports where there had been a qualified opinion, and that the more serious the qualification, the greater the delay in releasing the report (Soltani, 2002).

Krishnan (2005) found that the audit firm's degree of expertise has an effect on the timeliness of the publication of bad earnings news. Audit firms that specialize in the industry in which the company operates are timelier in reporting bad financial news than are audit firms that have less industry expertise.

33.2 Timeliness

One measure of transparency and quality of financial reporting is timeliness. The lapse of time between a company's year-end and the date when financial information is released to the public is related to the quality of the information reported. Issuing excellent, accurate, and comprehensive financial information 2 or 3 years after year-end is not as desirable as issuing less comprehensive and complete financial information a few months after year-end. Financial information becomes stale after a few months, and certainly after 2 or 3 years. The more stale it is, the less relevant it is to potential investors and creditors.

There are a number of reasons for the time lag between year-end and the issuance of the audit report and the publication of financial information. Ashton, Graul, and

Newton (1989) identified auditor size, industry classification, the presence or absence of extraordinary items, and the sign of net income as some factors that influence timeliness. To that one might add the cultural, political, and economic system of the country in which the particular firm is located. One purpose of the present study is to determine whether Russian companies are any less timely in the speed of financial reporting than companies in Western Europe and the United States.

In the not too distant past, some Russian enterprises were criticized for waiting too long to issue their financial reports. Some Russian companies did not issue their annual reports until a year or more after the end of the year. In some cases, Russian firms did not even have annual audits.

Measuring timeliness is relatively easy. The present study measures timeliness by computing the number of days that elapse between the company's year-end and the date of the auditor's report. Data for some large Russian companies in the energy sector are calculated and compared to those of selected non-Russian companies in the petroleum refining industry.

33.3 Comparing Russian and Non-Russian Company Data

Data were collected from company websites. The dates used were the dates of the auditor's report, which is not necessarily the same as the date the financial information was released to the public. However, it was not possible to determine when the annual financial reports were published, so the date of the audit opinion was selected as a surrogate. Using this date also made it possible to compare Russian and non-Russian company data.

Table 33.1 shows the number of days it took Russian companies to issue their audit report. The range was 81–181 days, with an average of 148.7 days. In other words, assuming the company's year-end was December 31, some companies published their audit opinion as early as 22 March while others took until 30 June. The average company from this group published its audit report on 29 May.

Non-Russian companies were taken from the *Fortune Global 500* list for 2005, which was published in the July 25, 2005 issue of *Fortune*. The *Fortune* article classified the selected companies as being in the petroleum refining industry. Data for the most recently reported year was chosen. Many companies had already issued their 2005 annual reports by the date this article was written but a few have not. The year in parentheses indicates the year of the annual report.

Table 33.2 shows the date of the most recent audit report for non-Russian companies in the petroleum refining industry. The range was 38–175 days, with an average of 78.6 days. In other words, assuming the company's year-end was December 31, some companies published their audit opinion as early as 7 February while others took until 24 June. The average company from this group published its audit report on 20 March, or in about 70 days before the average Russian energy company.

Chart 33.1 shows the differences between Russian and non-Russian companies graphically.

Is the difference significant? The Wilcoxon test says the difference is highly significant ($p < = 0.003941$).

Table 33.1 Russian oil, gas & energy companies

Company	Days delay in issuing audit report
Gazprom (2004) www.gazprom.ru	139
Lukoil (2004) www.lukoil.ru	144
RAO Unified Energy System of Russia (2004) www.rao-ees.ru/	179
Sibneft (2004) www.sibneft.ru	181
Tatneft (2004) www.tatneft.ru	178
Mosenergo (2004) www.mosenergo.ru/	109
Lenenergo (2004) www.lenenergo.ru/	126
Novatek (2004) www.novatek.ru	147
Irkutskenergo (2004) www.irkutskenergo.ru	81
TNK-BP (2004) www.tnk-bp.ru	180
Rosneft (2004) www.rosneft.ru	175
Transneft (2004) www.transneft.ru	145
Average	148.7

Table 33.2 Days delay in releasing financial information non-Russian companies in petroleum refining

Company	Days delay in issuing audit report
BP [UK] (2004) www.bp.com	38
Exxon Mobil [USA] (2005) www.exxonmobil.com	59
Royal Dutch/Shell Group [Netherlands] (2005) www.shell.com	67
Total [France] (2005) www.total.com	74
Chevron Texaco [USA] (2005) www.chevrontexaco.com	58
ConocoPhillips [USA] (2005) www.conocophillips.com	57
Sinopec [China] (2005) www.sinopec.com.cn	90
ENI [Italy] (2004) www.eni.it	175
Valero Energy [USA] (2005) www.valero.com	60
Marathon Oil [USA] (2005) www.marathon.com	62
Statoil [Norway] (2005) www.statoil.no	68
Repsol YPF [Spain] (2004) www.respol-ypf.com	91
Petrobras [Brazil] (2004) www.petrobras.com.br	123
Average	78.6

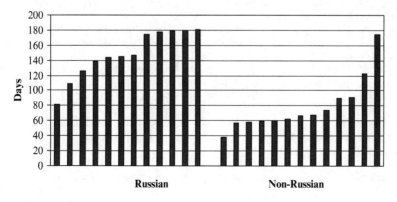

Chart 33.1 Days delay

33.4 Concluding Comments

Russian companies take more than 2 months longer to issue their financial statements than non-Russian companies, which makes their shares less desirable in the international marketplace. The information is not as fresh if its release is delayed by 149 days, which is the average delay. That is 89% longer than it takes non-Russian companies to issue their financial statements.

However, this lag in issuing financial statements may not be as bleak as first appears. Early release of financial information is extremely important in a country like the United States, where a large percentage of capital is equity capital. But many Russian companies rely more on debt capital for financing, which makes the timely release of audited financial statements somewhat less important.

Russian companies must satisfy a different audience – bankers rather than shareholders. Although the views, wants, and needs of shareholders are important in Russia, there is a tendency to pay more attention to bankers if that is where the capital is coming from. Bankers have access to financial information that shareholders do not. If bankers want financial information that is not reported in the annual financial statements, all they need do is demand it as a condition of giving the loan.

Another factor that reduces the importance of this difference in the timeliness of financial reporting is the attractiveness of investment in the industry. Energy has become an increasingly important industry in recent years. Profitability has increased and is expected to remain good for years to come. It is not likely that energy prices will drop significantly. That being the case, potential investors might not place as much emphasis on timely financial reporting as would be the case in a less profitable industry. Thus, although Russian energy companies need to make an effort to be timelier in their financial reporting, the fact that they are not as quick to report financial results as their non-Russian competitors is not necessarily fatal.

References

Accounting Principles Board. 1970. Basic Concepts and Accounting Principles Underlying Financial Statements of Business Enterprises – Statement No. 4. New York: American Institute of Certified Public Accountants.

Annaert, J., Marc J. K. DeCeuster, Ruud Polfliet & Geert Van Campenhout. 2002. To Be or Not Be ... 'Too Late': The Case of the Belgian Semi-annual Earnings Announcements. Journal of Business Finance & Accounting 29(3 & 4): 477–495.

Ashbaugh, H., Karla M. Johnstone & Terry D. Warfield. 1999. Corporate Reporting on the Internet. Accounting Horizons 13(3): 241–257.

Ashton, Robert H., Paul R. Graul & James D. Newton. 1989. Audit Delay and the Timeliness of Corporate Reporting. Contemporary Accounting Research 5(2): 657–673.

Atiase, Rowland K., Linda S. Bamber & Senyo Tse. 1989. Timeliness of Financial Reporting, the Firm Size Effect, and Stock Price Reactions to Annual Earnings Announcements. Contemporary Accounting Research 5(2): 526–552.

Ball, R., Kothari S. P. & Robin A. 2000. The Effect of International Institutional Factors on Properties of Accounting Earnings. Journal of Accounting and Economics 29(1): 1–51.

Ball, R. & Brown P. 1968. An Empirical Evaluation of Accounting Income Numbers. Journal of Accounting Research 6: 159–178.

Basu, Sudipta. 1997. The Conservatism Principle and the Asymmetric Timeliness of Earnings. Journal of Accounting & Economics 24: 3–37.

Bates, R. J. 1968. Discussion of the Information Content of Annual Earnings Announcements. Journal of Accounting Research 6 (Suppl): 93–95.

Beaver, W. H. 1968. The Information Content of Annual Earnings Announcements. Journal of Accounting Research 6 (Suppl): 67–92.

Blanchet, Jeannot. 2002. Global Standards Offer Opportunity. Financial Executive (March/April): 28–30.

Brown, P. & John W. Kennelly. 1972. The Information Content of Quarterly Earnings: An Extension and Some Further Evidence. Journal of Business 45: 403–415.

Chai, Mary L. & Samuel Tung. 2002. The Effect of Earnings-Announcement Timing on Earnings Management. Journal of Business Finance & Accounting 29 (9 & 10): 1337–1354.

Chambers, Anne E. & Stephen H. Penman. 1984. Timeliness of Reporting and the Stock Price Reaction to Earnings Announcements. Journal of Accounting Research 22(1): 21–47.

Davies, B. & Whittred G. P. 1980. The Association between Selected Corporate Attributes and Timeliness in Corporate Reporting: Further Analysis. Abacus 16(1): 48–60.

DeCeuster, M. & Trappers D. 1993. Determinants of the Timeliness of Belgian Financial Statements. Working Paper, University of Antwerp, cited in Annaert et al., 2002.

Dwyer, Peggy D. & Earl R. Wilson. 1989. An Empirical Investigation of Factors Affecting the Timeliness of Reporting by Municipalities. Journal of Accounting and Public Policy 8(1): 29–55.

Financial Accounting Standards Board. 1980. Statement of Financial Accounting Concepts No. 2, Qualitative Characteristics of Accounting Information. Stamford, CT: Financial Accounting Standards Board.

Gigler, Frank B. & Thomas Hemmer. 2001. Conservatism, Optimal Disclosure Policy, and the Timeliness of Financial Reports. The Accounting Review 76(4): 471–493.

Givoli, Dan & Dan Palmon. 1982. Timeliness of Annual Earnings Announcements: Some Empirical Evidence. The Accounting Review 57(3): 486–508.

Han, Jerry C. Y. & Shiing-wu Wang. 1998. Political Costs and Earnings Management of Oil Companies During the 1990 Persian Gulf Crises. The Accounting Review 73: 103–117.

Han, Jerry C. Y. & John J. Wild. 1997. Timeliness of Reporting and Earnings Information Transfers. Journal of Business Finance & Accounting 24 (3 & 4): 527–540.

Haw, In-Mu, Daquig Qi & Woody Wu. 2000. Timeliness of Annual Report Releases and Market Reaction to Earnings Announcements in an Emerging Capital Market: The Case of China. Journal of International Financial Management and Accounting 11(2): 108–131.

Hendriksen, Eldon S. and Michael F. van Breda. 1992. Accounting Theory, fifth edition, Burr Ridge, IL: Irwin.

Jindrichovska, Irina and Stuart Mcleay. 2005. Accounting for Good News and Accounting for Bad News: Some Empirical Evidence from the Czech Republic. European Accounting Review 14(3): 635–655.

Keller, Stuart B. 1986. Reporting Timeliness in the Presence of Subject to Audit Qualifications. Journal of Business Finance & Accounting 13(1): 117–124.

Kenley, W. John & George J. Staubus. 1974. Objectives and Concepts of Financial Statements. Accounting Review 49(4): 888–889.

Krishnan, Gopal V. 2005. The Association between Big 6 Auditor Industry Expertise and the Asymmetric Timeliness of Earnings. Journal of Accounting, Auditing & Finance 20(3): 209–228.

Kross, W. & Schroeder D. A. 1984. An Empirical Investigation of the Effect of Quarterly Earnings Announcement Timing on Stock Returns. Journal of Accounting Research 22(1): 153–176.

Kulzick, Raymond S. 2004. Sarbanes-Oxley: Effects on Financial Transparency. S.A.M. Advanced Management Journal 69(1): 43–49.

Lawrence, Janice E. & Hubert D. Glover 1998. The Effect of Audit Firm Mergers on Audit Delay. Journal of Managerial Issues 10(2): 151–164.

Leventis, S. & Pauline W. 2004. Timeliness of Financial Reporting: Applicability of Disclosure Theories in an Emerging Capital Market. Accounting and Business Research 34(1): 43–56.

Organisation for Economic Cooperation and Development. 1998. Global Corporate Governance Principles. Paris: OECD.

Pope, Peter F. & Walker M. 1999. International Differences in the Timeliness, Conservatism, and Classification of Earnings. Journal of Accounting Research 37 (Suppl): 53–87.

Prickett, Ruth. 2002. Sweet Clarity. Financial Management (September): 18–20.

Rees, William P. & Begona G. 2001. On the Asymmetric Recognition of Good and Bad News in France, Germany and the UK. Journal of Business Finance & Accounting 28 (9 & 10): 1285–1332.

Soltani, Bahram. 2002. Timeliness of Corporate and Audit Reports: Some Empirical Evidence in the French Context. The International Journal of Accounting 37: 215–246.

Trueman, Brett. 1990. Theories of Earnings-Announcement Timing. Journal of Accounting & Economics 13: 285–301.

Whittred, G.P. 1980. Audit Qualification and the Timeliness of Corporate Annual Reports. The Accounting Review 55(4): 563–577.

Whittred, G. & Zimmer I. 1984. Timeliness of Financial Reporting and Financial Distress. The Accounting Review 59(2): 287–295.

Chapter 34
The Timeliness of Financial Reporting and the Russian Banking System: An Empirical Study

Robert W. McGee and Thomas Tarangelo

34.1 Introduction

Transparency is one of those terms that have many facets. It is used in different ways. It can refer to the openness of governmental functions. It can refer to a country's economy. Or it can refer to various aspects of corporate governance and financial reporting. The OECD (1998) lists transparency as one element of good corporate governance. Kulzick (2004) and others (Blanchet, 2002; Prickett, 2002) view transparency from a user's perspective. According to their view, transparency includes the following eight concepts: accuracy, consistency, appropriateness, completeness, clarity, timeliness, convenience, and governance and enforcement. This paper focuses on just one aspect of transparency – timeliness.

The International Accounting Standards Board considers timeliness to be an essential aspect of financial reporting. In APB Statement No. 4, the Accounting Principles Board (1970) in the USA listed timeliness as one of the qualitative objectives of financial reporting disclosure. APB Statement No. 4 was later superseded but the Financial Accounting Standards Board continued to recognize the importance of timeliness in its Concepts Statement No. 2 (1980). The US Securities and Exchange Commission also recognizes the importance of timeliness and requires that listed companies file their annual 10-K reports by a certain deadline.

The issue of timeliness has several facets. There is an inverse relationship between the quality of financial information and the timeliness with which it is reported (Kenley and Staubus, 1974). Accounting information becomes less relevant with the passage of time (Atiase et al., 1989; Hendriksen and van Breeda, 1992; Lawrence and Glover, 1998).

R. W. McGee and T. Tarangelo
Florida International University

R. W. McGee (ed.), *Accounting Reform in Transition and Developing Economies,*
© Springer Science+Business Media LLC 2008

34.2   Review of the Literature

Studies show mixed conclusions regarding the relationship of quickness of reporting and the nature of the information being reported. Some studies show that good news is reported before bad news whereas other studies show that bad news is reported before good news.

There is some evidence to suggest that it takes more time to report bad news than good news (Bates, 1968; Beaver, 1968), both because companies hesitate to report bad news and because companies take more time to massage the numbers or resort to creative accounting techniques when they have to report bad news (Givoli and Palmon, 1982; Chai and Tung, 2002; Trueman, 1990). Stated differently, there seems to be a tendency to rush good news to press, such as better-than-expected earnings, and delay the reporting of bad news or less-than-expected earnings (Chambers and Penman, 1984; Kross and Schroeder, 1984). Dwyer and Wilson (1989) found this relationship to hold true for municipalities. Haw, Qi, and Wu (2000) found it to be the case with Chinese companies. Leventis and Weetman (2004) found it to be the case for Greek firms.

However, Annaert, DeCeuster, Polfliet, and Campenhout (2002) found that this was not the case for Belgian companies and Han and Wang (1998) found that this was not the case for petroleum refining companies, which delayed reporting extraordinarily high profits during the Gulf crisis of the 1990s, perhaps because political repercussions outweighed what would otherwise have been a good market reaction. Rees and Giner (2001) found that companies in France, Germany, and the UK tended to report bad news sooner than good news.

A study by Basu (1997) found that companies tend to report bad news quicker than good news, presumably because of conservatism. Gigler and Hemmer (2001) discuss this point in their study, which finds that firms with more conservative accounting systems are less likely to make timely voluntary disclosures than are firms with less conservative accounting systems.

Building upon the Basu study (1997), Pope and Walker (1997) found that there were cross-jurisdictional effects when extraordinary items were either included or excluded, using US and UK firms for comparison. Han and Wild (1997) examined the potential relationship between earnings timeliness and the share price reactions of competing firms. But Jindrichovska and Mcleay (2005) found that there was no evidence of conservatism in the Czech accounting system when it came to reporting bad news earlier than good news, presumably because the Czech tax system offers little incentive to do so. Ball, Kathari, and Robin (2000) found that companies in jurisdictions that have a strong shareholder orientation tend to disclose earnings information sooner than companies in countries operating under a legal code system.

There is also a relationship between the speed with which financial results are announced and the effect the announcement has on stock prices. If information is released sooner, the effect on stock prices is more pronounced. The longer the time lapse between year-end and the release of the financial information, the less effect there is on stock price, all other things being equal (Ball and Brown, 1968; Brown and Kennelly, 1972). This phenomenon can be explained by the fact that financial information seems to seep into the stock price over time, so the more time that elapses between year-end and the release of the financial reports, the more such information is already included in the stock price.

Some countries report financial results faster than other countries. DeCeuster and Trappers (1993) found that Belgian companies take longer to report their financial results than do Anglo-Saxon countries. Annaert, DeCeuster, Polfliet, and Campenhout (2002) found this to be the case for interim information as well. Companies can report financial results faster on the Internet and the information can be more widely disbursed but posting 2-year-old annual reports does nothing to improve timeliness (Ashbaugh et al., 1999).

Atiase, Bamber, and Tse (1989) found that large companies report earnings faster than small companies and that the reporting of earnings has a more significant market reaction for small firms than for large firms. In a study of Australian firms, Davies and Whittred (1980) found that small firms and large firms made significantly more timely reports than medium-sized firms and that profitability was not a significant variable.

Whittred (1980) found that the release of financial information for Australian companies is delayed the first time an audit firm issues a qualified report and that the extent of the delay is longer in cases where the qualification is more serious. Keller (1986) replicated that study for US companies and found the same thing to be true. Whittred and Zimmer (1984) found that it took Australian firms in financial distress a significantly longer time to publish their financial information. A study of more than 5,000 annual reports of French companies found that it took longer to release audit reports where there had been a qualified opinion, and that the more serious the qualification, the greater the delay in releasing the report (Soltani, 2002).

Krishnan (2005) found that the audit firm's degree of expertise has an effect on the timeliness of the publication of bad earnings news. Audit firms that specialize in the industry in which the company operates are timelier in reporting bad financial news than are audit firms that have less industry expertise.

A few studies have been published that compare the timeliness of financial reporting in transition economies and the more developed market economies. McGee (2006, 2007b) found that companies in the Russian energy sector take a significantly longer amount of time to report financial results than do non-Russian companies in the energy sector. Another study found the same thing to be true of the Russian telecom industry (McGee, 2007a). A comparative study of Chinese and non-Chinese companies found that Chinese companies took significantly longer to report than non-Chinese companies (McGee and Yuan, 2008). But a study comparing new EU countries that are also transition economies to EU countries that are not transition economies found no difference in timeliness (McGee and Igoe, 2008).

34.3 Methodology

Timeliness was determined by counting the number of days that elapsed between year-end and the date of the auditor's report. Some data was gathered from www.rustocks.com, a web site that contains a wealth of information on Russian companies.

Other data was gathered by going directly to the Russian company web sites or www.sec.gov.

Such a methodology is less than perfect for several reasons. For one, the date on the audit report might not be the same as the date the information was released to the general public. However, there is no way to obtain the date the information was released to the general public, so the date on the audit report acted as a surrogate for the actual release date.

Secondly, the sample only consisted of annual reports that were in the English language. However, this skewed sample does not constitute a fatal flaw, since it is likely that Russian banks that do not publish their financial statements in the English language are not seeking foreign investment anyway, so having a sample that consists of only English language annual reports actually does a good job of capturing the banks that are most likely looking for foreign capital. It is this group that is most likely to be concerned with the timeliness of financial reporting. Banks that are not trying to attract foreign capital have little or no pressure to publish their financial statements in any language, even though Russian law requires it, since the penalties for noncompliance are slight or none.

Another possible criticism of the present study is that some Russian banks report only 1 or 2 years worth of data while others publish 10 or more years of data. Analyzing data where the sample population differs by year is not as desirable as analyzing data where the sample sizes by year are about the same. However, the sample population was small to begin with, so the authors decided that it was better to enlarge the sample size even if that meant having sample sizes that differed by year. The alternative would have been to be forced to work with a much smaller sample size. In the few cases where banks reported more than 10 years of data, the authors selected only the 10 most recent years. Financial reporting practiced in Russia and other former Soviet republics has changed drastically since the implosion of the Soviet Union and it was thought that using data that was more than 10 years old would not provide a fair reflection of current accounting practices.

The data found was sometimes incomplete. Some annual reports disclosed the date of the audit report but not the auditor, or the auditor but not the date of the audit report. Some annual reports disclosed the accounting principles used while others did not. In cases where the company issued consolidated financial statements and also separate financial statements, the authors chose the date of the audit report for the consolidated financial statements.

34.4 Findings

34.4.1 Days Reporting Delay

Table 34.1 shows the data for all years. Data were found for 73 Russian banks. The sample size was 254, meaning that the authors could find 254 usable annual reports.

Table 34.1 Sample statistics – all years

Sample size	
Number of Banks	73
Years of Data	254
Measures of Central Tendency	
Range [January 18–December 12]	18–346 days
Mean [April 9]	98.8 days
Median [April 14]	104 days

The range was 18 to 346 days, meaning that one Russian bank had an audit report date that was 18 days after year-end while another Russian bank had an audit report dated 346 days after year-end. The arithmetic mean for all years was 98.8 days, which means that the average Russian bank with a December 31 year-end had an audit report dated April 9. The median for all years was 104 days, or April 14, meaning that half of the Russian banks had an audit report date before April 14 and half had a date after April 14.

To place things in perspective it would be useful to compare the measures of central tendency for Russian banks and non-Russian banks. We did not do that in the present study because of time constraints. However, studies that used this methodology to determine the timeliness of financial reporting for non-Russian companies found that it took fewer days for non-Russian companies to issue an audit report. The specifics are as follows:

145.5 days for Russian companies in the energy sector vs. 70.2 days for non-Russian energy companies (McGee 2007b)

138.3 days for Russian telecom companies vs. 63.2 days for non-Russian telecom companies (McGee 2007a)

136.6 days for Russian companies in various industries (McGee 2007c)

A few studies of non-Russian companies have also computed the number of days it takes to issue an audit report after year-end. The statistics for Chinese vs. non-Chinese companies and new EU entrants vs. old EU member countries are given below.

92.1 days for Chinese companies vs. 65.5 days for non-Chinese companies (McGee & Yuan 2008)

84.7 days for new EU entrants that are transition economies vs. 85.6 days for old EU member countries

Chart 34.1 shows the range of days for Russian banks.

Although no studies have ever been done to our knowledge that compute the number of days delay in issuing audit opinions for non-Russian banks, it would be useful to compare data for the studies of timeliness that have been done.[1] Table 34.2 summarizes the results of prior studies.

---

[1] The authors are working on such a study. The results will be published in Robert W. McGee, Corporate Governance in Transition Economies, New York: Springer (2008 or 2009).

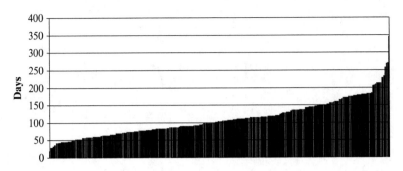

Chart 34.1 Range of days – Russian banks

Table 34.2 Days delay – findings from prior studies

Rank	Sample	Days delay
1	Non-Russian telecom (McGee 2007a)	63.2
2	Non-Chinese companies (McGee & Yuan 2008)	65.5
3	Non-Russian energy (McGee 2007b)	70.2
4	New EU countries (McGee & Igoe 2008)	84.7
5	Old EU countries (McGee & Igoe 2008)	85.6
6	Chinese companies (McGee & Yuan 2008)	92.1
7	Russian banks (present study)	98.8
8	Russian companies (McGee 2007c)	136.6
9	Russian telecom (McGee 2007a)	138.3
10	Russian energy (McGee 2007b)	145.5

It is not surprising that Russian companies in general take longer to report financial information, since they are relatively new to the financial reporting game. It is also not surprising that Russian banks do a better job of reporting financial information in a timely fashion than do Russian companies in other industries, since transition economies have a tendency to reform financial reporting practices in the banking sector first, before attention is paid to accounting reform in other sectors of the economy. What is slightly surprising is that Chinese companies in general are faster at reporting financial results than are Russian banks. If one were to do a study of the Chinese banking industry, this difference would likely be even more pronounced, since the banking industry in transition economies tend to have better financial reporting practices than the average industry.

Chart 34.2 shows the differences graphically.

The above data on Russian banks combines all the data collected. Some of that data is as old as 1998 while some is as recent as 2007. If there is any kind of trend it would be impossible to spot it, given the fact that the data are combined. If the data could be disaggregated it might be possible to spot a trend. One might assume that the timeliness of financial reporting for Russian banks would get better over time, but that is just an assumption. It can be tested by examining the data for each year individually. Table 34.3 does that.

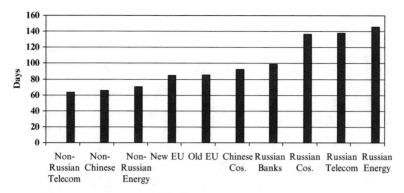

Chart 34.2 Days delay – study comparison (mean) scores

Table 34.3 Timeliness data for Russian banks by year

Year	Sample size	Low	High	Mean	Median
1998	2	113	182	147.5	147.5
1999	4	42	174	87.8	67.5
2000	9	45	180	89.3	73.0
2001	13	44	184	90.2	81.0
2002	25	45	232	108.9	100.0
2003	41	29	346	108.1	86.0
2004	53	18	270	113.5	98.0
2005	51	31	181	108.0	104.0
2006	56	51	258	118.6	117.0
2007	2	81	107	94.0	94.0

Sample sizes for some years are too small to draw any conclusions but the sample sizes for other years are sufficiently large to draw some tentative conclusions. Chart 34.3 shows the median scores graphically for all years that had a sample size larger than 10. It was thought that examining median scores would be more meaningful than looking at mean scores, since outliers could distort mean scores but would not distort median scores.

The results are somewhat surprising. One would think that the Russian banking sector, which is probably one of the most advanced sectors in terms of financial reporting, would become timelier in its financial reporting practices over time. But Chart 34.3 shows that just the opposite has happened. With the exception of 2002, it has taken more time to report financial results with each succeeding year.

By looking at the bar chart one might easily conclude that the trend is to take significantly more time to report financial results over time. However, one need not be content with a conclusion that is reached solely by visual inspection of the data. One may take a more scientific approach. Submitting the data to a nonparametric test such as the Wilcoxon Test could provide further evidence of a significant trend. Table 34.4 shows the results of those tests.

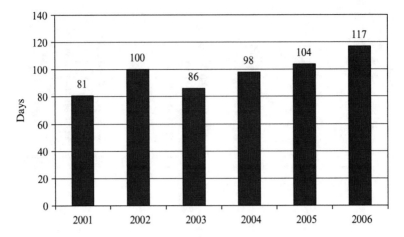

Chart 34.3 Timeliness trend (median scores)

Table 34.4 Tests of significance

Years compared	p Value
2001 vs. 2002	0.2301
2001 vs. 2003	0.3215
2001 vs. 2004	0.156
2001 vs. 2005	0.1167
2001 vs. 2006	0.01967*
2003 vs. 2004	0.4103
2003 vs. 2005	0.2907
2003 vs. 2006	0.04384*
2004 vs. 2005	0.9974
2004 vs. 2006	0.3013
2005 vs. 2006	0.1759

* Significant at 5% level

A statistical analysis shows that the trend, if measured from 2001 to 2006, is significant at the 5% level. The trend for the shorter period of 2003 to 2006 is also significant at the 5% level. Thus, it can be concluded that the trend in the Russian banking industry is to take more time to report financial results with each passing year.

34.4.2 Auditor

Another bit of data worth examining is which audit firms audit Russian banks. Prior studies have found that the Big-4 accounting firms have a dominant position in the audit of large Russian and Ukrainian companies (McGee and Preobragenskaya 2005, 2006). It is reasonable to expect that the Big-4 have a dominant position in the Russian banking industry. Table 34.5 shows the relative frequency for the various audit firms where information was available. In some cases the audit firm could not be determined.

Table 34.6 shows the concentration for the Big-4 accounting firms.

Table 34.6 shows that the Big-4 firms are clearly dominant with 85% of the banking market. However, these data do not report on the whole banking market but only that segment of the banking market that issues English language financial statements. This segment is also the segment represented by large international banks. Chart 34.4 shows the extent of Big-4 dominance graphically.

Table 34.5 Audit firm – all years

	#	%
Audit Ltd. (a Russian firm)	2	0.7
BDO Unicon	2	0.7
Deloitte & Touche	61	22.8
Ernst & Young	41	15.4
Grant Thornton	2	0.7
KPMG	52	19.5
OOO Audit (a Russian firm)	2	0.7
PKF (a large Russian firm)	4	1.5
PricewaterhouseCoopers	73	27.3
Other Russian	28	10.5
Total	267	

Table 34.6 Market share of big-4 firms

Firm	% Of total	Cumulative %
PricewaterhouseCoopers	27.3	27.3
Deloitte & Touche	22.8	50.1
KPMG	19.5	69.6
Ernst & Young	15.4	85.0

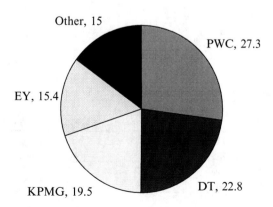

Chart 34.4 Big-4 market share (all years)

The above analysis of audit firm dominance used data for several years, some going back as far as 1998. Perhaps dominance for the most recent year is difference from the weighted average dominance analyzed above. Audit firm data for the most recent year is shown in Table 34.7. In a few cases the audit firm issuing the auditor's report could not be determined.

Table 34.8 shows the market share for each of the Big-4 firms for both the most recent year and on a weighted average basis. As can be seen, market dominance has declined somewhat, from 85% on a weighted average basis to 82.6% for the most current year reported. The relative market share increased for Deloitte & Touche and Ernst & Young and declined for the other two Big-4 firms. Chart 34.5 shows the relative market share of the Big-4 firms for the most recent year reported.

It is reasonable to expect that a decline in market share would occur over time. When the Russian banking system first opened up to the West, none of the Russian audit firms had sufficient expertise in International Accounting Standards to conduct audits of banks that issued financial statements using IAS. Banks had to go to the Big-4 (or Big-5 in the early days) or other international accounting firms like Grant Thornton or BDO Seidman. With the passage of time, Russian audit firms became more educated in IAS and were in a better position to audit banks and other companies that issue IAS-based financial statements.

Table 34.7 Audit firm – most recent year

	#	%
BDO Unicon	1	1.4
Deloitte & Touche	18	26.1
Ernst & Young	12	17.4
Grant Thornton	1	1.4
KPMG	12	17.4
PKF	1	1.4
PricewaterhouseCoopers	15	21.7
Other Russian	9	13.0
Total	69	

Table 34.8 Market share of big-4 firms – most current year and weighted average

Firm	% Of total (weighted average)	% Of total (current year)	Cumulative % (current year)
Deloitte & Touche	22.8	26.1	26.1
PricewaterhouseCoopers	27.3	21.7	47.8
KPMG	19.5	17.4	65.2
Ernst & Young	15.4	17.4	82.6

Chart 34.5 Big-4 market share (most recent years)

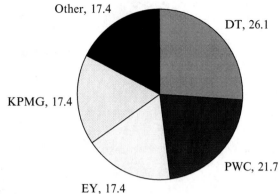

Other, 17.4

DT, 26.1

KPMG, 17.4

PWC, 21.7

EY, 17.4

Table 34.9 Accounting standards used – all years

Standard	#	%
IAS/IFRS	204	78.2
RAS	50	19.2
USGAAP	7	2.7
Total	261	

34.4.3   Accounting Standards Used

It is reasonable to expect that a high percentage of Russian banks that want to go into international capital markets would use one of the two internationally known and respected set of accounting standards – International Financial Reporting Standards (IFRS) or US generally accepted accounting principles (GAAP). With the world trend moving toward IFRS and away from US GAAP it could be expected that IFRS is taking on an increasingly dominant position over time. All Russian companies are required to use Russian Accounting Standards (RAS) for domestic purposes but there is no rule that precludes them from issuing financial statements using other accounting standards as well.

Table 34.9 shows the relative popularity of issuing English language financial statements for all the years under study. For some years it could not be determined which set of accounting standards were used to prepare the annual financial statements. As can be seen, issuing English language financial statements using IAS/IFRS is by far the most popular option.

Table 34.10 shows the relative popularity for the most recent year reported. As can be seen, the trend seems to be toward issuing financial statements using IFRS. The percentage of statements issued using either Russian or US accounting standards has declined over time, as might be expected. Chart 34.6 shows the relative frequencies for the most recent period graphically.

Table 34.11 shows the data used to make the present study.

Table 34.10 Accounting standards used – most recent year

Standard	#	%
IAS/IFRS	56	83.6
RAS	10	14.9
USGAAP	1	1.5
Total	67	

Chart 34.6 Use of accounting standards (most recent years)

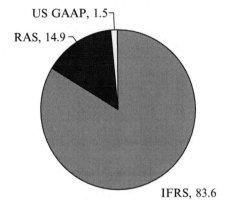

US GAAP, 1.5

RAS, 14.9

IFRS, 83.6

Table 34.11 Sample data

Company name	Year	Days	Auditor	Standards
ABSOLUT BANK	2006	60	PWC	IFRS
	2005	62	PWC	IFRS
	2004	73	PWC	IFRS
	2003	89	PWC	IFRS
	2002	79	PWC	IFRS
	2001	N/A	PWC	IAS
AK BARS BANK	2006	118	PWC	IFRS
	2005	174	PWC	IFRS
	2004	168	PWC	IFRS
ALFA BANK	2006	115	PWC	N/A
	2005	N/A	N/A	N/A
	2004	98	PWC	IFRS
	2003	111	PWC	IFRS
	2002	N/A	N/A	N/A
	2001	N/A	N/A	N/A
	2000	106	PWC	N/A
	1999	174	PWC	N/A

(continued)

Table 34.11 (continued)

Company name	Year	Days	Auditor	Standards
	1998	182	PWC	N/A
ALTA BANK	2005	157	KPMG	IFRS
	2004	171	KPMG	IFRS
APR BANK	2005	86	R	R
	2004	69	R	R
	2003	82	R	R
	2002	56	R	R
	2001	N/A	R	R
	2000	45	R	R
	1999	52	R	R
BANK AVANGARD	2006	117	DT	IFRS
	2005	97	DT	IFRS
	2004	91	DT	IFRS
	2003	86	DT	IFRS
	2002	94	DT	IAS
	2001	102	DT	IAS
	2000	73	DT	R
BANK ELECTRONIKA	2006	156	DT	IFRS
	2005	137	DT	IFRS
	2004	143	DT	IFRS
	2003	118	DT	IFRS
	2002	90	DT	IFRS
BANK OF MOSCOW	2006	86	BDO UNICON	IFRS
BANK PETROCOMMERCE	2006	102	PWC	R
	2005	104	PWC	R
	2004	N/A	PWC	N/A
	2003	146	KPMG	N/A
BANK SNORAS	2004	63	EY	N/A
BANK SOYUZ	2006	118	DT	IFRS
	2005	159	PWC	IFRS
	2004	178	PWC	IFRS
	2003	204	PWC	IFRS
BANK VOZROZHDENIYE	2006	82	PWC	IFRS
	2005	90	PWC	IFRS
	2004	144	PWC	IFRS
	2003	145	PWC	IFRS
	2002	118	PWC	IFRS
	2001	135	PWC	IAS
	2000	135	PWC	IAS
BIN BANK	2006	100	DT	IFRS
	2005	83	DT	IFRS
	2004	63	DT	IFRS
COMMERZBANK (EURASIJA)	2006	107	PWC	R
	2005	104	PWC	R
	2004	124	PWC	R
	2003	N/A	PWC	R
CONVERSBANK	2004	120	EY	IFRS

(continued)

Table 34.11 (continued)

Company name	Year	Days	Auditor	Standards
	2003	77	EY	R
CONVERSBANK FINANCIAL GROUP	2006	N/A	N/A	N/A
	2005	151	EY	IFRS
	2004	120	EY	IFRS
	2003	77	EY	IFRS
	2003	77	EY	R
CREDIT BANK OF MOSCOW	2006	110	KPMG	GAP/US
	2005/2004	97	KPMG	GAP/US
	2004/2003	82	KPMG	GAP/US
	2003/2002	76	KPMG	GAP/US
DENIZBANK FINANCIAL SERVICE GROUP	2005	47	KPMG	IFRS
	2004	47	KPMG	IFRS
	2003	29	R	IFRS
DENIZBANK MOSCOW (DEXIA BANK)	2005	31	GT	IAS
	2004	18	GT	IAS
	2003	42	R	IAS
EVROFINANCE MOSNARBANK	2006	160	DT	IFRS
	2005	N/A	N/A	N/A
	2004	63	AUDIT LTD	R
	2003	86	OOO AUDIT	R
	2002	79	AUDIT LTD.	R
	2001	70	OOO AUDIT	R
FUNDSERVICE BANK	2006	145	PWC	IFRS
	2005	156	PWC	IFRS
	2004	N/A	PWC	IFRS
GARANTI BANK OF MOSCOW	2006	58	KPMG	IFRS
	2005	52	KPMG	IFRS
	2004	63	KPMG	IFRS
	2003	71	KPMG	IFRS
GAZPROMBANK	2006	178	DT	IFRS
	2005	181	DT	IFRS
	2004	117	DT	IFRS
	2003	113	DT	IFRS
	2002	115	DT	IAS
	2001	81	KPMG	R
	2000	47	KPMG	R
	1999	83	KPMG	R
	1998	113	KPMG	R
GLOBEXBANK	2006	170	RA	IFRS
	2005	177	RA	IFRS
	2004	270	RA	IFRS
HOUSING FINANCE BANK	2004	74	N/A	IFRS
	2003	106	N/A	IFRS
	2002	152	N/A	IFRS
INTERNATIONAL INDUSTRIAL	2006	148	DT	IFRS

(continued)

Table 34.11 (continued)

Company name	Year	Days	Auditor	Standards
BANK	2005	N/A	DT	N/A
	2004	N/A	DT	N/A
INTERNATIONAL JOINT STOCK	2006	170	R	IFRS
BANK	2005	N/A	R	R
	2004	N/A	R	R
INTERNATIONAL MOSCOW	2006	53	EY	IFRS
BANK (IMB)	2005	53	EY	IFRS
(UniCredit Bank)	2004	46	EY	IFRS
	2003	49	EY	IFRS
	2002	45	KPMG	IAS
	2001	44	KPMG	IAC
	2000	45	KPMG	IAC
	1999	N/A	KPMG	IAC
INTERPROM BANK	2006	117	DT	R
	2005	N/A	N/A	N/A
	2004	35	DT	R
	2003	N/A	DT	R
	2002	N/A	N/A	N/A
	2001	63	PWC	R
INTERREGIONAL INVESTMENT	2006	258	R	R
BANK	2005	N/A	R	R
INVESTMENT TRADE BANK	2006	150	KPMG	IFRS
	2005	135	KPMG	IFRS
	2004	115	KPMG	IFRS
	2003	346	KPMG	IFRS
KMB BANK (SMALL BUSINESS	2006	61	EY	IFRS
CREDIT BANK)	2005	59	PWC	IFRS
	2004	60	PWC	IFRS
	2003	65	EY	IFRS
	2002	115	PWC	IFRS
	2001	70	PWC	IFRS
LANTA BANK	2006	N/A	R	R
	2005	107	R	N/A
	2004	94	EY	R
LOCKO BANK	2006	86	KPMG	IFRS
	2005	83	KPMG	IFRS
	2004	74	KPMG	IFRS
	2003	75	KPMG	IFRS
	2002	56	KPMG	IFRS
	2001	184	KPMG	IFRS
	2000	180	KPMG	IFRS
MDM BANK	2007	81	KPMG	IFRS
	2006	92	KPMG	IFRS
	2007	107	KPMG	IFRS
MDM FINANCIAL GROUP	2006	92	KPMG	IFRS
	2005	107	KPMG	IFRS

(continued)

Table 34.11 (continued)

Company name	Year	Days	Auditor	Standards
	2004	151	KPMG	IFRS
	2003	138	KPMG	IFRS
	2002	143	PWC	IFRS
	2001	116	PWC	IAS
MEZHTOPENERGOBANK	2006	178	KPMG	IFRS
	2005	177	KPMG	IFRS
	2004	227	KPMG	IFRS
	2003	208	KPMG	IFRS
	2002	232	KPMG	IFRS
MOSCOW BANK FOR	2006	118	DT	IFRS
RECONSTRUCTION & DEV'MENT	2005	69	DT	IFRS
(MBRR)	2004	98	DT	IFRS
	2003	64	DT	R
	2002	108	DT	R
	2001	N/A	DT	R
MOSKOMMERTSBANK	2006	73	DT	IFRS
	2005	59	DT	IFRS
	2004	28	N/A	IFRS
	2003	43	N/A	IFRS
MY BANK GROUP	2006	155	R	IFRS
NATIONAL FACTORING	2006	53	EY	IFRS
COMPANY	2005	46	EY	IFRS
	2004	213	EY	IFRS
NESHPROMBANK	2006	N/A	R	IFRS
	2005	N/A	R	IFRS
NOMOS-BANK	2006	136	DT	IFRS
(NOVAYA MOSKVA)	2005	82	DT	IFRS
	2004	81	DT	IFRS
	2003	72	DT	IFRS
	2002	66	DT	IAS
	2001	60	N/A	IAS
NOTA-BANK	2006	180	PWC	IFRS
ORGRESBANK	2006	110	PWC	IFRS
	2005	90	PWC	IFRS
PROMSVYAZBANK	2006	N/A	N/A	N/A
	2005	137	KPMG	N/A
ROS DOR BANK	2006	N/A	PWC	IFRS
ROSBANK	2006	114	DT	R
	2005	108	DT	R
	2004	N/A	N/A	N/A
	2003	72/118	DT	IFRS
	2002	66	DT	IAS
	2001	N/A	DT	R
	2000	58	DT	R
ROSSELKHOZBANK	2006	113	PWC	IFRS

(continued)

Table 34.11 (continued)

Company name	Year	Days	Auditor	Standards
(RUSSIAN AGRICULTURAL)	2005	116	PWC	IFRS
	2004	171	BDO UNICON	IFRS
	2003	212	PWC	IFRS
	2002	166	PWC	IFRS
	2001	105	PWC	IAS
ROSSIYSKIY KREDIT BANK	2006	180	KPMG	N/A
RUSS-BANK	2006	130	DT	IFRS
	2005	146	DT	IFRS
	2004	91	DT	IFRS
RUSSIAN BANK FOR	2006	71	DT	R
DEVELOPMENT	2005	104	DT	US
	2004	77	DT	US
	2003	51	DT	US
RUSSIAN DEVELOPMENT BANK	2006	166	EY	IFRS
	2005	118	RA	RA
	2004	56	RA	RA
	2003	N/A	N/A	N/A
RUSSIAN STANDARD BANK	2006	92	PWC	IFRS
	2005	100	PWC	IFRS
	2004	N/A	N/A	N/A
	2003	61	PWC	IFRS
	2002	90	PWC	IFRS
	2001	84	PWC	IAS
	2000	115	PWC	IAS
	1999	42	N/A	IAS
RUSSKY SLAVIANSKY BANK	2006	134	PWC	IFRS
(RUSSALBANK)	2005	137	PWC	IFRS
	2004	145	PWC	IFRS
SBERBANK (SAVINGS BANK OF	2006	115	IPWC	IFRS
THE RUSSIAN FEDERATION)	2005	110	PWC	IFRS
	2004	151	EY	IFRS
	2003	177	EY	IFRS
	2002	175	U	IFRS
SDM BANK	2006	92	PKF?	IFRS
	2005	130	PKF?	IFRS
	2004	183	PKF?	IFRS
	2003	212	PKF?	IFRS
SEVERO-VOSTOCHY ALLIANCE	2006	130	R	R
	2005	N/A	N/A	N/A
	2004	N/A	N/A	N/A
	2003	85	PWC	IFRS
	2002	74	PWC	IFRS
SOBINBANK	2006	N/A	RA	R
	2005	N/A	RA	R
	2004	110	RA	R
	2003	110	PWC	R

(continued)

Table 34.11 (continued)

Company name	Year	Days	Auditor	Standards
	2002	100	PWC	R
SOCGORBANK	2006	113	PWC	IFRS
	2005	90	PWC	IFRS
	2004	82	PWC	IFRS
SUDOSTROITELNY BANK	2006	51	DT	IFRS
(COMMERCIAL BANK)	2005	90	DT	IFRS
	2004	269	PWC	IFRS
	2003	182	PWC	IFRS
	2002	212	PWC	IFRS
SVIAZ-BANK	2006	127	DT	N/A
	2005	69	DT	IFRS
	2004	152	DT	IFRS
TEMBR-BANK (Commercial Fuel and Energy Bank for Reconstruction)	2004	91	N/A	N/A
TRANSCAPITAL BANK	2006	61	DT	IFRS
TRANSCREDIT BANK	2006	75	EY	IFRS
	2005	86	EY	IFRS
	2004	90	EY	IFRS
	2003	78	EY	IFRS
	2002	77	EY	IFRS
TRUST INVESTMENT BANK	2006	159	KPMG	IFRS
	2005	79	KPMG	IFRS
	2004	126	KPMG	IFRS
	2003	65	KPMG	IFRS
UNIASTRUM BANK	2005	174	KPMG	IFRS
	2004	207	KPMG	IFRS
	2003	86	N/A	N/A
URAL SIBERIAN BANK	2006	135	EY	IFRS
	2005	142	EY	IFRS
	2004	77	EY	IFRS
VNESHECONOMBANK	2006	127	EY	IFRS
	2005	95	EY	IFRS
	2004	98	EY	IFRS
	2003	N/A	N/A	N/A
	2002	N/A	N/A	N/A
	2001	59	EY	IAS
	2000	N/A	EY	IAS
	1999	N/A	N/A	N/A
	1998	N/A	EY	N/A
VNESHTORGBANK	2006	97	EY	IFRS
(BANK FOR FOREIGN TRADE)	2005	114	EY	IFRS
VTB GROUP	2004	136	EY	IFRS
	2003	128	EY	IFRS
	2002	108	PWC	IFRS
ZENIT BANK	2002	106	EY	IFRS

34.5   Concluding Comments

Some of the findings of the present study could be expected while others were surprising. Although the Russian banking industry does not report financial results as fast as do companies in the more developed market economies, it reports in a timelier manner than some other Russian industries. Newly admitted EU members, including former Soviet republics like Latvia, Lithuania, and Estonia, have advanced their financial reporting to the point where it is indistinguishable from that of the older EU member states. Financial reporting in the Russian banking sector seems to be moving backwards rather than forward in terms of timeliness. There seems to be a shift toward IFRS and the Big-4 accounting firms, while continuing to be dominant, have lost some market share in recent years.

References

Accounting Principles Board. 1970. Basic Concepts and Accounting Principles Underlying Financial Statements of Business Enterprises – Statement No. 4. New York: American Institute of Certified Public Accountants.

Annaert, Jan, Marc J.K. DeCeuster, Ruud Polfliet & Geert Van Campenhout. 2002. To Be or Not Be . . . 'Too Late': The Case of the Belgian Semi-annual Earnings Announcements. *Journal of Business Finance & Accounting* 29(3 & 4): 477–495.

Ashbaugh, Hollis, Karla M. Johnstone & Terry D. Warfield. 1999. Corporate Reporting on the Internet. *Accounting Horizons* 13(3): 241–257.

Ashton, Robert H., Paul R. Graul & James D. Newton. 1989. Audit Delay and the Timeliness of Corporate Reporting. *Contemporary Accounting Research* 5(2): 657–673.

Atiase, Rowland K., Linda S. Bamber & Senyo Tse. 1989. Timeliness of Financial Reporting, the Firm Size Effect, and Stock Price Reactions to Annual Earnings Announcements. *Contemporary Accounting Research* 5(2): 526–552.

Ball, R., Kothari S.P. & Robin A. 2000. The Effect of International Institutional Factors on Properties of Accounting Earnings. *Journal of Accounting and Economics* 29(1): 1–51.

Ball, R. & Brown P. 1968. An Empirical Evaluation of Accounting Income Numbers. *Journal of Accounting Research* 6: 159–178.

Basu, Sudipta. 1997. The Conservatism Principle and the Asymmetric Timeliness of Earnings. *Journal of Accounting & Economics* 24: 3–37.

Bates, R.J. 1968. Discussion of the Information Content of Annual Earnings Announcements. *Journal of Accounting Research* 6(Suppl): 93–95.

Beaver, W.H. 1968. The Information Content of Annual Earnings Announcements. *Journal of Accounting Research* 6(Suppl): 67–92.

Blanchet, Jeannot. 2002. Global Standards Offer Opportunity. Financial Executive (March/April): 28–30.

Brown, Philip & John W. Kennelly. 1972. The Information Content of Quarterly Earnings: An Extension and Some Further Evidence. *Journal of Business* 45: 403–415.

Chai, Mary L. & Samuel Tung. 2002. The Effect of Earnings-Announcement Timing on Earnings Management. *Journal of Business Finance & Accounting* 29(9 & 10): 1337–1354.

Chambers, Anne E. & Stephen H. Penman. 1984. Timeliness of Reporting and the Stock Price Reaction to Earnings Announcements. *Journal of Accounting Research* 22(1): 21–47.

Davies, B. & G.P. Whittred. 1980. The Association between Selected Corporate Attributes and Timeliness in Corporate Reporting: Further Analysis. *Abacus* 16(1): 48–60.

DeCeuster, M. & D. Trappers. 1993. Determinants of the Timeliness of Belgian Financial Statements. Working Paper, University of Antwerp, cited in Annaert et al., 2002.

Demos, Telis. 2006. The Russia 50: The Country's Largest Public Companies. Fortune 153(2): 70–71 [February 6].

Dwyer, Peggy D. & Earl R. Wilson. 1989. An Empirical Investigation of Factors Affecting the Timeliness of Reporting by Municipalities. *Journal of Accounting and Public Policy* 8(1): 29–55.

Financial Accounting Standards Board. 1980. Statement of Financial Accounting Concepts No. 2, Qualitative Characteristics of Accounting Information. Stamford, CT: Financial Accounting Standards Board.

Gigler, Frank B. & Thomas Hemmer. 2001. Conservatism, Optimal Disclosure Policy, and the Timeliness of Financial Reports. *The Accounting Review* 76(4): 471–493.

Givoli, Dan & Dan Palmon. 1982. Timeliness of Annual Earnings Announcements: Some Empirical Evidence. *The Accounting Review* 57(3): 486–508.

Han, Jerry C.Y. & Shiing-wu Wang. 1998. Political Costs and Earnings Management of Oil Companies during the 1990 Persian Gulf Crises. *The Accounting Review* 73: 103–117.

Han, Jerry C.Y. & John J. Wild. 1997. Timeliness of Reporting and Earnings Information Transfers. *Journal of Business Finance & Accounting* 24(3 & 4): 527–540.

Haw, In-Mu, Daquig Qi & Woody Wu. 2000. Timeliness of Annual Report Releases and Market Reaction to Earnings Announcements in an Emerging Capital Market: The Case of China. *Journal of International Financial Management and Accounting* 11(2): 108–131.

Hendriksen, Eldon S. and Michael F. van Breda. 1992. Accounting Theory, fifth edition, Burr Ridge, IL: Irwin.

Hoover's Most Viewed Company Directory by Country www.hoovers.com/free/mvc/country.xhtml

Jindrichovska, Irina and Stuart Mcleay. 2005. Accounting for Good News and Accounting for Bad News: Some Empirical Evidence from the Czech Republic. *European Accounting Review* 14(3): 635–655.

Keller, Stuart B. 1986. Reporting Timeliness in the Presence of Subject to Audit Qualifications. *Journal of Business Finance & Accounting* 13(1): 117–124.

Kenley, W. John & George J. Staubus. 1974. Objectives and Concepts of Financial Statements. *Accounting Review* 49(4): 888–889.

Krishnan, Gopal V. 2005. The Association between Big 6 Auditor Industry Expertise and the Asymmetric Timeliness of Earnings. *Journal of Accounting, Auditing & Finance* 20(3): 209–228.

Kross, W. & D.A. Schroeder. 1984. An Empirical Investigation of the Effect of Quarterly Earnings Announcement Timing on Stock Returns. *Journal of Accounting Research* 22(1): 153–176.

Kulzick, Raymond S. 2004. Sarbanes-Oxley: Effects on Financial Transparency. S.A.M. *Advanced Management Journal* 69(1): 43–49.

Lawrence, Janice E. & Hubert D. Glover 1998. The Effect of Audit Firm Mergers on Audit Delay. *Journal of Managerial Issues* 10(2): 151–164.

Leventis, Stergios & Pauline Weetman. 2004. Timeliness of Financial Reporting: Applicability of Disclosure Theories in an Emerging Capital Market. *Accounting and Business Research* 34(1): 43–56.

McGee, Robert W. (2006). Timeliness of Financial Reporting in the Energy Sector. *Russian/CIS Energy & Mining Law Journal* 4(2): 6–10.

McGee, Robert W. (2007a). Corporate Governance in Russia: A Case Study of Timeliness of Financial Reporting in the Telecom Industry, *International Finance Review* 7: 365–390.

McGee, Robert W. (2007b). Corporate Governance and the Timeliness of Financial Reporting: A Case Study of the Russian Energy Sector. Fifth International Conference on Accounting and Finance in Transition, London, July 12–14, 2007.

McGee, Robert W. (2007c). Transparency and Disclosure in Russia, in Tomasz Marek Mickiewicz (ed.), Corporate Governance and Finance in Poland and Russia 278–295, London: Palgrave Macmillan.

McGee, Robert W. and Danielle N. Igoe (2008). Corporate Governance and the Timeliness of Financial Reporting: A Comparative Study of Selected EU and Transition Countries. Proceedings of the 43rd Annual Western Regional Meeting of the American Accounting Association, San Francisco, May 1–3, 2008, pp. 74–87.

McGee, Robert W. and Galina G. Preobragenskaya (2005). Accounting and Financial System Reform in a Transition Economy: A Case Study of Russia. New York: Springer.

McGee, Robert W. and Galina G. Preobragenskaya (2006). Accounting and Financial System Reform in Eastern Europe and Asia. New York: Springer.

McGee, Robert W. and Xiaoli Yuan (2008). Corporate Governance and the Timeliness of Financial Reporting: An Empirical Study of the People's Republic of China. *International Journal of Business, Accounting and Finance* (forthcoming).

Organisation for Economic Cooperation and Development. 1998. Global Corporate Governance Principles. Paris: OECD.

Pope, Peter F. & Martin Walker. 1999. International Differences in the Timeliness, Conservatism, and Classification of Earnings. *Journal of Accounting Research* 37 (Suppl): 53–87.

Prickett, Ruth. 2002. Sweet Clarity. Financial Management (September): 18–20.

Rees, William P. & Begona Giner. 2001. On the Asymmetric Recognition of Good and Bad News in France, Germany and the UK. *Journal of Business Finance & Accounting* 28 (9 & 10): 1285–1332.

Soltani, Bahram. 2002. Timeliness of Corporate and Audit Reports: Some Empirical Evidence in the French Context. *The International Journal of Accounting* 37: 215–246.

Trueman, Brett. 1990. Theories of Earnings-Announcement Timing. *Journal of Accounting & Economics* 13: 285–301.

Whittred, G.P. 1980. Audit Qualification and the Timeliness of Corporate Annual Reports. *The Accounting Review* 55(4): 563–577.

Whittred, Greg & Ian Zimmer. 1984. Timeliness of Financial Reporting and Financial Distress. *The Accounting Review* 59(2): 287–295.

Chapter 35
Corporate Governance in the Slovak Republic

Jan Vravec and Radoslav Bajus

35.1 Introduction

Corporate governance is very important for long-term growth of Slovak companies as well as all segments of the Slovak economy. The main problems of Slovak corporate government are:

1. Quality of Contracts
2. Bankruptcies of Companies
3. Regulator of Financial Markets
4. High Level of Corruption

35.2 Quality of Contracts

The quality of a contract is governed not only by law but also by a gentlemen's agreement among partners. One segment of the managers of Slovak companies thinks that in Slovakia it is better to have very detailed contracts and not rely on common business practices. We cover more relations and details in agreements than G7 countries do.

The other view is that in G7 countries there are a larger number of relations covered by contracts because there exists more freedom in legislation of G7 countries. In Slovakia, the managers understand mostly that law enforcement is based on other than legislative and contractual relations. Slovak managers do not have the feeling that they have to incorporate everything in the contract because if the other party will break it, the legal redress is in any case difficult and slow to enforce.

Managers rely rather on other forms of enforcing their interests: payments in advance etc. Contracts in G7 countries are more detailed, as they try to solve ex-ante all the possible situations that can happen. It is not possible in Slovakia, because of

J. Vravec and R. Bajus
Technical University of Kosice

R. W. McGee (ed.), *Accounting Reform in Transition and Developing Economies,*
© Springer Science + Business Media LLC 2008

frequent changes in legislation. Sometimes, the imperfect contracts may have been caused by inadequate legal experience of managers.

Today's situation has improved compared to 2 or 3 years ago when many contracts were concluded knowing that they would not be kept. These tendencies have gradually been diminishing because the numbers of those involved and long-term relations between them in the respective industries have stabilized, and confidence and the space for gentlemen agreements grows as the parties get to know each other.

35.3   Corporate Bankruptcies

In Slovakia the slow drafting of bankruptcy-related legislation and backlogs of cases in the courts had threefold negative effects:

- Tunneling
- Capital stranding
- Stranding of labor

The tunneling itself was warranted by legislation and its enforcement. Also, corruption of the corresponding institutions played a role. Tunneling can never be a matter of a single company since all stakeholders, including employees, minority owners, suppliers, clients, the local community, and the state, pay for it.

Capital stranding is mostly understood mechanically. The company goes bankrupt, its assets are sold, by parts or (in the best case) as a whole to new owners, with the original production being at least discontinued and all the previous links being disrupted. Good legislation and a better institutional provision can be expected to result in bankruptcies, whereby enterprises are getting recovered under the administration of the biggest creditors and subsequently sold as a going concern with all their links and undisrupted production.

Stranding of labor in surviving enterprises is a big problem too. This makes creditors win since they achieve bigger yields; as do employees who do not have to discontinue work; and all the other stakeholders. The final effect is that this is better, since excess employment in a nonprospective enterprise or sector is addressed as soon as possible, so that the labor can look for other jobs, may invest into qualification (improvement or change), or establish its own enterprises (small trade licensees).

The amendment to the Act on Bankruptcy and Settlement attempts to resolve more trivial problems of the existent regulation. Among the major improvements, the liability of the administrator and courts has been laid down to respect the interests of the creditors. So far, the interaction of an administrator and a judge basically ignored the creditors (see the recent big case of the Deposits Protection Fund), and informal talks with companies and banks suggest that the bankrupt's estate would frequently be divided between them.

The classification of creditors has been made simpler, there are now fewer groups of them, and an automatic threshold has been introduced for bankruptcy to be opened, if payments are delayed for more than 30 days. The opportunity to exit the market is one of the most appreciated criteria of the efficiency of one market.

It is necessary to admit that it is very difficult to seize bankruptcies and insolvencies. Even G7 countries have problem doing it correctly. Another problem is the enforceability of such legislation, political will to pursue it, and the general culture of entrepreneurship. A brilliant example is that of German construction giant Philip Holzman saved by the State although it should have gone into bankruptcy.

On the other side of the ocean, bankruptcies are a common phenomenon. The bankruptcy of Enron illustrates the rapidity and effectiveness of the Anglo-Saxon way of bankruptcy. Bankruptcies are definitely assessed as one of the weakest parts of the Slovak entrepreneurial environment. They were practically not applied during some period and it was in paradox caused by the valid legal norm. In consequence of the nonexistence of effective bankruptcy and settlement, many companies continued to exist and do business in the market that would not able to survive in a competitive environment. The situation has been changing slowly in recent years [1].

35.4   Regulator of Financial Markets

The newly established Financial Market Commission (FMC) has a very short track record of existence, since January 2001. In their answers, questionnaire respondents (late 2000) therefore referred to the decade when the Ministry of Finance (MF) itself played this role and received a very bad reputation. As noted by several interviewed persons, instead of regulating the MF has in fact killed the market. Interviewees (late 2001/early 2002) could have also expressed their perception of the FMC. Although establishing the FMC was certainly the right decision, respondents feel that its real independence from the MF must be proven in practice and also unless the FMC is able to attract and employ the elite within the market, which it by now has not, it is not supposed to achieve good results anyway. This question received the highest ranking in the section.

Perception of the Slovak Central Bank has been twofold: conduct of monetary policy in general has been considered reliable and professional, backed up by relatively sound results in terms of inflation and the exchange rate. On the other hand, bank supervision has been rather negatively evaluated mainly because of the recent case of Devin Bank.

Results are therefore affected by the weight each respondent assigned to these two factors. The interviews were conducted after the scandalous bankruptcy of the Devin Bank, indicating political ties of the central bank supervision in this case. Devin Bank is the fourth bank to go bankrupt in the recent decade in Slovakia. This number is relatively low (as compared to, e.g., the Czech Republic) mainly due to a conservative bank license provision by the Slovak Central Bank.

The Central Bank in Slovakia presents a relatively successful story of a regulator in a transition country. As expressed by one of our interviewees since the very beginning, the Central Bank relied on international standards and rules, but could not have applied them strictly. Otherwise, it could have closed down most of the banks in the early 1990s. Nowadays, all these rules can be applied fully.

35.5 High Level of Corruption

According to the recently published corruption index (CPI 2001) assessed by the international anti-corruption organization Transparency International, Slovakia ranked 51–54th with a CPI 2001 index of 3.7 points (upper and lower bounds are 2.1–4.9). The level of corruption represented by the CPI index of 3.7 is measured on the scale of 0 (a completely corrupt country) to 10 (country without corruption) in 91 assessed countries [2].

As revealed by the World Bank study, enterprises encountered bribery during 1998–2000 mostly at customs, import and export licensing, the Certification Authority, construction permits, and State Business Supervision. The bribes reported by enterprises ranged from 40 to 500,000 SK, with the largest bribes being paid in the areas of banking services, import and export licenses, courts, telecommunications, and customs. The courts and banking services were the recipients of the highest average bribes and the highest median bribes [3].

References

1. INEKO (Institute for Economic and Social Reforms): Corporate Governance Risk in the Slovak Republic at http://www.ineko.sk
2. For more information on CPI index, please see http://www.transparency.sk
3. World Bank – USAID (2000): Corruption in Slovakia. Results of Diagnostic Surveys. Available at http://www.government.gov.sk

Part V
Public Finance

Chapter 36
Opinions on the Ethics of Tax Evasion: A Comparative Study of Ten Transition Economies

Robert W. McGee and Wendy Gelman

36.1 Introduction

This chapter reports on the results of an empirical study that examined the opinions of a wide range of individuals in ten transition economies. Data was taken from a wider study that gathered information on human beliefs and values in 85 different countries. The present study had a sample size of 12,320. The question posed was whether the respondent would cheat on taxes if it were possible to do so. Responses were measured on a 10-point Likert scale. Results are reported for the following categories: overall, gender, and age.

Tax evasion has been in existence ever since governments started imposing taxes. There is a large body of literature in the economics and public finance literature that discusses and analyzes various aspects of tax evasion. Economists render opinions on the reasons for tax evasion and the methods and policies that governments can adopt to reduce it. There is even a theory of optimal tax evasion (Davidson et al., 2005; Levaggi and Menoncin, 2007). Yet very few of these studies apply ethical theory in an attempt to determine when, and under what circumstances tax evasion might be ethical or unethical.

The present study does not take either of these approaches. It does not analyze tax evasion from the perspective of economics or public finance and it does not apply ethical theory to determine under what circumstances tax evasion might be considered ethical, although ethics is discussed. This study focuses on the attitudes toward tax evasion of a wide range of individuals in ten transition economies. The main goals of the present study are to determine general attitudes toward the ethics of tax evasion and to determine whether certain demographic variables, including gender and age, have a significant effect on attitude toward the ethics of tax evasion.

36.2 Review of the Literature

Although much has been written about tax evasion from the perspective of public finance, not many studies have focused on the ethical aspects of tax evasion. One of the most comprehensive early studies on the ethics of tax evasion was done by

R. W. McGee and W. Gelman
Florida International University

R. W. McGee (ed.), *Accounting Reform in Transition and Developing Economies,*
© Springer Science+Business Media LLC 2008

Martin Crowe (1944), a Catholic priest who surveyed the philosophical and religious (mostly Catholic) literature that had been written over the previous five centuries. Crowe found that three basic positions had emerged over the centuries. Tax evasion was considered to be: never ethical, always ethical, or ethical under certain facts and circumstances. McGee (2006b) expanded on this literature review.

More recent studies were done by Torgler (2003) and McGee (1994, 1998a). The Torgler study was mostly empirical but did not examine the philosophical and ethical literature in depth. The McGee studies examined the philosophical and ethical literature but did not conduct empirical investigations.

Although very few philosophical studies on the ethics of tax evasion have been performed, the ones that have been completed span all three viewpoints. Block (1989, 1993) surveyed the public finance literature but failed to find any adequate explanations or arguments to justify taxation. McGee (1994) applied Lysander Spooner's (1870) philosophy to the issue of tax evasion, which challenged the social contract theories of Hobbes (1651), Locke (1689), and Rousseau (1762).

At the other end of the spectrum, a few philosophical studies concluded that tax evasion is never justified. The literature of the Baha'i religion strictly prohibits tax evasion, the main argument being that individuals have a duty to obey the laws of the country in which they live (DeMoville, 1998). A study of the Mormon religious literature reached the same conclusion for exactly the same reason (Smith and Kimball, 1998).

Two philosophical studies of the ethics of tax evasion from a Jewish perspective (Cohn, 1998; Tamari, 1998) concluded that tax evasion is never, or almost never ethical according to the Jewish literature. A third Jewish study, which was both philosophical and empirical in nature (McGee and Cohn, 2008) found that although the Jewish literature was firmly against tax evasion on ethical grounds, the Jews who were surveyed were more flexible on the issue. An empirical study of Mormon views (McGee and Smith, 2006) found that many Mormons were also more flexible on the issue than their religious literature would suggest.

Several philosophical studies concluded that tax evasion could be ethical in certain situations. Pennock (1998) concluded that tax evasion was ethical in cases where the country collecting the taxes was engaged in an unjust war. Morales (1998) regarded a man's duty to feed his family was more important than feeding the state's coffers. Gronbacher (1998) and Schansberg (1998) concluded that the Catholic religious literature permits tax evasion in certain situations, a view that concurs with the Crowe (1944) study. Gronbacher's (1998) study of the Christian literature reached the same conclusion. Two Islamic scholars (Murtuza and Ghazanfer, 1998) examined their religious literature and reported that Muslims have a duty to God to contribute to the poor. They did not address the issue of the relationship of the individual to the state and the corresponding duty to pay taxes. A survey of the Islamic business ethics literature by a non-Muslim scholar (McGee, 1997, 1998b) found that tax evasion can be justified in cases where the effect of the tax is to increase prices or where the tax is on income.

A few empirical studies on the ethics of tax evasion have been conducted. Studies of Argentina (McGee and Rossi, 2006), Armenia (McGee and Maranjyan,

2006), Bosnia & Herzegovina (McGee et al., 2008), China (McGee and Guo, 2006; McGee and Noronha, 2008; McGee and An, 2006), Germany (McGee et al., 2005), Guatemala (McGee and Lingle, 2005), Hong Kong (McGee and Butt, 2008; McGee and Ho, 2006), Macau (McGee et al., 2006), Poland (McGee and Bernal, 2006), Romania (McGee, 2005a), Slovakia (McGee and Tusan, 2006), Thailand (McGee, 2006a), Ukraine (Nasadyuk and McGee, 2006), philosophy teachers (McGee, 2008a), and international business academics (McGee, 2005b) asked respondents to give their opinion on the ethics of tax evasion in various specific situations, using a 7-point Likert Scale. All these studies concluded that tax evasion may be ethically justified in certain situations, although some arguments were stronger than others. The Torgler (2003) study reached the same conclusion, using a different methodology.

The various McGee et al. studies found that tax evasion is more likely to be viewed as justifiable if the tax system is perceived as being unfair; if the government abuses human rights; if tax funds wind up in the pockets of corrupt politicians, their friends, or family; or if tax rates are too high. Another reason found in these studies is that tax evasion can be justified if there is an inability to pay. This finding corresponds closely with the Catholic theological literature on the topic (Crowe, 1944) and with a study of Mexican migrant workers (Morales, 1998). These studies also found that support for tax evasion is weak where individuals get something in return for their money.

A few studies have used the Inglehart et al. (2004) database to examine attitudes toward tax evasion for various subgroups. Torgler (2003) utilized it in his doctoral dissertation. McGee and Bose (2007) used it to compare attitudes of sample populations in Australia, New Zealand, and the United States. The database was also used for studies of Vietnam (McGee, 2008b), several Asian countries (McGee, 2007), and a longitudinal study of ten transition economies (McGee, 2008c). All of these studies found that there is some support for tax evasion but that support is weak.

36.3   Methodology

This study used the data that was compiled in a much larger and comprehensive study by Inglehart et al. (2004). The Inglehart study asked hundreds of questions to more than 200,000 people in 85 different countries. One of those questions (F116) was on the ethics of tax evasion. The question asked whether the respondent would cheat on taxes if there were an opportunity to do so. Responses were tallied using a 10-point Likert scale where 1 represented never justifiable and 10 represented always justifiable.

The ten transition economies chosen for the present study were China, the Czech Republic, Estonia, Hungary, Latvia, Lithuania, Poland, Russia, Vietnam, and Ukraine.

One criticism that could be made of the methodology is that the data was gathered in face-to-face interviews. Data gathered in this manner may not be highly representative of the real views of the people being interviewed, since there may be a tendency to give the interviewer the response that is expected, deemed to be moral, or least embarrassing. A better approach would have been to collect the data anonymously. However, the Inglehart et al. study is widely respected and face-to-face interviewing is an accepted research methodology. Furthermore, several studies of tax evasion using the Inglehart et al. data have been published, making it possible to compare results. The present study fills a gap in the literature by examining data from ten transition economies.

36.4   Findings

If one were to summarize the findings of the present study in a single sentence, it would be that there is some support for tax evasion but that support is weak and varies by country, gender, and age.

Table 36.1 lists the sample sizes and overall mean scores for each country. All of the mean scores were well below 4.0 which, on a scale of 1 to 10, indicates that there is not much support for evading taxes even when there is a possibility of doing so. This could be explained for a variety of reasons, including the threat of possible punishment, and the perceived notion that there is some moral duty, either to God, to the state or to some segment of the taxpaying community. The Inglehart et al. (2004) study did not ask for reasons for the various responses, so one can only speculate about the reasons for the responses, although several studies have addressed this issue (McGee, 2006b; McGee and Cohn, 2008) and found that all of these reasons have been given from time to time as reasons for not evading taxes.

Chart 36.1 compares the mean scores graphically and assembles them from the lowest (never justifiable) to the highest (always justifiable). The chart clearly shows that, although the mean scores are different, they are all rather low compared to the highest possible score of 10. The Vietnamese sample was most likely to hold that tax evasion is never justifiable. Lithuanians were most likely to view tax evasion as

Table 36.1 Sample size and overall mean scores (1 = never justifiable; 10 = always justifiable)

	Sample size	Mean score
China	985	1.57
Czech Republic	1,885	2.07
Estonia	974	3.15
Hungary	975	2.12
Latvia	989	2.36
Lithuania	968	3.77
Poland	1,066	2.23
Russia	2,381	3.09
Ukraine	1,108	3.45
Vietnam	989	1.32
Total	12,320	2.55

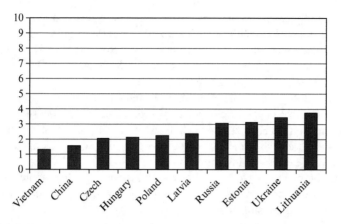

Chart 36.1 Mean scores

justifiable, although a mean score of only 3.77 indicates that there is not much support for this proposition even in Lithuania.

Curiously, the two lowest mean scores were in Asian countries – Vietnam and China – whereas the top five scores were from the former Soviet republics. The three scores that were higher than the Asian countries, but lower than those of former Soviet republics, were the Soviet block countries in Central Europe. If there is a correlation between these mean scores and respect for the government in general, one might tentatively conclude that the people who live in former Soviet republics have the least respect for the government whereas the people who live in Asia have the highest respect for the government.

36.5   Gender

Numerous studies have compared male and female attitudes and opinions on a variety of ethical issues. Some studies have concluded that females are more ethical than males (Boyd, 1981; Dawson, 1997; Ruegger and King, 1992) while other studies have concluded just the opposite (Barnett and Karson, 1987; Weeks et al., 1999). A third group of studies found no statistical difference between male and female attitudes (Loo, 2003; Posner and Schmidt, 1984; Stanga and Turpen, 1991).

A few studies have explored male and female attitudes toward the ethics of tax evasion. Women were found to be more strongly opposed than men to tax evasion in studies of Guatemala (McGee and Lingle, 2005), Hong Kong (McGee and Butt, 2006), Hubei, China (McGee and Guo, 2006), international business professors (McGee, 2005b), orthodox Jews (McGee and Cohn, 2008), Spain (Alm and Torgler, 2004), Thailand (McGee, 2006), and US business students in Utah (McGee and Smith, 2006). Men were found to be more opposed to tax evasion in studies of Romania (McGee, 2005a) and Slovakia (McGee and Tusan, 2006).

The views of men and women toward the ethics of tax evasion were found to be the same in studies of Argentina (McGee and Rossi, 2006), Beijing, China (McGee and An, 2006), Guangzhou, China (McGee and Noronha, 2008), Hong Kong (McGee and Ho, 2006), Macau (McGee et al., 2006), Poland (McGee and Bernal, 2006), and Ukraine (Nasadyuk and McGee, 2006).

Table 36.2 shows the results of the present study, based on gender. Male scores were higher in eight of ten cases, indicating that men are less opposed to evading taxes than are women. However, Wilcoxon tests found the differences to be significant only in five cases. In the two cases where women were less opposed to tax evasion, the difference was insignificant.

It would be premature to conclude from these findings that women are more ethical than men, however. In order to reach that conclusion one must begin with the premise that tax evasion is unethical, which might not be the case. The various studies cited above have shown that a significant portion of various populations believe that tax evasion is morally justified in certain cases. Some of the religious literature also supports this view (Crowe, 1944; Gronbacher, 1998; McGee, 1994, 1997, 1998a, b; Pennock, 1998; Schansberg, 1998), although the religious literature of Judaism (Cohn, 1998; Tamari, 1998), the Church of Jesus Christ of Latter-Day Saints (Smith and Kimball, 1998), and the Baha'i religion (DeMoville, 1998) do not. All that one may conclude from the present findings is that women generally tend to be more opposed to evading taxes.

Chart 36.2 shows the overall mean scores graphically. The graph clearly shows that, although men are more likely to evade taxes if they have an opportunity to do so, neither group is very likely to evade taxes.

Chart 36.3 shows the gender comparisons for each country. Men are usually less opposed to tax evasion, sometimes significantly so. But there is not much difference in the larger scheme of things. None of the mean scores are above 4 and some

Table 36.2 Gender mean scores (1 = never justifiable; 10 = always justifiable)

				Score larger by		
	Combined	Male	Female	Male	Female	p Value
China	1.57	1.53	1.61		0.08	0.6722
Czech Republic	2.07	2.23	1.92	0.31		0.001211*
Estonia	3.15	3.36	2.98	0.38		0.02518**
Hungary	2.12	2.26	1.99	0.27		0.2017
Latvia	2.36	2.62	2.14	0.48		0.008116*
Lithuania	3.77	3.93	3.64	0.29		0.1274
Poland	2.23	2.31	2.15	0.16		0.9153
Russia	3.09	3.40	2.83	0.57		4.309e-06*
Ukraine	3.45	3.69	3.23	0.46		0.008417*
Vietnam	1.32	1.28	1.36		0.08	0.2936
Averages	2.55	2.70	2.42	0.28		

* Significant at 1% level
** Significant at 5% level

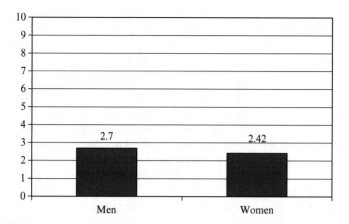

Chart 36.2 Overall mean score comparison

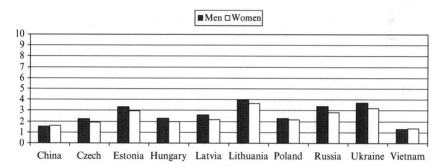

Chart 36.3 Gender comparisons

of them are below 2. Since the scale goes up to 10, one could interpret the results to mean that there is not much support for tax evasion, although support seems to be stronger among men in general and Lithuanian men in particular.

36.6   Age

A study by Ruegger and King (1992) found that people become more ethical as they get older. Their study divided respondents into the following four groups: 21 or less, 22–30, 31–40, and 40 plus. But Sims et al. (1996) found that older students had fewer qualms about pirating software than did younger students.

Babakus et al. (2004) also found that age made a difference, but what difference age makes sometimes depends on culture. Younger people from the UK, USA, and France tend to be less ethical consumers than do older people from these countries, whereas younger Austrians tend to be more ethical consumers than their elders. Age generally did not matter for Hong Kong consumers, except in the case of stealing towels from hotels and blankets from aircraft. Younger people tended to be less tolerant of these kinds of activities than older Hong Kong consumers. Brunei consumers showed mixed results. In some cases younger people were more ethical whereas in other cases older people were more ethical.

Table 36.3 summarizes the mean scores by age for the present study. The Inglehart et al. (2004) data separated the groups into three age categories. In nine out of ten countries, the mean scores declined with age, meaning that there is less support for tax evasion as people get older. If one were to equate respect for law with aversion to tax evasion, one could reasonably conclude that people have more respect for law as they get older. This finding supports the findings of some of the studies cited above.

Chart 36.4 shows the overall mean scores for each age group graphically. As can be seen, the mean score declines as people get older, indicating that people are less likely to evade taxes as they become older.

Table 36.3 Age mean scores (1 = never justifiable; 10 = always justifiable)

	Average	15–29	30–49	50+
China	1.57	1.73	1.55	1.50
Czech Republic	2.07	2.43	2.31	1.67
Estonia	3.15	3.90	3.47	2.45
Hungary	2.11	2.58	2.50	1.47
Latvia	2.36	3.32	2.43	1.92
Lithuania	3.77	4.67	4.06	2.87
Poland	2.23	2.92	2.12	1.92
Russia	3.09	4.25	3.23	2.20
Ukraine	3.45	4.45	3.66	2.64
Vietnam	1.32	1.31	1.31	1.33
Averages	2.55	3.27	2.64	2.02

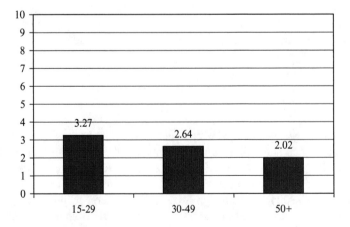

Chart 36.4 Mean scores by age

Chart 36.5 shows the age means by country. In almost all cases the mean score declines with age.

Table 36.4 shows the *p* values for each age group and each country. The decline in mean scores is significant in 22 of 30 cases. The most significant differences tended to be in the cases where the youngest and oldest age groups were being compared.

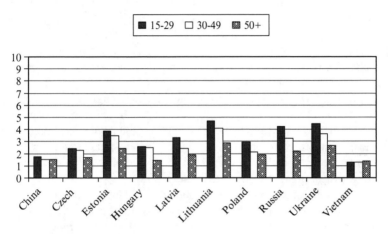

Chart 36.5 Age means by country

Table 36.4 *p* Values – Age

	15–29 vs. 30–49	15–29 vs. 50+	30–49 vs. 50+
China	0.1172	0.09004***	0.6488
Czech Republic	0.1643	3.507e-12*	1.675e-10*
Estonia	0.02819**	1.328e-13*	1.311e-09*
Hungary	0.4841	2.305e-11*	6.903e-11*
Latvia	2.153e-05*	1.037e-11*	0.003517*
Lithuania	0.01305**	2.948e-13*	2.7e-08*
Poland	3.387e-05*	2.163e-07*	0.1393
Russia	3.877e-11*	2.937e-39*	1.815e-16*
Ukraine	0.0006314*	9.195e-16*	2.44e-08*
Vietnam	0.3642	0.8723	0.2346

* Significant at 1% level	19
** Significant at 5% level	2
*** Significant at 10% level	1
Not significant	83

36.7   Concluding Comments

There are many explanations for why the attitudes toward cheating on taxes may differ (or not) by country. Some possible partial explanations are the influence certain demographics such as gender and age play in shaping one's opinions. The political system of the country where one lives is another. Income level, education, and religious preference, which are not examined in the present study, also probably play a role. It is reasonable to expect that people who earn more money tend to feel exploited if they are forced to pay a higher percentage of their marginal income in taxes than are people at lower income levels. The wealthier classes might resent being forced to pay relatively high tax rates, and this resentment may cause them to view cheating on taxes more favorably than individuals who receive benefits in exchange for their tax contributions.

People at the lower end of the economic spectrum might also resent paying taxes, but for entirely different reasons. Rather than feeling exploited compared to other income groups, they may feel that they have little or no moral obligation to pay because of inability. This reason was one of the dominant arguments to justify tax evasion in the Catholic literature (Crowe, 1944) and this view was supported by a study of Mexican migrant workers (Morales, 1998).

Culture also plays a role. Hofstede (1980, 1991, 1994a, b) examined power distance, collectivism versus individualism, uncertainty avoidance, masculinity verses femininity, and long-term orientation as factors that affect a wide range of attitudes and behaviors. Hall (1959, 1966, 1976) looked at culture from the perspectives of high and low context and compared monochromic cultures to polychromic cultures. All of these factors play a role, although it is not always clear what that role is, and a number of factors interact, making it difficult, if not impossible, to determine which factors play a dominant role.

The findings of the present study indicate that some people will cheat on taxes if they have an opportunity, but that many will not. Results vary by country, gender, and age. Further study is needed to determine the reasons for the differences.

References

Alm, J. and Torgler, B. (2004). 'Estimating the Determinants of Tax Morale.' National Tax Association – Tax Institute of America. Proceedings of the Annual Meeting, pp. 269–274.

Babakus, Cornwell, E.T., Mitchell, V. and Schlegelmilch, B. (2004). 'Reactions to Unethical Consumer Behavior across Six Countries', The Journal of Consumer Marketing 21(4/5): 254–263.

Barnett, J. H. and Karson, M.J. (1987). 'Personal Values and Business Decisions: An Exploratory Investigation', Journal of Business Ethics 6(5): 371–382.

Block, W. (1989). 'The Justification of Taxation in the Public Finance Literature: A Critique', Journal of Public Finance and Public Choice, 3: 141–158.

Block, W. (1993). 'Public Finance Texts Cannot Justify Government Taxation: A Critique', Canadian Public Administration/Administration Publique du Canada, 36(2): 225–262, reprinted in revised form under the title "The Justification for Taxation in the Economics Literature" in R. W. McGee (ed.), *The Ethics of Tax Evasion*. The Dumont Institute for Public Policy Research, Dumont, NJ, 1998, pp. 36–88.

Boyd, D P. (1981). 'Improving Ethical Awareness through the Business and Society Course', *Business and Society* 20, 21, 2, 1: 27–31.

Cohn, G. (1998). 'The Jewish View on Paying Taxes', *Journal of Accounting, Ethics & Public Policy*, 1(2): 109–120, reprinted in R. W. McGee (ed.), *The Ethics of Tax Evasion*. Dumont, NJ: The Dumont Institute for Public Policy Research, 1998, pp. 180–189.

Crowe, M. T. (1944). 'The Moral Obligation of Paying Just Taxes', The Catholic University of America Studies in Sacred Theology No. 84.

Davidson, C., L. Martin and J.D. Wilson (2005). Tax Evasion as an Optimal Tax Device. *Economics Letters* 86(2): 285–289.

Dawson, L. M. (1997). Ethical Differences between Men and Women in the Sales Profession, *Journal of Business Ethics* 16(11): 1143–1152.

DeMoville, W. (1998). The Ethics of Tax Evasion: A Baha'i Perspective, *Journal of Accounting, Ethics & Public Policy*, 1(3): 356–368, reprinted in R. W. McGee (ed.), *The Ethics of Tax Evasion*. Dumont, NJ: The Dumont Institute for Public Policy Research, 1998, pp. 230–240.

Gronbacher, G.M.A. (1998). Taxation: Catholic Social Thought and Classical Liberalism, *Journal of Accounting, Ethics & Public Policy*, 1(1): 91–100, reprinted in R. W. McGee (ed.), The Ethics of Tax Evasion, Dumont, NJ: The Dumont Institute for Public Policy Research, Dumont, NJ, 1998, pp. 158–167.

Hall, E.T. (1959). The Silent Language. Garden City, NY: Doubleday.

Hall, E.T. (1966). The Hidden Dimension. Garden City, NY: Doubleday.

Hall, E.T. (1976). Beyond Culture. Garden City, NY: Doubleday.

Hall, E.T. (1983). The Dance of Life. Garden City, NY: Doubleday.

Hobbes, T. (1651). Leviathan, Cambridge: Cambridge University Press.

Hofstede, G. (1980). Motivation, Leadership, and Organizational: Do American Theories Apply Abroad? *Organizational Dynamics* 10(1): 42–63.

Hofstede, G. (1991). Cultures and Organizations: Software of the Mind. New York: McGraw-Hill.

Hofstede, G. (1994a). Cultures and Organizations, Software of the Mind: Intercultural Cooperation and its Importance for Survival. London: McGraw-Hill.

Hofstede, G. (1994b). Management Scientists are Human. *Management Science* 40(1): 4–13.

Inglehart, R., Basanez, M., Diez-Medrano, J., Halman, L. and Luijkx, R. (eds.) 2004. Human Beliefs and Values: A Cross-Cultural Sourcebook based on the 1999–2002 values surveys. Siglo XXI Editores: Mexico.

Levaggi, R. and Menoncin, F. (2007). A Note on Optimal Tax Evasion in the Presence of Merit Goods. Available at http://ssrn.com/abstract=979687.

Locke, J. (1689). Two Treatises on Government, Cambridge: Canbridge University Press.

Loo, R. (2003). Are Women More Ethical Than Men? Findings from Three Independent Studies, *Women in Management Review* 18(3/4): 169–181.

McGee, R. W. (1994). Is Tax Evasion Unethical? *University of Kansas Law Review*, 42(2): 411–435. Reprinted at http://ssrn.com/abstract=74420.

McGee, R. W. (1997). The Ethics of Tax Evasion and Trade Protectionism from an Islamic Perspective, *Commentaries on Law & Public Policy* 1: 250–262. Reprinted at http://ssrn.com/abstract=461397.

McGee, R. W. (ed.). (1998a). The Ethics of Tax Evasion. Dumont, NJ: The Dumont Institute for Public Policy Research.

McGee, R. W. (1998b). The Ethics of Tax Evasion in Islam: A Comment, *Journal of Accounting, Ethics & Public Policy*, 1(2): 162–168, reprinted in R. W. McGee (ed.), The Ethics of Tax Evasion. Dumont, NJ: The Dumont Institute for Public Policy Research 1998, pp. 214–219.

McGee, R. W. (2005a). 'The Ethics of Tax Evasion: A Survey of Romanian Business Students and Faculty,' Andreas School of Business Working Paper Series, Barry University, Miami Shores, FL 33161, USA, September. Available at www.ssrn.com. Reprinted in R. W. McGee and G. G. Preobragenskaya, Accounting and Financial System Reform in Eastern Europe and Asia. New York: Springer, 2006.

McGee, R. W. (2005b). 'The Ethics of Tax Evasion: A Survey of International Business Academics.' Presented at the 60th International Atlantic Economic Conference, New York, October 6–9, 2005. Also available at www.ssrn.com.

McGee, R. W. (2006a). The Ethics of Tax Evasion: A Case Study of Opinion in Thailand. 2006 Academy of International Business Southeast Asia Regional Conference, Bangkok, December 7–9, 2006.

McGee, R.W. (2006b). Three Views on the Ethics of Tax Evasion. *Journal of Business Ethics* 67(1): 15–35.

McGee, R. W. (2007). Ethics and Tax Evasion in Asia. *ICFAI Journal of Public Finance* 5(2) (May 2007): 21–33. Reprinted in Business Ethics: A 360 Degree Appraisal. Hyderabad, India: ICFAI University Press.

McGee, R. W. (2008a). The Ethics of Tax Evasion: A Survey of Philosophy Teachers (forthcoming).

McGee, R.W. (2008b). A Survey of Vietnamese Opinion on the Ethics of Tax Evasion, in R. W. McGee (ed.), *Taxation and Public Finance in Transition and Developing Economies*. New York: Springer (forthcoming).

McGee, R.W. (2008c). Trends in the Ethics of Tax Evasion: An Empirical Study of 10 Transition Economies, in Robert W. McGee, editor, *Taxation and Public Finance in Transition and Developing Economies*. New York: Springer (forthcoming).

McGee, Robert W. and Yuhua An (2006). 'The Ethics of Tax Evasion: A Survey of Chinese Business and Economics Students.' Published in the Proceedings of the International Academy of Business and Public Administration Disciplines (IABPAD), 2006 Winter Conference, Orlando, Florida, January 3–6. Reprinted at www.ssrn.com.

McGee, R.W., Basic, M. and Tyler, M. (2008). 'The Ethics of Tax Evasion: A Survey of Bosnian Opinion.' *Journal of Southern Europe and the Balkans* 10(1): xxx–xxx, forthcoming.

McGee, R. W. and Bernal, A. (2006). The Ethics of Tax Evasion: A Survey of Business Students in Poland. Sixth Annual International Business Research Conference, co-sponsored by the Coggin College of Business, University of North Florida and the School of Management, Warsaw University, February 10–11, 2006, Jacksonville, Florida. Reprinted at www.ssrn.com.

McGee, R.W. and S. Bose (2007). The Ethics of Tax Evasion: A Comparative Study of Australian, New Zealand and USA Opinion. International Academy of Business and Public Administration Disciplines (IABPAD) Spring Conference, May 3–6, 2007, Dallas. Published in The IABPAD Conference Proceedings at pp. 951–964.

McGee, R. W. and Butt, Y.Y. (2008). The Ethics of Tax Evasion: A Survey of Hong Kong Opinion (forthcoming).

McGee, R. W. and Cohn, G. (2008). Jewish Perspectives on the Ethics of Tax Evasion, *Academy of Accounting and Financial Studies Journal* (forthcoming).

McGee, R. W. and Guo, Z. (2006). 'The Ethics of Tax Evasion: A Survey of Law, Business and Philosophy Students in China.' Published in the Proceedings of the International Academy of Business and Public Administration Disciplines (IABPAD), 2006 Winter Conference, Orlando, Florida, January 3–6. Reprinted at www.ssrn.com.

McGee, R. W. and Ho, S. S. M. (2006). 'The Ethics of Tax Evasion: A Survey of Accounting, Business and Economics Students in Hong Kong.' Published in the Proceedings of the International Academy of Business and Public Administration Disciplines (IABPAD), 2006 Winter Conference, Orlando, Florida, January 3–6. Reprinted at www.ssrn.com.

McGee, R. W. and Lingle, C. (2005). The Ethics of Tax Evasion: A Survey of Guatemalan Opinion. Presented at the 60th International Atlantic Economic Conference, New York, October 6–9, 2005. Also available at www.ssrn.com.

McGee, R. W. and Maranjyan, T.B. (2006). 'Tax Evasion in Armenia: An Empirical Study.' Presented at the Fourth Annual Armenian International Policy Research Group Conference, Washington, DC, January 14–15. Also available at www.ssrn.com.

McGee, R.W., Nickerson, I. and Fees, W. (2005). When Is Tax Evasion Ethically Justifiable? A Survey of German Opinion. Proceedings of the Academy of Legal, Ethical and Regulatory Issues 9(2): 35–38, Las Vegas.

McGee, R. W. and Noronha, C. (2008). The Ethics of Tax Evasion: A Survey of Opinion in Southern China (forthcoming).

McGee, R. W., Noronha, C. and Tyler, M. (2006). The Ethics of Tax Evasion: A Survey of Macao Opinion, Presented at the Fifteenth Annual World Business Congress of the International Management Development Association (IMDA), Sarajevo, Bosnia, June 18–21,

McGee, R. W. and Rossi, M.J. (2006). The Ethics of Tax Evasion: A Survey of Law and Business Students in Argentina. Sixth Annual International Business Research Conference, co-sponsored by the Coggin College of Business, University of North Florida and the School of Management, Warsaw University, February 10–11, 2006, Jacksonville, Florida. Reprinted at www.ssrn.com.

McGee, R. W. and Smith, S.R. (2006). 'The Ethics of Tax Evasion: An Empirical Study of Utah Opinion', Andreas School of Business Working Paper, Barry University, Miami Shores, FL 33161 USA, September.

McGee, R.W. and Tusan, R. (2006). 'The Ethics of Tax Evasion: A Survey of Slovak Opinion.' Andreas School of Business Working Paper, Barry University, September.

McGee, R.W. and Tyler, M. (2007). Tax Evasion and Ethics: A Comparative Study of 33 Countries. *Proceedings of the International Academy of Business and Public Administration Disciplines* 4(1): 709–729.

Morales, A. (1998). Income Tax Compliance and Alternative Views of Ethics and Human Nature, *Journal of Accounting, Ethics & Public Policy* 1(3): 380–399, reprinted in R. W. McGee (ed.), The Ethics of Tax Evasion. Dumont, NJ: The Dumont Institute for Public Policy Research, 1998, pp. 242–258.

Murtuza, A. and Ghazanfar, S.M. (1998). Taxation as a Form of Worship: Exploring the Nature of Zakat, *Journal of Accounting, Ethics & Public Policy* 1(2): 134–161, reprinted in R W. McGee (ed.), The Ethics of Tax Evasion. Dumont, NJ: The Dumont Institute for Public Policy Research, 1998, pp. 190–212.

Nasadyuk, I. and McGee, R.W. (2006). Lessons for Emerging Tax Regimes: The Ethics of Tax Evasion in the Ukraine, Open Society Institute, Higher Education Support Program, Regional Seminar for Excellence in Teaching, Odessa, July 23–August 4, 2006. Published in the Proceedings at 47–66.

Pennock, R. T. (1998). Death and Taxes: On the Justice of Conscientious War Tax Resistance, *Journal of Accounting, Ethics & Public Policy*, 1(1): 58–76, reprinted in R. W. McGee (ed.), *The Ethics of Tax Evasion*. Dumont, NJ: The Dumont Institute for Public Policy Research, 1998, pp. 124–142.

Posner, B. Z. and Schmidt, W.H. (1984). Values and the American Manager: An Update, *California Management Review* 26(3): 202–216.

Rousseau, J. J. (1762). The Social Contract. London: Penguin.

Ruegger, D. and King, E.W. (1992). A Study of the Effect of Age and Gender upon Student Business Ethics, *Journal of Business Ethics* 11(3): 179–186.

Schansberg, D. E. (1998). The Ethics of Tax Evasion within Biblical Christianity: Are There Limits to "Rendering Unto Caesar"? *Journal of Accounting, Ethics & Public Policy* 1(1): 77–90, reprinted in R. W. McGee (ed.), The Ethics of Tax Evasion. Dumont, NJ: The Dumont Institute for Public Policy Research, 1998, pp. 144–157.

Sims, R. R., Cheng, H.K. and Teegen, H. (1996). Toward a Profile of Student Software Piraters, *Journal of Business Ethics* 15(8): 839–849.

Smith, S. R. and Kimball, K.C. (1998). Tax Evasion and Ethics: A Perspective from Members of The Church of Jesus Christ of Latter-Day Saints, *Journal of Accounting, Ethics & Public Policy* 1(3): 337–348, reprinted in R. W. McGee (ed.), The Ethics of Tax Evasion. Dumont, NJ: The Dumont Institute for Public Policy Research, 1998, pp. 220–229.

Spooner, L. (1870). No Treason: The Constitution of No Authority, originally self-published by Spooner in Boston in 1870, reprinted by Rampart College in 1965, 1966 and 1971, and by Ralph Myles Publisher, Inc., Colorado Springs, Colorado in 1973.

Stanga, K. G. and Turpen, R.A. (1991). 'Ethical Judgments on Selected Accounting Issues: An Empirical Study', *Journal of Business Ethics* 10(10): 739–747.

Tamari, M. (1998). 'Ethical Issues in Tax Evasion: A Jewish Perspective', *Journal of Accounting, Ethics & Public Policy*, 1(2), 121–132, reprinted in R. W. McGee (ed.), *The Ethics of Tax Evasion*. Dumont, NJ: The Dumont Institute for Public Policy Research, 1998, pp. 168–178.

Torgler, B. (2003). Tax Morale: Theory and Empirical Analysis of Tax Compliance. Dissertation der Universität Basel zur Erlangung der Würde eines Doktors der Staatswissenschaften.

Weeks, W. A., Moore, C.W., McKinney, J.A. and Longenecker, J.G. (1999). 'The Effects of Gender and Career Stage on Ethical Judgment', *Journal of Business Ethics* 20(4): 301–313.

Index